Fiscal Policies and the World Economy

Fiscal Policies and the World Economy

Second Edition

Jacob A. Frenkel
Assaf Razin

The MIT Press
Cambridge, Massachusetts
London, England

This book was set in Palatino by Asco Trade Typesetting Ltd, Hong Kong and printed and bound in the United States of America.

Library of Congress Cataloging-in-Publication Data

Frenkel, Jacob A.
    Fiscal policies and the world economy / Jacob A. Frenkel, Assaf Razin. — 2nd ed.
        p.   cm.
    Includes bibliographical references and index.
    ISBN 0-262-06149-X. — ISBN 0-262-56068-2 (pbk.)
    1. Fiscal policy. 2. International economic relations.
    I. Razin, Assaf. II. Title.
    HJ141.F74   1992
    339.5′2—dc20   92-14463
                                                                         CIP

Contents

Preface to the Second Edition   ix
Preface to the First Edition   xi

I   **Prologue** xv

     1   Stylized Facts on Fiscal Policies and International Economic
        Interdependence   1

II   **Traditional Approaches to Fiscal Policies and International
Economic Interdependence**   17

     2   The Income-Expenditure Model: Fiscal Policies and the
        Determination of Output   19

     3   Fiscal Policies and International Capital Mobility in the Income-
        Expenditure Model   49

     Problems   103

III   **Elements of Intertemporal Macroeconomics**   109

     4   The Composite-Commodity World   111

     5   The Multiple-Good World   137

     Problems   151

IV   An Intertemporal Approach to Fiscal Policies in the World Economy   159

6   Government Spending   161

7   Budget Deficits with Nondistortionary Taxes: The Pure Wealth Effect   195

8   An Exposition of the Two-Country Overlapping-Generations Model   219

V   Distortionary Tax Incentives: Concepts and Applications   255

9   Equivalence Relations in International Taxation   257

10   Budget Deficits with Distortionary Taxes   277

11   Fiscal Policies and the Real Exchange Rate   291

12   Capital Income Taxation in the Open Economy   315

Problems   325

VI   Stochastic Fiscal Policies   331

13   International Stock Markets and Fiscal Policy   333

Problems   348

VII   International Spillovers of Tax Policies: A Simulation Analysis   353

14   Spillover Effects of International VAT Harmonization   355

15   Spillover Effects of Budget Deficits   391

VIII Epilogue 397

    16 Analytical Overview 399

    17 Bibliographical Notes 419

Index 449

Preface to the Second Edition

Since our book came out in 1987, there has been a continuing process of increased economic integration among the industrialised economies, which culminated in the unification of the European market in 1992. The globalization process has resulted in growing interest in fiscal policies in the integrated world economy.

Concurrently, scientific progress has been made in three important directions:

1. The ongoing interaction between international economics and public economics has resulted in deepening and refinement of the overlapping area of research, international taxation. This progress in research can shed light on key policy issues, such as international tax competition and tax harmonization, effects of taxes on the location and destination of production, investment and saving, and the like.

2. Calibration and dynamic simulation methods have been applied to tax and budget issues to assess the policy-relevant dimensions of the more analytical treatment based on the traditional as well as the intertemporal approaches.

3. The incorporation of stochastic elements into international macroeconomics has become more widespread. The new developments in theory have proven to be especially useful for a more rigorous interpretation of international time series data.

These recent developments are incorporated into the Second Edition of *Fiscal Policies and the World Economy*.

Our original objective remains the same, to provide a comprehensive and coherent treatment of the intertemporal approach to international macroeconomics. Part I provides an overview of the facts and developments in the world economy in the last decade. To offer a self-contained treatment we devote part II to the traditional approach to fiscal policies in the open economy and part III to a systematic analysis of the key elements of the intertemporal approach. Part IV applies the intertemporal approach to key issues of spending and debt-tax policies. Extensions of the analysis to incorporate the effects of distortionary taxation on labor-leisure, saving-consumption, and investment choices are developed in part V. In part VI we extend the intertemporal framework to incorporate into the analysis risk-sharing behavior. The implications of the intertemporal model are illustrated by means of dynamic simulations in part VII. The simulations highlight the role of international considerations in the design of tax policies. Theoretical overview, extensions, and bibliographical notes are provided in part VIII.

Some of the new material in the revised edition draws on our previous work: chapters 3 and 16 draw on Jacob A. Frenkel and Assaf Razin, "Fiscal Policy in the Open Economy," in *The New Pelgrave Dictionary of Money and Finance*, Macmillan, 1992; chapter 9 draws on Alan Auerbach, Jacob A. Frenkel, and Assaf Razin, "Notes on International Taxation," mimeo, February 1987; chapter 11 draws on Jacob A. Frenkel and Assaf Razin, *Spending, Taxes, and Deficits: International-Intertemporal Approach*, International Finance Section, Princeton University, 1988; chapter 12 draws on Assaf Razin and Efraim Sadka, "Vanishing Tax on Capital Income in the Open Economy," Working Paper NBER 3796, 1991; chapter 13 draws on Assaf Razin, "Fiscal Policies and the Integrated World Stock Market," *Journal of International Economics*, 1990; and chapter 14 draws on Jacob A. Frenkel, Assaf Razin and Steve Symansky, "International VAT Harmonization: Macroeconomic Effects," *IMF Staff Papers*, 1991. We are indebted to Alan Auerbach, Efraim Sadka, and Steve Symansky for agreeing to include in the book chapters drawing on our joint work.

By covering a full line of topics in international economics, the book has been used successfully in graduate courses in international economics, and recently has been translated to Japanese and Spanish. To increase its classroom usefulness, we include at the end of each analytical chapter a set of problems and exercises prepared by Tom Krueger and Jonathan Ostry. A companion manual, *Exercises in Intertemporal Open-Economy Macroeconomics*, by Thomas H. Krueger and Jonathan D. Ostry, contains a detailed analysis and solutions to the exercises.

We are indebted to numerous students and colleagues for useful comments on the revision. We wish to thank especially Alan Auerbach, Efraim Sadka, Tom Krueger, Jonathan Ostry, Steve Symansky, Steve Turnovsky, Alberto Giovannini, Torsten Persson, and Enrique Mendoza.

Preface to the First Edition

Recent theoretical developments in closed-economy macroeconomics have not yet been fully incorporated into the main corpus of international macroeconomics. This book aims at filling this void. We develop a unified conceptual framework suitable for the analysis of the effects of government expenditure and tax policies on key macroeconomic aggregates in the interdependent world economy.

The analysis is motivated by stylized facts characterizing recent major developments. These include unsynchronized changes in national fiscal policies resulting in large budgetary imbalances, volatile real rates of interest, sharp changes in real exchange rates, and significant imbalances in national current account positions. Associated with these developments were drastic changes in public-sector debt and in the international allocation of external debt. Although these real-world developments provide the impetus for the analysis, the orientation of the book is theoretical. Its purpose is to identify and clarify the main channels and the pertinent economic mechanisms through which government-spending and tax policies influence the world economic system. We develop a unified coherent theory capable of interpreting the stylized facts and at the same time, provide a framework for the analysis of the normative issues related to the welfare implications of fiscal policies in the world economy.

The main characteristic of the analysis is the detailed attention given to dynamic and intertemporal considerations. In contrast with the more traditional analyses, the modern approach is based on solid microeconomic foundations. These foundations "discipline" the analysis and impose constraints on the modeling of macroeconomic behavior. Specifically, an explicit account of temporal and intertemporal budget constraints and of the forward-looking behavior consistent with these constraints restrict the permissible behavior of households and governments and thereby sharpen the predictive content of the economic theory. Furthermore, by deriving the economic behavior from utility maximization, the modern analytical framework allows for meaningful treatment of issues in welfare economics.

The resulting macroeconomic model is capable of dealing with new issues in consistent manner. Among these issues are the effects of various time patterns of government spending and taxes. We can thus distinguish between temporary and permanent, as well as between current and expected future policies. Likewise, the model is capable of analyzing the macroeconomic consequences of alternative specifications of the tax structure, including the effects of different types of taxes (income tax, value-added tax, etc.).

By being grounded on solid microeconomic foundations, this approach to open-economy macroeconomics narrows the gap between the modes of analysis typical to the branch of international economics dealing with the pure theory of international trade and the branch dealing with open-economy macroeconomics.

To provide a self-contained treatment of the subject matter and to motivate the logical progression of the analysis, we devote a part of the book to a review and a synthesis of traditional approaches to open-economy macroeconomics. This part yields the rationale for the developments of the modern treatment which is the key contribution of the book. In addition it also provides the analytical continuity and completeness necessary for the use of this book as a text. Readers familiar with the traditional approach to international macroeconomics may skip part II (chapters 2 through 3).

The focus of this inquiry is the international dimensions of fiscal policies. This instrument of macroeconomic policy is placed at the center stage for two reasons. First, budget deficits in major industrial countries have played a leading role in the world economic scene in recent years. The prominance of, and the complex interactions among, budget policies and key macroeconomic variables in the world economy provide a justification for a book-length study that focuses on various aspects of this policy instrument. Second, even though we touch in various chapters on some issues of monetary policy, we believe that in contrast with fiscal policies, the state of the art of monetary economics is not yet ripe for an analogous unified comprehensive treatment of the international dimensions of monetary policies based on solid microeconomic foundations.

This book was written while J. A. Frenkel was the David Rockefeller Professor of International Economics at the University of Chicago and A. Razin was the Daniel and Grace Ross Professor of International Economics at Tel-Aviv University. Our joint work on the international dimensions of fiscal policies started at Tel-Aviv University in the fall of 1983. During this period, as well as during the summer of 1985, J. A. Frenkel was a fellow at the Sackler Institute of Advanced Studies and a Visiting Professor in the Department of Economics. Our collaboration continued during the winter of 1984 while A. Razin held a visiting professorship at Princeton University. The main work on the book was carried out at the University of Chicago during the spring, summer, and fall of 1986 while A. Razin was a visiting professor in the Department of Economics and the Graduate School of Business. Further work was done in Cambridge, Massachusetts, during our participation in the summer institute sessions of the National Bureau of Economic Research (1984 to 1986), as well as in Washington, D.C., during our visit to the World Bank in the summer of 1986. We wish to thank these institutions for providing a comfortable and stimulating environment which made this research and the preparation of the book possible.

Some of the chapters in this book draw on material contained in our joint articles. Chapter 4 is based on "The Mundell-Fleming Model: A Quarter Century Later" (*IMF Staff Papers*, forthcoming). Chapters 5, 7, and 8 draw on "Spending, Taxes and Deficits: International-Intertemporal Approach" (*Princeton Studies in International Finance*, forthcoming) and on "Deficits with Distortionary Taxes: International Dimensions" (NBER, Working Paper No. 2080, November 1986). Chapter 9 draws on "Fiscal Policies and Real Exchange Rates in the World Economy" (NBER, Working Paper No. 2065, November 1986). Chapters 10 through 13 draw on our articles, "Government Spending, Debt and International Economic Interdependence" (*Economic Journal* 95, September 1985:619–636); "Fiscal Expenditures and International Economic Interdependence" (in W. H. Buiter and R. C. Marston, eds., *International Economic Policy Coordination*, Cambridge: Cambridge University Press, 1985:37–73); "The International Transmission and Effects of Fiscal Policies" (*American Economic Review* 76, May 1986:330–335); "Fiscal Policies in the World Economy" (*Journal of Political Economy* 94, June 1986:564–594); "Real Exchange Rates, Interest Rates and Fiscal Policies" (*The Economic Studies Quarterly* 37, June 1986:99–113); and "The International Transmission of Fiscal Expenditures and budget Deficits in the World Economy" (in A. Razin and E. Sadka, eds., *Economic Policy in Theory and Practice*, London: Macmillan, 1987:51–96). Finally, some of the arguments in chapter 15 draw on "The Limited Viability of Dual Exchange-Rate Regimes" (NBER, Working Paper No. 1902, April 1986) and "Exchange-Rate Management Viewed as Tax Policies" (unpublished manuscript, 1987).

During the course of this research we have benefited from useful coments and suggestions by Joshua Aizenman, Alan Auerbach, Olivier Blanchard, William Branson, Willem Buiter, Guillermo Calvo, Avinash Dixit, Rudiger

Dornbusch, Martin Feldstein, Stanley Fischer, Robert Flood, John Geweke, Itzhak Gilboa, Jeremy Greenwood, Vittorio Grilli, Koichi Hamada, Elhanan Helpman, Peter Howitt, John Huizinga, Kent Kimbrough, Robert Lucas, Franco Modigliani, Michael Mussa, Maurice Obstfeld, Torsten Persson, Thomas Sargent, Don Schlagenhauf, Alan Stockman, Larry Summers, and Lars Svensson. During the past three years we have also received numerous suggestions in seminars and workshops at the Brookings Institution, the University of Chicago, CEPR (London), CEPREMAP (Paris), Columbia University, Duke University, Harvard University, Hebrew University, International House in Tokyo, the University of Michigan, MIT, NBER (Cambridge), New York University, Princeton University, Stanford University, Tel-Aviv University, University of Washington, University of Western Ontario, the World Bank, and the Latin-American Econometric Society meeting held in Cordoba.

In preparing the book we benefited from comments and efficient research assistance by our graduate students at the University of Chicago, including Ken Kasa, Thomas Krueger, Jonathan Ostry, and Kei-Mu Yi. We owe special thanks to Thomas Krueger who thoroughly read the entire manuscript and provided us with numerous comments and suggestions that improved the presentation and sharpened the arguments.

We wish to thank June Nason of the University of Chicago for her tireless efforts and high efficiency in cheerfully typing successive drafts of the manuscript. Her willingness to work long hours is deeply appreciated. Thanks are also due to Terry Vaughn, the economics editor at the MIT Press, for his remarkable professionalism and dedication in the various stages of this enterprise.

The writing of a jointly authored book under a very tight time schedule always entails complicated arrangements, coordination, and discipline. In our case the need for transatlantic communications added logistical difficulties that could not have been surmounted without the understanding, selflessness, and unfailing support of our wives, Niza Frenkel and Shula Razin. It is only appropriate that we dedicate this book to them.

J. A. F
A. R.
February 1987

I

Prologue

1

Stylized Facts on Fiscal Policies and International Economic Interdependence

This book deals with the international dimensions of fiscal policies. The opening chapter surveys key facts relevant for the analysis of the effects of government spending and tax policies in the world economy. The empirical regularities exhibited by the stylized facts serve to identify the issues and the macroeconomic variables that play central roles in the interdependent world economy. The main purpose of the discussion in this chapter is to motivate the theoretical analysis that follows.

We devote the first section of this chapter to a brief review of major developments related to the effects of public-sector spending policies and budget deficits during the 1980s. Relative to other recent periods, this decade stands out in terms of the major changes taking place in the fiscal policies of the major countries. To identify empirical relations among the key economic variables that are likely to be related to, and influenced by fiscal policies, we present in section 1.2 summary statistics pertaining to comovements among these variables. The summary statistics describe various combinations of temporal, intertemporal, and international correlations among the key variables. These correlations, together with the stylized facts outlined in section 1.1, can be useful in the construction of theoretical models. The final section of this chapter summarizes key characteristics emerging from the data. These characteristics provide a guide to the choice of variables incorporated into the analytical framework, and they highlight issues that need to be addressed by the theory.

1.1 Selected Facts

During the 1980s the world economy was subject to large and unsynchronized changes in fiscal policies, high and volatile real rates of interest, large fluctuations in real exchange rates and significant variations in private-sector spending. During this period national fiscal policies have exhibited large divergencies. The United States adopted an expansionary course while the other major countries taken together followed a relatively contractionary course. These policies undertaken by the major economies affected the rest of the world through the integrated goods and capital markets, and resulted in increased concern in each country over policy measures undertaken in the rest of the world.

Since the beginning of 1980 short- and long-term real rates of interest exhibited different patterns. As illustrated in figure 1.1, a weighted average of the annual short-term real interest rates in the five major industrial countries (the United States, Japan, France, West Germany, and the United Kingdom) rose from about 2.0 percent at the beginning of 1980 to about 5.0 percent in 1986; the short-term rate then fell to about 4.0 percent at the end of the decade. The corresponding long-term rates rose from about 0.5 percent in early 1980 to about 8.0 percent in 1984, to about 3–4 percent in 1989–90. Both rates peaked and surpassed 8 percent in mid-1982. Thus, during 1980 to 1985, real rates of interest were high (in comparison with early 1980) and the slope of the real yield curve, which was negative until the third quarter of 1981, turned positive starting from mid-1982; while real interest rates fell further in 1986, they rose again in 1987. Toward the end of the decade the slope of the real yield curve became negative.

The decade also witnessed sharp changes in real exchange rates. In the first quarter of 1985 the real effective value of the U.S. dollar (calculated on the basis of unit labor cost) was about 43 percent above its average value for the decade 1974 to 1983 and 57 percent above its low point of the third quarter of 1980. By the end of the decade the real effective value of the U.S. dollar was about 35 percent below the 1985 peak. Likewise, in the last quarter of 1985 the real effective value of the Japanese yen was about 50 percent above its low point in the first quarter of 1980. By 1989 the real effective value of the Japanese yen was about 35 percent higher than its mid-1980s level. The other major currencies (especially the British pound, the French franc, and the Italian lira) have also exhibited very large fluctuations. Figure 1.2 illustrates the extent of the changes in the effective nominal exchange rates of the U.S. dollar, Japanese yen, British pound, German mark, French franc, Canadian dollar, and Italian lira. The sharp changes in the real exchange rates (as measured by the relative GDP deflators and by the relative unit labor costs) are shown in figure 1.3. As shown by these figures, the U.S. dollar, after several years of consecutive appreciation, depreciated significantly beginning in March 1985. Its depreciation continued throughout 1988. Correspondingly, the currencies of other major

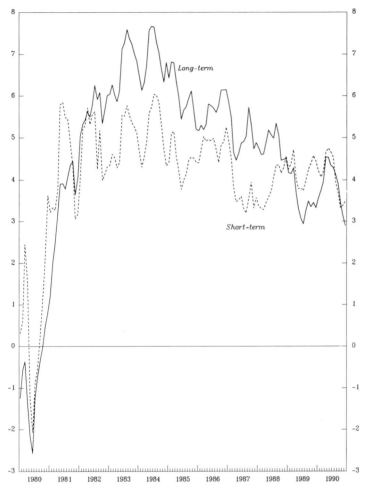

1/ Weighted by the average U.S. dollar value of GNP's over the preceding three years.

Figure 1.1
Five major industrial countries: Short- and long-term real interest rates, January 1980 to December 1990

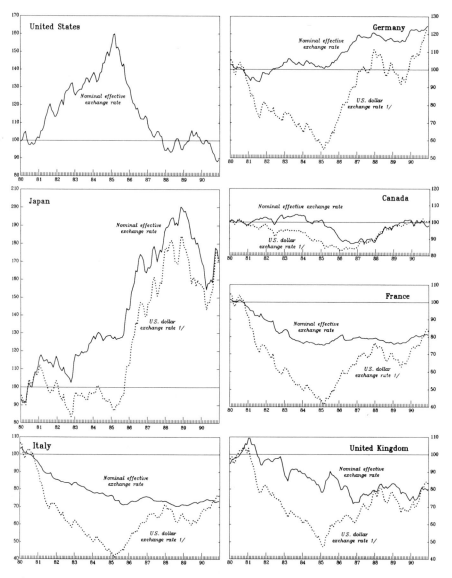

1/ U.S. dollar exchange rate is measured as the U.S. dollar value of the domestic currency.

Figure 1.2
Major industrial countries: Exchange rates vis-à-vis U.S. dollar and indexes of nominal effective exchange rates, January 1980 to December 1990

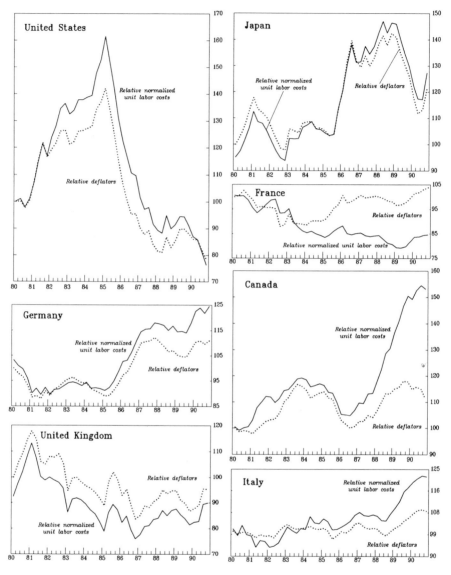

Figure 1.3
Major industrial countries: Indexes of real effective exchange rates, first quarter 1980 to
fourth quarter 1990

industrial countries, especially Japan and West Germany, appreciated in nominal and real terms throughout the decade.

Another key fact characterizing this period is the large and divergent pattern of the current-account positions of the major industrial countries. These divergencies are especially pronounced in the comparison between the developments of the current-account positions of the United States with that of Japan and Germany. For example, the U.S. current-account position switched from a surplus of about 0.25 percent of GNP in 1980 to a deficit of about 3 percent of GNP in 1985. The deficit in the U.S. current account remained throughout the 1980s, but declined to about 1.8 percent of GNP in 1990. During 1980–1986 the current-account position of Japan switched from a deficit of about 1 percent of GNP in 1980 to a surplus of about 4.4 percent of GNP in 1986. The Japanese surplus declined toward the end of the decade and reached the level of 1.7 percent of GNP in 1990. Likewise the current-account position of Germany also switched from a deficit of about 1.7 percent of GNP in 1980 to a surplus of about 4.4 percent of GNP in 1986 and then declined to 3.3 percent in 1990. These developments in the current accounts of the balance of payments reflected themselves in correspondingly large changes in the external debt position of these countries. (The source of the data used in this section is International Monetary Fund: *World Economic Outlook*.)

These developments in real interest rates, real exchange rates, and current-account positions were associated with large and divergent changes in world fiscal policies. The budget deficit of the general U.S. government as a fraction of GNP rose from about 1 percent in 1980 to about 3.5 percent in 1985 (after reaching a peak of 3.8 percent in 1983). The deficit stabilized at about 1.7 percent of GNP in 1986–90. At the same time the budget deficit as a fraction of GNP declined in Japan until 1986 and became a surplus of about 3 percent of GNP toward the end of the decade. Similarly the 1977–86 average budget deficit of about 3.7 percent of GNP in the United Kingdom turned into a surplus in 1987–90 of about 1 percent, on average. In Germany the 1977–88 deficit of about 2.4 percent, on average, turned to surplus in 1989 and then switched to a deficit of about 3–4 percent in 1990–91, following the unification of Germany. Similarly, since 1982, according to IMF measures, the fiscal impulse (which is a more exogenous measure of fiscal policy) has been expansionary for Canada, France, and the United States and contractionary for the other industrial countries taken together. This pattern is shown in figure 1.4, in which a positive fiscal impulse indicates injection of stimulus while a negative impulse indicates withdrawal of stimulus.

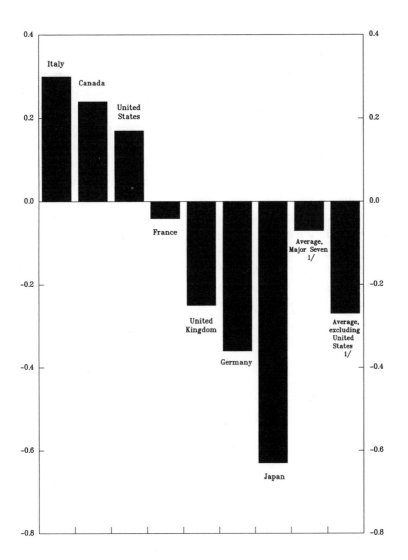

1/ Weighted by U.S. dollar GNP's in the preceding three years.

Figure 1.4
Fiscal impulses for the major industrial countries (in percent of GDP at annual rates, 1982–1990)

The cumulative implications of the budgetary imbalances are reflected in the size of public debt. The rapid rise in net public debt as a ratio of GNP in Germany and Japan leveled off toward the end of the first half decade of the 1980s (at around one-quarter of GNP). In the United Kingdom the same quantity remained relatively stable at around one-half of GNP. On the other hand, and in contrast with these countries, the ratio of net government debt to GNP in the United States rose sharply during the same period from about one-fifth of GNP to close to one-third of GNP. These developments are reflected in a relative rise of the debt-service burden imposed on the U.S. government budget.

Another indicator of the levels and divergencies among national fiscal policies is provided by a comparison among annual percentage changes in public-sector consumption. As seen in table 1.1, the percentage annual growth of U.S. public-sector consumption accelerated in the second part of the period, exceeding 7 percent in 1985, and then decelerating to 3.1 percent in 1989. During the late 1970s and early 1980s, public-sector consumption in Japan and Europe grew faster than in the United States (the difference for Japan reaching 3.3 percent in 1981, and for Europe 2.2 percent

Table 1.1
Differences in private and public consumption: United States, Japan, and Europe, 1977–1990 (in percent per annum)

	United States		United States minus Japan		United States minus Europe	
	Private	Public	Private	Public	Private	Public
1977	4.4	1.5	0.3	−2.6	1.4	0.2
1978	4.1	2.6	−1.3	−2.5	0.1	−1.3
1979	2.2	0.8	−4.3	−3.5	−1.9	−2.2
1980	−0.2	1.9	−1.3	−1.4	−2.0	−0.4
1981	1.2	1.5	−0.4	−3.3	0.6	−0.4
1982	1.3	1.9	−3.1	−0.1	0.4	0.6
1983	4.7	1.1	1.2	−1.9	2.8	−0.6
1984	4.8	4.4	2.1	1.7	3.3	2.7
1985	4.7	7.9	1.3	6.2	2.2	6.0
1986	3.9	4.2	0.5	−0.3	−0.4	2.0
1987	2.8	2.3	−1.4	1.9	−0.9	0.1
1988	3.6	0.2	−1.6	−2.0	−0.5	−2.0
1989	1.9	2.3	−2.4	0.1	−0.9	2.4
1990	0.9	2.8	−3.1	1.4	−2.0	0.4

Source: Computed from data in IMF, *World Economic Outlook*, May 1991; and IMF, *International Financial Statistics*.

in 1979), and during 1984–85, public-sector consumption in Japan and Europe grew more slowly (the difference in "favor'" of the United States reaching in 1985 6.2 percent in comparison with Japan and 5.9 percent in comparison with Europe). In the second half of the decade, public consumption in the United States and Japan exhibited roughly the same growth rates, but growth rate of the United States exceeded that of Europe.

Concomitantly, the anual percentage changes in real private-sector consumption also displayed large fluctuations that differed across countries. In the United States these changes ranged from −0.2 percent in 1980 to 4.8 percent in 1984, and, as seen in table 1.1, the growth of private-sector consumption in Japan exceeded that in the United States during 1979–82, fell short of it during 1983–86, and exceeded it during 1987–89. The growth of private-sector consumption in Europe exceeded that in the United States during 1978–81, fell short of it during 1982–85, and then exceeded the rate in the United States in 1986–89. As illustrated in table 1.2, the international differentials among growth rates of GNP and of fixed investment also displayed a similar pattern.

Table 1.2
Differences in real GNP and gross fixed investment: United States, Japan, and Europe, 1977–1990 (in percent per annum)

	United States		United States minus Japan		United States minus Europe	
	GNP	Investment	GNP	Investment	GNP	Investment
1977	4.7	14.1	−0.1	11.3	1.8	13.6
1978	5.3	9.8	0.3	2.0	1.8	7.1
1979	2.5	3.7	−3.2	−2.5	−1.5	−1.2
1980	−0.2	−7.9	−3.6	−7.9	−1.3	−10.0
1981	1.9	1.1	−1.5	−1.3	1.7	5.6
1982	−2.5	−9.6	−6.0	−9.4	−3.3	−7.8
1983	3.6	8.2	0.8	9.1	1.8	7.0
1984	6.8	16.8	2.5	12.1	4.5	14.7
1985	3.4	5.3	−1.8	0.0	1.0	3.5
1986	2.7	1.0	0.1	−3.8	−0.0	−2.2
1987	3.4	1.9	−0.9	−7.7	0.7	−3.2
1988	4.5	5.6	−1.8	−6.4	0.4	−2.6
1989	2.5	1.6	−2.2	−7.3	−0.7	−4.4
1990	1.0	−0.1	−4.7	−11.0	−1.7	−4.1

Source: Computed from data in IMF, *World Economic Outlook*, May 1991; and IMF, *International Financial Statistics*.

1.2 Comovements of Key Economic Variables in the World Economy: Summary Statistics

In this section we present stylized facts concerning the comovements of selected economic variables. These facts are based on data pertaining to the thirty-year period from 1955 to 1989 (obtained from IMF, *International Financial Statistics*). In so doing, we gain insight into some of the empirical regularities characterizing the international transmission mechanism of economic policies and exogenous shocks. We start by presenting figures showing the international comovements of some key variables and proceed with the presentation of summary statistics concerning the temporal, intertemporal, and international correlations among these variables. Throughout, we focus on the seven major industrial countries: Canada, United States, Japan, France, Germany, Italy, and the United Kingdom. We divide these countries into two blocks: the United States and the "rest-of-the-world" (comprised of the other six countries taken together as an aggregate). Our analysis of the stylized fact is based on this "two-country" world economy.

Figures 1.5 and 1.6 show, respectively, the international comovements of the rates of growth of government consumption and of (gross) tax revenue. The main features exhibited by these figures are the large amplitude of these series, the low contemporaneous international correlation between growth rates of government consumption, and the somewhat higher correlation between the growth rates of tax revenue (as reported in table 1.3, the correlation between growth rates of public consumption is 0.14, while we found that the tax-revenue correlation is 0.26 for the period 1955−85). As shown in figure 1.5, the largest changes in the growth rate of U.S. government consumption occurred in the second half of the 1960s in conjunction with the Vietnam War. It is relevant to note, however, that significant variations also took place in other years.

The pattern of tax revenue show in figure 1.6 reflects in large measure the growth rates of GNP shown in figure 1.7. Indeed, for 1955−85 the contemporaneous correlation between the growth rates of GNP and of tax revenue is 0.64 in the United States and 0.44 in the rest-of-the-world. The comovements of GNP growth rates reflect the outcomes of macroeconomic policies, as well as external and internal shocks. All these manifest themselves in the characteristics of the international transmission of business cycles. For example, the high correlation exhibited during the period 1973 to 1976 reflects the common external shock associated with the first oil crisis. On the other hand, the low correlation exhibited during the early part

Figure 1.5
Growth rates of government consumption: United States (thin line) versus rest-of-the-world (thick line)

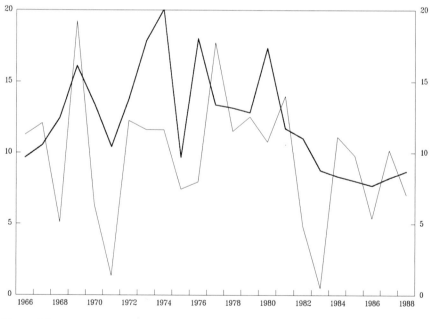

Figure 1.6
Growth rates of tax revenue: United States (thin line) versus rest-of-the-world (thick line)

Table 1.3
National and international contemporaneous correlations of growth rates, 1955–90 (in percent per annum)

	Y	I	C	G	Y*	I*	C*	G*	C + C*
Y	1.00								
I	0.92	1.00							
C	0.84	0.81	1.00						
G	0.10	−0.12	−0.01	1.00					
Y*	0.52	0.45	0.51	−0.10	1.00				
I*	0.43	0.34	0.34	−0.07	0.86	1.00			
C*	0.42	0.36	0.50	−0.21	0.89	0.77	1.00		
G*	0.09	−0.01	0.05	0.14	0.26	0.04	0.35	1.00	
C + C*	0.74	0.69	0.88	−0.12	0.80	0.63	0.85	0.22	1.00

Note: Y = GNP, I = private-sector investment, C = private-sector consumption, G = government consumption, and an asterisk (*) denotes "rest-of-the-world" variables, which are constructed as weighted averages of real growth rates. Each country's weight corresponds to the average over the previous three years of the U.S. dollar value of its GNP as a fraction of the six-country sum of the U.S. dollar values of GNP.

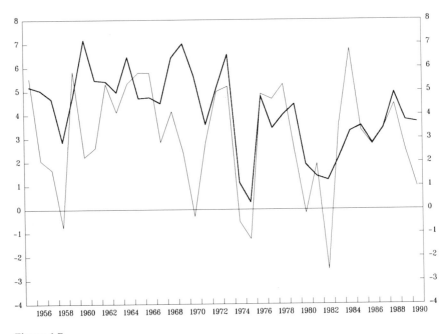

Figure 1.7
Growth rates of GNP: United States (thin line) versus rest-of-the-world (thick line)

Figure 1.8
Growth rates of private-sector consumption: United States (thin line) versus rest-of-the-world (thick line)

of the 1980s reflects the divergencies of internal policies (discussed in section 1.1). On the whole, as indicated in table 1.3, the international correlation between the gowth rates over the entire period is 0.55.

Changes in the fiscal stance (government spending and tax revenue) and the induced changes in GNP are associated with corresponding adjustments of private-sector spending (consumption and investment). Figure 1.8 shows the international comovements of the rates of growth of private-sector consumption. As revealed by this figure, in some years (especially during the first half of the period) the growth rates of private-sector consumption were negatively correlated internationally, whereas in other years (especially during the second half of the period) these growth rates were positively correlated. On the whole, as indicated by table 1.3, the international correlation over the entire period was 0.50. We also note that during the second half of the period, the amplitude of this series for the United States exceeds that of the rest of the world.

Finally, figure 1.9 shows the comovements of the rates of growth of investment. Typically, the amplitude of these series is very high (exceeding those of the other series), and the United States exhibits higher volatility than the rest-of-the-world. As for the international correlations, table 1.3

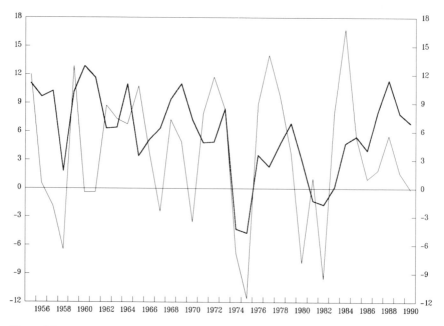

Figure 1.9
Growth rates of private-sector investment: United States (thin line) versus rest-of-the-world (thick line)

indicates that overall there is a (weak) positive correlation between the United States and the rest-of-the-world series. In general (as with tax revenue), the rates of growth of investment in both the United States and the rest-of-the world are highly correlated with the corresponding growth rates of GNP. As indicated in table 1.3, these correlations are 0.92 for the United States, and 0.86 for the rest-of-the-world.

The bilateral pairwise relations exhibited by figures 1.5 through 1.9 is supplemented by the national and international time-series correlations reported in tables 1.3 and 1.4. Noteworthy among these correlations is the persistence of growth rates of domestic and foreign government consumption as reflected by the magnitudes of the autocorrelation coefficients (0.55 for the United States and 0.37 for the rest-of-the-world). The other feature revealed by the correlations is the relatively high positive association between the growth rates of current (and lagged) government spending of the rest-of-the-world and the corresponding growth rates of foreign output, consumption, and investment. The association between the growth rate of current U.S. government spending and the corresponding growth rates of U.S. GNP and private-sector consumption is positive, but relatively weak.

Table 1.4
International and intertemporal correlations of growth rates: autocorrelations with one-year lag, 1955–1990 (in percent per annum)

	Y	I	C	G	Y*	I*	C*	G*	C + C*
Y^{-1}	0.18	0.06	0.05	0.35	0.36	0.31	0.32	0.02	0.21
I^{-1}	0.18	0.13	0.08	0.19	0.32	0.28	0.32	0.03	0.23
C^{-1}	0.40	0.32	0.30	0.19	0.51	0.41	0.45	0.02	0.44
G^{-1}	0.18	0.02	0.23	0.55	0.10	0.09	0.07	−0.03	0.18
Y^{*-1}	−0.01	−0.05	−0.15	0.03	0.49	0.41	0.48	0.31	0.18
I^{*-1}	−0.09	−0.13	−0.25	0.06	0.46	0.52	0.42	0.10	0.08
C^{*-1}	0.10	0.03	−0.05	−0.11	0.61	0.52	0.59	0.35	0.30
G^{*-1}	0.16	0.09	0.11	0.04	0.32	0.05	0.34	0.37	0.26
$C^{-1} + C^{*-1}$	0.30	0.21	0.16	0.06	0.64	0.54	0.59	0.21	0.43

Note: For identification of variables and explanation of weighting scheme, see table 1.3; the subscript $^{-1}$ indicates one-year lag.

However, the (positive) correlation between the growth rates, one-period lagged, of U.S. government spending and the growth rates of U.S. GNP and private-sector consumption are more sizable. Finally, it is relevant to note that the contemporaneous correlation between U.S. government spending and U.S. investment is negative (−0.12).

1.3 Facts and Theory

The selected facts from the 1980s, along with the correlations obtained from the more extended time period, serve as a guide for the selection of variables and for the identification of channels through which the effects of fiscal policy are transmitted throughout the world economy. Accordingly, the discussion in section 1.1 suggests that in modeling the international effects of fiscal policies, allowance should be made for the special role that real exchange rates, short- and long-term interest rates, current-account adjustment, and the size of foreign debt play in the international transmission mechanism. A proper theory of the effects of fiscal policy on the interdependent world economy should be capable of clarifying the mechanisms underlying the varying patterns of responses of these macroeconomic variables to such policies. Furthermore the theory should also illuminate and uncover the economic forces responsible for the large fluctuations and for the varying cross-country correlations of private-sector consumption, investment, and output growth rates.

The comovements of the key economic variables discussed in section 1.2 also indicate the significance of an additional consideration that should be incorporated into theoretical modeling of interdependencies. The correlations imply that the timing of the various fiscal measures plays a critical role. In this context the degree of persistence exhibited by the series measuring growth rates of government spending, and the lack of such a persistence in the growth rates of tax revenues suggest that the theory should distinguish between permanent and transitory policies.

The stylized facts reported in this chapter motivate the choice of topics and issues examined in this book. Although the various real-world developments provide the impetus for the analysis, the orientation of the book is theoretical. Its purpose is to identify and clarify the main channels and the pertinent mechanisms through which government-spending and tax policies influence the world economic system. The models that are developed are aimed at providing a coherent theory capable of interpreting the stylized facts, and at the same time, they provide a framework for the analysis of the normative issues related to the desirability of fiscal policies in the interdependent world economy.

In part II of this book we introduce the key issues and concepts within the traditional income-expenditure models of interdependent economies. These models attempt to clarify the factors underlying the patterns of co-movements of national outputs, consumption, investment, and fiscal policies observed in the data. Following the presentation of the traditional income-expenditure models, we review their limitations and proceed in parts III through VII to develop an approach that highlights important intertemporal considerations. Factors playing a critical role in this approach include forward-looking behavior, private and public-sectors' intertemporal solvency, and the specification of the precise time pattern of policies. This approach, which rests on solid microeconomic foundations, permits a meaningful analysis of the welfare implications of government-spending and tax policies.

II

Traditional Approaches to Fiscal Policies and International Economic Interdependence

2

The Income-Expenditure Model:
Fiscal Policies and the Determination
of Output

This chapter, along with chapter 3, is devoted to the presentation of the traditional income-expenditure approach to open-economy macroeconomics. Its focus on factors underlying the determination of output reflects a Keynesian heritage. The great depression of the 1930s, and the "beggar thy neighbor" policies adopted during that period by many countries, stimulated the development of this approach. Interest in this type of modeling is also stimulated by the observation (reported in tables 1.3 and 1.4 of chapter 1) on the cross-country correlations between private-sector absorption, government spending, and, in particular, national outputs.

In this chapter we outline the analytical framework of the income-expenditure model of the world economy. This framework is employed in the subsequent analysis of fiscal policies and income determination. Here we present a "Keynesian" two-country model in which prices are given while the levels of output and employment adjust in response to changes in aggregate demand. A similar framework could present a "classical" model in which the assumptions concerning the fixity of prices and the flexibility of output and employment are replaced by the assumption that prices are flexible while output is given at the full employment level. The analytical framework outlined in section 2.1 serves both of these analyses.

2.1 The Analytical Framework of the Income-Expenditure Model

Consider a two-country model of the world economy. The two countries are referred to as the home (domestic) country and the foreign country. Each country produces a distinct commodity: the domestic economy produces good x, and the foreign economy produces good m. The domestic level of output is denoted by Y_x, and the foreign level of output by Y_m^*. Throughout the analysis foreign variables are denoted by an asterisk. We assume that there is one noninterest-bearing asset—money, whose domestic and foreign quantities are denoted by M and M^*, respectively. The budget constraint requires that during each period, t, the value of the resources at the disposal of individuals equal the value of the uses of these resources. Accordingly, the domestic and foreign budget constraints are

$$Z_t^* + M_t = P_t(Y_{xt} - T_t) + M_{t-1}, \tag{2.1}$$

$$Z_t^* + M_t^* = P_t^*(Y_{mt}^* - T_t^*) + M_{t-1}^*, \tag{2.2}$$

where Z_t and P_t denote, respectively, nominal spending and the GDP deflator, and where Y_{xt} and T_t denote, respectively, real GDP and real taxes—both measured in terms of the domestic good. Equation (2.1) states that the individuals who allocate their resources between spending (Z_t) and asset holding (M_t) are constrained by the total available resources. These resources are the value of disposable income $[P_t(Y_{xt} - T_t)]$ and assets carried over from the previous period (M_{t-1}). As revealed by this formulation, money serves as a store of value facilitating the transfer of purchasing power from one period to the next. Similar notations (with an asterisk) and a similar interpretation apply to the foreign country budget constraint in equation (2.2).

In characterizing the behavior of domestic and foreign individuals, suppose that the desired levels of spending and asset holding depend only on the values of currently available resources. Thus, making use of the budget constraints, the *spending functions* are

$$Z_t = Z(P_t y_{xt}, M_{t-1}), \tag{2.3}$$

$$Z_t^* = Z^*(P_t^* y_{mt}^*, M_{t-1}^*), \tag{2.4}$$

where y_{xt} and y_{mt}^* denote, respectively, the values of domestic and foreign real disposable incomes ($Y_x - T$ and $Y_m^* - T^*$). Analogously, the implied money-demand functions are

$$M_t = M(P_t y_{xt}, M_{t-1}), \tag{2.5}$$

$$M_t^* = M^*(P_t^* y_{mt}^*, M_{t-1}^*). \tag{2.6}$$

In this formulation we have specified the spending and the money-demand functions in nominal terms. Naturally the choice of units of measurement should not affect individuals' behavior with respect to real spending and real money demand. It follows that the *nominal* spending and money-demand functions are homogeneous of degree one in their arguments. Accordingly, we can define the *real spending functions* by

$$E_t = E\left(y_{xt}, \frac{M_{t-1}}{P_t}\right), \tag{2.7}$$

$$E_t^* = E^*\left(y_{mt}^*, \frac{M_{t-1}^*}{P_t^*}\right), \tag{2.8}$$

where $E_t = Z_t/P_t$ denotes the real value of domestic spending measured in terms of the domestic good, and where $E_t^* = Z_t^*/P_t^*$ denotes the real value of foreign spending, measured in terms of the foreign good.

The marginal propensity to save out of income, s, is assumed to be positive but less than unity, and thus the marginal propensity to spend, $1 - s$, is a positive fraction. Likewise, the marginal propensity to spend out of assets is positive. Similar properties characterize the foreign-spending function.

The domestic private sector is assumed to allocate its spending between domestic goods, C_{xt}, and foreign goods, C_{mt}. Analogously, the foreign private sector also allocates its spending between these two goods, C_{xt}^* and C_{mt}^*. Thus the real values of domestic and foreign spending (each measured in terms of own GDP) are

$$E_t = C_{xt} + p_{mt}C_{mt}, \tag{2.9}$$

$$E_t^* = \frac{1}{p_{mt}}C_{xt}^* + C_{mt}^*, \tag{2.10}$$

where p_{mt} denotes the *relative* price of good m in terms of good x. This relative price is assumed to be equalized across countries through international trade. The relative share of domestic spending on good m (the foreign good) is denoted by $\beta_m = p_{mt}C_{mt}/E_t$. Likewise, the relative share of foreign spending on good x (the good produced by the home country) is denoted by $\beta_x^* = C_{xt}^*/p_{mt}E_t^*$. Thus β_m and β_x^* are the relative shares of domestic and foreign spending on their corresponding importable good. These expenditure shares are assumed to be constant.

The levels of real government spending in period t in each country (measured in terms of own GDP) are denoted by G_t and G_t^*, respectively. Analogously to the private sectors, the governments also allocate their spending between the two goods. Domestic government spending on importables (good m) is $\beta_m^g G_t/p_{mt}$, and foreign government spending on their importables (good x) is $\beta_x^{g*} p_{mt} G_t^*$, where β_m^g and β_x^{g*} denote, respectively, the domestic and foreign relative shares of government spending on importables.

The surplus in the domestic economy's *trade account* in period t, $(TA)_t$, is defined as the difference between its exports and imports. The economy's export equals the difference between domestic production and national consumption of exportables, where the latter consists of private-sector and government purchases. Here exports are $Y_{xt} - [(1 - \beta_m)E_t + (1 - \beta_m^g)G_t]$. Analogously, the economy's imports equal the difference between national consumption and production of importables. Here, since in the present formulation the importable good is not produced domestically, imports are $\beta_m E_t + \beta_m^g G_t$. It follows that the trade-balance surplus can be expressed as the difference between GDP and national spending (absorption):

$$(TA)_t = Y_{xt} - (E_t + G_t). \tag{2.11}$$

Equation (2.11) can be used together with the budget constraint (2.1) to yield

$$M_t - M_{t-1} = P_t[(TA)_t - (T_t - G_t)] \tag{2.12}$$

Equation (2.12) expresses private savings (the accumulation of assets by the private sector) as the difference between national savings (indicated by the trade-balance surplus) and government savings (indicated by the surplus in the government budget).

We assume that the economy operates under a fixed exchange-rate regime and that the exchange rate is pegged by the monetary authority. The absence of interest-bearing debt implies that discrepancies between government spending and taxes are met by corresponding changes in the money supply. Thus, abstracting from the commercial-banking system, changes in the money supply reflect two activities of the monetary authorities: those associated with pegging the exchange rate, and those associated with financing government budget deficits. The two terms on the right-hand side of equation (2.12) correspond to these two sources of changes in the money supply. The first is the surplus in the official settlements account of the balance of payments, indicating the official accumulation of international reserves induced by the exchange-rate-pegging operation of the monetary authorities. Since in the present stage of the analysis we do not allow for international borrowing and lending, the official settlements balance equals the trade-balance surplus, $P_t(TA)_t$. The second term on the right-hand side of equation (2.12) is the monetary change induced by the surplus in the government budget, $-P_t(T_t - G_t)$.

Similar considerations apply to the foreign economy. Therefore the foreign-country analogue to the trade-balance and the monetary-flow equations (2.11) and (2.12) is

$$(TA)_t^* = Y_{mt}^* - (E_t^* + G_t^*)$$ (2.13)

and

$$M_t^* - M_{t-1}^* = P_t^*[(TA)_t^* - (T_t^* - G_t^*)],$$ (2.14)

where the real magnitudes are measured in terms of the foreign good, m.

Equilibrium in the world economy requires that world demand for each good equals the corresponding supply. Accordingly,

$$(1 - \beta_m)E_t + (1 - \beta_m^g)G_t + p_{mt}(\beta_x^* E_t^* + \beta_x^{g^*} G_t^*) = Y_{xt},$$ (2.15)

$$\frac{1}{p_{mt}}(\beta_m E_t + \beta_m^g G_t) + (1 - \beta_x^*)E_t^* + (1 - \beta_x^{g^*})G_t^* = Y_{mt}^*.$$ (2.16)

The two equilibrium conditions (2.15) and (2.16), together with the definitions of the trade balance in equations (2.11) and (2.13), imply that in equilibrium the surplus in the home country's trade account is equal to the foreign country's deficit so that $(TA)_t = -p_{mt}(TA)_t^*$, where $(TA)_t$ is

$$(TA)_t = p_{mt}(\beta_x^* E_t^* + \beta_x^{g^*} G_t^*) - (\beta_m E_t + \beta_m^g G_t).$$ (2.17)

The relative price of good m in terms of good x, p_{mt}, which is assumed to be equal across countries, can be written as

$$p_{mt} = \frac{eP_t^*}{P_t},$$ (2.18)

where e is the nominal exchange rate expressing the price of the foreign currency in terms of the domestic currency. With this expression the equality between the surplus in the domestic trade balance and the deficit in the foreign trade balance (expressed in common units) states that $(TA)_t = -(eP_t^*/P_t)(TA)_t^*$. This equality together with equations (2.12) and (2.14) implies that

$$(M_t - M_{t-1}) + e(M_t^* - M_{t-1}^*) = P_t(G_t - T_t) + eP_t^*(G_t^* - T_t^*).$$ (2.19)

Equation (2.19) indicates that the change in the world money supply is the sum of the deficits in the domestic and the foreign governments' budget (all measured in terms of domestic currency units). This equality reflects the assumed fixity of the world stock of international reserves. As a result of this fixity changes in the foreign-exchange component of the monetary base in any given economy are fully offset by opposite changes in the rest of the world, and changes in the world money supply arise only from public-sector deficit finance.

It should be obvious that the automatic monetization of budget deficits reflects the absence of credit markets. If credit markets existed, then the governments could also finance their budget through borrowing. In chapter 3 we allow for both domestic and international credit markets. For the present analysis, in order to focus only on pure fiscal policies (rather than on monetary policies), we consider only balanced-budget changes in government spending. The analysis of the effects of budget deficits is relegated to chapter 3.

The analytical framework of the income-expenditure model outlined earlier is general in that it encompasses the Keynesian and the classical versions of the model. To simplify the exposition and to highlight the symmetry between the two versions, we conclude this section by presenting a simplified specification of the model. Accordingly, we assume that the marginal propensities to spend and save out of disposable income are the same as the corresponding propensities to spend and save out of assets. With this assumption, the spending and money-demand functions of equations (2.3) through (2.6) become

$$Z_t = Z(P_t Y_t - P_t T_t + M_{t-1}), \qquad Z_t^* = Z^*(P_t^* Y_t^* - P_t^* T_t^* + M_{t-1}^*),$$

$$M_t = M(P_t Y_t - P_t T_t + M_{t-1}), \qquad M_t^* = M^*(P_t^* Y_t^* - P_t^* T_t^* + M_{t-1}^*),$$

$$(2.20)$$

where we have suppressed the commodity subscripts x and m. With this specification the equilibrium conditions (2.15) and (2.16) become

$$\frac{1 - s - a}{1 - s} Z(P_t Y_t - P_t T_t + M_{t-1}) + (1 - a^g)P_t G_t$$

$$+ \frac{a^*}{1 - s^*} eZ^*(P_t^* Y_t^* - P_t^* T_t^* + M_{t-1}^*) + a^{g^*} eP_t^* G_t^* = P_t Y_t \qquad (2.15a)$$

$$\frac{a}{1 - s} Z(P_t Y_t - P_t T_t + M_{t-1}) + a^g P_t G_t$$

$$+ \frac{1 - s^* - a^*}{1 - s^*} eZ^*(P_t^* Y_t^* - P_t^* T_t^* + M_{t-1}^*) + (1 - a^{g^*})eP_t^* G_t^*$$

$$= eP_t^* Y_t^*, \qquad (2.16a)$$

where s and a denote, respectively, the domestic marginal propensities to save and import out of income (or assets), a^g denotes the government marginal propensity to import out of government spending, and where similar notations (with an added asterisk) apply to the foreign country. The relations between the propensities to save and spend out of income and the corresponding propensities to save and spend out of expenditures are stated in section 2.3. In the specification of the equilibrium conditions we have used the law-of-one-price according to which $p_{mt} = eP_t^*/P_t$.

The specification of equations (2.15a) and (2.16a) reveals the symmetry between the Keynesian and the classical versions of the income-expenditure model. Specifically, in the absence of government spending and taxes and for given levels of money holdings, the system determines the values of domestic and foreign *nominal* incomes, $P_t Y_t$ and $P_t^* Y_t^*$. In this system the specific values of output and prices generating the equilibrium values of nominal incomes are immaterial. The Keynesian version of the model postulates fixed prices. Thereby the equilibrium changes in nominal incomes are brought about through output adjustments. The classical version postulates fixed outputs and employment. Thereby the equilibrium changes in nominal incomes are brought about through price adjustments. Since both versions of the income-expenditure model generate the same paths of nominal incomes, they also generate the *same* paths of spending and balance-of-payments adjustments. Inspection of equations (2.15a) and (2.16a) also reveals that in the presence of government spending and taxes the relation between the two versions of the model depends on the specification of the paths of government spending and taxes.

2.2   The Keynesian Version

For the remainder of this chapter we analyze the Keynesian version of the income-expenditure model. Under this specification prices are given while the levels of output are determined by aggregate demand. For expository purposes we normalize units so that $e = P_t = P_t^* = p_{mt} = 1$, and accordingly, we suppress the commodity subscripts x and m. In this specification of the model the spending and money-demand functions of equation (2.20) become

$$E_t = E(Y_t - T_t + M_{t-1}), \qquad E_t^* = E^*(Y_t^* - T_t^* + M_{t-1}^*),$$

$$M_t = M(Y_t - T_t + M_{t-1}), \qquad M_t^* = M^*(Y_t^* - T_t^* + M_{t-1}^*). \tag{2.20a}$$

In the appendix to this chapter we analyze the more general system that corresponds to equations (2.5) through (2.8).

In the next three sections we analyze the equilibrium levels of output and the balance of payments for the short run, the long run, and the adjustment period characterizing the transition between the short and the long runs.

2.3   Short-Run Equilibrium Levels of Output

In order to characterize the short-run equilibrium of the system, we differentiate the equilibrium conditions (2.15a) and (2.16a) and obtain

$$
\begin{pmatrix} -(s+a) & a^* \\ a & -(s^*+a^*) \end{pmatrix} \begin{pmatrix} dY_t \\ dY_t^* \end{pmatrix}
$$

$$
= \begin{pmatrix} a^g - a - s \\ -(a^g - a) \end{pmatrix} dG + \begin{pmatrix} s - (1 - a - a^*) \\ -s^* + (1 - a - a^*) \end{pmatrix} dM_{t-1}, \tag{2.21}
$$

where we recall that in this specification $s = 1 - E_y = 1 - E_M$ and $a = \beta_m E_y = \beta_m E_M$ denote, respectively, the domestic marginal propensities to save and to import, $a^g = \beta_m^g$ denotes the government marginal propensity to import out of government spending (E_y and E_M denote the partial derivatives of private real spending, E, with respect to income and assets). In the derivation of the system (2.21) we have assumed that governments run balanced budgets, that the paths of government spending and taxes are stationary (i.e., $G_t = T_t = G = T$ and $G_t^* = T_t^* = G^* = T^*$), and that foreign policies are given. We have also made use of the implication of the balanced-budget assumption, according to which $dM_{t-1} = -dM_{t-1}^*$ (from equation 2.19).

The system shown in (2.21) indicates that changes in the levels of domestic and foreign GDP are induced by two distinct factors. The first corresponds to changes in the level and commodity composition of aggregate demand induced by fiscal policy; the second corresponds to dynamic changes in the distribution of the world money supply. As is evident, the (balanced-budget) changes in the level of government spending induce immediate changes in the levels of domestic and foreign outputs. On the other hand, the effects of redistributions of the world money supply only occur through time.

In what follows, we analyze the effects of balanced-budget changes in government spending on the equilibrium of the system. In the short run the international distribution of the world money supply is given. This distribution may change over time through surpluses or deficits in the official-settlements account of the balance of payments. Long-run equilibrium obtains when the dynamic process of the redistribution of world money reaches a halt.

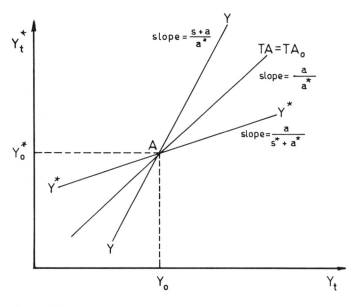

Figure 2.1
Short-run equilibrium outputs

The short-run equilibrium of the system is depicted in figure 2.1. The YY and the Y^*Y^* schedules are, respectively, the domestic and the foreign goods-market equilibrium schedules. Along the YY schedule world demand for domestic output equals domestic GDP, and along the Y^*Y^* schedule world demand for foreign output equals foreign GDP. The domestic schedule YY is positively sloped since a unit rise in domestic GDP raises domestic demand for the domestic good by $1 - s - a$, and thereby creates an excess supply of $1 - (1 - s - a) = s + a$ units. To restore equilibrium, foreign output must rise. A unit rise in foreign output raises foreign demand for the domestic good by a^* units, and therefore, to eliminate the excess supply of $s + a$ units, foreign output must rise by $(s + a)/a^*$. Thus the slope of the YY schedule is

$$\frac{dY^*}{dY} = \frac{s + a}{a^*} \qquad \text{along the } YY \text{ schedule.} \qquad (2.22)$$

Analogously, the foreign schedule Y^*Y^* is also positively sloped, and by similar reasoning, its slope is

$$\frac{dY^*}{dY} = \frac{a}{s^* + a^*} \qquad \text{along the } Y^*Y^* \text{ schedule.} \qquad (2.23)$$

As is evident, the YY schedule is steeper than the Y^*Y^* schedule. Both of these schedules are drawn for a given level of government spending and for a given distribution of the world money supply.

The equilibrium of the system obtains at point A at which domestic GDP is Y_0 and foreign GDP is Y_0^*; the trade balance associated with these levels of outputs can be inferred from equation (2.17). To complete the characterization of the equilibrium and to set the stage for the analysis of the dynamic effects of government spending, we differentiate the trade-balance equation (2.17) and obtain

$$d(TA)_t = (a^* dY_t^* - a dY_t) - (a^g - a)dG - (a + a^*)dM_{t-1}. \tag{2.24}$$

The three terms on the right-hand side of equation (2.24) correspond to the three factors governing trade-balance adjustments. The first reflects adjustments induced by (endogenous) changes in the levels of output, the second reflects the trade-balance implications of (balanced-budget) changes in government spending, and the third reflects the trade-balance implications of the dynamic process effecting the international distribution of the world money supply.

As seen from equation (2.24), for given values of government spending and the money supply, maintenance of a given level of the trade balance requires that domestic and foreign outputs move in the same direction. These considerations are embodied in the $TA = TA_0$ locus exhibited in figure 2.1. This schedule shows combinations of domestic and foreign outputs along which the balance of trade (which in our case is the official settlements balance) is constant. The TA locus is positively sloped since a unit rise in domestic GDP worsens the balance of trade by a units, and this worsening can be offset by a rise in foreign output. Since a unit rise in foreign output improves the domestic trade balance by a^* units, it follows that foreign output must rise by a/a^* units. Thus the slope of the $TA = TA_0$ schedule is

$$\frac{dY^*}{dY} = \frac{a}{a^*} \qquad \text{along the } TA = TA_0 \text{ schedule.} \tag{2.25}$$

As is evident, by comparison with equations (2.22) and (2.23), this slope falls in between those of the YY and the Y^*Y^* schedules. To the right of the $TA = TA_0$ locus the domestic economy's balance of trade worsens, and to the left of this locus the domestic trade balance improves.

The foregoing analysis implies that for a given level of government spending and for a given distribution of the world money supply, the *short-run* equilibrium is fully characterized by the intersection between the

YY and the Y^*Y^* schedules as at point A in figure 2.1. The trade balance, TA_0, associated with this short-run equilibrium, determines the direction of the international redistribution of the world money supply. If TA_0 is negative, the home country's money supply is falling over time while the foreign country's money supply is rising. In the long run, as seen from equations (2.12) and (2.14), with balanced budgets the trade account is balanced (so that $TA = 0$), and as a result the international distribution of the world money supply does not tend to change.

2.4   Long-Run Equilibrium Levels of Output

In this section we analyze the determinants of the long-run equilibrium. As was already indicated, in the long run, the endogenously determined distribution of the world money supply is such that international monetary flows cease and $TA = 0$. Thus in the long run, $M_t = M_{t-1} = M$ and $M_t^* = M_{t-1}^* = M^* = \overline{M} - M$, where $\overline{M}$ is the world money supply which is assumed to be given. Accordingly, using the money-demand equations from (2.20)—omitting the time subscripts of domestic and foreign GDPs and replacing the taxes, T and T^*, by the corresponding levels of government spending, G and G^* (due to the balanced-budget assumption which is necessary for the maintenance of the fixed world money supply)—yield equation (2.26) as the condition for world monetary equilibrium

$$M(Y - G + M) + M^*(Y^* - G^* + \overline{M} - M) = \overline{M}. \tag{2.26}$$

Similar considerations indicate that in the long run (in which the stocks of assets do not vary over time) the budget constraints (2.1) and (2.2) imply that private spending in each country equals the corresponding level of disposable income; in addition the balanced-budget assumption implies that in each country disposable income equals the level of GDP net of government spending. Hence, using (2.20), the long-run budget constraints are

$$E(Y - G + M) = Y - G, \tag{2.27}$$

$$E^*(Y^* - G^* + \overline{M} - M) = Y^* - G^*. \tag{2.28}$$

The system (2.26) through (2.28) yields the combinations of long-run Y and Y^* that are consistent with money-market equilibrium in the world economy. These combinations are depicted by the negatively sloped $\overline{MM}$ schedule in figure 2.2. The schedule is drawn for given levels of govern-

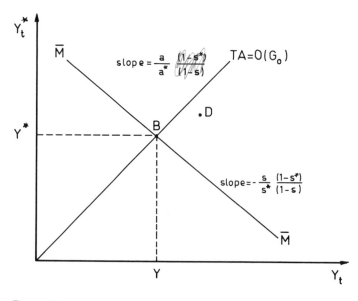

Figure 2.2
Long-run equilibrium outputs

ment spending and world money supply. The slope of the $\overline{MM}$ schedule is negative since a rise in domestic resources $(dY + dM)$ raises spending by $(1 - s)$ times this quantity, and since in the long run the rise in spending equals the rise in GDP, it follows that $(1 - s)(dY + dM) = dY$. Thus the rise in domestic GDP raises the domestic long-run demand for money by $[s/(1 - s)]dY$. Similarly, a fall in foreign output by dY^* induces a decline in foreign money demand by $[s^*/(1 - s^*)]dY^*$. With a given world money supply the maintenance of world monetary equilibrium necessitates that the rise in the domestic money demand equals the fall in the foreign demand. Hence

$$\frac{dY^*}{dY} = -\frac{s\,(1 - s^*)}{s^*\,(1 - s)} \qquad \text{along the } \overline{MM} \text{ schedule.} \qquad (2.29)$$

In addition to the requirement of world monetary equilibrium, the conditions for long-run equilibrium also require that the goods market clear. In the long run this requirement implies trade-balance equilibrium. Accordingly, since in the absence of monetary flows $M_t = M_{t-1} = M$ and $M_t^* = M_{t-1}^* = M^* = \overline{M} - M$, it follows that

$$\bar{a}^*E^*(Y^* - G^* + \overline{M} - M) + a^{g^*}G^* - [\bar{a}E(Y - G + M) + a^g G] = 0, \qquad (2.30)$$

where $\bar{a} = a/(1 - s)$ and $\bar{a}^* = a^*/(1 - s^*)$ are, respectively, the domestic and foreign marginal propensities to import out of *spending* (these propensities should be distinguished from a and a^* which are the corresponding propensities to import out of *income*). Equation (2.30) is the goods-market analogue to the monetary-equilibrium condition (2.26). The system (2.27), (2.28), and (2.30) yield the combinations of long-run values of domestic and foreign outputs that are consistent with goods-market equilibrium in the world economy. Formally, substituting (2.27) and (2.28) into (2.30) yields

$$\bar{a}^* Y^* - \bar{a}Y = (a^g - \bar{a})G - (a^{g^*} - \bar{a}^*)G^*. \tag{2.30a}$$

Equation (2.30a) is shown in figure 2.2 by the positively sloped $TA = 0$ schedule. This schedule is drawn for given levels of government spending and world money supply. Its slope is positive since a rise in domestic output worsens the trade balance, whereas a rise in foreign output improves it. Thus, analogously to equation (2.25), the slope of the $TA = 0$ schedule is

$$\frac{dY^*}{dY} = \frac{\bar{a}}{\bar{a}^*} \qquad \text{along the } TA = 0 \text{ schedule.} \tag{2.31}$$

Along the $\overline{MM}$ schedule the stationary distributions of the world money supply, M and $M^* = \overline{M} - M$, and world outputs, Y and Y^* (determined from the system 2.26 through 2.28), generate world demand for money that equals the existing stock, $\overline{M}$. However, the levels of output and the distribution of world money necessary to bring about such a monetary equilibrium may not be consistent with goods-market equilibrium. Analogously, along the $TA = 0$ schedule, the stationary distributions of world money supply and outputs (determined from the system 2.27, 2.28, and 2.30) generate world demand for each output that equals the corresponding supply. However, the levels of output and the distribution of world money necessary to bring about such an equilibrium in the goods market may not generate world money demand that is equal to the existing stock.

The long-run equilibrium obtains at the intersection of the $\overline{MM}$ and the $TA = 0$ schedules. At such an intersection both goods and money markets clear, and the levels of output and money holdings do not change over time. Point B in figure 2.2 depicts the long-run equilibrium. In the next section we complete the characterization of the equilibrium by analyzing the dynamic process that underlies the transition between short- and long-run equilibria.

2.5 Dynamics of Adjustment and the Balance of Payments

The short-run equilibrium depicted by point A in figure 2.1 is associated with an imbalance in the balance of payments equal to TA_0. The international monetary flows induced by this imbalance disturb the initial short-run equilibrium. As indicated by the goods-market equilibrium conditions (2.21), changes in the international distribution of the world money supply (as measured by dM_{t-1}) alter the positions of the YY and the Y^*Y^* schedules and result in a new short-run equilibrium associated with the prevailing new distribution of the world money supply. In this section we analyze the transition period characterized by a sequence of such short-run equilibria and show that this dynamic process converges to the long-run equilibrium. The impact of a given change in domestic money holdings, dM_{t-1}, on the goods-market equilibrium schedules is shown on the right-hand side of (2.21). Accordingly, a unit rise in the domestic money holdings, accompanied by a unit fall in the foreign money holdings, raises the domestic demand for home output by c units (where c denotes the domestic marginal propensity to spend on domestic goods, $c = 1 - s - a$) and lowers the foreign demand for home output by a^*. Hence, whether at the initial levels of output this change in the distribution of money holdings creates an excess demand or an excess supply of domestic output depends on whether $c - a^*$ is positive or negative. If it is positive, then the rise in domestic money holdings shifts the YY schedule to the right, and vice versa. Similarly, the fall in the foreign money holdings creates an excess supply of foreign output if $c^* - a$ is positive, and it creates an excess demand if $c^* - a$ is negative (where c^* denotes the foreign marginal propensity to spend on foreign goods, $c^* = 1 - s^* - a^*$). If it is positive, then the fall in foreign money holdings shifts the Y^*Y^* schedule downward, and vice versa.

The effects of a redistribution of the world money supply on the short-run equilibrium levels of domestic and foreign outputs are obtained by solving (2.21). Hence

$$\frac{dY_t}{dM_{t-1}} = \frac{s^*c - sa^*}{ss^* + sa^* + s^*a'}'' \tag{2.32}$$

$$\frac{dY_t^*}{dM_{t-1}} = \frac{s^*a - sc^*}{ss^* + sa^* + s^*a}. \tag{2.33}$$

As seen, the direction of the change in domestic output depends on whether the ratio of the domestic to the foreign saving propensities, s/s^*, exceeds or falls short of the ratio of the domestic to the foreign propensities to spend on *domestic* goods, c/a^*. Analogously, the direction of the change in foreign output depends on whether the ratio of the saving propensities, s/s^* exceeds or falls short of the ratio of the domestic to foreign propensities to spend on *foreign* goods, a/c^*. Thus the direction of the long-run changes in output depends on the saving propensities and on the commodity composition of spending. The role of the saving propensities is clarified by noting that if the domestic saving propensity, s, is small, then a redistribution of the world money supply toward the domestic economy raises the levels of output in both countries. On the other hand, if the foreign saving propensity, s^*, is small, then the same redistribution lowers the levels of output in both countries. The opposite pattern of output changes arises in the other extreme cases in which the corresponding saving propensities are large. The role of the commondity composition of spending is clarified by noting that if the import propensities, a and a^*, are relatively small (i.e., if c and c^* are relatively large so that expenditures in each country are biased toward locally produced goods), then the redistribution of world money toward the domestic economy diverts world demand toward the domestically produced good and away from the foreign-produced goods. This change in the pattern of world demand raises the equilibrium level of domestic output. The opposite holds if each country's demand is biased toward imported goods.

Thus far we have determined the changes in the international *distribution* of world output induced by the dynamic redistribution of world money. The dynamic process is also associated with changes in the *level* of world GDP, $Y_t + Y_t^*$. Accordingly, adding the results in (2.32) and (2.33) yields

$$\frac{d(Y_t + Y_t^*)}{dM_{t-1}} = \frac{s^* - s}{ss^* + sa^* + s^*a}. \tag{2.34}$$

The interpretation of equation (2.34) can be stated in terms of the "transfer-problem" criterion familiar from the theory of international transfers. Accordingly, at the prevailing levels of output the redistribution of the world money supply raises domestic spending by $(1 - s)$ times the rise in the domestic money supply and lowers foreign spending by $(1 - s^*)$ times the same quantity. Hence *world* spending rises if s^* exceeds s, and world spending falls if s^* falls short of s. In the former case the rise in world spending creates an excess demand for world output which, in order to restore equilibrium between world spending and output, necessitates a corresponding rise in world GDP. The opposite holds in the latter case for which s^* falls short of s.

The redistribution of the world money supply and the induced changes in the short-run equilibrium levels of output also alter the initial trade-balance position and bring about additional changes in the money supply. Specifically, substituting equations (2.32) and (2.33) into (2.24) yields

$$\frac{d(TA)_t}{dM_{t-1}} = -\frac{sa^* + s^*a}{ss^* + sa^* + s^*a},$$

and noting that $M_t = M_{t-1} + (TA)_t$, it follows that dM_t/dM_{t-1} is a positive fraction, where

$$\frac{dM_t}{dM_{t-1}} = \frac{ss^*}{ss^* + sa^* + s^*a} < 1. \tag{2.35}$$

Equation (2.35) shows that the additions to the domestic quantity of money induced by the sequence of balance-of-payments surpluses diminish over time. It follows that the dynamic process of the redistribution of the world money supply that is effected through balance-of-payment adjustments converges to the long-run equilibrium.

Figure 2.3 shows the path of adjustment and demonstrates the stability of the dynamic process. In this figure the initial equilibrium is indicated by point A along the M_t schedule at which the level of domestic money holding is M_{-1} and the associated surplus in the balance of payments is

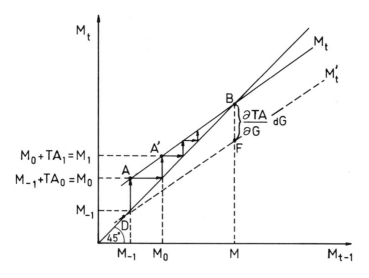

Figure 2.3
Balance-of-payments dynamics

TA_0. This initial short-run equilibrium corresponds to the one depicted in figure 2.1, and as before, the M_t schedule in figure 2.3 is drawn for a given level of government spending. The surplus in the balance of payments raises the domestic money supply from M_{-1} to M_0 and results in a new short-run equilibrium at point A' along the M_t schedule. In this equilibrium the trade surplus diminishes to TA_1. The sequence of short-run equilibria is associated with a path along which the positive increments to the money supply (associated with trade surpluses) diminish over time. This path converges to the long-run equilibrium at point B at which the long-run money holding by the home country is M. The long-run equilibrium shown in this figure corresponds to the one in figure 2.2.

Before concluding, we note that even though the direction of monetary flows during the adjustment process is clear cut, the directions of changes in domestic and foreign outputs depend on the relations between the marginal saving ratio, s/s^*, and the marginal consumption ratios of domestic goods, c/a^*, and of foreign goods, a/c^*. Independent, however, of the precise pattern of output adjustments, the system characterizing the world economy as a whole (including the level and the international distribution of world output) is dynamically stable.

2.6 Fiscal Policies and Outputs

In this section we use the results of the previous analysis to determine the short- and long-run effects of balanced-budget changes in the domestic government spending. For this purpose suppose that the world economy is initially in a long-run equilibrium, corresponding to point B in figures 2.2 and 2.3. At the prevailing levels of output, a unit rise in government spending raises the demand for domestically produced goods by $1 - a^g$, and the rise in taxes necessary to balance the budget lowers private demand for domestic output by $1 - a - s$. Thus the excess demand for domestic goods induced by this balanced-budget rise in government spending is $s + a - a^g$. By similar reasoning the excess demand for foreign goods induced by the unit rise in government spending is $a^g - a$ (these changes are represented by the coefficients of dG in the system of equations 2.21).

As is evident, the patterns of excess demands generated by the balanced-budget rise in government spending depend critically on the magnitude of the government propensity to import, a^g. For example, in the extreme case for which all government spending falls on domestic goods (so that $a^g = 0$), the excess demand for domestic goods is $(s + a)$, and the excess supply of foreign goods is a. In the other extreme case for which all government spending falls on importables (so that $a^g = 1$), the excess supply of domestic goods is $1 - (s + a)$, whereas the excess demand for foreign goods is $1 - a$.

The relative magnitudes of the government and the private sector marginal propensities to import also determine whether at the prevailing levels of output the trade balance improves or deteriorates. The unit rise in government spending raises imports by a^g, and the corresponding unit rise in taxes lowers private imports by a. Hence (as indicated by equation 2.24) at the prevailing levels of output the trade balance improves if a, the private import propensity, exceeds the government import propensity, a^g, and it deteriorates if a falls short of a^g. If the two import propensities are the same, then at the prevailing levels of output the redistribution of income between the private and the public sectors does not impact on the balance of trade.

In the diagrammatic analysis that follows, we consider the intermediate bench-mark case for which the private and the public sectors have the same marginal propensities to import (so that $a = a^g$). Consider figure 2.4, and let the initial long-run equilibrium be at point B. The equilibrium schedules YY and Y^*Y^* are drawn for the given initial level of government spending

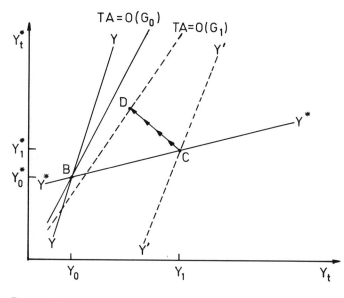

Figure 2.4
The short- and long-run effects of a balanced-budget rise in government spending

and for the initial distribution of the world money supply. The levels of output associated with this equilibrium are Y_0 and Y_0^*, and since the initial position is that of a long-run equilibrium, point B lies on the $TA = 0$ schedule along which the balance of payments is balanced.

A unit balanced-budget rise in the domestic government spending induces an excess demand for domestic goods by s units (in the bench-mark case for which $a = a^g$) and necessitates an equilibrating rise in domestic output by $s/(s + a)$ units (for a given level of foreign output). In terms of figure 2.4 the balanced-budget rise in government spending shifts the YY schedule rightward by $s/(s + a)$ units times the rise in government spending. This horizontal shift corresponds to the conventional balanced-budget foreign trade multiplier for a small open economy. The new equilibrium schedule is indicated by $Y'Y'$. Since with $a = a^g$ the balanced-budget rise in the domestic government spending does not generate an excess demand or an excess supply of foreign output, the Y^*Y^* schedule remains intact, and the new short-run equilibrium obtains at point C.

In the short-run equilibrium at point C, domestic and foreign outputs are higher than their initial levels. Thus, measured in terms of comovements of domestic and foreign outputs, the domestic fiscal expansion is transmitted positively to the rest of the world. It is also relevant to note that the magnitude of the equilibrium rise in domestic output exceeds the rise implied by the small-country foreign trade multiplier (a rise that is indicated by the rightward shift of the YY schedule).

In the more general case the private and public sectors' marginal propensities to import may differ from each other. In that case the short-run effects of the balanced-budget rise in government spending are obtained from the system in (2.21). Accordingly,

$$\frac{dY_0}{dG} = 1 - \frac{s^*a^g}{ss^* + sa^* + s^*a}, \tag{2.36}$$

$$\frac{dY_0^*}{dG} = \frac{sa^g}{ss^* + sa^* + s^*a}. \tag{2.37}$$

Equation (2.36) illustrates the negative dependence of the short-run equilibrium change in domestic output on the magnitude of the government import propensity. If the government import propensity, a^g, does not exceed the corresponding private-sector propensity, a, then the balanced-budget rise in government spending must raise domestic output. On the other hand, if a^g is relatively large, then domestic output may fall in the short run. This fall stems from the fact that the redistribution of income between the private and the public sectors diverts spending away from domestic output.

Equation (2.37) shows that in general foreign output rises. It also shows that this rise is proportional to the magnitude of the domestic government import propensity, a^g. In the extreme case for which all government spending falls on domestic goods (so that $a^g = 0$), foreign output does not change. In that case the rise in domestic output is maximized, and the balanced-budget multiplier is unity. The comparison between the directions of domestic and foreign output changes reveals that (in contrast with the bench-mark case) *the short-run international transmission of the effects of domestic balanced-budget fiscal policies may be positive or negative.*

Thus far we have characterized the nature of the international transmission mechanism in terms of the sign of the correlation between changes in domestic and foreign *outputs*. The focus on the levels of output reflects concern with respect to resource utilization and employment. An alternative measure characterizes the transmission mechanism in terms of the correlation between domestic and foreign *private-sector spending*. The latter is governed by changes in private disposable incomes. As is evident from equations (2.36) and (2.37), domestic disposable income falls, and foreign disposable income rises (in the limiting case in which $a^g = 0$ both disposable incomes remain unchanged). Thus, measured in terms of comovements of the domestic and the foreign private-sector spending, *the short-run international transmission of the effects of domestic balanced-budget fiscal policies is negative.*

The preceeding analysis examined the short-run effects of fiscal policies on the international *distribution* of world output and spending. The change in the *level* of world output is obtained by adding equations (2.36) and (2.37). Similarly, the change in the level of world private-sector spending reflects changes in each country's disposable income multiplied by the corresponding propensity to spend. Thus using equations (2.36) and (2.37) yields

$$\frac{d(Y_0 + Y_0^*)}{dG} = 1 + \frac{(s - s^*)a^g}{ss^* + sa^* + s^*a}, \tag{2.38}$$

$$\frac{d(E_0 + E_0^*)}{dG} = \frac{(s - s^*)a^g}{ss^* + sa^* + s^*a}. \tag{2.39}$$

Equation (2.38) shows that, in general, the direction of the change in world output depends on the relative magnitudes of the saving and import propensities. If, however, the government propensity to import, a^g, does not exceed the corresponding private-sector propensity, a, then world output must rise. The bench-mark case shown in figure 2.4 illustrates this result. Equation (2.39) shows that the direction of the change in world private-sector spending depends on whether the domestic economy's saving propensity exceeds or falls short of the foreign saving propensity. In the former case world spending rises, and in the latter case world spending falls.

The short-run effects of a balanced-budget rise in government spending are also reflected in the balance of payments. Using equation (2.24) along with the expressions for the equilibrium changes in outputs from equations (2.36) and (2.37) yields

$$\frac{d(TA)_0}{dG} = \frac{ss^* a^g}{ss^* + sa^* + s^* a}. \tag{2.40}$$

Thus, unless all government spending falls on the domestic goods, the rise in government spending induces a deficit in the home country's balance of payments. This deficit initiates the dynamic process by which the world money supply is redistributed over time from the domestic economy to the rest of the world.

In the bench-mark case shown in figure 2.4 the short-run equilibrium at point C is associated with a deficit in the balance of payments since it lies to the right of the $TA = 0$ schedule. (As seen from equation 2.24, this schedule is invariant with respect to government spending as long as $a = a^g$.) The fall in the domestic money supply, and the corresponding rise in the foreign money supply consequent on the payments imbalances lower domestic spending and raises foreign spending. As a result the $Y'Y'$ schedule shifts leftward, and the Y^*Y^* schedule shifts upward. Their new intersection yields a new short-run equilibrium. This process continues as long as the payments imbalances prevail. The location of this new short-run equilibrium relative to point C depends on whether the ratio of the domestic to the foreign-saving propensities, s/s^*, exceeds or falls short of the ratios of the domestic to the foreign propensities to consume domestic goods, c/a^*, and foreign goods, a/c^*.

Diagrammatically, the slope of the adjustment path characterizing the sequence of short-run equilibria is obtained by dividing equation (2.33) by equation (2.32). Accordingly,

$$\frac{dY_t^*}{dY_t} = \left(\frac{(a/c^*) - (s/s^*)}{(c/a^*) - (s/s^*)} \right) \frac{c^*}{a^*} \qquad \text{along the path of adjustment.} \tag{2.41}$$

As is evident, depending on the relative magnitudes of the parameters, this slope may be positive or negative. In figure 2.4 the path of adjustment is drawn with a negative slope corresponding to the case in which the spending patterns are such that the saving ratio, s/s^*, is bounded by the ratios of the two countries' propensities to spend on the domestic good, c/a^*, and on the foreign good, a/c^*. Accordingly, the sequence of short-run equilibria is described in figure 2.4 by the path connecting the initial short-run equilibrium point C with the long-run equilibrium point D. In general, as seen from equation 2.34, along the path of adjustment world output (and spending) rises or falls depending on whether the domestic saving propensity, s, exceeds or falls short of the foreign saving propensity, s^*.

The dynamics of adjustment can also be illustrated in terms of figure 2.3. In that figure the M_t schedule is drawn for a given level of government spending. The rise in government spending (at the initial distribution of the world money supply) worsens the trade account by $[\partial(TA)/\partial G]dG$ and shifts the M_t schedule downward to the position indicated by M_t' (since $M_t = TA_t + M_{t-1}$). This shift sets off the dynamic process (not drawn) that converges to the new long-run equilibrium point D (at which $M_t = M_{t-1}$ along the M_t' schedule). The new equilibrium point corresponds to the new international distribution of the world money supply.

The characteristics of the new long-run equilibrium can be examined with the aid of figure 2.2. The position of the new long-run equilibrium point depends on the effects of the balanced-budget rise in government spending on the world monetary-equilibrium schedule, $\overline{MM}$ and on the balance-of-payments equilibrium schedule, $TA = 0$. It is evident by in-spection of equations (2.26) through (2.28) that the $\overline{MM}$ schedule shifts rightward and that the extent of the horizontal shift equals the rise in government spending. The reason for the rightward shift of the $\overline{MM}$ schedule is that given the initial distribution of world money, the rise in domestic output is necessary in order to keep domestic disposable income unchanged for any given level of foreign output (and disposable income). Such a rise ensures the maintenance of world monetary equilibrium since, as long as the initial distribution of world money and the initial levels of disposable incomes do not change, the world demand for money remains intact.

By similar reasoning equation (2.30a) indicates that a unit balanced-budget rise in government spending induces a rightward shift of the $TA = 0$ schedule by $(\bar{a} - a^g)/a$ units. Given the initial distribution of world money, this change in domestic output ensures that the home country's total (private sector plus government) imports are unchanged. With unchanged imports the trade balance is also unchanged since, for a given level of foreign output, domestic exports are given. As is evident, the direction to which the $TA = 0$ schedule shifts depends on whether, at the prevailing situation, the redistribution of income between the domestic private sector and the government (consequent on the balanced-budget rise in government spending) raises or lowers long-run imports. If the private sector's marginal propensity to import out of spending, $\bar{a}$, exceeds the government propensity to import, a^g, then the balanced-budget rise in government spending improves the trade balance. Therefore, ceteris paribus, domestic output must rise in order to restore balanced trade. In this case the $TA = 0$ schedule shifts to the right. The opposite holds if a falls short of a^g.

The long-run equilibrium point D shown in figure 2.2 (as well as in figure 2.4) corresponds to the bench-mark case (used in the short-run analysis) in which the private sector's marginal propensity to import out of *income* equals that of the public sector (so that $a = a^g$). Under such circumstances the private sector's marginal propensity to import out of *spending*, $\bar{a}$, exceeds a^g, and therefore the balanced-budget rise in government spending shifts the $TA = 0$ schedule to the right.

In characterizing the long-run effects of fiscal policies, it is convenient to consider the case in which the initial $TA = 0$ schedule in figure 2.2 goes through the origin. As seen from equation (2.30a), this arises if the initial levels of domestic and foreign government spending are such that $(a^g - \bar{a})G = (a^{g^*} - \bar{a}^*)G^*$. This initial configuration is indicated in figure 2.2 by the parameteric value of G_0 which is held constant along the $TA = 0$ schedule. In that case a balanced-budget rise in domestic government spending is *neutral* in its long-run effects on the distribution of world outputs if $\bar{a} = a^g$ since it raises both domestic and foreign outputs equiproportionally. On the other hand, if $\bar{a}$ exceeds a^g, then the long-run output effects of the domestic fiscal expansion are *home-output biased*. In that case (indicated by point D in figure 2.2) the percentage long-run rise in domestic output exceeds the corresponding foreign rise. In the opposite case in which $\bar{a}$ falls short of a^g, the long-run output effects of the domestic fiscal expansion are *foreign-output biased*.

An additional factor determining whether the long-run effects are neutral or biased is the initial level of domestic and foreign government spending. For example, if initially foreign government spending is zero while the level of spending by the domestic government is positive, and if $\bar{a} = a^g$, then the $TA = 0$ schedule intersects the horizontal axis to the right of the origin. In that case a balanced-budget rise in domestic government spending biases the long-run distribution of outputs in favor of the foreign country.

The formal solutions for the long-run effects of the balanced-budget rise in government spending on outputs and on the distribution of the world money supply (as implied by equations A.14 through A.16 of the appendix) are

$$\frac{dY}{dG} = 1 - \frac{s^*(1-s)a^g}{sa^* + s^*a},$$

(2.42)

$$\frac{dY^*}{dG} = \frac{s(1-s^*)a^g}{sa^* + s^*a},$$

(2.43)

$$\frac{dM}{dG} = -\frac{ss^*a^g}{sa^* + s^*a},$$

(2.44)

Equation (2.42) indicates that the direction of the long-run effects of the fiscal expansion on domestic output depends on the magnitude of the government import propensity. As is evident, if the government import propensity, a^g, does not exceed the private-sector propensity, a, then domestic output must rise in the long run. Equations (2.43) and (2.44) show that in the long run foreign output rises, and the world money supply is redistributed toward the foreign country (unless government spending falls only on domestic goods).

Finally, we note that in the long run world output changes according to

$$\frac{d(Y + Y^*)}{dG} = 1 + \frac{(s - s^*)a^g}{sa^* + s^*a}.$$

(2.45)

Thus the balanced-budget multiplier of world output exceeds or falls short of unity according to whether the domestic saving propensity exceeds or falls short of the foreign saving propensity.

A comparison between the short-run responses (equations 2.36 through 2.38) and the corresponding long-run responses (equations 2.42, 2.43, and 2.45) reflects the dynamic path of outputs during the adjustment periods. As seen from equations (2.32) and (2.33), the characteristics of the path depend on whether the ratio of the two saving propensities exceeds or falls short of the ratios of the domestic to the foreign propensities to spend on a given good. Accordingly, the long-run level of domestic output falls short of the level obtained in the short run if $s/s^* < c/a^*$, and vice versa. Likewise, the long-run level of foreign output exceeds the level obtained in the short run if $s/s^* > a/c^*$, and vice versa.

So far we have focused mainly on the output effects of fiscal policies. These effects are of interest especially as indicators of employment levels. In order to obtain indicators for private-sector spending, we need to determine the long-run effects of fiscal policies on disposable incomes. Equation (2.42) implies that the balanced-budget rise in the domestic government spending lowers the long-run level of domestic disposable income. Since in the long run private-sector spending equals disposable income, it follows that the domestic private-sector spending also falls in the long run. On the other hand, the foreign private sector, whose taxes have not changed, enjoys (as indicated by equation 2.43) a rise in its long-run disposable income and spending. Finally, using equations (2.42) and (2.43), the effect of the balanced-budget rise in government spending on the long-run level of world spending:

$$\frac{d(E + E^*)}{dG} = \frac{(s - s^*)a^g}{sa^* + s^*a} . \tag{2.46}$$

As seen, in the long run world private spending rises if the domestic saving propensity, s, exceeds the foreign propensity, s^*, and vice versa. A comparison between equations (2.46) and (2.39) shows that the short-run changes in world private spending (which may be positive or negative) are magnified in the long run.

2.7   Summary

In this chapter we developed the analytical framework underlying the income-expenditure model of the interdependent world economy. Throughout the analysis it was assumed that there is a single noninterest-bearing asset (money) that is held by both countries. The international monetary system was assumed to operate under a fixed exchange-rate regime, and the international distribution of the world money supply was shown to be effected through international payments imbalances.

Following the outline of the analytical framework, we have adapted the extreme version of the Keynesian assumptions by which prices were assumed to be given while output was assumed to be demand determined. To focus on the pure effects of fiscal policies, we have assumed that the government (which in the absence of interesting-bearing debt instruments can not finance its spending through debt issue) finances its spending through taxes rather than through monetary creation. Thus we have analyzed the effects of balanced-budget changes in government spending.

Table 2.1
The effect of a unit balanced-budget rise in domestic government spending

	Y	Y^*	E	E^*	TA	M
Short run	$1 - \dfrac{s^*a^g}{\Delta}$	$\dfrac{sa^g}{\Delta}$	$-\dfrac{(1-s)s^*a^g}{\Delta}$	$\dfrac{(1-s^*)sa^g}{\Delta}$	$-\dfrac{ss^*a^g}{\Delta}$	—
Long run	$1 - \dfrac{(1-s)s^*a^g}{\Delta - ss^*}$	$\dfrac{(1-s^*)sa^g}{\Delta - ss^*}$	$-\dfrac{(1-s)s^*a^g}{\Delta - ss^*}$	$\dfrac{(1-s^*)sa^g}{\Delta - ss^*}$		$-\dfrac{ss^*a^g}{\Delta - ss^*}$

Note: $\Delta = ss^* + sa^* + s^*a > 0$, where s, s^*, a, and a^* are, respectively, the domestic and foreign marginal propensities to save and import out of income and a^g is the domestic government import propensity.

Throughout, we focused on the effects of fiscal policies on domestic output and private-sector spending as well as on foreign output and foreign spending. We drew a distinction between the short-run and long-run effects. In the short run the international distribution of the world money supply is given, whereas in the long run this distribution is endogenously determined so as to yield equality between income and spending in each country. Short-run discrepancies between income and spending yield international payments imbalances and generate a dynamic process by which the world money supply is redistributed internationally. We have demonstrated that the system of the world economy is dynamically stable. Thus the sequence of short-run equilibria converges to the long-run equilibrium.

The short-run and long-run effects of a unit balanced-budget rise in domestic government spending are summarized in table 2.1. It is seen that in the short run foreign output and spending rise while the level of the domestic private-sector spending falls. In the short run the balance of payments (which also equals the trade balance) deteriorates. This deterioration sets off the dynamic process of the redistribution of the world money supply toward the rest of the world. As is also shown in table 2.1, the short-run effects on the level of domestic output depend critically on the spending patterns of the government. If the import propensity of the government does not exceed that of the private sector, domestic output rises in the short run. If, on the other hand, government spending falls heavily on foreign goods, then domestic output may fall.

The second line in table 2.1 shows the long-run effects. A comparison between the two lines reveals that the long-run changes in domestic and foreign output may exceed or fall short of the short-run changes. The key factors determining whether the long-run changes magnify or dampen the corresponding short-run changes are the relations between the ratio of the two countries' saving propensities and the ratios of the two countries' spending propensities on domestic and foreign goods.

The comparison between the long- and the short-run changes in the levels of domestic and foreign private-sector spending shows that the short-run changes are always magnified in the long run. The mechanism responsible for this magnification is the redistribution of the world money supply occurring throughout the adjustment process. This dynamic process of the monetary flows is effected through payments imbalances. The cumulative imbalances characterizing the sequence of short-run equilibria are reflected in the long-run change in each country's money holding. The factor of magnification linking short-run and long-run changes in spending manifests itself in the link between the short-run payments imbalance and the ultimate long-run change in money holdings.

2.8   Appendix

In this appendix we derive the short-run and the long-run solutions for the income-expenditure model of output determination. The equilibrium conditions (2.15) and (2.16) (for fixed $p_{mt} = P_t = P_t^* = e = 1$) are

$$(1 - \beta_m)E(Y_t - G, M_{t-1}) + (1 - \beta_m^g)G$$

$$+ \beta_x^* E^*(Y_t^* - G^*, \overline{M} - M_{t-1}) + \beta_x^{g^*} G^* = Y_t, \tag{A.1}$$

$$\beta_m E(Y_t - G, M_{t-1}) + \beta_m^g G + (1 - \beta_x^*)E^*(Y_t^* - G^*, \overline{M} - M_{t-1})$$

$$+ (1 - \beta_x^{g^*})G^* = Y_t^*. \tag{A.2}$$

Differentiating this system yields

$$\begin{pmatrix} -(s + a) & a^* \\ a & -(s^* + a^*) \end{pmatrix} \begin{pmatrix} dY_t \\ dY_t^* \end{pmatrix} = \begin{pmatrix} a^g - a - s \\ a - a^g \end{pmatrix} dG$$

$$+ \begin{bmatrix} \dfrac{a^*}{1 - s^*} \gamma_z^* - \left(\dfrac{1 - s - a}{1 - s} \right) \gamma_z \\ \left(\dfrac{1 - s^* - a^*}{1 - s^*} \right) \gamma_z^* - \dfrac{a}{(1 - s)} \gamma_z \end{bmatrix} dM_{t-1}, \tag{A.3}$$

where γ_z and γ_z^* denote, respectively, the domestic and foreign marginal propensities to spend out of assets and where $\beta_m = a/(1 - s)$ and $\beta_x^* = a^*/(1 - s^*)$. In the case analyzed in the text, we have assumed that the marginal propensities to spend out of income and assets are equal to each other so that $\gamma_z = 1 - s$ and $\gamma_z^* = 1 - s^*$.

The Short Run

The *short-run* equilibrium changes in the values of domestic and foreign outputs in response to a balanced-budget change in domestic government spending are

$$\frac{dY_t}{dG} = 1 - \frac{s^* a^g}{\Delta_s},$$ (A.4)

$$\frac{dY_t^*}{dG} = \frac{s a^g}{\Delta_s} > 0,$$ (A.5)

where $\Delta_s = ss^* + sa^* + s^* a > 0$.

The short-run equilibrium responses of domestic and foreign outputs to a redistribution of the world money supply are

$$\frac{dY_t}{dM_{t-1}} = \frac{1}{\Delta_s}\left[a^*(\gamma_z - \gamma_z^*) + s^*\left(\frac{1-s-a}{1-s}\gamma_z - \frac{a^*}{1-s^*}\gamma_z^* \right) \right],$$ (A.6)

$$\frac{dY_t^*}{dM_{t-1}} = \frac{1}{\Delta_s}\left[a(\gamma_z - \gamma_z^*) + s\left(\frac{a}{1-s}\gamma_z - \frac{1-s^*-a^*}{1-s^*}\gamma_z^* \right) \right].$$ (A.7)

The balance-of-trade equation in a differentiated form (corresponding to equation 2.24) is

$$d(TA)_t = (a^* dY_t^* - a dY_t) - (a^g - a) dG$$

$$- \left(\frac{a^*}{1-s^*}\gamma_z^* + \frac{a}{1-s}\gamma_z \right) dM_{t-1}.$$ (A.8)

Substituting equations (A.4) and (A.5) into (A.8) yields

$$\frac{d(TA)_t}{dG} = -\frac{ss^* a^g}{\Delta_s} < 0.$$ (A.9)

Similarly, substituting equations (A.6) and (A.7) into (A.8) yields

$$\frac{d(TA)_t}{dM_{t-1}} = -\left(\frac{a}{1-s}s^*\gamma_z + \frac{a^*}{1-s^*}s\gamma_z^* \right)$$ (A.10)

Finally, using equation (A.10) along with the definition $M_t - M_{t-1} = (TA)_t$ yields

$$\frac{dM_t}{dM_{t-1}} = \frac{ss^* + sa^*[1 - \gamma_z^*/(1-s^*)] + s^* a[1 - \gamma_z/(1-s)]}{ss^* + sa^* + s^* a}.$$ (A.11)

Equation (A.9) implies that the impact effect of a (balanced-budget) rise in government spending is to worsen the trade account (as long as $a^g > 0$). Equation (A.11) is the stability condition of the system. As is evident for the case analyzed in the text ($\gamma_z = 1 - s$ and $\gamma_z^* = 1 - s^*$), dM_t/dM_{t-1} must be a positive fraction, and stability is ensured. In the general case of equation (A.11) a convergence to long-run stationary equilibrium requires that

$$2ss^* > sa^*\left(\frac{\gamma_z^*}{1 - s^*} - 1\right) + s^*a\left(\frac{\gamma_z}{1 - s} - 1\right). \tag{A.12}$$

Hence, if the spending propensities out of income do not fall short of the spending propensity out of assets, the sequence of short-run equilibria converges to the long-run equilibrium.

The Long Run

Long-run equilibrium requires that in addition to market clearing of domestic and foreign goods, the balance of payments is balanced so that $M_{t-1} = M_t = M$, $M_{t-1}^* = M_t^* = \overline{M} - M$ (where $\overline{M}$ denotes the given world money supply), and the levels of output are stationary so that $Y_t = Y$ and $Y_t^* = Y^*$. Imposing the requirement of trade-balance equilibrium into equation (A.8), and supplementing the system (A.3) with this additional condition, we obtain the differentiated form of the long-run equilibrium conditions. This system is

$$
\begin{bmatrix}
-(s + a) & a^* & \dfrac{1 - s - a}{1 - s}\gamma_z - \dfrac{a^*}{1 - s^*}\gamma_z^* \\[2ex]
a & -(s^* + a^*) & \dfrac{a}{1 - s}\gamma_z - \dfrac{1 - s^* - a^*}{1 - s^*}\gamma_z^* \\[2ex]
-a & a^* & -\left(\dfrac{a}{1 - s}\gamma_z + \dfrac{a^*}{1 - s^*}\gamma_z^*\right)
\end{bmatrix}
\begin{bmatrix}
dY \\[2ex]
dY^* \\[2ex]
dM
\end{bmatrix}
$$

$$
=
\begin{bmatrix}
a^g - a - s \\[2ex]
-(a^g - a) \\[2ex]
a^g - a
\end{bmatrix}
dG. \tag{A.13}
$$

The *long-run* changes in the values of domestic and foreign outputs and in the domestic money holdings (induced by the cummulative redistribution of the given world money supply) are

$$\frac{dY}{dG} = 1 - \frac{\gamma_z s^* a^g}{\Delta_L}, \tag{A.14}$$

$$\frac{dY^*}{dG} = \frac{\gamma_z^* s a^g}{\Delta_L} > 0, \tag{A.15}$$

$$\frac{dM}{dG} = -\frac{s s^* a^g}{\Delta_L} < 0, \tag{A.16}$$

where

$$\Delta_L = \frac{\gamma_z s^*}{1 - s} a + \frac{\gamma_z^* s}{1 - s^*} a^* > 0.$$

3

Fiscal Policies and International Capital Mobility in the Income-Expenditure Model

For the past three decades, the "workhorse" model of international macroeconomics has been the Mundell-Fleming model. The foundations of this model of international macroeconomics were laid during the 1960s by Mundell (1960, 1963), and Fleming (1962). It provides a systematic analysis of the role played by international capital mobility in determining the effectiveness of fiscal and monetary policies under alternative exchange rate regimes (for an exposition and evaluation, see Frenkel and Razin 1987a). The model extends the simple Keynesian approach to output determination by incorporating considerations of asset-market equilibrium.

To provide an overview consider the extreme case of capital market integration and suppose that arbitrage among identical assets denominated in domestic and foreign currencies ensures complete interest parity. Accordingly, $(1 + r) - (e^f/e)(1 + r_f)$, where r and r_f denote, respectively, the rates of interest on domestic and foreign securities identical in all respects except for the currency of denomination; and e and e^f denote, respectively, the current and the expected future exchange rates (the price of foreign exchange in terms of domestic currency).

Consider first the flexible exchange rate regime. Panel I of figure 3.1 shows the relation between the current exchange rate, e, and the domestic rate of interest, r, implied by interest arbitrage, for given values of the expected future exchange rate, e^f, and the foreign rate of interest, r_f. The positively sloped schedule, LM, in panel II, is the conventional money market equilibrium schedule, and the negatively sloped schedule, IS, is the goods market equilibrium schedule, adopted to the open economy and adjusted to incorporate the interest parity relation. A current transitory fiscal expansion that does not alter expectations concerning the future value of the exchange rate induces a rightward shift of the IS schedule, raises the level of output (under the Keynesian assumptions of price rigid-

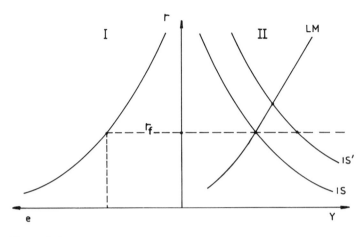

Figure 3.1
The Mundell-Fleming model

ity) and induces a rise in the domestic rate of interest. In order to maintain interest parity, the rise in the rate of interest results in an appreciation of the domestic currency (a fall in e). As is evident, the rise in the rate of interest (and the associated appreciation of the domestic currency) crowds out some domestic absorption, worsens the current account position, and mitigates the expansion of output. In contrast, if the fiscal expansion is permanent and expectations accordingly adjust, then the expected future exchange rate, e^f, falls to conform with the fall in e. Consequently, the IS schedule which has shifted rightward as a result of the fiscal expansion, is shifted back leftward due to the deterioration of the balance of trade caused by the appreciation of the future value of the currency. It follows that a fiscal expansion that is reflected in a current and future appreciation of the currency loses its effectiveness in altering the level of output. If both current and future exchange rates change in the same proportion, then the domestic rate of interest cannot deviate from the foreign rate and fiscal policy becomes completely ineffective. In the absence of debt revaluation effects the flexible exchange rate permits almost full insulation of the foreign economy from the consequences of the domestic tax-financed fiscal policies (see Frankel and Razin 1987b).

   Under a fixed exchange rate interest arbitrage ensures equality between domestic and foreign rates of interest (because $e = e^f$). Consequently, a fiscal expansion that induces a rightward shift of the IS schedule gains full potency in raising the level of output, because the offsetting force induced by currency appreciation is absent. The commitment to the maintenance of the fixed exchange rate ensures that the rise in the demand for money, caused by the rise in economic activity, is fully satisfied through a complete monetization of the capital inflows induced by the upward pressure on the domestic rate of interest. If the home country is relatively large in the world economy, then the rise in the demand for money would necessitate a rise in the world rate of interest which would mitigate the fiscally led expansion of domestic economic activity. The rise in the rate of interest under a fixed exchange rate regime is sharper than under a flexible exchange rate regime because in the latter the deterioration of the home country's competitive position (caused by its currency appreciation) reduces the expansionary effect of the fiscal policy and thereby diminishes the growth of money demand. It is also evident that a shift from a flexible to a fixed exchange rate regime amplifies the factors responsible for a negative transmission of domestic fiscal expansion to the output in the rest of the world.

The foregoing exposition of fiscal policies in open economies has aimed at highlighting key channels of international transmission under alternative exchange rate regimes. Other considerations relevant for the international effects of fiscal policies include debt versus tax-finance of government budgets, domestic and international debt-revaluation effects induced by the exchange rate changes, distinctions between short- and long-term multipliers, formulation of exchange rate expectations, the role of wage and price flexibility, risk and international capital mobility, and portfolio choice (for an incorporation of these elements, see Frenkel and Razin 1987b).

In this chapter we extend the analytical framework used in chapter 2 in two dimensions. First, we expand the menu of assets by adding interest-bearing bonds to the portfolio of assets. Second, we assume that the world capital markets are highly integrated and that all bonds are internationally tradable. The inclusion of interest-bearing bonds permits an analysis of the consequences of debt-financed changes in government spending. These consequences can then be compared with those of tax-financed changes in government spending. In conformity with the analysis in chapter 2 we continue to assume that the prices (GDP deflators) are fixed and that the levels of output are demand determined. In this context we analyze the short- and long-run effects of fiscal policies under fixed and flexible exchange-rate regimes.

As in chapter 2 the fixity of the GDP deflators implies that exchange-rate changes alter the relative prices of the domestically produced goods in terms of the foreign-produced goods (i.e., the terms of trade). Here, due to the expanded menu of assets traded in the integrated world capital market, exchange-rate changes impact on the economic system through two additional channels. First, they alter the real value of existing debts. Second, they influence expectations and thereby impact on the desired composition of the portfolio of assets. Thus the inclusion of interest-bearing assets and international capital mobility introduces new mechanisms governing the effects of fiscal policies and their international transmission.

3.1 The Analytical Framework

In specifying the behavioral functions, it is convenient to focus on the domestic economy. Accordingly, the budget constraint is

$$Z_t + M_t - B_t^p = P_t(Y_t - T_t) + M_{t-1} - R_{t-1}B_{t-1}^p, \tag{3.1}$$

where B_{t-1}^p denotes the domestic-currency value of private-sector's one-period debt issued in period t, and R_t denotes one plus the rate of interest. Analogously to equation (2.1) of chapter 2, the right-hand side of equation (3.1) states that in each period, t, the resources available to individuals are composed of disposable income, $P_t(Y_t - T_t)$—where for notational convenience we denote domestic output, Y_{xt}, by Y_t—and the net value of assets carried over from period $t - 1$. The latter consist of money, M_{t-1}, net of debt commitment $R_{t-1}B_{t-1}^p$ (including principal plus interest payments). For subsequent use we denote these assets by A_{t-1}, where

$$A_{t-1} = M_{t-1} - R_{t-1}B_{t-1}^p. \tag{3.2}$$

The left-hand side of equation (3.1) indicates the uses of these resources including nominal spending, Z_t, money holding, M_t, and bond holding, $-B_t^p$.

Throughout this chapter we assume that the GDP deflator, P_t, is fixed and normalized to unity. In that case nominal spending also equals real spending, E_t. Due to the absence of changes in prices we identify the real rate of interest, $r_t = R_t - 1$, with the corresponding nominal rate of interest (we return to this issue later in the chapter where we analyze the implications of exchange-rate changes).

Assuming that the various demand functions depend on the available resources and on the rate of interest, we express the spending and the money-demand function as

$$E_t = E(Y_t - T_t + A_{t-1}, r_t), \tag{3.3}$$

$$M_t = M(Y_t - T_t + A_{t-1}, r_t). \tag{3.4}$$

In specifying these functions, we have used a simplification similar to the one underlying equation (2.20) in chapter 2; we assume that the marginal propensities to spend and to hoard out of disposable income are the same as the corresponding propensities to spend and hoard out of assets. A similar specification underlines the demand for bonds which is omitted due to the budget constraint. We assume that desired spending and money holdings depend positively on available resources and negatively on the rate of interest.

A similar set of demand functions characterizes the foreign economy, where, as before, its variables are denoted by an asterisk and where its fixed GDP deflator, P^*, is normalized to unity. The specification of the equilibrium in the world economy depends on the exchange-rate regime. We start with the analysis of equilibrium under a fixed exchange-rate regime.

3.2   Capital Mobility with Fixed Exchange Rates

Equilibrium in the world economy necessitates that the markets for goods, money, and bonds clear. Under a fixed exchange rate, domestic and foreign money (in their role as assets) are perfect substitutes. Therefore money-market equilibrium can be specified by a single equilibrium relation stating that the world demand for money equals the world supply. Likewise, the assumptions that bonds are internationally tradable assets and that the current and future exchange rates are equal imply that in equilibrium these bonds command the same real return, $r_t = r_{ft}$, and that bond-market equilibrium can also be specified by a single equation pertaining to the unified world bond market. These considerations imply that the world economy is characterized by four markets: the markets for domestic output, foreign output, world money, and world bonds. By Walras's law we omit the bond market from the equilibrium specification of the two-country model of the world economy. Accordingly, the equilibrium conditions are

$$(1 - \beta_m)E(Y_t - T_t + A_{t-1}, r_t) + (1 - \beta_m^g)G + \beta_x^* \bar{e} E^*(Y_t^* + A_{t-1}^*, r_t) = Y_t, \tag{3.5}$$

$$\beta_m E(Y_t - T_t + A_{t-1}, r_t) + \beta_m^g G + (1 - \beta_x^*)\bar{e} E^*(Y_t^* + A_{t-1}^*, r_t) = \bar{e} Y_t^*, \tag{3.6}$$

$$M(Y_t - T_t + A_{t-1}, r_t) + \bar{e} M^*(Y_t^* + A_{t-1}^*, r_t) = \overline{M}, \tag{3.7}$$

where we continue to assume that foreign government spending and taxes are zero and where $\bar{e}$ denotes the fixed exchange rate expressing the price of foreign currency in terms of domestic currency. The (predetermined) value of foreign assets is measured in foreign-currency units so that $A_{t-1}^* = M_{t-1}^* + R_{t-1} B_{t-1}^p / \bar{e}$. Due to the assumed fixity of the GDP deflators, $\bar{e}$ also measures the relative price of importables in terms of exportables (defined in equation 2.18). As before, $\overline{M}$ denotes the world supply of money, measured in terms of domestic goods (whose domestic-currency price is unity); we continue to assume that the government does not finance its spending through money creation. Here it is relevant to note that in contrast with the analysis in chapter 2, the presence of capital markets permits discrepancies between spending and taxes which is made up for by debt issue.

The specification of the equilibrium system (3.5) through (3.7) embodies the arbitrage condition by which the yields on domestic and foreign bonds are equal. This equality justifies the use of the same rate of interest in the behavioral functions of the domestic and the foreign economies. The system (3.5) through (3.7) determines the short-run equilibrium values of domestic output, Y_t, foreign output, Y_t^*, and the world rate of interest, r_t, for given (predetermined) values of domestic and foreign net assets, A_{t-1} and A_{t-1}^*, and for given levels of government spending, G_t, and taxes, T_t.

The international distribution of the given world money supply associated with the short-run equilibrium is determined *endogenously* according to the demands. Thus

$$M_t = M(Y_t - T_t + A_{t-1}, r_t), \tag{3.8}$$

$$M_t^* = M^*(Y_t^* + A_{t-1}^*, r_t). \tag{3.9}$$

This equilibrium distribution obtains through international asset swaps.

A comparison between this short-run equilibrium system and the one used in chapter 2 reveals the significant role played by international capital mobility. In the absence of such mobility the short-run equilibrium determines the levels of domestic and foreign output from the goods-market equilibrium conditions (2.15) and (2.16) of chapter 2. Associated with these levels of outputs are equilibrium monetary *flows*, as shown by equations (2.12) through (2.14) and (2.19). These flows cease in the long run in which a stationary equilibrium distribution of the world money supply obtains, as indicated by the long-run equilibrium condition (2.26). In contrast, the equilibrium system (3.5) through (3.7) shows that with perfect capital mobility equilibrium in the world money market obtains through instantaneous asset swaps involving exchanges of money for bonds. This instantaneous *stock* adjustments is reflected in equation (3.7).

Fiscal Policies in a Small Country

To illustrate the effects of fiscal policies under a regime of fixed exchange rates with perfect capital mobility, it is convenient to begin with an analysis of a small country facing a given world rate of interest, $\bar{r}_f$, and a given world demand for its goods, $\bar{D}^* = \beta_x^* E^*$. Under these circumstances the equilibrium condition for the small economy reduces to

$$(1 - \beta_m)(E(Y_t - T_t + A_{t-1}, \bar{r}_f) + (1 - \beta_m^g)G + \bar{e}\bar{D}^* = Y_t. \qquad (3.5a)$$

This equilibrium condition determines the short-run value of output for the given (predetermined) value of assets and for given levels of government spending and taxes. As before, the money supply, M_t, associated with this equilibrium is obtained from the money-market equilibrium condition (3.8a):

$$M(Y_t - T_t + A_{t-1}, \bar{r}_f) = M_t. \qquad (3.8a)$$

This quantity of money is endogenously determined through instantaneous asset swaps at the prevailing world rate of interest.

To analyze the effects of fiscal policies, we differentiate equation (3.5a). Thus

$$\frac{dY_t}{dG} = \frac{1 - a^g}{s + a}, \quad \text{for } dT_t = 0, \qquad (3.10)$$

and

$$\frac{dY_t}{dG} = 1 - \frac{a^g}{s + a}, \quad \text{for } dT_t = dG, \qquad (3.11)$$

where, as before, $a^g = \beta_m^g$ is the government marginal propensity to import, and $1/(s + a)$ is the small-country foreign-trade multiplier. Equations (3.10) and (3.11) correspond, respectively, to a bond-financed and a tax-financed rise in government spending. As is evident, if all of government spending falls on domestic goods (so that $a^g = 0$), then the fiscal expansion that is financed by government borrowing raises output by the full extent of the foreign trade multiplier, while the balanced-budget fiscal expansion yields the closed-economy balanced-budget multiplier of unity. If, on the other hand, all of government spending falls on imported goods (so that $a^g = 1$), then the bond-financed multiplier is zero, whereas the balanced-budget multiplier is negative and equal to $(s + a - 1)/(s + a)$.

The changes in output induce changes in the demand for money. The induced changes in money holding can be found by differentiating equa-

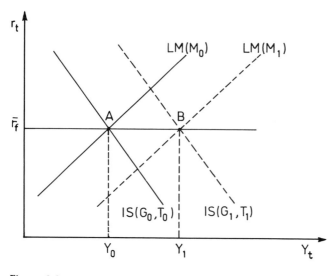

Figure 3.2
The short-run effects of fiscal policy under fixed exchange rates: the small-country case

tion (3.8a) and using (3.10) and (3.11). Accordingly, the debt-financed unit rise in government spending raises money holdings by $(1 - a^g)M_y/(s + a)$ units, and the balanced-budget rise in government spending lowers money holdings by $a^g M_y/(s + a)$.

This analysis is summarized by figure 3.2 in which the IS schedule portrays the goods-market equilibrium condition (3.5a). It is negatively sloped since both a rise in the rate of interest and a rise in output create an excess supply of goods. The initial equilibrium obtains at point A at which the rate of interest equals the exogenously given world rate, $\bar{r}_f$, and the level of output is Y_0. As indicated, the schedule IS is drawn for given levels of government spending and taxes, G_0 and T_0. The LM schedule passing through point A portrays the money-market equilibrium condition (3.8a). It is positively sloped since a rise in income raises the demand for money, whereas a rise in the rate of interest lowers the money demand. As indicated, the LM schedule is drawn for a given level of (the endogenously determined) money stock, M_0.

A unit rise in government spending creates an excess demand for domestic product (at the prevailing level of output). If it is bond financed, then the excess demand is $1 - a^g$ units, and if it is tax financed, then the excess demand is of $s + a - a^g$ units (which, depending on the relative magnitudes of the parameters, may be negative). The excess demand is reflected by a horizontal shift of the IS schedule from $IS(G_0)$ to $IS(G_1)$. As drawn, the IS schedule shifts to the right, reflecting the positive excess demand at the prevailing level of output. The new equilibrium obtains at point B, at which the level of output rises to Y_1. This higher level of output raises the demand for money, which is met instantaneously through an international swap of bonds for money that is effected through the world capital markets. The endogenous rise in the quantity of money from M_0 to M_1 is reflected in the corresponding rightward displacement of the LM schedule from $LM(M_0)$ to $LM(M_1)$.

The foregoing analysis determined the *short-run* consequences of an expansionary fiscal policy. The instantaneous asset swaps induced by the requirement of asset-market equilibrium alter the size of the economy's external debt. Specifically, if initially the economy was in a long-run equilibrium (so that $B_t^p = B_{t-1}^p = B^p$, $M_t = M_{t-1} = M$, $A_t = A_{t-1} = A$, and $Y_t = Y_{t-1} = Y$), then the fiscal expansion, which raises short-run money holdings as well as the size of the external debt, raises the debt-service requirement and (in view of the positive rate of interest) lowers the value of net assets $M_t - (1 + \overline{r}_f)B_t^p$ carried over to the subsequent period. This change sets in motion a dynamic process that is completed only when the economy reaches its new long-run equilibrium. We turn next to determine the long-run consequences of government spending.

The long-run equilibrium conditions can be summarized by the system (3.12) through (3.14):

$$E[Y - T + M - (1 + \overline{r})B^p, \overline{r}_f] = Y - \overline{r}_f B^p - T, \tag{3.12}$$

$$(1 - \beta_m)E[Y - T + M - (1 + \overline{r}_f)B^p, \overline{r}_f] + (1 - \beta_m^g)G + \overline{e}\,\overline{D}^* = Y, \tag{3.13}$$

$$M[Y - T + M - (1 + \overline{r}_f)B^p, \overline{r}_f] = M, \tag{3.14}$$

where the omission of the time subscripts indicates that in the long run the various variables do not vary over time. Equation (3.12) is obtained from the budget constraint (3.1) by using the spending function from equation (3.3) and by imposing the requirement that in the long run $M_t = M_{t-1}$ and $B_t^p = B_{t-1}^p$. This equation states that in the long run, private-sector spending equals disposable income, so that private-sector savings are zero. Equation (3.13) is obtained from (3.5a) and (3.8a) together with the long-run stationary requirement. This equation is the long-run market-clearing condition for domestic output. Finally, equation (3.14), which is the long-run counterpart to equation (3.8a), is the condition for long-run money-market equilibrium.

Up to this point we have not incorporated explicitly the government budget constraint. In the absence of money creation the long-run government budget constraint states that government outlays on purchases, G, and debt service, $\bar{r}_f B^g$ (where B^g denotes government debt), must equal taxes, T. Accordingly,

$$G + \bar{r}_f B^g = T. \tag{3.15}$$

Substituting this constraint into equation (4.12) yields

$$E[Y - G + M - B^p - \bar{r}_f(B^p + B^g), \bar{r}_f] + G$$

$$= Y - \bar{r}_f(B^p + B^g). \tag{3.12a}$$

Equation (3.12a) states that in the long run the sum of private-sector and government spending equals GNP. This equality implies that in the long run the current account of the balance of payments is balanced.

Using equations (3.12), (3.14), and (3.15), we obtain the combinations of output and debt that satisfy the long-run requirement of current-account balance as well as money-market equilibrium. These combinations are portrayed along the $CA = 0$ schedule in figure 3.2. Likewise, using equations (3.13) through (3.15), we obtain the combinations of output and debt that incorporate the requirements of goods- and money-market equilibrium. These combinations are portrayed along the YY schedule in figure 3.2. The slopes of these schedules are

$$\frac{dB^p}{dY} = -\frac{(s - M_y)}{(1 - s) - \bar{r}_f(s - M_y)} \quad \text{along the } CA = 0 \text{ schedule,} \tag{3.16}$$

$$\frac{dB^p}{dY} = -\frac{(s - M_y) + a}{(1 + \bar{r}_f)(1 - s - a)} \quad \text{along the } YY \text{ schedule.} \tag{3.17}$$

The term M_y is the marginal propensity to hoard (the inverse of the marginal income velocity) and $s - M_y$ represents the marginal propensity to save in the form of bonds. As is evident, the numerators in equations (3.16) and (3.17) are positive. The denominator of equation (3.17) is positive since $1 - s - a > 0$, and the denominator of equation (3.16) is positive on the assumption that $(1 - s) > \bar{r}_f(s - M_y)$. The latter assumption is a (partial) stability condition, ensuring that the perpetual rise in consumption $(1 - s)$ made possible by a unit rise in debt exceeds the perpetual return on the saving in bonds $\bar{r}_f(s - M_y)$ made possible by the initial unit rise in debt. (The condition for full stability is not explored). If this inequality does not hold, then consumption and debt rise overtime and do not

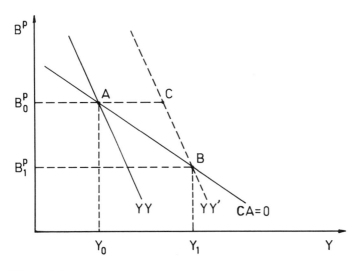

Figure 3.3
The long-run effects of a unit debt-financed rise in government spending under fixed exchange rates: The small-country case

converge to a long-run stationary equilibrium. The foregoing discussion implies that the slopes of both the $CA = 0$ and the YY schedules are negative. Further, since the numerator of (3.17) exceeds the one in (3.16) and the denominator of (3.17) is smaller than the one is (3.16), the YY schedule in figure 3.3 is steeper than the $CA = 0$ schedule. The initial long-run equilibrium is indicated by point A in figure 3.2 in which the levels of output and private-sector debt are Y_0 and B_0^p.

Consider the long-run effects of a *debt-financed* rise in government spending. As is evident by inspection of the system (3.12) through (3.14), as long as taxes remain unchanged, the $CA = 0$, which is derived from equations (3.12) and (3.14), remains intact. On the other hand, the rise in government spending influences the YY schedule, which is derived from equations (3.13) and (3.14). Specifically, to maintain goods-market equilibrium (for any given value of private-sector debt, B^p), a unit rise in government spending must be offset by $(1 - a^g)/(s + a)$ units rise in output. Thus, as long as some portion of government spending falls on domestic goods so that $a^g < 1$, the YY schedule in figure 3.3 shifts to the right. The new equilibrium is indicated by point B at which the level of output rises from Y_0 to Y_1 and private-sector debt falls to B_1^p. The new equilibrium is associated with a rise in money holdings, representing the cumulative surpluses in the balance of payments during the transition period.

A comparison between the short-run multiplier shown in equation (3.10) and the corresponding long-run multiplier (shown in equation A.7 of appendix A) reveals that the latter exceeds the former. In terms of figure 3.3, in the short run the output effect of the debt-financed rise in government spending is indicated by the point C, whereas the corresponding long-run equilibrium is indicated by point B.

Consider next the effects of a *tax-financed* rise in government spending. Such a balanced-budget rise in spending alters the positions of both the $CA = 0$ and the YY schedules. Using equations (3.12) and (3.14) together with the balanced-budget assumption that $dG = dT$, it can be shown that a unit rise in government spending induces a unit rightward shift of the $CA = 0$ schedule. By keeping the value of $Y - T$ intact and holding B^p constant, such a shift maintains the equality between private-sector spending and disposable income, and it also satisfies the money-market equilibrium condition. Likewise, using equations (3.13) and (3.14) together with the balanced-budget assumption, it is shown in appendix A that as long as the government import propensity, a^g, is positive, the YY schedule shifts to the right by less than one unit. The resulting new long-run equilibrium

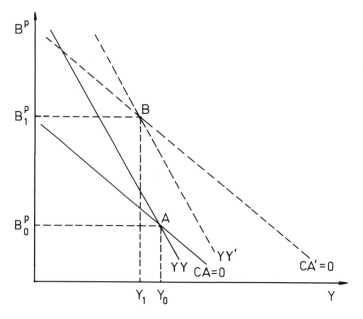

Figure 3.4
The long-run effect of a unit balanced-budget rise in government spending under fixed exchange rates: The small-country case

is indicated by point B in figure 3.4. For the case drawn, the long-run level of output falls from Y_0 to Y_1, and private-sector debt rises from B_0^p to B_1^p. Since government debt remains unchanged, the rise in private-sector debt corresponds to an equal rise in the economy's external-debt position. In general, however, depending on the parameters, domestic output may either rise or fall in the long run.

The size of the long-run multiplier of the balanced-budget rise in government spending depends on the government import propensity. At the limit, if all government spending falls on domestic output so that $a^g = 0$, the long-run balanced-budget multiplier is unity. In this case the YY schedule in figure 3.4 shifts to the right by one unit, the long-run level of output rises by one unit, and private-sector debt (and the economy's external debt) remains unchanged. At the other limit, if all government spending falls on foreign goods so that $a^g = 1$, the long-run balanced-budget multiplier is negative. In that case the rise in the economy's external debt is maximized.

The comparison between the short-run balanced-budget multiplier shown in equation (3.11) with the corresponding long-run multiplier (shown in equation A.10 of appendix A) highlights the contrasts between the two. If the government propensity to spend on domestic goods $(1 - a^g)$ equals the corresponding private-sector propensity $(1 - s - a)$, then the short-run multiplier is zero while the long-run multiplier is negative. On the other hand, if the government propensity $(1 - a^g)$ exceeds the private sector propensity $(1 - s - a)$, the short-run balanced-budget multiplier is positive, while the long-run balanced-budget multiplier is positive or negative. If both are positive, the short-run multiplier exceeds the long-run multiplier. Finally, if government spending falls entirely on domestically produced goods (so that $a^g = 0$), then the short-run and the long-run multipliers are equal to each other, and both are unity.

Fiscal Policies in a Two-Country World

In this section we return to the two-country model outlined in equations (3.5) through (3.7) and analyze the short-run effects of a debt and tax-financed rise in government spending on the equilibrium levels of domestic and foreign outputs as well as on the equilibrium world rate of interest. The endogeneity of the last two variables distinguishes this analysis from the one conducted for the small-country case. To conserve space, we do not analyze here the long-run effects; the formal system applicable to the long-run equilibrium of the two-country world is presented in appendix A.

The analysis is carried out diagrammatically with the aid of figures 3.4 and 3.5. In these figures the YY schedule portrays combinations of domestic and foreign levels of output that yield equality between the levels of production of domestic output and the world demand for it. Likewise, the Y^*Y^* schedule portrays combinations of output that yield equality between the level of production of foreign output and the world demand for it. The two schedules incorporate the requirement of equilibrium in the world money market. It is shown in appendix A that the slopes of these schedules are

$$\frac{dY_t^*}{dY_t} = \frac{1}{\bar{e}} \frac{(s+a)(M_r + \bar{e}M_r^*) + M_y H_r}{a^*(M_r + \bar{e}M_r^*) - M_y^*.H_r} \quad \text{along the } YY \text{ schedule,} \quad (3.18)$$

$$\frac{dY_t^*}{dY_t} = \frac{1}{\bar{e}} \frac{a(M_r + \bar{e}M_r^*) - M_y F_r}{(s^* + a^*)(M_r + \bar{e}M_r^*) + M_y^*.F_r} \quad \text{3along the } Y^*Y^* \text{ schedule,}$$

$$(3.19)$$

where H_r and F_r denote the partial (negative) effect of the rate of interest on the world demand for domestic and foreign outputs, respectively, and where E_r, M_r, E_r, and M_r^* denote the partial (negative) effects of the world rate of interest on domestic and foreign spending and money demand. As may be seen, the slopes of the two schedules may be positive or negative. To gain intuition, we note that the new element introduced in this chapter, which was absent from the analysis in chapters 2, is the role played by the market clearing world rate of interest in influencing spending. Indeed, in the special case for which spending does not depend on the rate of interest (so that $H_r = F_r = 0$), the slopes of the schedules indicated in equations (3.18) and (3.19) coincide with the slopes indicated in equations (2.22) and (2.23). Thus in that case both schedules must be positively sloped. If, on the other hand, the rate of interest exerts a strong negative effect on world spending, then the excess supply induced by a rise in one country's output may have to be eliminated by a fall in the other country's output. Even though this fall in foreign output lowers directly the foreign demand for the first country's exports, it also induces a decline in the world rate of interest which indirectly stimulates spending and may more than offset the direct reduction in demand. In that case market clearance for each country's output implies that domestic and foreign outputs are negatively related.

Even though the two schedules may be positively or negatively sloped, it may be verified (and is shown in appendix A) that if the two schedules have the same sign, then the YY schedule must be steeper than the Y^*Y^* schedule in absolute value. This restriction leaves four possible configura-

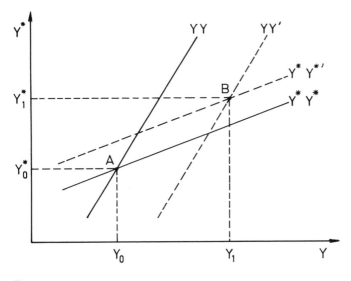

Figure 3.5
A unit debt-financed rise in government spending under fixed exchange rates: The two-country case

tions of the schedules. The common characteristic of these configurations is that starting from an initial equilibrium, if there is a rightward shift of the YY schedule that exceeds the rightward shift of the Y^*Y^* schedule, then the new equilibrium must be associated with a higher level of domestic output.

Two cases capturing the general pattern of world-output allocations are shown in figures 3.5 and 3.6. The other possible configurations do not yield different qualitative results concerning the effects of fiscal policies. In both figures the initial equilibrium is indicated by point A at which the domestic level of output is Y_0 and the foreign level is Y_0^*.

A debt-financed rise in government spending raises the demand for domestic output and induces a rightward shift of the YY schedule from YY to YY'. On the other hand, the direction of the change in the position of the Y^*Y^* schedule depends on the relative magnitudes of the two conflicting effects influencing world demand for foreign output. On the one hand, the rise in the domestic government spending raises the demand for foreign goods, but on the other hand, the induced rise in the world rate of interest lowers the demand. If the Y^*Y^* schedule is positively sloped, as in figure 3.5, then the rise in the domestic government spending induces a leftward (upward) shift of the Y^*Y^* schedule. The opposite holds if the Y^*Y^* schedule is negatively sloped as in figure 3.6. The formal expressions

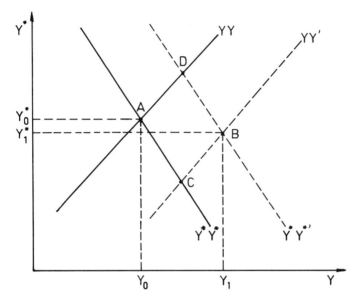

Figure 3.6
A unit debt-financed rise in government spending under fixed exchange rates: The
two-country case

indicating the magnitudes of the displacements of the schedules are provided in appendix A.

The new equilibrium obtains at point B at which domestic output rises
from Y_0 to Y_1. In the case shown in figure 3.5 (for which the interest-rate
effect on the world demand for foreign output is relatively weak) foreign
output rises. On the other hand, in the case shown in figure 3.6 (for which
the interest-rate effect on the world demand for foreign output is relatively
strong) foreign output may rise or fall depending on the magnitudes of the
parameters, especially the composition of government spending. For example, if government spending falls entirely on domestic output (so that
$a^g = 0$), the Y^*Y^* schedule does not shift, and the new equilibrium obtains
at a point like point C in figure 3.6 at which foreign output falls. In the
other extreme, if government spending falls entirely on foreign goods (so
that $a^g = 1$), then the YY schedule does not shift, and the new equilibrium
obtains at a point like point D at which foreign output rises.

It is shown in appendix A that independent of the direction of output
changes, the debt-financed rise in government spending must raise the
world rate of interest. The expressions reported in the appendix also reveal
that if the (negative) interest-rate effect on the world demand for domestic

output is relatively strong, then domestic output might fall. The balance-of-payments effects of the debt-financed rise in government spending are not clear cut, reflecting transfer-problem criteria. But, if the behavioral parameters of the domestic and foreign private sectors are equal to each other, and the government spending falls chiefly, on domestic output, then the balance of payments must improve, and the domestic money holdings are raised.

A tax-financed rise in government spending also alters the positions of the various schedules, as shown in the appendix A where we also provide the formal expressions for the various multipliers. In general, in addition to the considerations highlighted in the debt-financed case, the effect of a tax-financed fiscal spending also reflects the effects of the reduction in domestic disposable income on aggregate demand. This effect may more than offset the influence of government spending on domestic output. The effect on foreign output is also modified. If the interest-rate effect on world demand for foreign output is relatively weak (the case underlying figure 3.5), then the shift from a debt to a tax finance mitigates the expansion in foreign output. If, on the other hand, the interest-rate effect on the demand for foreign output is relatively strong (the case underlying figure 3.6), then the shift from debt to tax finance exerts expansionary effects on foreign output.

It is shown in appendix A that the direction of the change in the rate of interest induced by the tax-financed rise in government spending depends on a transfer-problem criterion, indicating whether the redistribution of world disposable income consequent on the fiscal policy raises or lowers the world demand for money. Accordingly, the rate of interest rises if the domestic-country ratio, s/M_y, exceeds the corresponding foreign-country ratio, $s^*/M_{y^*}^*$, and vice versa. Independent, however, of the change in the rate of interest, the tax-financed rise in government spending must deteriorate the domestic-country balance of payments and reduce its money holdings.

3.3 Capital Mobility with Flexible Exchange Rates

In this section we assume that the world economy operates under a flexible exchange-rate regime. With this assumption national monies become non-tradable assets whose relative price (the exchange rate, e) is assumed to be determined freely in the world market for foreign exchange. We continue to assume that in each country, the GDP deflators, P and P^*, are fixed and equal to unity. Under such circumstances the nominal exchange rates represent the terms of trade, and the nominal rates of interest in each country equal the corresponding (GDP-based) real rates. Further, as was traditionally postulated in the early literature on modeling macroeconomic policies in the world economy, we open the analysis by assuming that exchange-rate expectations are static. Under such circumstances the international mobility of capital brings about equality among national (GDP-based) real rates of interest. We return to the issue of exchange-rate expectations in a subsequent section.

Equilibrium in the world economy requires that world demand for each country's output equal the corresponding supply and that in each country the demand for cash balances equal the supply. Accordingly, the system characterizing the equilibrium in the two-country world economy is

$$(1 - \beta_m)E(Y_t - T_t + A_{t-1}, r_t) + (1 - \beta_m^g)G$$

$$+ e_t \beta_x^* E^*(Y_t^* + A_{t-1}^*, r_t) = Y_t, \tag{3.20}$$

$$\beta_m E(Y_t - T_t + A_{t-1}, r_t) + \beta_m^g G$$

$$+ e_t(1 - \beta_x^*)E^*(Y_t^* + A_{t-1}^*, r_t) = e_t Y_t^*, \tag{3.21}$$

$$M(Y_t - T_t + A_{t-1}, r_t) = M, \tag{3.22}$$

$$M^*(Y_t^* + A_{t-1}^*, r_t) = M^*. \tag{3.23}$$

Equations (3.20) and (3.21) are the goods-market equilibrium conditions (analogous to equations 3.5 and 3.6), and equations (3.22) and (3.23) are the domestic and foreign money-market equilibrium conditions, where M and M^* denote the supplies of domestic and foreign money. In contrast with the fixed exchange-rate system in which each country's money supply was determined endogenously, here it is determined *exogenously* by the monetary authorities. We also note that by Walras's law the world market equilibrium condition for bonds has been left out.

Finally, it is noteworthy that the value of securities may be expressed in terms of domestic or foreign currency units. Accordingly, the domestic-currency value of private-sector debt, B_t^p, can be expressed in units of foreign currency to yield $B_{ft}^p = B_t^p/e_t$. Arbitrage ensures that the expected rates of return on securities of different currency denomination are equalized. Accordingly, if r_t and r_{ft} are, respectively, the rates of interest on domestic- and foreign-currency-denominated bonds, then $1 + r_t = (\tilde{e}_{t+1}/e_t)(1 + r_{ft})$, where $\tilde{e}_{t+1}$ denotes the expected future exchange rate. By equating r_t to r_{ft}, the system (3.20) through (3.22) embodies the assumption of static exchange-rate expectations and perfect capital mobility. In appendix B we return to the issue of exchange-rate expectations.

Fiscal Policies in a Small Country

Analogously with our procedure in the analysis of fiscal policies under fixed exchange rates, we start the analysis of flexible exchange rates with an examination of the effects of fiscal policies in a small country facing a given world rate of interest, $\bar{r}_f$, and a given foreign demand for its goods, $\bar{D}^*$. The equilibrium conditions for the small country state that world demand for its output equals domestic GDP and that the domestic demand for money equals the supply. In contrast with the situation prevailing under a fixed exchange-rate regime where the monetary authorities, committed to peg the exchange rate, do not control the domestic money supply, under a flexible exchange-rate regime the supply of money is a policy instrument controlled by the monetary authorities.

The goods- and money-market equilibrium conditions are

$$(1 - \beta_m)E(Y_t - T_t + A_{t-1}, \bar{r}_f) + (1 - \beta_m^g)G + e_t\bar{D}^* = Y_t, \qquad (3.20a)$$

$$M(Y_t - T_t + A_{t-1}, \bar{r}_f) = M, \qquad (3.22a)$$

where

$$A_{t-1} = M_{t-1} - (1 + \bar{r}_f)e_tB_{f,t-1}^p.$$

As indicated, the valuation of the foreign-currency-denominated debt commitment, $(1 + \bar{r}_f)B_{f,t-1}^p$, employs the current exchange rate, e_t. These equilibrium conditions determine the short-run values of output and the exchange rate, and for comparison we recall that under the fixed exchange-rate regime the money supply rather than the exchange-rate was endogenously determined.

The equilibrium of the system is exhibited in figure 3.7. The downward-sloping IS schedule shows the goods-market equilibrium condition (3.20a). It is drawn for given values of government spending, taxes, and the exchange rate (representing the terms of trade). The upward-sloping LM schedule portrays the money-market equilibrium condition (3.22a). It is drawn for given values of the money supply, the exchange rate, and taxes. The initial equilibrium obtains at point A at which the rate of interest equals the world rate, $\bar{r}_f$, and the level of output is Y_0. The endogenously determined exchange rate associated with this equilibrium is e_0. It is relevant to note that in this system if the initial debt $B_{f,t-1}^p$ is zero, the LM

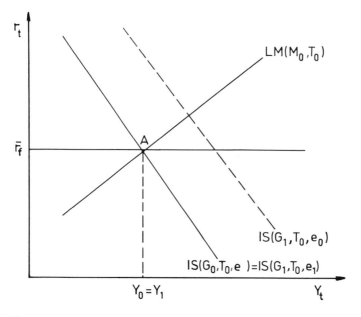

Figure 3.7
The short-run effects of a unit debt-financed rise in government spending under flexible exchange rates: The small-country case

schedule does not depend on the exchange rate and the level of output is determined exclusively by the money-market equilibrium condition, whereas (given the equilibrium level of output) the equilibrium exchange rate is determined by the goods-market equilibrium condition. This case underlies figure 3.7. Again a comparison with the fixed exchange-rate system is relevant. There, the equilibrium money stock is determined by the money-market equilibrium condition, whereas the equilibrium level of output is determined by the goods-market equilibrium condition.

Consider the effects of a debt-financed unit rise in government spending from G_0 to G_1, and suppose that the initial debt commitment is zero. At the prevailing levels of output and the exchange rate, this rise in spending creates an excess demand for domestic output and induces a rightward shift of the IS schedule by $(1 - a^g)/(s + a)$ units. This shift is shown in figure 3.7 by the displacement of the IS schedule from the initial position indicated by $IS(G_0, T_0, e_0)$ to the position indicated by $IS(G_1, T_0, e_0)$. Since with zero initial debt the LM schedule is unaffected by the rise in government spending, it is clear that given the world rate of interest, the level of output that clears the money market must remain at Y_0, corresponding to the initial equilibrium indicated by point A. To restore the initial equilibrium in

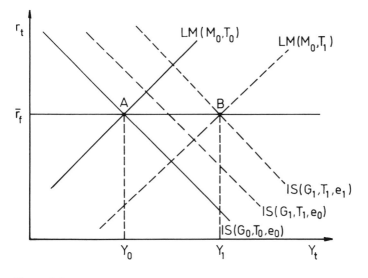

Figure 3.8
The short-run effects of a unit debt-financed rise in government spending under flexible
exchange rates: The small-country case

the goods market, the exchange rate must fall (i.e., the domestic currency
must appreciate). The induced improvement in the terms of trade lowers
the world demand for domestic output and induces a leftward shift of the
IS schedule. The goods market clears when the exchange rate falls to e_1 so
that the IS schedule indicated by $IS(G_1, T_0, e_1)$ also goes through point A.
We conclude that under flexible exchange rates with zero initial debt, a
debt-financed fiscal policy loses its potency to alter the level of economic
activity; its full effects are absorbed by changes in the exchange rate (the
terms of trade).

Consider next the effects of a tax-financed unit rise in government
spending from G_0 to G_1, shown in figure 3.8. In that case, at the prevailing levels of output and the exchange rate, the excess demand for domestic output induces a rightward displacement of the IS schedule by
$1 - a^g/(s + a)$ units to the position indicated by $IS(G_1, T_1, e_0)$. In addition
the unit rise in taxes lowers disposable income by one unit and reduces the
demand for money. To maintain money-market equilibrium at the given
world rate of interest, the level of output must rise by one unit so as to
restore the initial level of disposable income. Thus the LM schedule shifts
to the right from its initial position indicated by $LM(M_0, T_0)$ to the position indicated by $LM(M_0, T_1)$. With a zero level of initial debt (the case
assumed in the figure), the LM schedule does not depend on the value of

the exchange rate, and the new equilibrium obtains at point B, where the level of output rises by one unit from Y_0 to Y_1. Since at the initial exchange rate the horizontal displacement of the IS schedule is less than unity (as long as government spending falls in part on imported goods), it follows that at the level of output that clears the money market there is an excess supply of goods. This excess supply is eliminated through a rise in the exchange rate (i.e., a depreciation of the domestic currency) from e_0 to e_1. This deterioration in the terms of trade raises the world demand for domestic output and induces a rightward shift of the IS schedule to the position indicated by $IS(G_1, T_1, e_1)$. We conclude that under flexible exchange rates with zero initial debt, the tax-financed rise in government spending regains its full potency in effecting the level of economic activity.

Up to this point we have assumed that the initial debt position was zero. As a result the only channel through which the exchange rate influenced the system was through altering the domestic-currency value of the exogenously given foreign demand, $\bar{D}^*$. In general, however, with a nonzero level of initial debt, $B^p_{f,t-1}$ (denominated in units of foreign currency), the change in the exchange rate also alters the domestic currency value of the initial debt, and thereby of the initial assets, A_{t-1}. The revaluation of the debt commitment constitutes an additional channel through which the exchange rate influences the economic system. As a result the demand for money, and thereby the LM schedule, also depend on the exchange rate.

To appreciate the role played by debt-revaluation effects, we examine in figure 3.9 the implications of a nonzero level of initial debt. The various IS and LM schedules shown in the figure correspond to alternative assumptions concerning the level of initial debt $B^p_{f,-1}$; the rest of the arguments governing the position of the schedules are suppressed for simplicity. The initial equilibrium is shown by point A, and the solid schedules along which $B^p_{f,-1} = 0$ correspond to the cases analyzed in figures 3.7 and 3.8. With a positive value of initial debt, a rise in the exchange rate lowers the value of assets and lowers the demand for money. Restoration of money-market equilibrium requires a compensating rise in output. As a result in that case the LM schedule is positively sloped. By a similar reasoning, a negative value of initial debt corresponds to a negatively sloped LM schedule. The level of initial debt also influences the slope of the IS schedule. As shown in the figure, using similar considerations, the IS schedule is steeper than the bench-mark schedule (around point A) if $B^p_{f,-1} > 0$, and vice versa.

We can now use this figure to illustrate the possible implications of the initial debt position for the effects of fiscal policy in the figure we assume that the initial debt commitment falls short of foreign demand for the

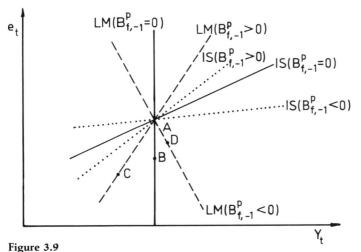

Figure 3.9
The short-run effect of a unit debt-financed rise in government spending under flexible
exchange rates: The debt-revaluation effect

domestic output. A debt-financed fiscal expansion induces a rightward shift
of the IS schedule and leaves the LM schedule intact. The short-run equilibrium of the system is changed from point A to point B if the level of initial
debt is zero, to point C if the level of initial debt is positive, and to point
D if this level is negative. Thus the debt revaluation effects critically
determine whether a debt-financed rise in government spending is contractionary or expansionary.

Using the system (3.20a) and (3.22a), the changes in the level of output
are

$$\frac{dY_t}{dG} = \frac{(1 - a^g)(1 + \overline{r}_f)B^p_{f,t-1}}{(1 + \overline{r}_f)B^p_{f,t-1} - \overline{D}^*}, \quad \text{for } dT_t = 0, \tag{3.24}$$

$$\frac{dY_t}{dG} = 1 - \frac{a^g(1 + \overline{r}_f)B^p_{f,t-1}}{(1 + \overline{r}_f)B^p_{f,t-1} - \overline{D}^*}, \quad \text{for } dT_t = dG. \tag{3.25}$$

Likewise, the induced changes in the exchange rates are

$$\frac{de_t}{dG} = \frac{1 - a^g}{(1 + \overline{r}_f)B^p_{f,t-1} - \overline{D}^*}, \quad \text{for } dT_t = 0, \tag{3.26}$$

and

$$\frac{de_t}{dG} = \frac{-a^g}{(1 + \overline{r}_f)B^p_{f,t-1} - \overline{D}^*}, \quad \text{for } dT_t = dG. \tag{3.27}$$

These results highlight the role played by the debt-revaluation effect of exchange-rate changes. Specifically, as is evident from equations (3.24) and (3.25), a rise in government spending may be contractionary if the initial debt commitment is positive. If, however, the private sector is initially a net creditor, then, independent of its means of finance, government spending must be expansionary. In the bench-mark case shown in figures 3.7 and 3.8, the initial debt position is zero, a tax finance is expansionary (yielding the conventional balanced-budget multiplier of unity), and a debt finance is not. The key mechanism responsible for this result is the high degree of capital mobility underlying the fixity of the rate of interest faced by the small country. With the given rate of interest and with a given money supply, there is in the short run a unique value of disposable income that clears the money market as long as the initial debt commitment is zero. Hence in this case a rise in taxes is expansionary, and a rise in government spending is neutral.

A comparison between the exchange-rate effects of government spending also reveals the critical importance of the means of finance and of the debt-revaluation effect. In general, for the given money supply the direction of the change in the exchange rate induced by a rise in government spending depends on whether the government finances its spending through taxes or through debt issue. If the initial debt commitment falls short of the (exogenously given) foreign demand for domestic output, then a debt-financed rise in government spending appreciates the currency, whereas a tax-financed rise in government spending depreciates the currency. The opposite holds if the initial debt commitment exceeds exports.

The foregoing analysis determined the short-run effects of government spending. We proceed to analyze the long-run effects of these policies. The long-run equilibrium conditions are shown in equations (3.28) through (3.30). These equations are the counterpart to the long-run fixed exchange-rate system (3.12) through (3.14). Accordingly,

$$E[Y - T + M - (1 + \bar{r}_f)eB_f^p, \bar{r}_f] = Y - \bar{r}_f eB_f^p - T, \tag{3.28}$$

$$(1 - \beta_m)E[Y - T + M - (1 + \bar{r}_f)eB_f^p, \bar{r}_f]$$
$$+ (1 - \beta_m^g)G + e\bar{D}^* = Y, \tag{3.29}$$

$$M[Y - T + M - (1 + \bar{r}_f)eB_f^p, \bar{r}_f] = M. \tag{3.30}$$

To set the stage for the analysis, consider first the bench-mark case for which the initial equilibrium was associated with a zero private-sector debt. For this case the long run is analyzed in figure 3.10. The $CA = 0$ schedule portrays combinations of private-sector debt and output that

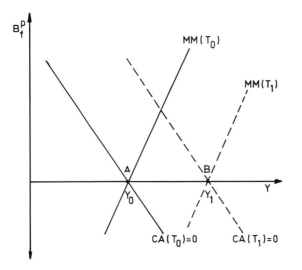

Figure 3.10
The long-run effects of a unit rise in government spending under flexible exchange rates: The small-country case

yield equality between spending and income, and thereby satisfy equation (3.28). In view of the government budget constraint shown in equation (3.15), this equality between private-sector income and spending also implies current-account balance. The MM schedule portrays combinations of debt and output that yield money-market equilibrium, and thereby satisfy equation (3.30). Around zero private-sector debt, both of these schedules are independent of the exchange rate. The slope of the $CA = 0$ schedule is $-s/e[1 - s(1 + \bar{r}_f)]$. Analogously to the previous discussion of the long-run equilibrium under fixed exchange rates, this slope is assumed negative for stability. The slope of the MM schedule is $1/(1 + \bar{r}_f)e$. It indicates that a unit rise in long-run private-sector debt raises debt commitment (principal plus debt service) by $(1 + \bar{r}_f)e$ and lowers the demand for money. To offset the reduction in disposable resources and restore the demand for money to its initial level, output must be raised by $(1 + \bar{r}_f)e$ units.

The initial long-run equilibrium is shown by point A, at which the level of private-sector debt is assumed to be zero and the level of output is Y_0. As is evident from equations (3.28) and (3.30), changes in the levels of government spending and government debt do not alter the $CA = 0$ schedule and the MM schedule. It follows that with zero private-sector debt a debt-financed rise in government spending does not alter the long-run equilibrium value of private sector debt indicated by point A in figure 3.10. In this long-run equilibrium the level of output remains unchanged, and the currency appreciates to the level shown in the short-run analysis of figure 3.7.

A rise in taxes alters both the $CA = 0$ and the MM schedules. As is evident from equations (3.28) and (3.30), a rise in output that keeps disposable income unchanged (at the given zero level of private-sector debt) maintains the initial current-account balance as well as money-market equilibrium intact. Thus a tax-financed unit rise in government spending induces a unit rightward displacement of both the $CA = 0$ and the MM schedules and yields a new long-run equilibrium at point B. At this point private-sector debt remains at its initial zero level. Also the level of output rises to Y_1, and the currency depreciates to e_1, as shown in the short-run analysis of figure 3.8.

The preceding discussion shows that under flexible exchange rates with zero initial private-sector debt, the long-run and the short-run effects of fiscal policies coincide. This characteristic is in contrast to the one obtained for fixed exchange rates, where the long-run effects of fiscal policies differ from the corresponding short-run effects. In interpreting these results, we note that due to the nontradability of national monies under a flexible exchange-rate regime, the mechanism of adjustment to fiscal policies does not permit instantaneous changes in the composition of assets through swaps of interest-bearing assets for national money in the world capital markets. As a result the only mechanism by which private-sector debt can change is through savings. Since with zero initial private-sector debt both debt-financed and tax-financed government spending do not alter disposable income (as seen from equations 3.24 and 3.25), it follows that these policies do not affect private-sector saving. Hence, if the initial position was that of a long-run equilibrium with zero savings and zero debt, the instantaneous short-run equilibrium following the rise in government spending is also characterized by zero savings. This implies that the economy converges immediately to its new long-run equilibrium.

The foregoing analysis of the long-run consequences of government spending abstracted from the debt-revaluation effect arising from exchange-rate changes. In general, if in the initial equilibrium the level of private-sector debt differs from zero, then the debt-revaluation effect breaks the coincidence between the short- and the long-run fiscal policy multipliers. Using the system (3.28) through (3.30), the long-run effects of a debt-financed rise in government spending are

$$\frac{dY}{dG} = 0, \quad \text{for } dT = 0, \tag{3.31}$$

$$\frac{dB_f^p}{dG} = \frac{(1 - a^g)B_f^p}{e\bar{D}^*}, \quad \text{for } dT = 0, \tag{3.32}$$

$$\frac{de}{dG} = -\frac{(1 - a^g)}{\bar{D}^*}, \quad \text{for } dT = 0. \tag{3.33}$$

Likewise, the long-run effects of a balanced-budget rise in government spending are

$$\frac{dY}{dG} = 1, \quad \text{for } dT = dG, \tag{3.34}$$

$$\frac{dB_f^p}{dG} = -\frac{a^g B_f^p}{e\bar{D}^*}, \quad \text{for } dT = dG, \tag{3.35}$$

$$\frac{de}{dG} = \frac{a^g}{\bar{D}^*}, \quad \text{for } dT = dG. \tag{3.36}$$

These results show that independent of the debt-revaluation effects, a rise in government spending does not alter the long-run level of output if it is debt financed, but the same rise in government spending raises the long-run level of output by a unit multiplier if it is tax financed. Thus, in both cases the long-run level of disposable income, $Y - T$, is independent of government spending. The results also show that if government spending is debt financed, and if the initial private-sector debt was positive, then in the long run it rises while the currency appreciates. The opposite holds for the case in which government spending is tax financed.

In comparing the extent of the long-run changes in private-sector debt with the corresponding changes in the exchange rate, we note that the *value* of debt, eB_f^p (measured in units of domestic output) remains unchanged. This invariance facilitates the interpretation of the long-run multipliers. Accordingly, consider the long-run equilibrium system (3.28) through (3.30), and suppose that government spending is debt financed. In that case as is evident from the money-market equilibrium condition (3.30), the equilibrium level of output does not change as long as the money supply, taxes, and the value of the debt commitment are given. Since, however, the rise in government spending creates an excess demand for domestic output, it is seen from equation (3.29) that the currency must appreciate (i.e., e must fall) so as to lower the value of foreign demand, $e\bar{D}^*$, and thereby maintain the same equilibrium output. Obviously, since e falls, (the absolute value of) private sector debt, B_f^p, must rise by the same proportion so as to maintain the product eB_f^p unchanged. Finally, these changes ensure that the zero-saving condition (3.28) is also satisfied. A similar interpretation can be given to the effects of a tax-financed rise in government spending, except that in this case the level of output rises in line with the rise in taxes so as to keep disposable income unchanged.

A comparison between these long-run effects and the corresponding short-run effects shown in equations (3.24) and (3.25) reveals that the relative magnitudes of these multipliers depend on the initial debt position. For example, if the initial debt commitment is positive but smaller than export earnings, then the short-run multiplier of tax finance is positive and larger than unity. In this case the long-run multipliers are more moderate than the corresponding short-run multipliers. If, however, the initial debt commitment exceeds export earnings, then the short-run debt-finance multiplier is positive (in contrast with the long-run multiplier), and the short-run tax-finance multiplier is smaller than unity, and could even be negative (in contrast with the unitary long-run balanced-budget multiplier).

Fiscal Policies in a Two-Country World

In this section we extend the analysis of the small-country case to the two-country model outlined in equations (3.20) through (3.23). To develop a diagrammatic apparatus useful for the analysis of fiscal policies, we proceed in three steps. First, we trace the combinations of domestic and foreign output levels that clear each country's goods market, incorporating the conditions of market clearing in the two national money markets (which under flexible exchange rates are the two nontradable assets). Second, we trace the combinations of domestic and foreign output levels that bring about a money-market equilibrium in each country and, at the same time, yield equality between the domestic and the foreign rates of interest, thereby conforming with the assumptions of perfect capital mobility and static expectations. Finally, in the third step, we find the unique combination of domestic and foreign levels of output that satisfy simultaneously the considerations underlying the first two steps.

Using the domestic money-market equilibrium condition (3.22), we can express the domestic money-market-clearing rate of interest, r_t, as a positive function of disposable resources, $Y_t - T_t + A_{t-1}$, and as a negative function of the domestic money stock, M; that is, $r_t = r(Y_t - T_t + A_{t-1}, M)$. Applying a similar procedure to the foreign country, we can express the foreign money-market-clearing rate of interest, r_t^*, as a function of foreign disposable resources and money stock; that is, $r_t^* = r^*(Y_t^* + A_{t-1}^*, M^*)$, where $A_{t-1}^* = M_{t-1}^* + R_{t-1}B_{t-1}^p/e_t$. By substituting these money-market-clearing rates of interest into the goods-market equilibrium conditions (3.20) and (3.21), we obtain the reduced-form equilibrium conditions (3.37) and (3.38):

$$(1 - \beta_m)\tilde{E}(Y_t - T_t + A_{t-1}, M) + (1 - \beta_m^g)G$$
$$+ e_t\beta_x^*\tilde{E}^*(Y_t^* + A_{t-1}^*, M^*) = Y_t, \tag{3.37}$$

$$\beta_m\tilde{E}(Y_t - T_t + A_{t-1}, M) + \beta_m^g G$$
$$+ e_t(1 - \beta_x^*)\tilde{E}^*(Y_t^* + A_{t-1}^*, M^*) = e_t Y_t^*, \tag{3.38}$$

where a tilde (˜) indicates a reduced-form function incorporating the money-market equilibrium conditions. For each and every value of the exchange rate, e_t, equations (3.37) and (3.38) yield the equilibrium combination of domestic and foreign output that clears the world market for both goods. The schedule ee in figure 3.11 traces these equilibrium output levels for alternative values of the exchange rate. The detailed derivation of this schedule is provided in appendix B, where it is shown that around balanced-trade equilibria with a zero initial private-sector debt (so that exchange-rate changes do not exert revaluation effects), this schedule is negatively sloped. In general, the ee schedule is negatively sloped if a rise in the exchange rate (a deterioration in the terms of trade) raises the world

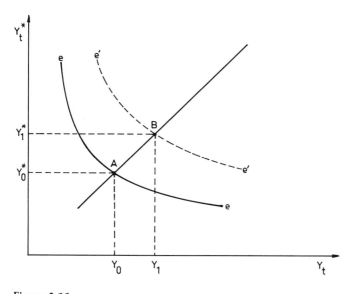

Figure 3.11
A debt-financed unit rise in government spending under flexible exchange rates: The two-country case

demand for domestic output and lowers the world demand for foreign output, allowing for the proper adjustments in each country's rate of interest so as to clear the national money market.

So far we have not yet incorporated the constraints imposed by the perfect international mobility of capital. To incorporate this constraint, the national money-market-clearing rates of interest, r_t and r_t^*, must be equal. This equally implies that

$$r(Y_t - T_t + A_{t-1}, M) = r^*(Y_t^* + A_{t-1}^*, M^*). \tag{3.39}$$

The combinations of domestic and foreign output levels conforming with the perfect capital-mobility requirement are portrayed by the rr^* schedule in figure 3.11. With a zero level of initial debt (so that the debt revaluation effects induced by exchange-rate changes are absent) this schedule is positively sloped since a rise in domestic output raises the demand for domestic money and the domestic rate of interest; international interest-rate equalization is restored through a rise in foreign output that raises the foreign demand for money and the foreign rate of interest.

The short-run equilibrium is indicated by point A in figure 3.11. At this point both goods markets clear, both national money markets clear, and the rates of interest are equalized internationally. The levels of output corresponding to this equilibrium are Y_0 and Y_0^*.

A debt-financed unit rise in government spending alters the position of the goods-market equilibrium schedule ee but does not impact on the capital-market equilibrium schedule, rr^*. It is shown in appendix B that for an initial trade-balance equilibrium with zero debt, the ee schedule shifts to the right by $1/\bar{s}$ units. The new equilibrium is indicated by point B in figure 3.11. Thus (in the absence of revaluation effects) in the new short-run equilibrium both the domestic and the foreign levels of output rise from Y_0 and Y_0^* to Y_1 and Y_1^*, respectively.

For the given supply of money and for the higher level of output (which raises the demand for money), money-market equilibrium obtains at a higher rate of interest (which restores money demand to its initial level). Finally, it is shown in appendix B that the exchange-rate effects of the debt-financed rise in government spending are not clear cut, reflecting transfer-problem criteria. These criteria reflect the relative pressures on the rates of interest in the domestic and foreign money markets induced by the changes in world demands for domestic and foreign outputs. If these pressures tend to raise the domestic rate of interest above the foreign rate, then the domestic currency must appreciate so as to lower the demand for domestic output and reduce the upward pressure on the domestic rate of

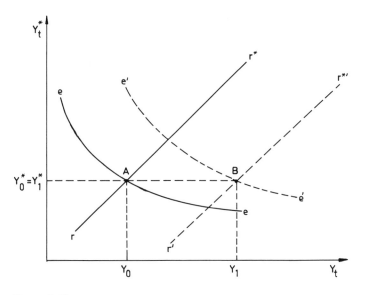

Figure 3.12
A tax-financed unit rise in government spending under flexible exchange rates: The two-country case

interest. The opposite follows in the converse circumstances. But, if the behavioral parameters of the two private sectors are equal to each other, and the government spending falls chiefly on domestic output, then the domestic currency must appreciate.

A tax-financed unit rise in government spending alters the positions of both the ee and the rr^* schedules. As is evident by inspection of equations (3.37) through (3.39), both schedules shift to the right by one unit. This case is illustrated in figure 3.12 where the initial equilibrium is indicated by point A and the new short-run equilibrium by point B. At the new equilibrium the domestic level of output rises by one unit so that disposable income remains unchanged. With unchanged levels of disposable income the demand for money is not altered, and the initial equilibrium rate of interest remains intact. As a result the initial equilibrium in the foreign economy is not disturbed, and the foreign level of output remains unchanged. Finally, in order to eliminate the excess supply in the domestic-goods market arising from the rise in domestic output and the unchanged level of disposable income, the currency must depreciate so as to raise the domestic-currency value of the given foreign demand. It follows that in the absence of revaluation effects, the flexible exchange-rate regime permits a full insulation of the foreign economy from the consequences of the domestic tax-financed fiscal policies. The more general results allowing for revaluation effects are provided in the appendix B. Analogously to the procedure adopted in the fixed exchange-rate case, we do not analyze explicitly the long-run equilibrium of the two-country world under the flexible exchange-rate regime. The formal equilibrium system applicable for such an analysis is presented in appendix B.

3.4   Summary and Overview

In this chapter we analyzed the effects of government spending under fixed and flexible exchange-rate regimes. Throughout we have assumed that the world capital markets are highly integrated so that capital is perfectly mobile internationally. To focus on the pure effects of fiscal policies, we assumed that there is no active monetary policy. In particular, we abstracted from money-financed government spending. Accordingly, we analyzed the short- and long-run consequences of debt-financed and of tax-financed changes in government spending. In this context we focused on the effects of fiscal policies on the levels of output, debt, and the rate of interest under the two alternative exchange-rate regimes. In addition, for the fixed exchange-rate regime, we examined the induced changes in the money supply, and for the flexible exchange-rate regime, we determined the induced change in the exchange rate.

The short- and long-run effects of a unit debt and tax-financed rise in government spending for a small country facing a fixed world rate of interest are summarized in table 3.1. In this table we show the various multipliers applicable to the fixed as well as to the flexible exchange-rate regimes. The output multipliers under the fixed exchange-rate regime are the typical simple foreign-trade multipliers. These results are of course expected since the rate of interest is exogenously given to the small country. The fixity of the rate of interest implies that the typical crowding-out mechanism induced by changes in the rate of interest are not present.

Under flexible exchange rates the short-run output multipliers of fiscal policies depend crucially on the debt-revaluation effect induced by exchange-rate changes. Indeed, in the absence of such an effect (as would be the case if the initial debt position is zero) fiscal policies lose their capacity to alter disposable income. Accordingly, with debt finance the output multiplier is zero, and with tax finance the corresponding multiplier is unity. In general, however, the signs and magnitudes of the *short-run* output multipliers depend on the size of the initial debt. In contrast, these considerations do not influence the *long-run* output multipliers. As seen in

Table 3.1
The short- and long-run effects of a unit rise in government spending under fixed and flexible exchange rates: the small-country case

	Debt financed		Tax financed	
	Short run	Long run	Short run	Long run
Fixed exchange rates: effects on				
Y	$\dfrac{1-a^g}{s+a}$	$\dfrac{1-a^g}{\Delta}[1-s-\bar{r}_f(s-M_y)]$	$1-\dfrac{a^g}{s+a}$	$1-\dfrac{a^g}{\Delta}[1-s-\bar{r}_f(s-M_y)]$
$B^p_{f,t-1}$	0	$-\dfrac{1-a^g}{\Delta}(s-M_y)$	0	$\dfrac{a^g}{\Delta}(s-M_y)$
M	$\dfrac{(1-a^g)M_y}{s+a}$	$\dfrac{1-a^g}{\Delta}M_y$	$-\dfrac{a^g}{s+a}M_y$	$-\dfrac{a^g}{\Delta}M_y$
Flexible exchange rates: effects on				
Y	$\dfrac{(1-a^g)R_fB^p_{f,t-1}}{R_fB^p_{f,t-1}-\bar{D}^*}$	0	$1-\dfrac{a^gR_fB^p_{f,t-1}}{R_fB^p_{f,t-1}-\bar{D}^*}$	1
$B^p_{f,t-1}$	0	$\dfrac{(1-a^g)B^p_f}{e\bar{D}^*}$	0	$-\dfrac{a^gB^p_f}{e\bar{D}^*}$
e	$\dfrac{(1-a^g)}{R_fB^p_{f,t-1}-\bar{D}^*}$	$-\dfrac{(1-a^g)}{\bar{D}^*}$	$\dfrac{-a^g}{R_fB^p_{f,t-1}-\bar{D}^*}$	$\dfrac{a^g}{\bar{D}^*}$

Note: $\bar{D}^*$ denotes export earnings measured in units of foreign currency, $R_f = 1 + \bar{r}_f$ and $\Delta = a - \bar{r}_f(s - M_y)$. $\Delta > 0$ under the assumption that a rise in income worsens the current account of the balance of payments. The term $1 - s - \bar{r}_f(s - M_y) > 0$ for stability.

the table, with perfect capital mobility and flexible exchange rates, the long-run value of disposable income cannot be affected by fiscal policies.

One of the important points underscored by the results reported in table 3.1 is the critical dependence of the direction of change in the key variables on the means of fiscal finance. Specifically, a shift from a debt finance to a tax finance reverses the signs of the multipliers of B_f^p, M, and e.

For example, a tax-financed rise in government spending under a fixed exchange-rate regime induces a balance-of-payments deficit and reduces both the short- and the long-run money holdings. On the other hand, a similar rise in government spending that is debt-financed induces a surplus in the balance of payments and raises money holdings in the short run as well as in the long run. Likewise, under a flexible exchange-rate regime the tax-financed rise in government spending depreciates the long-run value of the currency, whereas the debt-financed rise in government spending appreciates the long-run value of the currency. As indicated earlier, a similar reversal in the direction of the change in the exchange rate also pertains to the short-run, but whether the currency depreciates or appreciates in the short run depends on the size of the debt which in turn governs the debt-revaluation effect.

To study the characteristics of the international transmission mechanism, we extended the analysis of the small-country case to a two-country model of the world economy. The new channel of transmission is the world rate of interest which is determined in the unified world capital market. Table 3.2 summarizes the short-run effects of fiscal policies under the two alternative exchange-rate regimes. To avoid a tedious taxonomy, the summary results for the flexible exchange rates reported in the table are confined to the case in which the twin revaluation effects—debt revaluation and trade-balance revaluation—induced by exchange-rate changes are absent; accordingly, it is assumed that the initial debt is zero and that the initial equilibrium obtains with a balanced trade.

As shown, independent of the exchange-rate regime, a debt-financed rise in government spending raises the world rate of interest. Under the flexible exchange-rate regime the debt-financed rise in government spending stimulates demand for both domestic and foreign goods and results in an expansion of both outputs. Thus in this case the international transmission of the rise in government spending, measured by comovements of domestic and foreign outputs, is positive. On the other hand, under a fixed exchange-rate regime the rise in the world rate of interest may offset the direct effect of government spending on aggregate demand and may result in lower levels of output. But, if the (negative) interest-rate effect on

Table 3.2
The direction of the short-run effects of a rise in government spending under fixed and flexible exchange rates: the two-country world

	Debt financed	Tax financed
Fixed exchange rates: effects on		
Y	+ (for small H_r)	+ (for $a^g \leqslant a$)
Y^*	+ (for small F_r)	+
r	+	+ (for $A > 0$)
n	+ (for $B + C < 0$)	$-$
	$-$ (for $B + C > 0$)	$-$ (for $A < 0$)
Flexible exchange rates: effects on		
Y	+	+
Y^*	+	0
r	+	0
e	+ (for $\tilde{B} > 0$)	+
	$-$ (for $\tilde{B} < 0$)	

Note: The signs indicated in flexible exchange-rate part of the table are applicable to the case of an initial equilibrium with balanced trade and zero initial debt. H^r and F_r denote, respectively, the negative effect of the rate of interest on the world demand for domestic and foreign goods, $A = s\text{-}M_y - s^*\text{-}M_{y^*}^*$, $B = \bar{e}(M_y/M_r)[a^* + s^*(1 - a^g)] - (M_{y^*}^*/M_r^*)(a + sa^g)$, and $\tilde{B} = e_t(M_y/M_r)[\tilde{a}^* + \tilde{s}^*(1 - a^g)] - (M_{y^*}^*/M_r^*)(\tilde{a} + \tilde{s}a^g)$, correspond, respectively, to the fixed and flexible exchange-rate regimes and $C = M_y M_{y^*}^*.M_r M_r^*[F_r(1 - a^g) - H_r a^g]$.

aggregate demand is relatively weak, then both domestic and foreign outputs rise, thereby resulting in a positive international transmission. Finally, we note that there is no presumption about the direction of change in money holdings (under fixed exchange rates) and in the exchange rate (under flexible exchange rates) in response to the debt-financed fiscal expansion. As indicated, depending on the relative magnitudes of the domestic and foreign saving and import propensities, and the domestic and foreign sensitivities of money demand with respect to changes in the rate of interest and income, the balance of payments may be in a deficit or in a surplus, and the currency may depreciate or appreciate.

The results in table 3.2 also highlight the significant implication of alternative means of budgetary finance. Indeed, in contrast with debt finance, a tax-financed rise in government spending under a flexible exchange-rate regime leaves the world rate of interest unchanged, raises domestic output, and depreciates the currency. The reduction in the domestic private-sector demand for foreign output, induced by the depreciation of the currency, precisely offsets the increased demand induced by the rise in government spending. As a result, foreign output remains intact, and the flexible exchange rate regime fully insulates the foreign economy from the domestic tax-financed fiscal policy. In this case the analysis of the two-country world economy reduces to the one carried out for the small-country case. Therefore the long-run multipliers for the two countries operating under flexible exchange rates coincide with the short-run multipliers, the domestic short- and long-run output multipliers are unity, and the corresponding foreign output multipliers are zero.

In contrast with the flexible exchange-rate regime in which the currency depreciates to the extent needed to maintain world demand for (and thereby the equilibrium level of) foreign output, the fixed exchange-rate regime does not contain this insulating mechanism. As a result the tax-financed rise in the domestic government spending raises the world demand for (and thereby the equilibrium level of) foreign output. On the other hand, depending on the relative magnitude of the domestic-government import propensity, the domestic level of output may rise or fall. If, however, the government import propensity does not exceed the corresponding private-sector propensity, then domestic output rises, and the international transmission, measured by comovements of domestic and foreign outputs, is positive. Finally, since at the prevailing rate of interest domestic disposable income falls and foreign disposable income rises (as shown in chapter 2), these changes in disposable incomes alter the world demand for money and necessitate equilibrating changes in the world rate of interest. As shown in table 3.2, the change in the world demand for money (at the prevailing rate of interest) reflects a transfer-problem criterion. If the ratio of the domestic saving to hoarding propensities, s/M_y, exceeds the corresponding foreign ratio, s^*/M_y^*, then the international redistribution of disposable income raises the world demand for money and necessitates a rise in the world rate of interest. The opposite holds if s/M_y falls short of s^*/M_y^*. Independent, however, of the direction of the change in the interest rate, the tax-financed rise in government spending must worsen the balance of payments and lower the short-run equilibrium money holdings.

Throughout this chapter (except in the initial overview) we assume that expectations are static. Since under a flexible exchange-rate regime the actual exchange rates do change, the assumption that exchange-rate expectations are static results in expectation errors during the period of transition toward the long-run equilibrium. The incorporation of a consistent expectations scheme introduces an additional mechanism governing the short-run behavior. Aspects of this mechanism are examined in appendix B.

We conclude this summary with an overview of the income-expenditure model analyzed in chapters 2 and 3. The issues on which we focus are chosen so as to provide the motivation for, and the link to, the formulations and analyses carried out in the subsequent parts of the book.

A key characteristic of the formulation of the income-expenditure model used in this part of the book is the lack of solid micro-economic foundations underlying the behavior of the private and the public sectors, and the absence of an explicit rationale for the holdings of zero interest-bearing money in the presence of safe interest-bearing bonds. The latter issue is of relevance in view of the central role played by monetary flows in the international adjustment mechanism. Furthermore no attention was given to the intertemporal budget constraints, and the behavior of both the private and the public sectors was not forward-looking in a consistent manner. As a result there was no mechanism ensuring that the patterns of spending, debt accumulation, and money hoarding (which are the key elements governing the equilibrium dynamics of the economic system) are consistent with the relevant economic constraints. The implication of this shortcoming is that in determining the level and composition of spending, saving, and asset holdings, the private sector does not incorporate explicitly the intertemporal consequences of government policies.

To illustrate the significance of this issue, consider a debt-financed rise in current government spending. A proper formulation of the government's intertemporal budget constraint must recognize that to service the debt and maintain its solvency, the government must accompany this current fiscal expansion by either cutting down future spending or raising future (ordinary or inflationary) taxes. Furthermore a proper specification of the private sector's behavior must allow for the fact that the forward-looking individuals may recognize the future consequences of current government policies and incorporate these expected consequences into their current as well as planned future spending, saving, and asset holdings.

The neglect of the intertemporal budget constraints and of the consequences of forward-looking behavior consistent with these constraints are among the main deficiencies of the income-expenditure model as formulated in this part of the book. In the subsequent parts of the book we rectify these shortcomings. In doing so, we develop a unified model that is derived from optimizing behavior consistent with the relevant temporal and intertemporal economic constraints. The resulting macroeconomic model, which is grounded upon microeconomic foundations, is capable of dealing with new issues in a consistent manner. Among these issues are the effects of various time patterns of government spending and taxes. We can thus distinguish between temporary and permanent as well as between current and future policies. Likewise, the model is capable of analyzing the macroeconomic consequences of alternative specifications of the tax structure. We can thus distinguish between the effects of different types of taxes (e.g., income taxes, value-added taxes, and international capital flow taxes) used to finance the budget.

In this chapter as in chapter 2 we assumed that producer prices were given and that outputs were demand determined. In this framework nominal exchange-rate changes amounted to changes in the terms of trade. As a result the characteristics of the economic system were drastically different across alternative exchange-rate regimes. Throughout the subsequent parts of the book we relax the fixed-price assumption and allow for complete price flexibility. With this flexibility prices are always at their market-clearing equilibrium levels. Accordingly, changes in the terms of trade induced by equilibrium changes in prices trigger an adjustment mechanism that is analogous to the one triggered by nominal exchange-rate changes in the income-expenditure model. Therefore, we do not consider issues arising from nominal exchange-rate changes, yet we allow for the effects of terms of trade and real exchange-rate changes on the international adjustment mechanism.

Finally, it is noteworthy that an important feature of the intertemporal approach adopted in the rest of this book is its capability of dealing explicitly with the welfare consequences of economic policies and events. This feature reflects the basic attribute of the macroeconomic model: the economic behavior underlying this model is derived from, and is consistent with, the principles of individual utility maximization. Therefore, in contrast with the traditional approach underlying the discussion in this part of the book, the intertemporal optimizing approach to which we turn next provides a framework suitable for the normative evaluation of international macroeconomic policies.

3.5   Appendix A: Fixed Exchange Rates

Long-Run Equilibrium: The Small-Country Case

The long-run equilibrium conditions are specified by equations (3.12) through (3.15) of the text. Substituting the government budget constraint (3.15) into equations (3.12) through (3.14) yields

$$E[Y - G + M - B^p - \overline{r}_f(B^p + B^g), \overline{r}_f] + G = Y - \overline{r}_f(B^p + B^g), \quad \text{(A.1)}$$

$$(1 - \beta_m)E[Y - G + M - B^{p'} - \bar{r}_f(B^p + B^g), \bar{r}_f] + (1 - \beta_m^g)G + \bar{e}\bar{D}^*$$

$$= Y, \tag{A.2}$$

$$M[Y - G + M - B^p - \bar{r}_f(B^p + B^g), \bar{r}_f] = M. \tag{A.3}$$

Equations (A.1) and (A.3) yield the combinations of output and private-sector debt underlying the $CA = 0$ schedule, and equations (A.2) and (A.3) yield the combinations of these variables underlying the YY schedule. To obtain the slope of the $CA = 0$ schedule, we differentiate equations (A.1) and (A.3) and obtain

$$\begin{pmatrix} -s & s(1 + \bar{r}_f) - 1 \\ M_y & -(1 + \bar{r}_f)M_y \end{pmatrix} \begin{pmatrix} dY \\ dB^p \end{pmatrix} = \begin{pmatrix} -(1 - s) \\ 1 - M_y \end{pmatrix} dM, \tag{A.4}$$

where $s = 1 - E_y$ and $a = \beta_m E_y$. Solving (A.4) for dY/dM and dividing the resultant solutions by each other yields the expression for dB^p/dY along the $CA = 0$ schedule. This expression is reported in equation (3.16) of the text.

Likewise differentiating equations (A.2) and (A.3) yields

$$\begin{pmatrix} -(s + a) & -(1 + \bar{r}_f)(1 - s - a) \\ M_y & -(1 + \bar{r}_f)M_y \end{pmatrix} \begin{pmatrix} dY \\ dB^p \end{pmatrix} = \begin{pmatrix} -(1 - s - a) \\ 1 - M_y \end{pmatrix} dM. \tag{A.5}$$

Following a similar procedure, we obtain the expression for dB^p/dY along the YY schedule. This expression is reported in equation (3.17) of the text.

To obtain the horizontal displacements of the $CA = 0$ schedule following a balanced-budget rise in government spending, we differentiate equations (A.1) and (A.3), holding B^g and B^p constant. Accordingly, equation (A.1) implies that $(1 - s)(dY - dG + dM) = dY - dG$, and equation (A.3) implies that $dM = M_y(dY - dG)/(1 - M_y)$. Substituting the latter expression into the former reveals that $dY/dG = 1$. Thus a unit balanced-budget rise in government spending induces a unit rightward shift of the $CA = 0$ schedule.

Analogously, to obtain the horizontal shift of the YY schedule, we differentiate equations (A.2) and (A.3), holding B^g and B^p constant. Equation (A.2) implies that $(1 - s - a)(dY - dG + dM) + (1 - a^g)dG = dY$, where $a^g = \beta_m^g$, and equation (A.3) implies that $dM = M_y(dY - dG)/(1 - M_y)$. Substituting the latter into the former shows that the horizontal shift of the YY schedule is

$$1 - \frac{(1 - M_y)a^g}{s + a - M_y}.$$

Thus, in contrast with the unit rightward displacement of the $CA = 0$ schedule, the unit balanced-budget rise in government spending shifts the YY schedule to the right by less than one unit. These results underly the diagrammatic analysis in figures 3.3 and 3.4.

The long-run effects of fiscal policies are obtained by differentiating the system (3.12) through (3.14) of the text and solving for the endogenous variables. Accordingly,

$$
\begin{bmatrix}
-s & s(1 + \bar{r}_f) - 1 & 1 - s \\
-(s + a) & -(1 + \bar{r}_f)(1 - s - a) & 1 - s - a \\
M_y & -(1 + \bar{r}_f)M_y & -(1 - M_y)
\end{bmatrix}
\begin{bmatrix}
dY \\
dB^p \\
dM
\end{bmatrix}
$$

$$
= \begin{bmatrix}
0 \\
-(1 - a^g) \\
0
\end{bmatrix} dG + \begin{bmatrix}
-s \\
1 - s - a \\
M_y
\end{bmatrix} dT. \tag{A.6}
$$

Using this system, the long-run effects of a debt-financed rise in government spending (i.e., $dT = 0$) are

$$
\frac{dY}{dG} = \frac{1 - a^g}{\Delta}[1 - s - \bar{r}_f(s - M_y)] \geq 0, \quad \text{for } dT_t = 0, \tag{A.7}
$$

$$
\frac{dB^p}{dG} = -\frac{1 - a^g}{\Delta}(s - M_y) \leq 0, \quad \text{for } dT_t = 0, \tag{A.8}
$$

$$
\frac{dM}{dG} = \frac{1 - a^g}{\Delta}M_y \geq 0, \quad \text{for } dT_t = 0, \tag{A.9}
$$

where $\Delta = a - \bar{r}_f(s - M_y) > 0$ under the assumption that a rise in income worsens the current account of the balance of payments. Correspondingly, the long-run effects of a balanced-budget rise in government spending (i.e., $dG = dT$) are

$$
\frac{dY}{dG} = \frac{1}{\Delta}[a - \bar{r}_f(s - M_y) - a^g\{1 - s - \bar{r}_f(s - M_y)\}] \gtrless 0,
$$

$$
\text{for } dG = dT_t, \tag{A.10}
$$

$$
\frac{dB^p}{dG} = \frac{a^g}{\Delta}(s - M_y) \geq 0, \quad \text{for } dG = dT_t, \tag{A.11}
$$

$$
\frac{dM}{dG} = -\frac{a^g}{\Delta}M_y \leq 0, \quad \text{for } dG = dT_t. \tag{A.12}
$$

Short-Run Equilibrium: The Two-Country World

In this part of the appendix we analyze the short-run equilibrium of the system (3.5) through (3.7). This system determines the short-run equilibrium values of Y_t, Y_t^*, and r_t. The YY and Y^*Y^* schedules in figure 3.5 show combinations of Y_t and Y_t^* that clear the markets for domestic and foreign output, respectively. Both of these schedules incorporate the world money-market equilibrium condition (3.7) of the text. To derive the slope of the YY schedule, we differentiate equations (3.5) and (3.7). This yields

$$\begin{pmatrix} -(s+a) & \bar{e}a^* \\ M_y & \bar{e}M_{y^*}^* \end{pmatrix} \begin{pmatrix} dY_t \\ dY_t^* \end{pmatrix} = - \begin{pmatrix} H_r \\ (M_r + \bar{e}M_r^*) \end{pmatrix} dr_t, \tag{A.13}$$

where H_r denotes the partial (negative) effect a change in the rate of interest on the world demand for domestic output; that is, $H_r = (1 - \beta_m)E_r + \bar{e}\beta_x^* E_r^*$, where E_r, M_r, E_r^*, and M_r^* denote the partial (negative) effects of the rate of interest on domestic and foreign spending and money demand. To eliminate r_t from the goods-market equilibrium schedule, we solve (A.13) for dY_t/dr_t and for dY_t^*/dr_t, and divide the solutions by each other. This yields

$$\frac{dY_t^*}{dY_t} = \frac{1}{\bar{e}} \frac{(s+a)(M_r + \bar{e}M_r^*) + M_y H_r}{a^*(M_r + \bar{e}M_r^*) - M_{y^*}^* H_r} \quad \text{along the } YY \text{ schedule.} \tag{A.14}$$

Analogously, differentiating equations (3.13) and (3.14) yields

$$\begin{pmatrix} a & \bar{e}(s^* + a^*) \\ M_y & \bar{e}M_{y^*}^* \end{pmatrix} \begin{pmatrix} dY_t \\ dY_t^* \end{pmatrix} = - \begin{pmatrix} F_r \\ M_r + \bar{e}M_r^* \end{pmatrix} dr_t, \tag{A.15}$$

where $F_r = \beta_m E_r + \bar{e}(1 - \beta_x^*)E_r^*$ denotes the partial (negative) effect of the rate of interest on the world demand for foreign output. Applying a similar procedure as before, the slope of the Y^*Y^* schedule is

$$\frac{dY_t^*}{dY_t} = \frac{1}{\bar{e}} \frac{a(M_r + \bar{e}M_r^*) - M_y F_r}{(s^* + a^*)(M_r + \bar{e}M_r^*) + M_{y^*}^* F_r} \quad \text{along the } Y^*Y^* \text{ schedule.} \tag{A.16}$$

A comparison of the slopes in (A.14) and (A.16) shows that there are various possible configurations of the relative slopes of the YY and Y^*Y^* schedules. However, two configurations are ruled out: if both schedules are positively sloped, then the slope of the Y^*Y^* cannot exceed the slope of the YY schedule. This can be verified by noting that in the numerator of

(A.7) the negative quantity $a(M_r + \bar{e} M_r^*)$ is augmented by additional negative quantities, whereas the same negative quantity in the numerator of (A.16) is augmented by an additional positive quantity. A similar comparison of the denominators of (A.14) and (A.16) shows that the negative quantity $a^*(M_r + \bar{e} M_r^*)$ is augmented by additional negative quantities in (A.16) and by a positive quantity in (A.14). Likewise, if both schedules are negatively sloped, then, by substracting one slope from the other, it can be verified that the Y^*Y^* schedule cannot be steeper than the YY schedule. These considerations imply that for all situations in which there is a rightward shift of the YY schedule exceeding the rightward shift of the Y^*Y^* schedule, the new equilibrium must be associated with a higher level of domestic output.

A rise in the domestic government spending alters the position of both schedules. To determine the horizontal shift of the YY schedule, we use equations (3.5) and (3.7), holding Y^* constant and solving for dY/dG after eliminating the expression for dr/dG. A similar procedure is applied to determine the horizontal shift of the Y^*Y^* schedule from equations (3.6) and (3.7). Accordingly, the horizontal shifts of the schedules induced by a debt-financed rise in government spending are

$$\frac{dY}{dG} = \frac{1 - a^g}{s + a + [M_y H_r/(M_r + \bar{e} M_r^*)]} \geq 0 \quad \text{for the } YY \text{ schedule,} \quad (A.17)$$

$$\frac{dY}{dG} = \frac{-a^g}{a - [M_y F_r/(M_r + \bar{e} M_r^*)]} \geq 0 \quad \text{for the } Y^*Y^* \text{ schedule.} \quad (A.18)$$

The corresponding shifts for the tax-financed rise in government spending are

$$\frac{dY}{dG} = 1 - \frac{a^g}{s + a + [M_y H_r/(M_r + \bar{e} M_r^*)]} \quad \text{for the } YY \text{ schedule,} \quad (A.19)$$

$$\frac{dY}{dG} = 1 - \frac{a^g}{a - [M_y F_r/(M_r + \bar{e} M_r^*)]} \quad \text{for the } Y^*Y^* \text{ schedule.} \quad (A.20)$$

In equations (A.19) and (A.20), we assume that the government spending falls chiefly on domestic output. Comparisons of (A.17) with (A.18) and of (A.19) with (A.20) reveal the difference between the shifts of the YY and the Y^*Y^* schedules.

To compute the short-run multipliers of fiscal policies, we differentiate the system (3.5) through (3.7). Thus

$$\begin{bmatrix} -(s+a) & \bar{e}a^* & H_r \\ a & -\bar{e}(s^*+a^*) & F_r \\ M_y & \bar{e}M_{y^*}^* & M_r+\bar{e}M_r^* \end{bmatrix} \begin{bmatrix} dY_t \\ dY_t^* \\ dr_t \end{bmatrix}$$

$$= -\begin{bmatrix} 1-a^g \\ a^g \\ 0 \end{bmatrix} dG + \begin{bmatrix} 1-s-a \\ a \\ M_y \end{bmatrix} dT_t. \qquad (A.21)$$

With a debt-financed rise in government spending $dT_t = 0$, and thus the short-run effects are

$$\frac{dY_t}{dG} = \frac{1}{\Delta}\{[s^*(1-a^g)+a^*](M_r+\bar{e}M_r^*) + M_{y^*}^*[F_r(1-a^g)-a^gH_r]\},$$

$$\text{for } dT_t = 0, \quad (A.22)$$

$$\frac{dY_t^*}{dG} = \frac{1}{\bar{e}\Delta}\{(sa^g+a)(M_r+\bar{e}M_r^*) - M_y[F_r(1-a^g)-a^gH_r]\},$$

$$\text{for } dT_t = 0, \quad (A.23)$$

$$\frac{dr_t}{dG} = -\frac{1}{\Delta}\{[s^*(1-a^g)+a^*]M_y + (sa^g+a)M_{y^*}^*\} > 0, \quad \text{for } dT_t = 0,$$

$$(A.24)$$

where

$$\Delta = s[(s^*+a^*)(M_r+\bar{e}M_r^*) + M_{y^*}^*F_r] + a[s^*(M_r+\bar{e}M_r^*)$$

$$+ M_{y^*}^*(F_r+H_r)] + M_y[s^*H_r + a^*(F_r+H_r)] < 0.$$

Differentiating the domestic demand for money function (equation 3.8) and using (A.22) and (A.24) yields the short-run change in the domestic money holdings, that is, the balance of payments:

$$\frac{dM_t}{dG} = \frac{1}{M_rM_r^*\Delta}\left\{\frac{\bar{e}M_y}{M_r}[a^* + s^*(a-a^g)] - \frac{M_{y^*}^*}{M_r^*}(a+sa^g)\right.$$

$$\left. + M_yM_{y^*}^*M_rM_r^*[F_r(1-a^g)-H_ra^g]\right\}, \quad \text{for } dT_t = 0. \quad (A.25)$$

With a balanced-budget rise in government spending $dG = dT_t = dT$. Accordingly, the solutions of (A.21) are

$$\frac{dY_t}{dG} = \frac{1}{\Delta}\{s[(s^* + a^*)(M_r + \overline{e}M_r^*) + M_{y^*}^* F_r]$$

$$+ (a - a^g)[s^*(M_r + \overline{e}M_r^*) + M_{y^*}^*(F_r + H_r)]$$

$$+ M_y[s^* H_r + a^*(F_r + H_r)]\}, \quad \text{for } dG = dT_t, \tag{A.26}$$

$$\frac{dY_t^*}{dG} = \frac{a^g}{\overline{e}\Delta}[M_y(F_r + H_r) + s(M_r + \overline{e}M_r^*)] > 0, \quad \text{for } dG = dT_t, \tag{A.27}$$

$$\frac{dr_t}{dG} = \frac{a^g}{\Delta}(s^* M_y - s M_{y^*}^*), \quad \text{for } dG = dT_t. \tag{A.28}$$

Differentiating the domestic money demand function and using (A.26) and (A.28) yields

$$\frac{dM_t}{dG} = -\frac{a^g}{\Delta}[(s M_r M_{y^*}^* + s^* \overline{e} M_r^* M_y) + M_y M_{y^*}^*(F_r + H_r)] < 0,$$

$$\text{for } dG = dT_t. \tag{A.29}$$

Long-Run Equilibrium: The Two-Country World

The long-run equilibrium of the system is specified by equations (A.30) through (A.36), where the first five equations are the long-run counterpart to the short-run conditions (3.5) through (3.9) and the last two equations are the zero-savings requirements for each country implying (once the government budget constraint is incorporated) current account balances. By employing a common rate of interest, this long-run system embodies the assumption of perfect capital mobility.

$$(1 - \beta_m)E[Y - T + M - (1 + r)B^p, r] + (1 - \beta_m^g)G$$

$$+ \beta_x^* \overline{e} E^*\left[Y^* + M^* + (1 + r)\frac{B^p}{\overline{e}}, r\right] = Y, \tag{A.30}$$

$$\beta_m E[Y - T + M - (1 + r)B^p, r] + \beta_m^g G$$

$$+ (1 - \beta_x^*)\overline{e} E^*\left[Y^* + M^* + (1 + r)\frac{B^p}{\overline{e}}, r\right] = Y^*, \tag{A.31}$$

$$M[Y - T + M - (1 + r)B^p, r] + \overline{e}M^*\left[Y^* + M^* + (1 + r)\frac{B^p}{\overline{e}}, r\right]$$

$$= \overline{M}, \tag{A.32}$$

$$M[Y - T + M - (1 + r)B^p, r] = M, \tag{A.33}$$

$$M^*\left[Y^* + M^* + (1 + r)\frac{B^p}{\bar{e}}, r\right] = M^*, \tag{A.34}$$

$$E[Y - T + M - (1 + r)B^p, r] = Y - rB^p - T, \tag{A.35}$$

$$E^*\left[Y^* + M^* + (1 + r)\frac{B^p}{\bar{e}}, r\right] = Y^* + \frac{rB^p}{\bar{e}}. \tag{A.36}$$

By Walras's law one of the seven equations can be omitted, and the remaining six equations can be used to solve for the long-run equilibrium values of Y, Y^*, B^p, M, M^*, and r as functions of the policy variables.

3.6   Appendix B: Flexible Exchange Rates

Short-Run Equilibrium: The Two-Country World

In this appendix we analyze the short-run equilibrium of the two-country model under flexible exchange rates. Using the domestic money-market equilibrium condition (3.22), the domestic market-clearing rate of interest is

$$r_t = r(Y_t - T_t + A_{t-1}, M), \tag{A.37}$$

where a rise in disposable resources raises the equilibrium rate of interest while a rise in the money supply lowers the rate of interest. Similarly, using the foreign money-market-clearing condition (3.23) but not imposing yet an equality between the foreign rate of interest, r_t^*, and the domestic rate r_t, yields

$$r_t^* = r^*(Y_t^* + A_{t-1}^*, M^*). \tag{A.38}$$

Substituting (A.37) into the domestic expenditure future (3.3) and substituting (A.38) into the corresponding foreign expenditure function yields

$$E_t = \tilde{E}(Y_t - T_t + A_{t-1}, M), \tag{A.39}$$

$$E_t^* = \tilde{E}^*(Y_t^* + A_{t-1}^*, M^*). \tag{A.40}$$

Equations (A.39) and (A.40) are the reduced-form expenditure functions that incorporate the conditions of money-market equilibrium. A rise in disposable resources exerts two conflicting influences on the reduced-form expenditure function. On the one hand, it stimulates spending directly, but on the other hand, by raising the equilibrium rate of interest, it discourages spending. Formally, $\tilde{E}_y = E_y - (E_r/M_r)M_y$. In what follows we assume that the direct effect dominates so that $\tilde{E}_y > 0$. For subsequent use we note that the reduced-form saving propensity $\tilde{s} = 1 - \tilde{E}_y$ exceeds $M_y[1 + (E_r/M_r)]$. This follows from the assumption that bonds are normal goods (so that $1 - E_y - M_y > 0$) together with the former expression linking $\tilde{E}_y$ with E_y.

Substituting the reduced-form expenditure functions (A.39) and (A.40) into the goods-market-clearing conditions yields

$$(1 - \beta_m)\tilde{E}(Y_t - A_{t-1}, M) + (1 - \beta_m^g)G + e_t\beta_x^*\tilde{E}(Y_t^* + A_{t-1}^*, M^*) = Y_t,$$

(A.41)

$$\beta_m\tilde{E}(Y_t - T_t + A_{t-1}, M) + \beta_m^g G + e_t(1 - \beta_x^*)\tilde{E}^*(Y_t^* + A_{t-1}^*, M^*) = e_t Y_t^*,$$

(A.42)

where we recall that $A_{t-1} = M_{t-1} - (1 + r_{t-1})B_{t-1}^p$ and $A_{t-1}^* = M_{t-1}^* + (1 + r_{t-1})B_{t-1}^p/e_t$. Thus, though A_{t-1} is predetermined, the value of A_{t-1}^* depends on the prevailing exchange rate. Equations (A.41) and (A.42) are the reduced-form goods-market-clearing conditions. These conditions link the equilibrium values of domestic output, foreign output, and the exchange rate. In the first step of the analysis we derive the ee schedule of the text which portrays alternative combinations of Y and Y^* satisfying equations (A.41) and (A.42) for alternative values of the exchange rate (which is treated as a parameter). The slope of this schedule is obtained by differentiating equations (A.41) and (A.42) and solving for dY_t^*/dY_t. Accordingly,

$$\begin{pmatrix} -(\tilde{s} + \tilde{a}) & e_t\tilde{a}^* \\ \tilde{a} & -e_t(\tilde{s}^* + \tilde{a}^*) \end{pmatrix}\begin{pmatrix} dY_t \\ dY_t^* \end{pmatrix}$$

$$= \begin{pmatrix} -IM_t^* + \tilde{a}^*H \\ IM_t + (1 - \tilde{s}^* - \tilde{a}^*)H \end{pmatrix}de_t - \begin{pmatrix} 1 - a^g \\ a^g \end{pmatrix}dG + \begin{pmatrix} 1 - \tilde{s} - \tilde{a} \\ \tilde{a} \end{pmatrix}dT_t,$$

(A.43)

where $H = (1 + r_{t-1})B_{t-1}^p/e_t$ denotes the debt commitment of the home country, the reduced-form saving and import propensities are designated by a tilde ($\tilde{\ }$), and where $IM_t^* = \beta_x^*\tilde{E}^*$ and $IM_t = Y^* - (1 - \beta_x^*)\tilde{E}^*$ are, respectively, the foreign and the domestic values of imports expressed in units of foreign goods. The coefficient matrix in (A.43) is the counterpart of the system (2.21) shown in chapter 2. For given fiscal policies we obtain

$$\frac{dY_t}{de_t} = \frac{\tilde{s}^*IM_t^* + \tilde{a}^*(IM_t^* - IM_t) - \tilde{a}^*H}{\Delta},$$

(A.44)

$$\frac{dY_t^*}{de_t} = -\frac{\tilde{s}IM_t - \tilde{a}(IM_t - IM_t) + [\tilde{s}(1 - \tilde{s}^* - \tilde{a}^*) + \tilde{a}(1 - s^*)]H}{e_t\Delta},$$

(A.45)

where

$$\Delta = \tilde{s}\tilde{s}^* + \tilde{s}\tilde{a}^* + \tilde{s}\tilde{a} > 0.$$

To obtain the slope of the *ee* schedule, we divide (A.45) by (A.44), yielding

$$\frac{dY_t^*}{dY_t} = -\frac{\tilde{s}IM_t - \tilde{a}(IM_t^* - IM_t) + [\tilde{s}(1 - \tilde{s}^* - \tilde{a}^*) + \tilde{a}(1 - \tilde{s}^*)]H}{e_t[\tilde{s}^*IM_t^* + \tilde{a}^*(IM_t^* - IM_t) - \tilde{a}^*H]}$$

along the *ee* schedule.   (A.46)

Around a trade-balance equilibrium with zero initial debt (i.e., $IM_t = IM_t^*$ and $H = 0$) this slope is negative and is equal to $-\tilde{s}/e_t\tilde{s}^*$. With the negatively sloped *ee* schedule a downward movement along the schedule (i.e., a rise in Y_t and a fall in Y_t^*) is associated with higher values of e_t.

To determine the effects of changes in government spending, we compute the horizontal shift of the *ee* schedule by setting $dY_t^* = dT_t = 0$ in the system (A.43) and solving for dY_t/dG. This yields

$$\frac{dY_t}{dG} = \frac{IM_t + a^g(IM_t^* - IM_t) + [(1 - \tilde{s}^*)(1 - a^g) - \tilde{a}^*]H}{\tilde{s}IM_t - \tilde{a}(IM_t^* - IM_t) + [\tilde{s}(1 - \tilde{s}^* - \tilde{a}^*) + \tilde{a}(1 - \tilde{s}^*)]H}$$

for the *ee* schedule.   (A.47)

Thus around trade-balance equilibrium and zero initial debt, the schedule shifts to the right by $1/\tilde{s}$.

By setting $dY_t^* = dG = 0$ and following a similar procedure, the horizontal shift of the *ee* schedule induced by a unit rise in taxes is

$$\frac{dY_t}{dT_t} = -\frac{\tilde{a}(IM_t^* - IM_t) + (1 - \tilde{s})IM_t + \{(1 - \tilde{s})[1 - \tilde{s}^* - \tilde{a}^*(1 - \tilde{s}^*)]\}H}{-\tilde{a}(IM_t^* - IM_t) + \tilde{s}IM_t + [\tilde{s}(1 - \tilde{s}^* - \tilde{a}^*) + \tilde{a}(1 - \tilde{s}^*)]H}$$

for the *ee* schedule.   (A.48)

Thus around trade-balance equilibrium and zero initial debt, the schedule shifts to the left by $(1 - \tilde{s})/\tilde{s}$ units.

By combining the results in (A.47) and (A.48), we obtain the effect of a balanced-budget unit rise in government spending. Accordingly,

$$\frac{dY_t}{dG} = \frac{\tilde{s}IM_t + (a^g - \tilde{a})(IM_t^* - IM_t) + [\tilde{s}(1 - \tilde{s}^* - \tilde{a}^*) + (1 - \tilde{s}^*)(\tilde{a} - a^g)]H}{\tilde{s}IM_t - \tilde{a}(IM_t^* - IM_t) + [\tilde{s}(1 - \tilde{s}^* - \tilde{a}^*) + \tilde{a}(1 - \tilde{s}^*)]H}$$

for the *ee* schedule with $dG = dT_t$.   (A.49)

Thus around trade-balance equilibrium with zero initial debt, a balanced-budget unit rise in government spending shifts the ee schedule to the right by one unit.

In the second step of the diagrammatic analysis we assume that $H = 0$, and we derive the rr^* schedule portraying combinations of Y and Y^* along which the money-market-clearing rates of interest (under the assumption of static exchange-rate expectations) are equal across countries so that

$$r(Y_t - T_t + A_{t-1}, M) = r^*(Y^* + A^*_{t-1}, M^*). \tag{A.50}$$

The slope of this schedule is $r_y/r^*_{y^*}$ which can also be expressed in terms of the characteristics of the demands for money according to

$$\frac{dY^*_t}{dY_t} = \frac{M_y}{M^*_{y^*}} \frac{M^*_{r^*}}{M_r} > 0 \quad \text{along the } rr^* \text{ schedule.} \tag{A.51}$$

Obviously, around $r = r^*$, $M^*_{r^*} = M^*_r$. As is evident, the level of government spending does not influence the rr^* schedule, whereas a unit rise in taxes shifts the schedule to the right by one unit.

Formally, the effects of fiscal policies can be obtained by differentiating the system (A.41), (A.42), and (A.50). Thus

$$
\begin{bmatrix}
-(\tilde{s} + \tilde{a}) & e_t \tilde{a}^* & IM^*_t - \tilde{a}^* H \\[2mm]
\tilde{a} & -e_t(\tilde{s}^* + \tilde{a}^*) & -IM_t - (1 - \tilde{s}^* - \tilde{a}^*)H \\[2mm]
\dfrac{M_y}{M_r} & -\dfrac{M^*_{y^*}}{M^*_r} & \dfrac{HM^*_{y^*}}{e_t M^*_{r^*}}
\end{bmatrix}
\begin{bmatrix}
dY_t \\[2mm]
dY^*_t \\[2mm]
de_t
\end{bmatrix}
$$

$$
= -
\begin{bmatrix}
1 - a^g \\[2mm]
a^g \\[2mm]
0
\end{bmatrix}
dG +
\begin{bmatrix}
1 - \tilde{s} - \tilde{a} \\[2mm]
\tilde{a} \\[2mm]
\dfrac{M_y}{M_r}
\end{bmatrix}
dT_t. \tag{A.52}
$$

Solving (A.52), the short-run effects of a debt-financed rise in government spending are

$$\frac{dY_t}{dG} = \frac{M^*_{y^*}}{\Delta M^*_r}[IM_t(1 - a^g) + IM^*_t a^g + (1 - a^g)H], \quad \text{for } dT_t = 0, \tag{A.53}$$

$$\frac{dY^*_t}{dG} = \frac{M_y}{\Delta M_r}[IM_t + a^g(IM^*_t - IM_t)] + \frac{1}{\Delta}\left\{\frac{M^*_{y^*}}{M^*_r}(\tilde{a} + \tilde{s}a^g)\right.$$

$$\left. + \frac{M_y}{M_r}[(1 - a^g)(1 - \tilde{s}^*) - \tilde{a}^*]\right\}H, \quad \text{for } dT_t = 0, \tag{A.54}$$

$$\frac{de_t}{dG} = \frac{1}{\Delta}\left\{\frac{M_{y^*}^*}{M_r^*}(\tilde{a} + \tilde{s}a^g) - \frac{e_t M_y}{M_r}[\tilde{a}^* + \tilde{s}^*(1 - a^g)]\right\}, \quad \text{for } dT_t = 0,$$

(A.55)

where

$$\Delta = \frac{M_{y^*}^*}{M_r^*}[(\tilde{s} + \tilde{a})IM_t - \tilde{a}IM_t^*] + \frac{e_t M_y}{M_r}[(\tilde{s}^* + \tilde{a}^*)IM_t^* - \tilde{a}^*IM_t]$$

$$+ \left[(\tilde{s} + \tilde{a})\frac{M_{y^*}^*}{M_r^*} - e_t\tilde{a}^*\frac{M_y}{M_r}\right]H.$$

Thus with an initial balanced trade and with zero initial debt, $\Delta < 0$. Differentiating the money-market equilibrium condition (equation 3.8) and using (A.53), we obtain the equilibrium change in the rate of interest:

$$\frac{dr_t}{dG} = -\frac{M_y M_{y^*}^*}{M_r M_r^* \Delta}[IM_t + a^g(IM_t^* - IM_t) + (1 - a^g)H], \quad \text{for } dT_t = 0.$$

(A.56)

Likewise the short-run effects of a tax-financed rise in government spending are

$$\frac{dY_t}{dG} = \frac{1}{\Delta}\left\{\frac{M_{y^*}^*}{M_r^*}[\tilde{s}IM_t^* + (\tilde{a} - g^g)(IM_t - IM_t^*)] + \frac{e_t M_y}{M_r}[\tilde{s}^*IM_t^*\right.$$

$$\left. + \tilde{a}^*(IM_t^* - IM_t)] + \left[\frac{M_{y^*}^*}{M_r^*}(\tilde{s} + \tilde{a} - a^g) - \frac{e_t M_y}{M_r}\tilde{a}^*\right]H\right\},$$

for $dG = dT_t$, (A.57)

$$\frac{dY_t^*}{dG} = \frac{a^g}{\Delta}\left\{\frac{M_y}{M_r}(IM_t^* - IM_t) - \left[\frac{M_y}{M_r}(1 - \tilde{s}^*) - \frac{M_{y^*}^*}{M_r^*}\tilde{s}\right]H\right\},$$

for $dG = dT_t$, (A.58)

$$\frac{de_t}{dG} = \frac{a^g}{\Delta}\left(\frac{e_t M_y}{M_r}\tilde{s}^* + \frac{M_{y^*}^*}{M_r^*}\tilde{s}\right), \quad \text{for } dG = dT_t.$$

(A.59)

Using the money-market equilibrium condition together with (A.57) yields

$$\frac{dr_t}{dG} = -\frac{M_y}{M_r \Delta}\left\{a^g(IM_t^* - IM_t) + \left[\frac{M_{y^*}^*}{M_r^*}(\tilde{s} + \tilde{a} - a^g) + \frac{e_t M_y}{M_r}\tilde{a}^*\right]H\right\},$$

for $dG = dT_t$. (A.60)

Long-Run Equilibrium: The Two-Country World

The long-run equilibrium of the system is characterized by equations (A.61) through (A.65), where the first three equations are the long-run counterparts to equations (A.41), (A.42), and (A.50) and the last two equations are the requirements of zero savings in both countries implying (once the government budget constraint is incorporated) current-account balances. Embodied in the system are the requirements of money-market equilibria and perfect capital mobility.

$$(1 - \beta_m)\tilde{E}[Y - T + M - (1 + r)B^p, M] + (1 - \beta_m^g)G$$

$$+ e\beta_x^* \tilde{E}^* \left[Y^* + M^* + \left(\frac{1 + r}{e} \right) B^p, M^* \right] = Y, \tag{A.61}$$

$$\beta_m \tilde{E}[Y - T + M - (1 + r)B^p, M] + \beta_m^g G$$

$$+ e(1 - \beta_x^*)\tilde{E}^* \left[Y^* + M^* + \left(\frac{1 + r}{e} \right) B^p, M^* \right] = eY^*, \tag{A.62}$$

$$r[Y - T + M - (1 + r)B^p, M]$$

$$= r^* \left[Y^* + M^* + \left(\frac{1 + r}{e} \right) B^p, M^* \right], \tag{A.63}$$

$$\tilde{E}[Y - T + M - (1 + r)B^p, M] = Y - rB^p - T, \tag{A.64}$$

$$\tilde{E}^* \left[Y^* + M^* + \left(\frac{1 + r}{e} \right) B^p, M^* \right] = Y^* + \frac{rB^p}{e}. \tag{A.65}$$

This system, which determines the long-run equilibrium values of Y, Y^*, e, B^p, and r, can be used to analyze the effects of government spending and taxes on these endogenous variables.

Exchange-Rate Expectations

Up to this point we have assumed that the expectations concerning the evolution of the exchange rate are static. This assumption implied that the rates of interest on securities denominated in different currencies are equalized. Since, however, the actual exchange rate does change over time, it is useful to extend the analysis and allow for exchange-rate expectations that are not static. Specifically, in this part of the appendix we assume that expectations are rational in the sense of being self-fulfilling. We continue to assume that the GDP deflators are fixed. To illustrate the main implication of exchange-rate expectations, we consider a stripped-down version of the small-country flexible exchange-rate model, and for expository convenience, we present the analysis using a continuous-time version of the model.

The budget constraint can be written as

$$E_t + \dot{M}_t - e_t \dot{B}_{ft}^p = Y_t - T_t - \bar{r}_f e_t B_{ft}^p, \tag{A.66}$$

where a dot over a variable represents a time derivative. The spending and money-demand functions (the counterparts to equations 3.3 and 3.4) are

$$E_t = E(Y_t - T_t - \bar{r}_f e_t B_{ft}^p, M_t - e_t B_{ft}^p, \bar{r}_f), \tag{A.67}$$

$$M_t = M\left(Y_t - T_t - \bar{r}_f e_t B_{ft}^p, M_t - e_t B_{ft}^p, \bar{r}_f + \frac{\dot{e}_t}{e_t}\right), \tag{A.68}$$

where the demand for money is expressed as a negative function of the expected depreciation of the currency, $\dot{e}_t/e_t$. In what follows we simplify the exposition by assuming that the world rate of interest, $\bar{r}_f$, is very low (zero), and that the effect of assets $(M_t - e_t B_{ft}^p)$ on spending is negligible. With these simplifications the goods and money-market equilibrium conditions (the counterparts to equations 3.20a and 3.22a) are

$$(1 - \beta_m)E(Y_t - T_t) + (1 - \beta_m^g)G + e_t \bar{D}^* = Y_t, \tag{A.69}$$

$$M\left(Y_t - T_t, M - e_t B_{ft}^p, \frac{\dot{e}_t}{e_t}\right) = M. \tag{A.70}$$

Equation (A.69) implies that the level of output that clears the goods market depends positively on the level of the exchange rate and on government spending, and negatively on taxes. This dependence can be expressed as

$$Y_t = Y(e_t, G, T_t), \tag{A.71}$$

where $\partial Y_t/\partial e_t = \bar{D}^*/(s + a)$, $\partial Y_t/\partial G = (1 - a^g)/(s + a)$, and $\partial Y_t/\partial T_t = -(1 - s - a)/(s + a)$ are the conventional foreign-trade multipliers. Substituting the functional relation (A.71) into the money-market equilibrium condition and solving for the (actual and expected) percentage change in the exchange rate yields

$$\frac{\dot{e}_t}{e_t} = f(e_t, B_{ft}^p, G, T_t, M), \tag{A.72}$$

where

$$\frac{\partial f}{\partial e} = \frac{-M_y \bar{D}^*/(s+a) + M_A B_{ft}^p}{M_r},$$

$$\frac{\partial f}{\partial B_{ft}^p} = \frac{e_t M_A}{M_r},$$

$$\frac{\partial f}{\partial G} = -\frac{1 - a^g}{(s+a)M_r},$$

$$\frac{\partial f}{\partial T_t} = \frac{1 - s - a}{(s+a)M_r},$$

and where M_A and M_r denote, respectively, the derivatives of the demand for money with respect to assets $(M - e_t B_{ft}^p)$ and the rate of interest. The former is positive, and the latter negative. The interpretation of the dependence of the percentage change in the exchange rate, representing the money-market-clearing interest rate, on the various variables follows. A rise in the exchange rate raises the goods-market-clearing level of output and raises the demand for money. To restore money-market equilibrium, the rate of interest must rise; that is, $\dot{e}_t/e_t$ must rise. On the other hand, the rise in e raises the domestic-currency value of the debt B_{ft}^p. If the private sector is a net creditor, the depreciation of the currency raises the domestic-currency value of assets and raises the demand for money. This in turn also contributes to the rise in the rate of interest. If, however, the private sector is a net debtor, then the value of assets falls, and the demand for money is reduced, thereby contributing to a downward pressure on the rate of interest. The net effect on the rate of interest depends therefore on the net debtor position of the private sector; if, however, B_{ft}^p is zero, then the rate of interest must rise so that $\partial f/\partial e_t > 0$. Analogous interpretations apply to the other derivatives where it is evident that $\partial f/\partial B_{ft}^p < 0$, $\partial f/\partial G \gtrless 0$, and $\partial f/\partial T_t < 0$.

Equation (A.72) constitutes the first differential equation of the model governing the evolution of the exchange rate over time. The second variable whose evolution over time characterizes the dynamics of the system is the stock of private-sector debt. Substituting the goods-market equilibrium condition (A.71) into the budget constraint (A.66), and using the fact that in the absence of monetary policy $\dot{M}_t = 0$, we can solve for the dynamics of private-sector debt. Accordingly,

$$\dot{B}_{ft}^{p} = \frac{1}{e_t} h(e_t, G, T_t)$$

$$= \frac{1}{e_t} \{E_t[Y(e_t, G, T_t) - T_t] - Y(e_t, G, T_t) + T_t\}. \tag{A.73}$$

Equation (A.73) expresses the rate of change of private-sector debt as the difference between private-sector spending and disposable income. The previous discussion implies that $\partial h/\partial e_t = -\bar{D}^*s/(s + a) < 0$, $\partial h/\partial G = -(1 - a^g)s/(s + a) \lessgtr 0$, and $\partial h/\partial T_t = s/(s + a) > 0$.

In interpreting these expressions, we note that the function h represents the negative savings of the private sector. Accordingly, a unit rise in e_t or G raises savings by the saving propensity times the corresponding multiplier. Analogously, a unit rise in taxes that lowers disposable income lowers savings by the saving propensity times the corresponding disposable-income multiplier.

The equilibrium of the system is exhibited in figure 3A.1. The positively sloped $\dot{e}_t = 0$ schedule shows combinations of the exchange rate and private-sector debt that maintain an unchanged exchange rate. The schedule represents equation (A.72) for $\dot{e}_t = 0$. Its slope is positive around a zero level of private-sector debt, and its position depends on the policy variables G, T_t, and M. Likewise, the $\dot{B}_{ft}^p = 0$ locus represents equation (A.73)

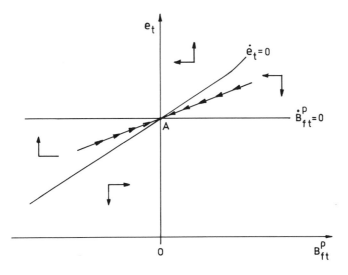

Figure 3A.1
The equilibrium exchange-rate dynamics and debt accumulation

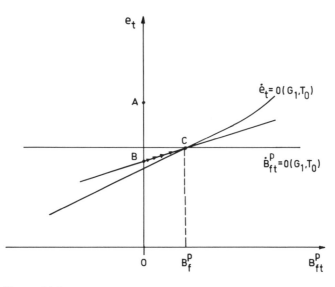

Figure 3A.2
The effects of a debt-financed rise in government spending on the paths of the exchange rate and private-sector debt

for $\dot{B}_{ft}^p = 0$. It is horizontal since, as specified, the rate of change of private-sector debt does not depend on the value of debt. The arrows around the schedules indicate the directions in which the variables tend to move, and the solid curve shows the unique saddle path converging toward a stationary state. As is customary in this type of analysis, we associate this saddle path with the equilibrium path. The long-run equilibrium of the system is shown by point A in figure 3A.1, where for convenience we show a case in which the long-run value of private-sector debt is zero.

The effects of a unit debt-financed rise in government spending from G_0 to G_1 are shown in figure 3A.2. Starting from an initial long-run equilibrium at point A, the rise in G shifts the $\dot{B}_{ft}^p = 0$ schedule from point A downward by $-(1 - a^g)/\bar{D}^*$, and it also shifts the $\dot{e} = 0$ schedule from point A downward by $-(1 - a^g)/M_y\bar{D}^*$. For $M_y < 1$, the vertical displacement of the $\dot{e} = 0$ schedule exceeds the corresponding displacement of the $\dot{B}_{ft}^p = 0$ schedule, and the new long-run equilibrium obtains at point C, at which the domestic currency has appreciated and private-sector debt has risen. The short-run equilibrium obtains at point B along the new saddle path, and transition toward the long run follows along the path connecting point B and C. As is evident, the initial appreciation of the currency overshoots the long-run appreciation.

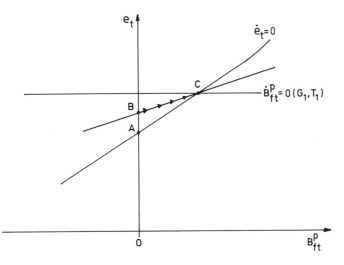

Figure 3A.3
The effect of a tax-financed rise in government spending on the paths of the exchange rate and private-sector debt

The effects of a unit tax-financed rise in government spending are shown in figure 3A.3. With $dG = dT$, the $\dot{B}^p_{ft} = 0$ schedule shifts upward by $a^g/\bar{D}^*$ while the $\dot{e} = 0$ schedule shifts vertically by $(s + a - a^g)/M_y\bar{D}^*$. The bench-mark case shown in figure 3A.3 corresponds to the situation in which the private sector and the government have the same marginal propensities to spend on domestic goods (i.e., $s + a = a^g$). In that case the $\dot{e} = 0$ remains intact, the short-run equilibrium is at point B, and the long-run equilibrium is at point C. As seen in this case the domestic currency depreciates, and the short-run depreciation undershoots the long-run depreciation. These results are sensitive to alternative assumptions concerning the relative magnitudes of $(s + a)$ and a^g.

Problems

1. Consider the fixed-price, fixed-exchange rate, flexible-output model of chapter 2. Assume that all demand functions are such that the propensities to spend and save out of assets are the same as the propensities to spend and save out of disposable income. Assume that government spending is constant and, without loss of generality, equal to zero in all periods.

a. What is the effect on domestic and foreign output in period zero, Y_0 and Y^*_0, of a unit increase in the domestic money supply, M_0, brought about by a unit decrease in domestic taxes in period zero, T_0, holding T_t constant and equal to 0, for all $t > 0$? What is the effect of this policy on the period zero trade balance, TA_0, and on the domestic money supply, M_0?

b. With taxes returning to their previous value of zero and all quantities stationary over time, what is the effect on the value of domestic and foreign output in the long run? Also, how is the distribution of the world money supply affected by this policy? In answering this part of the question, you may assume that expenditure and money demand functions are linear.

2. Consider the "dual" to the fixed-price Keynesian model of chapter 2, in which prices were fixed and output variable. Specifically, assume in this exercise that output is fixed at its full employment level, which is normalized to unity in both countries, and that the prices of all goods are perfectly flexible. As in chapter 2, we continue to assume that the exchange rate is fixed and set equal to unity. Finally, assume as in exercise 1b that all behavioral functions are linear, that the domestic and foreign governments run balanced budgets in all periods, and that government spending in the foreign country is equal to zero in all periods.

a. Write down the conditions that must be satisfied in the short-run equilibrium. Also write down an expression for the nominal trade balance.

b. Solve explicitly for the (short-run) equilibrium domestic and foreign price level in terms of the level of *nominal* government spending and the world money stock. Substitute these solutions into your expression for the nominal trade balance, and obtain an expression for the latter in terms of these exogenous variables. Using the expression for the trade balance and the relation $M_t = M_{t-1} + TA_t$, show that the coefficient multiplying M_{t-1} in the equation for M_t is positive and less than unity, and hence, that the changes in the domestic money supply that occur during the process of adjustment eventually come to a halt, i.e., the system converges to its long-run equilibrium.

c. Show that if the initial level of government spending is equal to zero, then a rise in M_{t-1} (consequent on a trade balance surplus) worsens the home country's terms of trade (i.e., raises P_t^*/P_t) if the sign of the parameter b is positive, where $b = a^*(s^*a - sc^*) - a(1 - s^*)(s^*c - sa^*)$.

d. Solve explicitly for the domestic and foreign price levels in the long run.

e. Show that the effect of a balanced-budget increase in government spending by the home country results in a negative comovement of domestic and foreign levels of nominal private sector spending in both the short run and the long run. Are short-run changes in nominal spending smaller or larger than the corresponding long-run changes? Why?

3. Consider the model with fixed output and flexible prices outlined in exercise 2.

a. Prove that a balanced budget increase in government spending improves the home country's long-run terms of trade if and only if the domestic private sector's propensity to import out of spending $(\bar{a} = a/(1 - s))$ exceeds the government import propensity, a^g.

b. Define the domestic consumer price index, P_c, as a geometric weighted average of the domestic and foreign GDP deflators, P and P^*, with weights equal to the domestic expenditure shares. Thus, the weight of domestic goods in P_c would be $\bar{c} = (1 - s - a)/(1 - s)$, and the weight of foreign goods would be $\bar{a} = a/(1 - s)$, and clearly $\bar{c} + \bar{a} = 1$. Define the level of domestic and foreign real spending as nominal spending in the particular country divided by the corresponding consumer price index, i.e., $E = Z/P_c$, and $E^* = Z^*/P_c^*$, where E and E^* denote real spending levels at home and abroad, respectively. Show that, from an initial position in which $G = G^* = 0$, the long-run proportional change in E^* from a balanced budget rise in government spending originating in the domestic economy is positive if and only if $a^g < \bar{a}$. Also show that the long-run proportional change in E caused by a balanced budget increase in G is always negative, independent of differences in the import propensities between the government and the private sector. In this last part, you will need to recall the restriction that $1 - s - a > 0$, i.e., that the marginal propensity to consume domestic goods is positive.

4. Consider the fixed exchange rate, perfect capital mobility model of chapter 3. Consider the case of a small country that takes foreign demand for its output (assumed for convenience to be zero) as given, and faces a given exogenous world rate of interest. Suppose that initial government spending, taxes, and debt are all zero, and that in the initial stationary equilibrium, this economy is neither a net borrower nor a net lender in world capital markets. Consider the effect of an exogenous increase in the world rate of interest.

a. What is the effect on output and the equilibrium money stock in the short run?

b. How does output behave in the long run? In signing your answer, you may assume, as in the chapter, that a rise in income worsens the current account of the balance of payments (namely, $a > r(s - M_y)$).

c. Compare your answers to a and b. Does output move in the same direction in the short run as in the long run? If so, does it move by more or less on impact than in the long run? If not, what accounts for the different behavior of output in the short run and long run?

d. Show that although the long-run effect on money holdings is ambiguous, a rise in the world rate of interest necessarily increases the private sector's holdings of financial assets, $M - B$, in the steady state.

5. Consider the small-country model of chapter 3 with flexible exchange rates and capital mobility. Assume that there is no government spending or taxes, nor government debt. Assume that initially the private sector is a net debtor, i.e., $B_{t-1} > 0$.

a. Compute the effects on output and the exchange rate in the short run of debt forgiveness in the amount of one unit, i.e., $dB_{t-1} = -1$.

b. Compute the effects on output in the case where the small country operates with a fixed exchange rate.

c. Suppose that export earnings D are approximately equal to the amount of initial debt, B (in 1990, external debt for all developing countries amounted to about 1 1/4 times annual export earnings, so this isn't too bad an approximation). Would you expect debt forgiveness of the type analyzed in parts a and b of this question to have a larger effect on output under fixed or flexible exchange rates?

6. Consider the Mundell-Fleming model of chapter 3. Compare the long-run effects of changes in the nominal supply of money for a small country with a flexible exchange rate regime to those of a change in the nominal exchange rate in the fixed exchange rate regime version of the model. Does the flexible exchange rate model exhibit long-run neutrality in the sense that a doubling of the money stock leads to a doubling of the exchange rate, with no change in real variables? In the case of the model with fixed exchange rates, does a doubling of the exchange rate lead to a doubling of the nominal quantity of money? Explain.

7. An important simplifying assumption in the model presented in chapter 3 was the assumption that the actual current and expected future values of the exchange rate would always be equal to one another (static expectations). Suppose, in contrast to chapter 3, that people do not necessarily expect the exchange rate to remain constant at its current level. If we denote by e_t^a the anticipated or expected future value of the exchange rate, then the assumption that domestic and foreign assets are identical in all

respects except for currency denomination implies that the following arbitrage condition holds at all times:

$$(1 + i_t) = (e_t^a/e_t)(1 + i_t^*),$$ (1)

where i_t and i_t^* are the domestic and foreign nominal interest rates at time t. Under the fixed-price assumption of chapter 3, the same arbitrage condition also holds with respect to real interest rates so that

$$(1 + r_t) = (e_t^a/e_t)(1 + r_t^*).$$ (1')

a. Consider the effects of a debt-financed increase in government spending on domestic goods under the assumption of fixed exchange rates, so that anticipated and actual exchange rates are always equal to one another (and may be assumed equal to unity). Assume that the country undertaking the fiscal expansion is small in world markets, that in the initial steady state the country is neither a net lender nor a net borrower in world capital markets, and that the effects of interest rate changes on domestic absorption are negligible so that the partial derivative, E_r, of the expenditure function with respect to the domestic interest rate is zero. Consider only the short-run effects.

b. Now consider the same policy experiment under flexible exchange rates, under the flexible exchange rates, under the assumption that the expected future exchange rate is constant. Is the effect on output larger or smaller than under fixed exchange rates?

c. Suppose now that the increase in government spending lasts for some time and that the expected exchange rate moves in the same direction as the actual exchange rate moved in part b. Is the rise in output larger or smaller than in b? If the expected exchange rate moves by the same proportion as the actual exchange rate, by how much does output change in response to the fiscal expansion?

III

Elements of Intertemporal Macroeconomics

4

The Composite-Commodity World

The main characteristic of the modern analysis of fiscal policies is the detailed attention given to dynamic and intertemporal considerations. In contrast with earlier analyses, the modern approach is based on more solid microeconomic foundations. These foundations "discipline" the analysis and impose constraints on the modeling of macroeconomic behavior. Specifically, an explicit account of temporal and intertemporal budget constraints restricts the permissible behavior of households and governments and sharpens the predictive content of the economic model. Furthermore, by deriving the private sector's *aggregate* behavior from the utility maximization behavior of *individuals*, the modern analytical framework allows for a meaningful treatment of normative issues. Hence within this framework a macroeconomic analysis is applicable for both positive economic issues as well as issues in welfare economics.

In this chapter we review basic elements of intertemporal open-economy macroeconomics. To motivate the discussion, we start in section 4.1 with a specification of a simple stylized two-period model of a small open economy that has free access to world capital markets and that produces and consumes a single aggregate tradable good. In this context we characterize the maximizing behavior of firms and households and determine the general equilibrium levels of investment, consumption, savings, and the various accounts of the balance of payments.

The intertemporal disparities between the paths of consumption and income are reflected in debt accumulation and decumulation. To highlight the central motives underlying the determination of intertemporal allocations of debt, we introduce in section 4.2 three basic concepts: consumption smoothing, consumption tilting, and consumption augmenting. These concepts are useful for interpreting the role that capital markets play in facilitating the adjustments of consumption paths over time.

In section 4.3 we illustrate the usefulness of the three concepts by applying the stylized model to the analysis of supply shocks. In this context we analyze the effects of temporary (current or anticipated future) and permanent supply shocks on the levels of consumption, investment, and the trade balance.

In section 4.4 we extend the analysis of the small open economy to the familiar home-country-foreign-country model of the world economy. The analysis identifies the factors that determine the equilibrium level of the world rate of interest and the associated international and intertemporal distribution of trade imbalances. The key factors governing the equilibrium are the relation between the home and the foreign marginal saving propensities (reflecting differences between marginal rates of time preference), the relation between the home and the foreign percentage rates of growth of GDP, the percentage rate of growth of world GDP, and the initial distribution of world debt. The impact of the initial distribution is illustrated through an analysis of the effects of international transfers on the equilibrium level of the world rate of interest.

In section 4.5 we extend the analysis of the small open economy to the analysis of stochastic supply shocks. In this context we demonstrate the effect of consumption smoothing on the variability of consumption compared to the variability of GDP.

4.1 A Stylized Model

Let us consider a small open economy producing and consuming one aggregate tradable good and facing a given world rate of interest. The aggregation of goods into a single aggregate commodity is done to focus attention on intertemporal trade, that is, on international borrowing and lending. Obviously, in designing a model that is suitable for intertemporal analysis, we need to extend the single-period perspective into a multi-period setting. In the context of the stylized model we adopt the minimal framework of a two-period model.

We start by specifying the supply side of the model. The economy is endowed with an initial stock of capital, K_0, and a production function that depends on capital, $F_0(K_0)$. We assume that the production function exhibits positive and diminishing marginal returns.

The investment technology is assumed to exhibit increasing average as well as marginal costs of investment due to adjustment costs. The latter, indicated by the coefficient $g \geqslant 0$, reflect installation, job reassignment, or training. To simplify we assume quadratic costs:

$$Z_0 = I_0 \left(1 + \frac{\frac{1}{2}gI_0}{K_0} \right), \tag{4.1}$$

where I_0 is the level of investment, and Z_0 is the cost of investment. Average costs of investment, $1 + \frac{1}{2}gI_0/K_0$, fall short of the marginal costs of investment, $1 + gI_0/K_0$, implying increasing average costs. Putting it differently, there are diminishing returns to capital formation.

The capital stock in period one, K_1, is augmented by the investment that takes place in period zero, according to

$$K_1 = I_0 + K_0, \tag{4.2}$$

where for simplicity we ignore depreciation.

The investment process modifies the intertemporal pattern of available outputs (GDP). Formally, output in period one, Y_1, is linked to the initial stock of capital, K_0, and the level of investment, I_0, through the production function

$$Y_1 = F_1(K_1) = F_1(I_0 + K_0). \tag{4.3}$$

Naturally, in the absence of investment the capital stock cannot be augmented, and future output is $Y_1 = F_1(K_0)$.

Firms are assumed to maximize the present value of profits. Formally, the firm's investment policy is determined by solving the maximization problem

$$\tilde{\pi} = \max_{I_0} \left\{ \alpha_1 [F_1(I_0 + K_0) + (I_0 + K_0)] - I_0 \left(1 + \frac{\frac{1}{2}gI_0}{K_0} \right) \right\}, \tag{4.4}$$

where $\alpha_1 = 1/(1 + r_0)$ denotes the present value or discount factor, and r_0 is the world rate of interest between periods one and zero. The formulation in (4.4) indicates that a unit of current investment, I_0, bears fruits, $F_1(I_0 + K_0)$, only in the subsequent period; this is reflected by the discounting in the profit function. Figure 4.1 illustrates the maximization problem and the firm's investment policy. In the absence of investment the output sequence is $(F_0(K_0), K_0 + F_1(K_0))$. This pair of outputs is denoted by point A, and the present value of this sequence of outputs is denoted by point D. The (absolute value of the) slope of the dashed line connecting points A and D is the intertemporal price $(1/\alpha_1) = 1 + r_0$. Point M represents the maximum level of investment, so that the domestic production that is allocated for present consumption is zero (i.e., $Z_0 = F_0(K_0)$). The schedule originating from point A and passing through point B specifies the trans-

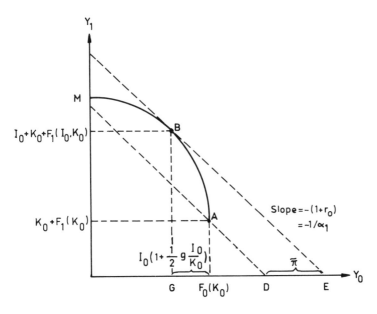

Figure 4.1
The determination of investment and profits

formation schedule linking current period production that is allocated for consumption with future period production that is allocated for consumption.

Diagrammatically, investment spending is measured in a leftward direction from $F_0(K_0)$. In the absence of investment, future profits are zero. Thus, the dashed line AD is a zero-profit locus. The profit-maximizing firm seeks to reach the highest isoprofit locus subject to its technological constraints. Point B in figure 4.1 represents the outcome of the firm's profit-maximizing investment policy. With such policy the present value of future profits, $\tilde{\pi}$, is measured by the distance DE, and the level of investment spending, Z_0, is measured by the distance from G to $F_0(K_0)$.

As is evident from figure 4.1, the firm will carry out positive investment only if the transformation function emerging at the initial endowment point, A, is steeper at that point than $1 + r_0$. At point B the present value of future profits is maximized, and the (absolute value of the) slope of the transformation function equals $1 + r_0$. More formally, we note from equation (4.4) that the first-order condition for profit maximization requires that

$$\frac{F_1'(I_0 + K_0) - gI_0/K_0}{q_0} = r_0, \tag{4.5}$$

where $q_0 = 1 + gI_0/K_0$ is the marginal adjustment cost. Diminishing returns, that is, $F_1''(I_0 + K_0) < 0$, and increasing marginal costs of adjustment, that is, $g > 0$, imply that a higher rate of interest lowers the profit-maximizing level of investment. In terms of figure 4.1, a higher rate of interest steepens the isoprofit loci and slides point B rightward along the transformation schedule toward point A. The new profit-maximization point is associated with a smaller level of investment.

We turn next to an analysis of the demand side of the model. Consider a representative consumer maximizing lifetime utility subject to budget constraints. The individual's resources are composed of the initial endowments, $F_0(K_0)$ and $K_0 + F_1(K_0)$, and profits, $F_1(I_0 + K_0) + (I_0 + K_0) - [F_1(K_0) + K_0]$, that firms distribute as dividends to share holders. These resources are used in the first period for consumption and saving. During the second (and last) period, total income is fully consumed. Hence, the first-period budget constraint is

$$C_0 = F_0(K_0) - Z_0 + B_0 - (1 + r_{-1})B_{-1}, \tag{4.6}$$

and the second-period budget constraint is

$$C_1 = F_1(K_0 + I_0) + (K_0 + I_0) - (1 + r_0)B_0. \tag{4.7}$$

In equations (4.6) and (4.7), C_0 and C_1 denote first- and second-period consumption; B_0 denotes first-period borrowing, which can be positive or negative; Z_0 denotes the initial investment spending corresponding to the losses of firms (negative dividends); and $(1 + r_{-1})B_{-1}$ is the historically given initial debt commitment of the representative individual corresponding to the economy's external debt. Finally, the term $-(1 + r_0)B_0$ in equation (4.7) indicates that in the second period individuals must repay debts incurred in the previous period. Obviously, in this two-period model the solvency requirement ensures that in the second period the individual does not incur new debt. Thus, in the final period all debt commitments are settled.

From national income accounting, the sum of consumption, investment, and the surplus in the current account of the balance of payments equals GNP. In terms of equation (4.6), GDP is $F_0(K_0)$, external debt payments are $r_{-1}B_{-1}$, GNP is $F_0(K_0) - r_{-1}B_{-1}$, and the current-account surplus (equal to the capital-account deficit) is $-(B_0 - B_{-1})$. Alternatively, the current-account surplus also equals savings $(F_0(K_0) - r_{-1}B_{-1} - C_0)$ minus investment (Z_0). Hence, the specification in equation (4.6) conforms with national income accounting. Similar considerations apply to the second-period budget constraint in equation (4.7).

Because the representative individual has free access to world capital markets, he or she can lend and borrow freely subject to the world rate of interest, r_0. This access to capital markets implies that the individual's choices are constrained by a consolidated present-value budget constraint rather than two separate periodic budget constraints. To derive the consolidated constraint, we divide equation (4.7) by $(1 + r_0)$, add the resulting equation to equation (4.6), and obtain

$$C_0 + \alpha_1 C_1 = F_0(K_0) + \alpha_1 [F_1(I_0 + K_0) + (I_0 + K_0)] - Z_0 - (1 + r_{-1}) B_{-1}$$

$$\equiv W_0. \tag{4.8}$$

The right-hand side of equation (4.8) defines the value of wealth in period zero, W_0. The consolidated budget constraint highlights the fact that the key decisions that individuals make concern the choices of C_0 and C_1. Implicit in these decisions is the magnitude of new borrowing, B_0, which appears explicitly in the temporal budget constraints (4.6) and (4.7).

It is relevant to note that intertemporal solvency implies that the discounted sum of the periodic surpluses in the trade account must equal the sum of the principal plus interest payments on the historically given initial debt. The trade-balance surplus in each period equals GDP minus domestic absorption (consumption plus investment). Formally, using equations (4.6) and (4.7)—or equivalently using the consolidated equation (4.8)—we note that

$$(TA)_0 + \alpha_1 (TA)_1 = (1 + r_{-1}) B_{-1}, \tag{4.9}$$

where $(TA)_i$ denotes the surplus in the trade balance in period $i = 0, 1$. Formally, $(TA)_0 = F_0(K_0) - C_0 - Z_0$, and $(TA)_1 = F_1(K_0 + I_0) + (K_0 + I_0) - C_1$. It follows therefore that the discounted sum of the periodic surpluses in the current account must equal the discounted sum of the trade balance surplus plus the discounted sum of the surplus in the debt-service account. Formally,

$$(CA)_0 + \alpha_1 (CA)_1 = (1 + r_{-1}) B_{-1} + (DA)_0 + \alpha_1 (DA)_1, \tag{4.9a}$$

where $(CA)_i$ denotes the surplus in the current account (equal to GNP minus domestic absorption), and DA_i denotes the surplus in the debt-service account (equal to minus interest payments on previous period debt) in period $i = 0, 1$. Hence, in our two-period model $(DA)_0 = -r_{-1} B_{-1}$ and $(DA)_1 = -r_0 B_0$. Equation (4.9) reveals that in the absence of initial debt, a trade-balance surplus in a given period must equal (in present-value terms) the trade-balance deficits in all other periods taken as a whole. As illustrated by equation (4.9a), a similar property does not apply to the inter-temporal pattern of the current account.

Let the representative individual's utility depend on the levels of consumption, and let his or her lifetime utility function be denoted by $U(C_0, C_1)$. As usual, we assume that the marginal utilities of consumption in each period are positive and that the marginal rate of substitution of consumption between two consecutive periods is diminishing along any given indifference curve (a quasi-concave U). The individual seeks to maximize lifetime utility subject to the consolidated lifetime budget constraint. Formally, the individual's maximization problem is

$$\tilde{U} = \max_{\{C_0, C_1\}} U(C_0, C_1), \tag{4.10}$$

subject to

$$C_0 + \alpha_1 C_1 = W_0.$$

The solution to this maximization problem is shown in figure 4.2, which incorporates the relevant information from the firm's profit maximization problem of figure 4.1. In this figure, point E measures the discounted sum of current and future GDPs, minus investment (Z_0), and W_0 measures the value of wealth in period zero. That is, E measures $F_0(K_0) + \alpha_1[F_1(K_0 + I_0) + (K_0 + I_0)] - Z_0$, whereas W_0 measures $F_0(K_0) +$

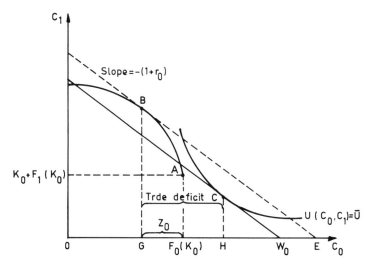

Figure 4.2
The general equilibrium of consumption, investment, and the trade balance

$\alpha_1[F_1(K_0 + I_0) + (K_0 + I_0)] - Z_0 - (1 + r_{-1})B_{-1}$. The horizontal distance between E and W_0 corresponds therefore to the initial external debt commitment $(1 + r_{-1})B_{-1}$. The maximized level of utility obtains at point C at the tangency of indifference curve $\bar{U} = U(C_0, C_1)$ with the budget line. The budget line in turn emerges from point W_0—corresponding to the value of wealth in period zero—and its slope (in absolute terms) equals $1/\alpha_1 = 1 + r_0$.

The equilibrium portrayed in figure 4.2 represents the general equilibrium of the small open economy incorporating both the profit maximization by firms and the utility maximization by households. The case shown in the figure corresponds to a situation in which period zero's absorption (consumption, OH, plus investment, $GF_0(K_0)$) exceeds that period's GDP, $F_0(K_0)$. As a result, the economy runs in period zero a trade-balance deficit that is equal to GH. Obviously, the corresponding current-account deficit is obtained by adding the debt service, $r_{-1}B_{-1}$, to the trade-balance deficit.

4.2   Three Determinants of Borrowing and Lending

The equilibrium pattern of consumption portrayed in figure 4.2 is associated with discrepancies between the periodic levels of consumption and incomes. The lack of a complete synchronization between the time series of consumption and income is reconciled by a reliance on the world capital markets. Accordingly, in obtaining the optimal time profile of consumption, individuals find it beneficial to incur debt during some periods of their life. In determining the extent of the optimal departure of the path of consumption from that of income, and thereby the optimal reliance on capital markets and debt accumulation, it is useful to identify three separate motives: the consumption-smoothing motive, the consumption-tilting motive, and the consumption-augmenting motive. These three motives govern the desired volume of borrowing and lending.

In introducing the three concepts we need to define the concept of the subjective discount factor, which plays a critical role in determining the intertemporal allocations. The subjective discount factor, δ, measures the marginal rate of substitution between consumption in two consecutive periods evaluated at the point of a flat time profile of consumption $(C_0 = C_1 = C)$. Thus,

$$\delta = \frac{\partial U(C, C)/\partial C_1}{\partial U(C, C)/\partial C_0}. \tag{4.11}$$

The subjective discount factor, δ, is related to the subjective marginal rate of time preference, ρ, according to $\delta = 1/(1 + \rho)$.

To facilitate the exposition, we suppose that the subjective discount factor is fixed and that the utility function is

$$U(C_0, C_1) = U(C_0) + \delta U(C_1), \tag{4.12}$$

where U exhibits diminishing marginal utilities (i.e., U is concave): As is evident from the first-order condition of the consumer's maximization problem of equation (4.10), utility maximization implies an equality between the intertemporal marginal rate of substitution and the discount factor. Hence,

$$\frac{U'(C_0)}{\delta U'(C_1)} = \frac{1}{\alpha_1}. \tag{4.13}$$

Armed with these preliminaries, we turn now to illustrate the basic concepts. To sharpen the exposition of each concept, we focus on special cases designed to isolate each factor separately. In all cases we assume that there is no initial debt. We consider first the consumption-smoothing motive. In figure 4.3 we assume that the subjective and the market discount factors are equal to each other (i.e., $\delta = \alpha_1$), that there is no investment, but that the periodic levels of income (endowments) differ from each other ($\overline{Y}_0 \equiv F_0(K_0) \neq K_0 + F_1(K_0) \equiv \overline{Y}_1$). In that case equilibrium consumption is described by point C along the 45° ray. As is evident, because of the

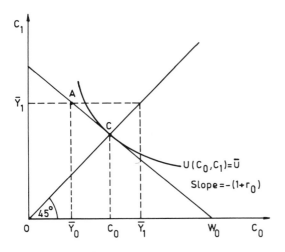

Figure 4.3
The consumption-smoothing effect

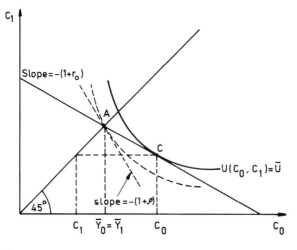

Figure 4.4
The consumption-tilting effect

equality between the subjective and the market discount factors, δ and α_1 (or equivalently, between the subjective rate of time preference, ρ, and the market rate of interest, r_0), individuals wish to smooth the time profile of consumption relative to the fluctuating levels of current income, and as seen in the figure, consumption (which is equal across periods) falls between $\bar{Y}_0$ and $\bar{Y}_1$. This consumption-smoothing motive is effected through borrowing in period zero and repaying the loan plus interest in the subsequent period.

We consider next the consumption-tilting motive. In figure 4.4 we assume that the subjective and the market discount factors differ from each other (i.e., $\alpha_1 \neq \delta$), that there is no investment, and that the periodic levels of income (endowments) are equal (i.e., $\bar{Y}_0 = \bar{Y}_1$). In that case the equilibrium consumption point C does not lie along the 45° ray. In the case drawn, $\delta < \alpha_1$, so that the subjective rate of time preference (ρ) exceeds the world rate of interest (r_0). As a result, individuals facing a flat time profile of income wish to tilt the time profile of consumption toward period zero. This consumption-tilting motive is also effected through the world capital markets in which the individuals borrow in period zero and settle their debts in period one.

Finally, we consider the consumption-augmenting motive. In figure 4.5 we assume equality between the subjective and the market discount factors (i.e., $\delta = \alpha_1$) and between the periodic levels of income (endowments) so that $\bar{Y}_0 = \bar{Y}_1$; we also assume that there is positive investment, because

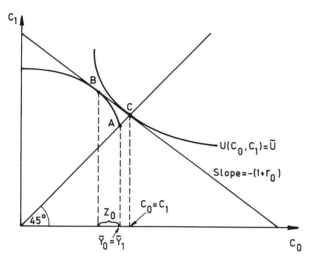

Figure 4.5
The consumption-augmenting effect

Table 4.1
Assumptions generating pure consumption-smoothing, consumption-tilting, and consumption-augmenting effects

	Smoothing	Tilting	Augmenting
Discount	$\delta = \alpha_1$	$\delta \neq \alpha_1$	$\delta = \alpha_1$
Endowments	$\bar{Y}_0 \neq \bar{Y}_1$	$\bar{Y}_0 = \bar{Y}_1$	$\bar{Y}_0 = \bar{Y}_1$
Investment profitability	$F_1'(K_0) \leq r_0$	$F_1'(K_0) \leq r_0$	$F_1'(K_0) > r_0$

$F_1'(K_0) > 1 + r_0$. In that case, equilibrium consumption is at point C. As seen, the investment opportunities, which tilt the time profile of income, augment the levels of consumption in each period without introducing variability to its time profile. As with the other cases, this consumption-augmenting motive is also effected through the world capital markets in which individuals borrow in period zero and repay debt commitment in period one. As is evident, in the absence of international capital markets the investment carried out in period zero would have crowded out private-sector consumption in that period. Access to the world capital markets facilitates the augmentation of consumption at a rate that is uniform over time.

The assumptions needed to generate the pure consumption-smoothing, consumption-tilting, and consumption-augmenting effects are summarized in table 4.1. In all cases these motives are expressed through borrowing and lending in the capital market. Although we have isolated each of the three effects, in general, it is likely that the three motives coexist and interact in generating the equilibrium patterns of consumption, investment, and debt accumulation.

4.3   The Intertemporal Adjustment to Supply Shocks

In this section we illustrate the operation of the three factors in the context of adjustment to supply shocks. To analyze the equilibrium response to supply shocks and to highlight the intertemporal considerations involved in such an adjustment, we distinguish between temporary and permanent shocks and between current and anticipated future shocks. The supply shocks are reflected in either a change in the endowment, $(\bar{Y}_0, \bar{Y}_1)$, or a change in the technological coefficient governing investment, g. Throughout we consider positive supply shocks that increase the endowment bundle or improve the technology of investment. To facilitate the exposition in this discussion, we assume that the utility function $U(C_0, C_1)$ is homothetic. This assumption implies that for a given rate of interest the ratio of consumption in different periods is independent of the level of wealth.

Figure 4.6 illustrates the effects of supply shocks. To focus on the essentials, we assume that the historically given debt, B_{-1}, is zero; that the subjective rate of time preference, ρ, equals the rate of interest, r_0; that initially the endowments are uniformly distributed over time (so that $\bar{Y}_0 = \bar{Y}_1$, and that initially there is no profitable investment. In that case the

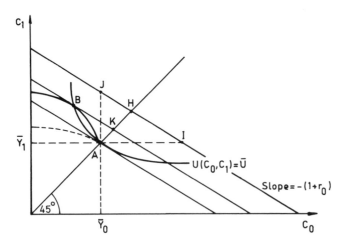

Figure 4.6
Supply shocks

initial equilibrium is described by point A along the 45° ray, and thus consumption in each period equals the corresponding level of the endowment. Hence, in the initial equilibrium the trade-balance deficit is zero. Furthermore, because there is no initial debt, the current account of the balance of payments is also balanced.

Consider first a permanent supply shock that raises the endowment in each period by the same proportion. In terms of figure 4.6 the new endowment is represented by point H. Because we have assumed that the utility function is homothetic, the consumption-expansion locus is the ray from the origin going through the initial equilibrium point. Hence, the new pattern of consumption coincides with the new endowment point H on the new higher budget line. In this case the permanent supply shock results in neither a surplus nor a deficit in the balance of trade. The supply shock yielding this outcome is referred to as a *neutral supply shock*.

Obviously, if the utility function is not homothetic, then the consumption-expansion locus would not be characterized by the 45° ray in figure 4.6; in that case a permanent supply shock is not neutral with respect to its effect on the current account of the balance of payments. For example, if the rate of time preference is high at low levels of wealth and falls as wealth rises, then the consumption-expansion locus is steeper than the 45° ray (it intersects point A in figure 4.6 from below), and a permanent positive supply shock induces a trade-account surplus in the early period.

We consider next a temporary supply shock that raises the endowment only in period zero to point I in figure 4.6. In the figure we have assumed that this temporary supply shock yields the same budget line as the one obtained in the previous case of a permanent shock. Because we are interested only in the qualitative effects of the various shocks, we make this assumption to simplify the diagrammatic exposition. With this shock, equilibrium consumption is described by point H. To bring about this pattern of consumption, the economy runs a surplus in its balance of trade equal to the difference between the new endowment in period zero (corresponding to point I) and the new consumption in period zero (corresponding to point H). Obviously the counterpart to this trade surplus is a trade deficit in the subsequent period in which consumption exceeds the endowment level.

Analogously, an expected future supply shock that raises the endowment in period one is illustrated by point J in figure 4.6 (which is again designed to yield the same budget as in the previous cases). As before, the consumption point is described by point H, and the economy runs a trade-balance deficit in period zero and a corresponding surplus in period one.

The key factor underlying the consumption response to the various supply shocks is the consumption-smoothing motive. Accordingly, the utility-maximizing consumers smooth the time profile of consumption and disregard the variability in the time profile of GDP. The mechanism that facilitates such consumption smoothing operates through the world capital market, and the variability of the stream of GDP is reflected in the time profile of the trade balance. If the (positive) supply shock is temporary, it leads to a trade-balance surplus in the period in which the shock occurs and to trade-balance deficits in all other periods. By analogy with our definition of a neutral (permanent) supply shock, we define a prolending supply shock as the situation in which the positive temporary shock occurs in the present, and we define a proborrowing supply shock as the situation in which the positive temporary shock is expected to occur in the future. Obviously the description of the shocks as being prolending or proborrowing is valid from the perspective of the current period.

The foregoing analysis examined the response of the economy to supply shocks that take the form of exogenous changes in the levels of GDP. Another possible (positive) supply shock may stem from a technological improvement in the process of investment. In terms of figure 4.6 suppose that under the initial technology the investment opportunities schedule is the dashed schedule emerging from point A. Because the marginal product of investment falls short of the rate of interest, no investment takes place at the initial equilibrium. The technological improvement is represented in figure 4.6 by the higher investment opportunities schedule emerging from point A and passing through point B. In that case, as shown earlier, the level of production is characterized by point B, and the level of consumption by point K. Thus, the current level of consumption rises even before the process of investment bears fruit. This represents both the consumption-smoothing and the consumption-augmenting effects. Following our previous definitions, this type of supply shock may be classified as a proborrowing shock.

4.4 The Determination of the World Interest Rate

In the previous sections the analysis of the stylized model treated the world rate of interest as given to the small open economy. In this section we analyze the determination of the equilibrium rate of interest in the world economy. For this purpose we consider the familiar home-country–

foreign-country model. As usual, we designate all variables pertaining to the foreign economy by an asterisk

In determining the world equilibrium intertemporal terms of trade (the rate of interest) and the associated patterns of intertemporal trade (trade-account surplus or deficit), it is convenient to separate the effects of three distinct factors: international differences in subjective rates of time preference, international differences in GDP growth rates, and the growth rate of world output. In the exposition of these three factors we abstract from initial debt and from endogenous investment.

We consider first the role of the subjective rates of time preference. To isolate this factor, let us suppose that home and foreign endowments are stationary and equal to each other; that is, let $\bar{Y}_0 = \bar{Y}_1 = \bar{Y}_0^* = \bar{Y}_1^*$. Also, suppose that the home subjective rate of time preference exceeds the foreign rate, so that $\rho > \rho^*$. The equilibrium of the world economy is portrayed by the Edgeworth box in figure 4.7. In that figure the horizontal axis measures world GDP in period zero, $\bar{Y}_0 + \bar{Y}_0^*$, and the vertical axis measures the corresponding quantity for period one $\bar{Y}_1 + \bar{Y}_1^*$. By construction the box is squared, and the international and intertemporal distribution of world outputs is specified by point A, the midpoint along the

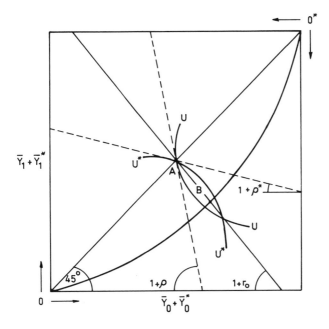

Figure 4.7
International differences in time preferences

diagonal OO^*. As usual, quantities pertaining to the home country are measured from point O as an origin, and quantities pertaining to the foreign country are measured from point O^* as an origin. At the initial endowment point A the slope of the domestic indifference curve, UU, equals one plus the domestic subjective rate of time preference $(1 + \rho)$, whereas the slope of the foreign indifference curve, U^*U^*, equals one plus the foreign subjective rate of time preference $(1 + \rho^*)$.

Because $\rho > \rho^*$, it follows that the equilibrium patterns of international and intertemporal consumption must be located to the southeast of point A, at a point like point B on the contract curve (the locus of tangencies between home and foreign indifference curves). At the equilibrium point B the rate of interest, r_0, is equalized across countries, and its magnitude must be bounded between the domestic and the foreign subjective rates of time preference; that is, $\rho > r_0 > \rho^*$. As is evident from a comparison of the patterns of consumption at point B with the patterns of GDPs at point A, in period zero the home country runs a deficit in its trade account while the foreign country runs a corresponding surplus of an equal magnitude. In the subsequent period this pattern of trade is reversed to ensure that the discounted sum of each country's trade balance is zero. This intertemporal pattern of international trade reflects the consumption-tilting effect operating in each country. Hence, the less patient country (the country with the higher rate of time preference) runs a trade deficit in the early period.

We consider next the role of international differences in GDP growth rates. To isolate this factor, let us suppose that the home and the foreign subjective rates of time preference are equal to each other, so that $\rho = \rho^*$. Our previous analysis implies that in equilibrium the rate of interest equals the common value of the subjective rates of time preference; that is, $\rho = r_0 = \rho^*$. Let us suppose further that world output is stationary, so that $\bar{Y}_0 + \bar{Y}_0^* = \bar{Y}_1 + \bar{Y}_1^*$, but let the growth rate of the home country GDP exceed the foreign growth rate. We denote the percentage growth of GDP by θ, where $\theta = (\bar{Y}_1 / \bar{Y}_0) - 1$, and a similar definition applies to the foreign growth rate, θ^*.

The equilibrium of the world economy is portrayed in figure 4.8, where the international and the intertemporal distributions of GDP are specified by point A. This point lies to the left of the diagonal OO^*, thereby reflecting the assumption that $\theta > \theta^*$. (Notice that because, by assumption, world output is stationary, it follows that $\theta > 0$, whereas $\theta^* < 0$). The international and intertemporal distribution of world output equilibrium consumption is specified by point B. This point lies on the diagonal OO^*, thereby reflecting the assumptions that the world output is stationary and

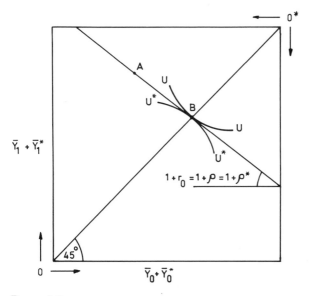

Figure 4.8
International differences in GDP growth rates

that $\rho = \rho^*$. As is evident, in this case the home country runs a trade deficit in the early period while the foreign country runs a corresponding surplus. Obviously this pattern of trade imbalances is reversed in the subsequent period. This intertemporal pattern of international trade reflects the consumption-smoothing effect operating in each country. Hence, the faster-growing country runs a trade deficit in the early period.

Finally, we consider the role of the rate of growth of world output. To isolate this factor we continue to assume that the domestic and the foreign subjective rates of time preference are equal, so that $\rho = \rho^*$. We also assume that world output is growing at the percentage rate, θ, that is common to the percentage growth rate of each country's GDP. Thus, let $\bar{Y}_1/\bar{Y}_0 = \bar{Y}_1^*/\bar{Y}_0^* = 1 + \theta$. The equalities between the home and the foreign marginal rates of time preference and between the home and the foreign growth rates imply that in this case the two factors analyzed here do not play a role in determining the rate of interest, nor do they determine the patterns of trade. If we assume that the home and the foreign utility functions are identical and homothetic, then we can specify the equilibrium without taking account of international differences in the levels of GDP.

The equilibrium of the world economy is shown in figure 4.9, in which point A describes the international and the intertemporal distributions of both GDP and consumption. Obviously, in that case, because of the equal-

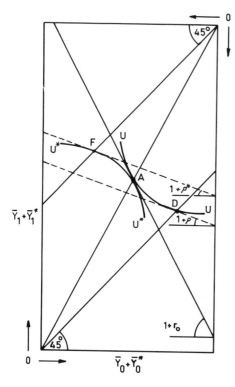

Figure 4.9
Growth of world output

ity between the patterns of production and consumption in each country, there are no trade imbalances. The main point that is demonstrated by the figure concerns the equilibrium value of the world rate of interest. As shown, the equilibrium rate of interest (corresponding to the common slope of the home and the foreign indifference curves at point A) exceeds the home and foreign common subjective rates of time preference (corresponding to the slopes of the domestic and the foreign indifference curves at points D and F on the 45° lines). The difference between the equilibrium rate of interest and the rates of time preference rises with the growth rate of world GDP. Hence, the higher the growth rate of the world economy, the higher the equilibrium world rate of interest.

To derive the precise relation between the equilibrium rate of interest and the rate of growth of the world economy, we denote the consumption ratio C_1/C_0 by c and the intertemporal elasticity of substitution by σ, where

$$\sigma = \frac{\partial \log c}{\partial \log[(\partial U/\partial C_0)/(\partial U/\partial C_1)]} > 0. \tag{4.14}$$

Assuming that the elasticity of substitution is constant and using these notations, we observe from figure 4.9 that

$$\log c(A) = \log c(D) + \sigma[\log(1 + r_0) - \log(1 + \rho)], \tag{4.15}$$

where $c(A)$ and $c(D)$ are the consumption ratios in figure 4.9 at points A and D, respectively. Because point D lies on the 45° line, $c(D) = 1$. Further, because point A lies on the diagonal OO^*, it is evident that $c(A) = 1 + \theta$. It follows that $\log(1 + \theta) = \sigma \log[(1 + r_0)/(1 + \rho)]$; therefore,

$$(1 + r_0) = (1 + \rho)(1 + \theta)^{1/\sigma}. \tag{4.16}$$

This means that $1/\sigma$ is the equilibrium elasticity of the rate of interest with respect to the percentage rate of growth of world GDP. Hence, the positive association between the equilibrium rate of interest and the percentage rate of growth of world GDP decreases with the elasticity of substitution between the levels of consumption in two consecutive periods.

The foregoing analysis presumed that the growth of world output stemmed from an exogenous rise in the levels of the endowments. A similar analysis also applies to the case in which the growth of world output (evenly distributed across countries) arises from an improved availability of investment opportunities. In that case, figure 4.9 applies, except that the dimensions of the box are endogenous. Specifically, although in the previous case the dimensions of the box reflected the exogenously given growth rate of world GDP, $1 + \theta = \bar{Y}_1/\bar{Y}_0 = \bar{Y}_1^*/\bar{Y}_0^*$, in the present case they reflect the endogenously determined growth rate of GDP net of investment:

$$1 + \theta = \frac{F_1(I_0(r_0) + K_0) + I_0(r_0) + K_0}{F_0(K_0) - I_0(r_0)(1 + (\tfrac{1}{2})gI_0(r_0)/K_0}$$

$$= \frac{F_1^*(I_0^*(r_0) + K_0^*) + I_0^*(r_0) + K_0^*}{F_0^*(K_0^*) - I_0^*(r_0)(1 + (\tfrac{1}{2})g^*I_0^*(r_0)/K_0^*)}, \tag{4.17}$$

where $I_0(r_0)$ and $I_0^*(r_0)$ denote desired investment as a function of the rate of interest. The equilibrium rate of interest is determined as the solution to equations (4.16) and (4.17), and as before, in equilibrium there are no trade imbalances.

If investment opportunities are not distributed evenly between the two countries, then the two (endogenous) growth rates of GDP also differ from

each other. In that case the total effect exerted by the investment opportunities on the rate of interest and on the patterns of trade reflects the
considerations underlying the cases analyzed in figures 4.8 and 4.9. Specifically, suppose that the home country faces a more profitable set of investment opportunities than the foreign country. Then the (endogenously
determined) growth rate of the home country's GDP, net of investment,
exceeds the corresponding growth rate of the foreign economy, and the
world rate of interest exceeds the subjective rate of time preference according to equation (4.16) in which the growth rate, θ, is now interpreted as
the weighted average of the two countries' growth rates. The resulting
patterns of trade are similar to those portrayed by figure 4.8, reflecting the
general principle that the faster-growing country runs a trade deficit in the
early period.

Up to now we have abstracted from the role that the historically given
initial debt position plays in determining the equilibrium world rate of
interest and the patterns of trade. To examine the consequences of the
initial debt position, it is useful to compare an equilibrium without an
initial debt commitment with another equilibrium in which the initial debt
commitment of the home country is positive. Hence, we consider an initial
zero-debt equilibrium that is disturbed by a transfer of $T = (1 + r_{-1}) B_{-1}$
units of current output from the home to the foreign country. The effects
of such a transfer are examined with the aid of figure 4.10, which is familiar
from the famous transfer-problem analysis.

Suppose that at the initial equilibrium the international and intertemporal
distributions of GDP are specified by point A and the corresponding
distributions of consumption by point B. Analogously to our discussion of
figure 4.7, this pattern of consumption reflects the assumption that the
home marginal propensity to save falls short of the foreign marginal
propensity. This difference between the two marginal saving propensities
is reflected in the relative slopes of the home and foreign consumption-
expansion loci, OGB and O^*BF, respectively. As shown in figure 4.10, at
the initial equilibrium the rate of interest is r_0, and the two expansion loci
are drawn for this rate of interest.

As a brief digression, we compute now the slopes of the expansion
loci. Using the representative individual's maximization problem of equation (4.8), we obtain the implied demand functions for current and future
consumption:

$$C_0 = C_0(\alpha_1, W_0), \tag{4.18}$$

$$C_1 = C_1(\alpha_1, W_0). \tag{4.19}$$

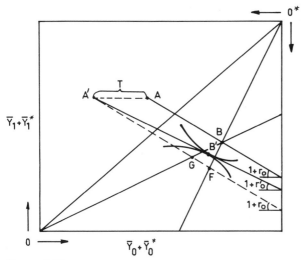

Figure 4.10
The effect of a redistribution of world debt

If we assume normality, we can invert equation (4.18) to read

$$W_0 = h(\alpha_1, C_0). \tag{4.20}$$

Substituting (4.20) into (4.19) yields

$$C_1 = C_1[\alpha_1, h(\alpha_1, C_0)]. \tag{4.21}$$

The slope of the consumption-expansion locus is obtained by differentiating equation (4.21) and noting that from (4.20) $\partial h/\partial C_0 = 1/(\partial C_0/\partial W_0)$. Thus,

$$\frac{dC_1}{dC_0} = \frac{\partial C_1/\partial W_0}{\partial C_0/\partial W_0} = \frac{1 - (\partial C_0/\partial W_0)}{\alpha_1(\partial C_0/\partial W_0}, \tag{4.22}$$

where the second quality follows from the budget constraint in equation (4.10).

It follows that if the foreign and the home residents face the same rate of interest, then the differences between the slopes of their consumption-expansion loci depend only on the relations between their marginal propensities to consume (or save) out of wealth. Our previous analysis of figure 4.7 indicates that in the absence of world output growth there is also a unique relation between the equilibrium pattern of the two countries' consumption ratios (C_1/C_0 and C_1^*/C_0^*) and the difference between their subjective rates of time preference. Specifically, as illustrated by point B in figure 4.7, if $\rho > \rho^*$, then $(C_1/C_0) < (C_1^*/C_0^*)$, and vice versa. Hence, in the absence of growth the pattern of consumptions exhibited in figure 4.10, and the analysis of the effects of a redistribution of world debt that is carried out with the aid of the same figure, can also be characterized in terms of differences between the subjective rates of time preference rather than differences between the marginal propensities to save. Finally, we note that if the utility functions are homothetic, then the difference between the home and foreign marginal propensities to save depends only on the difference between their subjective rates of time preference. In that case, the general-equilibrium configuration exhibited by figure 4.7 is also applicable to a situation in which there is growth.

We consider now the effects of a transfer from the home to the foreign country. Following the transfer, the net endowments of the two countries are specified in figure 4.10 by point A', where the horizontal distance between A and A' equals the size of the transfer, T. The new endowment alters the patterns of demand in both countries, and since the two subjective rates of time preference differ from each other, the new pattern of demand alters the rate of interest. Specifically, following the transfer at the initial rate of interest, the home demand for current and future goods is described by point G, and the corresponding foreign demand is described by point F, where points G and F lie on the consumption-expansion loci associated with the initial interest rate. Obviously this pattern of world demand creates an excess supply of current-period goods and an excess demand for future-period goods. To eliminate this disequilibrium, the relative price of current goods in terms of future goods (i.e., the rate of interest) must fall. Put differently, world savings rise because the transfer redistributes wealth from the home country (with the low saving propensity) to the foreign country (with the high saving propensity). The fall in the rate of interest is necessary to eliminate excess savings in the world economy. Diagrammatically, the fall in the rate of interest from r_0 to r_0' raises the desired consumption ratios C_0/C_1 and C_0^*/C_1^* and alters accordingly the slopes of both the home and the foreign consumption-expansion loci. The new equilibrium obtains at point B', at which the slopes of the two countries' indifference curves are equal to $1 + r_0'$, where $r_0' < r_0$. As is evident, point B' must be located inside the triangle BGF. It follows that if the foreign rate of time preference exceeds the home rate, the contract curve in figure 4.10 would be located above the diagonal OO^*, and the transfer from the home to the foreign country would necessitate a rise rather than a fall in the world rate of interest.

It is relevant to note that as is typical in transfer-problem analyses, the relevant criterion determining the effect of a redistribution of world debt on the rate of interest involves a comparison between the home and the foreign marginal propensities to save rather than the average saving propensities. In fact, the initial endowment in figure 4.10 could have been placed to the southeast of point B along the extension of the line segment AB. The analysis of the effect of the transfer on the rate of interest remains intact as long as the home marginal propensity to save is smaller than the foreign marginal propensity, even though in that case the (positive) home average propensity to save exceeds the (negative) foreign average propensity to save.

4.5 Extension: Random Shocks

To shed more light on the basic motives underlying saving decisions we now incorporate random shocks into the analysis. Consider a small open economy with perfect access to the world capital market. Output (net of investment) is subject to random shocks. If they reverse themselves, they can be viewed as *transitory shocks*. Alternatively, if they behave like a random walk, they can be viewed as *permanent shocks*. To simplify the exposition, we assume that time is continuous and the horizon is infinite. (See, for example, Faig 1991 and Pitchford and Turnovsky 1977.)

As usual, the household chooses a consumption path so as to maximize the expected utility over the infinite horizon:

$$U_t = E_t \int_t^\infty e^{-\delta(\tau-t)} u(c_\tau) \, d\tau, \tag{4.23}$$

subject to the flow-budget constraint

$$dA_t = (rA_t - c_t) \, dt + Y_t, \tag{4.24}$$

where E, δ, c, A, r, and Y denote the expectation operator, the discount rate, consumption level, asset position, the rate of interest, and the output level, respectively. Naturally, the initial value of assets is predetermined.

Transitory Shocks

The representative household does not know exactly when a transitory shock will occur, nor how long it will last. To fix ideas, assume that output shocks follow a Poisson process, so that each state of nature has a random duration which is distributed exponentially. To simplify, we consider a two-state distribution so that the high-output event lasts b_H units of time, on average, and the corresponding low-output event lasts b_L units of time. To obtain closed-form solutions, we assume that the Arrow-Pratt measure of absolute risk aversion is constant. Thus the von Neumann-Morgenstern utility function is specified as

$$u(c_t) = -\frac{1}{\eta} e^{-\eta c_t}, \tag{4.25}$$

where η denotes the measure of absolute risk aversion.

Denoting the value function (that is, the maximized utility as a function of the predetermined variables) in the low-output state by V^L, and the corresponding value function in the high-output state by V^H, the Bellman's equation must hold for each state. Accordingly (see the appendix), the maximization problem must satisfy

$$(\delta + b^L)V^L(A_t) - b^L V^H(A_t) = \underset{c_t}{\text{Max}} \left[u(c_t) + V_A^L(A_t)(rA_t - c_t) \right] \tag{4.26}$$

and

$$(\delta + b^H)V^H(A_t) - b^H V^L(A_t) = \underset{c_t}{\text{Max}} \left[u(c_t) + V_A^H(A_t)(rA_t - c_t) \right]. \tag{4.27}$$

A solution can be found by the method of undetermined coefficients, using the Bellman's equations and an initial guess for the high-output and low-output value functions. Our initial guess is

$$V^L(A) = -\frac{p^L}{q^L} e^{-q^L A}, \quad V^H(A) = -\frac{p^H}{q^H} e^{-q^H A}. \tag{4.28}$$

Solving the maximization problem in (4.26) and (4.27) yields

$$q^H = q^L = r\eta, \quad c^L = \frac{1}{\eta}(-\ln p^L + r\eta A), \quad c^H = \frac{1}{\eta}(-\ln p^H + r\eta A). \tag{4.29}$$

Finally, upon substituting (4.28) and (4.29) into (4.26) and (4.27), it can be shown that $p^L = p^H$ and the implied consumption function is

$$c_t = \frac{\delta - r}{r\eta} + rA_t. \tag{4.30}$$

The implication is that in a small open economy with perfect access to the world capital market, transitory output shocks do not affect current consumption. Thus, consumption is *perfectly* smoothed. In contrast, if the domestic capital market is completely closed, consumption must equal income (net of investment). By the general-equilibrium considerations in this case the output variance must be equal to the consumption variance, and consumption smoothing cannot be achieved.

Permanent Output Shocks

To analyze the effects of permanent shock (as in a random walk) we assume that the output process follows a Brownian motion. That is,

$$dY_t = \mu dt + \sigma dz, \tag{4.31}$$

where μ is a drift and z is a standard Weiner process with zero mean and unitary standard deviation. Asset accummulation is specified as $dA_t = (rA_t - c_t)\,dt + Y_t$. The Bellman's equation is

$$\delta V(A_t) - \mu V_A(A_t) - \tfrac{1}{2}\sigma^2 V_{AA}(A_t) = \underset{c_t}{\text{Max}}\,[u(c_t) + V_A(A_t)(rA_t - c_t)], \tag{4.32}$$

where use has been made of Ito's lemma to evaluate the expected rate of change in the value function (see chapter 13).

Following the same solution procedure as in the previous section, the implied consumption function is now given by

$$c_t = \left(\frac{\delta - r}{\eta} + \mu - \frac{\eta\sigma^2}{2}\right) + rA_t + Y_t. \tag{4.34}$$

The implication is that under permanent output shocks the conditional output variance (net of investment) is equal to the consumption variance.[1]

4.6   Appendix

In an approximate and discrete model, with time intervals of size Δt, the Bellman's equation for the low output state is given by

$$V^L(A_t) = \underset{c_t}{\text{Max}}\; u(c_t)\Delta t + [e^{-(\delta + b^L)\Delta t}]V^L(A_{t+\Delta t})$$

$$+ (e^{-\delta\Delta t} - e^{-(\delta + b^L)\Delta t})V^H(A_{t+\Delta t}), \tag{A.1}$$

where the evolution of assets is given by

$$A_{t+\Delta t} = A_t + (rA_t - c_t)\Delta t + Y_t. \tag{A.2}$$

In the limit as Δt goes to zero (as usual for a time derivative), the term $(1/\Delta t) [e^{-(\delta+b^L)\Delta t} V^L(A_{t+\Delta t}) - V(A_t)]$ approaches $(\delta + b^L) V^L(A_t) + V_A(A_t) (rA_t - c_t)$, while the term $(1/\Delta t) [e^{-\delta \Delta t} - e^{-(\delta+b^L)\Delta t}] V^H(A_{t+\Delta t})$ approaches $b^L V^H(A_t)$. The Bellman's equation for the high-output state is derived in a similar fashion. This limiting process underlies the Bellman's equations, (4.26)–(4.27), in the text.

5

The Multiple-Good World

The formulation of the stylized model discussed in the previous chapter adopted a high degree of commodity aggregation; it assumed a single composite-commodity world. With this level of aggregation the only price relevant for individual decision making was the relative price of consumption in different periods. This formulation enabled us to focus on the role played by the intertemporal terms of trade—the rate of interest. In this chapter we extend the stylized model to include multiple goods. This extension introduces the temporal terms of trade (the relative price of different goods in a given period) and facilitates the analysis of the interactions between *temporal* and *intertemporal* relative prices in influencing private-sector behavior and in determining the equilibrium of the system. In extending the model, we introduce the concepts of *consumption-based* real rate of interest and real wealth. We use the extended model to determine the effects of shocks to the commodity terms of trade on saving behavior, and thereby on current account adjustments. These results will prove useful in the subsequent analysis of the intertemporal effects of fiscal policies operating through the induced changes in temporal and intertemporal terms of trade.

5.1 The Analytical Framework

Consider a two-good-two-period model, and suppose that good X is exportable and good M is importable. For simplicity assume that there is no investment. Analogously to equations (4.6) and (4.7), the budget constraints of the representative individual (measured in terms of exportables) are

$$c_{x0} + p_0 c_{m0} = \overline{Y}_{x0} + p_0 \overline{Y}_{m0} + B_0 - (1 + r_{x,-1})B_{-1}, \tag{5.1}$$

$$c_{x1} + p_1 c_{m1} = \overline{Y}_{x1} + p_1 \overline{Y}_{m1} - (1 + r_{x0})B_0 \tag{5.2}$$

where c_{xt} and $\bar{Y}_{xt}$ denote, respectively, the levels of consumption and production of exportables in period t, c_{mt} and $\bar{Y}_{mt}$ denote, respectively, the levels of consumption and production of importables in period t, p_t denotes the relative price in period t of importables in terms of exportables, and $t = 0, 1$. The rate of interest, r_{xt}, and the levels of new borrowing, $B_t(t = -1, 0)$, are measured in units of exportables that serve as the numeraire throughout this section.

Before proceeding with the analysis, two points are worth noting. First, using the conventions of national income accounting, the budget constraints can also be expressed by the equality between the current-account surplus, $(CA)_t$, and the capital account deficit $-(KA)_t$. The trade-account surplus, $(TA)_t$, equals the difference between exports (the excess of production over consumption of exportables; i.e., $\bar{Y}_{xt} - c_{xt}$) and imports (the excess of the values of consumption over production of importables; i.e., $p_t[c_{mt} - \bar{Y}_{mt}]$); the current-account surplus is the difference between the surplus in the balance of trade and the deficit in the debt-service account; thus $(CA)_t = (TA)_t - (DA)_t$, where the debt-service account, $(DA)_t = r_{xt-1}B_{t-1}$, and finally, $(KA)_t = B_t - B_{t-1}$. Using these definitions, it can be verified that $(CA)_t + (KA)_t = 0$.

Second, our assumption that the debt commitment is denominated in units of good X may be material when there are unanticipated changes in the terms of trade yielding unanticipated capital gains or losses. Obviously, if all changes in the terms of trade are anticipated, interest-rate parity (across debt instruments denominated in units of different commodities) requires that $1 + r_{xt} = (p_{t+1}/p_t)(1 + r_{mt})$, where r_{mt} denotes the rate of interest in period t on debt denominated in units of importables. In that case the fully anticipated terms of trade changes do not alter the individuals' wealth position. It follows that an unexpected change in p_0 exerts different wealth effects depending on whether the initial debt commitment was $(1 + r_{x,-1})B_{-1}$ (as in equation 5.1) or $p_0/p_{-1}(1 + r_{m,-1})B_{-1}$. We will return to this issue in the subsequent analysis of terms of trade shocks.

The representative individual maximizes lifetime utility subject to the consolidated budget constraint (obtained by dividing equation 5.2 by $(1 + r_{x0})$ and adding the resultant expression to equation 5.1). The utility function is defined over the four goods $(c_{x0}, c_{m0}, c_{x1}, c_{m1})$. We assume that utility can be expressed as a function of two components, C_0 and C_1, which are in turn linearly homogeneous subutility functions of the consumption of goods in period zero (c_{x0}, c_{m0}) and in period one (c_{x1}, c_{m1}), respectively. Formally, the maximization problem is

$$\tilde{U} = \max_{\substack{\{c_{x1}, c_{m1}\} \\ c_{x0}}} U[C_0(c_{x0}, c_{m0}), C_1(c_{x1}, c_{m1})], \tag{5.3}$$

subject to

$$c_{x0} + p_0 c_{m0} + \alpha_{x1}(c_{x1} + p_1 c_{m1})$$

$$= \bar{Y}_{x0} + p_0 \bar{Y}_{m0} + \alpha_{x1}(\bar{Y}_{x1} + p_1 \bar{Y}_{x1}) - (1 + r_{x-1})B_{-1}$$

$$= W_0, \tag{5.4}$$

where $\alpha_{x1} = 1/(1 + r_{x0})$ is the discount factor applicable to consumption in period one.

The solution to the maximization problem can be decomposed into two parts. The first involves the *temporal* allocation of spending, $z_t = c_{xt} + p_t c_{mt}$, between the two goods so as to maximize the subutility $C_t(c_{xt}, c_{mt})$, and the second involves the *intertemporal* allocation of lifetime spending $(z_0 + \alpha_{x1} z_1 = W_0)$ so as to maximize the lifetime utility $U(C_0, C_1)$. In the first stage of the temporal maximization the consumer may be viewed as minimizing the cost, z_t, of obtaining a given level of subutility, C_t. The assumption that the subutility functions are linear homogeneous imply that the "cost" function is $z_t = P_t(p_t)C_t$, where $P_t(p_t)$ is the "marginal cost" of obtaining a unit of C_t (and the marginal cost depends on the relative price, p_t). In what follows we refer to P_t as the *consumption-based price index*. This price index exhibits the familiar properties of similar price indexes; in each period the elasticity of the price index, P, with respect to the price of importables, p, equals the expenditure share of this commodity in total spending.[1]

In the second stage the consumer, who has already optimized the temporal allocation of spending, attempts to optimize the intertemporal allocation. Formally, this maximization problem is

$$\tilde{U} = \max_{\{C_0, C_1\}} U(C_0, C_1), \tag{5.5}$$

subject to

$$P_0(p_0)C_0 + \alpha_{x1} P_1(p_1)C_1 = W_0. \tag{5.6}$$

For subsequent use it is convenient to normalize the budget constraint (6.6) and express it in *real* terms. For this purpose we divide both sides by the price index P_0 and obtain

$$C_0 + \alpha_{c1} C_1 = W_{c0}, \tag{5.6a}$$

where

$$\alpha_{c1} = \frac{P_1}{P_0}\alpha_{x1} \quad \text{and} \quad W_{c0} = \frac{W_0}{P_0}.$$

We refer to α_1 as the (consumption-based) real *discount factor* and to W_{c0} as the (consumption-based) *real wealth*. As seen, the real discount factor equals the discount factor expressed in terms of the numeraire (α_{x1}) adjusted by the "rate of inflation," that is, by the percentage change in the consumption-based price index.

The maximization of the utility function (5.5) subject to the normalized budget constraint (5.6a) yields conventional demand functions for the "goods" C_0 and C_1. As usual, these functions depend on the relevant relative price α_{c1}, and on the relevant concept of "income," which in our case is real wealth, W_{c0}. Thus the periodic demand functions (for $t = 0, 1$) are $C_t = C_t(\alpha_{c1}, W_{c0})$. These demand functions are the conventional consumption-based *real spending* functions. Obviously, we could also have used the previous analysis to define and characterize spending in terms of other baskets of goods, such as exportables, importables, or GDP; in these cases spending would have been measured by $P_t(p_t)C_t$, $P_t(p_t)C_t/p_{m,t}$, and $P_t(p_t)C_t/(\overline{Y}_{xt} + p_{m,t}\overline{Y}_{m,t})$, respectively. The choice of units is, of course, of prime importance in circumstances where relative prices change. In the subsequent analysis of the effects of terms of trade changes, we choose to express spending and the current account in terms of the consumption basket. This choice is made in order to obtain indicators useful for welfare evaluations. But first we digress briefly to define the consumption-based real rate of interest.

5.2   The Real Rate of Interest

Corresponding to the concept of the real discount factor, we can define the concept of the (consumption-based) *real rate of interest*. Accordingly, the real interest rate, r_{c0}, is

$$r_{c0} = \frac{1 + r_{x0}}{P_1/P_0} - 1. \tag{5.7}$$

As is evident, this consumption-based real rate of interest, r_{c0}, depends positively on the rate of interest in terms of the numeraire, r_{x0}, and negatively on the rate of "inflation," P_1/P_0, which in turn reflects the path of the relative price of importables, p_0 and p_1. In order to characterize the dependence of the real rate of interest on the path of the temporal terms of trade, p_0 and p_1, we differentiate equation (5.7) and obtain

$$\left(\frac{1}{1 + r_{c0}}\right) dr_{c0} = \left(\frac{1}{1 + r_{x0}}\right) dr_{x0} + \beta_{m0} \frac{dp_0}{p_0} - \beta_{m1} \frac{dp_1}{p_1}, \tag{5.8}$$

where β_{m1} denotes the expenditure share of importables in total spending in period t. Equation (5.8) reveals that, ceteris paribus, a temporary current deterioration in the commodity terms of trade (a rise in p_0) raises the real rate of interest while an expected future deterioration in the commodity terms of trade (a rise in p_1) lowers the real rate of interest. The effect of a permanent deterioration of the commodity terms of trade (so that p_0 and p_1 rise in the same proportion) depends on the intertemporal changes in the expenditure shares. If these shares do not vary over time, a permanent change in the commodity terms of trade is neutral in its effect on the real rate of interest.

5.3 The Terms of Trade and Real Spending

In this section we analyze the effects of transitory and permanent shocks to the commodity terms of trade on real spending, C, measured in terms of the consumption basket. This analysis will aid the subsequent discussion of currrent-account adjustments. As was shown previously, the periodic spending functions depend on the consumption-based real discount factor and on real wealth. Accordingly, the current-period-spending function is

$$C_0 = C_0(\alpha_{c1}, W_{c0}). \tag{5.9}$$

We use this function in order to analyze the effects of changes in the terms of trade.

Consider a temporary change in the *current*-period terms of trade. Differentiating the spending function with respect to p_0 and expressing the results in terms of elasticities, it can be shown that

$$\frac{\partial \log C_0}{\partial \log p_0} = \beta_{m0}\{-\eta_{ca} + [(1 - \gamma_s)\mu_{m0} - 1]\eta_{cw}\}, \tag{5.10}$$

where β_{m0} denotes the relative share of consumption of importables in current-period spending ($p_0 c_{m0}/z_0 = p_0 c_{m0}/P_0 C_0$), η_{ca} and η_{cw} denote the elasticities of C_0 with respect to α_{c1} and W_{c0}, respectively, $\gamma_s = \alpha_{c1} C_1/W_{c0}$ is the share of saving in wealth, and $\mu_{m0} = \bar{Y}_{m0}/c_{m0}$ is the ratio of production to consumption of importables, which ranges between zero and one. The two terms on the right-hand side of equation (5.10) reflect the effects of changes in the two variables appearing on the right-hand side of equation (5.19), α_{c1} and W_{c0}, induced by the current change in the commodity terms of trade, p_0. Equation (5.10) can be manipulated further by using the Slutsky decomposition (according to which $\eta_{ca} = \bar{\eta}_{ca} - \gamma_s \eta_{cw}$, where $\bar{\eta}_{ca}$ denotes the compensated demand elasticity) and noting that $\bar{\eta}_{ca} = \gamma_s \sigma$ (where σ, the intertemporal elasticity of substitution, is defined by equation 4.12). Hence

$$\frac{\partial \log C_0}{\partial \log p_0} = \beta_m[-\eta_{cw} + \gamma_s(\eta_{cw} - \sigma) + (1 - \gamma_s)\mu_{m0}\eta_{cw}]. \tag{5.11}$$

In interpreting the bracketed term on the right-hand side of equation (5.11), we note three channels through which changes in current-period terms of trade alter current-period spending. The first term represents the *deflator effect*, which operates through the change in the price index used to deflate wealth; the second term represents the *intertemporal-price effect*, which operates through the change in the real discount factor; and the third term represents the *wealth effect*, which operates through the change in real wealth induced by the change in the valuation of the output of importables.

The deterioration in the terms of trade raises the price index by β_{m0}; this lowers the real value of wealth equiproportionally and (assuming normality) lowers spending according to the elasticity η_{cw}—hence the negative term—η_{cw} on the right-hand side of equation (5.11). The intertemporal-price effect depends on the sign of $\eta_{cw} - \sigma$. Finally, the wealth effect is the product of η_{cw} and the percentage rise in wealth due to the appreciation of the output of importables. This can be verified by noting that $\partial \log W_0 / \partial \log p_0 = p_0 \bar{Y}_{m0} / W_0$ and that this can also be written as $(1 - \gamma_s)\beta_{m0}\mu_{m0}$. In interpreting this expression, we note that a given percentage rise in the price of importables appreciates the value of output of importables, but since their consumption exceeds production, the potential rise in the former is only a fraction μ_{m0} of the rise in price. To express the potential rise in consumption of importables in terms of lifetime spending, we need to multiply μ_{m0} by the share of consumption of importables in current spending, β_{m0}, times the share of current spending in lifetime spending $(1 - \gamma_s)$. Hence the last expression on the right-hand side of equation (5.11) is the wealth effect which, by normality, is positive.

The foregoing discussion indicated the signs of the deflator effects, the intertemporal-price effects, and the wealth effect. Combining these effects, we can rewrite equation (5.11):

$$\frac{\partial \log C_0}{\partial \log p_0} = -\beta_{m0}[(1 - \gamma_s)(1 - \mu_{m0})\eta_{cw} + \gamma_s\sigma]. \tag{5.11a}$$

As is evident, since γ_s and μ_{m0} are bound between zero and unity, the deterioration in the current terms of trade must lower current real spending.

To gain further insight into the factors governing the effects of changes in the terms of trade on spending, consider the extreme case in which $\mu_{m0} = 1$, so that in the current-period production and consumption of importables are equal to each other and imports are zero. In that case, as is evident from equation (5.11a), the negative change in spending arises only from the pure intertemporal substitution effect $(-\beta_{m0}\gamma_s\sigma)$. This case is of special interest since it highlights the importance of intertemporal considerations. It demonstrates that even though real income does not change (since net imports are zero), the utility-maximizing individual responds to the rise in the domestic consumption-based real rate of interest (induced by the temporary deterioration in the terms of trade) by substituting away from current spending toward future spending.

Consider next the effect of an expected *future* deterioration in the terms of trade (i.e., a rise in p_1) on current-period spending. Formally, differentiating equation (5.9) with respect to p_1, expressing in terms of elasticities and manipulating as before, yields

$$\frac{\partial \log C_0}{\partial \log p_1} = \beta_{m1}\gamma_s[(\sigma - \eta_{cw}) + \mu_{m1}\eta_{cw}]. \tag{5.12}$$

A comparison between the expressions showing the effects of current and future deteriorations in the terms of trade reveals that the deflator effect, $-\beta_{m0}\eta_{cw}$, which appears in equation (5.11), does not appear in equation (5.12). The other important difference concerns the direction of the intertemporal-price effect. As seen in equation (5.8), a rise in p_0 raises the real rate of interest, whereas a rise in p_1 lowers the real rate of interest. Because of these differences the effect of an anticipated future deterioration on spending is ambiguous. This should be contrasted with the unambiguous response of current spending to a current terms of trade change. The ambiguous effect depends, in part, on whether current consumption, C_0, and future consumption, C_1, are gross substitutes (i.e., $\eta_{ca} > 0$) or gross complements (i.e., $\eta_{ca} < 0$). This is indicated by the term $(\sigma - \eta_{cw})$ in equation (5.12).

The ambiguity of the effects of the expected future deterioration in the terms of trade can be clarified by considering a simple case in which the utility function is homothetic and the level of production of importables in the future is zero. Thus consider the case in which $\eta_{cw} = 1$ and $\mu_{m1} = 0$. Under these circumstances equation (5.12) becomes

$$\frac{\partial \log C_0}{\partial \log p_1} = \beta_{m1}\gamma_s(\sigma - 1), \tag{5.12a}$$

and as is evident, the response of current spending to an anticipated future deterioration in the terms of trade depends only on whether the intertemporal elasticity of substitution, σ, exceeds or falls short of unity.

The foregoing analysis of the effects of temporary (current or future) deteriorations in the terms of trade on current spending provides the ingredients necessary for determining the effects of a *permanent* deterioration. Formally, assuming that the percentage rise in p_0 equals the corresponding rise in p_1 so that $d \log p_0 = d \log p_1 = d \log p$, the effect of the permanent deterioration in the terms of trade on current spending is obtained by adding the expressions in equations (5.11) and (5.12). Hence

$$\frac{\partial \log C_0}{\partial \log p} = -\beta_{m0}\eta_{cw} + \gamma_s(\beta_{m0} - \beta_{m1})(\eta_{cw} - \sigma)$$
$$+ [(1 - \gamma_s)\beta_{m0}\mu_{m0} + \gamma_s\beta_{m1}\mu_{m1}]\eta_{cw}. \tag{5.13}$$

The three terms on the right-hand side of equation (5.13) correspond to the three channels through which a deterioration in the terms of trade affects spending. The first term—the *deflator effect*—represents exclusively the effects of the *current* deterioration in the terms of trade as it operates through the deflation of wealth; the second term—the *intertemporal-price effect*—operates through changes in the real rate of interest that occur only if the shares of expenditure on importables vary through time (as seen in equation 5.8); the third term—the *wealth effect*—operates through changes in the value of output occurring in both periods and stemming from the permanent rise in the price of importables. In general, these three effects exert conflicting influences on current spending.

The relation between the terms of trade and spending can be clarified, however, by considering the special case in which the utility function is homothetic and in which the expenditure shares, the output-consumption ratio of importables, and real spending (in present value) are all constant over time (i.e., let $\eta_{cw} = 1$, $\beta_{m0} = \beta_{m1} = \beta_m$, $\mu_{m0} = \mu_{m1} = \mu_m$, and $\gamma_s = 1 - \gamma_s$). In that case equation (5.13) becomes

$$\frac{\partial \log C_0}{\partial \log p} = -\beta_m(1 - \mu_m). \tag{5.13a}$$

Under these conditions (as long as $\mu_m < 1$) the permanent deterioration in the terms of trade lowers current spending. The fall in current spending arises exclusively from the reduction in real income (by the proportion

$\beta_m[1 - \mu_m])$ consequent on the deterioration in the terms of trade. Since this deterioration applies equally to both the current and the future periods, it does not alter the real rate of interest (as seen from equation 5.8), and therefore it does not induce intertemporal substitution. Finally, we note that in the limiting case for which production and consumption of importables are equal to each other (so that $\mu_m = 1$), real income is constant, and the permanent deterioration in the terms of trade does not alter spending.

5.4   The Terms of Trade and the Balance of Trade

The foregoing analysis determined the effects of temporary and permanent shocks to the commodity terms of trade on spending. In this section we use these results to determine the effects of such changes in the terms of trade on the balance of trade. This analysis highlights the principal mechanisms underlying the famous Laursen-Metzler-Harberger effect. Further the results provide the main ingredients necessary to determine the dynamics of the current account and of debt accumulation.

By definition, the balance of trade equals the difference between the value of production and spending. In what follows we express the balance of trade in terms of the consumption basket. Accordingly, we denote the consumption-based real balance of trade in period t by $(TA_c)_t$. Hence $(TA_c)_t = (TA)_t/P_t$, where, as before, $(TA)_t$ denotes the balance of trade in terms of exportables. Using the previous definitions, the consumption-based real balance of trade in the current period is

$$(TA_c)_0 = (GDP)_{c0} - C_0(\alpha_{c1}, W_{c0}), \qquad (5.14)$$

where

$$(GDP)_{c0} = \frac{(GDP)_0}{P_0(p_0)} = \frac{\bar{Y}_{x0} + p_0 \bar{Y}_{m0}}{P_0(p_0)}.$$

A given percentage deterioration in the terms of trade influences the balance of trade through its effects on the real value of output and on real spending. The proportional change in $(GDP)_{c0}$ is

$$\frac{\partial \log(GDP)_{c0}}{\partial \log p_0} = \frac{\beta_{m0}}{\mu_{c0}}(\mu_{m0} - \mu_{c0}), \qquad (5.15)$$

where $\mu_{c0} = (GDP)_{c0}/C_0$. Thus μ_{c0} exceeds or falls short of unity as the trade balance is in surplus or deficit, respectively; if the balance of trade is balanced, $\mu_{c0} = 1$.

The effects of temporary (current or future) and permanent changes in the terms of trade on the balance of trade can be obtained by differentiating equation (5.14). Substituting equations (5.11), (5.12), and (5.13), respectively, for the change in spending, and substituting equation (5.15) for the change in $(GDP)_{c0}$ yields

$$\frac{\partial(TA_c)_0}{\partial \log p_0} = \beta_{m0}[(\mu_{m0} - \mu_{c0}) + (1 - \gamma_s)(1 - \mu_{m0})\eta_{cw} + \gamma_s \sigma]C_0, \tag{5.16}$$

$$\frac{\partial(TA_c)_0}{\partial \log p_1} = -\beta_{m1}\gamma_s[(\sigma - \eta_{cw}) + \mu_{m1}\eta_{cw}]C_0, \tag{5.17}$$

$$\frac{\partial(TA_c)_0}{\partial \log p} = \{\beta_{m0}(\mu_{m0} - \mu_{c0}) + \beta_{m0}\eta_{cw} - (\beta_{m0} - \beta_{m1})\gamma_s(\eta_{cw} - \sigma)$$
$$- [(1 - \gamma_s)\beta_{m0}\mu_{m0} + \gamma_s\beta_{m1}\mu_{m1}]\eta_{cw}\}C_0. \tag{5.18}$$

Equations (5.16) through (5.18) reveal that the response of the balance of trade to current, future, and permanent deteriorations in the terms of trade depends on the key parameters of the economic system. These parameters are the expenditure share of importables (β_m), the ratio of production to consumption of importables (μ_m), the ratio of GDP to spending (μ_c), the average saving propensity (γ_s), the wealth elasticity of spending (η_{cw}), and the intertemporal elasticity of substitution (σ). The ratio of production to consumption of importables determines the changes in the real values of GDP and real income consequent on a given percentage deterioration in the terms of trade. The ratio of GDP to spending reflects the imbalance in the balance of trade; if this ratio exceeds unity, then the initial position is that of a trade-balance surplus, and vice versa. The average saving propensity influences both the extent of the intertemporal-price effect as well as the wealth effect consequent on the change in the terms of trade. The wealth elasticity of spending translates direct and indirect changes in wealth into spending. Finally, the intertemporal elasticity of substitution determines the pure substitution effect induced by changes in the real rate of interest consequent on the terms of trade change.

In order to clarify the precise role played by these parameters, consider the case of a permanent rise in the price of importables. As shown by the four terms on the right-hand side of equation (5.18), there are four effects that operate. The first is the real GDP effect—$\beta_{m0}(\mu_{m0} - \mu_{c0})$. The direction of this effect depends on the difference between two measures of imbalances: the import sector imbalance (μ_{m0}) and the trade-account imbalance (μ_{c0}); this real GDP effect is negative if the trade account is in surplus.

The second effect is the deflator effect—$\beta_{m0}\eta_{cw}$. This effect improves the trade balance due to the reduction in spending induced by the β_{m0} percent rise in the price index used to deflate wealth. This change in real wealth is translated into the reduction in spending through the spending elasticity. The third effect is the intertemporal-price effect—$(\beta_{m0} - \beta_{m1})\gamma_s(\eta_{cw} - \sigma)$. The direction of this effect depends on whether the rate of interest rises or falls as well as the response of spending to the change in the rate of interest. As is evident from equation (5.8), the permanent rise in the price of importables raises the rate of interest if β_{m0} exceeds β_{m1}, and vice versa. The change in the rate of interest in turn lowers or raises spending depending on whether the interest elasticity of spending—$\gamma_s(\eta_{cw} - \sigma)$—is positive or negative. Finally, the fourth effect is the wealth effect—which is the product of the wealth elasticity of spending, η_{cw}, and the percentage change in real wealth induced by the appreciated value of the domestic production of importables. This value of the domestic production of importables appreciates in each period t ($t = 0, 1$) by the magnitude $\beta_{mt}\mu_{mt}$. The rise in real wealth associated with each period appreciation is obtained by multiplying this magnitude by the weight of the corresponding period spending in real wealth (these weights are $1 - \gamma_s$ for period zero and γ_s for period one). Hence the percentage change in real wealth is a weighted average of $\beta_{mt}\mu_{mt}$ ($t = 0, 1$).

As is evident from equations (5.16) through (5.18), the net effect of changes in the terms of trade on the balance of trade depend on the relative magnitudes of the four aforementioned effects. To sharpen the analysis, consider the case in which the utility function is homothetic, and the expenditure shares and output-consumption ratios are constant over time (i.e., let $\eta_{cw} = 1$, $\beta_{m0} = \beta_{m1} = \beta_m$, and $\mu_{m0} = \mu_{m1} = \mu_m$). In that case equations (5.16) through (5.18) become

$$\frac{\partial(TA_c)_0}{\partial \log p_0} = \beta_m[(1 - \mu_{c0}) + \gamma_s(\mu_m + \sigma - 1)]C_0, \tag{5.16a}$$

$$\frac{\partial(TA_c)_0}{\partial \log p_1} = -\beta_m\gamma_s(\mu_m + \sigma - 1)C_0, \tag{5.17a}$$

$$\frac{\partial(TA_c)_0}{\partial \log p} = \beta_m(1 - \mu_{c0})C_0. \tag{5.18a}$$

In interpreting these results, consider first equation (5.18a) corresponding to a permanent deterioration in the terms of trade. This equation shows that the key criterion determining the direction of the change in the balance of trade is whether at the initial terms of trade the trade account is in deficit or surplus (i.e., whether μ_{c0}, exceeds or falls short of unity). If at the initial terms of trade the trade account is in deficit, then the permanent deterioration in the terms of trade improves the balance of trade, and vice versa. Finally, if initially the trade account is balanced, then the permanent deterioration in the terms of trade is neutral in its effect on the balance of trade. In that case the equiproportional fall in real GDP and in real spending implies that both fall by the same magnitude, and therefore the difference between them (the trade account) remains unchanged.

There are two key differences between the effects of permanent and temporary (current or future) deteriorations in the terms of trade. First, temporary changes alter the intertemporal pattern of real GDP in a manner similar to that of temporary negative supply shocks (analyzed in section 4.3). This change in the intertemporal pattern of real GDP, taken by itself, induces a trade-account deficit in the case of a current deterioration of the terms of trade and a trade-account surplus in the case of a future deterioration in the terms of trade. These trade-account adjustments are induced by the consumption-smoothing effects and are reflected by the term $\beta_m \gamma_s (1 - \mu_m)$ which appears negatively in equation (5.16a) and positively in equation (5.17a).

The second difference between the effects of permanent and temporary deteriorations in the terms of trade reflects the induced changes in the real rate of interest. If the terms of trade deteriorate permanently, then, with constant expenditure shares, the real rate of interest does not change. This is reflected in equation (5.18a) by the absence of terms relating to intertemporal substitution. In contrast, a current deterioration raises the rate of interest and induces substitution away from current spending toward future spending. This consumption-tilting effect is reflected by the positive term $\beta_m \gamma_s \sigma$ in equation (5.16a). Analogously, a future deterioration in the terms of trade lowers the real rate of interest and induces substitution toward current spending. This is reflected by the negative term $-\beta_m \gamma_s \sigma$ in equation (5.17a).

The foregoing analysis of the effects of temporary deteriorations in the terms of trade shows that the induced change in the intertemporal pattern of real GDP influences the trade account in a manner opposite to that of the induced change in the real rate of interest. As shown by equations (5.16a) and (5.16b), the net effect depends on whether the intertemporal elasticity of substitution, σ, exceeds or falls short of the ratio of imports to consumption of importables, $1 - \mu_m$. For values of σ smaller than this import-consumption ratio, the qualitative effects of temporary deteriorations in the terms of trade (starting from an initial balance in the trade account) are similar to those exerted by temporary negative supply shocks. On the other hand, for values of σ larger than this import-consumption ratio, the qualitative effects of temporary deteriorations in the terms of trade on the balance of trade are the opposite of those induced by negative supply shocks.

Before concluding, it is worth recalling that throughout the analysis we have expressed the balance of trade in terms of the consumption basket. Since changes in the terms of trade impact on the price index, the choice of the units of measurement is material. As an example, suppose that the trade account is measured in terms of exportables. By definition, the trade account measured in terms of exportable, TA, is related to its value measured in terms of the consumption basket, TA_c, according to $TA = P_0 TA_c$. Since the price index, P_0, depends only on the current price of importables, p_0, and not on the future price, p_1, it is obvious that changes in the two measures of the trade account may differ from each other only if the current terms of trade change. In that case, using our previous notations, the change in $(TA)_0$ is

$$\frac{\partial (TA)_0}{\partial \log p_0} = \left[\frac{\partial (TA_c)_0}{\partial \log p_0} + \beta_{m0}(\mu_{c0} - 1)C_0 \right] P_0. \tag{5.19}$$

Substituting equation (5.16) into (5.19) yields the expression indicating the effect of a current deterioration of the terms of trade on the trade account measured in terms of exportables. In order to derive the effect of a rise in p_1 on $(TA)_0$, we first note that a future deterioration in the terms of trade does not alter P_0. It follows that the expression (5.17), multiplied by P_0, yields the corresponding effect of a future rise in the price of importables. Obviously, the effect of a permanent deterioration in the terms of trade on the trade account measured in terms of exportables is the sum of these two expressions.

As is evident, changes in the current terms of trade may result in different inferences concerning the direction of the change in the two measures of the trade account only if at the initial terms of trade the trade account is unbalanced. For example, if the current rise in the price of importables worsens the trade account TA_c (measured in terms of the consumption basket), and if at the initial terms of trade there is a relatively large surplus in the trade account ($\mu_{c0} > 1$), then, as seen in equation (5.19), the trade account TA (measured in terms of exportables) improves. Obviously, under such circumstances the trade account measured in terms of importables must worsen. This phenomenon of a J-curve effect is exclusively an artifact of the arbitrary choice of units of measurements. As indicated previously, we have chosen to express the values of real spending, real GDP, and thereby the real trade balance in terms of the consumption basket in order to obtain information that is more amenable for a welfare analysis.

We note that an additional mechanism through which changes in the terms of trade influence the balance of trade operates through the effects of capital gains or losses on external debt commitments. These gains or losses depend on the units in terms of which debt is denominated. Specifically, unless the economy's external debt is fully linked to the consumption-based price index, any change in the terms of trade alters the real value of its initial debt commitment. This alters wealth and exerts an additional independent influence on spending and on the trade balance.

Figure 5.1 demonstrates the effects of a temporary deterioration in the terms of trade on the consumption-based trade balance. At the initial equilibrium point A, the current account is balanced. A current rise in the relative price of importables relocates the budget line: the consumption-based wealth falls and the consumption-based real rate of interest rises. The new endowment point is shown by B and the new consumption point is shown by A'. Thus, the trade account position is in a deficit.

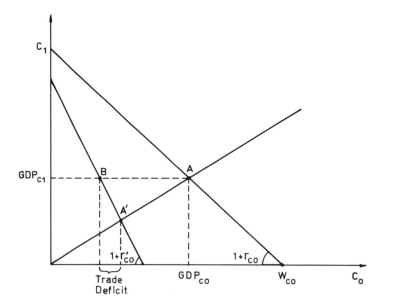

Figure 5.1

Table 5.1, based on Mendoza 1991a, illustrates the role of the trade balance as a shock absorber. The trade balance is more volatile than output and the terms of trade. Excluding Canada and the United States, the trade balance and the terms of trade are positively correlated, in line with the Harberger-Laursen-Metzler effect. However, the stylized relationships uncovered in the table yield no direct support for the prediction of the intertemporal model, since more persistent output and terms of trade shocks do not weaken the comovements between the trade balance and the terms of trade, or output. Consequently, a more structural econometric approach is required to assess the validity of the intertemporal approach.

Problems

1. Consider the small open economy model of chapter 4 in which there is a single aggregate tradable commodity. Agents receive endowments of this good in each period and for simplicity assume that the investment technology is such that it is never profitable to augment the endowment through investment. Consumers face an exogenous world discount factor, which we denote here by $R = 1/(1 + r)$, where r is the world interest rate prevailing between the two periods. For simplicity, we assume there is no historically given debt commitment so that initial trade and current account balances are equal. The utility function of the representative consumer is taken to be

$$U = [C_1^{1-1/\sigma} + DC_2^{1-1/\sigma}]/(1 - 1/\sigma),$$

where C_t denotes consumption in period t, D is the subjective discount factor, and σ is a positive parameter. The budget constraint of the consumer is

$$C_1 + RC_2 = Y_1 + RY_2 \equiv W,$$

where Y_t denotes the endowment in period t and W is the present value of the endowment stream or wealth.

a. Determine the levels of C_1 and C_2 that maximize utility, subject to the budget constraint.

b. Suppose the endowment in period 1 falls and the endowment in period 2 rises in such a way that W is unchanged. Find the effect on the current account balance between periods 1 and 2.

c. Suppose now the endowment in period 1 falls with no change in the endowment in period 2. Find the effect on the current account balance. How does it compare to your finding in part (b)?

Table 5.1
Statistical properties of output, the trade balance, and the terms of trade in the seven largest industrialized countries[1]

Country	GDP		Terms of Trade			Trade Balance			
	σ	ρ (persistence)	σ	ρ (persistence)	$\rho_{tot,y}$	σ	ρ	$\rho_{tb,y}$	$\rho_{tb,tot}$
United States	2.17	0.446	4.00	0.263	0.197	7.99	0.377	−0.277	−0.363
United Kingdom	1.98	0.524	4.41	0.551	−0.230	6.32	0.509	−0.538	0.731
France	1.49	0.654	3.46	0.341	0.287	4.43	0.132	−0.019	0.566
Germany	1.92	0.439	4.37	0.490	0.239	4.78	0.424	−0.299	0.346
Italy	2.17	0.537	5.03	0.504	0.112	8.73	0.305	−0.210	0.404
Canada	2.01	0.540	3.09	0.469	−0.034	4.75	0.394	−0.709	−0.102
Japan	3.58	0.812	10.98	0.583	0.559	10.99	0.275	0.054	0.527

1. Data for the terms of trade and the trade balance are for the period 1960–1989, and for GDP for the period 1965–1989, expressed in per-capita terms and detrended using the Hodrick-Prescott filter with the smoothing parameter set at 100. GDP is gross domestic product at constant domestic prices from National Income Accounts, the terms of trade are the ratio of U.S. dollar unit value of exports to U.S. dollar unit value of imports, the trade balance is exports minus imports of merchandise from the Balance of Payments expressed at constant import prices (the detrended trade balance corresponds to detrended exports minus detrended imports). Source: International Monetary Fund, *International Financial Statistics* and Data Base for the *World Ecomic Outlook*. σ is the percentage standard deviation, ρ is the first-order serial autocorrelation, $\rho_{tot,y}$ is the correlation of the terms of trade with GDP, $\rho_{tb,y}$ is the correlation of the trade balance with GDP, and $\rho_{tb,tot}$ is the correlation of the trade balance with the terms of trade.
Source: Mendoza 1991a.

d. Suppose there is an exogenous change in the world discount factor, R. Find the effect of such a change on the current account balance. What role does the parameter σ play in your answer? You may assume, in this part of the question, that the world discount factor R and the subjective discount factor D are equal in the initial equilibrium, and that the endowment is constant over time.

2. Consider a small open economy with preferences as described in the previous exercise, with a positive endowment in the second period only, and no endowment in period 1. As before, assume this economy has free access to the world capital market and faces a given world discount factor, which is taken to be equal to the subjective discount factor in the initial equilibrium. Assume also that, there is no investment or historically given debt commitment.

a. Write down the expression for the current account deficit in period 1.

b. The government decides to impose a (small) tax on international borrowing, i.e., on all loans taken out in period 1 for repayment in period 2. For simplicity assume that the interest rate inclusive of the tax on borrowing is r, with associated discount factor R, while the world interest rate is r^* with corresponding discount factor R^*. Assume that any revenue collected as a result of this tax is redistributed to private agents in a lump sum fashion. Also assume that in the initial equilibrium $R = R^* = D$. What is the budget constraint faced by the representative consumer in this case?

c. What is the effect of the tax on foreign borrowing on the current account balance?

3. Consider the two-country version of the model outlined in exercise 1. The representative consumer in the home country has preferences:

$$U = [C_1^{1-1/\sigma} + DC_2^{1-1/\sigma}]/(1 - 1/\sigma),$$

while the consumer in the foreign-country has the corresponding utility function:

$$U^* = [C_1^{*^{1-1/\sigma^*}} + D^*C_2^{*^{1-1/\sigma^*}}]/(1 - 1/\sigma^*),$$

where a superscripted asterisk denotes a foreign economy variable, and all other notation is as in exercise 1. As before, agents in each country receive endowments of the single aggregate consumption good in each period and we assume that there is no investment. There are no impediments to trade in goods or capital, and to simplify we assume no historical debt commitment. Initially, we assume that the subjective discount factors, D and D^*, are equal to one another. From the argument presented in chapter 4, the common value of the subjective discount factor must also be equal to the equilibrium world discount factor, which we denote as before by R. Finally, for the purpose of evaluating comparative statics results in the remainder of this exercise, it may be assumed that initially the profile of output (endowments) is flat in each country, i.e., $Y_1 = Y_2$ and $Y_1^* = Y_2^*$.

a. What is the effect on the world discount factor R of an increase in world output in period 1, $Y_1 + Y_1^*$? How does an increase in world output in the second period affect R? Prove that an increase in the growth rate raises the equilibrium interest rate. What role does intertemporal substitution play in your answer?

b. Suppose output both at home and abroad grows by a given percentage in period 1. How does this affect the home country's current account position in period 1? Provide a condition involving the relative magnitudes of σ and σ^* under which the home country's current account necessarily improves.

4. Consider the setup of the previous exercise. The utility functions of the representative agents in each country are, respectively

$$U = [C_1^{1-1/\sigma} + DC_2^{1-1/\sigma}]/(1 - 1/\sigma),$$

and

$$U^* = [C_1^{*\,1-1/\sigma^*} + D^*C_2^{*\,1-1/\sigma^*}]/(1 - 1/\sigma^*),$$

with notation as described previously. In addition, there is a government in each country that purchases goods and finances its expenditures via lump sum taxation.

a. Write down the budget constraint of the representative consumer and the government in each country.

b. Under the same simplifying assumptions as the previous exercise (no output growth, and subjective and world discount factors initially equal), find the effect of a transitory increase in government spending on the world discount factor. What is the effect of an anticipated future increase in government spending? Compare your answer to the one obtained in part (a) of the previous exercise. What is the intuition?

c. Suppose government spending is initially the same fraction of GDP in each economy and identical across periods. Suppose governments in both countries undertake a coordinated fiscal expansion whereby they raise their expenditures in proportion to GDP by the same amount in period 1 only.

Will the impact of such a policy be neutral insofar as the current account is concerned? What assumptions on the behavioral parameters would ensure that the current account neither worsens nor improves as a result of such a policy?

5. Consider a simplified version of the model of chapter 5 in which there is no domestic endowment of the importable good and no domestic consumption of the exportable good. Agents receive a constant endowment Y of the exportable good in each period which is sold in world markets at a constant price equal to unity. The import good is also purchased in world markets at a constant world price of unity. Agents can borrow and lend in world capital markets at a constant world interest rate equal to the domestic rate of time preference; the common value of the subjective and world discount factors is denoted by D. Agents have logarithmic utility given by

$$U = \log C_0 + D \log C_1, \tag{1}$$

where C_t denotes consumption of importables in period $t = 0, 1$.

a. Consider an initial equilibrium in which there is in place a constant ad valorem tariff at rate $t > 0$ levied on imports. Moreover, assume that the government rebates any collected tariff revenues in a lump sum fashion and there is no government consumption. Compare the utility level enjoyed by the representative agent in this case to a situation in which there is free trade, i.e., $t = 0$ in both periods. Note that this is not a comparative statics exercise; you are not asked to compute the effects on utility of small tariff changes. Rather, you need to solve for the utility level associated with a strictly positive tariff and the utility level associated with free trade. Explain the intuition of your answer.

b. Consider the situation with a strictly positive tariff t in both periods. The government decides to lower the tariff to zero in period 0 and maintain the same level t in period 1. Is the representative consumer better or worse off than when there is a constant tariff at rate t in both periods? (Note again this is not a comparative statics exercise.) Provide an intuitive explanation for the effect of a temporary liberalization on welfare.

6. Consider the model of chapter 5 in which agents consume importables and exportables and receive endowments of importables and exportables in each period. Assume there is no investment and that world prices are constant and for convenience equal to unity in each period. Assume that the world interest rate is equal to the domestic rate of time preference and denote the common value of the world discount factor and subjective

discount factor by D. Utility is assumed to be a logarithmic function of present and future consumption indices where the latter are themselves Cobb-Douglas functions of importables and exportables consumption in each period:

$$U = \log[c_{x0}^b c_{m0}^{1-b}] + D\log[c_{x1}^b c_{m1}^{1-b}], \tag{1}$$

where $0 < b < 1$.

Consider an initial equilibrium of free trade. Determine the effects on the trade balance measured in constant world prices of the following policies:

a. a temporary export tax imposed in period 0;

b. a temporary import tariff imposed in period 0;

c. a permanent export tax;

d. a permanent import tariff.

Assume in all cases that revenues from tax collections are rebated to consumers in a lump sum fashion and that there is no government consumption.

Are any of these policies equivalent? Lerner's symmetry theorem states that import and export taxes are equivalent policies. Is this theorem valid here?

7. Consider the model of chapter 5 where the representative agent consumes and receives endowments of importables and exportables in each period. There is no investment. Letting C_t denote the subutility index in period t, assume that agents maximize

$$U = [C_1^{1-1/\sigma} + DC_2^{1-1/\sigma}]/(1 - 1/\sigma),$$

where

$$C_t = [c_{xt}^{1-1/\varepsilon} + c_{mt}^{1-1/\varepsilon}]/(1 - 1-\varepsilon), \qquad t = 0, 1, \tag{2}$$

and where D is the subjective discount factor assumed to be equal to the world discount factor, and c_{xt} and c_{mt} denote, respectively, consumption of exportables and importables in period t, $t = 0, 1$. The parameter σ denotes the intertemporal elasticity of substitution while the parameter ε denotes the intratemporal elasticity of substitution between exportables and importables. The parameter σ denotes the intratemporal elasticity of substitution between exportables and im-portables.

In this economy, the government levies a constant ad valorem tariff on imports in amount T in each period. The government redistributes the revenues from tariff collections to consumers in a lump sum fashion. There is no government consumption.

a. Solve for the demands for C_t (the real spending functions) as a function of wealth, the discount factor, and the within-period consumer price indices.

b. Solve for the demands $c_{x,t}$ and $c_{m,t}$ as functions of within-period spending $P_t C_t$ and the within-period relative price. In this regard, you may assume that the world relative price is constant and equal to unity. You need not solve explicitly for P_t but you should recall from the chapter that its elasticity with respect to the within-period relative price is equal to the expenditure share.

c. Consider the effect on the period zero trade balance (measured in constant world prices) of an increase in the tariff in period zero (with no change in the tariff in period 1). You may assume that the initial equilibrium is stationary in the sense that the expenditure share on importables (denoted by $(1-b)$) and the price index P_t are constant through time. (Recall that the tariff rate T and world prices are constant in the initial equilibrium.) Does the temporary tariff cause the trade balance to "improve" or "deteriorate"? On what parameters of the utility function does your answer depend? Compare your answer to the one you got in the previous exercise in which the parameters σ and ε were both assumed to be equal to unity.

8. This exercise focuses on the effects of permanent terms of trade shocks on consumption, which is an important ingredient into the Laursen-Metzler effect, discussed in chapter 5. We extend the model of that chapter to a setting in which the terms of trade are subject to random shocks (see section 4.5 and appendix B of chapter 13 for further technical details). Since shocks are assumed to be of a permanent nature, and since it will prove convenient to work in a continuous-time framework, it is natural to think of the terms of trade as following the continuous-time version of a random walk, namely Brownian motion.

   Accordingly, consider a small open economy that receives a constant endowment y of an export good which, in order to simplify the analysis, we assume is not consumed domestically. The representative agent in this country consumes an imported good c (of which there is no domestic endowment) and the relative price of the export good in terms of the import good is called p and evolves according to

$$dp_t = \mu \, dt + \sigma \, dz, \tag{1}$$

where μ is a drift parameter and z is a standard Weiner process with zero mean and unitary standard deviation. The consumer has preferences:

$$U_t = E_t \int_t^\infty e^{-\delta(s-t)} u(c_s) \, ds, \tag{2}$$

where

$$u(c_s) = -\eta^{-1} e^{-\eta c_s}, \tag{3}$$

and η is the Arrow-Pratt measure of absolute risk aversion. Asset accumulation is specified as

$$dA_t = (rA_t - c_t) + yp_t, \tag{4}$$

where r is the constant (nonrandom) real interest rate.

a. Solve for the consumption function in this case.

b. How do innovations in the terms of trade (dz in equation 1) affect consumption and the trade balance?

IV

**An Intertemporal Approach
to Fiscal Policies in the
World Economy**

6

Government Spending

Up to now we have disregarded the role of government. In this chapter we extend the analysis by incorporating government into the model. There are various layers through which the introduction of government impacts on the economic system. First, from the perspective of the representative individual the public goods provided by the government enter directly into the utility function. Further, the taxes used to finance government spending enter directly into the individual's budget constraint. Second, from the perspective of the economy as a whole, the activities of the government absorb resources and provide public consumer and producer goods. Thereby the government alters the amount of resources available to the private sector, and the availability of public goods may alter the intertemporal pattern of private consumption and production. Third, from the perspective of the rest of the world, the activities of the government are transmitted internationally through its direct and indirect effects on world goods and capital markets. In what follows we examine the implications of government spending as they operate through the various layers. We start with the formal analytical framework.

6.1 The Analytical Framework

In the presence of government the representative individual's utility function, U, is $U(C_0, C_1, G_0, G_1)$, where G_0 and G_1 denote government spending in periods zero and one, respectively. For ease of exposition we assume that the utility function U takes the form of $U(C_0, G_0) + \delta U(C_1, G_1)$, where as before δ denotes the subjective discount factor. To highlight the pure effects of government spending, we abstract from possible distortionary effects arising from government finance. Thus throughout this chapter we assume that the government finances its budget with lump-sum taxes T_0 and T_1. Hence the individual seeking to maximize lifetime utility solves the following problem:

$$V(G_0, G_1, T_0, T_1) = \max_{\{C_0, C_1\}} U(C_0, G_0) + \delta U(C_1, G_1), \tag{6.1}$$

subject to

$$C_0 + \alpha_1^p C_1 = (\bar{Y}_0 - T_0) + \alpha_1^p(\bar{Y}_1 - T_1) - (1 + r_{-1}^p)B_{-1}^p = W_0, \tag{6.2}$$

where α_1^p denotes the present-value factor applicable to the private sector. The formulation in equation (6.1) indicates that, as usual, the individual who chooses the utility-maximizing path of consumption $\{C_0, C_1\}$ treats the paths of government spending $\{G_0, G_1\}$, and taxes $\{T_0, T_1\}$ as given. The function $V(\cdot)$ denotes the maximized value of utility given the paths of spending and taxes. The lifetime constraint in equation (6.2) indicates that the discounted sum of life-time consumption equals the discounted sum of lifetime disposable income net of initial private debt commitment $(1 + r_{-1}^p)B_{-1}^p$. For simplicity we assume that there is no investment.

The specification of equation (6.2) indicates that as long as the discounted sum of taxes $(T_0 + \alpha_1^p T_1)$ remains unchanged, the timing of taxes does not influence the individual's behavior.

As usual, the first-order condition for utility maximization requires that the marginal rate of substitution between consumption in two consecutive periods equals the reciprocal of the market discount factor applicable to the private sector. It is important to emphasize, however, that in the present case the marginal rate of substitution also reflects the interaction between government spending and private consumption. Hence

$$\frac{U_c(C_0, G_0)}{\delta U_c(C_1, G_1)} = \frac{1}{\alpha_1^p}, \tag{6.3}$$

where U_c denotes the marginal utility of consumption. It can also be shown (using the envelope relations obtained by constructing the Lagrangian form associated with equation 6.1 and the implied first-order conditions) that

$$\frac{\partial V(\cdot)}{\partial G_0} = U_G(C_0, G_0), \qquad \frac{\partial V(\cdot)}{\partial G_1} = \delta U_G(C_1, G_1),$$

$$\frac{\partial V(\cdot)}{\partial T_0} = -U_c(C_0, G_0), \qquad \frac{\partial V(\cdot)}{\partial T_1} = -\delta U_c(C_0, G_0). \tag{6.4}$$

These equalities state that the change in the maximized level of utility induced by a marginal change in government spending and by a marginal change in taxes equals, respectively, the marginal utility of public goods and the negative of the marginal utility of ordinary consumption.

The foregoing analysis treated the levels of government spending and taxes as given. The two, however, are linked to each other through the requirement that the government in its various activities must be solvent. The government budget constraints specify that in each period government outlays be financed by taxes or by debt issue, and solvency requires that in the last period all debt be repaid without issuing new liabilities. In our two-period model these constraints are

$$G_0 = B_0^g + T_0 - (1 + r_{-1}^g)B_{-1}^g,$$

$$G_1 - T_1 - \frac{1}{\alpha_1^g}B_0^g,$$

(6.5)

where B^g denotes government debt, and thus $(1 + r_{-1}^g)B_{-1}^g$ is the government debt commitment on the historically given initial government debt position. The formulation in (6.5) embodies the possibility that the rate of interest applicable to the government may differ from the one applicable to the private sector. Hence the government budget constraint is specified in terms of the present-value factor applicable to the government, α_1^g, rather than in terms of α_1^p.

Analogously to the procedure applied previously to consolidate the private sector's periodic budget constraints into a single present-value budget constraint, we can also consolidate the government constraints into a single present-value constraint. Applying this procedure to the constraints in (6.5) yields

$$G = G_0 + \alpha_1^g G_1 = T_0 + \alpha_1^g T_1 - (1 + r_{-1}^g)B_{-1}^g,$$

(6.6)

where G denotes the discounted sum of government spending.

The fully informed forward-looking individuals are presumed to "see through" the government budget constraint and thereby to recognize the precise dependence between the levels of government spending and the implied tax liabilities. Hence they incorporate the implications of the government budget constraint into their own. Incorporating the government budget constraint (6.6) into the private-sector constraint (6.2) yields

$$C_0 + \alpha_1^p C_1 = (\overline{Y}_0 + \alpha_1^p \overline{Y}_1) - (G_0 + \alpha_1^p G_1) - (\alpha_1^g - \alpha_1^p)(G_1 - T_1)$$

$$+ (r_{-1}^p - r_{-1}^g)B_{-1}^g - (1 + r_{-1}^p)B_{-1},$$

(6.7)

where B_{-1} denotes the historically given value of the economy's external debt position, which in turn equals the sum of the corresponding private-sector and government debts (i.e., $B_{-1} = B_{-1}^p + B_{-1}^g$). The right-hand side of equation (6.7) specifies the value of private-sector wealth which incorporates the government budget constraints as perceived (correctly) by the private sector. As may be seen, the value of wealth is composed of three items: the discounted sum of GDP net of government spending (discounted by the private sector's market interest rates), terms that are proportional to the discrepancy between private and government interest rates, and finally the historically given value of the economy's external debt commitment.

Equation (6.7) reveals that changes in taxes that satisfy the government budget constraint and that are not associated with changes in government spending alter private-sector wealth if the discount factors applicable to the private and to the public sectors differ from each other. Likewise, changes in the historical value of government debt that are not associated with corresponding changes in the economy's external debt position or in government spending alter private-sector wealth if there is a discrepancy between the historical rates of interest applicable to the private and to the public sectors.

Consider, for example, the effect of a government budget deficit arising from a current tax cut. Obviously, as indicated by the government budget constraint (6.6), a deficit arising from a fall in T_0, as long as it is not accompanied by a change in government spending, must be accompanied by an equal future surplus (in present-value terms) arising from a rise in future taxes, T_1. Equation (6.7) shows that if for reasons such as finite life the discount factor applicable to the government exceeds the discount factor applicable to the private sector (i.e., $\alpha_1^g - \alpha_1^p > 0$), then the deficit raises private-sector wealth, and thereby influences behavior and alters the real equilibrium of the system. The opposite holds if $\alpha_1^g < \alpha_1^p$. These examples highlight the considerations underlying the famous *Ricardian equivalence* proposition, according to which the timing of taxes and the size of government debt do not influence private sector's behavior and the real equilibrium as long as government spending and the size of foreign debt remain unchanged. In our case the Ricardian proposition emerges if the private and the public rates of interest are equal to each other (i.e., if $\alpha_1^g = \alpha_1^p = \alpha_1$ and $r_{-1}^g = r_{-1}^p = r_{-1}$). With such equalities the private-sector budget constraint (6.7) becomes

$$C_0 + \alpha_1 C_1 = (\overline{Y}_0 - G_0) + \alpha_1 (\overline{Y}_1 - G_1) - (1 + r_{-1})B_{-1}. \qquad (6.8)$$

Equation (6.8) shows that if both the private and the public sector can lend and borrow freely in the world capital market (at the same terms) and if all taxes are nondistortionary, then private-sector's wealth consists of the discounted sum of GDP net of government spending and of the initial external debt commitment. This is the case in which the internalization of government activities by the private sector eliminates the influence of the details of public finance.

6.2 Government Spending in a Small Open Economy

The foregoing analysis examined the factors underlying the effects of public finance (with nondistortionary taxes) on private-sector wealth. We turn next to analyze the effects of changes in government spending, starting with the case of a small open economy facing a given world rate of interest. In this context we highlight the role of timing by distinguishing between changes in government spending that are temporary (current or future) and changes that are permanent.

As indicated earlier, government spending influences the private sector through two channels. First, government activities absorb resources that otherwise would have been available to the private sector, and second, government spending may influence the marginal evaluations of private goods. The first channel is reflected in the terms $(\bar{Y}_0 - G_0)$ and $(\bar{Y}_1 - G_1)$ on the right-hand side of the budget constraint (6.8). We refer to this channel as the resource-withdrawal channel. The second channel is reflected in equation (6.3) by the dependence of the marginal rate of substitution between consumption in two consecutive periods on the levels of government spending. We refer to this channel as the consumption-tilting channel.

In operating through the resource-withdrawal channel, the influence of government spending is similar to that of supply shocks: both alter the size of *net* GDP (GDP net of government spending). Therefore our previous analysis of temporary (current or future) and permanent positive supply shocks (in section 4.3) also applies to the effects of temporary (current or future) and permanent reductions in government spending, operating through the resource-withdrawal channel.

In analyzing the effects of government spending as they operate through the consumption-tilting channel, we note that the dependence of the marginal rate of substitution of consumption in two consecutive periods on the levels of government spending reflects the characteristics of the utility function. If private consumption and government spending are complements (i.e., if the marginal utility of consumption rises with the level of government spending), then a temporary rise in current government spending raises the marginal rate of substitution in equation (6.3), whereas a temporary rise in future government spending lowers the marginal rate of substitution. In the former case the consumption expansion locus tilts toward current consumption, and in the latter case it tilts toward future consumption. The opposite holds if private consumption and government spending are substitutes. In the neutral case the marginal utility of private consumption (and therefore the marginal rate of substitution of consumption between consecutive periods) is independent of the level of government spending. In that case government spending does not induce consumption-tilting effects. Finally, we note that the effect of a permanent change in government spending on the marginal rate of substitution in consumption combines the effects of current and future changes in government spending. As was shown (except for the neutral case), the two effects tend to tilt the intertemporal consumption patterns in opposite directions. In fact, as is evident from equation (6.3), if the initial patterns of consumption and government spending are stationary, then the two effects exactly offset each other. It follows that in that case a permanent change in government spending does not induce a tilt in the intertemporal pattern of consumption. We conclude that the influence of the intertemporal pattern of government spending on the marginal rate of substitution of consumption are akin to the consumption-tilting effects analyzed in section 6.3.

In summary, the impact of government spending on the eqilibrium of the system reflects the combination of the effects operating through the resource-withdrawal channel and through the consumption-tilting channel. In the neutral case, in which the marginal rate of substitution of consumption in two consecutive periods is independent of the level of government spending, the impact of government spending operates only through the resource-withdrawal channel. In that case our analysis of the effects of supply shocks (in section 4.2) is fully applicable to the analysis of the effects of government spending.

6.3 Government Spending and the World Rate of Interest

Up to now we considered the case in which the economy is small in the world capital markets. To examine the effects of government spending on the rest of the world, we turn now to an extension of the analysis to a two-country model of the world economy. To simplify exposition, we consider the case in which government spending enters the utility function in a separable way and the utility functions are homothetic. The separability assumption implies that the marginal rate of substitution between consumption in different periods does not depend on the level of government spending. Thus in what follows government spending operates only through the resource-withdrawal channel, and not through the consumption-tilting channel.

Consider, first, the effects of a current transitory rise in the home country's government spending. At the initial rate of interest this rise in spending creates an excess demand for current-period goods. This excess demand arises from the fact that the private sector (whose taxes have risen in order to finance government spending) lowers its demand for current goods by less than the rise in government demand since the private sector's marginal propensity to spend is smaller than unity. This excess demand is eliminated by a rise in the relative price of present goods in terms of future goods, that is, by a rise in the rate of interest. This analysis is illustrated in figure 6.1 in which it is assumed that the home country's propensity to consume present goods relative to future goods exceeds the foreign country's corresponding propensity. As before, the dimensions of the box measure the present and the future levels of world GDP. At the initial equilibrium the international and intertemporal pattern of world consumption is represented by point A which denotes the intersection between the home and the foreign countries' consumption-expansion loci OA and O^*A, respectively. These loci correspond to the equilibrium rate of interest, r_0.

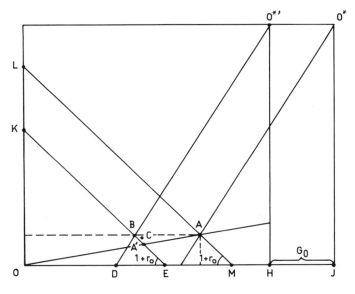

Figure 6.1
The effect of a temporary rise in current government spending on the world rate of interest

If the level of government spending on present goods is G_0, then the size of the box (corresponding to world GDP net of government spending) diminishes. Accordingly, in figure 6.1 the length of the horizontal axis measuring the supply of current goods net of government spending is reduced from OJ to OH. At the prevailing interest rate foreign demand remains unchanged, as represented in figure 6.1 by point B. This point is located on the foreign consumption-expansion locus displaced to the new origin $O^{*\prime}$. By construction, the parallel line segments $O^{*\prime}B$ and O^*A are of equal length. Analogously, as long as the initial rate of interest remains unchanged, the consumption-expansion locus of the domestic residents remains unchanged, but in view of the lower level of wealth (induced by the fall in disposable income), the new level of desired consumption is represented by point A' instead of point A. Diagrammatically, point A' designates the intersection of the domestic consumption-expansion locus and the line KE; the latter is obtained by a leftward (parallel) shift of the initial budget line LM by the magnitude of government spending G_0 (i.e., by construction, $HJ = EM$). As seen, the desired bundles of domestic and foreign consumption (indicated by points A' and B, respectively) represent an excess world demand for current goods and a corresponding excess world supply of future goods. Therefore the rate of interest (the relative price of current goods) must rise. The higher rate of interest induces substitution away from current consumption and toward future consumption. This substitution rotates both countries' consumption-expansion loci toward future goods and results in a new equilibrium (corresponding to their intersection) at a point such as C. Because of this rotation the new equilibrium point must lie to the left of point A' and to the right of point B. It follows that foreign current consumption must fall. Hence part of the rise in domestic government spending is "financed" through the crowding out of foreign consumption.

If we characterize the international transmission mechanism in terms of the correlations between contemporaneous levels of domestic and foreign private-sector consumption, then the temporary rise in current government spending is transmitted *positively* to the rest of the world. This inference follows since both domestic and foreign private-sector consumption fall. It is also noteworthy that this conclusion concerning the effects of a temporary rise in government spending does not depend on the assumption (implicit in figure 6.1) that the domestic subjective rate of time preference exceeds the foreign rate. Independent of the relation between the domestic and foreign subjective rate of time preference the temporary rise in current government spending must raise the rate of interest and must crowd out both domestic and foreign private-sector consumption of current goods.

The rise in the world rate of interest transmits the effects of the rise in government spending to the rest of the world. The higher rate of interest lowers the discounted sum of foreign disposable incomes, and thereby lowers foreign wealth. These changes in the interest rate and in wealth alter foreign consumption and impact on welfare. In the case shown in figure 6.1, point C indicates a fall in foreign welfare since in the initial eqilibrium the bundle of goods represented by point C was affordable but B was chosen. Hence by the principle of revealed preference we conclude that in the case shown, the rise in the home country's government spending lowers foreign welfare. This result, however, is not general since point C could have been located to the southwest of the line segment $A'B$. In that case foreign welfare would have risen. The key factor determining whether the rise in the rate of interest lowers or raises foreign welfare is the initial current account position, reflecting the initial differences between domestic and foreign *average* saving propensities. A rise in the rate of interest lowers foreign welfare if the foreign country was a net borrower in the world economy (i.e., if it ran a current account deficit), and vice versa. In addition to these considerations the impact of government spending on the home country's welfare also depends on both the reduced consumption of private goods and the increased consumption of public goods.

A similar analysis applies to the effects of a transitory rise in *future* government spending. In that case, however, the change in government spending induces an excess world demand for future goods and a corresponding excess supply of current goods. To restore equilibrium, the relative price of current goods—that is, the rate of interest—must fall. The fall in the rate of interest initiates the mechanism that transmits the effects of government spending to the rest of the world. It induces a rise in foreign wealth and impacts on foreign consumption and welfare in a manner opposite to the one discussed earlier when government spending rose in the present.

The analyses of the effects of transitory increases in current or in future government spending provide the ingredients relevant for determining the effects of a *permanent* rise in government spending. Since in that case there is a rise in government demand for both current and future goods, the rate of interest may rise or fall depending on the relative change in private-sector demand for current and future goods. In general, if the extent of the fall in private-sector demand for current goods is large relative to the fall in the demand for future goods, then the rate of interest falls, and vice versa. The key factor determining the relative reductions in private-sector demands for current and future goods is the difference between the domestic and the foreign marginal saving propensities. If the domestic saving propensity falls short of the foreign propensity (i.e., if the domestic subjective rate of time preference exceeds the foreign rate), then, at the prevailing rate of interest, the permanent rise in government spending raises world savings and necessitates a fall in the rate of interest. On the other hand, if the domestic saving propensity exceeds the foreign, the permanent rise in government spending lowers world savings and induces a rise in the rate of interest.

These results are illustrated in figure 6.2a and b. Panel a corresponds to the case in which the domestic subjective rate of time preference exceeds the foreign rate ($\rho > \rho^*$), and panel b corresponds to the opposite case in which $\rho^* < \rho$. The initial equilibrium is specified by point A. The permanent rise in government spending withdraws resources from the world economy in both the present and the future periods. Diagrammatically, this rise in the share of world output, which is absorbed by the government, is reflected in an equiproportional decline in the dimensions of the box. Hence, following the permanent rise in domestic government spending, the foreign country's origin shifts along the diagonal of the box from point O^* to point $O^{*\prime}$. At the prevailing rate of interest foreign consumption (measured from $O^{*\prime}$) is represented by point B (where the distance $O^*A = O^{*\prime}B$), and domestic consumption is represented by point A' along the initial consumption-expansion locus. Point A' is obtained by subtracting from the domestic private-sector budget the resources needed to finance the rise in government spending, G_0 and G_1, respectively. Geometrically, we note that by construction the distance $O^*O^{*\prime}$ equals the distance AB and that the slope of the line connecting points A' and B is one plus the prevailing rate of interest. As is evident, the consumption bundles represented by points A' and B indicate an excess supply of current goods in panel a and an excess demand for current goods in panel b. It follows that in the former case the rate of interest must fall, but in the latter case the rate of interest must rise.

As an interpretation of this result, we note that for the case in which $\rho > \rho^*$ (shown in figure 6.2a), the intertemporal pattern of spending of the domestic private sector (relative to the pattern of the foreign private sector) is biased toward current goods. The permanent rise in government spending lowers domestic private disposable income and reduces the relative weight of domestic private spending in world private spending. As a result world private spending is less biased toward current goods, and

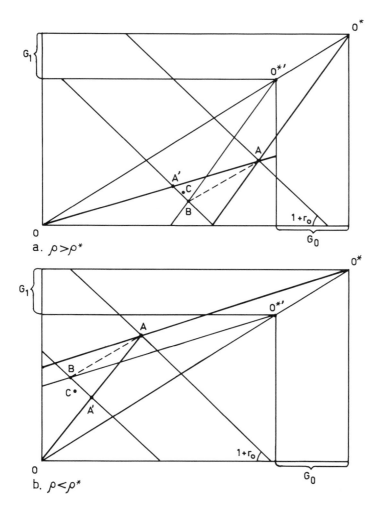

a. $\rho > \rho^*$

b. $\rho < \rho^*$

Figure 6.2
The effect of a permanent rise in government spending on the world rate of interest

the rate of interest must fall. An analogous interpretation pertains to the case in which $\rho < \rho^*$ (shown in figure 6.2b) in which the pattern of the intertemporal spending of the domestic private sector is relatively biased toward future goods.

As already indicated, the international transmission mechanism operates through the integrated world capital market, and the change in the rate of interest serves to transmit the effects of the rise in government spending to the rest of the world. The change in the rate of interest induced by the permanent rise in government spending rotates both countries' consumption-expansion loci and brings about a new equilibrium at a point like point

C. This new equilibrium point must lie inside the rectangle whose opposite vertexes are A' and B, implying a rise in foreign current consumption and a fall in foreign future consumption; the opposite holds in panel b in which point C must lie to the southeast of point B.

The effects of changes in domestic government spending on the level of foreign private-sector consumption are summarized in table 6.1 (which also contains a summary of the other results). As may be seen, depending on its timing and on the relation between the domestic and the foreign marginal propensities to save (which is governed by the relation between ρ and ρ^*), the rise in government spending may crowd out or crowd in foreign private consumption. Since domestic private consumption must always be crowded out, it follows that the sign of the correlation between changes in domestic and foreign private-sector consumption induced by changes in domestic government spending also depends on the time pattern of government spending and on the difference between the two private sectors' subjective rates of time preference.

6.4   Government Spending and the Terms of Trade in a Two-Country World

The preceding analysis of government spending was conducted under the assumption of a single composite-commodity world. As a result government spending influenced the world economy only through its impact on the *intertemporal* terms of trade (the rate of interest). In general, of course, if the economy is large enough in the world markets for goods, then changes in the level and commodity composition of government purchases also alter the *temporal* terms of trade (the relative price of importables in terms of exportables). Such changes in the temporal terms of trade provide an additional mechanism through which the effects of government spending are transmitted internationally.

In this section we extend the analysis by considering the effects of government spending on both the temporal and the intertemporal terms of trade. In order to identify the key principles, we first analyze the effects that government spending exert on the commodity terms of trade in isolation from the intertemporal repercussions induced by possible changes in the rate of interest. We then consider the other extreme by reexamining the effects that government spending exerts on the intertemporal terms of trade in isolation from the temporal repercussions induced by possible changes in the commodity terms of trade. Finally, we consider some as-

Table 6.1
Effects of a rise in domestic government spending on the world rate of interest, levels of consumption, and the trade account

Rates of time perference	Effects of a current rise in government spending on				Effects of a future rise in government spending on				Effects of a permanent rise in government spending on			
	r_0	C_0	C_0^*	$(TA)_0$	r_0	C_0	C_0^*	$(TA)_0$	r_0	C_0	C_0^*	$(TA)_0$
$\rho > \rho^*$	+	−	−	−	−	−	+	+	−	−	+	+
$\rho < \rho^*$	+	−	−	−	−	−	+	+	+	−	−	−

Note: The case in which $\rho > \rho^*$ indicates that the domestic marginal propensity to save out of wealth falls short of the foreign propensity, and vice versa.

pects of the interactions between the temporal and the intertemporal terms of trade.

We start by focusing on the relation between the temporal terms of trade and the commodity composition of government spending. For this purpose consider a bench-mark case in which the transmission mechanism operates exclusively through the commodity terms of trade and not through the rate of interest. Accordingly, we assume that the utility functions are homothetic, that in each country the composition of outputs (net of government purchases) does not vary over time, and that the domestic and foreign subjective rates of time preference are equal to each other. Also we assume that the time profiles of government and private consumption spendings are identical. These assumptions ensure (as implied by the analysis in chapter 5) that the domestic and the foreign (consumption-based) real rates of interest are equal to each other and that both are equal to the common rate of time preference (adjusted for growth, as in equation 4.14). As a result, in each country income equals spending. Thus in this benchmark case a *permanent* rise in government spending does not impact on the world rate of interest, and its effects are absorbed exclusively by induced changes in the (temporal) relative price of goods.

The diagrammatic analysis of the effects of a rise in government spending in this bench-mark case can be carried out with the aid of a relabeled version of figure 6.2. The relabeling replaces the two periods by the two commodities, the intertemporal terms of trade by the temporal terms of trade, and the international differences between the marginal propensities to spend out of wealth in the two periods (indicated by the difference between the domestic and the foreign marginal rates of time preference) by the international differences in the marginal shares of expenditures on the two goods. Thus in figure 6.2 the dimensions of the box correspond to the world supply of the two goods net of government spending on these goods. The vertical axis measures good x—the home country's exportables—and the horizontal axis measures good m—the home country's importables. In the initial equilibrium the commodity composition of the domestic and foreign private-sector demands are indicated by the slopes of the rays OA and O^*A, respectively. The initial equilibrium obtains at point A, at which the relative price of importables, p_m, is the common slope of the domestic and foreign indifference curves at point A (not drawn). Thus the angle indicated by $1 + r_0$ in figure 6.2 now measures the relative price of goods, p_m. The case shown in panel a differs from the one shown in panel b. Panel a corresponds to a situation in which the domestic pattern of the commodity composition of spending is relatively biased toward importables so that the domestic expenditure share β_m exceed the foreign share, β_m^*, whereas panel b corresponds to the opposite case in which the domestic spending patterns are relatively biased toward exportables so that $\beta_m < \beta_m^*$. (In that case the composition of domestic output is even more biased in favor of good x, which therefore is the export good.)

Consider first the case of an equiproportional rise in government spending on both goods (indicated in figure 6.2 by G_0 on importables and G_1 on exportables). This lowers world output net of government spending and reduces the dimensions of the box. It changes the foreign-country origin along the diagonal from point O^* to point $O^{*'}$. At the initial terms of trade the desired domestic consumption basket is indicated by point A', and the corresponding foreign consumption basket (measured from the origin $O^{*'}$) is indicated by point B. As is evident, if β_m exceeds β_m^* (as in panel a), this configuration represents excess supply of importables and a corresponding excess demand for exportables, and vice versa if β_m falls short of β_m^* (as in panel b). In the former case p_m falls so that the terms of trade of the domestic country improve, and in the later case p_m rises so that the domestic terms of trade worsen. These changes in the terms of trade bring about a new equilibrium pattern of world consumption as indicated in figure 6.2 by a point located within the square whose opposite vertexes are points B and A', such as point C.

This example of the terms-of-trade effects of an equiproportional rise in government spending indicates the analogy between the intertemporal analysis of the effects of permanent government spending and the temporal analysis of an equiproportional rise of government purchases of goods. In order to derive the general principle governing the effects of government spending on the terms of trade, we define the marginal share of government expenditure on importables by $\beta_m^g = p_m G_m/(p_m G_m + G_x) = 1/[1 + (G_x/p_m G_m)]$, where G_m and G_x denote the rise in government purchases of importables and exportables, respectively (from an initial position where both quantities are zero). With this definition the basic criterion determining the effects of a rise in government spending on the terms of trade involves a comparison between the expenditure shares of the private sector and of the government. If β_m^g exceeds β_m, *then the rise in government spending induces a deterioration of the terms of trade, and conversely if β_m^g falls short of β_m.*

The dependence of the change in the terms of trade on the relative magnitudes of β_m and β_m^g is shown in figure 6.3, which illustrates the case of a borderline situation in which the change in government spending does not alter the terms of trade. In the case shown, the government expenditure

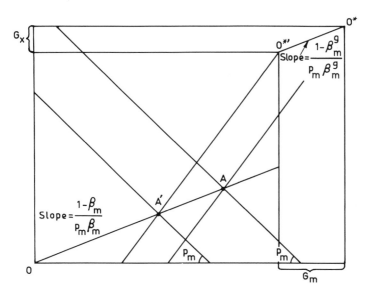

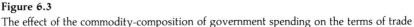

Figure 6.3
The effect of the commodity-composition of government spending on the terms of trade

share β_m^g is assumed to be equal to the domestic expenditure share β_m. The rise in government spending shifts the origin O^* to $O^{*\prime}$ and alters the equilibrium point from point A to point A'. In the figure the rays OA and $O^*O^{*\prime}$ are drawn parallel to each other due to the assumed equality between β_m^g and β_m. As is evident, in the move from the initial equilibrium point, A, to the new equilibrium point, A', the terms of trade have not changed.

The interpretation of this result is given in terms of the transfer-problem criterion. In the present case the transfer of income from the domestic private sector to the government (a transfer associated with the taxes levied to finance the rise in government spending) does not alter the commodity composition of the domestic *national* spending (private sector plus government) since it involves a transfer of income between units with identical spending patterns. Therefore the transfer does not alter the levels of world demand and supply, and the terms of trade do not change. This borderline case implies that if β_m^g exceeds β_m, then the rise in government spending tilts the composition of national spending toward importables and results in a deterioration of the domestic terms of trade. Conversely, if $\beta_m^g < \beta_m$, the rise in government spending tilts the composition of national spending toward exportables, and the terms of trade improve.

We turn next to reexamine the effects of the time profile of government spending on the intertemporal terms of trade, and we consider another bench-mark case in which the transmission mechanism operates exclusively through the intertemporal terms of trade and not through the commodity terms of trade. For that reason we assume that the composition of output (net of government purchases) does not vary over time and that the government as well as the domestic and the foreign expenditure shares are equal to each other. These assumptions ensure that the commodity terms of trade are fixed and do not depend on the time pattern of government spending. Under these assumptions we can aggregate the two goods into a single composite commodity. This aggregation reduces the multiple good model to its single-good counterpart of section 6.3.

As in the previous analysis of the effects of government spending on the temporal terms of trade, there is a general principle that governs the effects of government spending on the intertemporal terms of trade. This principle can also be stated in terms of a transfer-problem criterion; it involves a comparison between the saving propensities of the private sector and the government. For this we define the government marginal propensity to save out of government "wealth" (the discounted sum of government spending) by $\gamma_s^g = \alpha_{x1} G_1 / (G_0 + \alpha_{x1} G_1)$; we recall that the private sector marginal propensity to save out of wealth is $\gamma_s = \alpha_{x1} z_1 / (z_0 + \alpha_{x1} z_1)$, where z_t ($t = 0, 1$) denotes private-sector spending in terms of good x. The effect of a rise in government spending on the rate of interest depends on whether the time profile of the rise in government spending is such that the implied saving propensity, γ_s^g, exceeds or falls short of the private saving propensity, γ_s. *If γ_s^g exceeds γ_s, then a rise in government spending lowers the rate of interest (raises α_{x1}), and conversely if γ_s^g falls short of γ_s.* As with the analysis of the temporal terms of trade, the transfer-problem criterion provides the interpretation of this result. Accordingly, if γ_s^g exceeds γ_s, the rise in government spending transfers wealth from a low saver (the private sector) to a higher saver (the government), and thereby raises *national* (private-sector plus government) saving. This induces excess world savings and necessitates a fall in the rate of interest. The opposite holds if $\gamma_s^g < \gamma_s$. Finally, in the borderline case in which $\gamma_s^g = \gamma_s$, the rise in government spending redistributes wealth between economic units with identical saving propensities. Therefore in that case national and world saving do not change, and the rate of interest remains intact.

Before proceeding, it is relevant to note that the definitions of saving used in the preceding analysis, which provided the key criterion for determining the effect of government spending on the intertemporal terms of trade, differ from those used in the national income accounts. In particular, we have defined the government propensity as the ratio of future government spending (in present value) to the discounted sum of current and future taxes. In contrast, the national income accounts define government saving in terms of the difference between contemporaneous taxes and spending. A similar remark applies to the definition of private saving.

It is noteworthy that the analysis of the effects of temporary (current or future) and permanent changes in government spending (conducted in the previous sections) can be viewed as specific illustrations of the general principle. Accordingly, a transitory current rise in government spending corresponds to the case $\gamma_s^g = 0$ (and hence $\gamma_s > \gamma_s^g$). An anticipated future rise in government spending corresponds to the case $\gamma_s^g = 1$ (and hence $\gamma_s < \gamma_s^g$). Finally, a permanent rise in government spending (which raises permanently the relative share of government spending in world output) corresponds to the case in which the government-saving propensity, γ_s^g, equals the world private-sector-saving propensity, γ_s^w, which is defined as the ratio of the discounted sum of future net world output to the discounted sum of current and future world net output. Thus

$$\gamma_s^w = \frac{\alpha_1(\overline{Y}_1 - G_1 + \overline{Y}_1^* - G_1^*)}{[(\overline{Y}_0 - G_0) + (\overline{Y}_0^* - G_0^*)] + \alpha_1[(\overline{Y}_1 - G_1) + (\overline{Y}_1^* - G_1^*)]}.$$

We further note that γ_s^w is a weighted average of the saving propensities of the domestic and foreign private sectors, γ_s and γ_s^*. It follows that if $\gamma_s^* > \gamma_s$, then $\gamma_s^g > \gamma_s$—and conversely, if $\gamma_s^* < \gamma_s$, then $\gamma_s^g < \gamma_s$. Our previous analysis showed that the effects of a permanent change in government spending depend on differences between the saving propensities of the domestic and the foreign private sectors. This dependence, however, reflects the more general principle stated in terms of the relation between the saving propensities of the domestic government and the *domestic* private sector, since with a permanent change in government spending the relation between γ_s^g and γ_s can be cast in terms of the relation between γ_s^* and γ_s.

The foregoing analysis isolated the two mechanisms through which the effects of government spending are transmitted to the rest of the world. These two mechanisms operate through the induced changes in the temporal terms of trade (the relative price of exportables in terms of importables) and through the induced changes in the intertemporal terms of trade (the rate of interest). The two bench-mark cases were designed to distinguish between the two mechanisms of adjustment. In general, however, if the subjective rates of time preference and the expenditure shares differ across countries, changes in government spending alter both the temporal and the intertemporal terms of trade. In that case the generalization of the transfer-problem analysis implies that the changes in the two terms of trade are governed by a multitude of transfer-problem criteria involving comparisons between the private-sector and the government temporal spending propensities—indicated by the expenditure shares β_m and β_m^g—and intertemporal spending propensities—indicated by the saving ratios γ_s and γ_s^g.

To illustrate the interactions between the temporal and the intertemporal terms of trade, consider the logarithmic utility function

$$U = [\beta_{m0} \log c_{m0} + (1 - \beta_{m0}) \log c_{x0}]$$
$$+ \delta[\beta_{m1} \log c_{m1} + (1 - \beta_{m1}) \log c_{x1}]. \tag{6.9}$$

With this utility function it is shown in the appendix that for each period the consumption-based temporal price index (defined in section 5.1) can be written as

$$P_0 = (p_{m0})^{\beta_{m0}} \quad \text{and} \quad P_1 = (p_{m1})^{\beta_{m1}}. \tag{6.10}$$

Using these price indexes, the (consumption-based) real discount factor $\alpha_{c1} = \alpha_{x1}(P_1/P_0)$ is

$$\alpha_{c1} = \frac{1}{1 + r_{c0}} = \frac{1}{1 + r_{x0}} \frac{P_1}{P_0}, \tag{6.11}$$

and the (consumption-based) wealth deflator, P_w (the intertemporal "true" price index) is defined by

$$P_w = P_0^{(1-\gamma_s)}(\alpha_{x1} P_1)^{\gamma_s}. \tag{6.12}$$

In general, government spending influences both the temporal and the intertemporal terms of trade, and thereby alters both the (consumption-based) real discount factor and the real wealth deflator. In the appendix we show that, in general, the effects of government spending can be characterized in terms of a multitude of transfer-problem criteria. Accordingly, at the prevailing prices a rise in government spending alters the temporal and the intertemporal pattern of the domestic national demand (private sector plus government) only if the saving propensity and the expenditure shares of the government differ from the corresponding magnitudes of the domestic private sector. In the absence of such differences, changes in government spending do not create an excess demand or supply and do not necessitate a change in the initial equilibrium prices.

It is shown in the appendix that the rise in government spending creates excess demands only if the government's marginal propensities to spend on importables out of government wealth (i.e., government lifetime spending) differ from that of the domestic private sector. Formally, the rise in government spending does not create excess demands only if

$$\beta_{m0}(1 - \gamma_s) = \beta_{m0}^g(1 - \gamma_s^g) \qquad (6.13)$$

and

$$\beta_{m1}\gamma_s = \beta_{m1}^g\gamma_s^g. \qquad (6.14)$$

In the absence of such equalities, the induced excess demands must alter the prevailing prices. The precise changes in the equilibrium prices depend on differences among the saving propensities of the domestic and foreign private sectors, on differences among the temporal expenditure shares of the two private sectors, and on the relative shares of the two private sectors in world demands and supplies.

As is evident, the complex structure of the model implies that, in general, the effects of government spending on the temporal and the intertemporal terms of trade—and thereby on the (consumption-based) real rates of interest and wealth deflator—depend on numerous transfer-problem criteria involving comparisons among the value of parameters characterizing the behavior of the domestic government, the domestic private sector, and the foreign private sector. In order to focus on the differences between the private and the public sectors, we examine the special case in which in the initial equilibrium the domestic and the foreign economies are identical in terms of production and consumption patterns. In this case the effects of the rise in the domestic government spending reflect only the differences in the behavioral patterns of the domestic private and public sectors.

Table 6.2 summarizes the effects of government spending on the (consumption-based) real rate of interest, r_{c0}, and on the real wealth deflator, P_w. The results reported in the table are based on the analysis in the appendix. It shows that if the government propensity to spend on exportables in the current period, $(1 - \gamma_s^g)(1 - \beta_s^g)$, falls short of the corresponding private-sector saving propensity, $(1 - \gamma_s)(1 - \beta_m)$, then the rise in the domestic government spending raises the real wealth deflator (which is the "true" price of lifetime spending). Conversely, if the government propensity to spend on exportables in the current period exceeds the corresponding private sector's propensity, then the rise in government spending lowers the real wealth deflator. If the two spending propensities

Table 6.2
The effects of a rise in government spending on the (consumption-based) real rate of interest and real wealth deflator

Effects on	Relation between private and public spending propensities		
	$(1 - \beta_m)(1 - \gamma_s) > (1 - \beta_m^g)(1 - \gamma_s^g)$	$(1 - \beta_m)(1 - \gamma_s) = (1 - \beta_m^g)(1 - \gamma_s^g)$	$(1 - \beta_m)(1 - \gamma_s) < (1 - \beta_m^g)(1 - \gamma_s^g)$
P_w	+	0	—
r_{c0}	$\gamma_s > \gamma_s^g$ +	$\gamma_s = \gamma_s^g$ 0	$\gamma_s < \gamma_s^g$ —

Note: r_{c0} is the (consumption-based) real rate of interest, and P_w is the (consumption-based) real wealth deflator (the intertemporal price index). The symbols +, 0, and — indicate, respectively, that the rise in the domestic government spending raises, leaves unchanged, or lowers P_w or r_{c0}. The underlying assumption is that the private sectors in the two countries are identical, that the initial equilibrium is autarkic, and that initially government spending in both countries is zero.

are equal to each other, then the transfer-problem criterion implies that the rise in government spending does not alter the real wealth deflator.

The second row (r_{c0}) in table 6.2 shows the effects of the rise in government spending on the (consumption-based) real rate of interest. As is evident, in this multicommodity world the key factor governing the direction of the induced change in the real rate of interest remains the transfer-problem criterion applied to a comparison between the saving propensities of the domestic government and the domestic private sector. Accordingly, if the private-sector-saving propensity, γ_s, exceeds the government-saving propensity, γ_s^g, then (at the prevailing prices) a rise in government spending redistributes wealth from the private to the public sectors and lowers national savings. To restore equilibrium, the level of savings must be raised. The necessary rise in savings is brought about through changes in the temporal and in the intertemporal prices. These price changes yield a higher (consumption-based) real rate of interest. The opposite holds if the saving propensity of the private sector falls short of the corresponding propensity of the domestic government. In the borderline case for which the two saving propensities are equal to each other so that $\gamma_s = \gamma_s^g$, the transfer-problem criterion implies that the rise in government spending does not alter national savings, and therefore the (consumption-based) real rate of interest remains intact.

Finally, it is relevant to note that the assumed similarity between the two countries' private sectors implies that the changes in the foreign (consumption-based) real rate of interest and real wealth deflator are the same as those occurring in the domestic economy.

6.5 Government Spending and Investment

Up to this point our analysis of the effects of government spending on the world economy abstracted from investment. The stylized facts, on the other hand, suggest a close correlation between public-sector spending and investment. In what follows we extend the analysis and allow for endogenous investment. In order to focus on the essentials, we return to the single composite-commodity world. As seen earlier, government spending influences the level of the eqilibrium rates of interest. These changes in interest rates alter the profitability of domestic and foreign investment and influence the evolution of world output.

The analysis is conducted with the aid of figure 6.4, in which the upward-sloping schedule, S^w, describes the ratio, z, of current to future world GDP net of investment and government spending as an increasing

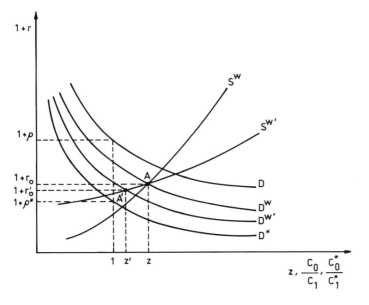

Figure 6.4
The effect of a permanent rise in domestic government spending on the rate of interest
and investment

function of the rate of interest. Formally, using the previous notation,

$$z = \frac{\bar{Y}_0 - I_0(r_0) + \bar{Y}_0^* - I_0^*(r_0) - G_0 - G_0^*}{\bar{Y}_1 + F[I_0(r_0)] + \bar{Y}_1^* + F^*[I_0^*(r_0)] - G_1 - G_1^*}. \tag{6.15}$$

The positive dependence of z on the rate of interest reflects the fact that
investment falls when the rate of interest rises.

The downward-sloping schedules in figure 6.4 plot the desired ratio of
current to future consumption as a decreasing function of the rate of
interest. The assumption that the utility functions are homothetic enables
us to express the various demand schedules in terms of desired consumption ratios. The domestic and foreign private-sector relative demands are
denoted by D and D^*, and their values at the point in which $(C_0/C_1) =
(C_0^*/C_1^*) = 1$ indicate, respectively, the subjective rates of time preference
ρ and ρ^*. The elasticities of the relative demand schedules are the corresponding intertemporal elasticities of substitution in consumption. The
world relative demand, D^w, is a weighted average of the two private
sectors' relative demands, D and D^*. That is,

$$\frac{C_0 + C_0^*}{C_1 + C_1^*} = \mu \frac{C_0}{C_1} + (1 - \mu) \frac{C_0^*}{C_1^*}, \tag{6.16}$$

where

$$\mu = \frac{C_1}{C_1 + C_1^*}.$$

The initial equilibrium is described by point A in figure 6.4, at which the rate of interest is r_0.

Consider the effect of a permanent rise in domestic government spending. This permanent rise alters both the supply schedule and the world demand schedule in figure 6.4. We define a permanent rise in government spending as an equal rise in the relative share of the domestic government in world net output in both the present and the future. It follows that such a change in current and future government spending does not alter the initial ratio on the supply schedule. As a matter of arithmetic it is obvious that this rise in government spending rotates the supply schedule around the initial equilibrium of point A. As a result the supply schedule associated with the permanently higher level of government spending is $S^{w'}$ instead of S^w. The rise in government spending also alters the world demand schedule. Specifically, since at the prevailing rate of interest domestic disposable income must fall (in order to finance the growth of government), it follows that the relative weight μ attached to the domestic schedule D falls. This change in relative weights shifts the world (weighted-average) demand schedule closer to D^* and results in a new world demand schedule $D^{w'}$.

The new equilibrium obtains at point A'. The equilibrium rate of interest falls from r_0 to r_0', and as may be seen, in the new equilibrium the world rate of interest is closer to the foreign rate of time preference ρ^*. In the new equilibrium aggregate private spending is less biased toward present goods, reflecting the lower weight attached to the lower saving pattern of the home country's private demand. The lower rate of interest encourages investment in both countries according to the properties of the investment functions $I_0(r_0)$ and $I_0^*(r_0)$. This rise in investment raises future outputs according to the properties of the investment opportunity functions $F(\cdot)$ and $F^*(\cdot)$.

It is relevant to note that the effect of the permanent rise in government spending on the balance of trade is ambiguous since it reflects the possibly different responses of domestic and foreign investment and future outputs. This should be contrasted with the situation analyzed earlier in figure 6.2a in which investment was absent. In that case the permanent rise in government spending lowered interest rates and induced a deficit in the first-period balance of trade.

Table 6.3
The effects of a rise in domestic government spending on the levels of investment

Rates of time preference	Current rise	Future rise	Permanent rise
$\rho > \rho^*$	−	+	+
$\rho < \rho^*$	−	+	−

Note: The case in which $\rho > \rho^*$ indicates that the domestic marginal propensity to save out of wealth falls short of the foreign propensity, and vice versa.

The foregoing analysis of the effects of permanent changes in government spending was conducted under the assumption that (in comparison with the rest of the world) the home country's spending patterns are biased toward the consumption of present goods. This relative bias reflected the assumption that the domestic rate of time preference, ρ, exceeds the corresponding foreign rate, ρ^*. In the opposite case, for which $\rho < \rho^*$, the permanent rise in government spending raises the (weighted-average) world relative demand curve in figure 6.4 and results in a higher world rate of interest and in lower levels of investment.

Similar principles can be applied to the analysis of the effects of transitory (current or future) changes in the levels of government spending. Corresponding to our previous analysis, it follows that a transitory rise in current government spending lowers domestic and foreign investment since it raises the rate of interest, whereas a transitory rise in future government spending raises domestic and foreign investment since it lowers the rate of interest. These results are summarized in table 6.3. The key point underscored by this table is that whether government spending crowds out or crowds in private investment depends on the timing of government spending and on the difference between the domestic and the foreign private sectors' marginal propensities to save. Alternatively, cast in terms of the general rule, if γ_s exceeds γ_s^g, then, by raising the world rate of interest, government spending crowds out domestic and foreign private-sector investment, and conversely if γ_s falls short of γ_s^g.

6.6 The Optimal Size of Government

Throughout the previous analysis we have treated the level of government spending as exogenous, and we have examined the effects of various changes in the time profile of spending. In this section we extend the analysis and examine the optimal path of government spending. This extension facilitates a more complete analysis of the welfare implications of fiscal policies.

In order to determine the optimal size of government, we use the private sector's utility function and recognize that the provision of public goods influences the level of welfare. Thus we use the maximized level of utility (defined in equation 6.30) together with the government budget constraint (defined in equation 6.35). In order to focus on the determination of the optimal path of government spending and abstract from issues concerning the optimal path of taxes, we assume that the private and the public sectors face the same world rate of interest so that $\alpha_1^g = \alpha_1^p = \alpha_1$. This assumption introduces the Ricardian irrelevance property into the model. Formally, the government maximization problem is

$$\tilde{V} = \max_{\{G_0, G_1, T_0, T_1\}} V(G_0, G_1, T_0, T_1) \tag{6.17}$$

subject to

$$G_0 + \alpha_1 G_1 = T_0 + \alpha_1 T_1 - (1 + r_{-1})B_{-1}^g.$$

Carrying out the maximization and using the conditions specified in equation (6.4) yields the first-order conditions:

$$\frac{U_G(C_0, G_0)}{U_C(C_0, G_0)} = \frac{U_G(C_1, G_1)}{U_C(C_1, G_1)} = 1. \tag{6.18}$$

As usual for a two-good economy, equation (6.18) states the requirement that in each period the marginal rate of substitution between the two goods equals the marginal rate of transformation (which in the present specification equals unity). Since the two goods are a private good and a public good, the equality between the marginal rate of substitution and the marginal rate of transformation reflects the implicit assumption of a single-consumer economy; in general, the Samuelson condition requires equality between the *sum* of the individual marginal rates of substitution and the economy's marginal rate of transformation.

The formal specification of the government maximization problem embodies the utility-maximizing conditions of the private sector. Hence in addition to the *temporal* condition (6.18) the solution contains the inter-temporal condition (6.3) stating the *intertemporal* marginal rate of substitution between consumption of private goods as well as between consumption of public goods equals one plus the rate of interest. These equilibrium conditions along with the economy's consolidated budget constraint (5.3) determine the optimal path of government spending as part of the general equilibrium solution of model.

The symmetric treatment of private and public goods suggests that the question of the optimal size of government can also be cast in terms of the utility-maximizing demand functions for current and future consumption of private and public goods. As usual, these demand functions are expressed as functions of prices and wealth. In our case the relevant temporal price of public goods in terms of private goods is unity, the intertemporal price is α_1, and the relevant concept of wealth is the discounted sum of GDP net of the historically given initial external debt commitment; that is, $\overline{Y}_0 + \alpha_1 \overline{Y}_1 - (1 + r_{-1})B_{-1}$. Formally, these demand functions are

$$C_t = C_t[\alpha_1; \overline{Y}_0 + \alpha_1 \overline{Y}_1 - (1 + r_{-1})B_{-1}],$$

$$G_t = G_t[\alpha_1; \overline{Y}_0 + \alpha_1 \overline{Y}_1 - (1 + r_{-1})B_{-1}], \quad t = 0, 1,$$

(6.19)

where we have suppressed the temporal prices that are equal to unity.

The equations in (6.19) can be used to analyze the effects of supply shocks on the optimal path of government spending. For this purpose we assume that the private and the public goods are normal goods. Consider the effect of a temporary supply shock that raises the value of current GDP, $\overline{Y}_0$. Since all goods (including future goods) are normal, it is obvious that in order to "finance" a rise in future consumption (C_1 and G_1), the induced rise in current consumption of both goods (C_0 and G_0) must be smaller than the rise in $\overline{Y}_0$. Thus, since not all new output is absorbed by current consumption, it follows that the current-period supply shock induces an improvement in the economy's balance of trade. Analogously, if the temporary supply shock is expected to occur in the future, normality implies that the rise in $\overline{Y}_1$ raises consumption of all four goods, including current goods. In that case the economy's trade balance deteriorates in the early period. The foregoing examples demonstrate that the consumption-smoothing motive that characterizes private consumption in the absence of public goods also extends to the broader concept of consumption that includes both private and public goods, if the supply of the latter is optimal. Consequently the qualitative trade-balance effects of temporary supply shocks also remain intact.

Finally, consider the effects of a permanent supply shock. For ease of exposition suppose that the historically given initial external debt position, B_{-1}, is zero, that the utility function over all four goods is homothetic, and that the level of GDP is stationary. In that case the initial trade balance is zero, and an equiproportional rise in current and future GDP raises the consumption of all goods (including public goods) by the same proportion and leaves the trade balance unchanged. This outcome is the analogue to the neutral-supply shock analyzed in figure 4.3 for the case in which public goods were absent.

A key proposition of the foregoing analysis is that in the presence of both private and public goods, supply shocks induce a positive correlation between the levels of consumption of private and public goods if the latter are optimally supplied. The symmetric treatment of private and public goods reveals that the optimal supply of public goods (as reflected by the level of government spending) responds to expected future events in a manner similar to that of the consumption of private goods. Therefore the optimal level of government spending need not be synchronized with supply shocks, and as a result the contemporaneous correlation between government spending and GDP may be low. This property reflects the role of government as a supplier of public goods and not as an instrument of stabilization policies. Allowance for the latter role would introduce countercyclical elements to the path of government spending and would thereby contribute to a negative correlation between contemporaneous changes in GDP and government spending.

6.7   Summary

In this chapter we incorporated the government into the model. For this purpose we extended the specification of the utility function and the budget constraints so as to include public goods and taxes. We showed that there are two channels through which government spending influences the equilibrium of the economic system: the resource-withdrawal channel and the consumption-tilting channel. The former reflects the combination of changes in net output (induced by government purchases of goods and services) and in private-sector wealth (induced by the nondistortionary taxes used for government finance). The latter reflects the temporal-intertemporal substitution-complementarity relations between public and private consumption and production.

In analyzing the effects of domestic government spending on the two-country world economy, we focused on the induced changes in the temporal and intertemporal terms of trade and on the cross-country comovement of private sectors' spending. We cast the analysis in terms of various transfer-problem criteria familiar from the theory of international transfers. In the present context these criteria involve comparisons between the domestic country's private and public sector's saving and spending propensities. Accordingly, if the government's propensity to spend on importables (out of expenditure) exceeds the corresponding private-sector propensity, then a rise in the domestic government's spending raises the relative price of importables, and thereby worsens the domestic country's temporal terms of trade, and vice versa. Likewise, if the domestic government's saving propensity exceeds the corresponding private-sector propensity, then the rise in the domestic government's spending lowers the world rate of interest—the intertemporal terms of trade, and vice versa. In this context both the private and the public sector's saving propensities reflect the relation between the present value of future consumption and the discounted sum of current and future consumption. This transfer-problem criterion underscores the significance of the timing of government spending, being transitory or permanent.

In our multicommodity world there is a complex interaction between the temporal and the intertemporal terms of trade. To allow for this interaction, we defined the appropriate (consumption-based) real rate of interest and real wealth deflator, and applied the transfer-problem criterion to determine the effects of the commodity composition and the time pattern of government spending on these variables.

In regards to investment, we showed that the key factor determining whether government spending crowds in or crowds out private-sector investment at home and abroad is again the relation between the domestic private and public sector's saving propensities.

The chapter concluded with a brief analysis of the optimal size of government. In this context we showed that the consumption-smoothing motive characterizing private consumption in the absence of public goods extends to the broader concept of consumption that includes both private and public goods, if the supply of the latter is optimal. A key proposition emerging from this consumption-smoothing feature is that with an optimal provision of public goods, supply shocks induce a positive correlation between the levels of consumption of private and public goods.

6.8   Appendix

In this appendix we provide a formal analysis of the effects of government spending on the temporal and the intertemporal terms of trade. Throughout we assume logarithmic utility functions. We start with a derivation of the consumption-based price indexes corresponding to the specific utility function.

The maximization problem is

$$\tilde{U} = \max_{\substack{\{c_{m0}, c_{x0}\} \\ \{c_{m1}, c_{x1}\}}} \beta_{m0} \log c_{m0} + (1 - \beta_{m0}) \log c_{x0}$$

$$+ \delta[\beta_{m1} \log c_{m1} + (1 - \beta_{m1}) \log c_{x1}] \tag{A.1}$$

subject to

$$z_0 + \alpha_{x1} z_1 = W_0,$$

where

$$z_0 = (p_{m0} c_{m0} + c_{x0}),$$

$$z_1 = (p_{m1} c_{m1} + c_{x1}).$$

The solution to this maximization problem yields the following demand functions:

$$c_{m0} = \frac{\beta_{m0} W_0}{(1 + \delta) p_{m0}}, \qquad c_{m1} = \frac{\beta_{m1} W_0}{(1 + \delta) \alpha_{x1} p_{m1}},$$

$$c_{x0} = \frac{1}{1 + \delta} (1 - \beta_{m0}) W_0, \quad c_{x1} = \frac{\delta(1 - \beta_{m1}) W_0}{(1 + \delta) \alpha_{x1}}. \tag{A.2}$$

Substitution of the demand functions into the utility function yields the indirect utility function

$$\tilde{U} = a + \log\left(\frac{W_0^{(1+\delta)}}{p_{m0}^{\beta_{m0}} p_{m1}^{\beta_{m1} \delta} \alpha_{x1}^{\delta}}\right), \tag{A.3}$$

where a is a constant.

Recalling the definition of γ_s—the private sector propensity to save out of wealth—and using the definitions of spending and the demand functions from (A.2) yields

$$\gamma_s = \frac{\alpha_{x1} z_1}{z_0 + \alpha_{x1} z_1} = \frac{\delta}{1 + \delta}. \tag{A.4}$$

Substituting (A.4) for δ into (A.3) yields

$$\tilde{U} = a + \log \frac{W_0^{(1/(1-\gamma_s))}}{P_w^{(1/(1-\gamma_s))}} = a + \left(\frac{1}{1 - \gamma_s}\right) \log\left(\frac{W_0}{P_w}\right), \tag{A.5}$$

where

$$P_w = (P_0)^{1-\gamma_s} (\alpha_{x1} P_1)^{\gamma_s} \tag{A.6}$$

and where

$$P_0 = p_{m0}^{\beta_{m0}}, \quad P_1 = p_{m1}^{\beta_{m1}}.$$

Equation (A.6) defines the "true" utility-based *temporal* price indexes P_0 and P_1 and the "true" utility-based *intertemporal* price index P_w. As seen from (A.5), P_w is the price index relevant for welfare analysis.

Equilibrium in the world economy requires that in each period world private-sector demand for the two goods equals the corresponding supply net of government purchases. Thus

$$\beta_{m0} \frac{1}{1+\delta} W_0 + \beta_{m0}^* \frac{1}{1+\delta} W_0^*$$

$$= p_{m0}[\bar{Y}_{m0} - G_{m0} + (\bar{Y}_{m0}^* - G_{m0}^*)], \tag{A.7}$$

$$(1 - \beta_{m0}) \frac{1}{1+\delta} W_0 + (1 - \beta_{m0}^*) \frac{1}{1+\delta^*} W_0^*$$

$$= (\bar{Y}_{x0} - G_{x0}) + (\bar{Y}_{x0}^* - G_{x0}^*). \tag{A.8}$$

$$\beta_{m1} \frac{\delta}{1+\delta} W_0 + \beta_{m1}^* \frac{\delta^*}{1+\delta^*} W_0^*$$

$$= \alpha_{x1} p_{m1}[(\bar{Y}_{m1} - G_{m1}) + (\bar{Y}_{m1}^* - G_{m1}^*)], \tag{A.9}$$

$$(1 - \beta_{m1}) \frac{\delta}{1+\delta} W_0 = (1 - \beta_{m1}^*) \frac{\delta^*}{1+\delta^*} W_0^*$$

$$= \alpha_{x1}[(\bar{Y}_{x1} - G_{x1}) + (\bar{Y}_{x1}^* - G_{x1}^*)], \tag{A.10}$$

where

$$W_0 = p_{m0}(\bar{Y}_{m0} - G_{m0}) + (\bar{Y}_{x0} - G_{x0})$$

$$+ \alpha_{x1}[p_{m1}(\bar{Y}_{m1} - G_{m1}) + (\bar{Y}_{x1} - G_{x1})]$$

and

$$W_0^* = p_{m0}(\bar{Y}_{m0}^* - G_{m0}^*) + (\bar{Y}_{x0}^* - G_{x0}^*)$$

$$+ \alpha_{x1}[p_{m1}(\bar{Y}_{m1}^* - G_{m1}^*) + (\bar{Y}_{x1}^* - G_{x1}^*)].$$

By Walras's law we omit, in what follows, equation (A.10).

Differentiating totally the system (A.7) through (A.9) around $G = 0$ yields

$$[\lambda_{m0}(1 - \gamma_s)\beta_{m0}\mu_{m0} + \lambda_{m0}^*(1 - \gamma_s^*)\beta_{m0}^*\mu_{m0}^* - 1]\hat{p}_{m0}$$

$$+ [\lambda_{m0}\gamma_s\beta_{m1}\mu_{m1} + \lambda_{m0}^*\gamma_s^*\beta_{m1}^*\mu_{m1}^*]\hat{p}_{m1}$$

$$+ [\lambda_{m0}\gamma_s\mu_1 + \lambda_{m0}^*\gamma_s^*\mu_1^*]\hat{\alpha}_{x1}$$

$$= g_{m0}[\beta_{m0}(1 - \gamma_s) - \beta_{m0}^g(1 - \gamma_s^g)] dG, \tag{A.11}$$

$$[\lambda_{x0}(1 - \gamma_s)\beta_{m0}\mu_{m0} + \lambda_{x0}^*(1 - \gamma_s)\beta_{m0}^*\mu_{m0}^*]\hat{p}_{m0}$$

$$+ [\lambda_{x0}\gamma_s\beta_{m1}\mu_{m1} + \lambda_{x0}^*\gamma_s^*\beta_{m1}^*\mu_{m1}^*]\hat{p}_{m1}$$

$$+ [\lambda_{x0}\gamma_s\mu_1 + \lambda_{x0}^*\gamma_s^*\mu_1^*]\hat{\alpha}_{x1}$$

$$= g_{x0}[(1 - \beta_{m0})(1 - \gamma_s) - (1 - \beta_{m0}^g)(1 - \gamma_s^g)] dG, \tag{A.12}$$

$$[\lambda_{m1}(1 - \gamma_s)\beta_{m0}\mu_{m0} + \lambda_{m1}^*(1 - \gamma_s^*)\beta_{m0}^*\mu_{m0}^*]\hat{p}_{m0}$$

$$+ [\lambda_{m1}\gamma_s\beta_{m1}\mu_{m1} + \lambda_{m1}^*\gamma_s^*\beta_{m1}^*\mu_{m1}^* - 1]\hat{p}_{m1}$$

$$+ [\lambda_{m1}\gamma_s\mu_1 + \lambda_{m1}^*\gamma_s^*\mu_1^* - 1]\hat{\alpha}_{x1}$$

$$= g_{m1}[\beta_{m1}\gamma_s - \beta_{m1}^g\gamma_s^g] dG, \tag{A.13}$$

where λ denotes the share of spending on a given good by the corresponding unit in world net output of the given good (net of government purchases). For example, λ_{m0} denotes the share of domestic private-sector spending on good m (in period zero) in world net output of good m in period zero; that is, $\lambda_{m0} = c_{m0}/[(\bar{Y}_{m0} - G_{m0}) + \bar{Y}_{m0}^* - G_{m0}^*)]$. Initially, with $G = 0$, $\lambda_{m0} = c_{m0}/(\bar{Y}_{m0} + \bar{Y}_{m0})$, and in this case $\mu_{m1} = \bar{Y}_{m1}/c_{m1}$. The terms g_{m0}, g_{x0}, and g_{m1} denote, respectively, the reciprocals of the world production of good m_0, x_0, m_1 (net of government purchases of the good). The rest of the variables are defined in the text.

The system (A.11) through (A.13) can be solved to yield the effects of G on p_{m0}, p_{m1}, and α_{x1}. As is obvious by inspection of the coefficients of dG in equations (A.11) through (A.13), changes in the level of domestic government spending influence the temporal and the intertemporal terms of trade according to the principles known from the analysis of transfers. Thus changes in government spending influence the equilibrium only if the various spending propensities of the. private sector differ from the corresponding propensities of the government. Indeed, in the special case in which these propensities are equal to each other so that $\beta_{m0} = \beta_{m0}^g$, $\beta_{m1} = \beta_{m1}^g$, and, $\gamma_s = \gamma_s^g$, changes in government spending do not influence the equilibrium temporal and intertemporal prices.

As is evident, the complex structure of the model implies that, in general, the effects of government spending on the temporal and intertemporal terms of trade depend on a multitude of transfer-problem criteria, involving comparisons among the marginal propensities to save of the private sector and of the government as well as comparisons among the periodic expenditure shares of the domestic and the foreign private sectors and the government.

In order to focus on differences between the private and the public sectors, suppose that the various shares do not vary over time and that the domestic and the foreign private sectors are identical in their marginal propensities to save, in their expenditure shares, and in their relative shares in world private demand. In that case $\lambda_m = \lambda_m^*$, $\beta_m = \beta_m^*$, and $\gamma_s = \gamma_s^*$, where the time subscript is omitted due to the assumption that the various propensities and shares are constant over time. We further assume that initially the ratios of output to private-sector spending are equal across countries so that $\mu_m = \mu_m^*$ and $\mu_1 = \mu_1^*$. This implies that the initial equilibrium is autarkic, so that $\mu_1 = \mu_m = 1$. With these assumptions the solution for the effect of government spending on the consumption-based intertemporal price index (the utility-based wealth deflator), P_w, is

$$\frac{d\log P_w}{dG} = \frac{1}{\overline{Y}_x + \overline{Y}_x^*}[(1 - \beta_m)(1 - \gamma_s) - (1 - \beta_m^g)(1 - \gamma_s^g)]. \qquad (A.14)$$

Equation (A.14) shows that, as usual, the direction of the effect of a rise in government spending on the utility-based wealth deflator depends only on the various transfer-problem criteria.

Similarly, under the same assumptions the effect of a rise in government spending on the consumption-based real discount factor, $\alpha_{c1} = \alpha_{x1}P_1/P_0$, is

$$\frac{d\log \alpha_{c1}}{dG} = \frac{\beta_m}{\gamma_s p_m(\overline{Y}_m + \overline{Y}_m^*)}[\beta_m(1 - \gamma_s) - \beta_m^g(1 - \gamma_s^g)]$$

$$+ \frac{(1 - \beta_m)c_m}{\gamma_s c_x(\overline{Y}_m + \overline{Y}_m^*)}[(1 - \beta_m)(1 - \gamma_s) + (1 - \beta_m^g)(1 - \gamma_s^g)].$$

Using the equality $p_m c_m/c_x = \beta_m/(1 - \beta_m)$ yields

$$\frac{d\log \alpha_{c1}}{dG} = \frac{\beta_m}{\gamma_s p_m(\overline{Y}_m + \overline{Y}_m^*)}(\gamma_s^g - \gamma_s). \qquad (A.15)$$

Equations (A.14) through (A.15) underlie the results reported in table 6.2 of the text.

7

Budget Deficits with Nondistortionary Taxes: The Pure Wealth Effect

In this chapter we develop an analytical framework for the analysis of the effects of budget deficits in an undistorted economy. In such a framework, it is the induced wealth effects that constitute the primary mechanism by which budget deficits influence the economy. This mechanism supplements the one outlined in chapter 10 where we allowed for distortionary taxes. With such taxes budget deficits influence the economy through temporal and intertemporal substitution effects induced by the distortions.

To conduct a meaningful analysis of budget deficits in the absence of distortions, our analytical framework departs from the pure Ricardian model in which the timing of taxes and government debt issue plays no role as long as the path of government spending is given. We depart from that model by allowing for differences between the time horizons relevant for individual decision making and for the society at large. These differences result in discrepancies between the private and public sectors' costs of borrowing, which in turn implies that the equilibrium is no longer invariant with respect to the timing of taxes. The specification that we use to yield differences between the horizons relevant for the individual and the society relies on the assumption that individuals have finite life. In contrast, the society at large has an infinite horizon due to the continuous entry of newly born generations.

A significant portion of this chapter is devoted to the development of the analytical framework underlying the overlapping-generations model. In this context we specify in detail the procedure by which the individual behavioral functions are aggregated into the corresponding aggregate behavioral functions. This procedure constitutes a key building block which is used in subsequent chapters.

Following the development of the model, we devote the remainder of this chapter to the analysis of the effects of budget deficits on aggregate consumption and debt accumulation in an economy facing given world rates of interest. The wealth effects induced by budget deficits stem from differences between the effective interest rates that individuals use in discounting future taxes and the corresponding market interest rates that govern public sector behavior.

7.1 The Aggregate Consumption Function

We start with a specification of the individual decision problem and derive the individual consumption function. The dynamic character of the overlapping-generations society necessitates great care in the specification of the aggregate behavior. Accordingly, we discuss in detail the procedures underlying the aggregation of the individual consumption functions into the aggregate private-sector consumption function.

Let $c_{a,t}$ denote the level of consumption in period t of an individual of age a, and suppose that the utility function of this individual in period t is

$$U = \frac{1}{1-\theta} \sum_{v=0}^{\infty} \delta^v c_{a+v,t+v}^{1-\theta}, \tag{7.1}$$

where δ denotes the subjective discount factor and θ is the reciprocal of the intertemporal elasticity of substitution, σ (thus $\theta = 1/\sigma$). Assume that the individual maximizes *expected utility*, which is computed on the basis of his or her probability of survival. We denote the probability that an individual survives from one period to the next by γ, which, in order to facilitate the aggregation, is assumed to be independent of the individual's age. Thus the probability that an individual survives the next v periods is γ^v. Accordingly, the probability as of period t that an individual of age a will be alive in period $t + v$ and enjoy the utility level $[1/(1 - \theta)]c_{a+v,t+v}^{1-\theta}$ is γ^v. Therefore, using equation (7.1), the expected utility can be written as

$$\frac{1}{1+\theta} E_t \sum_{v=0}^{\infty} \delta^v c_{a+v,t+v}^{1-\theta} = \frac{1}{1-\theta} \sum_{v=0}^{\infty} (\gamma\delta)^v c_{a+v,t+v}^{1-\theta}. \tag{7.2}$$

Equation (7.2) is the *certainty equivalent* utility function with an effective discount factor that is equal to $\gamma\delta$. Thus, by reducing the effective discount factor, the probability of death raises the effective subjective discount rate and (in and of itself) tilts consumption toward the present period.

We assume that because of uncertain lifetime, all loans require in addition to regular interest payments a purchase of life insurance. In case of death, the estate is transferred to the life insurance company which, in turn, guarantees to cover outstanding debts. It is assumed that there is a large number of individuals in each cohort so that the frequency of those who survive equals the survival probability, γ. Furthermore we assume that there is competition among insurance companies. Under such circumstances the zero-profit condition ensures that the percentage insurance premium equals the probability of death, $1 - \gamma$. To verify this relation, consider a given population composed of many individuals who, in the aggregate, borrow one dollar. The insurance company's income associated with this loan transaction is the percentage premium, π, which, if invested at the market rate of interest, r, yields at the end of the period $\pi(1 + r)$. On the other hand, since a fraction $(1 - \gamma)$ of this population does not survive, the commitment to cover the outstanding debts costs the company $(1 - \gamma)(1 + r)$ dollars. The zero-profit condition guarantees that $\pi = 1 - \gamma$. An alternative institutional arrangement to the requirement that each loan is associated with a purchase of life insurance is a direct surcharge imposed on the loan. Under such an arrangement it is assumed that in case of death the lender has no claim on the outstanding debt. In this case, in order to secure a safe retun, $1 + r$, on a given one-dollar loan, the competitive lender charges $(1 + r)/\gamma$ dollars. Since the fraction of the borrowers who survive to repay the loan is γ, the safe return is $\gamma[(1 + r)/\gamma] = 1 + r$. Thus the *effective* cost of borrowing relevant for individual decision making is $(1 + r)/\gamma$.

Consider an individual who is of age a in period zero. His periodic budget constraints are

$$c_{a,0} = y_0 + b_{a,0} - \left(\frac{1 + r_{-1}}{\gamma}\right) b_{a-1,-1},$$

$$c_{a+1,1} = y_1 + b_{a+1,1} - \left(\frac{1 + r_0}{\gamma}\right) b_{a,0}, \tag{7.3}$$

$$c_{a+2,2} = y_2 + b_{a+2,2} - \left(\frac{1 + r_1}{\gamma}\right) b_{a+1,1}, \quad \text{etc.,}$$

where the budget constraint applicable to period t is

$$c_{a+t,t} = y_t + b_{a+t,t} - \frac{1 + r_{t-1}}{\gamma} b_{a+t-1,t-1} \tag{7.3a}$$

and where y_v and $b_{a+v,v}$ are the individual's disposable income and new (one-period) borrowing in period v ($v = 0, 1, \ldots$). The formulation in (7.3) also presumes that disposable income is the same across all individuals regardless of age. This assumption is made to facilitate the aggregation.

Following procedures similar to those in previous chapters, the periodic budget constraints can be consolidated into a single present-value lifetime constraint. For this purpose we define a present-value factor. The present-value factor, whose inverse is composed of one-period rates of interest compounded from period zero up to period $t - 1$, is denoted by α_t, and therefore the ratio α_t/α_{t+1} is the *market* discount factor, which is equal to one plus the market rate of interest in period t (i.e., $1 + r_t$). Accordingly, $\alpha_0 = 1$. Analogously, the market risk rate is $\gamma^t/\gamma^{t+1} = 1/\gamma$. It follows that the *effective* interest factor faced by individuals is $\alpha_t/\gamma\alpha_{t+1}$, and correspondingly the effective interest rate is $[(1 + r_t)/\gamma] - 1$.

Using this notation, the consolidated present-value constraint is

$$\sum_{v=0}^{\infty} \gamma^v \alpha_v c_{a+v,v} = \sum_{v=0}^{\infty} \gamma^v \alpha_v y_v - \frac{1 + r_{-1}}{\gamma} b_{a-1,-1} = w_{a,0}, \tag{7.4}$$

where $w_{a,0}$ is the wealth of an individual of age a at period zero. Finally, in deriving equation (7.4), we have made use of the solvency requirement that in the limit, as v approaches infinity, the present value of debt commitment is zero. That is,

$$\lim_{v \to \infty} \gamma^v \alpha_v b_{a+v,v} = 0. \tag{7.5}$$

As seen from the consolidated budget constraint in equation (7.4), the individual's wealth is composed of two components. The first, which is the discounted sum of income, is referred to as *human* wealth, and the second, which is the interest plus principal payments on past debt (which may be positive or negative), is referred to as *financial* (nonhuman) wealth. The key characteristic of human wealth is that it is attached to a specific individual. As a result the individual's human wealth disappears from the system once the individual is not alive.

The individual's problem is to maximize the expected utility, given by equation (7.2), subject to the budget constraint (7.4). Formally, the maximization problem can be written as

$$\max_{\{c_{a+v,v}\}} \frac{1}{1 - \theta} \sum_{v=0}^{\infty} (\gamma\delta)^v c_{a+v,v}^{1-\theta} + \lambda\left(w_{a,0} - \sum_{v=0}^{\infty} \gamma^v \alpha_v c_{a+v,v}\right), \tag{7.6}$$

where λ denotes the Lagrange multiplier associated with the budget constraint. The first-order condition of maximization implies that

$$(\gamma\delta)^v c_{a+v,v}^{-\theta} - \lambda(\gamma^v \alpha_v) = 0, \quad \text{for } v = 0, 1, \ldots. \tag{7.7}$$

Equation (7.7) shows that the finiteness of life, reflected by γ, influences both the subjective and the market-effective present-value factors, $(\gamma\delta)^v$ and $\gamma^v\alpha_v$, in the *same* manner. It follows therefore that the marginal rates of substitution between the levels of consumption in two consecutive periods equal the *market* (risk-free) discount factor, $1/(1 + r)$, independent of γ. It follows that even though there is a discrepancy between the effective (risk-adjusted) rates of interest applicable to the individual choice and the market (risk-free) rate of interest applicable to the society at large, this discrepancy does not distort the intertemporal allocations of consumption. This property ensures that in the absence of other distortions, the equilibrium obtained is Pareto efficient. In the subsequent discussion we assume that taxes are nondistortionary. As a result the mechanism through which budget deficits influence the real equilibrium does not operate through the distortion effects analyzed in chapter 10. We will return to these issues later on.

Using the budget constraint (7.4) and substituting the solution for $c_{a+v,v}$ from (7.7) yields $w_{a,0} = \sum_{v=0}^{\infty} \gamma^v\alpha_v c_{a+v,v} = \lambda^{-\sigma} \sum_{v=0}^{\infty} \gamma^v\alpha_v(\delta^v/\alpha_v)^\sigma$, where we recall that the elasticity of substitution, σ, is equal to $1/\theta$. Accordingly, the solution for the value of the marginal utility of wealth is

$$\lambda = [(1 - s_0)w_{a,0}]^{-1/\sigma}, \tag{7.8}$$

and the consumption function is

$$c_{a+t,t} = (1 - s_0)\left(\frac{\delta^t}{\alpha_t}\right)^\sigma w_{a,0}, \quad \text{for } t = 0, 1, \ldots, \tag{7.9}$$

where

$$1 - s_0 = \left\{ \sum_{v=0}^{\infty} (\gamma^v\alpha_v)^{1-\sigma}[(\gamma\delta)^v]^\sigma \right\}^{-1}.$$

In equation (7.9) the term $(1 - s_0)$ denotes the marginal propensity to consume out of wealth in period zero. Thus for $t = 0$, $c_{a,0} = (1 - s_0)w_{a,0}$. It is seen that, in general, the propensity to consume depends on the *entire path* of effective rates of interest (indicated by the effective present-value factor $\gamma^v\alpha_v$) and on the effective present-value factor $(\gamma\delta)^v$. In the special case for which the utility function is logarithmic, the elasticity of substitution is unity, and the marginal propensity to spend depends only on the effective subjective discount factor, $\gamma\delta$, and not on the path of the effective rates of interest. In that case $1 - s_0 = 1 - \gamma\delta$. This special case may be viewed as intermediate between two extreme cases. In one extreme case the elasticity of substitution is zero, and in the other extreme case the elasticity of substitution is infinite. With no substitution, the marginal propensity to spend depends only on the effective present-value factor $\gamma^v \alpha_v$. In that case consumption is fixed over time (so that the consumption smoothing motive is absolute), and using the budget constraint, the marginal propensity to spend is $1/\sum_{v=0}^{\infty} \gamma^v \alpha_v$. In the other extreme case, with perfect substitution, the marginal propensity to spend is zero if δ^v exceeds α_v, and it is unity if δ^v falls short of α_v. In the general case, as seen from equation (7.9), the spending propensity falls with the rate of interest if the elasticity of substitution exceeds unity, and vice versa if the elasticity of substitution is smaller than unity.

The saving propensity, s_0, is the key parameter linking the value of wealth in period zero with the value of wealth in period one. Analogous to the definition of period-zero wealth of an individual who is of age a at period zero, $w_{a,0}$ (equation 7.4), the value of wealth in period one of the same individual, $w_{a+1,1}$, is defined as

$$w_{a+1,1} = \sum_{v=1}^{\infty} \gamma^{v-1}(1 + r_0)\alpha_v y_v - \frac{1 + r_0}{\gamma} b_{a,0}. \tag{7.10}$$

Using the fact that consumption in period zero is proportional to period zero wealth (with $1 - s_0$ being the proportionality factor), it follows from the definitions of $w_{a,0}$ and $w_{a+1,1}$, and from the budget constraint applicable to period zero (equation 7.3), that

$$w_{a+1,1} = \frac{1 + r_0}{\gamma} s_0 w_{a,0}. \tag{7.11}$$

Equation (7.11) shows that if the individual survives from period zero to period one, then his wealth equals the fraction of wealth not consumed in period zero, $s_0 w_{a,0}$ adjusted by the *effective* rate of interest.

Thus far we have specified the utility-maximizing saving propensity for period zero, s_0, as derived from period-zero maximization problem (7.6). A similar maximization problem can be formulated for an individual of age a in period t. With this formulation the resultant utility-maximizing consumption function for period t, $c_{a,t}$, is

$$c_{a,t} = (1 - s_t)w_{a,t}, \tag{7.12}$$

where

$$1 - s_t = \left\{ \sum_{v=t}^{\infty} \left(\gamma^{v-t} \frac{\alpha_v}{\alpha_t} \right)^{1-\sigma} [(\gamma\delta)^{v-t}]^{\sigma} \right\}^{-1},$$

and

$$w_{a,t} = \sum_{v=1}^{\infty} \gamma^{v-t} \frac{\alpha_v}{\alpha_t} y_t - \frac{1 + r_{-1}}{\gamma} b_{a-1,t-1}.$$

The spending propensity $1 - s_t$ is the generalization of the expression for period-zero propensity, $1 - s_0$, in equation (7.9), and as is evident, it depends on the entire path of the rates of interest. In general, if the rates of interest vary over time, the saving propensity s_t is not constant, except for the special case in which the elasticity of substitution, σ, is unity. In that case the spending propensity is a constant (equal to $1 - \gamma\delta$). Independent, however, of whether the elasticity of substitution equals to or differs from unity, the spending propensity does not depend on the *age* of the individual. This property (which reflects the assumption that the probability of survival does not depend on age) permits a simple aggregation of the *individual* consumption functions into the *aggregate* consumption function.

We now turn to the derivation of the *aggregate* consumption function. Population is normalized so that at birth every cohort consists of one individual who is assumed to be born without debt. Due to death the size of each cohort of age a becomes γ^a. The equality between the probability of survival of a given cohort and its frequency relative to its initial size stems from the law of large numbers. Since at each period there are γ^a members of a cohort of age a, the (constant) aggregate size of population is

$$\sum_{a=0}^{\infty} \gamma^a = \frac{1}{1 - \gamma}.$$

Aggregate consumption in period t is the sum of consumption of individuals from all cohorts. Since consumption of a cohort of age a is $\gamma^a c_{a,t}$, per-capita aggregate consumption, C_t, is

$$C_t = (1 - \gamma) \sum_{a=0}^{\infty} \gamma^a c_{a,t}. \tag{7.13}$$

Disposable income, y_t, is assumed to be the same across all individuals regardless of age. Therefore the per-capita value of aggregate income, Y_t, is equal to the individual disposable income, y_t. In what follows Y_t is referred to as per-capita income. The per-capita aggregate consumption function (7.13) together with the individual consumption function and the definition of wealth from equation (7.12) yields

$$C_t = (1 - s_t) W_t, \tag{7.14}$$

where

$$W_t = H_t - (1 + r_{-1})B^p_{t-1},$$

$$H_t = (1 - \gamma) \sum_{a=0}^{\infty} \gamma^a \sum_{v=t}^{\infty} \gamma^{v-t} \frac{\alpha_v}{\alpha_t} y_v = \sum_{v=t}^{\infty} \gamma^{v-t} \frac{\alpha_v}{\alpha_t} y_v,$$

$$B^p_{t-1} = (1 - \gamma) \sum_{a=0}^{\infty} \gamma^{a-1} b_{a-1,t-1}.$$

Equation (7.14) is the per-capita *aggregate* consumption function in which W_t, H_t, and B^p_{t-1} denote, respectively, the per-capita values of aggregate total wealth, aggregate human wealth, and aggregate private sector indebtedness. The per-capita value of aggregate human wealth is defined as the discounted sum of per-capita income computed by using the effective (risk-adjusted) rates of interest. As formulated in equation (7.14), the per-capita value of total aggregate wealth in period t, W_t, equals the value of human wealth in that period net of interest and principal payments on past private-sector per-capita debt. As is evident, the rate of interest applicable to the (per-capita value of) aggregate private-sector debt is the (risk-free) market rate of interest. This should be contrasted with the formulation of the *individual* wealth in equation (7.12) in which the rate of interest applicable to the computation of individual debt service is the (risk-adjusted) effective rate. We also note that as indicated earlier, the invariance of the individual spending propensity with respect to age is reflected in the equality between the individual and the aggregate spending propensities in equations (7.12) and (7.14). Finally, the specification in equation (7.14) defines the per-capita magnitudes of aggregate consumption and wealth. Obviously, as long as the demographic parameter, γ, is given, the size of the population is constant, and therefore the distribution between per-capita and aggregate quantities is inconsequential. In the limit, as γ approaches unity, the magnitude of the aggregate quantities (e.g., population, consumption, and wealth) is boundless, but the per-capita quantities are well defined according to equation 7.14).

7.2   Aggregate Wealth and Its Composition

The analysis of per-capita aggregate consumption specified the behavior of the economy at a point in time as a function of per-capita aggregate wealth. In order to characterize the behavior of the economy over time so as to be able to deal with the dynamic effects of fiscal policies, we need to determine the evolution of per-capita aggregate wealth through time. Since, as will be shown later, the two components of wealth (human and nonhuman wealth) are governed by different laws of motion, we need to study them separately. Throughout, we analyze the evolution of the per-capita aggregate quantities, but, for short, we omit in what follows an explicit mention of the term "per capita." We start with an analysis of the dynamics of human wealth. Lagging the expression for H_t from equation (7.14) by one period yields an analogous expression for H_{t-1} which, together with equation (7.14), yields

$$H_t = \frac{1 + r_{t-1}}{\gamma}(H_{t-1} - Y_{t-1}). \tag{7.15}$$

Equation (7.15) describes the evolution of aggregate human wealth as a function of the difference between its own lagged value and the lagged value of aggregate income Y_{t-1}. It is important to note that both the definition of aggregate human wealth and its law of motion employ the *effective* rates of interest that include the life insurance premium associated with the probability of death. This feature is specific to the human wealth component and does not play a role in the computation of the other component of wealth to which we turn next.

The evolution of aggregate private debt, B_t^p, can be obtained by aggregating equation (7.3a) across individuals. Accordingly,

$$B_t^p = C_t - Y_t + (1 + r_{t-1})B_{t-1}^p. \tag{7.16}$$

In contrast with the law of motion governing the accumulation of human wealth (in equation 7.15) and *individual* debt (in equation 7.3a), the accumulation of *aggregate* private debt is governed by the *market* rate of interest $(1 + r_{-1})$ rather than the *effective* rate of interest $(1 + r_{t-1})/\gamma$. The absence of the life-insurance premium from the law of motion governing aggregate debt accumulation in equation (7.16) stems from the fact that from the perspective of the society at large, the life-insurance premia represent transfers within the society which do not alter the social rates of return.

Having determined the evolution of the human and financial components of wealth, we can now combine the two in order to characterize the evolution of aggregate wealth. Substituting equations (7.15) and (7.16) into the definition of wealth in equation (7.14), and using the consumption function $C_{t-1} = (1 - s_{t-1})W_{t-1}$, we obtain

$$W_t = (1 + r_{t-1})s_{t-1}W_{t-1} + (1 - \gamma)H_t. \tag{7.17}$$

Equation (7.17) expresses the value of wealth in period t in terms of its value in period $t - 1$ and in terms of its human wealth component. The dependence of the path of aggregate wealth on its composition reflects the asymmetry between human and nonhuman wealth. This asymmetry, which arises from the uncertainty concerning the length of life, disappears if the probability of survival is unity. Thus, with $\gamma = 1$, the value of wealth becomes

$$W_t = (1 + r_{t-1})s_{t-1}W_{t-1}. \tag{7.18}$$

In this case the evolution of wealth depends on its *aggregate* value and not on its *composition*.

As indicated by the aggregate consumption function, for any given path of the rate of interest, the evolution of aggregate consumption depends exclusively on the evolution of aggregate wealth. Thus we can use equations (7.14) and (7.17) in order to characterize the evolution of aggregate consumption. Accordingly, the dependence of current consumption on the lagged value thereof is characterized by

$$C_t = s_{t-1}(1 + r_{t-1})\frac{1 - s_t}{1 - s_{t-1}}C_{t-1} + (1 - \gamma)(1 - s_t)H_t. \tag{7.19}$$

Thus, analogously to the characteristics of the evolution of aggregate wealth, aggregate consumption in period t depends on its lagged value as well as on the composition of wealth. In the special case for which $\gamma = 1$, equation (7.19) reduces to

$$C_t = \left[s_{t-1}(1 + r_{t-1})\frac{1 - s_t}{1 - s_{t-1}} \right]C_{t-1}. \tag{7.19a}$$

In that case (for a given path of the rates of interest) aggregate consumption in period t depends only on its lagged value. The comparison between (7.19) and (7.19a) reveals the role that the finiteness of the individual's horizon plays in determining the dynamics of aggregate consumption. As seen in (7.19a), given the rates of interest, the only variable relevant for predicting future consumption is current consumption. In particular, once current consumption is known, knowledge of wealth is not required for the prediction of future consumption. In the general case, however, as indicated by equation (7.19), once $\gamma < 1$, knowledge of current consumption is not sufficient for the prediction of future consumption, and one needs to know the detailed path of the composition of wealth. In the appendix we modify assumptions underlying equation (7.19) and obtain an empirically estimable form. In the next section we analyze in greater detail the factors governing aggregate consumption. This analysis will then be used in interpreting the effects of fiscal policies.

7.3   Dynamics of Aggregate Consumption

To facilitate the exposition, we assume in this section that the world rate of interest faced by the small economy is stationary so that $r_t = r$. In this case the saving propensity defined in equation (7.12) is constant, and can be written as

$$s = \left(\frac{\gamma}{R}\right)^{1-\sigma}(\gamma\delta)^{\sigma} = \gamma\delta^{\sigma}R^{\sigma-1}, \tag{7.20}$$

where $R = 1 + r$. As is evident, the saving propensity is a function of the effective cost of borrowing, γR, and the effective subjective discount factor, $\gamma\delta$; the weights of these two factors are $1 - \sigma$ and σ, respectively. In the special case in which the intertemporal elasticity of substitution is unity, the saving propensity equals $\gamma\delta$; in that case the saving propensity is independent of the cost of borrowing.

To determine the dynamics of consumption, we need to characterize the dynamics of wealth. For expositional simplicity suppose that the path of future disposable incomes is stationary so that $Y_t = Y$ for $t > 0$. In that case current and future human capital can be written with the aid of equation (7.14) as

$$H_0 = Y_0 + \frac{\gamma}{R - \gamma}\,Y,$$
$$\tag{7.21}$$
$$H_t = \frac{R}{R - \gamma}\,Y, \quad \text{for } t > 0.$$

Accordingly, using equations (7.14), (7.19), and (7.21), the levels of current and future consumption are

$$C_0 = (1 - s)\left[\left(Y_0 + \frac{\gamma}{R - \gamma}\,Y\right) - RB_{t-1}^p\right],$$
$$\tag{7.22}$$
$$C_t = RsC_{t-1} + (1 - \gamma)(1 - s)\frac{R}{R - \gamma}\,Y, \quad \text{for } t > 0.$$

The equations in (7.22) characterize the evolution of consumption through time. These consumption dynamics are illustrated in figure 7.1. The schedule $C_{t+1}(C_t)$ plots the values of C_{t+1} as a function of C_t. The equation of this schedule is shown in (7.22). As seen, the slope of the schedule is Rs, and the case drawn in figure 7.1 corresponds to the situation in which $Rs < 1$. In this case the system converges to a steady state with

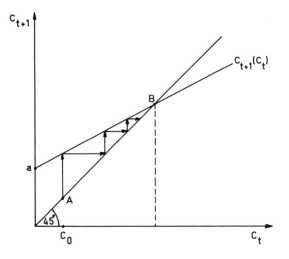

Figure 7.1
Consumption dynamics in the overlapping-generations model: The stable case

positive consumption. Accordingly, if the initial equilibrium is associated with consumption level C_0 (shown by point A in figure 7.1), the long-run equilibrium is associated with a steady-state level of consumption C (shown by point B in figure 7.1). The arrows in the figure indicate the path along which the level of consumption evolves through time.

To clarify the role played by the finiteness of the horizon, we note that the intercept of the $C_{t+1}(C_t)$ schedule (indicated by point a) depends on the value of γ. Specifically, with infinite lifetime, $\gamma = 1$ and $a = 0$. In that case the $C_{t+1}(C_t)$ schedule emerges from the origin, and the system does not converge to a long-run steady state with positive consumption. In that case the saving propensity is $\delta^\sigma R^{\sigma-1}$, and the slope of the consumption schedule is $(R\delta)^\sigma$. Thus, if $R\delta$ exceeds unity, consumption grows without a bound, and if $R\delta$ falls short of unity, consumption shrinks to zero. It follows that in order to allow for the possibility of a steady-state equilibrium with positive levels of consumption, the model must allow for a finite horizon.

The steady-state trade-balance surplus depends on the discrepancy between output, Y, and consumption C. Using (7.22), the steady-state level of consumption is

$$C = \left(\frac{1-\gamma}{R-\gamma}\right)\left(\frac{1-s}{1-Rs}\right)RY. \tag{7.23}$$

Using this equation along with equation (7.20), the steady-state trade-balance surplus is

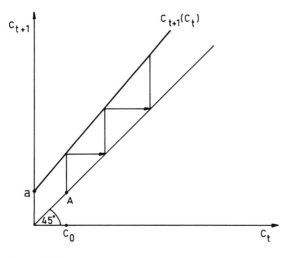

Figure 7.2
Consumption dynamics in the overlapping-generations model: The unstable case

$$(Y - C) = \frac{\gamma(R - 1)Y}{(R - \gamma)(1 - Rs)}[1 - (R\delta)^\sigma].$$

It can be seen that the economy runs a steady-state trade-balance surplus if $R\delta < 1$. This surplus is necessary in order to service the debt accumulated during the transition toward the steady state during which (on average) the economy consumed in excess of its GDP. On the other hand, if $R\delta$ exceeds unity, then the transition toward the steady state is characterized by trade-balance surpluses as the economy produces (on average) in excess of its consumption. In that case the economy reaches the steady state as a net creditor. As a result its steady-state level of consumption exceeds its GDP, and the steady-state trade balance is in deficit.

The foreoing analysis presumed that Rs is smaller than unity so that the economy converges to a long-run equilibrium with a positive level of consumption. To complete the analysis, we show in figure 7.2 the case in which Rs exceeds unity. In that case consecutive increments to the levels of consumption rise over time, and as a result consumption increases without a bound.

The level of consumption can be solved (by forward iteration of equations 7.22) to yield

$$C_t = (Rs)^t(C_0 - C) + C, \tag{7.24}$$

where C_0 and C are defined in equation (7.22) and (7.23). As seen, if

$Rs < 1$, the first term in equation (7.24) approaches zero with the passage of time, and consumption converges to its steady-state level C. On the other hand, if $Rs > 1$, the level of consumption grows over time without bound since in that case (as indicated by equations 7.22 and 7.23) $C_0 - C$ must be positive.

The foregoing analysis of the dynamics of consumption will prove useful in the subsequent section where we analyze the effects of budget deficits.

7.4   Wealth Effects of Budget Deficits

In this section we use the analytical framework of the small open economy for the analysis of the effects of a budget deficit arising from a current cut in lump-sum taxes. In order to focus on the essentials underlying aggregate saving and current-account adjustments, we abstract from capital accumulation and from multiple goods. We continue to assume that government spending is financed by taxes or by debt issue. Accordingly, the government budget constraint for period t is

$$G_t = T_t + B_t^g - (1 + r_{t-1})B_{t-1}^g, \tag{7.25}$$

where G_t, T_t, and B_t^g denote, respectively, the per-capita values of government spending, lump-sum taxes, and new government borrowing in period t. As is evident from equation (7.25), in analogy with the evolution of aggregate private debt in equation (7.16), the law of motion governing the accumulation of government debt depends on the *market* rate of interest.

Consolidating the temporal budget constraints (7.25) and imposing the requirement that over time government spending obeys the intertemporal solvency constraint implies that

$$\sum_{v=0}^{\infty} \alpha_v(T_v - G_v) = (1 + r_{t-1})B_{-1}^g. \tag{7.26}$$

Equation (7.26) states that the value of government debt commitment (interest plus principal payments) at the beginning of period zero must equal the discounted sum of current and future budget surpluses.

Prior to analyzing the effects of current budget deficits, we note for future use that the sum of private debt, B^p, and government debt, B^g, equals the value of the economy's external debt, B. Hence, using equations (7.16) and (7.25), the evolution of the external debt is governed by the current account position according to

$$B_t - B_{t-1} = (C_t + G_t - Y_t) + r_{t-1}B_{t-1}. \tag{7.27}$$

To examine the role of government budget deficits, suppose that the government changes the time pattern of taxes and debt issue while holding the path of spending unchanged. Specifically, consider the situation in which taxes are reduced in period j but are raised in a more distant period u so as to satisfy the government intertemporal solvency constraint. To find the effects of the change in the time profile of taxes on the level of current (period-zero) consumption and thereby on the trade balance, we need to determine the change in current wealth, W_0. Since the only component of wealth affected by the tax policy is the current value of human wealth, H_0, it is sufficient to determine the effect of the change in the timing of taxes on curent human wealth. Using equation (7.14), current human wealth is

$$H_0 = \sum_{v=0}^{\infty} \gamma^v \alpha_v (Y_v - T_v), \tag{7.28}$$

and the change in current value of human wealth is

$$dH_0 = -(\gamma^j \alpha_j dT_j + \gamma^u \alpha_u dT_u). \tag{7.29}$$

From the government solvency requirement (7.26) we note that

$$dT_u = \frac{\alpha_j}{\alpha_u} dT_j. \tag{7.30}$$

and therefore the change in current human wealth is

$$dH_0 = -(1 - \gamma^{u-j})\gamma^j \alpha_j dT_j. \tag{7.31}$$

Equation (7.31) shows that a tax cut in period j (followed by a corresponding tax rise in the more distant period, u; i.e., $dT_j < 0$ and $u > j$) raises the current value of human wealth. This positive wealth effect is stronger, the longer the period of time elapsing between the tax cut and the corresponding tax hike. The key factor responsible for the positive wealth effect induced by the tax policy is the finiteness of the individual horizon. At the limit, as γ approaches unity, the wealth effects disappear. In that case the Ricardian proposition reemerges, and once the path of government spending is given, the time pattern of taxes and government debt issue is irrelevant.

The foregoing analysis demonstrated that both a current budget deficit or an anticipated future deficit must raise current period wealth as long as it is financed by a subsequent rise in taxes. The rise in wealth stimulates current period consumption and worsens the trade balance.

The explanation for this result can be given as follows. If the probability of survival, γ, is unity, then the rise in future taxes which is equal in present value to the reduction in current taxes leaves wealth unchanged. On the other hand, the same change in the pattern of taxes raises wealth if each individual knows that there is a positive probability that he or she will not survive to pay these higher future taxes. Under such circumstances the current reduction in taxes constitutes net wealth. Equivalently, the explanation can be stated in terms of the difference between the market and the effective interest factors. For example, in the case of a current tax cut the government solvency requirement implies that changes in current taxes must be made up for by α_u times the offsetting change in future taxes. On the other hand, individuals discount these future taxes by $\gamma^u \alpha_u$. Therefore, as long as $\gamma < 1$, the current budget deficit raises human wealth. Yet another interpretation may be given in terms of a transfer-problem criterion familiar from the theory of international transfers. Accordingly, the budget deficit exerts real effects because it redistributes wealth from those who have not yet been born, and whose marginal propensity to consume current goods is obviously zero, to those who are currently alive, and whose marginal propensity to consume current goods is positive. As a result the budget deficit raises private-sector spending.

The foregoing analysis showed that a change in the time profile of taxes in favor of the present generation raises current consumption and worsens the balance of trade. To characterize the dynamic effects of the tax policy, we use the formulation of section 7.3 and examine the dynamic effects of a current tax cut which is accompanied by a permanent rise in future taxes. Using equation (7.30), the implied changes in current and future disposable incomes are

$$d(Y_0 - T_0) = -\frac{1}{R-1}d(Y - T). \tag{7.32}$$

With such changes in the time profile of disposable income, the change in current consumption (obtained from equation 7.22) is

$$\frac{dC_0}{dT_0} = -\frac{(1-\gamma)(1-s)R}{R-\gamma}. \tag{7.33}$$

Similarly, if the steady state exists (i.e., if $Rs < 1$), then the change in the steady-state level of consumption (obtained from equation 7.23) is

$$\frac{dC}{dT_0} = (R - 1)\frac{(1 - \gamma)(1 - s)R}{(R - \gamma)(1 - Rs)}.$$ (7.34)

As is evident from inspection of (7.33) and (7.34), the current budget deficit raises current consumption, C_0, and lowers the long-run level of consumption, C.

The changes in current and future consumption can be illustrated in terms of figure 7.1. Accordingly, a unit rise in current disposable income resulting from a tax cut induces a downward displacement of the $C_{t+1}(C_t)$ schedule by the magnitude $(R - 1)(1 - \gamma)(1 - s)R/(R - \gamma)$. As seen in figure 7.1, such a displacement lowers the long-run level of consumption and displaces the long-run equilibrium point B leftward along the 45° line. In addition, by raising current consumption, the budget deficit displaces the initial equilibrium point, A, rightward along the 45° line. The fall in long-run consumption is necessary in order to finance the larger steady-state debt service resulting from the tilting of the path of consumption in favor of the current generation.

The precise effect of the budget deficit on the level of consumption in any period, t, is obtained from equation (7.24) along with equations (7.33) and (7.34). Accordingly,

$$\frac{dC_t}{dT_0} = -\frac{(1 - \gamma)(1 - s)R}{(R - \gamma)(1 - Rs)}[R(1 - s)(Rs)^t - (R - 1)].$$ (7.35)

As is evident, the current budget deficit raises the levels of consumption in periods that are close to the present, but it lowers the levels of consumption in periods that are more distant from the present. It can be shown from equation (7.35) that the period $\bar{t}$, in which the level of consumption following the tax policy equals the level obtained in the absence of such policy, is

$$\bar{t} = \frac{\log[(R - 1)/(1 - s)R]}{\log Rs}.$$ (7.36)

Equation (7.36) shows that a higher saving propensity (induced by a higher value of γ or δ) lowers the length of time during which the level of consumption exceeds the level obtained in the absence of the tax policy. Finally, we note that in the periods immediately following the tax cut, the level of consumption exceeds the level obtained in the absence of such policy, even through disposable income is lower. This consumption pattern reflects the consumption-smoothing motive of the members of the generation enjoying the rise in wealth consequent on the tax cut. Mortality reduces the size of this generation, and birth of new generations implies that the weight in aggregate consumption of the generation benefiting from the tax cut falls over time. Hence aggregate consumption is increasingly dominated by the reduced wealth of the future generations' incurring the rise in taxes, and eventually, after period $\bar{t}$, aggregate consumption falls below the level obtained prior to the tax policy.

7.5 Summary

In this chapter we developed an analytical framework suitable for the analysis of the effects of budget deficits in an undistorted economy. In that framework the principal mechanism through which tax policy influences economic behavior operates through the induced wealth effects. These wealth effects stem from the difference between the *effective* interest rate that individuals use in discounting future taxes and the corresponding *market* interest rates governing government behavior. In the present analysis the specific reason responsible for the difference between the two interest rates arises from differences between the time horizons relevant for private and public-sector decisions. This provides a rationale for our formulation in chapter 6 where we allowed for differences between the private and the public sectors' rates of interest. It is relevant to note that in contrast with the formulation in chapter 10, in which the difference between the intertemporal terms of trade governing the private and the public sectors arises from distortionary taxes, here the interest differential neither reflects nor results in a distortion.

   To gain an intuitive feel into the quantitative implications of the finiteness of the horizon, it is instructive to examine the effects of a current tax cut on current consumption for alternative assumptions concerning the life expectancy of the economic decision maker. Consider a current period unit tax cut lasting for $s - 1$ periods and followed by a permanent rise in taxes that maintains the discounted sum of taxes. The rise in wealth induced by this tax-shift policy equals $[R/(R - \gamma)](1 - \gamma^s)$, and the change in current consumption equals the marginal propensity to consume $(1 - \gamma\delta)$ times this change in wealth. The resulting consumption multiplier is shown in table 7.1 for alternative values of life expectancy and of length of tax-cut period. As is evident, with immortality the multipliers are zero, and the Ricardian proposition emerges. On the other hand, with low life expectancy, for example, twenty years, the multipliers associated with tax cuts lasting one and three periods are, respectively, 0.36 and 0.59. The relatively low life expectancy would seem to correspond to economies in which the average age of the economic decision maker (being roughly the

Table 7.1
Current-consumption multiplier for alternative length of current tax-cut periods

Length of current tax-cut period	Life expectancy			
	∞ ($\gamma = 1$)	90 ($\gamma = 0.90$)	38 ($\gamma = 0.85$)	20 ($\gamma = 0.80$)
1	0	0.19	0.28	0.36
3	0	0.35	0.49	0.59
5	0	0.48	0.63	0.75
7	0	0.58	0.74	0.84

Note: The multipliers reported are equal to $(1 - \gamma\delta)[(R/(R - \gamma)](1 - \gamma^s)$, where s is one plus the length of the period for which the current tax cut is in effect. Life expectancy of the economic decision maker equals $\sum_{a=1}^{\infty} a\gamma^a = \gamma/(1 - \gamma)^2$. The computations assume that $R = 1.05$.

difference between life expectancies at birth and at that age) is relatively high.

An implicit assumption underlying the analytical framework is the absence of a bequest motive. Accordingly, each individual's utility function does not contain as arguments the levels of utility of the subsequent generations. Otherwise, individuals could be thought of as immortal through their offspring up to the indefinite future. In that case the Ricardian proposition reemerges, and budget deficits arising from changes in the time profile of taxes do not alter the real equilibrium. We could of course allow for a bequest motive as long as it does not extend into the indefinite future or, alternatively, as long as there is uncertainty about survival of each dynastic family. In that case the effective life expectancy of the dynastic family decision-making unit may be significantly longer than that of any given individual.

Finally, we note that a similar (nondistorting) mechanism by which budget deficits exert pure wealth effects on the existing generation could also be present under circumstances in which individuals are immortal or, equivalently, are endowed with a bequest motive linking them to their offspring up to the indefinite future. This would be the case if over time there is growth in the number of individuals and entry of new families. Under such circumstances the future tax base is broader, and the burden of the future tax hike associated with the current deficit falls in part on the new members of the society that do not enter into the bequest considerations of the existing families. With this mechanism, the growth-adjusted rates of interest of the society at large (i.e., of the government) is lower than the corresponding rates used by individuals and families.

In case of growth the interest differential depends on the growth rate in a similar manner to its dependence on the mortality rate in the case of finite horizons. In both cases the wealth effects induced by budget deficits are similar.

The analysis in this chapter illustrates the wealth effects induced by changes in the timing of taxes for a given path of the world rates of interest. In the next chapter we use this model to determine the effects of budget deficits on the world rates of interest. Such changes in the world rate of interest constitute the key mechanism for the international transmission of budget deficits in an undistorted world economy.

7.6 Appendix

In this appendix we modify three of the assumptions underlying the consumption equation (7.19) of the text. We allow for an uncertain income stream and for durable goods, and we replace the homothetic utility function by a quadratic function. These modifications yield on empirically estimable form of the consumption equation. Accordingly, the individual's objective function on the right-hand side of equation (7.2) of the text is replaced by

$$E_t \sum_{v=0}^{\infty} (\gamma\delta)^v u(c_{a+v,t+v}), \tag{A.1}$$

where E_t is the conditional-expectation operator reflecting the uncertain income stream. With durable goods, we modify the periodic budget constraint (7.3a) of the text to become

$$c_{a+t,t} = (1 - \phi)c_{a+t-1,t-1} + x_{a+t,t} \tag{A.2a}$$

$$x_{a+t,t} = y_t + b_{a+t,t} - \frac{R}{\gamma}b_{a+t-1,t-1}, \tag{A.2b}$$

where c denotes the *stock* of consumer goods, x denotes the *flow* of consumption purchases, ϕ denotes the rate of depreciation of the stock, and $R = 1 + r_{t-1}$ is assumed to be constant. The flow of income, y_t, is stochastic. Equations (A.2) and (A.2b) reduce to (7.3a) in the special case for which $\phi = 1$ and y_t is deterministic. The utility function is assumed to be quadratic:

$$u(c_{a+v,t+v}) = \alpha c_{a+v,t+v} - \tfrac{1}{2}c^2_{a+v,t+v}, \tag{A.3}$$

where $\alpha > 0$ and $c_{a+v,t+v} < \alpha$. This ensures that the marginal utility of consumption is positive and diminishing. To simplify the notation, we suppress in what follows the subscripts a and v; thus we replace $c_{a+v,t+v}$ by c_t, etc.

The maximization problem can be expressed in dynamic programming terms by the value function v as

$$v\left(y_t - \frac{R}{\gamma}b_{t-1}\right) = \max_{x_t} \left\{u[x_t + (1 - \phi)c_{t-1}]\right.$$

$$\left. + \gamma\delta E_t v\left[y_{t+1} + \frac{R}{\gamma}\left(y_t - x_t - \frac{R}{\gamma}b_{t-1}\right)\right]\right\}. \tag{A.4}$$

Differentiating the right-hand side of (A.4) and equating to zero yields

$$u'(c_t) - \delta RE_t v'(\cdot) = 0, \tag{A.5}$$

where the primes denote derivatives. Totally differentiating (A.4) yields

$$v'\left(y_t - \frac{R}{\gamma}b_{t-1}\right) = [u'(c_t) - \delta RE_t v'(\cdot)]\frac{dx_t}{dy_t} + \delta RE_t v'(\cdot)$$

$$= \delta RE_t v'(\cdot), \tag{A.6}$$

where use has been made of (A.5). Equations (A.5) and (A.6) imply that

$$u'(c_t) = \delta RE_t u'(c_{t+1}). \tag{A.7}$$

Using the specification in (A.3), we can express (A.7) as

$$\alpha - c_t = \delta RE_t(\alpha - c_{t+1}). \tag{A.8}$$

Expected human wealth is expressed as

$$E_t h_t = E_t \sum_{v=0}^{\infty} \left(\frac{\gamma}{R}\right)^v y_{t+v}. \tag{A.9}$$

From equation (A.9) we obtain

$$y_t = E_t h_t - \frac{\gamma}{R}E_t h_{t+1}. \tag{A.10}$$

For the purpose at hand, it is convenient to define expected (durability-adjusted) wealth as

$$E_t \tilde{w}_t = E_t h_t - \frac{R}{\gamma}b_{t-1} + (1 - \phi)c_{t-1}. \tag{A.11}$$

The constraints (A.2a) and (A.2b), together with (A.10), imply that

$$ac_t = E_t \tilde{w}_t - \left(\frac{\gamma}{R}\right) E_t \tilde{w}_{t+1}, \tag{A.12}$$

where

$$a = 1 - \left(\frac{\gamma}{R}\right)(1 - \varphi).$$

We proceed by postulating that the solution to the maximization problem is of the form

$$c_t = \beta_0 + \beta_1 E_t \tilde{w}_t) \tag{A.13}$$

In what follows we show that this is indeed the solution, and we provide explicit expressions for the coefficients β_0 and β_1. We first note that equations (A.12) and (A.13) imply that

$$E_t \tilde{w}_{t+1} = \frac{R}{\gamma}[-\beta_0 a + (1 - \beta_1 a) E_t \tilde{w}_t]. \tag{A.14}$$

Substituting (A.13) into (A.8) yields

$$\alpha - (\beta_0 + \beta_1 E_t \tilde{w}_t) = \delta R[\alpha - (\beta_0 + \beta_1 E_t \tilde{w}_{t+1})]. \tag{A.15}$$

Likewise, substituting (A.14) into (A.15) yields

$$\alpha - (\beta_0 + \beta_1 E_t \tilde{w}_t)$$

$$= \delta R \left[\alpha - \left\{ \beta_0 + \beta_1 \frac{R}{\gamma}[-\beta_0 a + (1 - \beta_1 a) E_t \tilde{w}_t] \right\} \right]. \tag{A.16}$$

Rearranging terms in equation (A.16) yields

$$\left\{ (1 - \delta R)\alpha - \left[1 - \delta R \left(1 - \frac{R}{\gamma} \beta_1 a \right) \right] \beta_0 \right\}$$

$$+ \left[-1 + \frac{\delta R^2}{\gamma}(1 - \beta_1 a) \right] \beta_1 E_t \tilde{w}_t = 0. \tag{A.17}$$

The solution specified in equation (A.13) is confirmed if (A.17) holds for all $E_t \tilde{w}_t$. This requirement is fulfilled if each of the bracketed terms in (A.17) equals zero. Thus equating these terms to zero yields

$$\beta_1 = \frac{1}{a}\left(1 - \frac{\gamma}{\delta R^2} \right), \tag{A.18}$$

$$\beta_0 = \alpha \frac{\gamma(1 - \delta R)}{\delta R(R - \gamma)},$$

where from (A.12) the parameter a (and thus β_1) depends on the depreciation coefficient, ϕ. The consumption function (A.13) whose coefficients are given in equations (A.18) and (A.19) is the analogue to the consumption function in equation (7.8).

We turn next to derive a consumption equation suitable for empirical estimations. Using (A.11) in (A.13), aggregating the resultant individual consumption function over all cohorts, and dividing by the size of population yields the per-capita aggregate consumption C_t, where

$$C_t = \beta_0 + \beta_1 \left[E_t \sum_{v=0}^{\infty} \left(\frac{\gamma}{R} \right)^v Y_{t+v} - RB_{t-1}^p + \gamma(1 - \phi)C_{t-1} \right]. \tag{A.20}$$

Aggregating (A.2b) over all cohorts, the per-capita flow aggregate budget constraint (in period $t - 1$) is

$$B_{t-1}^p = X_{t-1} - Y_{t-1} + RB_{t-2}^p, \tag{A.21}$$

where X_t denotes aggregate per-capita purchases. This equation is the analogue to equation (7.16). Substituting (A.2a), (A.10), and (A.20) into (A.21) yields

$$B_{t-1}^p = \beta_0 + (\beta_1 - 1)E_{t-1}h_{t-1} + \frac{\gamma}{R}E_{t-1}h_t + R(1 - \beta_1)B_{t-2}^p$$

$$+ \gamma(1 - \phi)(\beta_1 - 1)C_{t-2}. \tag{A.22}$$

Define

$$E_t \tilde{W}_t = E_t h_t - RB_{t-1}^p + \gamma(1 - \phi)C_{t-1}$$

$$= E_{t-1}h_t - RB_{t-1}^p + \gamma(1 - \phi)C_{t-1} + \varepsilon_t^*, \tag{A.23}$$

where $\varepsilon^* = (E_t h_t - E_{t-1}h_t)$. Substituting (A.22) into (A.23) yields

$$E_t \tilde{W}_t = (1 - \gamma)E_{t-1}h_t - R\beta_0 - R(\beta_1 - 1)E_{t-1}\tilde{W}_{t-1}$$

$$+ \gamma(1 - \phi)C_{t-1} + \varepsilon_t^*. \tag{A.24}$$

Equation (A.20) can be rewritten as

$$C_t = \beta_0 + \beta_1 E_t \tilde{W}_t. \tag{A.20a}$$

Lagging (A.20a) and rearranging yields

$$E_{t-1}\tilde{W}_{t-1} = \frac{1}{\beta_1}(C_{t-1} - \beta_0). \tag{A.25}$$

Substituting (A.25) into (A.24) yields

$$E_t \tilde{W}_t = (1 - \gamma)E_{t-1}h_t + \gamma(1 - \phi)C_{t-1} - R\beta_1$$

$$- \frac{R(\beta_1 - 1)}{\beta_1}(C_{t-1} - \beta_0) + \varepsilon_t^*, \tag{A.26}$$

which can be substituted into (A.20a) to yield

$$C_t = \beta_0(1 - R) + \beta_1(1 - \gamma)E_{t-1}h_t + [\gamma(1 - \phi)\beta_1 - R(\beta_1 - 1)]C_{t-1} + \varepsilon_t,$$

where $\varepsilon_t = \beta_1\varepsilon_t^*$ is a stochastic (zero-mean) residual term.

Equation (A.27) is the analogue to equation (7.19). Using the facts that aggregate consumption purchases, X_t, are related to the aggregate stock, C_t, according to $X_t = C_t - (1 - \phi)C_{t-1}$, while $C_{t-1} = \sum_{\tau=0}^{\infty}(1 - \phi)^{\tau}X_{t-1-\tau}$, we can express (A.27) in terms of the current and the lagged values of *observable* purchases. This form therefore is readily applicable for empirical estimation of the key parameters, particularly, the finite-horizon coefficient γ.

8

An Exposition of the Two-Country Overlapping-Generations Model

In this chapter we extend the overlapping-generations model of chapter 7 to a two-country model of the world economy. We develop a simple diagrammatic exposition which is used in the analysis of the international effects of fiscal policies. The key channel through which the effects of fiscal policies are transmitted internationally is the world rate of interest. As in chapter 7, in the absence of distortionary taxes, the mechanism responsible for the real effects of budget deficit operates through the pure wealth effects. These effects stem from the intergenerational redistribution of income consequent on budget deficits.

We also extend the analysis by allowing a more refined commodity aggregation, distinguishing between tradable and nontradable goods. The incorporation of nontradable goods permits an examination of the consequences of budget deficits on the real exchange rate, as they operate through the mechanism of the pure wealth effect.

The exposition in this chapter is based on the assumption that the utility function is logarithmic. Under this assumption, as shown in chapter 7 the marginal propensity to save is $\gamma\delta$ (where γ denotes the survival probability and δ denotes the subjective discount factor.) Accordingly, the per-capita aggregate consumption function is

$$C_t = (1 - \gamma\delta)W_t, \tag{8.1}$$

where, as before, per-capita aggregate wealth, W_t, equals the sum of human wealth and financial wealth. Human wealth is the discounted sum of disposable income, computed by using the *effective* rates of interest. Since this chapter deals with the interaction between the domestic economy and the rest of the world, we need to specify the behavioral functions of the foreign economy. In what follows variables pertaining to the foreign economy are denoted by an asterisk (*), and it is assumed that the foreign consumption function has the same form as the domestic consumption function.

8.1 World Equilibrium

In this section we analyze the determination of the equilibrium path of world rates of interest in the two-country world economy. As before, we assume that world capital markets are fully integrated and therefore individuals and governments in both countries face the same *market* rates of interest. This feature provides for the key channel through which policies undertaken in one country affect economic conditions in the rest of the world.

World equilibrium requires that in each period the given supply of world output equals the demand. To facilitate the exposition, we divide the horizon into two periods: the present, which is denoted by $t = 0$, and the future ($t = 1, 2, \ldots$). The detailed procedure of time aggregation is specified in the appendix. In aggregating the future into a composite single period, we need to compute the present values of the various flows. Assuming that outputs, government spending, and taxes do not vary across future periods ($t = 1, 2, \ldots$), we define an *average* interest rate, r. This average interest rate, which may be thought of as the yield on current investment lasting up to the indefinite future, represents the entire path of rates of interest that actually *do change* over time. For further reference r may be termed a "constancy-equivalent" interest rate.

The equilibrium conditions include the specification of the initial values of domestic and foreign wealth as well as the requirement that present and future goods-markets clear. These conditions are given in equation (8.2) through (8.5):

$$W_0 = (Y_0 - T_0) + \frac{\gamma}{R - \gamma}(Y - T)$$

$$+ (1 + r_{-1})(B^g_{-1} - B_{-1}), \tag{8.2}$$

$$W_0^* = (Y_0^* - T_0^*) + \frac{\gamma}{R - \gamma}(Y^* - T^*)$$

$$+ (1 + r_{-1})(B^{g*}_{-1} + B_{-1}), \tag{8.3}$$

$$(1 - \gamma\delta)W_0 + (1 - \gamma\delta^*)W_0^* = (Y_0 - G_0) + (Y_0^* - G_0^*) \tag{8.4}$$

$$\left[\gamma\delta W_0 + \frac{(1 - \gamma)}{(R - 1)}\frac{R}{(R - \gamma)}(Y - T)\right]$$

$$+ \left[\gamma\delta^* W_0^* + \frac{(1 - \gamma)}{(R - 1)}\frac{R}{(R - \gamma)}(Y - T)\right]$$

$$= \frac{1}{R-1}[(Y-G)+(Y^*-G^*)], \tag{8.5}$$

where $R = 1 + r$, and where we have assumed that $\gamma = \gamma^*$.

Equations (8.2) and (8.3) specify the initial equilibrium values of domestic and foreign wealth owned by the existing population. In this specification private wealth is expressed as the sum of present values of current and future disposable incomes plus the net asset positions. In these equations the term $\gamma/(R - \gamma)$ denotes the present value of an annuity (commencing at period $t = 1$) evaluated by using the effective constancy-equivalent interest rate. These equations also embody the requirement that the home country's initial external indebtedness, B_{-1}, equals the foreign country's initial net creditor position.

Equation (8.4) is the requirement that world demand for goods in period $t = 0$ equal world supply. The left-hand side of this equation shows the sum of domestic and foreign per-capita private sector consumption (as implied by equation 8.1 and its foreign counter-part), and the right-hand side is the sum of per-capita domestic and foreign outputs (Y_0 and Y_0^*) net of government spending. The equality between γ and γ^* ensures that sizes of the population of the two countries are equal to each other. As a result aggregate world demand and supply can be expressed in terms of an equality between the *unweighted* sum of the individual country per-capita demand and the unweighted sum of the corresponding per-capita supply.

Equation (8.5) specifies the requirement that the discounted sum of per-capita domestic and foreign private demand for future goods equal the discounted sum of per-capita future world outputs net of government spending. These discounted sums are computed as of period $t = 0$ with the aid of the constancy-equivalent interest rate. The interpretation of the various terms follows. Consider the first bracketed term on the left-hand side of equation (8.5). In this expression the term $\gamma \delta W_0$ represents the per-capita savings of the population *present* in $t = 0$; these savings ultimately must be spent on future goods. The second term represents the per-capita wealth of those who will be born in all *future* periods from $t = 1$ onward; this wealth will be spent on future goods. To verify that this is indeed the meaning of the second term, we note that $(Y - T)$ is the disposable income of each individual at the time of birth and its product with $R/(R - \gamma)$ is the present value of such an annuity. Therefore the term $[R/(R - \gamma)](Y - T)$ denotes each individual's wealth at the time of birth, and since by our normalization the size of each cohort at birth is one individual, this term also represents the cohort's wealth at birth. Since in each period in the future there is a new cohort whose wealth at birth is computed similarly, the discounted sum of all future cohorts' welath (as of period $t = 1$) is obtained by multiplying the term $[R/(R - \gamma)](Y - T)$ by $R/(R - 1)$, which denotes the present value of an annuity (commencing at $t = 1$) evaluated by using the constancy-equivalent interest rate. The resulting expression is then discounted to the present (period $t = 0$) through a division by R. This yields $[R/(R - 1)(R - \gamma)](Y - T)$. Multiplying this term by $(1 - \gamma)$ converts this aggregate wealth into the corresponding per-capita wealth. Equivalently, the first bracketed term on the left-hand side of equation (8.5) can also be obtained as the discounted sum of per-capita consumption, expressed by an equation analogous to equation (7.24). A similar interpretation applies to the second bracketed term on the left-hand side of equation (8.5). Finally, the right-hand side of equation (8.5) is the discounted sum of all future domestic and foreign outputs net of government spending. As a manifestation of Walras's law the system (8.2) through (8.5) is linearly dependent. This property is used in the subsequent analysis.

In addition to equations (8.1) through (8.5) the equilibrium conditions also include the requirements that both governments be solvent. Expressed in terms of the constancy-equivalent interest rate, these requirements are

$$(T_0 - G_0) + \frac{1}{R - 1}(T - G) = (1 + r_{-1})B^g_{-1} \tag{8.6}$$

and

$$(T^*_0 - G^*_0) + \frac{1}{R - 1}(T^* - G^*) = (1 - r_{-1})B^{g*}_{-1}. \tag{8.7}$$

This system of equations can be solved for the equilibrium values of W_0 and W^*_0 and R for any given values of the parameters. As shown in the appendix, the solutions obtained for the equilibrium values of wealth, W_0 and W^*_0, are the same as those that may be obtained from the original system (without the specific time aggregation) for which the rates of interest within the future may now vary. The use of the constancy-equivalent interest rate thus simplifies the analysis considerably, and it provides complete information about the impact of policies on the precise *current* values of all key variables including wealth, consumption, and debt accumulation, as well as on the average value of the rate of interest (computed as of time zero).

Using the government budget constraints, substituting $C_0/(1 - \gamma\delta)$ for W_0, and omitting equation (8.2) by Walras's law, the complete system of equations can be reduced to two basic market-clearing equilibrium conditions, one for present goods and another for future goods. These conditions are

$$
C_0 + (1 - \gamma\delta^*)\left[(Y_0^* - G_0^*) + \frac{\gamma}{R - \gamma}(Y^* - T^*)\right.
$$

$$
\left. + \frac{1}{R - 1}(T^* - G^*) + (1 + r_{-1})B_{-1}\right]
$$

$$
= [(Y_0 - G_0) + (Y_0^* - G_0^*)], \tag{8.8}
$$

$$
\left[\frac{\gamma\delta}{(1 - \gamma\delta)}C_0 + \frac{(1 - \gamma)}{R - 1}\frac{R}{(R - \gamma)}(Y - T)\right] + \left\{\gamma\delta^*\left[(Y_0^* - G_0^*)\right.\right.
$$

$$
+ \frac{\gamma}{R - \gamma}(Y^* - T^*) + \frac{1}{R - 1}(T^* - G^*) + (1 + r_{-1})B_{-1}\right]
$$

$$
\left. + \frac{(1 - \gamma)}{R - 1}\frac{R}{(R - \gamma)}(Y^* - T^*)\right\}
$$

$$
= \frac{1}{R - 1}[(Y - G) + (Y^* - G^*)]. \tag{8.9}
$$

Equation (8.8) is the reduced-form market-clearing condition for present goods, with the left-hand side showing the sum of domestic and foreign private sector demands and the right-hand side showing the world supply of outputs net of government spending. Equation (8.9) is the reduced-form market-clearing condition for future goods, with analogous interpretations applied to the terms on its left and right-hand sides. These market-clearing conditions are used later in the diagrammatic exposition of the world equilibrium.

Throughout we assume that the foreign government follows a balanced-budget policy and that initially the domestic budget is balanced. This ensures that changes in world rates of interest that result from domestic fiscal deficits do not impact on the solvency of the foreign government and therefore do not necessitate secondary changes in fiscal policies.

Figure 8.1 shows the equilibrium of the system. In panel I the *PP* schedule describes combinations of R and C_0 that maintain equilibrium in the market for *present* goods. It is positively sloped since, as seen from equation (8.8), a fall in the rate of interest raises foreign wealth and induces a rise in foreign spending on present goods; therefore domestic consumption must fall in order to induce an offsetting reduction in demand. The *FF*

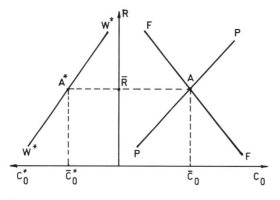

Figure 8.1
Equilibrium consumption and the rate of interest in the world economy

schedule describes combinations of R and C_0 that maintain equilibrium in the market for *future* goods. Its slope is negative since a fall in R creates an excess supply of world future output which is eliminated by an offsetting rise in demand induced by a rise in domestic wealth that is associated with the rise in C_0. Panel II of figure 8.1 portrays the negatively sloped W^*W^* schedule describing the equilibrium relationship between R and C_0^* as implied by the foreign consumption function and by the negative dependence of W^* on R (from equation 8.3). The equilibrium is described by points A and A^* at which the values of the variables are $\bar{C}_0$, $\bar{C}_0^*$, and $\bar{R}$.

8.2 Effects of Current Budget Deficits

In this section we analyze the effects of budget deficits on the world rates of interest and on the levels of domestic and foreign private-sector spending. To focus on the impact of deficits rather than the impact of government spending, we assume that the deficits result from changes in taxes and that the path of government spending is given. Since government spending remains unchanged, solvency requires that current changes in taxes be accompanied by offsetting changes in future taxes. The present value of these tax changes must equal each other. The initial balance in the domestic budget ensures (from equation 8.6) that a change in current taxes, dT_0, must be related to the future change, dT, according to

$$dT_0 = -\frac{1}{R-1}dT, \tag{8.10}$$

where $1/(R-1) = 1/r$ is the annuity value of a unit tax change com-

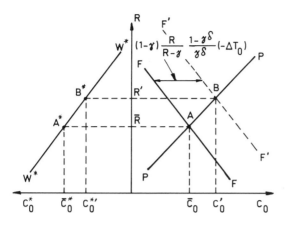

Figure 8.2
The effects of a current budget deficit

mencing from period $t = 1$ and evaluated in period $t = 0$. The rate of interest used in computing this annuity value is the constancy-equivalent rate of interest.

Figure 8.2 is used to determine the effects of a budget deficit. A deficit induced by a current tax cut of $-\Delta T_0$ necessitates (as long as government spending remains unchanged) a corresponding rise in future taxes by $(R - 1)\Delta T_0$ according to equation (8.10). These tax changes do not impact on the PP schedule, but as seen from equation (8.9), they induce a fall in demand for future goods. To restore equilibrium at the given rate of interest, W_0 must rise so as to raise demand for future goods. Associated with such a rise in wealth is a rise in current consumption C_0. Thus the FF schedule shifts to the right by $(1 - \gamma)R(1 - \gamma\delta)/[\gamma\delta(R - \gamma)]\Delta T_0$. As a result the new equilibrium is reached at points B and B^* and $C_0' > \bar{C}_0$, $R' > \bar{R}$, and $C_0^{*\prime} < \bar{C}_0^*$.

Thus a budget deficit arising from a reduction in domestic taxes raises the world interest rate. Likewise, the domestic budget deficit raises the equilibrium value of domestic consumption, C_0, and lowers the corresponding value of foreign consumption, C_0^*. It follows that domestic budget deficits are transmitted *negatively* to the rest of the world. The international transmission mechanism is effected through the rate of interest. The rise in the world interest rate lowers foreign wealth and mitigates the initial rise in domestic wealth. These changes in wealth raise domestic spending, lower foreign spending, and worsen the domestic current account of the balance of payments. In the present context the direction of the international transmission is measured in terms of the comovements of current levels of domestic and foreign spending. It is relevant to note, however, that the level of current spending may not be a sufficient indicator for welfare changes.

As may be seen, if the probability of survival, γ, is unity, then budget deficits do not alter interest rates and consumption. In that case the model yields the familiar Ricardian proposition according to which the timing of taxes, and thereby the timing of deficits, do not influence the real equilibrium of the system as long as the path of government spending remains intact. In terms of figure 8.2, in that case the FF schedule does not shifts in response to such tax changes. In the general case, however, with $\gamma < 1$, budget deficits exert real effects.

8.3 Effects of Current and Future Government Spending

The diagrammatic apparatus developed in the previous section can also be applied to illustrate the effects of government spending. In order to focus on the effect of changes in the level of government spending rather than on the effects of budget deficits, we assume (as in earlier chapters) that government budgets are balanced. The basic mechanism through which balanced-budget changes in government spending influence the economy do not depend, of course, on whether or not the model conforms with the Ricardian equivalence proposition. Accordingly, the results illustrated in this section are similar to those shown in chapter 5. These results are repeated here as a useful application of the diagrammatic apparatus.

Anticipating the results we recall from chapter 5 that, in general, the effects of balanced-budget changes in government spending on private-sector spending and on the world rate of interest depend on the comparison between the time pattern of government spending, as reflected by its saving propensity and the time pattern of domestic private-sector spending, as reflected by its saving propensity. Specifically, if the saving propensity of the government, γ_s^g, exceeds the private-sector saving propensity, γ_s, then a rise in the discounted sum of government spending creates an excess demand for future goods and necessitates a fall in the rate of interest, and vice versa. In the present case the government saving propensity is the fraction of the discounted sum of government spending that falls on future goods. That is,

$$\gamma_s^g = \frac{G/(R-1)}{G_0 + G/(R-1)}. \tag{8.11}$$

Likewise, the corresponding private-sector-saving propensity, γ_s, is the fraction of the discounted sum of private-sector spending that falls on future goods. Using the terms pertaining to domestic private-sector spending from equations (8.4) and (8.5), we obtain

$$\gamma_s = \frac{\gamma\delta W_0 + [(1 - \gamma)R]/[(R - 1)(R - \gamma)](Y - T)}{W_0 + [(1 - \gamma)R]/[(R - 1)(R - \gamma)](Y - T)}. \tag{8.12}$$

The expression in (8.11) and (8.12) define the average saving propensities, while our general principle is stated in terms of a comparison between the *marginal* saving propensities. If, however, the initial levels of debt, government spending, and taxes are zero, if the initial path of output is stationary and if the government maintains balanced budgets then the average and the marginal propensities are equal to each other. In the following exposition we identify the expressions in equations (8.11) and (8.12) with the corresponding marginal saving propensities.

The implications of this general principle are illustrated in figure 8.3 where we analyze the effects of alternative time patterns of government spending. In figure 8.3 the initial equilibrium obtains at points A and A^* at which the levels of domestic and foreign consumption are $\bar{C}_0$ and $\bar{C}_0^*$ and the rate of interest is indicated by $\bar{R}_0$. A transitory balanced-budget rise in *current* government spending of ΔG_0 creates an excess demand for present goods and necessitates a corresponding fall in private-sector spending. As

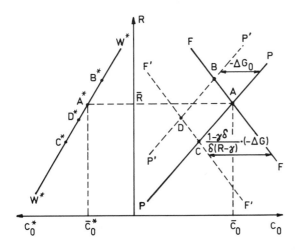

Figure 8.3
The effects of current, future, and permanent government spending on domestic and foreign consumption and the world rate of interest.

implied by equation (8.8), the PP schedule shifts to the left by ΔG_0 to $P'P'$, and the new equilibrium obtains at points B and B^*. In that case the equilibrium world rate of interest rises and the levels of domestic and foreign private-sector consumption fall. This result conforms with the general principle since, as seen from equations (8.11) and (8.12), with a transitory rise in current government spending, the saving propensity of the government, γ_s^g, is zero while the corresponding propensity of the domestic private sector is positive.

Consider next a transitory balanced-budget rise in *future* government spending by ΔG. Such a rise creates an excess demand for future goods and necessitates a corresponding fall in private-sector demand for future goods. Such a reduction results from a decline in wealth that also induces (for any given rate of interest) a corresponding reduction in C_0. As implied by equation (8.9), the FF schedule shifts to the left by $(1 - \gamma\delta)/[\delta(R - \gamma)]\Delta G$ to the position indicated by $F'F'$. The new equilibrium obtains at points C and C^*. In that case the equilibrium world rate of interest falls, domestic private-sector consumption falls, and foreign consumption rises. This result also illustrates the general principle since, as seen from equations (8.11) and (8.12), with a transitory rise in future government spending, γ_s^g is unity while γ_s is smaller than unity.

The foregoing analysis provides the ingredients necessary for determining the effects of a *permanent* balanced-budget rise in government spending. Such a rise in government spending (with $\Delta G_0 = \Delta G$) raises demand for *both* present and future goods and shifts both schedules in figure 8.3 leftward. The impact on the rate of interest depends on the *relative* excess demands in both markets. Diagrammatically, the difference between the horizontal leftward shifts of the PP and the FF schedules is $(\delta R - 1)/[\delta(R - \gamma)]\Delta G$. Accordingly, if δR falls short of unity, then the leftward shift of the FF schedule exceeds that of the PP schedule. This situation is shown in figure 8.3 where the new equilibrium obtains at point D and D^*. At this equilibrium the world rate of interest falls, and domestic private-sector consumption falls while foreign consumption rises. If, on the other hand, δR exceeds unity, then the leftward shift of the PP schedule exceeds that of the FF schedule. In that case the world rate of interest rises and the levels of domestic and foreign private-sector consumption fall.

In interpreting these results, we note that if δR exceeds unity, then the desired level of consumption by individuals in the domestic economy rises over time. In and of itself this contributes to a surplus in the current account of the domestic balance of payments during the early periods. Of course the counterpart to this surplus is a corresponding deficit in the foreign current account of the balance of payments. Thus, if $\delta R > 1$, then (at the margin) the domestic economy is a net saver in the world economy and the permanent rise in government spending raises the world rate of interest. The opposite holds if the domestic economy is a net dissaver in the world economy, that is, if δR falls short of unity.

The dependence of the interest-rate effects of a permanent rise in government spending on whether δR exceeds or falls short of unity conforms with the general principle expressed in terms of a comparison between the domestic private- and public-sector-saving propensities. To verify this conformity, we substitute equation (8.2) for W_0 into equation (8.12); assuming the absence of initial debt as well as balanced budgets and stationary paths of output and government spending, it can be shown that γ_s^g exceeds or falls short of γ_s according to whether δR falls short or exceeds unity.

To gain further insights, we apply the relative demand—relative supply diagrammatic apparatus of chapter 5 to determine the effects of balanced-budget changes in government spending on the rates of growth of domestic and foreign per-capita consumption. Since the qualitative effects of the analysis do not depend on whether the survival probability is unity or not, we assume that the value of γ is unity so that individuals have an infinite horizon. This assumption permits the use of this diagrammatic device.

Figure 8.4 shows the domestic (D), the foreign (D^*), and the world (D^w) relative demand schedules as functions of the rate of interest. In the figure,

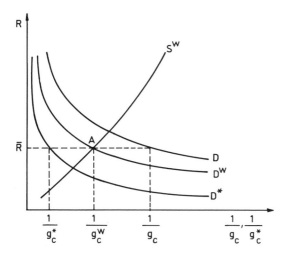

Figure 8.4
Government spending: Domestic, foreign, and world growth rates of consumption, and the world rate of interest

g_c, g_c^*, and g_c^w denote the ratios of the discounted sum (as of period one) of future consumption to current consumption of the domestic, the foreign, and the world private sector, respectively. These magnitudes are indicators of the corresponding growth rates of consumption. The model contained in equations (8.1) through (8.5) implies that if $\gamma = 1$ then $g_c = \delta R$ and $g_c^* = \delta^* R$. Hence in the present case the downward-sloping relative demand schedules are rectangular hyperbolas. As in the previous chapters, the D^w schedule is a weighted average of D and D^*. Accordingly,

$$\frac{1}{g_c^w} = \mu \frac{1}{g_c} + (1 - \mu)\frac{1}{g_c^*}, \tag{8.13}$$

where μ is the fraction of the discounted sum of future domestic consumption in the discounted sum of world future output net of government spending.

The S^w schedule in figure 8.4 portrays the ratio of current to (the discounted sum of) future world output net of government spending. This schedule is positively sloped since a rise in the rate of interest lowers the discounted sum of future outputs. The initial equilibrium is shown by point A at which the world relative demand equals the corresponding supply. At this point the equilibrium rate of interest is indicated by $\bar{R}$, and the relative world consumption is indicated by $1/g_c^w$. Associated with this rate of interest, the corresponding values of domestic and foreign relative consumption are indicated by $1/g_c$ and $1/g_c^*$, respectively.

A transitory balanced-budget rise in current government spending lowers the relative supply and induces a leftward displacement of the S schedule. Further the rise in taxes that is necessary to balance the budget lowers private-sector consumption and, as indicated by equation (8.13), reduces the weight of the domestic relative demand in the world relative demand. This induces a displacement of the D^w schedule toward the foreign schedule D^* (whose relative weight has risen). The case shown in figure 8.4 corresponds to the situation in which $\delta < \delta^*$ so that the domestic saving propensity falls short of the foreign one. In that case the domestic schedule D lies to the right of D^*, and the rise in the domestic government spending induces a leftward displacement of the D^w schedule. Specifically, if the relative supply schedule shifts leftward by 1 percent, then the world relative demand schedule shifts leftward by only μ percent. As a result the equilibrium rate of interest rises, and the growth rates of consumption in both countries rise. The same qualitative results apply to the situation in which the saving-propensities condition is reversed so that $\delta > \delta^*$. In that case the D schedule lies to the left of the D^* schedule and the rise in the domestic government induces a right-ward shift of the D^w schedule. In that case the rate of interest rises to a larger extent.

A similar analysis applies to the effects of a transitory rise in future government spending. In that case the relative supply schedule shifts to the right, and as before, the world relative demand schedule shifts to a position closer to that of the foreign relative demand schedule. The new equilibrium is associated with a lower rate of interest and a higher growth rate of domestic and foreign consumption. These qualitative results are independent of the relative magnitudes of δ and δ^* since even if the relative world demand shifts in the same direction as the supply, the proportional horizontal displacement of the S schedule, exceeds the corresponding displacement of the D^w schedule.

Finally, a permanent rise in government spending that does not alter the relative share of government spending in world GDP leaves the S schedule intact and displaces the D^w schedule toward the foreign schedule D^*. Hence, if δ exceeds δ^*, the world relative demand schedule shifts to the right, the rate of interest rises, and the growth rates of consumption fall. The opposite holds for the case in which δ falls short of δ^*. Since the equilibrium value of $1/R$ lies in between δ and δ^*, it is evident that the dependence of the effects of a permanent rise in government spending on the saving-propensities condition (i.e., on whether δ exceeds or falls short of δ^*) can be expressed equivalently in terms of whether δR exceeds or falls short of unity. Indeed, the previous analysis in this section was cast in terms of the latter condition.

8.4   Effects of Past Government Spending

We proceed with the exposition in this chapter by applying the diagrammatic apparatus to the analysis of the effects of past balanced-budget rises in government spending. Other things equal, the higher level of past transitory government spending was associated with a worsened past current-account position. Therefore, from the perspective of the current generations, the higher level of past government spending is reflected in a larger size of the initial external debt.

To analyze the effect of the size of the initial external debt position, consider a redistribution of world debt from the home country to the rest of the world. Suppose that this transfer is represented by increasing $(1 + r_{-1})B_{-1}$ by ΔB. This redistribution of world debt lowers domestic demand for both present and future goods and induces a corresponding rise in foreign demand. From equation (8.8) it is seen that the PP schedule

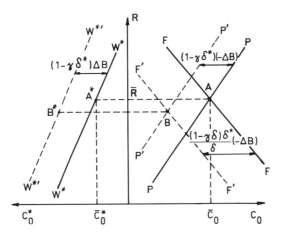

Figure 8.5
Changes in external debt, domestic and foreign consumption, and the world rate of interest

shifts to the left by $(1 - \gamma\delta^*)\Delta B$, and from equaton (8.9) it is seen that the
FF schedule shifts to the left by $(1 - \gamma\delta)(\delta^*/\delta)\Delta B$. From equation (8.3) and
the foreign consumption function the transfer also shifts the W^*W^* sched-
ule to the left by $(1 - \gamma\delta^*)\Delta B$. As a result the equilibrium of the system
shifts from points A and A^* to points B and B^*.

The effect of the transfer on the new equilibrium rate of interest reflects
the usual considerations underlying the transfer-problem criterion. In terms
of figure 8.5 the rate of interest falls if the horizontal displacement of the
FF schedule exceeds the corresponding displacement of the *PP* schedule,
and vice versa. As can be seen, the difference between the horizontal shifts
of the *FF* and the *PP* schedules is proportional to $(\delta^* - \delta)/\delta$. If the saving-
propensities condition is such that $\delta < \delta^*$, then the transfer raises world
savings and necessitates a fall in the rate of interest so as to restore the
initial level of world savings. This is the case illustrated in figure 8.5. If,
however, $\delta > \delta^*$, then the transfer lowers world savings and induces a rise
in the world rate of interest. In general, independent of the direction of
the change in the rate of interest, the redistribution of world debt in favor
of the foreign country lowers domestic consumption and raises foreign
consumption.

8.5   Welfare Aspects

The analysis in the preceding sections indicated the effects of fiscal
policies on interest rates and wealth. Knowledge of these effects was

sufficient for determining the impact of policies on the paths of aggregate consumption which, in turn, govern the evolution of the key economic variables in the world economy. It is obvious, however, that because of the structure of the overlapping-generations model, the analysis of *normative* questions is much more complex. Specifically, it is evident that the welfare effects of fiscal policies cannot be inferred from knowledge of the resulting changes in aggregate private wealth. In the first place changes in intertemporal prices (rates of interest) also impact on the level of welfare in addition to their effects on wealth. More important, complexities arise from the fact that not all generations share equally in the benefits of tax cuts and in the burdens of tax levies. Furthermore, in designing optimal fiscal policies, one needs to define a social welfare function. This raises the conceptual issues concerning the proper weighting of current and prospective generations in the social welfare function and the possible implication for the time consistency of government policies.

In this section we illustrate some of these issues by examining the effects of a current budget deficit on the welfare of the population existing in the period of the tax cut. It is convenient to focus the analysis on the individual born in the period of the tax cut, but since the survival probability is the same for all individuals, the direction of the change in welfare is the same for everyone else who is alive during the period of the tax cut. Therefore the qualitative results apply to the entire population that is alive during the period of the deficit. Recalling that each individual is born with no debt and that therefore his wealth consists of the properly discounted value of lifetime disposable income, the per-capita wealth is

$$w_0 = (Y_0 - T_0) + \frac{\gamma}{R - \gamma}(Y - T). \tag{8.14}$$

With the assumed logarithmic utility function, the individual's expected utility is given by

$$\sum_{t=0}^{\infty} (\gamma\delta)^t \log c_t, \tag{8.15}$$

and correspondingly, his consumption (computed with the aid of the constancy-equivalent interest rate) is

$$c_t = (1 - \gamma\delta)(\delta R)^t w_0. \tag{8.16}$$

Using these expressions, it can be shown that the individual's *indirect* expected utility, v, is represented by

$$v = \log \frac{w_0}{R^{-\gamma\delta/(1-\gamma\delta)}} = \log \left[\frac{(Y_0 - T_0) + \gamma/(R - \gamma)(Y - T)}{R^{-\gamma\delta/(1-\gamma\delta)}} \right], \qquad (8.17)$$

where the second equality follows from equation (8.14) and $R^{-\gamma\delta/(1-\gamma\delta)}$ is
the real-wealth deflator which is the intertemporal price index (in terms of
current consumption) appropriate for evaluating the real value of wealth.
Thus, utility is a function of *real* wealth. As seen in equation (8.17), current
budget deficits impact on the level of utility directly through the effects of
the reduction in T_0 and the accompanying rise in T and, indirectly through
the effect of changes in the rate of interest. The latter in turn operates
through its impact on the present value of future disposable income and on
the intertemporal price index. As is evident, in the extreme case with
$\gamma = 1$, the direct effects induced by the changes in current and future taxes
offset each other (since $dT_0 + dT/[R - 1] = 0$), and since with $\gamma = 1$ the
rate of interest does not change, the indirect effect of the tax shift is also
zero. Obviously, in that case a budget deficit does not impact on the
individual's utility level. In the other extreme for which γ is very small, the
individual is concerned mainly with his or her current level of income and
consumption and therefore changes in the rate of interest exert small effects
on his welfare. In that case the weight, $\gamma\delta/(1 - \gamma\delta)$, of future prices in the
real-wealth deflator as well as the weight of future disposable income in w_0
are small, and therefore a current tax cut raises welfare. In general, since the
budget deficit raises both the value of wealth and the rate of interest (as
shown formally in the appendix), it follows that it raises the level of welfare
of the existing population. The preceding analysis examined the impact of
current budget deficits on the level of welfare of the existing population.
Of course the future rise in taxes and the associated changes in the rates of
interest also impact on the utility level of the yet unborn generations.

Turning to the evaluation of foreign welfare, we note that the changes
in the rates of interest impact on the welfare of the existing foreign population according to whether the foreign country is a net saver or dissaver.
Thus, as far as the existing foreign population is concerned, the direction
of changes in their current wealth and consumption (which was emphasized
in our preceding positive analysis) is not the relevant indicator for welfare
changes. Therefore, in assessing whether the international transmission
mechanism is positive or negative, a distinction should be drawn between
positive measures of transmission expressed in terms of current consumption and wealth and normative measures expressed in terms of welfare.

In concluding this section, it is relevant to note that throughout the
discussion we have not inquired into the motives underlying the adaption

of a budget-deficit policy. In this context the possibility that the existing population gains from current deficits raises the question as to what factors limit the introduction of further tax cuts at the expense of future generations, and possibly at the expense of foreigners (if they are net borrowers). In general, considerations that may operate to limit current tax cuts include (1) governments that are also concerned with future generations' welfare, (2) the possibility that the welfare loss imposed on foreigners through the domestic tax cuts may stimulate retaliation and result in a costly "fiscal war," (3) the existence of an upper limit to the feasible rise in future taxes, (4) the existence of distortionary taxes and costly fiscal management that sets an upper limit to the benefits that current tax cuts yield to the future population, and (5) the possibility that a significant rise in debt introduces the probability of default and may raise the cost of external borrowing. In connection with this final consideration we recall that throughout the analysis individuals were assumed to be mortal, whereas government commitments were implicitly assumed to be immortal. In general, of course, the probability that governments and their commitments survive indefinitely is also less than unity. Under such circumstances the interest-rate differential on private and public sectors' loans, and thereby the impact of budget deficits, is governed by the relation between the default probabilities of individuals and government commitments. It is noteworthy, however, that allowing for the possibility that governments renege on their commitments (in the context of designing optimal policies) introduces to the analysis new dimensions associated with the issues of time-consistent policies.

8.6 Budget Deficits and Real Exchange Rates: The Two-Country World

In this section we extend the analysis to the two-country case. As in previous chapters such an extension illuminates the nature of the international transmission mechanism of tax policies. In our analysis we continue to assume that all taxes are nondistortionary. As a result the mechanism responsible for the real consequences of budget deficits operates through the wealth effects. We adopt the general features of the model outlined in section 8.1 but modify the classification of commodities so as to allow for the existence of nontradable goods at home and abroad. This extension introduces the domestic and foreign real exchange rates as key variables adjusting to the budget deficits. Thus, by emphasizing the wealth effects of tax policies, the present analysis supplements the one presented in chapter

11 in which due to distortionary taxes the intertemporal substitution effects were emphasized.

To simplify the exposition, we follow a similar procedure as in section 8.1 and divide the horizon into two: the current period and the future period. All quantities pertaining to the current period are indicated by a zero subscript, and the paths of the exogenous variables are assumed stationary across future periods.

Equilibrium necessitates that in the current period world output of tradable goods is demanded and the discounted sum of future outputs of tradable goods equals the discounted sums of future domestic and foreign demands. Likewise, in each country current and future period outputs of nontradable goods must be demanded. In what follows we outline the complete two-country model. The aggregate consumption functions at home and abroad are $Z_t = (1 - s)W_t$ and $Z_t^* = (1 - s^*)W_t^*$, where as before the propensities to save, s and s^*, are equal to $\gamma\delta$ and $\gamma\delta^*$ (where the survival probability, γ, is assumed to be equal across countries). Domestic and foreign wealth are defined as

$$W_0 = (\overline{Y}_{x0} + p_{n0}\overline{Y}_{n0} - T_0) + \frac{\gamma}{R - \gamma}(\overline{Y}_x + p_n\overline{Y}_n - T)$$

$$+ (1 + r_{x,-1})(B_{-1}^g - B_{-1}) \tag{8.18}$$

and

$$W_0^* = (\overline{Y}_{x0}^* + p_{n0}^*\overline{Y}_{n0}^* - T_0^*) + \frac{\gamma}{R - \gamma}(\overline{Y}_x^* + p_n^*\overline{Y}_n^* - T^*)$$

$$+ (1 + r_{x,-1})(B_{-1}^{*g} + B_{-1}). \tag{8.19}$$

As seen, equations (8.18) and (8.19) express wealth as the sum of the present values of current and future disposable incomes plus net asset positions. Also it is recalled that in these equations the term $\gamma/(R - \gamma)$ denotes the present value of an annuity (commencing at period $t = 1$) evaluated by using the discount factor relevant for private decision making, γ/R.

The market-clearing conditions for the domestic nontradable goods require that

$$\beta_n(1 - s)W_0 = p_{n0}[\overline{Y}_{n0} - \beta_n^g(1 - \gamma_s^g)G] \tag{8.20}$$

and

$$\beta_n \left[sW_0 + \frac{1-\gamma}{R-1} \frac{R}{R-\gamma} (\bar{Y}_x + p_n \bar{Y}_n - T) \right]$$

$$= \frac{1}{R-1} [p_n \bar{Y}_n - \beta_n^g \gamma_s^g G], \tag{8.21}$$

where, as before, G denotes the discounted sum of government spending and where β_n^g and γ_s^g indicate the government's temporal and intertemporal spending pattern. Equation (8.20) specifies the equilibrium condition in the current-period market, and question (8.21) states that the discounted sum of domestic demand for future nontradable goods equals the discounted sum of future supply net of government absorption.

Analogously, equations (8.22) and (8.23) describe the corresponding equilibrium conditions in the foreign markets for nontradable goods.

$$\beta_n^*(1 - s^*) W_0^* = p_{n0}^* \bar{Y}_{n0}^* - \beta_n^{*g}(1 - \gamma_s^{*g})G^* \tag{8.22}$$

and

$$\beta_n^* \left[s^* W_0^* + \frac{1-\gamma}{R-1} \frac{R}{R-\gamma} (\bar{Y}_x^* + p_n^* \bar{Y}_n^* - T^*) \right]$$

$$= \frac{1}{R-1} [p_n^* \bar{Y}_n^* - \beta_n^{*g} \gamma_s^{*g} G^*]. \tag{8.23}$$

Finally, the equilibrium conditions in the *world* market for tradable goods are specified in equations (8.24) and (8.25), where the first of the two pertains to the current period and the second pertains to the discounted sums of demand and supply in all future periods:

$$(1 - \beta_n)(1 - s)W_0 + (1 - \beta_n^*)(1 - s^*)W_0^*$$

$$= \bar{Y}_x - (1 - \beta_n^g)(1 - \gamma_s^g)G + \bar{Y}_x^* - (1 - \beta_n^{*g})(1 - \gamma_s^{*g})G^* \tag{8.24}$$

and

$$(1 - \beta_n) \left[sW_0 + \frac{1-\gamma}{R-1} \frac{R}{R-\gamma} (\bar{Y}_x + p_n \bar{Y}_n - T) \right]$$

$$+ (1 - \beta_n^*) \left[s^* W_0^* + \frac{1-\gamma}{R-1} \frac{R}{R-\gamma} (\bar{Y}_x^* + p_n^* \bar{Y}_n^* - T^*) \right]$$

$$= \frac{1}{R-1} [\bar{Y}_x - (1 - \beta_n^g)\gamma_s^g G + \bar{Y}_x^* - (1 - \beta_n^{*g})\gamma_s^{*g}G^*]. \tag{8.25}$$

The system of equations (8.18) through (8.25) can be solved for the equilibrium values of the domestic and foreign current-period wealth, W_0 and W_0^*, current and future prices of nontradable goods (the inverse of the corresponding real exchange rates), p_{n0}, p_{n0}^*, p_n, p_n^*, and for the world rate of interest, $R - 1$. As usual, the eight-equation system (8.18) through (8.25) is linearly dependent, and thus, by Walras's law, one of these equations can be left out. In what follows we leave out equation (8.18) specifying the equilibrium value of domestic wealth.

Analogously to our analysis in chapter 11, we can reduce the complete model to two basic equilibrium conditions. These conditions state that the world markets for tradable goods clear in both the current period as well as in the (consolidated) future period. These equations, derived explicitly in the appendix, are reduced-form equations—they incorporate the requirement that in each country and in all periods the markets for nontradable goods clear. Accordingly,

$$(1 - \beta_n)(1 - \gamma\delta)W_0 + (1 - \beta_n^*)(1 - \gamma\delta^*)W_0^* = \overline{Y}_x + \overline{Y}_x^*, \tag{8.26}$$

$$(1 - \beta_n)\left[\gamma\delta W_0 + \frac{(1 - \gamma)R}{(R - 1)(R - \gamma)} I(R, W_0, T) \right]$$

$$+ (1 - \beta_n^*)\left[\gamma\delta^* W_0^*(R) + \frac{(1 - \gamma)R}{(R - 1)(R - \gamma)} I^*(R) \right]$$

$$= \frac{1}{R - 1}(\overline{Y}_x + \overline{Y}_x^*), \tag{8.27}$$

where we replaced s and s^* by $\gamma\delta$ and $\gamma\delta^*$, respectively.

Equation (8.26) states that the sum of world private demand for current tradable goods equals world supply. In this equation $(1 - \beta_n)(1 - \gamma\delta)W_0$ is the home country's private demand, and $(1 - \beta_n^*)(1 - \gamma\delta^*)W_0^*$ is the corresponding foreign demand. The foreign wealth is expressed as a negative function of the rate of interest reflecting the role of the latter in discounting future incomes and in influencing the real exchange rate used to evaluate the income streams. It is noteworthy that this reduced-form functional dependence of wealth on the rate of interest is not shown explicitly for the domestic wealth since we have omitted the explicit domestic-wealth equation (8.18) by Walras's law. This choice makes the equilibrium determination of domestic wealth (along with the world rate of interest) the focus of the subsequent analysis.

The second reduced-form equation (8.27) states that the discounted sum of domestic and foreign demands for future tradable goods equals the discounted sum of future world supply. The first term is the product of the consumption share of tradable goods $(1 - \beta_n)$ and total domestic future consumption. The latter equals the sum of the savings of those alive in period zero, $\gamma\delta W_0$, and the discounted sum of the demand for future goods of those who will be born in the future and whose disposable income in each period is I. This reduced-form future disposable income (in terms of tradable goods) is expressed as a negative function of future taxes, T, and a positive function of the future relative price of nontradable goods. The latter in turn depends negatively on R (through its effect on future wealth of those yet unborn) and positively on W_0 (through its effect on the demand of those alive). An analogous interpretation applies to the foreign disposable income, I^*. The dependence of I^* on R only reflects the assumption that foreign taxes are zero and incorporates the negative dependence of W_0^* on R. Before proceeding, it is relevant to note that in the absence of nontradable goods, $\beta_n = \beta_n^* = 0$, $I(R, W_0, T) = Y - T$, $I^*(R) = Y^*$, $\overline{Y}_n = \overline{Y}_n^* = 0$, and $W^*(R) = Y^* + Y^*/(R - 1) + R(B_{-1}^g + B_{-1})$. Thus in this special case equations (8.26) and (8.27) reduce to equations (8.8) and (8.9).

Equations (8.26) and (8.27) yield the equilibrium values of the home country's initial wealth, W_0, and the world rate of interest, $r_x = R - 1$, for any given values of the parameters. In equilibrium the demand for nontradable goods $\beta_n(1 - \gamma\delta)W_0$ equals the value of the supply, $p_{n0}\overline{Y}_n$. Hence the equilibrium price (the inverse of the real exchange rate) is

$$p_{n0} = \frac{\beta_n(1 - \gamma\delta)W_0}{\overline{Y}_n}. \tag{8.28}$$

The equilibrium of the system is analyzed by means of figure 8.6. The PP schedule drawn in panel I of figure 8.6 shows combinations of r_x and p_{n0} that clear the market for present tradable goods. It is positively sloped since a rise in the rate of interest lowers foreign demand (by lowering W_0^*), and a rise in p_{n0} raises domestic demand (by raising W_0). The future tradable-goods market clears along the FF schedule. This schedule is negatively sloped since a rise in the rate of interest creates an excess demand for future tradable goods which must be offset by a fall in W_0 (and therefore p_{n0}). Panel II of the figure shows the negative relation between the equilibrium rate of interest and the foreign relative price of nontradable goods. This relation is based on equation (8.29) which is the foreign-country analogue to equation (8.28):

$$p_{n0}^* = \frac{\beta_n^*(1 - \gamma\delta^*)}{\overline{Y}_n} W_0^*(R). \tag{8.29}$$

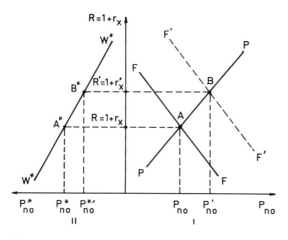

Figure 8.6
Budget deficits, the real exchange rate, and the real rate of interest

The equilibrium of the system is shown by point A in panel I and point A^* in panel II of figure 8.6. Accordingly, the current equilibrium relative price of domestic tradable goods is p_{no}, the foreign equilibrium relative price is p_{no}^*, and the corresponding equilibrium rate of interest is r_x. In what follows we analyze the effects of a domestic budget deficit on the world rate of interest and on the equilibrium real exchange rates. The formal derivations of the results are contained in the appendix.

A domestic budget deficit arising from a current tax cut necessitates a corresponding rise in future taxes, T. As seen from equation (8.27), the rise in future taxes lowers future domestic disposable income, I, and thereby lowers the demand for future goods. For a given world rate of interest the fall in demand can be eliminated by a rise in W_0. As implied by equation (8.28) the rise in W_0 is associated with a rise in p_{no}. Thus the FF schedule shifts to the right to F'F'. As is evident the horizontal shifts of the FF schedule is proportional to $(1 - \gamma)$; if $\gamma = 1$ the position of the schedule as well as the characteristics of the initial equilibrium remain intact (the Ricardian equivalence case). In general, as indicated in panel I, the new equilibrium obtains at point B with a *higher rate of interest, a higher domestic relative price of nontradable goods, p_{no}, and a higher level of domestic wealth and consumption. The new equilibrium is indicated in panel II by point B^*, where it is seen that the higher rate of interest lowers foreign wealth and consumption and reduces the foreign relative price of nontradable goods.* Thus on the basis of the correlations between domestic and foreign private-sector spending and between domestic and foreign real exchange rate, *the international transmission of the budget deficit is negative.* As an interpretation we note that the wealth effects induced by the domestic budget deficit creates an excess demand for present tradable goods resulting in a rise in their *intertemporal* relative price—the rate of interest. Likewise, it creates an excess demand for domestic nontradable goods and an excess supply of foreign nontradable goods. These excess demands and supplies alter the *temporal* relative price of these goods—the real exchange rates.

8.7   Summary

In this chapter we provided an exposition of the two-country overlapping-generations models of the world economy. We developed a simple diagrammatic exposition of the model by focusing on the markets for present and future goods. To reduce the high dimensionality of the model, we have constructed a composite of future goods and defined the concept of a constancy-equivalent rate of interest used in the definition of this composite good. This procedure facilitated the exposition and simplified the analysis considerably without loss of pertinent information.

The diagrammatic apparatus was applied to the analysis of the effects of current budget deficits and to the effects of various time patterns of balanced-budget changes in government spending. In this context we focused on the effects of these fiscal policies on the world rate of interest and on the levels and growth rates of domestic and foreign private-sector spending.

The diagrammatic exposition provided in this chapter illustrates the general principles of the various transfer-problem criteria developed in previous chapters. It illustrates that the interest-rate effects of various time patterns of government spending can be determined by simple comparison between the properly defined marginal saving propensities of the domestic private and public sectors. Likewise, the effects of changes in the time profile of taxes are interpreted in terms of a comparison between the marginal spending propensities of current and future generations. Finally, the effects of a redistribution of world debt arising from past balanced-budget changes in government spending depend on the relative magnitudes of the marginal saving propensities of domestic and foreign residents.

We followed the exposition with a brief analysis of welfare implications of budget deficits. This discussion was cast in terms of the effects of budget deficits on wealth and on the wealth deflator. It was shown that the budget deficit raises the level of welfare of the existing domestic population. The welfare of the foreign population rises if the foreign economy is a net saver in the world economy, and vice versa. We also outlined some of the checks that may limit the incentives for the adoption of budget deficits.

We concluded the exposition with an analysis of the consequences of budget deficits on the real exchange rate operating through the mechanism of the pure wealth effect. To focus on this mechanism rather than the mechanism of substitution effects, we assumed that all taxes are non-distortionary. In that case the finiteness of the horizon implies that budget deficits induce a positive wealth effect.

Our analysis of the two-country case focused on the consequences of budget deficits on the domestic and the foreign real exchange rates. In this case the international transmission mechanism operates through the effects of the budget deficit on the world rate of interest. Accordingly, the wealth effect induced by the budget deficit raises the domestic demand for present-period goods, and thereby lowers the domestic real exchange rate and raises the world rate of interest. This rise transmits the effects of the domestic deficit to the rest of the world: it lowers foreign spending and raises the foreign real exchange rate. Accordingly, the budget deficit induces negative cross-country correlations between the levels of private-sector spending as well as between the real exchange rates.

The pattern of the cross-country correlations between real exchange rates and the effects of budget deficits on the world rate of interest reflect the mechanism of the pure wealth effect set in place in the absence of distortionary taxes. These results should be contrasted with those obtained in chapter 11 where it was shown that with distortionary taxes the effects of budget deficits depend on the specific taxes that are altered. In this context we also note that the interest-rate and real exchange-rate effects of a balanced-budget rise in government spending (analyzed in chapter 11) carry over to the infinite-horizon model used here.

Finally, the analysis can be reinterpreted by viewing leisure as the nontradable good and the real wage as the reciprocal of the real exchange rate. With such a reinterpretation the analysis in this chapter yields insights into the effects of budget deficits on real-wage dynamics, and on cross-country correlations of real wages.

8.8   Appendix

The Time-Aggregation Procedure

The aggregation procedure and the use of the constancy-equivalent rate of interest which underlie equations (8.2) through (8.5) is justified as follows.

From equation (7.14) and its foreign-country counterpart, the market-clear-ing condition for period $t = 0$ is shown in equation (A.1) and the corresponding definitions of wealth are shown in equations (A.2) and (A.3). Thus

$$(1 - s_0)W_0 + (1 - s_0^*)W_0^* = (Y_0 - G_0) + (Y_0^* - G_0^*), \tag{A.1}$$

$$W_0 = \sum_{t=0}^{\infty} \gamma^t \alpha_t (Y_t - T_t) + (1 + r_{-1})(B_{-1}^g - B_{-1}), \tag{A.2}$$

$$W_0^* = \sum_{t=0}^{\infty} (\gamma^*)^t \alpha_t (Y_t^* - T_t^*) + (1 + r_{-1})(B_{-1}^{g*} + B_{-1}), \tag{A.3}$$

where

$$s_0 = 1 - \left\{ \sum_{t=0}^{\infty} (\gamma^t \alpha_t)^{1-\sigma}[(\gamma\delta)^t]^\sigma \right\}^{-1},$$

$$s_0^* = 1 - \left\{ \sum_{t=0}^{\infty} [(\gamma^*)^t \alpha_t]^{1-\sigma^*}[(\gamma^*\delta^*)^t]^{\sigma^*} \right\}^{-1}.$$

The value of s_0 is taken from equation (7.9), and s_0^* is the corresponding foreign-country counterpart.

Under the conditions that $Y_t - T_t = Y - T$, $Y_t^* - T_t^* = Y^* - T^*$ (for $t = 1, 2, \ldots$), $\sigma = \sigma^* = 1$, and $\gamma = \gamma^*$, equations (A.1) through (A.3) can be solved for the equilibrium values of W_0, W_0^*, and $\sum_{t=1}^{\infty} \gamma^t \alpha_t$. In the text we define $\sum_{t=1}^{\infty} \gamma^t \alpha_t$ by $\gamma/(R - \gamma)$, where $r = R - 1$ is the constancy-equivalent rate of interest. With these substitution equations (A.1) through (A.3) become equations (8.2) through (11.4).

It can be readily verified that adding equation (8.5) to the system (8.2) through (8.4) yields a linearly dependent system of equations. Therefore, as a manifestation of Walras's law the *equilibrium* values of W_0, W_0^*, and R can be solved from any subset of three equations from the four-equation system.

The Impact of Budget Deficits

In this part of the appendix we consider the impact of current budget deficits. The quantitative impacts of changes in domestic taxes on R, W_0, and W_0^*, (evaluated around an initial balanced budget and initial stationary paths of output, taxes, and government spending) can be obtained from any three equations of the system (8.2) through (8.5) along with the implications of the government budget constraint (8.10). These changes are

$$\frac{dW_0}{dT_0} = -(1 - \gamma)(1 - \gamma\delta^*)\lambda^* \frac{R^2}{(R - \gamma)^2} < 0, \tag{A.4}$$

$$\frac{dW_0^*}{dT_0} = (1 - \gamma)(1 - \gamma\delta)\lambda^* \frac{R^2}{(R - \gamma)^2} > 0, \tag{A.5}$$

$$\frac{dR}{dT_0} = -(1 - \gamma)\frac{(1 - \gamma\delta)\lambda^* R^2}{\gamma(Y^* - G^*)} < 0, \tag{A.6}$$

where λ^* is the relative share of foreign output net of government spending in the corresponding world quantity; that is,

$$\lambda^* = \frac{Y^* - G^*}{Y - G + Y^* - G^*},$$

and where use has been made of the market-clearing condition by which

$$(1 - \gamma\delta)\frac{R}{R - \gamma}(Y - T) + (1 - \gamma\delta^*)\frac{R}{R - \gamma}(Y - T)$$

$$= Y - G + Y^* - G^*.$$

Thus a current budget deficit arising from a reduction of domestic taxes ($dT_0 < 0$) raises the rate of interest and domstic wealth and lowers foreign wealth. Multiplying these changes in wealth by the propensities to consume, $(1 - \gamma\delta)$ and $(1 - \gamma\delta^*)$, yields the corresponding changes in domestic and foreign consumption. These changes vanish if $\gamma = 1$.

In this part of the appendix we first derive the reduced-form equations (8.26) and (8.27). Throughout we omit equation (8.18) by Walras's law. Using equations (8.21) and (8.23) and solving for the future values of production of nontradable goods yields

$$p_n \overline{Y}_n = A[(R - 1)sW_0 + \frac{(1 - \gamma)R}{R - \gamma}(\overline{Y}_x - T)], \tag{A.7}$$

$$p_n^* \overline{Y}_n^* = A^*[(R - 1)s^*W_0^* + \frac{(1 - \gamma)R}{R - \gamma}(\overline{Y}_x^* - T^*)], \tag{A.8}$$

where

$$\theta = \frac{\beta_n^g \gamma_s^g G}{p_n \overline{Y}_n}, \qquad \theta^* = \frac{\beta_n^* \gamma_s^{*g} G^*}{p_n^* \overline{Y}_n^*}$$

$$A = \frac{\beta_n}{(1 - \theta) - \beta_n(1 - \gamma)R/(R - \gamma)},$$

$$A^* = \frac{\beta_n^*}{(1 - \theta^*) - \beta_n^*(1 - \gamma)R/(R - \gamma)}.$$

The requirement that in equilibrium there is positive consumption of non-tradable goods that command a positive price imposes the feasibility condition according to which

$$A \geqslant 0, \quad A^* \geqslant 0. \tag{A.9}$$

Substituting (A.8) and equation (8.22) into equation (8.29) yields

$$W_0^* = D^*\left[\bar{Y}_x^* - T_0^* + \frac{\gamma}{R - \gamma}\left(1 + A^*\frac{(1 - \gamma)R}{R - \gamma}\right)(\bar{Y}_x^* - T^*)\right.$$

$$\left. + (1 + r_{x,-1})(B_{-1}^{*g} + B_{-1})\right], \tag{A.10}$$

where

$$D^* = (1 - \theta^*)\left\{(1 - \theta^*)\right.$$

$$\left. - \beta_n^*\left[\frac{(R - 1)\gamma s^*}{(1 - \theta^*)(R - \gamma) - \beta_n^*(1 - \gamma)R} + \frac{1 - s^*}{1 - \theta^*}\right]\right\}^{-1}.$$

The requirement that in equilibrium wealth is positive imposes the additional feasibility constraint according to which

$$D^* \geqslant 0.$$

Substituting equation (A.10) into equation (8.24) yields

$$(1 - \beta_n)(1 - s)W_0 + (1 - \beta_n^*)D^*\left\{\bar{Y}_x^* - T_0^*\right.$$

$$+ \frac{\gamma}{R - \gamma}\left[1 + A^*\frac{(1 - \gamma)R}{R - \gamma}\right](\bar{Y}_x^* - T^*)$$

$$\left. + (1 + r_{x,-1})(B_{-1}^{*g} + B_{-1})\right\}$$

$$= \bar{Y}_x - (1 - \beta_n^g)(1 - \gamma_s^g)G + \bar{Y}_x^* - (1 - \beta_n^{*g})(1 - \gamma_s^{*g})G^*. \tag{A.12}$$

Substituting equations (A.7) and (A.8) for $p_n\bar{Y}_n$ and $p_n^*\bar{Y}_n^*$ into equation (8.25) yields

$$(1 - \beta_n) \left[sW_0 + \frac{(1 - \gamma)R}{(R - 1)(R - \gamma)} \right.$$

$$\times \left\{ A(R - 1)sW_0 + \left[1 + A\frac{(1 - \gamma)R}{R - \gamma} \right](\bar{Y}_x - T) \right\} \right]$$

$$+ (1 - \beta_n^*) \left[s^*W_0^* + \frac{(1 - \gamma)R}{(R - 1)(R - \gamma)} \right.$$

$$\times \left\{ A^*(R - 1)s^*W_0^* + \left[1 + A^*\frac{(1 - \gamma)R}{R - \gamma} \right](\bar{Y}_x^* - T^*) \right\} \right]$$

$$= \frac{1}{R - 1} [\bar{Y}_x - (1 - \beta_n^g)\gamma_s^g G + \bar{Y}_x^* - (1 - \beta_n^{*g})\gamma_s^{*g}G^*]. \tag{A.13}$$

The system of equations (A.10), (A.12), and (A.13) can be used to solve for the equilibrium values of W_0, W_0^*, and R.

To derive the more compact formulation of the reduced-form equilibrium conditions of the text, we focus on the role of domestic tax policy by assuming that $G = G^* = T^* = 0$. We first note that for a given value of the parameters the equilibrium value of foreign wealth shown in equation (A.10) can be expressed implicitly as

$$W_0^* = W_0^*(R), \quad \frac{\partial W_0^*}{\partial R} < 0. \tag{A.14}$$

Equation (A.14) expresses foreign current wealth as a negative function of the rate of interest. This reduced-form relationship incorporates the equilibrium conditions in the markets for current and future nontradable goods. The negative dependence on the rate of interest reflects the role of the rate of interest in discounting future incomes and in influencing the real exchange rates used to evaluate the income streams. Next we define the domestic and foreign reduced-form future disposable incomes

$$I(R, W_0, T) = (R - 1)A\gamma\delta W_0 + \left[1 + \frac{(1 - \gamma)RA}{R - \gamma} \right](\bar{Y}_x - T) \tag{A.15}$$

and

$$I^*(R) = (R - 1)A^*\gamma\delta^*W_0^*(R) + \left[1 + \frac{(1 - \gamma)RA^*}{R - \gamma} \right]\bar{Y}_x^*. \tag{A.16}$$

Equation (A.15) expresses disposable income (in terms of tradable goods) as a negative function of future taxes, T, and a positive function of the relative price of nontradable goods, p_n. The latter in turn depends negatively on R through its effect on future wealth of those yet unborn) and positively on W_0 (through its effect on the demand of those alive). An analogous interpretation applies to the foreign disposable income, I^*, where in (A.47) we incorporate the functional dependence of W_0^* on R and the assumption that foreign taxes are zero.

Substituting equations (A.15) and (A.16) into (A.12) and (A.13) together with the assumption that $G = G^* = T^* = 0$ yields

$$(1 - \beta_n)(1 - \gamma\delta)W_0 + (1 - \beta_n^*)(1 - \gamma\delta^*)W_0^*(R) = \bar{Y}_x + \bar{Y}_x^*, \tag{A.17}$$

$$(1 - \beta_n)\left[\gamma\delta W_0 + \frac{(1 - \gamma)R}{(R - 1)(R - \gamma)} I(R, W_0, T)\right]$$

$$+ (1 - \beta_n^*)\left[\gamma\delta^* W_0^*(R) + \frac{(1 - \gamma)R}{(R - 1)(R - \gamma)} I^*(R)\right]$$

$$= \frac{1}{R - 1}(\bar{Y}_x + \bar{Y}_x^*). \tag{A.18}$$

Equations (A.17) and (A.18) are the reduced-form equilibrium conditions (8.26) and (8.27). These equations underlied the diagrammatical analysis of the text.

We turn next to a more formal analysis of he comparative statics results reported in the text. For this purpose we return to the complete model outlined in equations (8.18) through (8.24), omitting equation (8.25) by Walras's law. We continue to assume that $G = G^* = T^* = 0$. Substituting (A.7) and equation (8.20) into equation (8.19) yields

$$W_0 = D\left\{\bar{Y}_x - T_0 + \frac{\gamma}{R - \gamma}\left[1 + A\frac{(1 - \gamma)R}{R - \gamma}\right](\bar{Y}_x - T)\right.$$

$$\left. + (1 + r_{x,-1})(B_{-1}^g - B_{-1})\right\}, \tag{A.19}$$

where

$$D = \left\{1 - \beta_n\left[\frac{(R - 1)\gamma^2\delta}{(R - \gamma) - \beta_n(1 - \gamma)R} + (1 - \gamma\delta)\right]\right\}^{-1}.$$

Likewise, with zero foreign government spending and taxes equation (A.10) becomes

$$W_0^* = D^* \left\{ \overline{Y}_x^* + \frac{\gamma}{R - \gamma} \left[1 + A^* \frac{(1 - \gamma)R}{R - \gamma} \right] \overline{Y}_x^* \right.$$

$$\left. + 1(+ r_{x,-1})(B_{-1}^{*g} + B_{-1}) \right\}, \tag{A.20}$$

where

$$D^* = \left\{ 1 - \beta_n^* \left[\frac{(R - 1)\gamma^2 \delta^*}{(R - \gamma) - \beta_n^*(1 - \gamma)R} + (1 - \gamma\delta^*) \right] \right\}^{-1},$$

and feasibility requires that $D \geqslant 0$ and $D^* \geqslant 0$. Finally, using equation (8.24), we get

$$(1 - \beta_n)(1 - \gamma\delta)W_0 + (1 - \beta_n^*)(1 - \gamma\delta^*)W_0^* = \overline{Y}_x + \overline{Y}_x^*. \tag{A.21}$$

The system of equations (A.19) through (A.21) solves for the equilibrium values of W_0, W_0^*, and R. Differentiating this system, and noting that from the government budget constraint $dT_0 = -[1/(R - 1)]dT$, yields

$$\frac{dW_0}{dT} = -(1 - \gamma)\frac{J_1 J_2}{\Delta}(1 - \beta_n^*)(1 - \gamma\delta^*) > 0, \tag{A.22}$$

$$\frac{dW_0}{dT} = (1 - \gamma)\frac{J_1 J_2}{\Delta}(1 - \beta_n)(1 - \gamma\delta) < 0, \tag{A.23}$$

$$\frac{dR}{dT} = -(1 - \gamma)\frac{J_2}{\Delta}(1 - \beta_n)(1 - \gamma\delta) > 0, \tag{A.24}$$

where

$$\Delta = -\left\{ (1 - \beta_n^*)^2(1 - \gamma\delta^*)\frac{\gamma[1 - \beta_n^*(1 - \gamma)]\overline{Y}_x^* D^{*2}}{[(R - \gamma) - \beta_n^*(1 - \gamma)R]^2} \right.$$

$$\left. + (1 - \beta_n)^2(1 - \gamma\delta)\frac{\gamma[- \beta_n(1 - \gamma)]\overline{Y}_x D^2}{[(R - \gamma) - \beta_n(1 - \gamma)R]^2} \right\} < 0,$$

$$J_1 = \frac{(1 - \beta_n^*)\gamma[1 - \beta_n^*(1 - \gamma)]\overline{Y}_x^* D^{*2}}{[(R - \gamma) - \beta_n^*(1 - \gamma)R]^2} > 0,$$

$$J_2 = \frac{(1 - \beta_n)RD}{(R - 1)[(R - \gamma) - \beta_n(1 - \gamma)R]} > 0.$$

Using (A.22) and (A.24) together with equation (8.28) and (8.29) yields

$$\frac{dp_{n0}}{dT} = -(1 - \gamma)\frac{J_1 J_2}{\Delta \overline{Y}_n}\beta_n(1 - \gamma\delta)(1 - \beta_n^*(1 - \gamma\delta^*)) > 0, \tag{A.25}$$

$$\frac{dp_{n0}^*}{dT} = (1 - \gamma)\frac{J_1 J_2}{\Delta \overline{Y}_n^*}\beta_n^*(1 - \gamma\delta^*)(1 - \beta_n)(1 - \gamma\delta) < 0. \tag{A.26}$$

The results reported in (A.22) through (A.26) justify the diagrammatic analysis of the text. They show that a current budget deficit (necessitating a future rise in taxes so that $dT > 0$) raises domestic wealth, lowers foreign wealth, raises the world rate of interest, lowers the domestic current real exchange rate (the reciprocal of p_{n0}), and raises the foreign current real exchange rate. All of these real effects vanish if the value of γ approaches unity. In that case the pure wealth effects of budget deficits do not exist.

A similar computation reveals that the effects of the budget deficit on the future value of the real exchange rates are ambiguous. This ambiguity reflects the conflicting forces exercised by the wealth and substitution effects induced by the change in the rate of interest that in the home country supplements the direct wealth effects of the tax policy. It can be shown, however, that the budget deficit decelerates the rate of increase of the foreign real exchange rate between the present and the future period.

Problems

1. Consider a two-country model of the world economy as in chapter 6. In each period t, the home country is completely specialized in the production of good X_t and similarly, the foreign country is completely specialized in the production of good M_t, $t = 1, 2$. Let p_t denote the relative price of good X_t, i.e., the terms of trade of the home country and let M_t serve as numeraire throughout. Let R denote the world discount factor in terms of the foreign good. The budget constraint of the representative consumer living in the home country is

$$p_1 c_{x1} + c_{m1} + R(p_2 c_{x2} + c_{m2})$$
$$= p_1(X_1 - I_1 - T_1) + Rp_2[X_2(K_1 + I_1) - T_2], \tag{1}$$

where I_1 represents the level of domestic investment; c_{xt} and c_{mt} denote consumption of home and foreign goods in period t; K_1 is the initial capital stock and the technology $X_2(.)$ satisfies $X_2' > 0$ and $X_2'' < 0$. Tax liabilities in period t are denoted T_t. A corresponding constraint holds for the representative consumer living in the foreign country:

$$p_1 c_{x1}^* + c_{m1}^* + R(p_2 c_{x2}^* + c_{m2}^*)$$

$$= (M_1 - I_1^* - T_1^*) + R[M_2^*(K_1^* + I_1^*) - T_2^*], \tag{2}$$

where an asterisk denotes a corresponding foreign variable and where the technology $M_2(.)$ satisfies $M_2' > 0$ and $M_2'' < 0$.

a. Show that I_1 is an increasing function of the domestic discount factor Rp_2/p_1 while I_1^* is an increasing function of the foreign discount factor R.

b. Suppose that the representative consumer in the home country has the following utility function:

$$U = [C_1^{1-1/\sigma} + DC_2^{1-1/\sigma}]/(1 - 1/\sigma), \tag{3}$$

where $C_t = c_{xt}^b c_{mt}^{1-b}$ and D is the subjective discount factor. The utility function in the foreign country is also CES and the period-utility function is also Cobb-Douglas. Assume further that preferences are identical so that $D = D^*$, $\sigma = \sigma^*$, and $b = b^*$ (where b^* denotes the expenditure share on good x). Consider an initial equilibrium in which government spending levels in both countries are optimally set (i.e., government spending is zero in both countries). What is the effect of a temporary current period increase in government spending undertaken by the home country on domestic and foreign investment levels? Consider both the case where the government spends on domestic and foreign goods.

2. Consider the two-country model developed in the previous exercise. Can a temporary fiscal expansion lead to a negative comovement between consumption growth rates at home and abroad? Discuss.

3. Consider a two-country model of the world economy. In each period t, each country receives endowments of two goods X_t and M_t for the home country X_t^* and M_t^* for the foreign country, where the first good is assumed to be exported by the home country and the second is imported by the home country, and $t = 1, 2$. The world relative price of importables is denoted p_t and the world discount factor is R. The numeraire is the home country's exportable. There is no investment. The budget constraint of the representative consumer living in the home country is

$$c_{x1} + p_1(1 + \tau_1)c_{m1} + R[c_{x2} + p_2(1 + \tau_2)c_{m2}]$$

$$= [X_1 + p_1(1 + \tau_1)M_1 + G_1] + R[X_2 + p_2(1 + \tau_2)M_2 + G_2] = W, \tag{1}$$

where τ_t is an ad valorem tariff levied by the government of the home country on imports $(c_{mt} - M_t)$ and G_t denotes government spending on transfers, which consumers take as given. The government's budget constraint satisfies

$$G_1 + RG_2 = \tau_1 p_1 c_{m1} + R\tau_2 p_2 c_{m2}. \tag{2}$$

In the foreign country, the consumer's budget constraint is given by

$$c_{x1}^* + p_1 c_{m1}^* + R(c_{x2}^* + p_2 c_{m2}^*) = (X_1^* + p_1 M_1^*) + R(X_2^* + p_2 M_2^*) = W^*, \tag{3}$$

where it has been assumed that there is no tariff in the foreign country, and where an asterisk denotes a corresponding foreign-economy variable. Suppose preferences in the home country are given by

$$U = \log[c_{x1}^b c_{m1}^{1-b}] + D\log[c_{x2}^b c_{m2}^{1-b}], \tag{4}$$

where $0 < b < 1$ and D is the subjective discount factor. Assume that preferences in the foreign country are of the same form and that $b = b^*$ and $D = D^*$.

a. Beginning from an initial equilibrium of free trade (i.e., $\tau_2 = \tau_2 = 0$), find the effect on relative prices p_1 and p_2 of the imposition of a permanent tariff, i.e., $d\tau_1 = d\tau_2 = d\tau > 0$.

b. Find the effect on the period 1 trade balance of the permanent tariff. You may assume that initially the trade account balance is equal to zero. How does your answer compare to the answer you got in exercise 6 in chapter 5 for the case of a small country? Discuss.

4. Consider an endowment economy where dynasties, in contrast to the model in chapter 7, have infinite lives. Suppose that new cohorts enter the economy in each period, say due to immigration, and that the total population grows at a constant rate n. While new entrants have no initial debt they are otherwise identical to existing dynasties. In particular, all agents have identical endowments ("labor incomes") and are subject to the same lump-sum taxes. Suppose that preferences of an agent born at time s can be described by a log-utility function:

$$U(s) = \sum_{\delta}^{\infty} \delta^t \ln\{c(s, t)\}, \tag{1}$$

where δ denotes the subjective discount factor ($0 < \delta < 1$) and $c(s, t)$ is consumption in period t of an agent born at time s ($s \geqslant t$).

a. Describe the optimal consumption path and debt allocation for agents born in period s.

b. Find the *aggregate* consumption path and the law of motion for the different types of wealth. Explain why the relevant private-sector discount rates are different for human capital and financial assets/debt.

c. Show that, for $n > 0$, Ricardian neutrality does not hold even though agents have infinite horizons.

5. Consider the infinite horizon overlapping generations model with non-zero population growth that was developed in exercise 4. Suppose the government enacts a temporary taxcut followed by future tax increases that leave government's spending path unchanged. Calculate the value of the current-consumption multiplier for alternative length of the tax-cut period and different values of the population growth rate. Assume that the interest rate factor $R = 1.05$, the subjective discount factor $\delta = .95$ and let the time interval for the tax cut range from 1 to 7 periods. Compare the results to the effects of varying life expectancies in the model of chapter 7.

6. Consider the overlapping generations model of chapter 7 where agents have a constant survival probability (γ). In extension to the model, suppose that new cohorts arrive each period as described in exercise 4. Consequently, total population is growing at a constant rate n. For simplicity, assume that an agent's preferences can be described by a logarithmic expected utility function.

a. Derive the optimal consumption path and the laws of motion for different types of wealth.

b. Explain the conditions for debt neutrality. Show that the results in chapter 7 and exercise 4 emerge as special cases.

7. Consider the two-country overlapping generations model of chapter 8. Suppose that preferences of domestic and foreign agents can be represented by logarithmic utility functions and that the planning horizon is identical for individuals in both countries ($\gamma = \gamma^* < 1$). Let the foreign government's budget be balanced in all periods. Also assume that the path of domestic government expenditure remains unaffected by the following modifications to the budget deficit.

a. Suppose that all future periods are aggregated into a single period. In this two-period model derive the effects of an anticipated future budget deficit on the "constancy equivalent" interest rate.

b. Let future periods be divided into two separate intervals, a "near" future and a "distant" future. Suppose that the domestic government alters taxes in the near future and offsets the revenue effects by changing taxes in the distant future, leaving current period taxes unchanged. For simplicity assume initial debt, taxes, and government spending are zero and that outputs are stationary. Show that a deficit in the near future will increase the future interest rate. Also demonstrate that the effect on the interest rate between the current period and the near future depends on a familiar transfer criterion.

8. Consider a small open economy version of the model in chapter 8. Suppose that the country produces both tradable and nontradable goods and that the output levels of either good are fixed over time. Agents have a finite planning horizon as a result of their finite lifespan and incomplete bequest motives. Also assume that the consumer's preferences can be represented by a logarithmic expected utility function. The government buys tradable and nontradable goods and its purchases are financed with lump-sum taxes. Finally, assume that the small country faces a constant interest rate, r_x, in terms of the tradable good, the numeraire in the analysis.

a. Show that the private propensity to save is independent of the real exchange rate.

b. Suppose that the government implements an unanticipated tax cut in the current period followed by a tax increase in the subsequent period leaving government spending patterns unchanged. Prove that the unanticipated current-period tax cut leads to an increase in today's nontradable price and a lower nontradable goods price in the next period. Also describe the effects of the unanticipated deficit on consumption and the economy's external debt.

9. Consider a monetary version of the model in Chapter 8. Assume that domestic and foreign goods are internationally tradable and perfect substitutes. At the *beginning* of each period financial markets are open and agents acquire their desired asset portfolios. As part of these transactions they purchase domestic and foreign currencies based on the planned consumption purchases *during* the period, i.e., at a time when the financial markets are closed. Accordingly, goods purchases are subject to a cash-in-advance constraint. It is assumed that cash payments have to be conducted in terms of the seller's country currency. At the end of each period, which is equivalent to the beginning of the next period, domestic firms redistribute their receipts to domestic residents and foreign firms to foreign residents. For simplicity assume that the domestic country pegs its exchange rate at a unified level for all transactions and faces a given interest rate and rice level in terms of the foreign currency. As in Chapter 8, individuals have

finite lives with a constant probability of survival (γ), and their preferences are characterized by a logarithmic expected utility function.

a. Describe the equilibria in the goods and asset markets.

b. Show that exchange-rate interventions affect the individual's wealth (for $\gamma < 1$) and thereby the consumption opportunity set, but leave inter-temporal prices unchanged. Thus, one can interpret exchange-rate management as a lump-sum tax policy.

V

Distortionary Tax Incentives: Concepts and Applications

9

Equivalence Relations in International Taxation

This chapter is about equivalence relations among different combinations of fiscal instruments.[1] Taxes themselves may vary in many apparently significant respects, such as who pays them, what country collects them, when the taxes are collected, and whether the fiscal instruments are even thought of as taxes, yet many of these differences vanish with the households and firms. The resulting equivalences have an important bearing on the design and effectiveness of tax policy. They suggest that a given objective may be accomplished in a variety of ways, some perhaps more feasible or politically acceptable than others. Another implication, however, is that a tax policy may be subverted by the failure to coordinate such equivalent channels. These implications can have considerable economic significance, and there is ample evidence that they, as well as the equivalences themselves, are of prime relevance for policymaking.

For example, one fundamental equivalence we discuss is of combinations of trade-based (border) taxes on exports and imports and domestic taxes on production and consumption. A second equivalence concerns *direct* and *indirect* taxation. As Anthony Atkinson (1977) puts it, direct taxes are taxes that can be based on specific characteristics of individuals and households (e.g., marital status, number of dependents, or age) or businesses (e.g., type of industry). The main forms of direct taxes are personal and corporate income taxes, wealth taxes, and inheritance taxes. Indirect taxes are taxes based on *transactions* such as consumption, exports, or imports.

As we argue below, the relevance of these tax equivalences can be demonstrated using the economic integration of the countries of the European Community (EC). Among the goals of the 1992 process of economic integration in Europe is a harmonization of national tax systems, aimed at eliminating the adverse incentives for the movement of capital, goods, and production activity that may derive from the conflicting national objectives of independently designed national tax systems.

Economic integration obviously requires limits on the ability of countries to tax or subsidize exports or imports within the integrated community. In addition, in recognition of the relevance of domestic taxation to
export and import incentives, two types of domestic indirect taxation are
dealt with in the harmonization provisions. An important indirect tax used
in the EC is the value-added tax (VAT) that applies to the domestic
consumption of goods and services. The coverage, rates, and method of
calculation of such taxes vary extensively among the member countries.
The difference in tax rates gives rise to incentives to move reported sales
from high-tax to low-tax countries. Because of differences in tax base
definitions, some sales across national borders may be taxed in more than
one country. The harmonization proposals would attack these problems by
reducing the extent of tax rate variation and standardizing the tax base
definition. In addition, the excise duties currently levied at very different
rates among countries on specific commodities such as alcoholic beverages,
cigarettes, and gasoline would be entirely harmonized at uniform tax rates
for each commodity.

The apparent motivation for these provisions is that they will facilitate
the elimination of fiscal frontiers with the EC. This exclusive focus on
indirect taxation is also found in the provisions of the General Agreements
on Tariffs and Trade, (GATT), which restrict tax-based trade barriers. The
discussion in this chapter implies, however, that there is little theoretical
basis for such an approach. Just as domestic and trade-based indirect taxes
have similar effects that require coordination, so too do direct and indirect
taxes.

To provide the intuition for certain tax equivalences, we begin with a
simple model in which many different types of tax policy are assumed to
be the same and then show the conditions under which some of these very
basic equivalences carry over to much more refined models that are better
suited for guiding policy actions.

9.1 One-Period Model

We consider a one-period model of a small open economy with a single
representative consumer. The country produces two goods in domestically
owned industries, and both goods are consumed domestically. One good,
X, is exported as well as being domestically consumed. The other good, M,
is imported as well as being domestically produced. Each good is produced
using two factors of production, labor, L, and capital, K. Let C_i be the
domestic consumption of good i; L_i and K_i the levels of labor and capital

allocated to industry i, respectively; w and r the factor returns of labor and capital, respectively; and π_i the pure profits generated for the household sector by industry i, $(i = X, M)$. Let the world price of the export good be normalized to unity, with the relative world price of the imported good equal to p_M. In the absence of taxes the household's budget constraint is

$$C_X + p_M C_M = wL_X + wL_M + rK_X + rK_M + \pi_X + \pi_M. \tag{9.1}$$

Equation (9.1) states, simply, that spending equals income.

This budget constraint may be derived in an alternative way via the production and trade sectors of the economy. Starting with the production sector accounts, which require that production in sector i, Z_i, equal factor payments plus profits, we obtain

$$p_i Z_i = wL_i + rK_i + \pi_i, \qquad (i = X, M). \tag{9.2}$$

To this we add the requirement that trade must be balanced; that is, exports must equal imports:

$$p_M(C_M - Z_M) = Z_X - C_X. \tag{9.3}$$

Equation (9.3) is a requirement imposed by the model's single-period assumption. No country will be willing to "lend" goods to the rest of the world by running a trade surplus; because there will be no subsequent period in which the debt can be repaid via a trade deficit. Using equation (9.2) in equation (9.3) yields equation (9.1), which can be then viewed as the overall budget constraint of the economy.

Let us now introduce to this model a variety of taxes including consumption taxes, income taxes, and trade taxes. In practice, consumption taxes may take a variety of forms, including retail sales taxes and VATs on consumption goods. In this simple model, with no intermediate production, the two types of taxes are identical. One could also impose a direct consumption tax at the household level. Although there has been considerable theoretical discussion of personal consumption taxes, no country has yet adopted such a tax.

Simple Equivalences

Let the tax on good i be expressed as a fraction τ_i of the producer price. (A basic and familiar feature concerning excise taxes is that it is irrelevant whether the tax is paid by the producer or the consumer). The tax appears on the left-hand side of the budget constraint (9.1), and the export good's domestic consumer price becomes $1 + \tau_x$, and the import good's domestic consumer price becomes $(1 + \tau_M)p_M$. The producer domestic prices are $p_x = 1$ and p_M, respectively.

The first very simple equivalence to note is that the taxes could also be expressed as fractions $(\tau'_i, i = X, M)$ of the consumer prices, in which case the consumer prices would become $p_i/(1 - \tau'_i)$. This distinction is between a tax, τ, that has a *tax-exclusive* base and one, τ', that has a *tax-inclusive* base. If $\tau' = \tau/(1 + \tau)$, then the two taxes have identical effects on the consumer and producer and provide the same revenue to the government. Yet, when tax rates get reasonably high, the nominal difference between tax-exclusive and tax-inclusive rates becomes quite substantial. A tax-inclusive rate of 50 percent, for example, is equivalent to a tax-exclusive rate of 100 percent.

We consider now income taxes on profits and returns to labor and capital. Rather than raising consumer prices, these taxes reduce the resources available to consume. In practice, such taxes are assessed both directly and indirectly. There are individual and business income taxes, but also payroll taxes, for example. By the national income identity, a uniform VAT on all production is simply an indirect tax on domestic factor incomes, both payrolls and returns to capital and profits.

We note, as in the case of consumption taxes, that it does not matter whether the supplier of a factor, in this case the household, or the user, in this case the firm, must actually remit the tax. A factor tax introduced in equation (9.2) or (9.1) has the same effect. The same point holds in regard to tax-exclusive versus tax-inclusive tax bases. We also observe from inspection of (9.1) that a uniform tax on income is equivalent to uniform tax on consumption. Each tax reduces real income. Imposition of a tax-inclusive consumption tax at rate τ divides the left-hand side of (9.1) by the factor $(1 - \tau)$, whereas a tax-inclusive income tax (the way an income tax base is normally defined) at the same rate multiplies the right-hand side of (9.1) by $(1 - \tau)$. Because dividing one side of an equation by a certain factor is equivalent to multiplying the other side by the same factor, the equivalence between a uniform consumption tax and a uniform income tax is established in a one-period model.

Despite their simplicity, these basic equivalences are useful in understanding the potential effects of various policies. For example, the EC tax harmonization provisions would narrow differences in rates of VAT among member countries, but these provisions say nothing about income taxes. But our results suggest that a uniform consumption tax or any type of uniform income tax would be equivalent to a uniform VAT. Thus, a country with a VAT deemed too high could accede to the provisions of the harmonization process by lowering its VAT and raising other domestic taxes, with no impact on its own citizens nor, moreover, on the citizens of other countries either. We must conclude that either these proposals have not taken adequate account of simple equivalences or that the simple equivalences may break down in more complicated situations, a possibility we explore next.

International Trade Equivalences

We turn now to taxes explicitly related to international trade. We say *explicitly*, of course, because an obvious theme of this chapter is to recognize the equivalences that make some policies, not specifically targeted at trade, perfect substitutes for others that are.

Tax-based trade policies may involve border taxes, such as tariffs on imports or export subsidies, but may also be industry-specific taxes aimed, for example, at making trade-sensitive industries more competitive. It is well known that quantity restrictions may in some cases be used to replicate the effects of trade-based taxes. The most familiar case is the use of import quotas instead of tariffs. Other alternatives to explicit tax policies are discussed later.

The first equivalence we note among trade-based tax policies is between taxes on exports and taxes on imports. One might imagine that these policies would work in opposite directions, because the first appears to encourage a trade deficit (a decline in exports not of imports), whereas the second appears to discourage one. However, it must be remembered that this one-period model *requires* balanced trade. Hence, there can be no trade deficit or surplus; only the *level* of balanced trade may be influenced. Once this is recognized, the equivalence of these two policies can be more rapidly understood; each policy discourages trade by driving a wedge between the buyer's and seller's prices of one of the traded goods. This is the well-known Lerner's symmetry proposition.

Algebraically, the equivalence is straightforward. An import tax at a tax-exclusive rate of τ causes the domestic price of the imported good to equal the world price, p_M, multiplied by the factor $1 + \tau$. Note that because the import tax does not apply to the domestic producer, then $p_M(1 + \tau)$ is the domestic price not only for the consumer but also for the domestic producers. If we denote by w and r the equilibrium factor returns to labor and capital, respectively, the four-tuple

$$(p_M(1 + \tau); 1, w, r) \tag{9.4}$$

is an equilibrium domestic price vector with an import tax at a tax-exclusive rate of τ. On the other hand, an export tax at the same tax-exclusive rate of τ causes the exporting firm to receive only $1/(1 + \tau)$ for every unit of the export good sold at the export price of one. The rest, $\tau/(1 + \tau)$, equals what the tax exporters must pay, whch is the tax rate times the net price received, $1/(1 + \tau)$. Note that $1/(1 + \tau)$ becomes also the domestic price of the export good, as an exporter can either sell domestically or abroad and must therefore receive the same net price at home and abroad. Multiplying the price vector (9.4) by $1/(1 + \tau)$, we obtain another price vector

$$\left(p_M, \frac{1}{(1 + \tau)}, w', r' \right),   \tag{9.5}$$

where $w' = w/(1 + \tau)$, and $r' = r/(1 + \tau)$. Notice that the price vectors (9.4) and (9.5) represent the same *relative* prices. As only relative prices matter for economic behavior, the two price vectors, (9.4) and (9.5), support the same equilibrium allocation. Put differently, multiplying p_M on the left-hand side of the household's budget constraint by $1 + \tau$ (an import tax) is equivalent to multiplying all other prices in that equation (and the profits π_M and π_X) by $1/(1 + \tau)$ (an export tax). Thus, the equivalence between an import tax at a tax-exclusive rate of τ (which generates the equilibrium price vector (9.4)) and an export tax at the same tax-exclusive rate of τ (which generates the equilibrium price vector (9.5)) is established.

It is important to point out that this symmetry of trade taxes makes no assumption about whether the taxing country is small or large, that is, whether its policies can affect the relative world price of the two goods. The equivalence indicates that these two policies are really one.

Equivalences Between Trade and Domestic Policies

The next class of policy equivalences we study is between trade policies and combinations of domestic policies. We have already shown that an import tariff at a tax-exclusive rate τ causes the domestic price of the imported good to equal the world price, p_M, multiplied by the factor $1 + \tau$. We also noted that $p_M(1 + \tau)$ is the domestic price for both the consumer and the producer. If instead of an import tax at a tax-exclusive rate of τ, the government imposes an excise (consumption) tax at the same tax-exclusive rate of τ, then the consumer price of the import good becomes $p_M(1 + \tau)$, but the producer price remains the world price of p_M. However, the pro-

ducer will be indifferent between the import tax [which generates a producer price of $p_M(1 + \tau)$] and the excise tax (which generates a producer
price of only p_M) if the excise tax is accompanied by a subsidy at a rate τ
to domestic production that raises the price for the producer back to
$p_M(1 + \tau)$. An immediate implication is that one cannot control tax-based
trade barriers without also controlling domestic taxes and that controlling
only domestic sales or consumption taxes alone is still not enough. It is
possible to convert a perfectly domestic sales tax into an import tariff by
subsidizing domestic production of the commodity in question at the rate
of consumption tax already in place.

9.2   Multiperiod Model

Many of the equivalences just demonstrated hold in very general models.
Even those that do not may "break down" in much more limited ways than
one might think. Furthermore, the conditions under which such equivalences do fail provide insight into the channels through which different tax
policies operate. Perhaps the most important extension of the simple model
we have used is the addition of several periods during which households
may produce and consume. This permits the appearance of saving, investment, and imbalances of both the government and trade accounts, the "two
deficits."

In fact, we may go quite far toward such a model simply by reinter-
preting the previous one. We consider once again the basic model of
equations (9.1)–(9.3). We originally interpreted this as a one-period model,
with capital and labor as primary factors supplied to the production process
and p_M, w, and r the one-period relative prices of imports, labor, and
capital. Let us suppose, instead, that we wished to consider a multiperiod
economy. What would the budget constraint of a household choosing
consumption and labor supply over several periods look like? We know
that the household planning no bequests would equate the present value of
its lifetime consumption to the present value of its lifetime labor income
plus the initial value of its tangible wealth. What is this initial wealth? It
equals the present value of all future profits plus the value of the initial
capital stock. The value of the initial capital stock, in turn, may also
be expressed as the present value of all future earnings on that capital.
Thus, we may replace expression (9.1) with

$$PV(C_X + p_M C_M) = PV(wL_X + wL_M) + PV(rK_X + rK_M) + PV(\pi_X + \pi_M),$$
$$(9.6)$$

where $PV(\ )$ represents the present value of a future stream rather than a single period quantity, K_i is the initial capital stock of industry i, and L_i and π_i are the flows of industry i's labor input and profits in period i.

In (9.6) we have made the transition to a multiperiod budget constraint. Note that this budget constraint no longer requires that income equal consumption in any given period, only that lifetime income (from labor plus initial wealth) equal lifetime consumption, in present value. Thus, there may be saving in some periods and dissaving in others.

Similar adjustments are needed to equations (9.2) and (9.3) to complete the transition to a multiperiod model. Just as a household need not balance its budget in any given year, a country need not have balanced trade in any given year. Over the entire horizon of the model, however, trade must be balanced in present value, following the argument used for balance in the one-period model. That is, each country will give up no more goods and services, in present value, than it receives. The dates of these matching exports and imports may be different, of course, and this is what causes single-period trade deficits and surpluses. Thus, equation (9.3) becomes

$$PV[p_M(C_M - Z_M)] = PV[Z_X - C_X]. \tag{9.7}$$

The last equation in need of reinterpretation is (9.2). The natural analogue in the multiperiod context is

$$PV(p_i Z_i) = PV(wL_i) + PV(rK_i) + PV(\pi_i) \qquad (i = X, M), \tag{9.8}$$

which says that the present value of output in each industry equals the present value of the streams of payments to labor and profits plus the payments to the *initial* capital stock. However, this condition requires further explanation, because one might expect returns to all capital over time, and not just the initial capital stock, to appear on the right-hand side of the expression.

The explanation is that new investment and its returns are subsumed by the "final form" relationship between final outputs and primary inputs given in (9.8). Stated differently, Z_i is interpreted as the output that is available for final uses outside the production sector, that is, Z_i is output that is available for either domestic consumption or exports. We may think of capital goods produced after the initial date and then used in production as intermediate goods. Normal production relations represent each stage of production. In a two-period model, for example, we would depict first-period capital and consumption as being produced by initial capital and first-period labor, and second-period consumption as being produced by initial capital plus capital produced during the first period, and second-period labor. Inserting the first-period production relation into the second-period production relation allows us to eliminate first-period capital from the equation, giving us a single "final form" relating each period's consumption to each period's labor input and the initial stock of capital. This approach may be applied recursively in the same manner for multiperiod models, leading to the type of relationship given in (9.8). In fact, if the capital goods produced in one industry are used in the other, then (9.8) does not hold for each industry separately—only when the two conditions are summed together. This is still consistent with conditions (9.6) and (9.7).

Given the similarity of the multiperiod model (9.6)–(9.8) and the single-period model (9.1)–(9.3), it is not surprising that several of the one-period equivalences carry over to the multiperiod model. First, a permanent tax on consumption is equivalent to a permanent tax on labor income plus profits plus the returns to the initial capital stock. A permanent consumption tax at a tax-exclusive rate of τ causes expression (9.6) to become

$$PV[(1 + \tau)(C_X + p_M C_M)] = PV(wL_X + wL_M) + PV(rK_X + rK_M)$$

$$+ PV(\pi_X + \pi_M). \tag{9.9}$$

Multiplying this equation by $1 - \tau' = 1/(1 + \tau)$, we obtain

$$PV(C_X + p_M C_M) = PV[wL_X + wL_M)(1 - \tau')] + PV[(rK_K + rK_M)(1 - \tau')]$$

$$+ PV[\pi_M + \pi_X)(1 - \tau')]. \tag{9.10}$$

Equation (9.10) is obtained from (9.6) when a permanent tax at a tax-inclusive rate of τ' is imposed on labor income plus profits plus the returns to the initial stock of capital. Thus, the equivalence between the latter tax and a consumption tax is established. Clearly, this equivalence holds only if the tax rates are *constant* over time, so that the tax terms can be taken outside the present value operators $PV(\ )$. One may be tempted to interpret this result as showing that consumption taxes and income taxes are equivalent in multiperiod models with saving, but it is important to recognize that the type of income tax imposed here is not the income tax as normally conceived. The tax here is on wage income plus capital income attributable to initial wealth. It excludes from the tax base the income attributable to capital generated by saving done during the model's periods. Were such income also taxed, there would be an additional change to both sides of (9.6): the present-value operator, $PV(\ )$, which aggregates future streams of income and consumption, would now be based on the after-tax interest rate, $r(1 - \tau')$, rather than on the market interest rate, r. Transferring resources from one period to a subsequent one would now increase the household's tax burden. Indeed, this *double taxation* of saving has traditionally been emphasized in distinguishing income taxation from consumption taxation.

On the other hand, it is also no longer true that labor-income taxation and consumption taxation are equivalent. The equivalence we have uncovered is between consumtion taxation, and labor-income taxation *plus* taxes on profits and the returns to the initial capital stock. This distinction between consumption taxes and labor-income taxes has been misleadingly termed a "transition" issue by some, because only the capital income from initial assets is concerned. However, such income is large, even in present value. For example, if the economy's capital to output ratio is 3, and the ratio of output to consumption is 1.5 (realistic values for the United States), then a permanent consumption tax of, say, 20 percent, which attaches 20 percent of these assets' flows and hence 20 percent of their value, will raise additional revenue equal to 90 percent ($0.2 \times 3 \times 1.5$) of one year's consumption.

The equivalence between export and import taxes also carries over to the multiperiod case. Inspection of (9.7) shows that the imposition of a permanent import tariff at rate τ multiplies the terms inside the present-value operator on the left-hand side by $(1 + \tau)$, whereas an export tax divides each of the terms inside the present-value operator on the right-hand side by $(1 + \tau)$. Again, if the tax rates are constant over time, one may take them outside the present-value operators, and the logic of the one-period model then applies. Clearly, the equivalence would not hold for time-varying tax rates. For example, a single-period import tax would be expected not only to discourage trade overall but also to shift imports to other periods. Likewise, an export tax would not only discourage trade but also shift exports to other periods. Thus, one would expect the first policy to lead to a greater trade surplus *in the period of taxation* than the second.

A similar outcome for temporary taxation would hold in the previous case of consumption taxes and taxes on labor income plus returns to initial assets. It has been argued that a VAT should be more favorable to the development of trade surpluses because of its use of the destination principle rather than the origin principle of taxation. Indeed, for a one-period tax, this will be so, because a one-period consumption tax (destination-based VAT) will shift consumption to other periods, whereas a one-period income tax will shift production to other periods.

Thus, the primary requirements for the basic one-period equivalences to carry over to the multiperiod context are that rates be permanent and the returns to savings not be taxed. (Even the basic equivalences depend on our implicit assumption that there are no additional nominal constraints on the system—for example, that it is just as easy for a real wage reduction to be accomplished through a fall in the nominal wage as a rise in the price level.) Yet, it is unrealistic to assume that governments wish to keep taxes constant over time or that, even if they did, they could bind themselves to do so. Likewise, the taxation of new saving and investment plays an extremely important role not only in the domestic policy context but also increasingly in the international area, as world capital markets become more integrated and the transactions and information costs to investment abroad decline. It is important that we go beyond the previous analysis to consider the effects of changing tax rates and the taxation of savings and investment.

9.3   Tax Equivalences in a Two-Period Model and Cash-Flow Taxation

To allow a tractable treatment of more general tax policies and yet maintain the dynamic aspect of the multiperiod model, we consider a two-period model with a single consumption good, no pure profits, and fixed labor supply, with the input in each period normalized to unity. In such a model there can no longer be exports and imports in the same period, but issues of trade can still be discussed because there can be exports in one period and imports in another. Because we wish to consider time-varying tax policies and capital-income taxation, we must explicitly treat capital accumulation, including foreign as well as domestic investment. This is most easily exposited by representing separately the budget constraints the household faces in each of the two periods, taking account of first-period savings decisions.

In the absence of taxes the household's budget constraints in periods zero and one for this model are

$$C_0 = w_0 + \rho_0 K_{D0} + \rho_0^* K_{F0} - K_{D1} - K_{F1}, \tag{9.11}$$

$$C_1 = w_1 + \rho_1 K_{D1} + \rho_1^* K_{F1}, \tag{9.12}$$

where C_i is period i consumption, w_i is the wage in period i, ρ_i is the return to capital in the home country in period i, ρ_i^* is the return to capital in the foreign country in period i, K_{Di} is the stock of domestic capital owned by the household in period i, and K_{Fi} is the stock of foreign capital owned by the household in period i. In terms of the multiperiod model previously considered, K_{D1} and K_{F1} are stocks of initial capital. Capital fully depreciates in each period. There are no costs of adjustment of investment. The only savings decisions involve the levels of second-period capital purchased.

Now let us introduce taxes to this model. In addition to the consumption taxes and labor income taxes discussed previously, we consider several taxes on capital income. We make three important distinctions with respect to these capital-income taxes: whether they are assessed at home or abroad, whether they are assessed on the firm or the household, and whether they apply to capital investment or capital income. These three binary distinctions give rise to eight types of capital-income tax. Although such a number of tax instruments may seem excessive, each of these taxes has different economic effects, and all have significant real-world representations. Indeed, there are still important restrictions implicit in this characterization.

The eight instruments are denoted τ_{RD}, τ_B, τ_{RF}, τ^*_{NB}, τ_{HS}, τ_I, τ_{RFC}, and τ^*_I. The first four apply to capital income, and they may be different in periods zero and one. The last four apply to capital investment and hence are relevant only in period zero. We now define each of these taxes and offer real-world examples:

τ_{RD} — household-level domestic tax on income from domestic investment; taxes on interest an dividend income from domestic sources;

τ_B — firm-level domestic tax on income from domestic investment; domestic corporate income taxes;

τ_{RF} — household-level domestic tax on income from foreign investment; taxes on interest and dividend income from foreign sources (net of foreign tax credits);

τ^*_{NB} — firm level foreign tax on income from foreign investment; foreign corporate income taxes;

τ_{HS} — household-level domestic rate of deduction for domestic investment;

τ_I — firm-level domestic rate of deduction for domestic investment; domestic investment tax credit;

τ_{RFC} — household-level domestic rate of deduction for foreign investment; tax-deductible pension saving abroad;

τ_I^* —   firm-level foreign rate of deduction for foreign investment; foreign investment tax credit;

Note that the two tax instruments denoted by an asterisk are applied by foreign governments to investment and capital income owned by the domestic household in the foreign countries. This tax classification scheme does not include domestic taxes on foreign corporate income. For simplicity we assume that all investment abroad is portfolio investment by domestic households rather than foreign direct investment by corporations. We adopt this restriction not because foreign direct investment is unimportant empirically (for this is not the case) but because the effects of taxation on foreign investment can be described adequately using the instruments already specified. Likewise, we ignore the fact that such portfolio income may in some countries be taxed by the host country at the individual as well as firm levels before being repatriated.

In any particular country several of these eight capital tax instruments might be absent. For example, if a country integrated its personal and corporate income tax systems, a policy often recommended but never fully adopted, all separate firm-level taxes would vanish. If a country's tax rules called for taxation of foreign-source capital income, the tax rate τ_{RF} could be low or even zero if the home country credited foreign taxes on such income. In such a scheme the tax on foreign-source income is

$$\tau_{RF} = \frac{(\tau - \tau^*)}{(1 - \tau^*)},$$

where τ and τ^* are the statutory rates of income tax in the home and foreign countries, respectively. Thus, if $\tau = \tau^*$, $\tau_{RF} = 0$.

To introduce these taxes into the budget constraints (9.11) and (9.12) in a realistic manner, we need one additional element of notation. Most countries that tax household capital income emanating from firms do so only on a *realization* basis. Households are taxes on dividends and interest received, but not on corporate retained earnings. This has important implications concerning the cost of capital and the market value of corporate assets. To represent the fact that retained earnings are not taxed at the household level, we let R_0 and R_0^* be earnings retained in period 0 by domestic and foreign corporations owned by domestic households and assume that household-level taxes on corporate income are levied on earnings net of these values.

Letting τ_{ci} be the tax-exclusive consumption tax and τ_{Li} the labor income tax in period i, we may rewrite the budget constraints (9.11) and (9.12) to account for the capital-income tax treatment just considered:

$$(1 + \tau_{C0})C_0 = (1 - \tau_{L0})w_0 + (1 - \tau_{RD0})[(1 - \tau_{B0})\rho_0 K_{D0} - R_0]$$

$$+ (1 - \tau_{RF0})[(1 - \tau_{NB0}^*)\rho_0^* K_{F0} - R_0^*]$$

$$- (1 - \tau_{HS})[(1 - \tau_I)K_{D1} - R_0]$$

$$- (1 - \tau_{RFC})[(1 - \tau_I^*)K_{F1} - R_0^*], \tag{9.13}$$

and

$$(1 + \tau_{C1})C_1 = (1 - \tau_{L1})w_1 + (1 - \tau_{RD1})(1 - \tau_{B1})\rho_1 K_{D1}$$

$$+ (1 - \tau_{RF1})(1 - \tau_{NB1}^*)\rho_1^* K_{F1}. \tag{9.14}$$

Despite its apparent complexity, this system is useful in demonstrating a variety of tax equivalences.

We begin with a special case. Suppose there are no taxes at the firm level, and that tax rates that apply to deductions for investment at home and abroad, τ_{HS} and τ_{RFC}, equal the corresponding taxes on investment income, τ_{RD} and τ_{RF}, respectively. The budget constraints (9.13) and (9.14) then become

$$(1 + \tau_{C0})C_0 = (1 - \tau_{L0})w_0 + (1 - \tau_{RD0})(\rho_0 K_{D0} - K_{D1})$$

$$+ (1 - \tau_{RF0})(\rho_0^* K_{F0} - K_{F1}), \tag{9.15}$$

and

$$(1 + \tau_{C1})C_1 = (1 - \tau_{L1})w_1 + (1 - \tau_{RD1})\rho_i K_{D1} + (1 - \tau_{RF1})\rho_1^* K_{F1}. \tag{9.16}$$

Note that in this case the consumption tax in each period is equivalent to a combination of taxes in the same period at the same rate on labor income, domestic capital income, and foreign capital income, net of domestic and foreign investment. This is a new result, but it is closely related to one derived in the previous section. If, in addition, we assume that the tax rates are constant over time, and the rates of return ρ_1 and ρ_1^* are equal (as would be the case if foreign and domestic investments were taxed at the same rate and investors chose to hold each), we may combine (9.15) and (9.16) to obtain

$$(1 + \tau_C)\left(C_0 + \frac{C_1}{\rho_1}\right) = (1 - \tau_L)\left(w_0 + \frac{w_1}{\rho_1}\right)$$

$$+ (1 - \tau_{RD})\rho_0 K_{D0} + (1 - \tau_{RF})\rho_0^* K_{F0}, \tag{9.17}$$

which gives the previous multiperiod result, confirming the equivalence of a constant consumption tax to taxes at the same rate on labor income and the income from initial assets.

Even when tax rates differ across periods, we have identified an important period-by period equivalence between consumption and income taxes. A consumption tax can be replicated by a tax on labor income plus taxes on domestic plus foreign capital income, net of new investment. This is in no way inconsistent with our previous intuition that a consumption tax does not impose a tax on new savings: a constant tax on capital income, net of investment, imposes no tax in present value on the income from new investment. Although the entire return from such investment is taxed, its entire cost is deducted at the same rate. Thus, the government is simply a fair partner in the enterprise (although because of its passive role in the actual operation of the firm it is sometimes called a "sleeping" partner). Only income from capital already in place at the beginning of period one is subject to a true tax, and this tax was previously seen to be part of the income tax-equivalent scheme.

These foreign and domestic taxes on capital income less investment are sometimes called *cash-flow* taxes, because they are based on net flows from the firm. In the case of the foreign tax, the cash-flow tax is a tax on net capital inflows. In this sense it is equivalent to a policy of taxing foreign borrowing and interest receipts and subsidizing foreign lending and payments of interest. In the domestic literature on taxation much has been made of the equivalence between labor-income taxes plus business cash-flow taxes and consumption taxes. But in an open economy this equivalence also requires the taxation of cash flows from abroad; otherwise, the destination-based consumption tax will include an extra piece that is absent from the tax on labor and domestic capital income net of domestic investment.

We turn next to issues related to the level of capital-income taxation, business versus household. In the real world, some payments by firms to suppliers of capital are taxed only at the investor level, without being subject to a business-level tax. These are interest payments, which are treated as tax-deductible business expenses. Other payments—dividends—are typically either partially deductible or not deductible at all. One may think of the tax rates τ_B and τ_{NB}^* as representing weighted-average tax rates of the positive tax rate on dividends and the zero tax rate on interest. (Again, it is typical for the *individual* tax rates on these two forms of capital income to differ, but not as significantly. We ignore such differences in our model.)

One would expect these tax provisions to affect firms' incentives with respect to retained earnings, R and R^*. Indeed, it is clear from the budget constraint (9.13) that the optimal policy will be to maximize (minimize) R if $\tau_{RD} > (<) \tau_{HS}$; likewise, for foreign investment R^* should be maximized (minimize) if $\tau_{RF} > (<) \tau_{RFC}$. In the "normal" case that savers do not receive a full immediate deduction for funds supplied to the firm, firms will retain earnings until constrained from doing so. This would presumably be when they had financed all their investment, $(1 - \tau_I)K_{D1}$, or exhausted all available internal funds, $(1 - \tau_B)\rho_0 K_{DO}$. Were τ_{RD} to equal τ_{HS}, households would be indifferent: payments made to them by the firm and then immediately sent back would have no tax consequences. Following the same logic, a more generous rate of savings deduction would lead firms to distribute as much as possible to allow savers the opportunity to return the funds and reduce their net taxes. The lower limit on retentions would be zero, as dividends cannot be negative.

We thus have three cases domestically (and analogously three cases with respect to foreign savings):

(a) $\tau_{RD} > \tau_{HS}$ and $R = \min[(1 - \tau_I)K_{D1}, (1 - \tau_B)\rho_0 K_{DO}]$;

(b) $\tau_{RD} = \tau_{HS}$ and $\min[(1 - \tau_I)K_{D1}, (1 - \tau_B)\rho_0 K_{DO}] > R > 0$;

(c) $\tau_{RD} < \tau_{HS}$ and $R = 0$.

For each of these cases we may substitute the optimal value of R into equation (9.13) to obtain a budget constraint in which R does not explicitly appear. In the normal case (a) and the intermediate case (b) this procedure yields

$$(1 + \tau_{CO})C_0 = (1 - \tau_{LO})w_0$$

$$+ (1 - \tau_{DSO})[1 - \tau_{BO})\rho_0 K_{DO} - (1 - \tau_I)K_{D1}]$$

$$+ (1 - \tau_{FLO})[1 - \tau_{NB}^*)\rho_0^* K_{FO} - (1 - \tau_I^*)K_{F1}], \qquad (9.13a)$$

where

$$\tau_{DS} = \begin{cases} \tau_{HS} & \text{if } (1 - \tau_{BO})\rho_0 K_{DO} < (1 - \tau_I)K_{D1} \\ \tau_{RD} & \text{if } (1 - \tau_{BO})\rho_0 K_{DO} > (1 - \tau_I)K_{D1} \end{cases}$$

$$\tau_{FL} = \begin{cases} \tau_{RFC} & \text{if } (1 - \tau_{NB}^*)\rho_0^* K_{FO} < (1 - \tau_I^*)K_{F1} \\ \tau_{RF} & \text{if } (1 - \tau_{NB}^*)\rho_0^* K_{FO} > (1 - \tau_I^*)F_{F1}. \end{cases}$$

The value of τ_{DS} depends on whether the firm is in a regime in which it is paying dividends at the margin and hence financing marginal investment from retained earnings, τ_{RD}, or not paying dividends and financing new investment through issues of new shares, τ_{HS}. In either case, however, the behavior of the optimizing firm induces a household-level cash-flow tax. This implies that the economy may be closer to cash-flow taxation than might appear from the statutory tax treatment of household capital income. In particular, the *effective* tax burden on capital income at the household level is zero in present value, even if there are dividends and $\tau_{RD} > \tau_{HS}$. This is another equivalence, of existing systems of household capital income taxation to household cash-flow taxation.

A final equivalence involving the two levels of capital income taxation is *between* taxes at the two levels. In a variety of situations a tax at the firm level is equivalent to one at the household level. Consider, for example, the case in which all capital income taxes are cash-flow taxes. This is like the situation considered in equation (9.15) but with cash-flow business taxes added. In this case the first-period budget constraint is

$$(1 + \tau_{C0})C_0 = (1 - \tau_{L0})w_0 + (1 - \tau_{RD0})(1 - \tau_{B0})(\rho_0 K_{D0} - K_{D1})$$

$$+ (1 - \tau_{RF0})(1 - \tau_{B0}^*)(\rho_0^* K_{F0} - K_{F1}). \tag{9.13b}$$

(The second-period budget constraint [9.14] is unaffected.) It is clear from this equation that it is irrelevant from the household's viewpoint whether taxes are collected from firms or individuals. The tax rate τ_B is a perfect substitute for τ_{RD}, and τ_B^* is one for τ_{RF}. In the first case, with both taxes collected by the same government, the equivalence is complete; government is indifferent as well. In the second case this would not be so, unless a tax treaty existed that directed capital income taxes collected on specific assets to specific countries regardless of who actually collected the taxes.

Even in the domestic case, the taxes might *appear* to have different effects due to their different collection points. For example, measured rates of return from the corporate sector would be net of tax were the taxes collected from firms, but gross of tax were they collected from households.

9.4 Present-Value Equivalences

In discussing cash-flow taxation, we have made a point that has a more general application: that tax policies may change the timing of tax collections without changing their burden, in present value. A constant-rate cash-flow tax exerts no net tax on the returns to marginal investment, giving investors an initial deduction equal in present value to the ultimate tax on positive cash flows the investment generates.

In our two-period model, a cash-flow tax at a constant rate collects revenue equal in present value only to the cash flows from the first-period capital stock. Thus, an initial wealth tax on that stock would be equivalent from the viewpoint of both household and government. For example, consider the simple case with no firm-level taxes and constant tax rates examined previously. This is the example in which the first-period and second-period budget constraints can be combined as in the multiperiod model of the previous section. These three budget constraints (first-period, second-period, and combined) are under cash-flow taxation (assuming that $\rho = \rho^*$):

$$(1 + \tau_C)C_0 = (1 - \tau_L)w_0 + (I - \tau_{RD})(\rho_0 K_{D0} - K_{D1})$$

$$+ (1 - \tau_{RF})(\rho_0^* K_{F0} - K_{F1}), \tag{9.15a}$$

$$(1 + \tau_C)C_1 = (1 - \tau_L)w_1 + (1 - \tau_{RD})\rho_1 K_{D1} + (1 - \tau_{RF})\rho_1^* K_{F1}, \tag{9.16a}$$

and

$$(1 + \tau_C)\left(C_0 + \frac{C_1}{\rho_1}\right) = (1 - \tau_L)\left(w_0 + \frac{w_1}{\rho_1}\right)$$

$$+ (1 - \tau_{RD})\rho_0 K_{D0} + (1 - \tau_{RF})\rho_0^* K_{F0}. \tag{9.17a}$$

Here, if the terms K_{D1} and K_{F1} appearing in the first- and second-period budget constraints were no longer multiplied by $1 - \tau_{RD}$ and $1 - \tau_{RF}$, respectively, cash-flow tax would be replaced by a first-period tax on the returns to existing capital—a wealth tax—yet there would be no impact at all on the household's combined budget constraint. Its *measured* saving would be affected, but not its consumption.

Just as measured household saving would be affected, so would there also be apparent differences between the levels of government debt in the two cases. In the cash-flow tax case the government's revenue would be lower in the first and higher in the second period, and it would have a smaller first-period budget deficit. At the same time, firm values would be lower, to account for the larger impending second-period cash-flow tax payments. Indeed, these differences exactly offset each other. One could imagine the cash-flow tax policy as being a combination of the wealth tax policy plus a decision by the government to lend in the first period and force firms to accept loans of equal value at the market interest rate, to be repaid in the same period. Firms would require fewer funds from the household sector, leaving households just enough extra money to purchase the bonds floated by the government.

Thus, the explicitly measured government debt is not an accurate indicator of policy, because it may vary considerably between the two equivalent situations. One may think of the "forced loans" of the cash-flow tax system as being off-budget assets that cause the deficit to be overstated, assets that can be brought on budget by recalling the loans, paying back the debt, and shifting to the wealth tax.

One can imagine many similar examples of present-value equivalences, none of which go beyond the bounds of the realistic tax policies we have already considered. The government can arbitrarily change the measured composition of a household's wealth between government debt and tangible capital (and indeed between government debt and human capital, through changes in the time pattern of labor-income taxation) simply by introducing offsetting levels of debt and forced loans attached to these other assets. This is true whether or not the asset owners are domestic residents or not. Foreign owners of a domestic corporation that is suddenly hit with a cash-flow tax on *new* investment (i.e., excluding the wealth-tax effect on preexisting capital) will spend less of their funds on the domestic firms and the remainder on other assets—quite possibly the government debt—but not on the country's external debt, that is, the aggregate value of domestic assets owned by foreigners.

It is noteworthy that the government's ability to shift such asset values of foreigners is more circumscribed than its ability with respect to domestic residents. It cannot, for example, cause a reduction in the value of a foreigner's human capital offset by a loan to the foreigner (by cutting labor-income taxes today and raising them in the future), because it cannot tax the foreigner's labor income. All adjustments with respect to external debt must be through the tax treatment of foreign-owned domestic assets.

10

Budget Deficits with Distortionary Taxes

Up to chapter 9 we have assumed that all taxes are lump sum and non-distortionary. As a result we have focused on the effects of government spending rather than on the means of government finance; in fact we have used a model in which budget deficits arising from changes in the timing of taxes do not affect the real equilibrium. The assumption that all taxes are nondistortionary may, however, miss important features characterizing actual taxes. In this chapter we replace this assumption with the assumption that taxes are distortionary. Under these circumstances the real equilibrium is sensitive to alternative specifications of the time profile of taxes and public-debt issue. Hence the equilibrium is not invariant with respect to budget deficits.

In the analysis that follows we examine the effects of budget deficits under alternative assumptions about the taxes that are reduced. We consider consumption taxes, taxes on income from domestic investment, taxes on income from foreign lending, and taxes on labor income.

The analysis reveals that the various taxes may exert different quantitative and qualitative effects on the real equilibrium, and therefore the impact of a budget deficit and its international transmission may depend critically on the mix of taxes used to generate the deficit. Furthermore in the presence of distortionary taxes the wealth effects, which traditionally serve as the principal mechanism through which budget deficits influence the equilibrium, are supplemented by another important mechanism operating through intertemporal substitution. In fact it is shown that there are circumstances under which the wealth effects are weak and of ambiguous sign while the intertemporal substitution effects of distortionary taxes are the main driving force of budget deficits.

10.1   The Analytical Framework

To incorporate the effects of taxes, consider a one-good stylized model. The private sector's periodic budget constraints are

$$(1 + \tau_{c0})C_0 = (1 - \tau_{y0})(\overline{Y}_0 - I_0) + (1 - \tau_{b0})B_0^P - (1 + r_{-1} - \tau_{b0})B_{-1}^P$$

$$(10.1)$$

and

$$(1 + \tau_{c1})C_1 = (1 - \tau_{y1})[\overline{Y}_1 + F(I_0)] - (1 + \mathbf{r}_0 - \tau_{b1})B_0^P, \qquad (10.2)$$

where τ_{ct}, τ_{yt}, and τ_{bt} ($t = 0, 1$) denote, respectively, the ad valorem tax rates in period t on consumption, income, and new borrowing. In equation (10.1), the coefficient of C_0 indicates that the unit cost of consumption is unity plus the corresponding ad-valorem tax. The coefficient of the level of income $(\overline{Y}_0 - I_0)$ is unity minus the corresponding ad-valorem tax, reflecting taxes on income from existing capital and inelastic labor supply($\overline{Y}_0$) and a tax rebate on negative income from current investment (I_0). This tax is a cash-flow capital income tax (with full expensing of investment, I_0) Our formulation of the tax on international borrowing assumes that the tax applies to new net private-sector borrowing—$(B_0^P - B_1^P)$. This assumption can be verified by noting that the last two terms on the right-hand side of equation (10.1) could also be written as $(1 - \tau_{b0})(B_0^P - B_{-1}^\mu) - r_{-1}B_{-1}^P$. In this formulation, debt service is exempt from the tax. An analogous interpretation applies to the second budget constraint in equation (10.2). We note that in the second period there is negative new net borrowing (since past debt is repaid and no new debt is issued); therefore, the term $\tau_{b1}B_0^P$ corresponds to a tax rebate. As is evident from the formulation of equations (10.1) and (10.2), the three taxes are linked though an equivalence relation. This equivalence implies that the effect on the real equilibrium of any combination of the three taxes can be duplicated by a policy consisting of any two of them. Our formulation reveals that the celebrated equivalence between consumption and income taxes developed in the closed-economy context (see Auerbach and Kotlikoff 1987) does not carry over to the open-economy context.[1] In what follows, we use the equivalence property to suppress the tax on international borrowing. Thus, we set $\tau_{b0} = \tau_{b1} = 0$.

   With consumption and income taxes, the periodic budget constraints of the government are

$$G_0 = B_0^g + \tau_{c0}C_0 + \tau_{y0}(\overline{Y}_0 - I_0) - (1 + r_{-1})B_{-1}^g \qquad (10.3)$$

and

$$G_1 = \tau_{c1} C_1 + \tau_{y1}[\overline{Y}_1 + F(I_0)] - (1 + r_0)B_0^g. \qquad (10.4)$$

The private sector periodic budget constraints can be combined in order to yield the consolidated lifetime budget constraint.[2] Adding equation (10.2), multiplied by α_1, to equation (10.1) and dividing the resultant equation by $(1 + \tau_{c0})$ yields

$$C_0 + \alpha_{\tau1} C_1 = \frac{(1 - \tau_{y0})}{(1 + \tau_{c0})}\overline{Y}_0 + \frac{(1 - \tau_{y1})}{(1 + \tau_{c0})}\alpha_1 \overline{Y}_1$$

$$+ \frac{(1 - \tau_{y0})}{(1 + \tau_{c0})}[\alpha_n F(I_0) - I_0] - \frac{(1 + r_{-1})}{(1 + \tau_{c0})}B_{-1}^P, \qquad (10.5)$$

where $\alpha_{\tau1} = [(1 + \tau_{c1})/(1 + \tau_{c0})]\,\alpha_1$, $\alpha_{I1} = [(1 - \tau_{y1})/(1 - \tau_{y0})]\,\alpha_1$. For subsequent use we recall that the world discount factor is denoted by $\alpha_1 = 1/(1 + r_0)$.

Equation (10.5) is the private sector consolidated budget constraint, which incorporates the role of taxes. The key point is that it is the tax-inclusive discount factors that are applicable to future period quantities. These are the *effective discount factors* relevant for private sector decisions. Accordingly, $\alpha_{\tau1}$ measures the effective intertemporal price of C_1 in terms of C_0. This price reflects the prevailing tax structure. It is governed by the time profiles of the consumption tax [reflected by the ratio $(1 + \tau_{c1})/(1 + \tau_{c0})$].

Analogously, the effective discount factor applicable for investment decisions is α_{I1}. This effective discount factor is governed by the time profiles of the taxes on income. It does not depend on the time profile of the tax on consumption.

This dependence of the effective discount factors on the time profiles of the various taxes reflects the non-Ricardian feature of the model. A budget deficit arising from a current tax cut must be followed by a future tax hike in order to ensure government solvency. This change in the time profile of taxes alters the effective discount factors, opening up the principal channel through which budget deficits affect the intertemporal allocation of consumption and investment.

Finally, we note that if the time profile of any given tax is flat (so that $\tau_{c0} = \tau_{c1}$, or $\tau_{y0} = \tau_{y1}$), then this tax is nondistortionary, and its effect is similar to that of a lump-sum tax. This property underlies our choice of a cash-flow formulation of the income tax.

10.2 Deficits with Consumption Taxes

Next, the effects of a budget deficit induced by a cut in the tax on consumption are considered. We note in passing that this consumption tax is equivalent to a value-added tax (VAT) system under which investment and exports are exempt. To isolate the effect of this tax cut, we assume that all other taxes are zero. We also assume that the paths of foreign taxes are flat (so that the foreign tax system does not introduce a distortion) and that the foreign government runs a balanced budget (so that changes in the world rate of interest do not affect the foreign government's solvency).

The initial equilibrium is described in figure 10.1 by point A. The downward-sloping schedules portray the desired ratio of current-period to future-period consumption. We assume that the utility functions are homothetic and, therefore, the desired consumption ratios depend only on the rate of interest. The world relative demand is denoted by D^w, where $D^w = C_0^w/C_1^w = (C_0 + C_0^*)/(C_1 + C_1^*)$. This quantity is a weighted average of the two countries' relative demands, $D = C_0/C_1$, and $D^* = C_0^*/C_1^*$. Accordingly,

$$D^w = \mu_d D + (1 - \mu_d)D^*,$$

where the domestic country's weight is

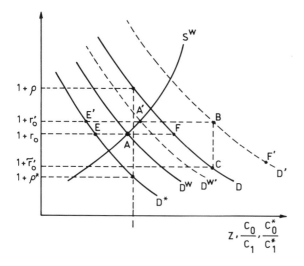

Figure 10.1
Effects of a budget deficit arising from a cut in consumption taxes

$$\mu_d = \frac{C_1}{C_1 + C_1^*}.$$

The upward-sloping S^w schedule is the world relative supply of (current-period to future-period) output net of investment and government spending. Its positive slope reflects the fact that investment falls when the rate of interest rises. This relative supply is denoted in figure 10.1 by the letter z. In figure 10.1, the vertical axis measures the (tax-free) world rate of interest, which is initially r_0. The schedules pertaining to the initial equilibrium $(D, D^*, D^w$, and $S^w)$ are drawn for the given initial configuration of taxes. A reduction in the current tax on consumption from τ_{c0} to τ'_{c0}, with a corresponding rise in the future tax from τ_{c1} to τ'_{c1} (necessary to restore government solvency), raises the effective discount factor applicable to consumption, $\alpha_{\tau 1}$ (that is, it lowers the effective rate of interest), and induces a substitution toward current consumption. Thus, for every value of the world rate of interest, the domestic (relative) demand schedule shifts to the right from D to D'. The proportional vertical displacement of the schedule equals the proportional rise in the effective discount factor. This proportion is $[(1 + \tau'_{c1})/(1 + \tau_{c1})][(1 + \tau_{c0})/(1 + \tau'_{c0})]$. Associated with the new domestic relative demand, the new world relative demand, $(C_0 + C_0^*)/(C_1 + C_1^*)$, also shifts to the right from D^w to $D^{w'}$ in fiure 10.1. This shift reflects the substitution from future to current-period consumption in the domestic economy.[3] Furthermore, the proportional displacement of the world relative demand schedule is smaller than the corresponding displacement of the domestic relative demand schedule.[4]

A rise in the effective discount factor applicable to consumption decisions, from $\alpha_{\tau 1}$ to $\alpha'_{\tau 1}$, does not affect the effective discount factor applicable to investment decisions. Therefore, the relative supply schedule in figure 10.1 remains intact, and the equilibrium world rate of interest rises from r_0 to r'_0. This higher rate discourages domestic investment as well as investment in the foreign country and therefore results in a positive cross-country correlation of investment.

To determine the incidence of this change in the time profile of taxes on the domestic effective rate of interest, we recall that the proportional vertical displacement of the D schedule equals the tax-induced percentage change in the effective discount factor. This change is represented by the distance BC in figure 10.1. Accordingly, in order to determine the new equilibrium value of the domestic effective rate of interest, we subtract from $1 + r'_0$ the distance BC. This yields $1 + \tilde{r}'_0$ in figure 10.1. Evidently the new equilibrium effective rate of interest $\tilde{r}'_0$ is lower than the initial rate

r_0, since the vertical displacement of D^w is smaller than BC and the percentage fall in the world discount factor is even smaller than the vertical displacement of D^w.

The rise in the world rate of interest in the new equilibrium induces intertemporal substitution in foreign consumption toward the future, resulting in a higher growth rate of foreign consumption (represented by the move from point E to point E' in figure 10.1). Similarly, the fall in the domestic effective rate of interest induces intertemporal substitution of domestic consumption toward the current period, thereby lowering the growth rate of domestic consumption (represented by the move from point F to point B in figure 10.1). Finally, we note that even though the growth rate of foreign consumption rises, the growth rate of world consumption falls (as represented by the move from point A to point A' in figure 10.1). This decline reflects the fall in world investment.

Through its influence on the world rate of interest, the domestic budget deficit is transmitted internationally. In general, because of possible conflicts between income and substitution effects induced by the tax policy and by the interest rate changes, the effects of the budget deficit on the *levels* of consumption and the trade balance are not clear cut. However, if the foreign economy has a flat tax profile, then—ruling out a backward-bending saving function—the rise in the world rate of interest operates to reduce current foreign consumption. In this case, since world investment falls while output is unchanged, the market-clearing condition for world output implies that domestic consumption rises. We conclude that, on the one hand, if the intertemporal elasticities of substitution between current and future consumption are relatively low, then the correlation between changes in domestic and foreign consumption consequent on the budget deficit may be positive or negative. On the other hand, if the elasticities of substitution are relatively high, then the budget deficit results in a negative correlation between domestic and foreign levels of consumption.

Finally, in the case in which the foreign saving function does not bend backwards, foreign absorption (consumption plus investment) falls, and therefore the foreign economy's trade account improves. The counterpart of this improvement is a corresponding deterioration in the domestic balance of trade.

10.3 Deficits with Income Taxes

We now consider the effects of a deficit arising from a current cut in taxes on income. Under the assumption that all other taxes are zero, this tax cut

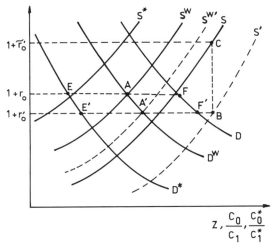

Figure 10.2
Effects of a budget deficit arising from a cut in income tax: Inelastic labor supply

must be accompanied by a corresponding rise in future taxes. Accordingly, suppose that the time profile of taxes is changed from (τ_{y0}, τ_{y1}) to a steeper profile (τ'_{y0}, τ'_{y1}). The initial equilibrium is described by point A in figure 10.2. Since the taxes τ_{y0} and τ_{y1} do not influence the effective discount factor applicable to consumption decisions α_{t1}, changes in the time profile of this tax do not alter the desired ratio of intertemporal consumption. Therefore, the relative demand schedules in figure 10.2 remain intact.

Turning to the supply side, we note that, like the world relative demand schedule, the world relative supply schedule is also a weighted average of the two countries' schedules, S and S^*. Accordingly, $S^w = \mu_s S + (1 - \mu_s)S^*$, where the domestic country weight is

$$\mu_s = \frac{\overline{Y}_1 + F(I_0) - G_1}{\overline{Y}_1 + F(I_0) - G_1 + \overline{Y}_1^* + F^*(I_0^*) - G_1^*} = \frac{\overline{Y}_1 + F(I_0) - G_1}{C_1 + C_1^*}.$$

By lowering the effective discount factor relevant for investment decisions α_{I1}, the budget deficit displaces the domestic relative supply schedule downward from S to S'. The proportional displacement is equal to $(1 - \tau'_{y1})(1 - \tau_{y0})/(1 - \tau_{y1})(1 - \tau'_{y0})$, which measures the percentage change in α_{I1}. The proportional downward displacement of the *world* relative supply schedule is smaller than the corresponding displacement of the domestic relative supply schedule.[5]

The new equilibrium obtains at the intersection of the (unchanged) world relative demand schedule, D^w, and the new world relative supply schedule, $S^{w'}$. This equilibrium is indicated by point A', at which the world rate of interest falls, from r_0 to r_0', and (one plus) the effective interest rate applicable to domestic investment rises by the proportion $(1 + \tilde{r}_0)/(1 + r_0')$. This rise is indicated by the distance BC corresponding to the vertical displacement of the domestic relative supply schedule. In the new equilibrium the rates of growth of domestic and foreign consumption fall, as indicated by the respective moves from point F to point F' and from point E to point E'. As a result, the rate of growth of world consumption must also fall. In view of the fall in the world rate of interest from r_0 to r_0', foreign investment rises, and, in view of the rise in the effective domestic rate of the interest from r_0 to $\tilde{r}_0$, domestic investment falls. Thus, a deficit arising from a cut in taxes on income crowds out domestic investment and crowds in foreign investment. These changes result in a negative correlation between domestic and foreign rates of growth of consumption.

The effects of this cut in taxes on the level of domestic consumption are unambiguous if the initial equilibrium is undistorted (that is, if the initial tax profile is flat). The reason is that the fall in the world rate of interest raises current consumption by increasing wealth (through the increased value of the discounted sum of gross domestic product (GDP)) and by inducing intertemporal substitution of consumption toward the current period. Similarly, if the time profile of foreign taxes is also flat, the fall in the world rate of interest raises foreign consumption for the same reasons. It follows that under these circumstances the domestic budget deficit crowds in both domestic and foreign private sector consumption and results in a positive cross-country correlation between the levels of consumption.

It is also noteworthy that, in contrast to the effects of a cut in consumption taxes, the reduction in taxes on income improves the domestic country trade balance. This improvement is the counterpart to the deterioration in the foreign trade account consequent on the rise in foreign absorption (consumption plus investment).

The foregoing analysis demonstrated that consumption tax policies influence the equilibrium in the world economy by altering the relative demand schedules, whereas capital income tax policies influence the equilibrium by altering the relative supply schedules. With a fixed labor supply, a tax on international borrowing is equivalent to a combination of consumption and income taxes (as can be seen from the budget constraints—equations (10.1) and (10.2). It follows that such a tax policy influences the equilibrium by altering both the relative demand and the relative supply schedules. The effects of a deficit arising from a cut in taxes on international borrowing are, therefore, a combination of the effects of cuts in both consumption and income taxes.

10.4 Budget Deficits with Variable Labor Supply

In this section we extend the stylized model to allow for a variable labor supply. The response of labor supply to changes in wages net of taxes adds an additional dimension to the intertemporal elasticity of the relative supply schedule. To highlight the supply-side effect induced by income taxes, we abstract from other taxes.

As in the previous sections, the individual who has access to the world capital market maximizes lifetime utility subject to the consolidated lifetime budget constraint. With variable labor supply, it is convenient to include in the definition of lifetime spending the imputed spending on leisure. Correspondingly, the definition of wealth includes the imputed value of labor endowment. Thus, the lifetime budget constraint is

$$C_0 + (1 - \tau_{y0})(1 - l_0)w_{l0} + \alpha_1[C_1 + (1 - \tau_{y1})(1 - l_1)w_{l1}]$$

$$= (1 - \tau_{y0})(w_{l0} + r_{k0}K_0 - I_0) + \alpha_1(1 - \tau_{y1})$$

$$\cdot \{w_{l1} + r_{kl}[K_0 + K(I_0)]\} - (1 + r_{-1})B^p_{-1} = W_0, \tag{10.6}$$

where τ_{yt}, w_{lt}, and r_{kt} denote, respectively, the tax rates on income, the wage rate, and the rental rate on capital in period t ($t = 0, 1$), where K_0 denotes the initial endowment of capital, and where l_t denotes the fraction of time spent on labor in period t ($t = 0, 1$); total endowment of time in each period is normalized to unity.[6] As indicated in equation (10.6), the individual lifetime (full) income—that is, the individual wealth (W_0)—is the discounted sum of the value of time endowment and capital income (net of taxes and of the initial debt commitment). Captial income in the current period is the rental on existing capital, $r_{k0}K_0$, minus investment, I_0; correspondingly, the stock of capital in the subsequent period is $K_0 + K(I_0)$.

Maximization of the utility function subject to the lifetime budget constraint yields the demand functions for ordinary consumption and for leisure in each period. These demand functions depend on the three relative prices (net wages in each of the two periods and the discount factor) and on wealth. Assuming that the amounts of leisure consumed in two consecutive periods are gross substitutes implies that for a given level of wealth a current tax cut lowers future labor supply, and a future tax cut lowers current labor supply. Furthermore, assuming that the utility function is separable between ordinary consumption and leisure implies that the utility-maximizing ratio of consumption in the two consecutive periods depends *only on the rate of interest* and not on the wage structure.

In each period the level of outputs Y_0 and Y_1 depends on labor and capital inputs. Under the assumptions that factor markets are competitive, and that the production functions are linear (the latter assumption being made for simplicity of exposition), the relative supply of world ordinary consumption is again denoted by z, which, as before, measures the ratio of world GDP net of investment and government spending in the two consecutive periods. That is,

$$z = \frac{(a_0 I_0 + b_0 K_0 - I_0 - G_0) + (a_0^* I_0^* + b_0^* K_0^* - I_0^* - G_0^*)}{\{a_1 l_1 + b_1[K_0 + K(I_0)] - G_1\} + \{a_1^* l_1^* + b_1^*[K_0^* + K^*(I_0^*)] - G_1^*\}}, \tag{10.7}$$

where a_t and b_t ($t = 0, 1$) denote, respectively, the marginal products of labor and capital in the home country in period t, and where a_t^* and b_t^* denote the corresponding foreign magnitudes.

The initial equilibrium of the system is described by point A in figure 10.3. As before, the downward-sloping schedules D and D^* denote the domestic and foreign relative demands for (ordinary goods) consumption in the two periods, and the schedule D^w is the weighted average of the

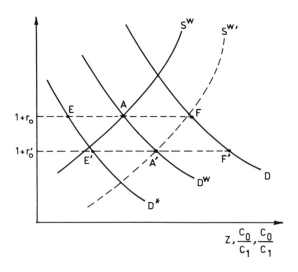

Figure 10.3
Effects of a budget deficit arising from a cut in income tax: Variable labor supply

domestic and foreign relative demands. The negative slopes of the schedules reflect the intertemporal substitution arising from changes in the rate of interest. The positively sloped schedule, S^w, reflects the response of z to the rate of interest.[7]

Consider now the effect of a budget deficit arising from a current reduction in the tax (τ_{y0}) on labor income (accompanied by a future rise in the tax (τ_{y1}). On the other hand, the assumption that the homothetic utility functions are separable between leisure and ordinary consumption implies that for a given rate of interest the change in the time profile of wages (net of taxes) does not alter the desired ratios of ordinary consumption in the two consecutive periods. Thus, the budget deficit does not alter the position of the relative demand schedules in figure 10.3.

On the other hand, the assumption that the amounts of leisure consumed in the two periods are gross substitutes ensures that the rise in the current net wage raises the current labor supply, l_0, and the fall in the future net wage lowers the future labor supply, l_1. These movements and the negative effect on investment cause the domestic relative supply schedule (not drawn) to shift to the right. Thus, as seen from equation (10.7), this change in the time profile of taxes raises the value of z for any given rate of interest. This is shown by the rightward shift of the world relative supply schedule from S^w to $S^{w'}$ in figure 10.3.

The new equilibrium shifts from point A to point A', the world rate of interest falls from r_0 to r'_0, and the rates of growth of domestic, foreign, and world consumption fall. The lower rate of interest induces a positive correlation between growth rates of consumption. It also stimulates investment in both countries and, therefore, induces a positive correlation between domestic and foreign rates of investment.

A budget deficit arising from the change in the time profile of taxes on labor income also alters the levels of consumption in both countries. In the domestic economy the changes in the level of consumption reflect the combination of the induced changes in labor supply, the wealth and substitution effects induced by changes in the world rate of interest, and the response of investment. The fall in the world rate of interest raises the discounted sum of foreign GDP (provided that the foreign labor supply is not greatly reduced by the fall in the rate of interest). In addition (ruling out a backward-bending saving function), the fall in the rate of interest induces substitution of current consumption for future consumption. Hence, in this case, foreign consumption rises.

Finally, in the present framework the budget deficit may cause an improvement in the balance of trade. For example, if the foreign labor supply does not respond appreciably (positively) to the fall in the rate of interest and, correspondingly, if the foreign GDP (net of government spending) does not rise much, then the rise in foreign absorption (consumption plus investment) worsens the foreign trade balance and, correspondingly, improves the domestic balance of trade. Thus, in this case the budget deficit causes an improvement in the trade account. This improvement reflects the rise in current period output induced by the stimulative policy of the lower taxes on labor income.

10.5   Budget Deficits: Overview

The important role attached to the intertemporal substitution effects suggests that the various distortionary taxes can be usefully categorized according to whether they induce excess demand for current goods or for future goods or, equivalently, whether they stimulate current external borrowing (national dissaving) or lending (national saving). Tax policy that induces an excess demand for current goods by raising current consumption or investment, or by lowering current GDP relative to future GDP, is classified as a *proborrowing* policy; and tax policy that creates an excess supply of current goods by discouraging current consumption or investment, or by raising current GDP relative to future GDP, is classified as a *prolending* policy. Alternatively, the various tax policies associated with the budget deficit can be classified into expansionary *supply-shift* policies and expansionary *demand-shift* policies. Accordingly, a deficit arising from a cut in taxes on income reflects supply-shift policies, whereas a deficit arising from a cut in the consumption tax (value-added tax) reflects demand-shift policy. The former is a prolending policy; the latter is a proborrowing policy. From this classification we note that a budget deficit arising from a cut in taxes on international borrowing contains elements of both supply- and demand-shift policies. It can be shown, however, that the demand-shift component dominates, so that a cut in the tax on international borrowing is a proborrowing policy.

The results of the analysis are summarized in table 10.1. It is seen that the effects of the budget deficit on the world rate of interest, r_0, depend on whether the deficit arises from a proborrowing or a prolending tax cut. A cut in current taxes on consumption and on international borrowing is a proborrowing tax policy that raises the world rate of interest; a cut in current taxes on capital income and on labor income is a prolending tax policy that lowers the world rate of interest. The table also shows that in the case of consumption and income taxes, domestic investment falls,

Table 10.1
Effects of budget deficits arising from tax cuts

Tax cut	Affected variables									
	g_c^w	r_0	$\bar{r}_0$	g_c	g_c^*	I_0	I_0^*	C_0	C_0^*	$(TA)_0$
On consumption	−	+	−	−	+	−	−	+	−	−
On international borrowing	$+^a$ $-^b$	+	−	−	+	+	−	?	−	−
On income	−	−	+	−	−	−	+	?	+	+

Note: g_c^w, g_c, and g_c^* denote, respectively, world, domestic, and foreign growth rates of consumption; $\bar{r}_0$ denotes the effective domestic rate of interest applicable to consumption. This effective rate also governs domestic investment decisions (excpet for the case of consumption taxes for which domestic investment depends on the world rate of interest r_0). The ambiguities in the effects of taxes on domestic consumption reflect conflicting substitution and weath effects. Domestic consumption rises if the substitution effect dominates the wealth effect. The latter depends on the initial borrowing-needs position. The assumption underlying the direction of the two changes in the *levels* of consumption and the trade account is the absence of backward-bending saving functions.
a. If $\mu_s > \mu_d$
b. If $\mu_s < \mu_d$

whereas in the case of taxes on international borrowing, domestic investment rises.

The results reported in the table show that whether the tax cut is proborrowing or prolending, the budget deficit always lowers the growth rate of domestic consumption, $g_c = (C_1/C_0) - 1$. However, the international transmission of the effects of the deficit does depend on whether the deficit arises from a proborrowing or prolending tax policy. If the tax policy is a proborrowing policy, then the growth rate of foreign consumption rises and foreign investment falls; a prolending tax policy will have the opposite effect.

Table 10.1 also reports the changes in the growth rates of world consumption, $g_c = (1/z) - 1$ (which is equal to the growth rate of world GDP net of investment and government spending). As has been shown, the direction of the change in the growth rate of world consumption depends on the characteristics of the taxes that are changed. Since the various taxes influence the levels of current and future consumption, investment, and GDP, the net effect reflects the interactions among these changes. Accordingly, on the one hand, the growth rate of world consumption rises if the (second-period) domestic trade account is in surplus and the budget deficit arises from a cut in taxes on international borrowing. On the other hand, the growth rate of world consumption falls if the tax cut on international borrowing occurs in the presence of a (second-period) domestic trade account deficit, or if the budget deficit stems from a cut in the other taxes.

Expressed in terms of correlations, table 10.1 reveals that a budget deficit arising from a proborrowing tax policy results in *negative* cross-country correlations between growth rates of consumption. A budget deficit arising from a prolending tax policy results in *positive* cross-country correlations between the growth rates of consumption. The cross-country correlations between levels of investment are shown to be positive if the deficit arises from a cut in taxes on consumption or labor income, and negative if the budget deficit stems from a cut in taxes on international borrowing and capital income.

The effects of the budget deficit on the *levels* of domestic and foreign consumption and on the balance of trade depend in general on the shape of the initial time profile of taxes, on the initial borrowing needs of the country (being positive or negative), and on the size of the intertemporal elasticity of substitution. The signs of the effects indicated in the last three columns in table 10.1 are based on the assumption that the initial tax profile is flat and that the saving functions are not backward bending. Under these assumptions, a budget deficit arising from a proborrowing tax policy lowers foreign consumption and worsens the domestic balance of trade, whereas a budget deficit arising from a prolending tax policy raises foreign consumption and improves the domestic balance of trade.

11

Fiscal Policies and the Real Exchange Rate

Up to this point in this part we have assumed that all goods are internationally tradable in world markets. This characteristic implies that fiscal policies that alter the relative price of goods impact directly on the rest of the world. In this section we extend the analysis by allowing for goods that are nontradable internationally, and whose relative prices are determined exclusively in the domesic economy. In that case the domestic effects of fiscal policies and their international transmission also operate through changes in the relative price of nontradable goods (the inverse of the real exchange rate). In what follows we examine the role of the real exchange rate in the analysis of fiscal policies. After introducing the analytical framework, we study the effects of government spending and then analyze the implications of budget deficits arising from tax cuts.

11.1   The Analytical Framework

The analytical framework employs a general-equilibrium intertemporal approach for a two-country model of the world economy. Throughout we assume that there are two composite goods: an internationally tradable good denoted by x, and a nontradable good denoted by n. To allow for intertemporal considerations we assume, for simplicity, a two-period model, period 0 and period 1. The relative price of the nontradable good (the inverse of the real exchange rate) in period t is p_{nt}, the exogenously given output of that good is Y_{nt}, government purchases of the nontradable good are G_{nt}, and private-sector demand is c_{nt} ($t = 0, 1$). The private-sector lifetime budget constraint is

$$(c_{x0} + p_{n0} c_{n0}) + \alpha_{x1}(c_{x1} + p_{n1} c_{n1}) = (\bar{Y}_{x0} + p_{n0} \bar{Y}_{n0}) + \alpha_{x1}(\bar{Y}_{x1} + p_{n1} \bar{Y}_{n1})$$

$$- (T_0 + \alpha_{x1} T_1) - (1 + r_{x, -1}) B^p_{-1} \equiv W_0, \tag{11.1}$$

where $\alpha_{x1} = 1/(1 + r_{x0})$ denotes the discount factor in terms of tradable goods and where T_t, c_{xt}, and $\bar{Y}_{xt}$ denote, respectively, the level of lump-sum taxes, the level of consumption, and the exogenously given level of production of tradable goods in period t ($t = 0, 1$). W_0 denotes wealth, r_{xt} ($t = -1, 0$) denotes the world interest rate, and B_t^p denotes private-sector debt in period t ($t = -1, 0$). The values of taxes, wealth, debt, and the interest rates are measured in terms of tradable goods.

The individual maximizes lifetime utility subject to the lifetime budget constraint (11.1). We assume that the lifetime utility function can be expressed as a function of two linearly homogeneous subutility functions $C_0(c_{x0}, c_{n0})$ and $C_1(c_{x1}, c_{n1})$. Hence, lifetime utility is $U(C_0, C_1)$. The maximization of this utility function subject to the lifetime budget constraint (11.1) is carried out in two stages, where the first stage optimizes the composition of spending within each period and the second stage optimizes the intertemporal allocation of spending between periods.

The optimization of the intertemporal allocation of the (consumption-based) real spending yields the demand functions for real spending in each period, $C_t = C_t(\alpha_{c1}, W_{c0})$, where α_{c1} is the (consumption-based) real wealth. Expressed in terms of tradable goods, the level of spending in each period is $P_t C_t$, where P_t is the consumption-based price index (the "true" price deflator). Thus, $\alpha_{c1} = \alpha_{x1} P_1 / P_0$ and $W_{c0} = W_0 / P_0$. Clearly, the price index in each period depends on the temporal relative price p_{nt} with an elasticity that equals the relative share of expenditure on nontradable goods, β_{nt}. Within each period, the utility-maximizing allocation of spending between goods depends on the relative price p_{nt}. (See chapter 6.)

The market for nontradable goods must clear in each country during each period. Accordingly,

$$c_{n0}[p_{n0}, P_0 C_0(\alpha_{c1}, W_{c0})] = \bar{Y}_{n0} - G_{n0} \qquad (11.2)$$

and

$$c_{n1}[p_{n1}, P_1 C_1(\alpha_{c1}, W_{c0})] = \bar{Y}_{n1} - G_{n1}, \qquad (11.3)$$

where the left-hand sides of these equilibrium conditions show the demand functions and the right-hand sides show the supply net of government purchases.[1] As we have seen, the demand functions depend on the relative price, p_{nt}, and on spending, $P_t C_t$, where P_t is the (consumption-based) price index, and C_t is (consumption-based) real spending. Real spending, in turn, depends on the (consumption-based) real discount factor, α_{c1}. We assume that the utility function is homothetic, so that the elasticity of consumption demand with respect to spending, as well as the elasticity of spending with respect to wealth, is unity.

11.2 Spending Policies

In analyzing the effects of government spending, we obtain the equilibrium value of wealth, W_0, by substituting the government present-value budget constraint (from footnote 1) into the corresponding private-sector budget constraint. Accordingly,

$$W_0 = [p_{n0}(\bar{Y}_{n0} - G_{n0}) + (\bar{Y}_{x0} - G_{x0})] + \alpha_{x1}[(\bar{Y}_{n1} - G_{n1})$$
$$+ (\bar{Y}_{x1} - G_{x1})] - (1 + r_{x,-1})B_{-1}. \qquad (11.4)$$

Thus, as usual, government spending absorbs resources that otherwise would have been available to the private sector. We assume that the public goods generated by these policies do not tilt the private-sector relative demand for private goods.

Next we determine the effects of government spending on the path of private-sector consumption of tradable goods. Analogously to the previous specification, the demand function for tradable goods in period t is

$$c_{xt} = c_{xt}[p_{nt}, P_t C_t(\alpha_{c1}, W_{c0})], \qquad t = 0, 1. \qquad (11.5)$$

Clearly, in contrast to the markets for nontradable goods, the consumption of tradable goods in any given period is not limited by the available domestic supply. It is shown in appendix A that the *intertemporal-consumption ratio* of tradable goods, c_{x0}/c_{x1}, depends on the world discount factor according to

$$\frac{d\log(c_{x0}/c_{x1})}{d\log\alpha_{x1}} = \frac{\sigma_{nx}\sigma}{\beta_n\sigma + (1 - \beta_n)\sigma_{nx}}, \qquad (11.6)$$

where β_n denotes the relative share of private-sector spending on non-tradable goods and σ and σ_{nx} denote, respectively, the intertemporal and the temporal elasticities of substitution.[2] Equation (11.6) (which incorporates the induced change in the path of the real exchange rate) shows that the only factors governing the change in the intertemporal-consumption ratio are pure temporal and intertemporal substitution effects. The absence of wealth effects reflects the homotheticity assumption. The foreign economy is assumed to be characterized by a structure of demand and supply similar to that of the domestic economy.

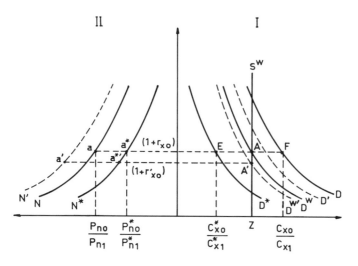

Figure 11.1
The effects of government spending on the world interest rate and on the paths of real exchange rates

To determine the equilibrium in the world economy, we need to consider the factors governing world demand and world supply of tradable goods. The analysis is carried out with the aid of figure 11.1. Panel I of figure 11.1 shows the *relative* intertemporal domestic, D, foreign, D^*, and world D^w, demands for tradable goods. The world relative demand is a weighted average of the domestic and foreign relative demands. That is,

$$D^w = \frac{c_{x0} + c_{x0}^*}{c_{x1} + c_{x1}^*} = \mu_d \frac{c_{x0}}{c_{x1}} + (1 - \mu_d)\frac{c_{x0}^*}{c_{x1}^*}, \tag{11.7}$$

where $\mu_d = c_{x1}/(c_{x1} + c_{x1}^*)$. The relative-demand schedules relate the desired consumption ratio of tradable goods to the interest rate. Their slope reflects the negative relationship embodied in equation (11.6). These demand schedules are drawn for a given level of government spending. Analogously, the relative world supply of tradable goods net of government purchases, z, is

$$z = \frac{(\bar{Y}_{x0} - G_{x0}) + (\bar{Y}_{x0}^* - G_{x0}^*)}{(\bar{Y}_{x1} - G_{x1}) + (\bar{Y}_{x1}^* - G_{x1}^*)}. \tag{11.8}$$

The relative-supply schedule, S^w, is drawn with a zero interest elasticity, since we abstract from investment. This schedule is also drawn for a given level of government spending.

The schedules N and N^* in panel II of figure 11.1 show the relationship between the world interest rate and the internal relative-price structure (the path of the real exchange rate) in each country. The elasticity of these schedules is given by equation (11.9), which is derived in appendix A:

$$\frac{d\log(p_{n0}/p_{n1})}{d\log\alpha_{x1}} = \frac{\sigma}{\beta_n\sigma + (1-\beta_n)\sigma_{nx}}. \tag{11.9}$$

Equation (11.9) indicates that changes in the world interest rate influence the path of the real exchange rate only through the intertemporal substitution effect. Accordingly, a rise in the world interest rate (a fall in α_{x1}) induces intertemporal substitution of spending toward the future. It thereby lowers the current price of nontradable goods relative to the future price (i.e., it decelerates the rate of increase in the real exchange rate from period 0 to period 1). As before, the homotheticity assumption accounts for the absence of the wealth variable in equation (11.9).

The initial equilibrium is described in panel I by point A, in which the world interest rate is r_{x0}. The domestic and foreign intertemporal consumption ratios are indicated by points F and E. The periodic percentage changes of the domestic and the foreign real exchange rates associated with the initial equilibrium are shown in panel II by points a and a^*.

Consider the effects of a rise in the level of domestic-government spending.[3] This change alters the domestic relative demand and the domestic country weight, μ_d (and, thereby, the world relative demand), as well as the world relative supply. A rise in the level of domestic-government spending influences world relative demand in two ways: (11.1) through its effect on domestic relative demand, and (11.2) through its effect on the domestic-country weight, μ_d. The effect of the rise in government spending on the domestic relative demand (derived in appendix A) is given by

$$\frac{d\log(c_{x0}/c_{x1})}{dG} = \frac{\beta_n\beta_n^g 0_n(1-\gamma_s)(\sigma_{nx}-\sigma)}{\beta_n\sigma + (1-\beta_n)\sigma_{nx}}\left[\frac{(1-\gamma_s^g)}{(1-\gamma_s)} - \frac{\gamma_s^g}{\gamma_s}\right], \tag{11.10}$$

where ϕ_n denotes the inverse of the value of private consumption of nontradable goods in period 0, that is, $\phi_n = 1/p_{n0}c_{n0}$. The intertemporal and temporal allocations of government spending are governed by the government saving propensity, γ_s^g, defined as the ratio of future government spending (in present-value terms) to the discounted sum of spending, and by the relative share of government spending on nontradables in total government spending in period t, β_n^g. Finally, γ_s, defined as the ratio of private-sector future consumption (in present-value terms) to the discounted sum of private-sector spending, denotes the private-sector saving propensity.

As shown in equation (11.10), the direction of the change in the relative-demand schedules depends on the *government-induced bias* in the intertemporal net supply of nontradable goods and on the *temporal-intertemporal substitution bias* in private-sector demand. Indeed, if either σ equals σ_{nx} or γ_s equals γ_s^g, the change in government spending does not alter the position of the relative-demand schedule.

The direction of the change in the world demand due to the induced change in the weight μ_d, while maintaining c_{x0}/c_{x1} constant, is equal to

$$\frac{d \log[(c_{x0} + c_{x0}^*)/(c_{x1} + c_{x1}^*)]}{dG} = \frac{1}{(c_{x0} + c_{x0}^*)}(1 - \mu_d)(1 - \beta_n)\gamma_s$$

$$\cdot \left[\frac{1 - \gamma_s^*}{\gamma_s^*} - \frac{1 - \gamma_s}{\gamma_s}\right]. \tag{11.11}$$

Note that this effect vanishes if γ_s equals γ_s^*.

To determine the direction of the change in the relative-supply schedule, we differentiate equation 11.8 with respect to government spending. Accordingly,

$$\frac{d \log z}{dG} = \lambda_x^g(1 - \beta_n^g)(1 - \gamma_s^g)$$

$$\cdot \frac{\gamma_s^g}{1 - \gamma_s^g} - \mu_d \frac{\gamma_s}{1 - \gamma_s} - (1 - \mu_d)\frac{\gamma_s^*}{1 - \gamma_s^*}, \tag{11.12}$$

where λ_x^g denotes the reciprocal of the world output of tradable goods net of government purchases of these goods in period 1. Thus, $\lambda_x^g = 1/[(\bar{Y}_x - G_x) + (\bar{Y}_x^* - G_x^*)]$. Equation 11.12 indicates that the direction of the change in the relative supply reflects the bias in the intertemporal allocation of government spending on tradable goods. For example, a temporary *current* rise in government spending ($\gamma_s^g = 0$) induces a leftward shift of the relative-supply schedule, whereas a temporary *future* rise in government spending ($\gamma_s^g = 1$) induces a rightward shift of the relative supply.

Similar considerations apply to the effects of government spending on the paths of the domestic and foreign real exchange rates. For a given value of the world interest rate (measured in terms of tradable goods), the effects of the rise in government spending on the time path of the real exchange rate, p_{n0}/p_{n1}, is found by differentiating equations (11.2) and (11.3) around

$G = 0$, subtracting the resulting equations from each other, and using the Slutsky decomposition. This yields

$$\frac{d\log(p_{no}/p_{n1})}{dG} = \frac{\beta_n^g \phi_n (1 - \gamma_s)}{\beta_n(\beta_n \sigma + (1 - \beta_n)\sigma_{nx})} \left[\frac{1 - \gamma_s^g}{1 - \gamma_s} - \frac{\gamma_s^g}{\gamma_s}\right]. \tag{11.13}$$

Equation (11.13) reveals that the direction of the change in the path of the real exchange rate depends on the temporal and the intertemporal allocations of government demand for nontradable goods relative to the corresponding allocations of private-sector demand. If the ratio of the relative share of government spending on nontradable goods in the current period, $\beta_n^g(1 - \gamma_s^g)$, to the private-sector share, $\beta_n(1 - \gamma_s)$, exceeds the corresponding ratio in the future period, $\beta_n^g \gamma_s^g / \beta_n \gamma_s$, then a rise in government spending raises the percentage rate of change of the real exchange rate, and vice versa.

This result can be interpreted in terms of a transfer-problem criterion relating the temporal and intertemporal spending patterns of the government and the domestic private sector. Accordingly, the rise in government spending raises the current price of nontradable goods relative to its future price if the pattern of government spending is biased toward current nontradable goods in comparison with the pattern of private-sector spending. As indicated by equation (11.12), depending on the temporal and intertemporal spending patterns of the government, the rise in government spending may induce a rightward or leftward shift of the N schedule in panel II of figure 11.1.

To illustrate the working of the model, we consider in figure 11.1 the effects of government spending for a benchmark case in which the intertemporal elasticity of substitution, σ, exceeds the temporal elasticity, σ_{nx}; the ratio of the shares of government spending to private spending in the current period, $(1 - \gamma_s^g)/(1 - \gamma_s)$, exceeds the corresponding ratio of future spending, γ_n^g/γ_s; government spending falls entirely on nontradable goods (so that $\beta_n^g = 1$); and the domestic private sector's saving propensity equals the foreign propensity. As indicated by equation (11.10), in this benchmark case the domestic, and thereby the world, relative-demand schedules shift leftward from the position indicated by D and D^w to the position indicated by D' and $D^{w'}$, respectively. Further, as indicated by equation (11.12), with $\beta_n^g = 1$ the relative supply of world tradable goods does not change. It follows that in this case the equilibrium point shifts from point A to point A' in panel I of figure 11.1, and the world interest rate falls from r_{x0} to $\tilde{r}_{x0}'$.

In panel II of figure 11.1 we show the effects of the rise in government spending on the paths of the domestic and foreign real exchange rates. As indicated by equation (11.13), in this benchmark case the N schedule shifts outward and, given the new lower world interest rate, the domestic and foreign equilibrium points shift from a and a^* to a' and $a^{*'}$, respectively. Accordingly, the percentage change (per unit of time) in the real exchange rates increases in both countries. In concluding the presentation of this benchmark case, we note that since the world interest rate (measured in terms of tradable goods) falls, and since in both countries the time paths of the real exchange rates steepen, it follows that in both countries the consumption-based real interest rates fall (even though, in general, the magnitude of this decline need not be the same for both countries).

We chose this specific benchmark case in which the rise in government spending lowers the world interest rate in order to highlight the implications of government spending on nontradable goods. In fact, if government spending falls entirely on tradable goods (so that $\beta_n^g = 0$), then the rise in spending does not alter the relative-demand schedules in figure 11.1, as seen from equation (11.10) with $\beta_n^g = 0$, but it induces a leftward shift of the relative-supply schedule, as seen from equation (11.12) for the case $\gamma_s^g < \gamma_s$, $\beta_n^g = 0$. Thus, under such circumstances, the rise in government spending raises the equilibrium interest rate. This case underlies the simple transfer-problem criterion described in the introduction to this chapter.

The more general configurations of the effects of government spending on the world interest rate, as implied by equations (11.8) and (11.10), are summarized in table 11.1, where we assume that initially $\gamma_s = \gamma_s^*$. The table demonstrates that if the commodity composition of government spending is strongly biased toward goods that are internationally tradable (so that β_n^g is small), then the key factor determining the direction of the change in

Table 11.1
The effects of a rise in government spending on the world interest rate in a model with nontradable goods

Relationship between temporal and intertemporal elasticities of substitution	Intertemporal and temporal allocations of government spending			
	$\gamma_s > \gamma_s^g$		$\gamma_s < \gamma_s^g$	
	$\beta_n^g = 0$	$\beta_n^g = 1$	$\beta_n^g = 0$	$\beta_n^g = 1$
$\sigma_{nx} > \sigma$	+	+	−	−
$\sigma_{nx} = \sigma$	$\geqq$	0	−	0
$\sigma_{nx} < \sigma$	+	−	−	+

Note: The world rate of interest is measured in terms of internationally tradable goods. This table assumes that initially $\gamma_s = \gamma_s^*$.

the world interest rate is the intertemporal allocation of government and private-sector spending. If government spending is biased toward the current period relative to private-sector spending, so that γ_s exceeds γ_s^g, then the world interest rate rises, and vice versa. On the other hand, if the commodity composition of government spending is strongly biased toward nontradable goods (so that β_n^g is close to unity), then the direction of the change in the interest rate depends on the interaction between the intertemporal allocation of government spending relative to the private sector and the difference between the temporal and the intertemporal elasticities of substitution of the domestic private sector. In fact, since in this case the effects of government spending operate only through changes in the relative-demand schedules, the interest rate rises if $(\sigma_{nx} - \sigma)(\gamma_s - \gamma_s^g)$ is positive, and vice versa.

The various possibilities concerning the relative magnitudes of the key parameters also imply that the effects of government spending on the time path of the domestic and foreign real exchange rates are not clear-cut. The possible outcomes are summarized in table 11.2. The results show that if the commodity composition of government spending is strongly biased toward internationally tradable goods (so that β_n^g is about zero), then, as implied by equation (11.13) the change in government spending does not materially displace the N schedule in panel II of figure 11.1. Therefore, the induced change in the path of the domestic real exchange rate mirrors only the change in the interest rate, since it involves a movement along the

Table 11.2
The effects of a rise in government spending on the paths of domestic and foreign real exchange rates

Relationship between temporal and intertemporal elasticities of substitution	The real exchange rate in the	Intertemporal and temporal allocations of government spending			
		$\gamma_s > \gamma_s^g$		$\gamma_s < \gamma_s^g$	
		$\beta_n^g = 0$	$\beta_n^g = 1$	$\beta_n^g = 0$	$\beta_n^g = 1$
$\sigma_{nx} > \sigma$	domestic economy	−	?	+	?
	foreign economy	−	−	+	+
$\sigma_{nx} = \sigma$	domestic economy	−	+	+	−
	foreign economy	−	0	+	0
$\sigma_{nx} < \sigma$	domestic economy	−	+	+	−
	foreign economy	−	+	+	−

Note: The paths of the real exchange rates are measured by p_{n0}/p_{ni} and p_{n0}^*/p_{n1}^*. This table assumes that initially $\gamma_s = \gamma_s^*$.

given N schedule. It follows that, with a small β_n^g, the change in the time path of the domestic real exchange rate is inversely related to the change in the world interest rate. This inverse relationship is verified from a comparison between the entries appearing in tables 11.1 and 11.2 in the columns corresponding to the case of $\beta_n^g = 0$. Indeed, in this case the direction of the change in the path of the real exchange rate depends only on the simple transfer-problem criterion involving the saving propensities of the domestic private and public sectors.

In the other extreme case, in which government spending falls mainly on nontradable goods (so that β_n^g is close to unity), then, as long as the temporal elasticity of substitution, σ_{nx}, does not exceed the intertemporal elasticity of substitution, σ, the key factor determining whether the path of the real exchange rate steepens or flattens is the intertemporal allocation of government spending. If government spending is biased toward the current period relative to private-sector spending, so that γ_s exceeds γ_s^g, the rise in spending accelerates the time path of the real exchange rate, and vice versa. On the other hand, if σ_{nx} exceeds σ, the time path of the real exchange rate is influenced by two conflicting forces, the one operating through a movement along the N schedule (induced by the change in the interest rate) and the other operating through a shift in the N schedule (induced by the direct effect of government spending on the relative supply of nontradable goods).

Finally, note that the foreign schedule, N^*, is not affected by domestic-government spending, so that the time path of the foreign real exchange rate, p_{n1}^*/p_{n1}^*, is always related negatively to the world interest rate. But since the correlation between the time path of the domestic real exchange rate and the world interest rate may be positive, zero, or negative (as can be verified by comparing the results reported in tables 11.1 and 11.2), it follows that the cross-country correlations between the paths of the real exchange rates and between the (consumption-based) real interest rates may also be negative, zero, or positive. The analysis underlying tables 11.1 and 11.2 identifies the main factors governing the signs of the various cross-country correlations.

11.3 Tax Policies

Heretofore, we have analyzed the effects of government spending under the assumption that taxes are nondistortionary. We next analyze the effects of tax policies by examining the effects of changes in distortionary taxes under the assumption that government spending remains intact. To focus on tax policies, we set government spending at zero. To isolate the key mechanism through which tax policies influence private-sector behavior, we incorporate taxes into the definition of the discount factor and consider two tax systems: a consumption tax system and an income tax system. We analyze two forms of tax policies: tax-reduction policies resulting in budget deficits and tax-conversion policies that do not alter the path of government revenue.

Budget Deficits

The key proposition here is that the effects on the world economy of budget deficits arising from tax cuts depend critically on the tax system. To demonstrate this point, we examine first the effects of a consumption tax cut and then the effects of an income tax cut.

Consider a value-added tax system (VAT) under which exports are exempt. Clearly, this tax is equivalent to a consumption tax. In the presence of such a tax, the effective (tax-adjusted) discount factor is denoted by $\alpha_{x\tau1}$, which is related to the undistorted world discount factor, α_{x1}, according to $\alpha_{x\tau1} = [(1 + \tau_{c1})/(1 + \tau_{c0})]\alpha_{x1}$, where τ_{ct} is the ad valorem consumption tax rate in period t ($t = 0, 1$). Correspondingly, the effective (consumption-based) real discount factor is denoted by $\alpha_{c\tau1}$, where $\alpha_{c\tau1} = (P_1/P_0)\alpha_{x\tau1}$. With such a tax, private-sector demands depend on $\alpha_{c\tau1}$ rather than on α_{c1}, and therefore changes in the time profile of taxes alter private-sector behavior. To simplify, we assume that foreign-government spending and taxes are zero.

A budget deficit arising from a current-period tax cut (a reduction in τ_{c0}) must be accompanied by a corresponding rise in future taxes (a rise in τ_{c1}) so as to maintain government solvency as long as government spending policies remain intact. The effects of such a change in the time profile of taxes are analyzed with the aid of figure 11.2. The initial equilibrium is described in panel I by point A, in which the world interest rate is r_{x0}. For convenience of exposition we assume that initially the time profile of taxes is "flat" ($\tau_{c0} = \tau_{c1}$), so that the domestic and foreign interest rates (in terms of tradable goods) are equal. Thus, the flat tax system is neutral with respect to the real equilibrium. The time paths of the domestic and foreign real exchange rates associated with the initial equilibrium are indicated in panel II by points a and a^* along the N and the N^* schedules. Thus, the initial equilibrium is identical to the one portrayed in figure 11.1.

Consider the effects of a budget deficit arising from a tax cut. Such a tax policy breaks the "flatness" of the tax system. Given the initial value of the

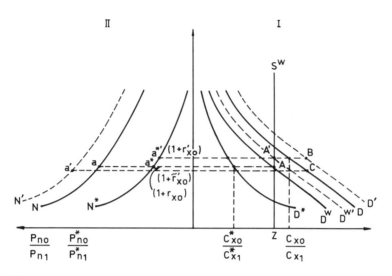

Figure 11.2
The effect of a budget deficit arising from a cut in a value-added tax on the world interest
rate and on the paths of the real exchange rates

world interest rate, r_{x0}, the reduction in τ_{c0} and the increase in τ_{c1} (implied
by the government budget constraint) raise the domestic effective discount
factor, $\alpha_{x\tau 1}$, and induce an upward displacement of the domestic relative-
demand schedule from D to D'. Assuming that initially γ_s equals γ_s^*, so that
the change in the domestic-country weight in the world relative demand
does not affect the world relative demand, the proportional vertical displacement of the schedule equals the proportional change in the effective
discount factor. This displacement is necessary in order to offset the effect
of the tax-induced reduction in the effective interest rate on the desired
domestic consumption ratio. Corresponding to the new domestic schedule
D', the world relative-demand schedule shifts from D^w to $D^{w'}$. The new
equilibrium is described by point A' in panel I of figure 11.2. Hence the
world interest rate rises from r_{x0} to r_{x0}'. The proportional vertical displacement of the world relative-demand schedule, D^w (indicated by the distance
AA'), is smaller than the corresponding displacement of the domestic
schedule, D (indicated by the distance BC), since the world schedule is a
weighted average of the domestic and the (given) foreign schedules. It
follows that the domestic effective interest rate must fall from r_{x0} to a lower
level such as $\tilde{r}_{x0}'$.

The change in the time profile of taxes, which (for any given level of the
world interest rate) raises the effective discount factor, also alters the
position of the domestic schedule N in panel II of figure 11.2. By analogy

to the previous analysis of the displacement of the relative-demand schedule, the proportional vertical displacement of the N schedule equals the
percentage change in the effective discount factor. As indicated by equation (11.9), this displacement is necessary in order to offset the effects of
the tax-induced reduction in the effective interest rate on the time path of
the domestic real exchange rate. Hence, given the new domestic effective
interest rate $\tilde{r}'_{x0}$, the rate of increase in the domestic real exchange rate from
period 0 to period 1 accelerates (as p_{n0}/p_{n1} rises). Likewise, given the new
world interest rate, r'_{x0}, the rate of increase in the foreign real exchange rate
decelerates (as p^*_{n0}/p^*_{n1} falls). These changes are indicated in panel II of
figure 11.2 by the displacement of the equilibrium points a^* and a to $a^{*'}$ and
a', respectively.

The foregoing analysis focused on the effects of budget deficits arising
from a change in consumption taxes. We now examine the effects of a
corresponding change in income taxes. For this purpose, the analytical
framework, which allows for tradable and nontradable goods, can be reinterpreted and applied to the analysis of the effects of income tax policies
on *real wages* in a model with variable labor supply. The reinterpretation of
the model treats leisure as the nontradable good, the real wage as the real
exchange rate, and the temporal elasticity of substitution as the (compensated) elasticity of labor supply. With this interpretation, government hir-
ing of labor is viewed as government purchases of nontradable goods, and
the relative share of government expenditure on nontradable goods, β^q_n,
corresponds to the relative share of wages in the government budget.
Likewise, the private-sector expenditure share, β_n, is viewed as the relative
share of leisure in private-sector total spending (inclusive of the imputed
value of leisure).[4] With this interpretation, an income tax operates like a tax
on tradable goods only (since leisure—the nontradable good—is not
taxable).

To provide a meaningful analysis of the effects of income tax policies,
we relax the assumption that labor is inelastically supplied. To simplify,
we suppose that the production functions are linear, that preferences are
homothetic, that the leisure and ordinary goods (in our case, the tradable
goods) are separable in the utility function, and that the amounts of leisure
(the nontradable good) consumed in two consecutive periods are gross
substitutes. These assumptions imply that the effective discount factor
governing the relative supply of tradable goods, $S = Y_{x0}/Y_{x1}$, is $\alpha_{n\tau1} =$
$[(1 - \tau_{y1})/(1 - \tau_{y0})]\alpha_{c1}$, which measures the price of future leisure in terms
of current leisure. As is evident, the relative supply depends negatively on
the effective discount factor $\alpha_{n\tau1}$.

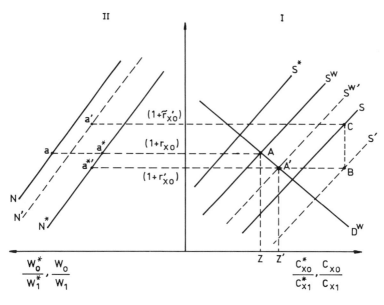

Figure 11.3
The effect of a budget deficit arising from a cut in income tax on the world interest rate and
on the path of real wages (real exchange rates)

The positively sloped S schedule in figure 11.3 reflects the positive
dependence of the relative supply on the interest rate. A higher interest
rate (measured in terms of tradable goods) corresponds to a higher consumption-based real interest rate which, in turn, induces substitution of
current-period labor for future-period labor, resulting in a higher relative
supply of tradable goods. The positively slope S^* schedule is derived in an
analogous manner for the foreign economy. The relative-supply schedule
pertaining to the world, S^w, is a weighted average of the domestic and
foreign relative supplies, so that $S^w = \mu_s S + (1 - \mu_s)S^*$, where the domestic country weight μ_s corresponds to the relative share of domestic output
of tradable goods in world output in the second period. That is, $\mu_s =
Y_{x1}/(Y_{x1} + Y^*_{x1})$.[5] Finally, in figure 11.3, the world relative-demand sched-
ule, D^w, as well as the nontradable goods market equilibrium schedules N
and N^*, are analogous to the corresponding schedules in figures 11.1 and
11.2, where the real wages w and w^* are identified wih the relative price of
nontradable goods. The initial equilibrium is shown in figure 11.3 by point
A, at which the world interest rate is r_{xo}, and the world relative quantities
of tradable goods are indicated by point z. The paths of the domestic and
foreign real wages (the reciprocals of the real exchange rates) are indicated
by points a and a^*, respectively.

A budget deficit arising from a current cut in the income tax rate, τ_{y0} which is compensated by a corresponding rise in the future income tax rate τ_{y1}, lowers the effective discount factor $\alpha_{n\tau1}$ at any given level of α_{c1}. This change induces an equiproportional downward displacement of the domestic relative-supply schedule (drawn against the reciprocal of the world discount factor) from S to S'. Since the world relative-supply schedule is a weighted average of the corresponding domestic and foreign schedules, and assuming that initially $\gamma_s = \gamma_s^*$, so that the change in the domestic-country weight, μ_s, does not affect the world relative supply, the displacement of the domestic schedule induces a smaller displacement of the world schedule from S^w to $S^{w'}$. Unlike the effect of this shift in the timing of income taxes on the relative-supply schedules, the reltive-demand schedules remain intact since relative demand for tradable goods depends on the consumption discount factor, α_{c1}, which is not influenced by income taxes. As seen in figure 11.3, the new equilibrium obtains at point A', at which the world interest rate falls from r_{x0} to r'_{x0} and the relative quantity of tradable goods rises from z to z'. In the new equilibrium, the domestic effective interest rate (applicable to the intertemporal labor-supply decision) rises to $\tilde{r}'_{x0}$. The wedge between the world and the domestic effective interest rates is indicated by the distance BC, reflecting the existence of income taxes.

The change in the time profile of income taxes also alters the position of the domestic market-clearing schedule for nontradable goods, from N to N' in panel II of figure 11.3. This downward shift in the schedule is necessary in order to eliminate the excess supply of current-period labor induced by the change in the time profile of taxes, because a lower interest rate raises current demand for leisure relative to future demand and thereby eliminates the current excess supply of labor. Hence, given the new lower world interest rate, the rate of growth in the foreign real wage decelerates, as indicated by the move from point a^* to point $a^{*'}$ along the N^* schedule. Analogously, given the new higher domestic effective interest rate, the rate of growth of the domestic wage accelerates, as indicated by the move from point a, along the N schedule, to point a', along the N' schedule.

The key consequences of the budget deficits are summarized in table 11.3, which highlights the contrast between the consumption and the income tax systems.

Revenue-Neutral Tax Conversions

The foregoing analysis can also be cast to illuminate key international effects of tax reforms that involves revenue-neutral tax conversions. For this purpose, we consider an economy undertaking a tax reform that substitutes a consumption tax system for an income tax system. To maintain revenue neutrality, we assume that consumption tax rate are adjusted so as to keep intact total tax revenue in each period. As an analytical matter, the tax reform can be thought of as consisting of two components. First, it involves a permanent reduction in the prevailing income tax and a permanent equiproportional rise in the consumption tax. Clearly, since this component of the reform does not alter the time profile of tax rates, it keeps intact the effective discount factors governing intertemporal decisions concerning consumption and labor supply.[7] Second, to maintain revenue neutrality in each period, the periodic consumption tax rates may need further adjustment. The extent and direction of this additional adjustment depend on whether the first component of the reform generates a budgetary surplus or a deficit. Since the offsetting changes in tax *rates* are equiproportional to each other, it follows that the only factor governing the change in the tax revenue is the size of the *consumption tax base* relative to that of the *income tax base*. If the consumption tax base exceeds the income tax base, the first component of the conversion from an income tax system to a consumption tax system generates a budgetary surplus, and vice versa.

In an open economy, the relative size of these two tax bases reflects the economy's current-account position. Specifically, if the domestic economy runs an initial-period trade-balance deficit, then the level of its consumption exceeds income and the equiproportional conversion from income to consumption tax generates a corresponding *initial-period* budgetary surplus. By the same token, the economy's intertemporal solvency necessitates a future trade-balance surplus so that consumption falls short of income. It follows that the same equiproportional tax conversion generates a *future-period* budgetary deficit. These departures from revenue neutrality imply that the second component of the reform involves a reduction in the current-period consumption tax rate, τ_{c0}, and a corresponding rise in the future-period tax rate, τ_{c1}. These changes raise the effective discount factor, $\alpha_{x\tau1}$ (applicable to consumption decisions), while keeping intact the effective discount factor, $\alpha_{n\tau1}$ (applicable to intertemporal labor-supply decisions).

Note that the change in the effective discount factors arising from the tax changes in the conversion from an income tax system to a consumption tax system are always in the same direction as in our analysis of budget deficits arising from consumption tax cuts. Thus, figure 11.2 can also be used to determine the effects of this tax conversion. Accordingly, as indicated

Table 11.3
The effects of domestic budget deficits arising from a cut in taxes on consumption and income

	r_{x0}	$\tilde{r}_{xc}$	r_{x1}	g_w	g_w^*
Consumption taxes	+	−	+	−	+
Income taxes	−	−	+	+	−

Note: r_{x0}, r_{xc} and r_{x1} denote, respectively, the world rate of interest and the domestic effective rates of interest applicable to decisions concerning consumption of tradable goods and leisure; g_w and g_w^* denote, respectively, the growth rates of the reciprocals of the corresponding real exchange rates). This table assumes that initially $\gamma_s = \gamma_s^*$.

by the first row in table 11.3, if the conversion takes place in an economy running a current-account deficit, the world interest rate rises, the effective interest rate governing domestic consumption decisions falls, and the corresponding interest rate governing labor-supply decisions also falls. In addition, the growth rate of domestic real wages declines while the corresponding foreign rate rises. Using the same arguments, the opposite pattern prevails if the tax conversion takes place in an economy running a current-account surplus.

The same reasoning can be used to analyze the opposite tax conversion, from a consumption tax system to an income tax system. In that case, the first component of the conversion yields a budgetary surplus if the initial-period current-account position was in surplus (so that income exceeds consumption). The restoration of revenue neutrality therefore involves a reduction in the initial-period income tax rate, τ_{y0}, and a corresponding rise in the future-period income tax rate, τ_{y1}. These changes in the time profile of income taxes lower the effective discount factors governing consumption decisions, $\alpha_{n\tau 1}$, while keeping intact the effective discount factors governing consumption decisions, $\alpha_{n\tau 1}$.

These changes are qualitatively similar to those obtained in our previous analysis of a budget deficit arising from income tax cuts, shown in figure 11.3. As indicated in the figure and shown in the second row of table 11.3, with this tax conversion both the world interest rate and the effective interest rate governing consumption decisions fall, and the effective interest rate governing domestic labor-supply decisions rises. In addition, the growth rate of domestic real wages rises, while the corresponding foreign growth rate falls. The opposite changes take place if the initial current-account position was in deficit.

The principal result derived from this section is that the direction of change in key macroeconomic variables (such as the world interest rate) caused by revenue-neutral tax reforms depends critically on the economy's current-account position.

Summary

We have dealt here with the effects of government spending and tax policies on the world economy. Using the modern international-intertemporal approach, our analysis has shown the precise manner in which the effects of government spending depend critically on two biases: the bias in the *intertemporal* allocation of government spending relative to the domestic private sector, and the bias in the commodity *composition* of government purchases relative to the domestic private sector. When government spending is strongly biased toward purchases of tradable goods, the key factor determining whether the world interest rate rises or falls is the intertemporal pattern of government spending relative to the private sector: if the government intertemporal pattern is biased toward current spending, the interest rate rises, and vice versa.

The analysis has also provided information about the time paths of the domestic and foreign real exchange rates. When the share of government spending on tradable goods is relatively high, a rise in government spending decelerates the rates of change of the domestic and foreign real exchange rates if the intertemporal allocation of government spending (relative to the private sector) is biased toward the present. But if the intertemporal allocation of government spending (relative to the private sector) is biased toward the future, the rates of change of the real exchange rates accelerate. It follows that, in this case, government spending induces positive cross-country correlations between the time paths of the real exchange rates as well as between the (consumption-based) real interest rates.

In contrast, if the commodity composition of government spending is strongly biased toward purchases of nontradable goods, the interest-rate effects depend on the interaction between the bias in the intertemporal allocation of government spending relative to the private sector and the temporal-intertemporal substitution bias of the domestic private sector. It is important to emphasize that, even though there is no presumption concerning the precise effects of government spending on the world interest rate and on the time paths of the real exchange rates, we identify the key (estimatable) parameters whose relative magnitudes determine these effects.

After analyzing government spending policies, we examined the effects of tax policies under alternative tax systems—consumption tax and income tax systems. We showed that with consumption taxes a budget deficit raises the world interest rate and lowers the domestic effective interest rate applicable to domestic consumption decisions. In addition, the deficit decelerates the rate of change of the domestic real exchange rate and accelerates the corresponding foreign rate of change. The deficit thereby lowers the domestic (consumption-based) effective real interest rate and raises the corresponding foreign real interest rate. These changes result in a negative cross-country correlation between the (consumption-based) real effective interest rates. In contrast, under an income tax system, the same budget deficit *lowers* the world interest rate and raises the domestic effective rate applicable to intertemporal labor-supply decisions. We showed that the deficit accelerates the rate of growth of the domestic real wage and decelerates the corresponding foreign growth rate.

Our analysis of budget deficits arising from tax cuts was designed to illuminate the effects of revenue-neutral tax-conversion schemes. We demonstrated that the effects of such shifts between income and consumption tax systems *raise* the world interest rate if the current-account position is in deficit. The revenue-neutral tax conversions *lower* the world interest rate if the current-account position is in surplus.

We conclude by reiterating one of the principal implications of this study. A proper analysis of the effects of fiscal policies on the world economy cannot be carried out on the basis of a single aggregate measure of the fiscal stance such as the budget deficit. It must be based on more detailed and specific information on government spending and taxes. On the spending side, such information must specify the distribution of spending between tradable and nontradable goods and its intertemporal allocation. On the revenue side, the information must specify the characteristics of the tax system, including the timing of taxes and the types of taxes used to finance the budget.

11.1 Appendix A: The World Interest Rate, Tradable-Goods Consumption, and the Real Exchange Rate

In this appendix, we derive the effects of the world discount factor on the growth rate of consumption of tradable goods and on the path of the real exchange rate. Recall that the market for nontradable goods must clear during each period. The equilibrium conditions indicated by equations (11.2) to (11.3) of the text are

$$c_{n0}[p_{n0}, P_0 C_0(\alpha_{c1}, W_{c0})] = \bar{Y}_{n0} - G_{n0} \tag{A.1}$$

and

$$c_{n1}[p_{n1}, P_1 C_1(\alpha_{c1}, W_{c1})] = \bar{Y}_{n1} - G_{n1} \tag{A.2}$$

Using these equations and the Slutsky decomposition, the percentage changes in $p_{nt}(t = 0, 1)$ for a given percentage change in the world discount factor are

$$\hat{p}_{n0} = \left[\frac{\gamma_s \sigma}{\beta_n \sigma + (1 - \beta_n)\sigma_{nx}} + \frac{\gamma_s(\mu_1 - 1)}{(1 - \beta_n)\sigma_{nx}} \right] \hat{\alpha}_{x1} \tag{A.3}$$

and

$$\hat{p}_{n1} = \left[\frac{-(1 - \gamma_s)\sigma}{\beta_n \sigma + (1 - \beta_n)\sigma_{nx}} + \frac{\gamma_s(\mu_1 - 1)}{(1 - \beta_n)\sigma_{nx}} \right] \hat{\alpha}_{x1}, \tag{A.4}$$

where a circumflex (^) denotes percentage change of a variable, and where μ_1 denotes the ratio of future net output to private consumption. Subtracting (A.4) from (A.3) yields equation (A.5), which is equation (11.9) of the text:

$$\frac{d \log(p_{n0}/p_{n1})}{d \log \alpha_{x1}} = \frac{\sigma}{\beta_n \sigma + (1 - \beta_n)\sigma_{nx}}. \tag{A.5}$$

In determining the percentage change in c_{xt} $t = 0, 1$), we differentiate equation (11.5) in the text and use the Slutsky decomposition. This yields

$$\hat{c}_{x0} = \beta_n(\sigma_{nx} - \gamma_s\sigma)\hat{p}_{n0} + \beta_n\gamma_s\sigma\hat{p}_{n1} + \gamma_s(\sigma + \mu_1 - 1)\hat{\alpha}_{x1} \tag{A.6}$$

and

$$\hat{c}_{x1} = \beta_n(1 - \gamma_s)\sigma\hat{p}_{n0} + \beta_n[\sigma_{nx} - (1 - \gamma_s)\sigma]\hat{p}_{n1}$$
$$- [(1 - \gamma_s\sigma - \gamma_s(\mu_1 - 1)]\hat{\alpha}_{x1}. \tag{A.7}$$

We can use these equations to determine the elasticity of the consumption ratio, c_{x0}/c_{x1}, with respect to the growth rate of the real exchange rate, p_{n0}/p_{n1}. This yields

$$\frac{d \log(c_{x0}/c_{x1})}{d \log(p_{n0}/p_{n1})} = \beta_n(\sigma_{nx} - \sigma). \tag{A.8}$$

Equation (A.8) shows that the qualitative effects of the changes in the price ratio p_{n0}/p_{n1} on the consumption ratio of tradable goods, c_{x0}/c_{x1}, depend only on whether the temporal elasticity of substitution, σ_{nx} exceeds or falls short of the intertemporal elasticity of substitution, σ. A rise in the relative price of nontradable goods, p_{nt}, induces substitution of consumption of tradable goods for nontradable goods *within* period t. The magnitude of this temporal substitution is indicated by σ_{nx}. Further, if p_{n0} rises by more than p_{n1} (so that the ratio p_{n0}/p_{n1} also rises), the extent of the temporal substitution within the current period exceeds the corresponding substitution within the future period. As a result, the ratio of current to future consumption of tradable goods rises. This is reflected by the positive term $\beta_n \sigma_{nx}$ in equation (A.8). The same rise in the intertemporal price ratio p_{n0}/p_{n1} raises the (consumption-based) real interest rate (and lowers the corresponding real discount factor, α_{c1}). This rise in the real interest rate induces substitution of spending *between* periods: from the present to the future period. The magnitude of this intertemporal substitution is indicated by the negative term $-\beta_n \sigma$ in equation (A.8). Finally, we note that the change in the intertemporal consumption ratio does not depend on private wealth. This reflects the homotheticity assumption, which implies that the tax-induced fall in wealth lowers current and future demand for tradable goods by the same proportion.

To determine the elasticity of tradable-goods consumption with respect to the discount factor we substitute equations (A.3) and (A.4) into (A.6) and (A.7), and obtain

$$\hat{c}_{x0} = \gamma_s \left[\frac{\sigma_{nx}\sigma}{\beta_n \sigma + (1 - \beta_n)\sigma_{nx}} + \frac{\mu_1 - 1}{1 - \beta_{nx}} \right] \hat{\alpha}_{x1} \tag{A.9}$$

and

$$\hat{c}_{x1} = \left[\frac{-(1 - \gamma_s)\sigma_{nx}\sigma}{\beta_n \sigma + (1 - \beta_n)\sigma_{nx}} + \frac{\gamma_s(\mu_1 - 1)}{1 - \beta_n} \right] \hat{\alpha}_{x1}. \tag{A.10}$$

Subtracting (A.10) from (A.9) yields equation (A.11), which is equation (11.6) of the text:

$$\frac{d\log(c_{x0}/c_{x1})}{d\log \alpha_{x1}} = \frac{\sigma_{nx}\sigma}{\beta_n \sigma + (1 - \beta_n)\sigma_{nx}}. \tag{A.11}$$

Finally, combining equations (11.13) and (A.8) yields equation (11.10) of the text.

11.6   Appendix B: The Multiperiod Simulation Model

In this appendix, we present the analytical framework underlying the illustrative simulation model of chapters 14 and 15. For this purpose, suppose that the utility function is

$$U = \sum_{t=0}^{T} \delta^t \log C_t + \sum_{t=0}^{T} \delta^t V(G_{nt}, G_{xt}) \tag{B.1}$$

and

$$C_t = [\beta_n c_{nt}^\rho + (1 - \beta_n)c_{xt}^\rho]^{1/\rho}, \tag{B.2}$$

where T denotes the time horizon, δ denotes the subjective discount factor, and where β_n and ρ are parameters of the utility function. Equation (B.1) implies that the intertemporal elasticity of substitution, σ, is unity and equation (B.2) implies that the temporal elasticity of substitution, σ_{nx}, is $1/(1 - \rho)$. As formulated in equation (B.1), the utility derived from government spending is indicated by the function $V(G_{nt}, G_{xt})$, which enters separably into the utility function. This separability assumption implies that the private-sector demand functions are independent of government services.

The private-sector wealth constraint, analogous to the text equation (11.4), is

$$W_0 = \sum_{t=0}^{T} \alpha_{xt}[\overline{Y}_{xt} - G_{xt} + p_{nt}(\overline{Y}_{nt} - G_{nt})] - (1 + r_{x,-1})B_{-1}, \tag{B.3}$$

where α_{xt} denotes the world present-value factor.

Maximization of the utility function subject to the wealth constraint yields the demand functions for tradable and nontradable goods, c_{xt} and c_{nt}, as well as the consumption-based price index P_t and the expenditure function $E_t = P_t C_t$, where C_t denotes the consumption-based real expenditure (i.e., real consumption):

$$c_{xt} = \frac{(1 - \beta_n)^{\sigma_{nx}}}{[(1 - \beta_n)^{\sigma_{nx}} + \beta_n^{\sigma_{nx}} p_{nt}^{1 - \sigma_{nx}}]} E_t, \tag{B.4}$$

$$c_{nt} = \frac{\beta_n^{\sigma_{nx}} p_{nt}^{-\sigma_{nx}}}{[(1 - \beta_n)^{\sigma_{nx}} + \beta_n^{\sigma_{nx}} p_{nt}^{1 - \sigma_{nx}}]} E_t, \tag{B.5}$$

$$P_t = [(1 - \beta_n)^{\sigma_{nx}} + \beta_n^{\sigma_{nx}} p_{nt}^{1 - \sigma_{nx}}]^{1/(1 - \sigma_{nx})}, \tag{B.6}$$

and

$$E_t = \frac{\delta^t}{\alpha_{xt}} \frac{(1 - \delta)}{(1 - \delta^T)} W_0. \tag{B.7}$$

Analogous functions pertain to the foreign economy, with asterisks denoting foreign quantities. The market-clearing conditions for nontradable goods are

$$c_{nt} = \overline{Y}_{nt} - G_{nt} \tag{B.8}$$

and

$$c_{nt}^* = \overline{Y}_{nt}^* - G_{nt}^*, \tag{B.9}$$

and the corresponding condition for the world tradable-good market is

$$c_{xt} + c_{xt}^* = (\overline{Y}_{xt} - G_{xt}) + (\overline{Y}_{xt}^* - G_{xt}^*). \tag{B.10}$$

The system of equations (B.4) to (B.7), along with their foreign-economy counterparts, and the market-clearing conditions (B.8) to (B.10) can be used to generate the simulations; see Frenkel, Razin, and Sadka 1991.

12

Capital Income Taxation in the Open Economy

The increased integration of the world capital markets has strong implications for the taxation of income from capital.[1] In general, if factors become more mobile they are potentially less desirable as a source of government revenue. In fact, in the extreme case, such as the federal system, the ability of individual states to tax capital income is severely constrained, since capital can move freely across state borders.

To provide public goods and services, the government needs to purchase goods and services from the private sector and to employ labor. Thus, there is no escape for the government but to resort to tax finance of its outlays. In the short run, the government may borrow, internally or externally, to finance its outlays. But, eventually, in the long run the government has to resort to taxes to pay for past, present, and future outlays. Taxes, however, are distortive. Thus, a key issue in the design of the tax system is how to reduce the amount of distortions imposed by the system.

To illustrate this point, consider in figure 12.1 a one-consumer closed economy endowed with one unit of leisure or labor time. The labor is employed to produce goods. The consumption possibility set is bounded from above and from the right by the line TT. Obviously, with no government the tax burden issue does not arise and a competitive equilibrium must yield an efficient allocation of resources, say point A in figure 12.1. At this point, as usual, the indifference curve of a representative household is tangent to the consumption possibilities' frontier, TT.

Assume that the government purchases private goods to provide public services. Suppose that these needs amount to the equivalent of g units of the produced good. In this case the relevant frontier for private uses of the produced goods and leisure becomes $T'T'$. If the government could obtain all the resources required for public uses by resorting to lump-sum taxes, which do not distort economic decisions, the ensuing equilibrium is the

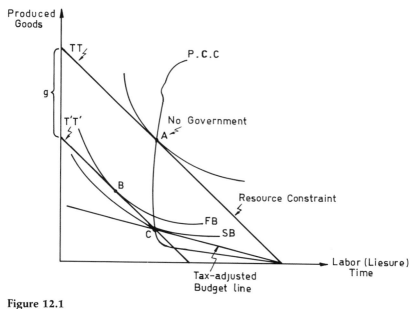

Figure 12.1
The deadweight loss of taxation

first-best allocation represented by point B. If, however, a flat-rate income tax is available to finance expenditures, the government must be restricted to a private consumption bundle which lies on the private sector's price-consumption curve (P.C.C.). The resulting (second-best) equilibrium is represented by point C. The difference between the indifference curve FB (associated with the first-best equilibrium) and the indifference curve SB (associated with second-best equilibrium) is called the *deadweight loss* (or the excess burden) of the tax system. At the heart of the tax design problem is the attempt to reduce, as much as possible, the deadweight loss.

12.1 Second-Best (Ramsey) Taxation

To demonstrate the analytical principles of the Ramsey tax design consider a stylized economy, consuming n goods (the nth good is leisure). The technology is linear. One unit of each one of the n goods can be produced by using one unit of leisure. Assume that the economy is endowed with just one unit of leisure but with no endowments of good i, $i = 1, 2, \ldots,$ $n - 1$. Accordingly, the resource constraint is

$$\sum_{i=1}^{n-1} (x_i + g_i) \leq 1 - x_n, \tag{12.1}$$

where

x_i = consumption of private good i

g_i = consumption of public good i, $i = 1, \ldots, n$.

To simplify, let the private component of the utility function be logarithmic:

$$U = \sum_{i=1}^{n} \alpha_i \ln x_i, \quad 0 < \alpha_i < 1, \quad \sum_{i=1}^{n} \alpha_i = 1. \tag{12.2}$$

Denote the post-tax price of good i by p_i and its pretax price by q_i, $i = 1, \ldots, n$. The representative household's budget constraint is

$$\sum_{i=1}^{n} p_i x_i - p_n \leqslant 0. \tag{12.3}$$

First-order conditions for utility maximization are

$$0 = \frac{\alpha_i}{x_i} - \lambda p_i, \quad i = 1, \ldots, n, \tag{12.4}$$

where λ denotes the Lagrange multiplier associated with the budget constraint in the household maximum problem.

The second-best optimum tax problem can be cast in terms of a choice of quantities (x_i, $i = 1, \ldots, n$) which have to satisfy the constraint in order to be implementable through the market economy.

Substituting the first-order conditions into the budget constraint yields the *implementability constraint*, as follows:

$$\sum_{i=1}^{n-1} \left(\frac{\alpha_i}{x_i} \right) x_i + \frac{\alpha_n}{x_n} (x_n - 1) = 0. \tag{12.5}$$

The implementability constraint is a restriction on the optimum tax problem due to the decentralized nature of the market-based economy. An obvious additional restriction is the resource constraint, (12.1).

Thus, the optimum tax problem is

$$\operatorname*{Max}_{\{x_i\}} \sum_{i=1}^{n} \alpha_i \ln x_i \tag{12.6}$$

subject to

(a) $\displaystyle\sum_{i=1}^{n} (x_i + g_i) \leqslant 1$

(b) $\sum_{i=1}^{n-1} \frac{\alpha_i}{x_i} x_i + \frac{\alpha_n}{x_n}(x_n - 1) \leqslant 0.$

Simple calculations yield the solution to (12.3) as follows:

$$x_n^{SB} = \alpha_n \qquad (12.7)$$

$$x_i^{SB} = \alpha_i \left(\frac{1 - \alpha_n - G}{1 - \alpha_n} \right), \quad i = 1, \ldots, n - 1, \qquad (12.8)$$

where

$$G = \sum_{i=1}^{n} g_i.$$

Given the linear technology, producer prices are obtained directly from the fixed production coefficients:

$$q_i = 1, \quad i = 1, \ldots, n. \qquad (12.9)$$

Consumer prices, derived from the first-order conditions, are

$$p_n = 1$$
$$p_i = \frac{1 - \alpha_n}{1 - \alpha_n - G}, \quad i = 1, \ldots, n - 1. \qquad (12.10)$$

Consequently, the implied tax on labor income is

$$\tau = 1 - \frac{p_n}{p_i} = \frac{G}{1 - \alpha_n}. \qquad (12.11)$$

The corresponding first-best optimum, implementable only if lump-sum taxes are available, is given by

$$\max_{\{x_i\}} \sum_{i=1}^{n} \alpha_i \ln x_i \qquad (12.12)$$

subject to

$$\sum_{i=1}^{n} x_i + g_i \leqslant 1.$$

The solution is given by

$$x_i^{FB} = \alpha_i (1 - G), \quad i = 1, \ldots, n. \qquad (12.13)$$

The comparison of (12.13) and (12.7)–(12.8) reveals that the first-best consumption of leisure is smaller than the second-best consumption, while consumption of marketable goods in the first-best allocation is larger than that in the second-best allocation. Excess burden, B, is implicitly given by the solution to

$$\sum_{i=1}^{n} \alpha_i \ln x_i^{FB} = \sum_{i=2}^{n} \alpha_i \ln x_i^{SB} + \alpha_1 \ln(1 + B)x_1^{SB}. \tag{12.14}$$

$$B = \left[(1 - G)\left(\frac{1 - \alpha_n}{1 - \alpha_n - G}\right)^{1-\alpha_n} \right]^{1/\alpha_1} > 0. \tag{12.15}$$

That is, the excess burden increases with G.

12.2   Principles of International Taxation

The diverse structures of the national tax systems have important implications for the direction and magnitude of international flows of goods and capital and, consequently, for the world-wide efficiency of resource allocation in the integrated world economy. Although there is probably no country that adheres strictly to a pure principle of international taxation, it seems nevertheless that two polar principles with a wide application can be detected, both in the area of direct taxation and in the area of indirect taxation. The two polar principles of international income taxation are the *residence* (of taxpayer) principle and the *source* (of income) principle. According to the residence principle, residents are taxed on their world-wide income uniformly, regardless of the source of income (domestic or foreign), while nonresidents are not taxed on income originating in the country.[2] According to the source principle all types of income originating in the country are taxed uniformly, regardless of place of residence of the recipients of income. Thus, residents of the country are not taxed on their foreign-source income and nonresidents are taxed equally as residents on income originating in the country.

To highlight the issue of tax arbitrage that arises under the integration of capital markets, consider the familiar two-country model ("home" country and "foreign" country) with perfect capital mobility. Denote interest rates in the home country and in the foreign country by r and r^* respectively. In general, the home country may have three different effective tax rates applying to capital (interest and dividend) income:

τ_D —   tax rate levied on residents on domestic source income;

τ_A —   effective rate of the *additional* tax levied on residents on foreign-source income (over and above the tax paid in the foreign country);

τ_N —   tax levied on income of nonresidents.

Correspondingly, the foreign country levies similar taxes, denoted by τ_D^*, τ_N^*.[3]

At the equilibrium, the home country residents must be indifferent between investing at home or abroad. This must imply that

$$r(1 - \tau_D) = r^*(1 - \tau_N^* - \tau_A). \tag{12.16}$$

Similarly, at the equilibrium, the residents of the foreign country must be indifferent between investing in their home country (the "foreign country") or investing abroad (the "home" country), so that

$$r^*(1 - \tau_D^*) = r(1 - \tau_N - \tau_A^*). \tag{12.17}$$

Hence, for the interest rates, r and r^*, to be positive (in which case we say that the capital market equilibrium is viable), the two equations (12.16) and (12.17) must be linearly dependent. That is,

$$(1 - \tau_D)(1 - \tau_D^*) = (1 - \tau_N - \tau_A^*)(1 - \tau_N^* - \tau_A). \tag{12.18}$$

This constraint, which involves tax rates of the two countries, implies that even though the two countries do not explicitly coordinate their tax systems between them, each one nevertheless must take into account the tax system of the other in designing its own tax system.[4]

It is noteworthy that if both countries adopt one of the two aforementioned polar principles of taxation, residence and source, then condition (12.18) is fulfilled. To see this, observe that if both countries adopt the residence principle, then

$$\tau_D = \tau_A, \quad \tau_D^* = \tau_A^*, \quad \tau_N = \tau_N^* = 0. \tag{12.19}$$

If both countries adopt the source principles, then

$$\tau_D = \tau_N, \quad \tau_D^* = \tau_N^* \quad \text{and} \quad \tau_A = \tau_A^* = 0. \tag{12.20}$$

Evidently, the joint constraint (12.18) is fulfilled if either (12.19) or (12.20) holds. However, if the two countries do not adopt the same polar principle (or do not adopt either one of the two polar principles), then, in general, condition (12.18) is not met, and a viable equilibrium may not exist.

The structure of taxation has also important implications for the international allocation of investments and savings. If all countries adopt the residence principle (that is, condition 12.19 holds), then it follows from either (12.16) or (12.17), the rate-of-return arbitrage conditions, that $r = r^*$. That is, the pretax rates of return to capital are equated internationally. As the gross return to capital is equal to the marginal product of capital, it follows that the marginal product of capital is equated across countries. Thus, the world (future) output is maximized and worldwide production efficiency prevails.[5] If, however, the tax rate on capital income is not the same in all countries (i.e., $\tau_D \neq \tau_D^*$), then the after-tax return on capital would vary across countries.

As the net return to capital is equal to the consumer's (intertemporal) marginal rate of substitution, it follows that the intertemporal marginal rates of substitution are not equated internationally. Thus, the international allocation of world savings is inefficient.

Alternatively, if all countries adopt the source principle (that is, condition 12.20 holds), then it follows from either (12.16) or (12.17) that $r(1 - \tau_D) = r^*(1 - \tau_D^*)$. Thus, the intertemporal marginal rate of substitution is equated internationally and the allocation of world savings is efficient. If, however, the tax rate on income from capital is not the same in all countries, then $r \neq r^*$. That is, the marginal product of capital varies across countries and the worldwide allocation of investment is inefficient.

12.3   Optimal Taxation in the Open Economy

Optimal taxation of capital income is usually subject to two conflicting forces. On the one hand, the income from existing capital is a pure rent, and taxing all of it away must be efficient. On the other hand, the taxation of the returns on current and future investment in capital may retard growth and may thus be an inefficient policy.

Following Diamond and Mirrlees (1971) and Lucas (1990), consider a small open economy with an infinitely-lived representative agent, endowed with one unit of leisure and K_0 units of capital. The maximization problem of the representative agent is specified by

$$\max_{(c_t, x_t)} \sum_{t=0}^{\infty} \beta^t u(c_t, x_t) \tag{12.21}$$

subject to

$$\sum_{t=0}^{\infty} P_t[\bar{w}_t(1 - x_t) - c_t] \geq 0,$$

where β denotes the subjective discount factor, c_t and x_t denote consumption of goods and leisure at period t, respectively, P_t denotes the consumer (post-tax) present value factor from period t to period 0, $\bar{w}_t$ denotes the post-tax wage rate at period t, and u is the instantaneous utility

function of the household. The Lagrangean expression for this problem is
$L = \sum_{t=0}^{\infty} [\beta^t u(c_t, x_t) + \lambda P_t[\bar{w}_t(1 - x_t) - c_t])$, where $\lambda \geq 0$ is a Lagrange
multiplier.

Underlying the specification in (12.21) is the idea that the household
sells its endowment of capital to the firm, at $t = 0$, and at this point of time
the government confiscates this income, since it amounts to a lump-sum
income. Consequently, the lifetime budget constraint implies that the discounted flow of consumption must be equal to the discounted flow of labor
income. In other words, income originating from the existing capital should
appear nowhere in the household problem while income originating from
new capital should appear only in the representative firm's problem.

First-order conditions are given by

(a) $\beta^t u_c(c_t, x_t) - \lambda P_t = 0$, (12.22)

and

(b) $\beta^t u_x(c_t, x_t) - \lambda P_t \bar{w}_t = 0$.

These conditions, substituted into the budget constraint in (12.21) generates the household implementability constraint for the optimum tax problem, as follows:

$$\sum_{t=0}^{\infty} \beta^t [u_x(c_t, x_t)(1 - x_t) - u_c(c_t, x_t)c_t] = 0. \qquad (12.23)$$

Assume that the representative firm is equipped with a constant return
to scale production function, $F(K_t, L_t)$, where K_t denotes the capital stock
and L_t denotes the employment of labor at period t. Denote the rate of
corporate income tax at period t by τ. The firm's objective is to maximize
the present value of its net cash flows. Thus, the firm chooses (K_t, L_t) so as
to maximize

$$\sum_{t=0}^{\infty} q_t((1 - \tau_t)F(K_t, L_t) - [K_{t+1} - (1 - \delta)K_t] + \tau_t \delta K_t - (1 - \tau_t)w_t L_t)$$

(12.24)

where q_t denotes the tax-adjusted present value factor from period t to
period 0, δ denotes the rate of depreciation, and w_t denotes the pre-tax
wage rate at period t. The net cash flow of the firm at period t consists of
the after-tax value of output $(1 - \tau_t)F( )$, minus gross investment, $K_{t+1} - (1 - \delta)K_t$, plus the depreciation allowance, $\tau \delta K_t$, minus the tax-adjusted
wage bill $(1 - \tau)w_t L_t$. The present value factor, q_t, associated with the

tax-adjusted domestic rate of interest, evolves according to the familiar relationship.

$$q_t/q_{t+1} = 1 + (1 - \tau_{t+1})r_{t+1} \tag{12.25}$$

where r is the pre-tax rate of interest from period t to period $t + 1$. Notice that the corporate income tax in this setting works essentially as a cash-flow tax (because capital used in the production process in period t is cashed on in that same period). Consequently, the corporate tax does not affect the investment behavior, as can be seen from the following first-order conditions for the firm's optimization problem:

$$F_L(K_t, L_t) = w_t \tag{12.26}$$

and

$$F_K(K_t, L_t) - \delta = r_t. \tag{12.27}$$

These last two conditions generate the firm implementability constraint for the optimum tax problem.

The optimal tax problem for our benevolent government can now be specified as follows. The government chooses c_t, $1 - x_t = L_t$, K_t, w_t and r_t so as to maximize the household utility function $\sum_{t=0}^{\infty} \beta^t u(c_t, x_t)$, subject to the present-value resource constraint of the small open economy,

$$\sum_{t=0}^{\infty} (1 + r^*(1 - \tau_N^*))^{-t}(F(K_t, 1 - x_t) - [K_{t+1} - (1 - \delta)K_t] - c_t - g_t) = 0,$$

and to the implementability conditions (12.23), (12.26), and (12.27) where g_t denotes government spending in period t. Notice that in this optimal tax problem w_t and r_t appear only in constraints (12.26)–(12.27). Hence, the two control variables w_t and r_t and the two constraints (12.26)–(12.27) may be omitted initially from the tax optimization problem. Once the problem is solved, one can then employ (12.26)–(12.27) to set w_t and r_t. The Lagrangean expression for the optimal tax problem is then

$$L = \sum_{t=0}^{\infty} \beta^t u(c_t, x_t) + \phi \sum_{t=0}^{\infty} \beta^t [u_x(c_t, x_t)(1 - x_t) - u_t(c_t, x_t)c_t]$$

$$+ \mu \sum_{t=0}^{\infty} [(1 + r^*(1 - \tau_N^*))^{-t}(F(K_t, 1 - x_t)$$

$$- [K_{t+1} - (1 - \delta)K_t] - c_t - g_t)] \tag{12.28}$$

where $\phi \geqslant 0$ and $\mu \geqslant 0$ are Lagrange multipliers. The resource constraint for the small open economy is equal to the discounted sum (using the world net of tax rate of interest $r^*(1 - \tau_N^*)$) of output flows, $F(\ )$, minus the discounted sum of gross investment, $K_{t+1} - (1 - \delta)K_t$, private consumption, c_t, and public consumption, g_t.

Setting the derivative of (12.28) with respect to K_t equal to zero, yields

$$[1 + r^*(1 - \tau_N^*)]^{-t+1} + [1 + r^*(1 - \tau_N^*)]^{-t}[F_k(K_t, 1 - x_t) + 1 - \delta) = 0.$$

Hence,

$$F_k(K_t - x_t) - \delta = r^*(1 - \tau_N^*). \tag{12.29}$$

Equation (12.24) implies that under the optimum tax regime the net (after depreciation), marginal product of capital must be equal to the world rate of interest (net of foreign tax) at each period of time. As was already pointed out in the preceding section, if individual residents can freely invest abroad, they must earn the same net return whether investing at home or abroad. That is,

$$r_t(1 - \tau_{tD}) = r^*(1 - \tau_N^* - \tau_{tA}). \tag{12.30}$$

Matching up conditions (12.27), (12.29), and (12.30), it follows that under the optimal tax regime the government in the small open economy must let capital move freely in and out of the country and must employ the *residence principle* of taxation (i.e., $r_t = r^*(1 - \tau_N^*)$ and $\tau_{tD} = \tau_{tA}$). Thus, at the optimum, investment is *efficiently* allocated between the home country and the rest of the world: the familiar production efficiency result.[6]

Other first-order conditions for the optimal tax problem are given by

$$\beta^t(u_c(c_t, x_t) - \phi[u_{cc}(c_t, x_t)c_t + u_c(c_t, x_t) - u_{cx}(c_t, x_t)(1 - x_t)])$$
$$+ \mu[1 + r^*(1 - \tau_N^*)]^{-t} = 0 \tag{12.31}$$

and

$$\beta^t(u_x(c_t, x_t) - \phi[u_{cx}(c_t, x_t)c_t - u_{xx}(c_t, x_t)(1 - x_t) + u_x(c_t, x_t)]$$
$$+ \mu[1 + r^*(1 - \tau_N^*)]^{-t}F_L(K_t, 1 - x_t) = 0. \tag{12.32}$$

Consider now a unique parameter configuration that yields a *steady state* for the optimal tax problem. For a small open economy this requires a specific relationship between the discount factor and the (net-of-tax) world rate of interest, that is,

$$\beta[1 + r^*(1 - \tau_N^*] = 1 \tag{12.33}$$

or

$$r^*(1 - \tau_N^*) = \beta^{-1} - 1. \tag{12.34}$$

Notice that $\beta^{-1} - 1$ is the intertemporal marginal rate of substitution in the steady state (where $c_{t+1} = c_t$ and $x_{t+1} = x_t$). Utility maximization implies that $\beta^{-1} - 1$ is equated to

$(P_t/P_{t+1}) - 1 = (1 - \tau_D)r_t$ (see condition 12.22).

Thus,

$$(1 - \tau_D)r = \beta^{-1} - 1 = r^*(1 - \tau_N^*),$$

by equation (12.24). Hence, $\tau_D = \tau_A = 0$.

Thus, we conclude that in the steady state the tax on capital income, from either domestic or foreign sources, *vanishes* entirely from the second-best tax menu. The tax burden falls entirely on consumption and labor income.

12.4 Summary

This chapter developed the Ramsey tax rules for an open economy that is fully integrated into the world capital market. We verify that the optimum tax rules call for the application of the residence principle and that at a steady state the capital income tax vanishes.

Problems

1. Consider a two-period model of a small country as in chapter 11. Agents receive endowments of a tradable (Y_T) and a nontradable (Y_N) good in each period t ($t = 0, 1$). Agents' preferences are given by

$$U = [C_0^{1-1/\sigma} + DC_1^{1-1/\sigma}]/(1 - 1 - \sigma), \tag{1}$$

where $C_t = c_{Tt}^{1-b} c_{Nt}^b$, c_T, c_N are consumption levels of tradable and non-tradable goods, and D denotes the subjective discount factor. There is perfect capital mobility—agents can borrow or lend at the world interest rate r^*, measured in terms of tradable goods, the numeraire.

a. Suppose that agents receive, in period zero only, an exogenous increase in their endowment of tradable goods, Y_{T0}. What will be the impact of this increase on: the real exchange rate in each period; the real (consumption based) discount factor; the trade balance (both in terms of tradables and consumption based index); and welfare? In your answer, you may assume that initially trade is balanced and that there is no initial debt.

b. How would your answers change if, instead, agents had no access to the world capital market?

2. Consider an economy consisting of a representative consumer who derives utility in period t ($t = 1, 2$) by consuming N_t units of a nontraded good and M_t units of an imported consumption good. The utility function is

$$U(N_t, M_t) = [1/(1 - \theta)][N_t^\beta M_t^{(1-\beta)}]^{(1-\theta)}, \qquad \theta \geqslant 0, 0 < \beta < 1. \tag{1}$$

When $\theta = 1$, the utility function takes the logarithmic form. Letting the constant $\rho > 0$ denote the subjective rate of time preference, the consumer's welfare is given by

$$V = U(N_1, M_1) + [1/(1 + \rho)]U(N_2, M_2). \tag{2}$$

On the production side, resources are competitively allocated between the nontraded goods sector and the export sector, where they produce N_t and X_t units of output, respectively. The economy's production possibilities are given by

$$X_t = f(N_t), \qquad f' < 0, f'' \leqslant 0. \tag{3}$$

We assume that X_t is not consumed domestically. All units of X_t are sold on world markets in exchange for M_t (which is not produced at home) or an internationally traded bond whose return is equal to r. We consider a small open economy which takes the world interest rate (r) and the terms of trade as given. For simplicity, we set the terms of trade to be equal to unity in both periods.

a. The representative consumer's objective is to maximize (2) subject to the intertemporal budget constraint:

$$f(N_1) + [1/(1 + r)]f(N_2) = M_1 + [1/(1 + r)]M_2. \tag{4}$$

Write down the first order conditions for the consumer's problem. Show that if $\rho = r$, the agent consumes the same bundle in both periods.

b. Suppose now that an unanticipated binding quota is imposed in period 1, limiting imports of good M to $\overline{M}$, and scheduled to be lifted in period 2, returning the economy to a free trade position. Assume that the import license is granted to consumers free of charge and also that $\rho = r$. What are the first order conditions for the consumer's problem in this case? Show that if $\theta = 1$, the quota generates an improvement in the trade balance in period 1 that is smaller than the reduction in imports. Show that if θ is sufficiently large, the temporary quota will actually cause the current account in period 1 to deteriorate.

3. Consider a two-period model of a small open economy. In each period, agents receive an endowment of a nontraded and an exportable good, where the latter is assumed not to be consumed domestically. Agents consume nontradables and importables, of which there is no domestic endowment. There is perfect capital mobility. Preferences are given by

$$U^{1-1/\sigma} = [C_1^{1-1/\sigma} + DC_2^{1-1/\sigma}], \tag{1}$$

where

$$C_t^{1-1/\varepsilon} = [c_{nt}^{1-1/\varepsilon} + c_{mt}^{1-1/\varepsilon}], \qquad t = 0, 1, \tag{2}$$

and where D is the subjective discount factor, and c_{nt} and c_{mt} denote, respectively, consumption of nontradables and imports in period t, $t = 0, 1$. The parameter σ denotes the intertemporal elasticity of substitution while the parameter ε denotes the intratemporal elasticity of substitution beteween nontradables and importables.

a. Find the effect on the consumption rate of interest of a temporary deterioration in the terms of trade. What role does the parameter ε play in your answer? How is the behavior of the real interest rate affected by the adjustment of the real exchange rate? In deriving your results, you may assume that the initial equilibrium is stationary in the sense that subjective and world discount factors are equal and expenditure shares are constant through time.

b. Does a deterioration in the terms of trade worsen or improve the (real) trade balance? What roles do the parameters ε and σ play in your answer? In your answer, you may assume that the trade account is initially balanced.

4. Consider a two-period, two-country model with four goods: m (the home country importable); x (the home country exportable); n (the home country nontradable); and n^* (the foreign country nontradable). Agents in each country receive endowments of the two tradable goods as well as the country-specific nontradable good. They also consume the two tradable goods and the country-specific nontradable. There is perfect capital mobility.

Consider the effects on domestic and foreign consumption rates of interest of the imposition of a small temporary tariff by the home country, assuming lump sum redistribution of the tariff revenue. In deriving your results, you may assume that preferences are identical in the two countries and are characterized by constant intratemporal elasticities of substitution (denoted by ε) and intertemporal elasticities of substitution (denoted by σ), and that the initial equilibrium is stationary so that expenditure shares are constant over time. You may also assume that the initial endowments and wealth levels are such that consumption interest rates and expenditure shares are equated across countries and, therefore, that transfer-problem criteria relating to cross-country differences in intratemporal or inter-temporal spending propensities play no role in determining the effects of tariffs.

6. Consider a one-period model of a small open economy with two sectors and two consumption goods. Goods are internationally tradable and domestic production employs a constant-returns-to-scale technology. The two inputs, labor and capital, are mobile across sectors but not across countries. Also assume that the economy is endowed with a fixed quantity of capital, K, while the quantity of labor input is part of the consumer's decision problem. There are six possible taxes available to the government: on the two consumption goods, the two factors of production, and trade taxes on imports and exports. Suppose that the government selects taxes to maximize consumer welfare for a given government expenditure profile and subject to external constraints and the production possibility set.

a. Show that zero tax rates on trade are an optimum for the small open economy.

b. Derive the rules for optimal consumption taxes.

7. Consider a two-period model of a small open endowment economy with one consumption good. Suppose the government chooses the distribution of consumption taxes over time to maximize consumer welfare for a given level of government expenditure. Also assume that the government has initially no domestic and foreign debt or assets and that government expenditures are constant across periods. Derive the conditions under which the optimal intertemporal tax policy would imply a budget deficit in the first period followed by a budget surplus in the second period.

8. Consider the open economy model with distortionary taxes presented in Chapter 10. Assume that the path of government expenditure remains unchanged by modifications of the tax regime. Describe the effects of a

budget deficit arising from the combined changes in the rates of taxation on labor and capital income.

a. What are the effects of a reduction in labor income tax rates today accompanied by an offsetting change in future capital income taxes?

b. What are the effects of a reduction in capital income tax rates today accompanied by an offsetting change in future labor income taxes?

9. Consider a small open economy version of the overlapping generations model in Chapter 7. Assume that individuals have a constant probability to survive each period (γ) and that their preferences can be described by a logarithmic expected utility function. Government spending is financed by a consumption tax with proportional tax rates. Describe the effects of a budget deficit arising from a current cut in taxes. To maintain the government's solvency condition and original pattern of government purchases, assume that the current-period tax cut is offset by a corresponding rise in future taxes.

VI

Stochastic Fiscal Policies

13

International Stock Markets
and Fiscal Policy

13.1 Introduction

Recent large swings in security prices that have taken place simultaneously throughout the OECD stock markets indicate the close international links existing among various stocks as a result of the integration of the world capital markets. They motivate the assumption of an integrated world stock market.

To address issues concerning the effects of fiscal shocks on the international allocation of consumption, saving, and risk, this chapter develops a two-country stochastic general-equilibrium model of the world economy. The analytical framework is used to study the effects of government spending and tax policies on private-sector consumption, spending, and asset portfolios.

In the preceding chapters the open-economy macroeconomic analysis under perfect foresight focused mainly on the international and intertemporal allocation of consumption and investment and their manifestations in trade imbalances. In such a framework the terms of trade and the world rate of interest are the main channels through which fiscal policies in one country are transmitted to the rest of the world. The present chapter extends the analysis to stochastic environments in which the main channel of transmission is the stock prices, determined within the integrated world stock market.

The stochastic extension of the international-intertemporal framework specifies a stock market model as in Diamond 1967, Helpman and Razin 1978, and Lucas 1978. (A recent application of the model to international trade in assets is contained in Svensson 1988).

In section 13.2 we set out the stochastic-intertemporal analytical framework. Section 13.3 considers the issue of government-finance neutrality, the stochastic analogue of the Ricardian neutrality proposition. Section

13.4 contains the analysis of spending policies in the case of complete markets for risk sharing. Following this benchmark case, sections 13.5 and 13.6 investigate how pro- and counter-cyclical behavior of government spending affects the stock market valuation of equities in the context of incomplete markets. The analysis highlights the role played by the cross-country correlations between the country-specific shocks and government spending shocks in the international transmission of fiscal policies. Section 13.7 extends the analysis to the infinite horizon. The appendixes, which follow the text, include algebraic derivations of key characteristics of the asset-demand functions under uncertainty, and some elementary properties of infinite-horizon valuations of stochastic consumption streams.

13.2 An Intertemporal Stochastic Model

Consider a two-period (nonmonetary) model of an open economy producing and consuming a single aggregate tradable good.[1] The economy is endowed with a sequence of outputs, $\theta_0 Y_0$ and $\theta_1(\gamma) Y_1$, where subscripts zero and one designate periods zero and one. The latter period is also indexed by the state of nature, γ. $\theta_1(\gamma)$ represents a productivity coefficient corresponding to the state of technology, $\gamma = 1, 2, \ldots S$, where S denotes the number of states of nature. We assume that the quantities $\theta_0 Y_0$ and Y_1 are predetermined.

As in Helpman and Razin 1978, we denote by q the period zero price of a unit of real equity issued by the representative home firm, in terms of units of the aggregate consumption good, (a security which pays $\theta(\gamma)$ units of output in state γ). Home firms produce Y_1 units of these equities while their value in the stock market is equal to $q \cdot Y_1$. Foreign firms produce the sequence $\theta_0^* Y_0^*$ and $\theta_1^*(\gamma) Y_1^*$ in periods zero and one, respectively; the price of a unit of foreign real equity is denoted by q^* and the stock-market value of foreign firms is equal to $q^* \cdot Y_1^*$. As before, an asterisk denotes foreign variables. The periodic budget constraints are

$$C_{HO} + q z_{H1} + q^* z_{H1}^* = q z_{H0} + q^* z_{H0}^* + \theta_0 z_{H0} + \theta_0^* z_{H0}^* - T_0, \tag{13.1}$$

and

$$C_{H1}(\gamma) = \theta_1(\gamma) z_{H1} + \theta_1^*(\gamma) z_{H1}^* - T_1(\gamma). \tag{13.2}$$

C_{HO} and $C_{H1}(\gamma)$ denote first- and second-period (state-γ) consumption and z_{Ht} and z_{Ht}^* denote period t shares of stocks that are issued by home and foreign firms ($t = 0, 1$). The productivity parameters, θ_t and θ_t^*, indicate the amount of dividends, per share, paid by domestic and foreign firms, respectively, while T_t denotes lump-sum net taxes in period t ($t = 0, 1$). First-period disposable income is specified as the sum of current dividends from the historically given portfolio (z_{H0}, z_{H0}^*), and the market value of this portfolio, net of taxes, T_0. Household income can be spent on consumption, C_{H0}, and on the new portfolio, (z_{H1}, z_{H1}^*). Second-period disposable income, derived from the dividends on the pre-existing portfolio (net of taxes), includes no resale value of stocks and no acquisition of new stocks, since it is the last period.

Let $u(C_{Ht})$ and $M(G_t)$ be concave von Neumann-Morgenstern private and public components of the representative individual utility function, respectively, and let δ denote the corresponding subjective discount factor. The expected utility is

$$U = u(C_{H0}) + \delta Eu[C_{H1}(\gamma)] + M(G_0) + \delta EM(G_1(\gamma)), \tag{13.3}$$

where E is the expectation operator.

The consumption-portfolio choice problem is to maximize the private component of the expected utility function (equation 13.3), subject to the budget constraints (equations 13.1 and 13.2), given common beliefs about the probability distribtution of states of nature. Financing its outlays through taxes or borrowing, the government's objective is to choose G_0 and G_1, so as to maximize the representative household expected utility.

13.3 Government Finance Neutrality

To prepare the ground for focusing on spending policies in the subsequent analysis, this section specifies conditions for a benchmark case in which government finance does not have real consequences. This is, of course, the stochastic counterpart to the Ricardian neutrality proposition. The consolidated private-sector budget constraint (derived from equations 13.1 and 13.2) is

$$C_{H0} + (q/\theta_1(\gamma))C_{H1}(\gamma) = [(q\theta_1^*(\gamma)/\theta_1(\gamma)) - q^*]z_{H1}^*$$
$$+ [(q + \theta_0)z_{H0} + (q^* + \theta_0^*)z_{H0}^*]$$
$$- [T_0 + (q/\theta_1(\gamma))T_1(\gamma)]. \tag{13.4}$$

It is evident from equation (13.4) that any tax shift policy that maintains $T_1(\gamma)/T_0 = -\theta_1(\gamma)/q$, so that the last bracketed term in equation (13.4) is equal to zero, does not affect the consumption possibilities set. Thus, if tax policies fulfill such a condition, the returns on the tax asset (namely the claim of government on private sector income) become proportional to returns on the privately issued domestic security, in every state. Accordingly, the government financial activities introduce effectively no new security into the stock market. Essentially, the government uses the proceeds from the current-period taxes to buy domestic equities while the next period state-dependent dividend revenue from the government financial investment would replace second-period transfers. These financial transactions have no effect on the private sector.

This means that the claim of the private sector on taxes can be viewed as a negative asset. Whether or not tax-shift policies are relevant must depend on whether or not the induced distribution of returns on such an asset is spanned by the equilibrium returns on the prevailing market assets.

13.4 Spending, International Allocation of Risk, and Stock Valuations

To highlight the effects of government spending on the international allocation of risk, and specifically on the relative price of the domestic security (in terms of the foreign security), we assume in this section that markets are *complete*. Since there are only two securities, the complete-market assumption implies that there must exist, at most, two states of nature (denoted by 0 and 1).

Expected utility maximization yields

$$\frac{\pi(0)u'(0)\theta_1^*(0) + \pi(1)u'(1)\theta_1^*(1)}{\pi(0)u'(0)\theta_1(0) + \pi(1)u'(1)\theta_1(1)} = \tilde{q}^*, \tag{13.5}$$

where $\tilde{q}^*$ is the relative price of the foreign security in terms of the domestic security. We denote the ratio of the price of state one contingent good, P_1, to state zero contingent good, P_0, by $p \ (= P_1/P_0)$. As usual, the marginal rate of substitution must be equal to this relative price, in equilibrium. That is,

$$\frac{\pi(1)u'(1)}{\pi(0)u'(0)} = p. \tag{13.6}$$

Equations (13.5) and (13.6) imply a specific relationship between p and $\tilde{q}^*$:

$$\frac{\theta_1^*(0) + p\theta_1^*(1)}{\theta_1(0) + p\theta_1(1)} = \tilde{q}^*. \tag{13.7}$$

Accordingly,

$$\text{sign} \frac{\partial \tilde{q}^*}{\partial p} = \text{sign} \left[\frac{\theta_1^*(1)}{\theta_1^*(0)} - \frac{\theta_1(1)}{\theta_1(0)} \right]. \tag{13.8}$$

In words, the sign of the derivative of the price of the foreign equity with respect to state one contingent-commodity price is equal to the sign of the difference between the foreign relative productivity in state one and the corresponding domestic productivity. That is if the good becomes more scarce in state 1 so that p goes up, then the asset whch pays off relatively more in state 1 will become more expensive.

The equilibrium in the world economy is portrayed by the Edgeworth box in figure 13.1. The vertical axis measures world output in state one $[\theta(1)Y + \theta^*(1)Y^*]$ while the vertical axis measures the corresponding state zero output. The cross-country allocation of claims to world output is specified by the point E. As usual, quantities pertaining to the home country are measured from point OH as the origin, and quantities pertaining to the foreign country are measures from point OF as the origin. The equilibrium obtains at point A, where the slopes of the domestic and foreign indifference curves are both equal to the single world relative price, p. Using equation (13.7) we can then derive the equilibrium relative price of the foreign security, $\tilde{q}^*$.

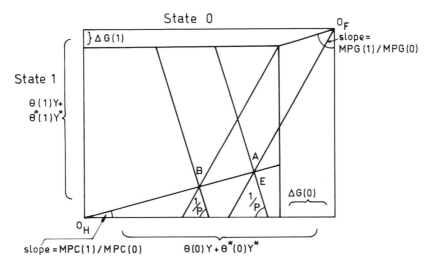

Figure 13.1
The effect of a rise in government spending on the relative state-contingent price

The *government* propensity to spend in the first and second state is determined by maximizing the public component of the expected utility function, $M(G_0) + \delta\pi(0) \cdot M(G_1(0)) + \delta\pi(1)M(G_1(1))$, subject to the budget constraint $G_0 + P(0)G_1(0) + P(1)G_1(1) = G$, where G denotes the present value of the domestic tax revenue. Optimization yields the endogenously determined propensities to spend for the government. Naturally, they depend, in general, on the probabilities (the π's), on the relative price (p), and on the government's overall resources (G).[2]

As in chapter 7, the basic criterion that determines the effect of a rise in government spending on the relative price of goods involves a comparison between the ratio of government marginal propensities to spend, $MPG(1)/MPG(0)$ (where $MPG(i)$ is the government propensity to spend in state i, $i = 1, 2$), and the corresponding ratio of the domestic private sector propensities to consume, $MPC(1)/MPC(0)$. A rise in government spending and a corresponding fall in the disposable income of the domestic private sector creates an excess demand for state one goods and an excess supply of state zero goods if the public sector propensity ratio exceeds the corresponding private sector ratio. As a result p must rise. If, on the other hand, the government propensity ratio falls short of the corresponding private propensity ratio, the equilibrium relative price, p, must fall.

The rise in government spending is indicated in figure 13.1 by the post-shock diminished size of the box. In a borderline case in which the relative propensities of the public and the private sector are equal (shown in the figure), the new equilibrium obtains at point B with no necessary changes in the market-clearing state-contingent prices. In this case there is also no change in the relative price of the domestic security (see equation 13.8).

However, if the public-private propensity configuration is such that following a rise in government spending the state one relative price, p, goes up, then the relative price of the domestic security must also rise if the domestic economy is relatively more productive in that state and vice versa.

13.5 Spending and International Allocation of Risk with Incomplete Markets

To highlight the effects of spending policies in the case of incomplete markets we abstract in this section from issues of government finance assuming that the government runs a balanced budget ($G_0 = T_0$, $G_1(\gamma) = T_1(\gamma)$). From the maximization of the expected utility (equation 13.3) subject to the budget constraints (equations (13.1) and (13.2)) we can derive the consumption and asset demand functions, which depend on the security prices, q and q^*, the entire distribution of second-period taxes, $\{T_1\}$, and the level of wealth, W_0:

$$C_{H0} = C_{H0}[q, q^*, \{T_1\}; W_0], \qquad z_{H1} = z_{H1}[q, q^*, \{T_1\}; W_0], \qquad (13.9)$$

and

$$z^*_{H1} = z^*_{H1}[q, q^*, \{T_1\}; W_0],$$

where wealth is defined by

$$W_0 = (q + \theta_0)z_{H0} + (q^* + \theta_0^*)z^*_{H0} - T_0.$$

The model is closed by the world market-clearing conditions for current-period consumption and equities of firms located in each of the two countries. Thus, world equilibrium is given by

$$C_{H0}[q, q^*, \{T_1\}, W_0] + C_{F0}[q, q^*, W_0^*] = \theta_0 Y_0 + \theta_0^* Y_0^* - G_0, \qquad (13.10)$$

$$z_{H1}[q, q^*, \{T_1\}, W_0] + z^*_{F1}[q, q^*, W_0^*] = Y_1 - G_1, \qquad (13.11)$$

and

$$z^*_{H1}[q, q^*, \{T_1\}, W_0] + z_{F1}[q, q^*, W^*] = Y_1^*. \qquad (13.12)$$

In describing the world equilibrium we can omit the current consumption market-clearing condition, equation (13.10), by invoking Walras' law. The remaining equilibrium conditions in equation (13.11) and (13.12) can then used to solve for the market-clearing prices q and q^*.

In the absence of uncertainty, all assets are perfect substitutes and they must command a single rate of return, the rate of interest. Recall from chapter 7 that the effect of government spending on the rate of interest is governed by a simple transfer-problem criterion. To derive this criterion we define in chapter 7 government 'wealth' by $G = G_0 + \Sigma_1 \alpha_1 G_1$, and the discounted flow of its *future* spending, $\Sigma_1 \alpha_1 G_t$, as the government "savings." If the marginal propensity to save out of wealth by the home country private sector exceeds the corresponding saving propensity of the home country government, the world interest rate, linking the present to the future, must rise with a permanent increase in government spending (since the rise in government spending and taxes amounts to a transfer from a high saver, the private sector, to a low saver, the government), and vice versa. In the presence of uncertainty, however, assets are imperfect

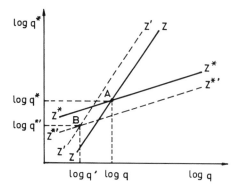

Figure 13.2
The effect of a transitory balanced-budget rise in current government spending

substitutes and the returns on different assets need not be equal to the rate of interest.

The nature of the world equilibrium, under the regime of free financial capital movements, is analyzed with the aid of figure 13.2. The upward-sloping schedule, ZZ, describes different combinations of the security prices (q and q^*) which are required to clear the domestic asset market. Likewise, the upward-sloping schedule Z^*Z^* describes different combinations of prices q and q^* which are required to clear the foreign security market.

A useful benchmark case for the analysis is a stationary equilibrium in which the portfolio composition does not change over time (analogously to the steady state in the infinite horizon problem). Observe that in such an equilibrium income effects associated wih price changes vanish entirely; only substitution effects remain. Formally, in the steady state, $Z_{H1} = Z_{H0}$, $Z_{H1}^* = Z_{H0}^*$, $Z_{F1} = Z_{F0}$, $Z_{F1}^* = Z_{F0}^*$, $Y_0 = Y_1$, and $Y_0^* = Y_1^*$. The ZZ schedule is steeper than the Z^*Z^* schedule around such an equilibrium point. To verify, we differentiate equations (13.11) and (13.12) (by using the definition of wealth given in equation (13.9). Rearranging, and using the Slutsky decomposition yields

$$\frac{q}{q^*}\frac{d\log q^*}{d\log q} = \frac{[Z_{H1q}^s - (Z_{H1} - Z_{H0})Z_{H1W}] + [Z_{F1q}^s - (Z_{F1} - Z_{F0})Z_{F1W}]}{[Z_{H1q^*}^{*s} - (Z_{H1}^* - Z_{H0}^*)Z_{H1W}] + [Z_{F1q^*}^{*s} - (Z_{F1}^* - Z_{F0}^*)Z_{F1W}]}. \tag{13.13}$$

along the ZZ schedule, and

$$\frac{q}{q^*}\frac{d\log q^*}{d\log q} = \frac{[Z_{H1q}^{*s} - (Z_{H1} - Z_{H0})Z_{H1W}^*] + [Z_{F1q}^{*s} - (Z_{F1} - Z_{F0})Z_{F1W}^*]}{[Z_{H1q^*}^{*s} - (Z_{H0}^* - Z_{H1}^*)Z_{H1W}] + [Z_{F1q^*}^{*s} - (Z_{F1}^* - Z_{F0}^*)Z_{F1W}^*}} \tag{13.14}$$

along the Z^*Z^* schedule, where a subscript denotes partial derivates (e.g., $Z_{H1q} = \partial Z_{H1}/\partial q$) and a superscript s indicates the price effect which applies to the compensated asset demand. From the theory of decisions under uncertainty we know that with a *time separable utility* function, assets z *and z^* must be net substitutes and the own price elasticity is larger (in absolute value) than the cross price elasticity* (see appendix A). Formally.

$$Z^s_{j1q} < 0, \qquad Z^s_{j1q^*} = Z^{*s}_{j1q} > 0, \qquad Z^{*s}_{j1q^*} < 0,$$

$$q^* Z^s_{j1q^*} < -q Z^s_{j1q}, \qquad q Z^{*s}_{j1q} < -q^* Z^{*s}_{j1q^*}, \qquad j = H, F.$$

Combining these properties of asset-demand functions with the right-hand sides of equations(13.13) and (13.14), and evaluating at the stationary portfolio equilibrium point (the benchmark case), it then follows that the ZZ and Z^*Z^* schedules must be upward-sloping, and that the former must be steeper than the latter. Consider the initial equilibrium point A in figure 13.2. A rise in the domestic-security price, due to substitution effects, generates an excess supply of domestic securities and an excess demand for foreign securities. To restore equilibrium in the market for foreign securities, the foreign security price, q^*, must rise. To clear the domestic security market the foreign country price, q^*, must rise as well, but proportionally more, since the changes in q have a stronger effect on the demand for domestic securities than on foreign securities, and the converse is true with regard to changes in q^*.

Consider now the effect of a *current-period transitory rise in the home country's government spending*. The rise in the current period spending (associated with a corresponding tax hike) must create an excess supply of domestic securities and necessitates a corresponding rise in private sector demand. As implied by equation (13.11) , this causes a leftward shift in the ZZ schedule to Z'Z'. The same rise in government spending creates also an excess supply of foreign securities and necessitiates a corresponding increase in demand for these securities that is reflected in the downward shift of the Z^*Z^* schedule, to $Z^{*\prime}Z^{*\prime}$. Thus, in the new equilibrium the prices of domestic and foreign securities must fall. This result obviously conforms with the nonstochastic analysis, in which a transitory rise in government spending raises the equilibrium world rate of interest. In direct analogy, following the rise in government spending the expected yields on both assets rise in the present stochastic case.

Consider now the effect of a stochastic *future* rise in the home country's government spending. Since the future output becomes relatively scarce, it must be more highly valued. As a result, private consumption in the future period must fall while saving must rise. In other words, through the consumption-smoothing mechanism the fall in future disposable income must enhance current-period savings. But even though the demand for assets as a group rises, we cannot ascertain that the demand for each and every asset necessarily rises. To characterize the effects on relative stock prices, we therefore need more information about the parameters of the demand functions and rates-of-return correlations. We now turn to an analytical framework that can shed light on the role played by the correlation between government spending and rates of return in the international transmission mechanism of fiscal policies.

13.6 Spending Policies and the CAPM Valuation

The role played by the correlations of government spending and asset returns is conveniently analyzed for the Capital Asset Pricing Model (CAPM) equilibrium valuations. We also introduce into the analysis a safe tradable bond with a return, R_0. Accordingly, incorporating bonds into the consolidated budget constraint, the relation between future consumption and current consumption is given by

$$C_{H1}(\gamma) = R_0 W_0 - G_1(\gamma) - R_0 C_{H0} + (\theta_1(\gamma) - R_0 q) z_{H1}$$
$$+ (\theta_1^*(\gamma) - R_0 q^*) z_{H1}^*$$

where W_0 is defined as in equation (13.9). Assume that $\theta_1(\gamma)$ and $\theta_1^*(\gamma)$ are normally distributed and let the private component of the expected utility function be

$$U = -e^{-bC_{H0}} - \delta E e^{-bC_{H1}(\gamma)}$$
$$= -e^{-bC_{H0}} - \delta e^{-b[EC_{H1}(\gamma) - (b/2)\mathrm{var}(C_{H1}(\gamma))]}, \qquad (13.15)$$

where b is the constant absolute risk-aversion parameter and $\mathrm{var}(\cdot)$ denotes the variance.

Deriving the first-order conditions for each country and adding them up yields

$$q = \frac{Y_1 - B\,\mathrm{cov}(\theta_1(\gamma)Y_1, C_{H1}(\gamma) + C_{F1}(\gamma))}{R_0 Y_1}, \qquad (13.16)$$

$$q^* = \frac{Y_1 - B\,\mathrm{cov}(\theta_1^*(\gamma)Y_1^*, C_{H1}(\gamma) + C_{F1}(\gamma))}{R_0 Y_1^*}, \qquad (13.17)$$

where $B = 1/[(1/b) + (1/b^*)]$ is the world market risk-aversion coefficient.

Using the equilibrium condition $C_{H1} + C_{F1} + G = \theta_1^* Y_1^* + \theta_1 Y_1$, the covariance terms can be expressed explicitly as follows:

$$\text{cov}(\theta_1(\gamma) Y_1, C_{H1}(\gamma) + C_{F1}(\gamma)) = Y_1^2 \sigma_{\theta\theta} + Y_1^* \sigma_{\theta\theta^*} - Y_1 \sigma_{\theta G},$$

and

$$\text{cov}(\theta_1^*(\gamma) Y_1^*, C_{H1}(\gamma) + C_{F1}(\gamma)) = Y_1 Y_1^* \sigma_{\theta\theta^*} + Y_1^{*2} \sigma_{\theta^*\theta^*} - Y_1^* \sigma_{\theta^* G},$$

where σ_{xy} denotes the covariance between x and y.

The remaining (first-order) condition, associated with bonds, can be derived similarly for each country. Adding up the latter conditions yields

$$\frac{1}{\delta}\log R_0 = (Y_1 + Y_1^* - EG_1(\gamma)) - (Y_0 + Y_0^*) - \left[\frac{1}{b}\log\delta + \frac{1}{b^*}\log\delta^*\right]$$
$$- \frac{1}{2}B[Y_1^2\sigma_{\theta\theta} + 2Y_1 Y_1^*\sigma_{\theta\theta^*} + Y_1^{*2}\sigma_{\theta^*\theta^*}] + \frac{1}{2}B(Y_1^*\sigma_{\theta^*\cdot G} + Y_1\sigma_{\theta G}).$$
(13.18)

It is evident from the equilibrium-valuation conditions in equations (13.16)–(13.18) that as long as the average level of government spending, $EG_1(\gamma)$, remains constant, a change in the distribution of government spending across states raises or lowers the equilibrium prices of equities, q and q^*, according to whether the covariances $\sigma_{\theta G}$ and $\sigma_{\theta^* G}$ are positive or negative, respectively. Thus, a procyclical fiscal policy, which tends to generate a positive correlation between government spending and productivity, raises the stock-market value and lowers the rate of interest. Thus, in this stylized case the correlation between the marginal changes in government spending and the country-specific productivity shock critically determines the effects of the fiscal policy on the equilibrium valuations in the integrated world stock market.

13.7   The Infinite Horizon

We consider in this section a small open economy in which the representative household solves an infinite-horizon problem. As in section 4.6, we assume that time is a continuous variable and we consider *permanent* productivity and fiscal shocks (see also Merton 1971). Accordingly, the consumer chooses the consumption stream and portfolio composition so as to maximize the expected intertemporal utility:

$$U = E_t \int_t^\infty e^{-\delta(\tau-t)} u(c_t)\, d\tau.$$
(13.19)

Starting with time intervals of size Δt our approximate specification for the flow budget constraint is given by

$$A_{t+\Delta t} = (A_t - c_t \Delta t)(\theta(1 + r\Delta t) + (1 - \theta)(1 + \rho_t \Delta_t)) + Y\Delta t - g_t.$$

$$(13.20)$$

Thus, at time t, an amount of consumption, $c_t \Delta t$, is taken from assets, A_t. The remaining assets, $A_t - c_t \Delta t$, are invested in a portfolio in which a share θ is invested in the safe asset with a fixed rate of return, r, and a risky asset with a stochastic rate of return, ρ_t, which follows a Brownian motion with mean ρ ($> r$) and standard deviation σ_ρ. In addition, asset accumulation between period t and period $t + \Delta t$ is augmented by the assumed fixed labor income, $Y\Delta t$, and is reduced by taxes, g, assumed to be equal to government spending, state by state. Government spending is assumed to follow a Brownian motion. At the limit Δg approaches dg such that

$$dg = \mu \, dt + \sigma_g \, dz \qquad (13.21)$$

where, μ represents the drift in government spending and z is a standard Wiener process so that dz has a zero mean and a unitary standard deviation.

The moments of the stochastic return, ρ_t, are given by

$$E(\rho_t) = \rho \, dt, \qquad \text{Var}(\rho_t) = \sigma_\rho^2 \, dt, \qquad \text{Cov}(\rho_t, g_t) = \sigma_{g\rho} \, dt. \qquad (13.22)$$

Appendix B demonstrates that at the limit the Bellman's equation for the consumption-portfolio choice problem is

$$0 = \underset{\{\theta, c\}}{\text{Max}} \, [u(c_t) - \delta V(A_t) + V_A(A_t)(A_t(\theta r + (1 - \theta)\rho) - c_t + Y - \mu)$$

$$+ \frac{1}{2} V_{AA}(A_t)(A_t^2(1 - \theta)^2 \sigma_\rho^2 + \sigma_g^2 - 2(1 - \theta)A_t \sigma_{g\rho})]. \qquad (13.23)$$

The first-order conditions are

$$0 = u_c(c_t) - V_A(A_t) \qquad (13.24)$$

$$0 = V_A(A_t)(r - \rho) + \frac{1}{2} V_{AA}(A_t)(-2(1 - \theta)\sigma_\rho^2 + 2A_t \sigma_{g\rho}). \qquad (13.25)$$

Equation (13.25) can be used to solve for the portfolio share, $1 - \theta$:

$$(1 - \theta) = \left(-\frac{V_A(A_t)}{A_t V_{AA}(A_t)}\right) \frac{1}{\sigma_\rho^2}(\rho - r) + \frac{1}{A_t} \frac{\sigma_{g\rho}}{\sigma_\rho^2}. \qquad (13.26)$$

Assume that the measure of absolute risk aversion is constant, which implies that the utility function is exponential:

$$u(c_t) = -\frac{1}{\eta} e^{-\eta c_t} \tag{13.27}$$

A solution to equations (13.24)–(13.25) can then be found by the method of undetermined coefficients and a guess for the value function $V(A_t)$ (see appendix B).

The solution for the consumption function and the portfolio shares yields

$$c_t = Y - \mu + rA_t + \frac{\delta - r}{r\eta} + (\rho - r)\frac{(r - \rho) + r\eta\sigma_{g\rho}}{r\eta\sigma_\rho^2} \tag{13.28}$$

$$(1 - \theta)A_t = \frac{\rho - r}{\sigma_\rho^2 r\eta} + \frac{\sigma_{g\rho}}{\sigma_\rho^2}. \tag{13.29}$$

Thus, the resulting linear consumption function depends negatively on government spending through the fiscal drift parameter, μ, and positvely on the correlation between government spending and the risky rate of return, $\sigma_{g\rho}/\sigma_\rho^2$. The amount invested in the risky asset, $(1 - \theta)A_t$, depends positively on the correlation between the fiscal and the productivity shocks, reflecting the fact that the risky asset provides an hedge against tax change risks.

13.8 Summary

This section extended the analysis of the effects of fiscal policies on the world equilibrium to uncertain environments, in which the key channel of transmission is the world stock market. The analysis shows that following a rise in government spending if the state-contingent marginal propensity to spend by the government exceeds the corresponding domestic private sector propensity, the equilibrium state-contingent price must rise. In such a case the domestic equity price rises relative to the foreign equity price if the domestic economy is relatively productive in this state and vice versa. Whether equity prices, (in terms of current-period consumption) rise or fall would depend on the cross-country correlations between productivity and fiscal shocks.

13.9 Appendix A: Characteristics of Asset Demands

In this appendix we derive the key characteristics of the asset-demand functions that underlie the slopes of schedules ZZ and Z*Z* in figure 13.2. To simplify the notation we suppress all period and country subscripts.

Using equations (13.2) and (13.3), the private component of the utility function can be expressed as a function of C_0, z, z^*, and $\{T_1(\gamma)\}$ as follows:

$$U(C_0, z, z^*, \{T_1(\gamma)\}) = u(C_0) + \delta E\{u[\theta(\gamma)z + \theta^*(\gamma)z^* - T(\gamma)]\}$$

$$= u(C_0) + v(z, z^*, T_1(\gamma)). \tag{A.1}$$

Consider the inverse of the function $u(C_0)$, that is, $C_0 = u^1(u) = \phi(u)$, the expenditure function $\mu(q, q^*, \{T_1(\gamma)\}, v)$ associated with $u = v(z, z^*, \{T_1(\gamma)\})$, and the expenditure function $m[1, q, q^*, \{T_1(\gamma)\}, U]$ associated with $U = U(C_0, z, z^*, \{T_1(\gamma)\})$. They are related to each other as follows:

$$m[1, q, q, \{T_1(\gamma)\}, U] = \min_{u, v} \{1 \cdot \phi(u) + \mu(q, q^*, (\{T_1(\gamma)\}, v) \text{ s.t.u} + v = U\}$$

$$= \min_{v} [1 \cdot \phi(U - v) + \mu(q, q^*, \{T_1(\gamma)\}, v)]. \tag{A.2}$$

The first-order condition of the optimization problem in (13.20) is

$$-1 \cdot \phi'(U - v) + \mu_v(q, q^*, \{T_1(\gamma)\}, v) = 0.$$

As usual, the compensated-asset demands are the partial derivatives of the expenditure function with respect to prices $(1, q, q^*)$. To obtain explicit expressions for v_1, v_{q^*}, we differentiate the first-order condition, and rearrange terms to yield

$$v_1 = \frac{\phi'}{\phi'' + \mu_{vv}} > 0, \qquad v_q = -\frac{\mu_{qv}}{\phi'' + \mu_{vv}} < 0,$$

and

$$v_{q^*} = -\frac{\mu_{q^*v}}{\phi'' + \mu_{vv}} < 0.$$

Substituting these expressions into the second-order derivatives of $m(\cdot)$ yields

$$m_{q1} = \mu_{qv} \frac{\phi'}{\phi'' + \mu_{vv}} > 0, \qquad m_{qq} = \mu_{qq} - \frac{\mu_{qv}^2}{\phi'' + \mu_{vv}} < 0,$$

and

$$m_{qq^*} = \mu_{qq^*} - \frac{\mu_{qv}\mu_{q^*v}}{\phi'' + \mu_{vv}} > 0.$$

The sign of m_{qq} must be negative since $\mu_{qq} < 0$ (because the demand for the domestic asset falls when the domestic security price rises while holding the welfare level, v, constant). The positive sign of m_{qq^*} is implied by the convexity of the expenditure function (so that $\mu_{vv}\mu_{qq^*} > \mu_{qv}\mu_{q^*v}$), since $\mu(\cdot)$ is homogeneous of degree zero in (q, q^*), it follows that μ_{qq} must be negative, and μ_{qq^*} must be positive; thus, $\phi''\mu_{qq^*} > 0$. The condition $m_{q1} > 0$ implies that the demand for the domestic security is positively related to the price of period zero consumption good, and the condition $m_{qq^*} > 0$ implies that the assets z and z^* must be net substitutes.

Multiplying the expression for m_{qq} by q and adding to it m_{qq^*} multiplied by q^*, yields

$$q^* m_{qq^*} + q m_{qq} = -\frac{\mu_v \mu_{qv}}{\phi'' + \mu_{vv}} < 0, \tag{A.3}$$

where use has been made of elementary properties of the expenditure function: (1) μ_q is homogeneous of degree zero in prices, q and q^*, and (2) μ_v is homogeneous of degree one in prices. The negative sign in (A.3) implies that $q^* m_{q^*q} < -q m_{qq}$. This means that a rise in the domestic security price, q, exerts a stronger effect on the demand for the domestic security compared to the demand for the substitute security. Similarly, it can be verified that a rise in q^* exerts a weaker effect on z^s than on z^{*s}.

13.10 Appendix B: Consumption and Portfolio Selection for the Infinite Horizon Case

The discrete-time version of the Bellman's equation, with time intervals of size Δt, is

$$V(A_t) = \text{Max } E_t \left[\int_t^{t+\Delta t} e^{-\delta(t-s)} u(c_s)\, ds + e^{-\delta \Delta t} V(A_{t+\Delta t}) \right] \tag{B.1}$$

where the asset-accumulation equation is given by

$$A_{t+\Delta t} = (A_t - c\Delta t)(\theta(1 + r\Delta t) + (1-\theta)(1 + \rho_t \Delta t) + Y\Delta t - g_t \tag{B.2}$$

where, ρ follows a Brownian motion, $d\rho_t = \rho\, d_t + \sigma_\rho\, dz$, and z is a Wiener process. A second-order expansion of $V(\cdot)$ by Taylor's theorem yields

$$e^{-\delta \Delta t} V(A_{t+\Delta t}) = V(A_t) - \delta V(A_t)\Delta t + V_A(A_t)\Delta A_t$$

$$+ \frac{1}{2} V_{AA}(A_t)(\Delta A_t)^2 + \frac{1}{2}\delta^2 V(A_t)(\Delta t)^2$$

$$- \delta V_A(A_t)\Delta t \Delta A_t. \tag{B.3}$$

Taking the expectations of (B.3) and eliminating terms of small order of magnitude (such as $\Delta t \Delta A_t$) yields

$$E_t[e^{-\delta\Delta t}V(A_{t+\Delta t})] = V(A_t) - \delta V(A_t)\Delta t$$

$$+ V_A(A_t)E_t(\Delta A_t) + \frac{1}{2}V_{AA}(A_t)E_t(\Delta A_t)^2. \tag{B.4}$$

With g_t following a Brownian motion, the asset-accumulation equation, (B.2), has the following stochastic properties:

$$E_t(\Delta A_t) = -c\Delta t + A_t[\theta r + (1 - \theta)\rho]\Delta t + (Y - \mu)\Delta t$$

$$\text{Var}(\Delta A_t) = [A_t^2(1 - \theta)^2\sigma_\rho^2 + \sigma_g^2 - 2(1 - \theta)A_t\sigma_{g\rho}]\Delta t, \tag{B.5}$$

Substituting (B.5) into (B.4), and the resulting expression into equation (B.1) while ignoring small order terms, yields the Bellman's equation, (13.23), in the text.

To solve the consumption-portfolio problem, our initial guesses are

$$V(A_t) = -\frac{p}{q}e^{-qA_t}, \qquad c_t = h + rA_t, \quad \text{and} \quad q = \eta r. \tag{B.6}$$

Substituting (B.6) into the first-order condition $u_c(c) = V_A(A)$ yields $\log p = -r\eta$. Substituting (B.6) into (13.25) we get

$$0 = \text{Max}\left\{-\frac{1}{\eta}e^{-\eta c} + \frac{\delta p}{q}e^{-qA} + pe^{-qA}(A(\theta r + (1 - \theta)\rho) + Y - c - \mu)\right.$$

$$\left. -\frac{1}{2}pqe^{-qA}[A^2(1 - \theta)^2\sigma_\rho^2 + \sigma_g^2 - 2(1 - \theta)A\sigma_{g\rho}]\right\}. \tag{B.7}$$

Setting the partial derivative of (B.7) with respect to θ equal to zero yields

$$\theta A = A - [(\rho - r)/q + \sigma_{g\rho}]/\sigma_\rho^2. \tag{B.8}$$

Substituting (B.8) into (B.9) yields

$$c_t = Y - \mu + rA_t + \frac{\delta - r}{r\eta} + (\rho - r)\frac{(r - \rho) + r\eta\sigma_{g\rho}}{r\eta\sigma_\rho^2}. \tag{B.9}$$

Equations (B.8) and (B.9) represent the solution for the portfolio selection and consumption determination problem.

Problems

1. Consider the infinite horizon model of a small open economy introduced in section 13.7. Assume that stochastic innovations (dz) of the returns (q_i)

in risky assets are increments of a standard Wiener process (z):

$$q_i = \mu_i \, dt + \sigma_i \, dz_i, \quad i = 1, 2, \ldots, n, \tag{1a}$$

so that asset i has mean μ_i and standard deviation σ_i. For simplicity, suppose that households receive no labor income. Also assume that the government follows a balanced budget policy and taxes households in proportion to their beginning-of-period wealth and at a constant tax rate τ. The stochastic innovations in τ are modelled as increments of a Wiener process with

$$\tau = \mu_g \, dt + \sigma_g \, dz_g. \tag{1b}$$

a. What determines a household's allocation of wealth among different risky assets? Are the optimal portfolio shares independent of a household's wealth? Show that if some risky assets had identical means and variances, domestic households would hold a larger share of the asset whose return has a higher covariance with government spending.

b. Assume domestic households have a power utility function of the form

$$u(c) = (1/\eta)c^{\eta}, \quad \text{and } 0 < \eta < 1. \tag{2}$$

Show that under the optimal consumption rule, if it exists, a household consumes a constant fraction of beginning-of-period wealth in each period. In this case, are the portfolio allocations independent of a household's wealth? What are the necessary transversality conditions for a well-defined solution? Suppose there is only one risky asset and define a countercyclical (procyclical) fiscal policy as one where, ceteris paribus, government spending is negatively (positively) correlated with asset returns. What are the effects of countercyclical and procyclical fiscal policies on the optimal consumption level?

2. Consider a two-country two-period stock market model. In the first period agents allocate their initial wealth among three assets: a riskless bond offering a return R, a domestic equity offering an uncertain pre-tax return R_1, and foreign equity with stochastic pre-tax return R_2. Aside from the equity returns, domestic and foreign taxes form a second source of uncertainty. These are levelled on dividends from equity holdings in the second period with tax rates based on the country in which the equity was issued (source principle).

For simplicity, and unlike the model in chapter 13, suppose that consumption of a single consumer good is confined to the second period. Also assume that the agents expected utility function can be represented by a mean-variance preference function (see Levy and Markowitz 1979):

$$E\{V_h\} - \frac{1}{2\tau_h} \text{Var}\{V_h\}, \tag{1}$$

where E denotes the expectation operator, Var the variance, and V_h is the home country's after-tax return on its portfolio. A similar function characterizes the foreign consumer's preferences. The parameter τ_j ($j = h, f$ and $\tau_j > 0$) may differ across countries and is a measure of the agent's "risk tolerance," the marginal rate of substitution between variance and expected return.

a. Derive the necessary equilibrium conditions for the world stock market. Show that the after-tax excess returns can be described by a Capital Asset Pricing Model (CAPM) relationship.

b. Demonstrate that domestic and foreign agents will hold shares in the same world market portfolio. Also prove that if domestic agents have a higher risk tolerance ($\tau_h > \tau_f$) and if the riskless asset is in zero net supply, the domestic agent will be a net borrower of the riskless asset.

c. Discuss how asset returns respond to changes in the stochastic properties of domestic taxes.

3. Consider the two-country two-period open economy model of chapter 13. Assume that there are two assets, a domestic and a foreign equity share, and that markets are complete.

a. Describe the government's optimal resource allocation across time and states if it maximizes a separable part of the private agent's expected utility function.

b. Assume that preferences of the representative domestic consumer can be described by the following expected utility function:

$$U = \frac{1}{1 - \sigma} [c_{h0}^{1-1/\sigma} + \delta\pi_0 c(0)_{h1}^{1-1/\sigma} + \delta\pi_1 c(1)_{h1}^{1-1/\sigma}] + U_g, \tag{1}$$

where U_g represents the utility derived from government consumption and π_s is the probability of state $s = 0, 1$. Assume that U_g and the representative foreign consumer's preferences are also described by power utility functions, although with possibly different substitution parameters σ, with $\sigma > 1$. Derive the optimal consumption plans for private agents and the government. Explain the implications for state-contingent prices of a redistribution of incomes from the private sector to the government.

c. Describe the effects of alternative tax paths across time and states on asset prices.

4. Consider a two-country two-period stock market model. In the first period agents allocate their initial wealth among three assets: a riskless bond offering a return R, a domestic equity offering an uncertain return R_1, and foreign equity with stochastic return R_2. Aside from the equity returns, domestic and foreign taxes form a second source of uncertainty. These are levelled on dividends from equity holdings in the second period with tax rates based on the country of residence of the investor (destination or residence principle).

For simplicity, suppose that consumption of a single consumer good is confined to the second period. Also assume that the agent's expected utility function can be represented by a mean-variance preference function:

$$E\{V_h\} - \frac{1}{2\tau_h} \text{Var}\{V_h\}, \tag{1}$$

where E denotes the expectations operator, Var the variance, and V_h is the home country's after-tax return on its portfolio. A similar function characterizes the foreign consumer's preferences. The parameter τ_j ($j = h, f$ and $\tau_j > 0$) may differ across countries and is a measure of the agent's risk "tolerance," the marginal rate of substitution between variance and expected return.

a. Derive the necessary equilibrium conditions for the stock market.

b. Demonstrate that domestic and foreign agents will, in general, *not* hold shares in the same world market portfolio. Compare this result with exercise 2 where, under otherwise the same set-up, taxation was based on the source principle.

c. As a special case, suppose that the domestic tax factor is a constant fraction of the foreign tax factor: $(1 - \tau_1) = \gamma(1 - \tau_2)$, where $\gamma > 0$ and τ_i ($i = h, f$) denotes the tax rate for the domestic or foreign resident. Also assume that the riskless after-tax return differs by the same factor γ across countries. Show that under these conditions domestic and foreign agents will hold shares in the same world market portfolio.

VII

International Spillovers
of Tax Policies:
A Simulation Analysis

14

Spillover Effects of International VAT Harmonization

A major challenge facing the move toward the single market in Europe in 1992 lies in the fiscal front.[1] The increased degree of international economic interdependence stimulated interest in the international coordination of fiscal policies, in general, and of tax policies in particular. A central issue in the discussion of fiscal policy convergence within Europe in 1992 involved the harmonization of value-added taxes (VAT). The increased integration of markets for goods and services within the European Community has contributed to the urgency of VAT harmonization among member countries. Such harmonization is designed to reduce tax revenue losses induced by cross-border arbitrage. In addition, in countries with high tax rates, industry puts pressures for lower tax rates aimed at restoring competitiveness and maintaining market shares. Furthermore, the increased integration of capital markets makes the tax base associated with internationally mobile capital highly elastic. All these factors imply that the process of European integration may require significant restructuring of tax systems. The purpose of this paper is to highlight key macroeconomic issues pertinent for the understanding of the international and the domestic effects of VAT harmonization.

In section 14.1, we outline the elements of the policies of VAT harmonization envisaged for Europe of 1992. In section 14.2, we present the basic tax model. The model, grounded on microeconomic foundations, is neoclassical in nature and is therefore suitable for the analysis of the incentive effects of various tax policies and their welfare implications. It allows for a rich tax structure and contains a detailed specification of public and private sector behavior. The analytical framework used in the paper adopts the saving-investment balance approach to the analysis of international economic interdependence. It thus emphasizes the effects of changes in the *time profile* of the various taxes on the intertemporal allocations of savings investment and labor. These dynamic effects are supplemented by the more conventional effects of the *level* of the flat rate taxes on the margins governing labor-leisure choice (such as the negative effect of consumption and income taxes on labor supply), the consumption-saving choice (such as the negative double taxation effect of income tax on saving) and the choice of investment plans (such as the negative effect of the corporate income tax on investment). Our formulation focuses on the roles played by the levels and the time profile of taxes on income (wage tax and capital income tax), investment and saving incentives (investment tax credit and saving tax credit), taxes on consumption (value-added tax), and on international borrowing.

In section 14.3, we apply the tax model of section 14.2 to examine the effects of international VAT harmonization. Throughout the analysis we ensure that the tax restructuring is constrained by the requirement that government solvency be maintained. Accordingly, changes in the value-added tax rates are accompanied by compensatory changes in other taxes. The effects of VAT harmonization are illustrated by means of dynamic simulations. The simulations reveal that the effects of such tax changes on the domestic and foreign levels of output, employment, investment, consumption, and other key macroeconomic variables depend critically on the degree of substitution governing temporal and intertemporal allocations as well as on the tax system. Furthermore, it is shown that these characteristics of the economic system also govern the precise welfare implications of VAT harmonization. We show that the policy of VAT harmonization may generate significant conflicts of interest within each country as well as between countries.

In section 14.4, we analyze the dynamic mechanism associated with changes in the time profile of taxes. Since VAT harmonization involves changes in the composition of taxes, in this section we examine the dynamic consequences of revenue-neutral tax conversions between income and consumption (VAT) tax systems undertaken by a single country. The revenue neutrality requirement is motivated by inflationary fears or debt aversion. Reflecting our emphasis on the saving-investment balance, we demonstrate analytically that the effects of such changes in the composition of taxes depend critically on international differences in saving and investment propensities, which in turn govern the time profile of the current account of the balance of payments. These issues are examined by means of dynamic simulations in section 14.5, in which the role of current imbalances in global tax restructuring is analyzed. Section 14.6 contains a summary.

14.1   VAT Harmonization: Europe 1992

In this section, we outline elements of the policies of VAT harmonization envisaged for Europe of 1992. Such policies form an important ingredient of the wide ranging measures associated with the move toward the single European market in 1992. In the fiscal area the European Commission has drawn up various proposals on the approximation of the rates and the harmonization of the structures of VAT.

The process of harmonization of the VAT systems has started with the First Council Directive of April 1967 and has proceeded thereafter through consecutive directives. The process involved the adoption of VAT in various member countries and the continuous convergence of rates and structures among members of the community. Much of the discussion surrounding the practical implementation of the approximation of the VAT rates concerned the width of bands within which various VAT rates should be placed, the products to which a reduced rate would be applicable, and the problem of zero-rated products.[2] For 1992 the commission envisaged a standard VAT rate ranging between 14 and 20 percent, and a reduced rate (applied to selected categories, such as foodstuffs) ranging between 4 and 9 percent.[3] The commission proposes to abolish the higher rate that presently exists in some member countries on certain categories of goods. In subsequent discussions an alternative proposal was considered according to which the standard rate band would be replaced by a minimum rate applicable from January 1, 1993. Each member state would choose a rate at least equal to the minimum rate, with due regard to the budgetary implications and to the "competitive pressures" arising from the rates chosen by other neighboring states and main trading partners. Table 14.1 provides summary information on VAT in the European Community. It illustrates the disparities between the various member country VAT rates.[4]

One of the central issues that needs to be addressed is the budgetary consequence of the harmonization in the VAT systems. A few member states (notably Denmark and Ireland) would suffer considerable tax revenue losses, while others (notably Spain, Luxembourg, and Portugal) would see their tax revenue go up considerably.

The increased integration of markets for goods and services within the European Community has contributed to increased pressures for VAT harmonization among member states. In the absence of such harmonization, cross-border arbitrage results in tax revenue losses in countries with high tax rates and tax revenue gains in countries with low rates. In addition, faced with reduced competitiveness, industry in countries with high tax

Table 14.1
VAT rates in the European Community

Country (year of VAT introduction)	Statutory rates (1990, percent)			Revenue contribution as percentage of total tax revenue (1987)	Revenue contribution as percentage of GDP (1987)
	Reduced rate	Standard rate	Higher rate		
Belgium (1971)	1, 6 and 7	19	25 and 33	16.3	7.2
Denmark (1967)	0	22	—	26.9	9.8
France (1968)	5.5, and 7	18.6	25	20.9	8.7
Germany (1968)	7	15	—	13.1	3.8
Greece	3 and 6	16	36	20.9	7.8
Ireland (1972)	0, 2.2, and 10	23	—	18.9	8.0
Italy (1973)	2 and 9	18	38	13.1	4.7
Luxembourg (1970)	3 and 6	12	—	13.3	6.0
Netherlands (1969)	6	18.5	—	15.2	7.9
Portugal (1986)	8	17	30	18.8	7.7
Spain (1986)	6	12	33	16.0	5.3
United Kingdom (1973)	0	15	—	16.3	6.0
Commission proposal					
A:	4 to 9	14 to 20	abolished		
B:	4 to 9	minimum rate	abolished		

Sources: Table 2.1 in Cnossen and Shoup (1987) and table 3.5.1 in *European Economy* (March 1988). EC: "The Evolution of VAT Rates Applicable in the Member States of the Community," *Inter-tax*, 1987/3, pp. 85–88, International Bureau of Fiscal Documentation, *Tax News Services*, various issues: IMF, *Government Finance Statistics Yearbook* (1989), and OECD, *Revenue Statistics of OECD Member Countries, 1966–1988*, Paris, 1989.

rates puts pressures for lower rates. These forces have provided some of the impetus for the movement toward narrowing the intra-European gaps among VAT rates.

One of the key issues addressed in the deliberations concerns the specification of the value-added tax: whether it would be a *destination-based* VAT (as is traditionally the case in Europe) or whether it would be a *source-based* VAT. The problem arises since the removal of fiscal frontiers through the abolishment of border controls may complicate the administration of destination-based VAT, which requires the levying VAT on imports and rebating the VAT on exports. These administrative difficulties, however, can be overcome through a variety of methods such as those used for cross-border transactions among the Benelux countries since 1969 as well as between Ireland and the United Kingdom until 1984. The key feature of the various methods involves computing border tax adjustment from books of accounts verified through written records (in the absence of border controls). An alternative method to protect the tax revenue of the country of destination is the establishment of a clearance mechanism among the various tax authorities.[5]

In the subsequent section we develop a tax model to assess the global implications of the move toward VAT harmonization. Throughout, we specify the tax system as being destination based. This formulation conforms with the prevailing system even though the future system is envisaged to be source-based. However, the European Commission proposed in May 1990 (following the guidelines set by the council of its economics and finance ministers in 1989) to maintain the present destination principle until January 1997. Our analysis, however, can also be used to shed light on the implications of harmonization with a source based VAT system.

14.2   The Tax Model

We start with a formulation of the budget constraint.[6] As usual, this serves to focus attention on key economic variables and tax policy parameters that play a central role in the analysis. The home country's private sector (full-income) budget constraint applicable to period t ($t = 0, 1, \ldots, T - 1$) is

$$(1 + \tau_{ct})C_t + (1 - \tau_{wt})w(1 - l_t)$$

$$= (1 - \tau_{wt})w + (1 - \tau_{kt})((r_k - \theta)K_t) - (1 - \tau_{It})I_t\left(1 + \frac{b}{2}\frac{I_t}{K_t}\right)$$

$$+ (B_t^p - B_{t-1}^p) - (1 - \tau_{kt})(1 + \tau_{st})r_{t-1}B_{t-1}^p \qquad (14.1)$$

where τ_{ct}, τ_{wt}, and τ_{kt} denote the tax rates on consumption (VAT), labor income, and capital income, respectively; all taxes are residence based. The terms τ_{It} and τ_{st} denote investment tax credit and saving tax credit, respectively. The levels of consumption, labor supply, capital stock, investment and the private sector international borrowing are denoted, respectively, by C_t, l_t, K_t, I_t, and B_t^P. The wage rate, the capital-rental rate, and the interest rate are denoted, respectively, by w, r_k, and r_t, and θ denotes the rate of depreciation. For convenience we normalize the endowment of leisure to unity and assume costs of adjustment in capital formation of the form $(\frac{1}{2})bI_t^2/K_t$. We note that in the final period (period T) the private sector settles its debt commitments and no new investment or new borrowing occurs so that $I_T = B_T^P = 0$[7]. To sum up, the left hand side of equation (14.1) represents the value of consumption of ordinary goods and leisure; the right hand side of this equation represents the value of labor endowment, capital income (net of investment), and new borrowing (net of debt service). All of these quantities are evaluated at the after-tax prices. To simplify the exposition we assume a linear production function with fixed coefficients. Thus, the competitive equilibrium conditions imply that the wage rate and the capital-rental rates, w and r_k, are constant.

The periodic (full income) budget constraints specified in equation (14.1) can be consolidated to yield the lifetime present-value budget constraint governing the decisions of the private sector. To facilitate the diagrammatic analysis that follows we illustrate the lifetime present value budget constraint for a two-period case ($t = 0, 1$). Accordingly,

$$
\begin{aligned}
C_0 + \alpha_c C_1 = & \left\{\frac{1 - \tau_{w0}}{1 + \tau_{c0}}\right\} \{wl_0 + \alpha_L wl_1\} + \left\{\frac{1 - \tau_{I0}}{1 + \tau_{c0}}\right\} \{\alpha_I (r_k - \theta) \\
& - \left(1 + \frac{b}{2}\frac{I_0}{K_0}\right)\right\} I_0 + \left\{\left(\frac{1 - \tau_{b0}}{1 + \tau_{c0}}\right)(r_k - \theta_k)\left[1 - \tau_{k0}\right.\right. \\
& \left.\left.+ \frac{1 - \tau_{k1}}{1 - \tau_{b1} + (1 - \tau_{k1})(1 + \tau_{s1})r_0}\right]\right\} K_0 \\
& - \left\{\frac{1 + (1 - \tau_{k0})(1 + \tau_{s0})r_{-1}}{1 + \tau_{c0}}\right\} B_{-1}^P
\end{aligned}
\tag{14.2}
$$

where

$$
\alpha_c = \frac{(1 + \tau_{c1})}{(1 + \tau_{c0})} \frac{1}{1 + (1 - \tau_{k1})(1 + \tau_{s1})r_0},
$$

$$\alpha_I = \frac{(1 - \tau_{k1})}{(1 - \tau_{I0})} \frac{1}{1 + (1 - \tau_{k1}(1 + \tau_{s0})r_0}$$

$$\alpha_L = \frac{(1 - \tau_{w1})}{(1 - \tau_{w0})} \frac{1}{1 + (1 - \tau_{k1})(1 + \tau_{s1})r_0} \quad \text{and} \quad \gamma_0 = \frac{1 - \tau_{w0}}{1 + \tau_{c0}}.$$

As indicated, the discount factors α_c, α_L, and α_I are the effective (tax-adjusted) discount factors governing *intertemporal* consumption, leisure, and investment decisions, respectively[8]. The *intratemporal* choice between labor supply (leisure) and consumption of ordinary goods is governed by the prevailing effective intratemporal tax ratio $\gamma = (1 - \tau_w)/(1 + \tau_c)$.

The expressions in equation (14.2) show the key factors operating on the various margins of substitution. The intratemporal tax ratio, γ, shows the conventional negative effect of labor income tax and consumption tax on labor supply. The effective discount factor governing consumption, α_c, shows the conventional negative effect of capital income tax, τ_k (through double taxation), on saving. Likewise, the effective discount factor governing investment, α_I, shows the negative effects of capital income tax, τ_k, on investment. In addition to these conventional channels, the expressions in equation (14.3) highlight the dynamic channels of tax policies. Specifically, as can be seen, the effective discount factors depend on the *time path* of the various taxes.

To understand the dynamic mechanisms underlying the effective discount factors it is useful to define a benchmark case in which the double-taxation of savings is eliminated. In that case, the tax incentive rates on savings and investment are equalized and the common rate is equal to the capital income tax. Accordingly, these equalities imply that $\tau_k = \tau_I = \tau_s/(1 + \tau_s)$. Such a configuration of taxes yields the *cash flow* income tax system[10]

It is noteworthy that such a cash flow income tax system is equivalent to a value-added tax system that is source based[11]. We note that in this benchmark case the effective discount factor governing *intertemporal* consumption decisions, α_c, is independent of the income tax, whereas the effective discount factor governing investment and leisure decisions, α_I and α_L, are independent of the consumption tax[12]. Since with such a cash flow tax system the effective discount factors depend only on the time path of the various taxes rather than on their levels, it follows that if the various tax rates do not vary over time, then the effective discount factors α_c, α_L, and α_I are equal to the undistorted tax-free factor $\alpha = 1/(1 + r_0)$. In that case in which the time paths of the various tax rates are "flat," the *intertemporal* allocations are undistorted. Of course, as indicated earlier, the intratemporal are distorted if the intratemporal tax ratio γ differs from unity.

Having discussed the budget constraint, we turn next to the specification of the utility function. To facilitate the simulation analysis in subsequent sections, we need to adopt a specific form of the multi-period utility function. Accordingly, we assume that the intraperiod utility function between consumption of ordinary goods and leisure is

$$u_t = \{\beta C_t^{(\sigma-1)/\sigma} + (1-\beta)(1-l_t)^{(\sigma-1)/\sigma}\}^{\sigma/(\sigma-1)}, \tag{14.3}$$

while the interperiod utility function is

$$U_0 = \sum_{t=0}^{T} \delta^t \log(u_t), \tag{14.4}$$

where σ is the temporal elasticity of substitution between leisure and consumption of ordinary goods, β is the distributive parameter of consumption, and δ is the subjective discount factor. This formulation implies a unitary intertemporal elasticity of substitution.

Maximizing the utility functions in equations (14.3) and (14.4) subject to the lifetime present value budget constraint (the multi-period analogue to equation 14.2) yields the consumption function and the labor supply function. The formal solutions are presented in appendix A, where it is shown that consumption demand and labor supply depend on wealth (which is defined, as usual, as the discounted sum of tax-adjusted income, net of investment, minus the initial debt commitment), on the path of the tax-adjusted rates of interest and on the intratemporal and intertemporal tax structure. The maximization of wealth yields the investment function. It is shown in appendix A that, in addition to the conventional technological characteristics, investment depends on the path of the tax-adjusted rates of interest. As is evident, in this model economic welfare as well as the key behavioral relations (consumption, labor supply, investment, and output) are determined within a dynamic context. Accordingly, the paths of saving and investment and thereby the current account of the balance of payments are also governed by dynamic considerations. In the present context the model highlights the central role played by the dynamics of the tax structure. The dynamics are reflected by the temporal and intertemporal substitutions captured by the various tax-adjusted discount factors. It follows, of course, that a proper evaluation of positive and normative implications of trends in savings, investment, and the current account cannot be complete without an assessment of the expected paths of taxes and the other economic variables influencing income and spending[13].

The foregoing discussion focused on the various channels and margins of substitution through which taxes impact on economic behavior. Such changes in economic behavior also influence economic welfare. The welfare implications depend, as always, on the distorted margins of substitution arising from the tax wedges, and on the elasticities of response to the implied changes in incentives. The behavioral response to changes in the tax wedges are shown in the consumption demand, labor supply, and investment in apendix A. Our formulation in equation (14.2) shows that in addition to their effects on the margins of substitution, the various taxes also contain elements that resemble lump-sum taxes. These elements are found in the taxes that fall on inelastic tax bases. For example, the capital income and consumption tax rates, τ_k and τ_c, are also applied (directly and indirectly) to the value of initial assets (K_0 and (B^p_{-1})), which are obviously inelastic tax bases. These elements of the tax structure are nondistortive. Our simulation analysis of the welfare implications of alternative tax instruments incorporates these attributes of the tax system.

The tax model developed in this section and its formal solution presented in appendix A are used in subsequent sections for the dynamic simulations of the effects of international tax harmonization.

14.3   Simulations of VAT Harmonization

In this section we present dynamic simulations of the effects of international harmonization of VAT. We use our two-country model and presume that prior to the VAT harmonization, the two countries use very different tax systems. The home country tax revenue stems from high income tax, while the foreign country revenue stems from high VAT. The harmonization of VAT entails a rise in the home country VAT rate and an equivalent reduction in the foreign rate. The narrowing of international disparities between VAT rates captures the commission's proposal of reducing the disparities of VAT rates among member countries and categories of goods. Furthermore, to maintain fiscal solvency, we assume that (in the absence of changes in government spending) changes in the VAT rates are accompanied in each country by opposite changes in income tax rates.

In performing the simulations we consider first a benchmark case in which the saving and investment propensities do not differ internationally, so that $\delta = \delta^*$ and $r_k = r_k^*$. These assumptions ensure that the current account positions (that is, the saving-investment gaps) are zero and, thereby, the tax restructuring in and of itself does not affect the world rate of interest. In subsequent sections, we depart from this benchmark case.

We first computed a baseline equilibrium. This equilibrium was then perturbed by the assumed VAT harmonization. The various figures presented below show the effects of the tax restructuring measured as percentage deviations from the baseline levels. Throughout, the home country was assumed to raise its VAT by 6 percent and restores fiscal solvency by a corresponding reduction of its income tax. We considered various tax systems: cash flow income tax, labor income tax, capital income tax, capital income tax combined with saving incentives, and capital income tax combined with investment incentives. The results of these simulations are shown in figures 14.1–14.5 and are summarized in table 14.2, which also reports the implied welfare implications of the VAT harmonization. To capture the essence of the dynamic evolution of the various variables, we report in table 14.2 the direction of changes for both the short run (SR) and the medium run (MR).

The multiplicity of mechanisms and channels operating on the various tax incentives result in a variety of configurations of the response of the other key economic variables as illustrated for the cases shown in table 14.2. Of special interest are the welfare effects indicated by the utility index in the simulations. The percentage factor by which the welfare change is measured by path of consumption must be raised in order to bring utility up to the preharmonization level. As always, the welfare consequences of tax policies can be decomposed into two components: first, those arising from changes in excess burden, and second, those arising from terms of trade effects. The changes in the degree of excess burden induced by VAT harmonization depend on the elasticity of the tax base as well as on the magnitude of the existing distortion. In the cases illustrated by the simulations, we have chosen parameters that result in relatively low investment and labor supply elasticities, and a relatively high consumption elasticity.[14] This choice suggests that in the case considered, the excess burden associated with a consumption tax is relatively high in comparison with the corresponding excess burden associated with an income tax.

The assumption that the saving and investment propensities do not differ internationally implies that the initial current account positions are balanced. As a result, the international VAT harmonization does not alter the world rate of interest. The dynamics of adjustment in this case arise only from the effects of the tax wedges on the various incentives.

In summarizing the results presented in figures (14.1)–(14.5) and table 14.2, we first note that with a labor income tax system, the VAT harmonization does not induce any change in the time path of domestic and foreign investment.

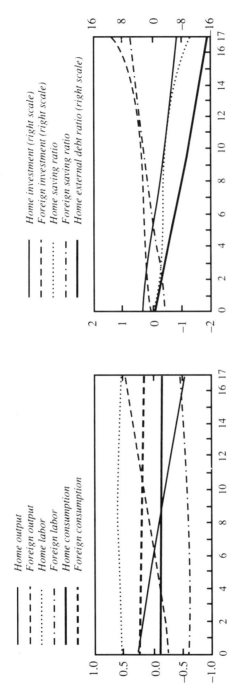

Figure 14.1
VAT harmonization: 6 percent permanent increase in home country VAT and 6 percent permanent reduction in foreign country VAT under cash flow tax system

Note: Assuming a permanent increase of 6 percent in home country VAT and a permanent reduction of 6 percent in foreign country VAT.

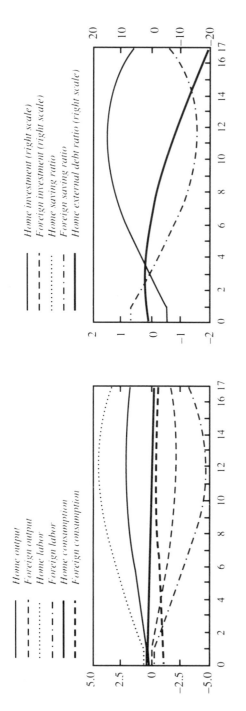

Note: Assuming a permanent increase of 6 percent in home country VAT and a permanent reduction of 6 percent in foreign country VAT.

Figure 14.2
VAT harmonization: 6 percent permanent increase in home country VAT and 6 percent permanent reduction in foreign country VAT under wage tax system

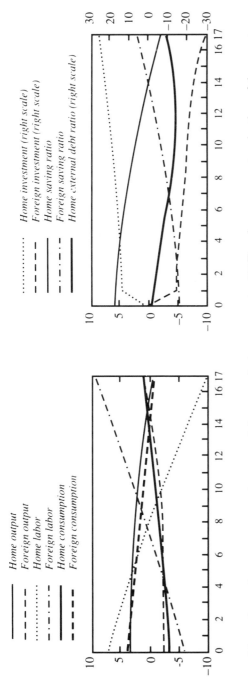

Note: Assuming a permanent increase of 6 percent in home country VAT and a permanent reduction of 6 percent in foreign country VAT.

Figure 14.3
VAT harmonization: 6 percent permanent increase in home country VAT and 6 percent permanent reduction in foreign country VAT under capital tax system

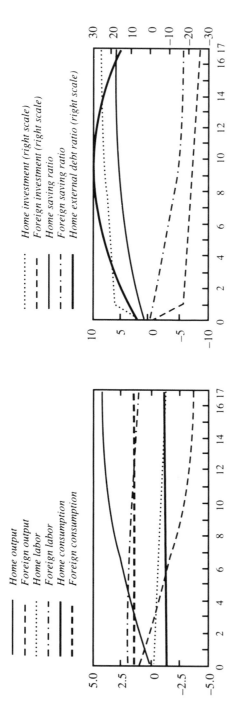

Note: Assuming a permanent increase of 6 percent in home country VAT and a permanent reduction of 6 percent in foreign country VAT.

Figure 14.4
VAT harmonization: 6 percent permanent increase in home country VAT and 6 percent permanent reduction in foreign country VAT under capital tax and saving incentive system

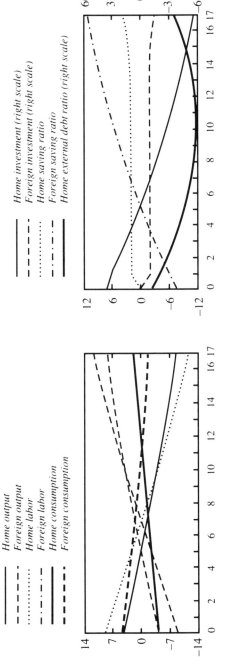

Figure 14.5
VAT harmonization: 6 percent permanent increase in home country VAT and 6 percent permanent reduction in foreign VAT under capital tax and investment incentive system

Note: Assuming a permanent increase of 6 percent in home country VAT and a permanent reduction of 6 percent in foreign country VAT.

Table 14.2
Effects of VAT harmonization under alternative tax systems (deviations from baseline)

Variable	Cash flow income tax		Labor income tax		Capital incomes tax		Capital income tax and saving incentives		Capital income tax and investment incentives	
	SR	MR	SR	MR	SR	MR	SR	MR	SR	MR
r	0	0	0	0	0	0	0	0	0	0
I	−	−	0	0	+	+	+	+	−	−
I^*	+	+	0	0	−	−	−	−	+	+
L	+	+	+	+	+	+	+	+	+	−
L^*	−	−	−	−	−	−	−	−	−	−
Y	+	+	+	+	+	+	+	+	+	+
Y^*	−	−	−	−	−	−	−	−	−	−
C	+	+	+	+	−	+	+	+	−	+
C^*	+	+	+	+	+	−	+	+	+	+
S	+	−	+	+	+	−	+	+	+	−
S^*	−	+	+	−	−	+	−	−	−	+
B	−	−	+	−	−	−	+	+	−	−
U	0.3	−7.8	0.0	−12.5	1.4	−7.0	1.2	−3.0	1.0	−7.8
U^*	−0.3	8.7	0.1	14.6	−1.0	7.3	−0.8	2.2	−0.8	8.4

Note: The VAT harmonization obtains through a permanent 6% rise in r_c and a fall in r_c^*. Budgetary balance obtains through appropriate adjustments in the periodic rates of cash flow, labor income, and capital income taxes (with and without saving incentives). The technology and preference parameters of the two countries are assumed to be equal (so that the current account position is balanced). SR and MR are defined as short run and medium run, respectively. The welfare change is measured by the percentage factor by which the post-harmonization consumption path must be raised in order to bring utility up to the preharmonization level. For the utility index the SR pertains to the discounted sum of utilities over the entire period except the final one, while MR pertains to the final period utility (reflecting the entire period beyond the simulation period).

Second, whenever the income tax system contains an investment incentive component, it dominates in its effect on the paths of investment. Indeed, under the cash flow income tax system (which obviously contains an investment incentives component), and under a system of capital income tax combined with investment incentives, the path of domestic investment consequent on the reduced income tax is lowered for both the short and the medium runs. The opposite occurs in the foreign country. This pattern is reversed under the income tax systems that do not contain incentives to investment.

Third, and analogously to the foregoing reasoning, whenever the income tax system contains a saving incentive component (like the IRA system in the United States, which eliminates the double taxation of savings) its effect dominates the changes in consumption. Thus, under the cash flow income tax system and under a system of capital-income tax combined with saving incentives, the path of domestic consumption consequent on the VAT harmonization is lowered for both the short and the medium runs. The opposite occurs in the foreign country. This pattern is reversed under the labor tax system.

Fourth, whenever, the income tax system contains a tax on labor income, changes in that tax dominate the effect of the VAT harmonization on employment. Thus, under the cash flow income tax system and under the system of labor income tax, the path of domestic employment consequent on the reduced income tax is raised for both the short and the medium runs. The opposite occurs in the foreign country in which income taxes rise. Finally, by inspecting the figures, one could infer the effects of the VAT harmonization under alternative tax systems on the growth rates of domestic and foreign output and on the path of external debt.[15].

An examination of figures 14.1–14.5 and table 14.2 indicates a potential for international conflicts of interest with respect to the implementation of VAT harmonization. In fact, as is evident, under all tax systems considered, the direction of changes in domestic and foreign employment, output, consumption, savings, and investment consequent on the international VAT harmonization are opposite to each other in both the short and the medium runs. The same phenomenon emerges from an examination of the utility indices of economic welfare. In all cases the domestic and foreign SR utility indices (given by the discounted sums of utilities over the entire period except for the final one) move in opposite directions. In general, the same holds for the MR utility indices, reflecting the entire future beyond the simulation period. Furthermore, the cases considered the VAT harmonization results in a redistribution of welfare between generations. This is evident by the opposite direction of changes in the SR and MR utility indices within each country. The various simulations show that the changes in the utility indices reflect, by and large, a *redistribution* of world welfare since the *sum* of the domestic and foreign utility indices does not change appreciably. This result underscores the notion that the resolution of international conflicts of interest in implementing the VAT harmonization may necessitate a compensation mechanism from gainers to losers.

14.4 Tax Conversions: Revenue Neutrality and Current Account Imbalances

In this section we focus on a reform that introduces a consumption tax (VAT) system instead of the prevailing income-tax system, allowing for current account imbalances[16]. To simplify, we consider a two-period case with a cash flow tax system. With such a tax system the effective discount factors governing consumption, investment, and labor supply decisions (indicated in equation 14.2) become

$$\alpha_c = \frac{1 + \tau_{c1}}{1 + \tau_{c0}}\alpha, \qquad \alpha_I = \frac{1 - \tau_{k1}}{1 - \tau_{k0}}\alpha, \qquad \alpha_L = \frac{1 - \tau_{w1}}{1 - \tau_{w0}}\alpha \qquad (14.5)$$

where $\alpha = 1/(1 + r_0)$ denotes the undistorted discount factor[17].

The tax conversion can be thought of as consisting of two components. First, it involves a permanent reduction of the income tax and a permanent equiproportional rise in VAT. Second, it involves further adjustments in the income tax aimed at restoring the initial level of the revenue in each period. As is evident from equation (14.5) with a cash flow income tax system, the *first component* of the tax conversion does not alter the effective discount factors governing decisions concerning the rate of growth of consumption and the level of investment. As a result, the dynamic characteristics of the real equilibrium (involving the levels of investment and the rates of growth of output and consumption) remain intact.[18] However, to the extent that the equiproportional changes in the tax rates alter government revenue, further adjustments in income taxes are necessary. The key factor determining whether the tax conversion results in a shortfall or an excess of tax revenue is the economy's initial current account position. The conversion from an income tax system to a VAT system broadens the tax base if the level of consumption exceeds the level of output plus net investment, that is, if the country runs a deficit in the current account of its baance of payments.[19] In that case the first component of the tax conversion raises government revenue. To ensure revenue neutrality the second component involves a downward adjustment in the present-period income tax rate. Since intertemporal solvency implies that the economy runs a current account surplus in the future period, restoration of future revenue neutrality necessitates an upward adjustment of the future-period income tax rate. Opposite adjustments in the current and future income tax rates would be necessary if the economy's present-period current account position was in surplus so that the first-component of the conversion toward a VAT system narrows the tax base.

We now apply the analysis to a two-country model of the world economy. We carry out the analysis with a simple diagrammatic apparatus that portrays the rates of gowth of consumption and output (net of investment) as functions of the corresponding tax-adjusted discount factors. In figure 14.6 the upward-sloping schedule, S^w, describes the ratio of future to present world output net of investment as an increasing function of the discount factor. The positive slope reflects the fact that a rise in the discount factor (a fall in the rate of interest) raises current investment and induces

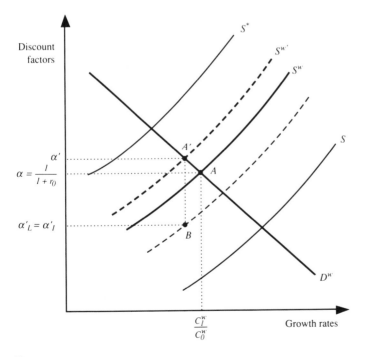

Figure 14.6
The effects of international tax conversion on saving and investment

substitution away from present-period labor supply toward a future-period labor supply. These changes raise the ratio of future-to present-period output net of investment. This world relative supply schedule is a weighted average of the corresponding domestic, S, and foreign. S^* relative supply schedules. The downward-sloping schedule, D^w, shows the world desired ratio of future to current consumption as a decreasing function of the discount factor. This world relative demand is weighted average of the two countries' relative demand schedules (not drawn). As shown in figure 14.6 the initial equilibrium obtains at point A, at which the world rate of interest is r_0.

Suppose that the domestic economy runs a present-period current account deficit. Under such circumstances, the shift toward a VAT broadens the tax base. To maintain revenue neutrality, the current income taxes τ_{k0} and τ_{w0}, fall, while future income taxes, τ_{k1} and τ_{w1}, rise. As seen from equation (14.5), the new configuration of income tax rates lowers the effective discount factors applicable to investment and labor decisions, α_J and α_L. However, since the intertemporal ratio of consumption taxes remains unchanged, the effective discount factor applicable to consumption decisions, α_c, remains intact.

The fall in the effective discount factors applicable to investment and labor supply induces an intertemporal substitution in the domestic economy toward current period output (net of investment). Thus, for each and every value of the world discount factor the domestic relative supply schedule shifts to the left from S to S'. The proportional vertical displacement of the schedule equals the proportional tax-induced fall in the effective discount factor. Associated with the new level of domestic relative supply, the new world relative supply schedule also shifts to the left from S^w to $S^{w'}$. We note that the proportional displacement of the world relative supply schedule is smaller than the corresponding displacement of the domestic relative supply schedule. The new equilibrium obtains at the intersection of the (unchanged) world relative demand schedule, D^w, and the new world relative supply schedule $S^{w'}$. This equilibrium is indicated by point A', at which the world discount factor has risen from α to α'. To determine the incidence of this change on the domestic discount factors, we subtract from α' the tax wedge and obtain the new lower domestic effective discount factors α'_I and α'_L. Thus, by raising the world discount factor this tax conversion reduces the rates of growth of domestic and foreign consumption and crowds in foreign investment. On the other hand, the induced fall in the domestic tax-adjusted discount factor, governing investment and labor supply, crowd out domestic investment and the rate of growth of domestic employment falls.

Using similar reasoning it is evident that if the country adopting the tax reform has a present-period current account surplus, then the tax conversion toward a VAT system narrows the present-period tax base and lowers tax revenue. Restoration of revenue neutrality necessitates intertemporal adjustments of income tax rates in directions opposite to those underlying figure 14.6. In that case the world discount factor falls and the domestic tax adjusted factors α_I and α_L rise. In that case the tax reform increases the rates of growth of domestic and foreign consumption, crowds out foreign investment, and crowds in domestic investment.[20]

14.5   Simulation of VAT Harmonization:
Current Account Imbalances

In what follows, we present dynamic simulations of the consequences of international harmonization of VAT in the presence of current account imbalances. We use our two-country model and as in section 14.3 presume that prior to the VAT harmonization, the two countries use very different tax systems. The home country tax revenue stems from high income tax while the foreign country revenue stems from high VAT. The harmonization of VAT entails a rise in the home country VAT rate and an equivalent reduction in the foreign VAT rate.

Our analysis can be illuminated by the analytical results obtained in the previous section on tax conversions. In fact, our specification of VAT harmonization entails various tax conversions which take place simultaneously in all countries. To avoid the budgetary imbalances consequent on the changes in the VAT rates we ensure revenue neutrality by adopting the same procedure used in the analysis of tax conversions in section 14.4. Accordingly, the induced budgetary imbalances are corrected through changes in income tax rates.

In performing the simulations as in section 14.3 we first computed a baseline equilibrium. This equilibrium was then perturbed by the assumed VAT harmonization. The various figures presented below show the effects of the tax restructuring measured as percentage deviations from the baseline levels. As indicated by the analysis in section 14.4, one of the key factors governing the effects of revenue-neutral tax conversions is the time pattern of the current account position. Since the current account positions can be expressed in terms of the saving-investment gap, they reflect intercountry differences in either saving propensities, induced for example by differences between the subjective discount factors, δ and δ^*, or in investment patterns induced, for example, by differences between the productivities of capital, r_k and r_k^*. In figure 14.7–14.10 we plot the simulation results for cases distinguished according to the time pattern of current account imbalances. In these figures, we assume that the income tax used in both countries is of the cash flow variety. Throughout we assume that the home country raises permanently its VAT by 6 percent and restores its tax revenue by lowering its cash flow income tax rates; the foreign country (whose initial VAT rate is assumed to be high) lowers permanently its VAT by 6 percent and restores its tax revenue by raising its cash flow income tax rates. The figures show the paths of domestic and foreign output, labor supply, savings, investment, and consumption as well as the paths of the world rate of interest and the home country's external debt consequent on the VAT harmonization. All paths are expressed as percentage deviations from baseline (except for the rate of interest, whose deviation is expressed in basis points). The simulations reveal that the international VAT harmonization triggers a dynamic response in all the key macroeconomic variables. The specific nature of the dynamic response reflects international differences in the parameters governing saving and investment patterns.

The key features of the simulation analysis of tax harmonization underlying figures 14.7–14.10 are summarized in table 14.3, which also reports the implied welfare implications of the VAT harmonization. To capture the essence of the dynamic evolution of the various variables we reported in table 14.3 the direction of changes for both the short run (SR) and the medium run (MR).

In conformity with the tax conversion analysis of section 14.5, the results in table 14.3 demonstrate the key role played by the current account position. Specifically, if in the early stage the home country runs a current account deficit due to low saving or high investment (e.g., if $\delta < \delta^*$ or $r_k > r_k^*$), then the paths of domestic and foreign income tax rates over time so as to maintain tax revenue. As a result, the world rate of interest falls.[21] In that case, the rates of growth of domestic and foreign consumption (g_c and g_c^* respectively) fall, both in the short and in the medium runs.

If on the other hand the configuration of saving and investment propensities is such that the home country runs a current account surplus in the early stage, then the dynamic effects of the VAT harmonization on these variables are reversed. Specifically, if in the home country saving is high or investment is low (e.g., if $\delta > \delta^*$ or $r_k < r_k^*$), then the paths of domestic and foreign income tax rates fall while the world rate of interest rises. In that case the rates of growth of domestic and foreign consumption rise. Thus, under the present cash flow income tax system the direction of changes in

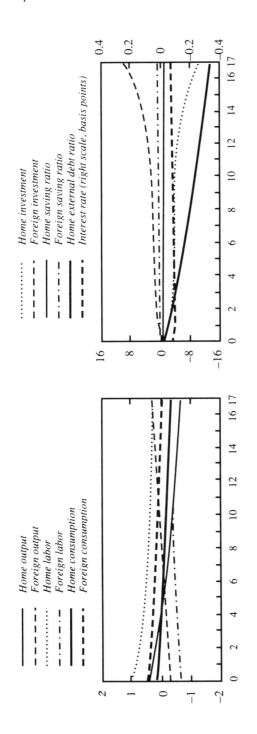

Home investment
Foreign investment
Home saving ratio
Foreign saving ratio
Home external debt ratio
Interest rate (right scale, basis points)

Home output
Foreign output
Home labor
Foreign labor
Home consumption
Foreign consumption

Note: Assuming a permanent increase of 6 percent in home country VAT and a permanent reduction of 6 percent in foreign country VAT.

Figure 14.7
VAT harmonization: 6 percent permanent increase in home country VAT and 6 percent permanent reduction in foreign country VAT.

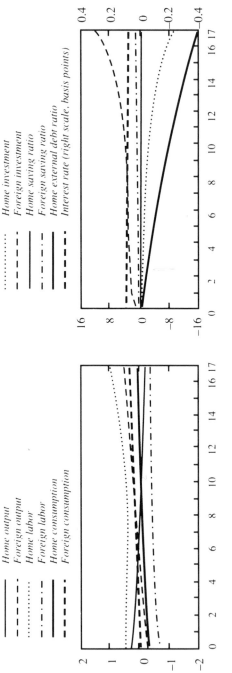

Figure 14.8
VAT harmonization: 6 percent permanent increase in home country VAT and 6 percent reduction in foreign country VAT

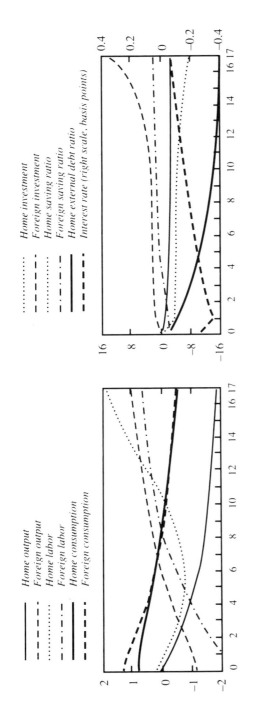

Figure 14.9

VAT harmonization: 6 percent permanent increase in home country VAT and 6 percent permanent reduction in foreign country VAT

Note: Assuming a permanent increase of 6 percent in home country VAT and a permanent reduction of 6 percent in foreign country VAT.

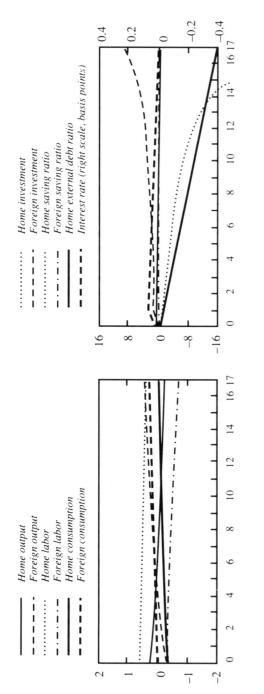

Figure 14.10

VAT harmonization: 6 percent permanent increase in home country VAT and 6 percent permanent reduction in foreign country VAT

Note: Assuming a permanent increase of 6 percent in home country VAT and a permanent reduction of 6 percent in foreign country VAT.

Table 14.3
Effects of VAT harmonization under alternative current account positions (deviations from baseline)

| Variable | Home country current account deficit | | | | Home country current account surplus | | | |
| | $\delta < \delta^*$ $r_k = r_k$ | | $\delta - {}^{d*}$ $r_k > r_k$ | | $\delta > \delta^*$ $r_k = r_k$ | | $\delta - {}^{d*}$ $r_k < r_k$ | |
	SR	MR	SR	MR	SR	MR	SR	MR
Path of r_y	rising		rising		falling		falling	
Path of r_y^*	rising		rising		falling		falling	
r	−	−	−	−	+	+	+	+
g_c	−	−	−	−	+	+	+	+
g_c^*	−	−	−	−	+	+	+	+
I	−	−	−	−	−	−	−	−
I^*	+	+	+	+	+	+	+	+
L	+	+	−	+	+	+	+	+
L^*	−	−	−	−	−	−	−	−
Y	+	−	−	−	+	−	+	+
Y^*	−	+	−	+	−	+	−	+
C	+	−	+	−	−	+	−	−
C^*	+	−	+	−	−	+	+	+
S	+	−	−	−	+	−	+	−
S^*	−	+	−	+	−	+	−	+
B	−	−	−	−	−	−	−	−
U	0.2	−8.2	−0.1	−6.7	0.3	−7.6	+0.3	−8.5
U^*	−0.3	+8.4	−0.3	10.9	−0.3	9.2	−0.3	7.5

Note: The VAT harmonization obtains through a permanent 6% reduction in r_c and a rise in r_c^*. Budgetary balance obtains through appropriate adjustments in the periodic income tax rates, r_y and r_y^*. SR and MR denote, respectively, the short run and the medium run. The tax system is a cash flow system. In general, the short-run pertains to the first few periods while the medium-run pertains to the remaining periods in the simulation. The welfare change is measured by the percentage factor by which the postharmonization consumption path must be raised to bring utility up to the preharmonization level. For the utility index SR pertains to the discounted sum of utilities over the entire periods except for the final one, while MR pertains to the final period utility (reflecting the entire future beyond the simulation period).

the world rate of interest and in the growth rates of consumption consequent on international VAT harmonization depend exclusively on the paths
of the saving-investment gap.

The lower panel of table 14.3 summarizes the corresponding short- and
medium-run changes in other key economic variables. As can be seen, in
the cases considered, the international VAT harmonization crowds out
domestic investment and crowds in foreign investment independent of the
current account positions. These investment responses reflect the induced
changes in the domestic and foreign tax incentives and the world rate of
interest. These changes yield two conflicting effects: the effect of the change
in the world rate of interest and the opposite effect of the change in the tax
wedges induced by the alteration of the time paths of income tax rates.

The welfare effects of terms of trade changes depend on the magnitude
of the change in the terms of trade and on the gap between purchases and
sales of the good whose relative price has changed. In our intertemporal
context the terms of trade correspond to the world of interest, and the gap
between purchases and sales correspond to the current account position. As
illustrated by table 14.3, in all cases the change in the terms of trade
operates in favor of the country that raises its VAT. When the country runs
a current account deficit (i.e., when it borrows in the world economy) its
intertemporal terms of trade improve since the rate of interest falls. Likewise, if the country's current account position is in surplus its intertemporal
terms of trade also improve since the rate of interest rises. As illustrated by
the table, this improvement in the home country welfare induced by the
changes in the world rate of interest can be mitigated (or even offset) by
the excess-burden effects of the VAT harmonization. Similar considerations
apply to the welfare consequences of the reduction in VAT in the foreign
economy.

A comparison between the effects of the international VAT harmonization on the domestic and the foreign economies reveal that in the two
countries the levels of foreign employment, investment, output, and some
other key macroeconomic indicators change in opposite directions. In fact,
in most cases the utility index indicates that domestic and foreign welfare
move in opposite directions. These phenomena suggest the possibility that
international VAT harmonization may induce international conflicts of
interest. A resolution of such conflicts may necessitate international fiscal
transfers from countries benefiting from the VAT harmonization to countries that lose. The potential difficulties arising from international conflicts
of interest may be augmented by internal conflicts of interest associated

with redistributions of income between labor and capital in the short and medium runs.[22]

The foregoing analysis was confined to the case in which the income taxes used to restore budgetary balance following the international VAT harmonization were of the cash flow variety. Under such circumstances, in conformity with the analytical results of section 14.5, the current account positions played the key role in determining the direction of changes in the world rate of interest and the growth rates of domestic and foreign consumption. As indicated by the simulations in figures 14.7–14.10 and in the summary results in the lower panel of table 14.3, the dynamic effects of the international VAT harmonization on the path of the other key macroeconomic variables do not depend only on the current account positions. In fact, for the cases shown in these simulations, domestic investment, foreign employment, foreign savings (in the short run), and the level of the domestic country's external debt are reduced independent of the current account positions, while foreign investment and foreign savings (in the medium run) always rise.

14.6 Summary

One of the major developments in the world economy during the 1990s is likely to be the move toward the single market of Europe in 1992. The removal of barriers to trade and factor movements, the unification of markets, the developments of new monetary arrangements, the increased harmonization of fiscal policies, and tax structures are all key factors in a process that is likely to shape the global economic system for years to come.

One of the elements of the move toward tax harmonization in the European Community involves a convergence of the various VAT systems. In this paper we have analyzed the global effects of such an international VAT harmonization. For this purpose we have developed a model that encompasses a rich menu of tax systems. The model contains two countries and therefore is capable of highlighting the spillover effects of taxes across countries. The analytical framework is grounded on microeconomic foundations and therefore is suitable for an examination of the incentive effects as well as the welfare consequence of tax policies.

To examine the quantitative implications of international VAT harmonization, we have performed dynamic simulations. The analysis as well as simulations demonstrate that the effects of VAT harmonization on the key macroeconomic variables (such as output, employment, investment, consumption, interest rates, the current account, and the value of external debt) are very significant. Furthermore, these effects (quantitatively and qualitatively) are not spread evenly across income groups, generations, and countries. As a result, such a VAT harmonization may give rise to internal conflicts of interest within each country (arising from changes in the distribution of income among members of each generation as well as among generations) and between countries. The international differences in the incidence of the VAT harmonization arise from differences in the current account positions (reflecting underlying differences in saving and investment propensities) as well as from differences in the tax structures. The resolution of the various conflicts of interest regarding the adoption of VAT harmonization may give rise to the developments of a fiscal mechanism by which gainers compensate losers within countries as well as between countries.

Throughout, we have emphasized the dynamic features of the interactions among economies as they operate through the integrated world capital market. Accordingly, we have focused on the intertemporal terms of trade—the rate of interest. Obviously, an additional channel through which the effects of tax policies spill over to the rest of the world is the temporal commodity terms of trade—the relative price of tradable to nontradable goods and the relative price of exportables to importables. A useful extension would allow for a more refined aggregation of commodities. With such a refinement, the model could also shed light on the effects of international VAT harmonization on the structures of industry and trade as well as on the sectoral distribution of employment and investment.

Finally, our analysis of the world economy has been conducted within a two-country model. Since the effects of VAT harmonization among a subset of the countries may impact on the rest of the world, it would be useful to extend the analysis to more than two countries to allow for a more complete examination of the international spillovers of the VAT harmonization. Such an extension would facilitate an analysis of "trade creation" and "trade diversion" in both goods and capital markets associated with the establishment of the single market in Europe in 1992.[23]

14.7   Appendix A: The Solution of the Model

In this appendix we present the formal solution to the model. The maximization of the utility functions subject to the lifetime present-value budget constraint yields

$$u_t = \left[\sum_{s=0}^{T} \delta^s \right]^{-1} \frac{W_0}{P_t} \frac{\delta^t}{d_t},$$ (A.1)

$$P_t = [\beta^\sigma \{1 + \tau_{ct}\}^{1-\sigma} + (1 - \beta)^\sigma ((1 - \tau_{wt})w)^{1-\sigma}]1/(1 - \sigma),$$ (A.2)

$$C_t = \frac{\beta^\sigma (1 + \tau_{ct})^{-\sigma} P_t u_t}{\beta^\sigma (1 + \tau_{ct})^{1-\sigma} + (1 - \beta)^\sigma ((1 - \tau_{wt})w)^{1-\sigma}},$$ (A.3)

$$1 - l = \frac{(1 - \beta)^\sigma ((1 - \tau_{wt})w)^{-\sigma} P_t u_t}{\beta^\sigma (1 + \rho_{ct})^{1-\sigma} + (1 - \beta)^\sigma ((1 - \tau_{wt})w)^{1-\sigma}},$$ (A.4)

where u is the utility-based real spending, P denotes the associated price index, C denotes consumption of ordinary goods, and $1 - l$ denotes leisure. In these equations $t = 1, 2, \ldots, T$, d_t is the tax-adjusted present-value factor applicable to period t; that is, $d_t = (1 + (1 - \tau_{k1})(1 + \tau_{s1})r_0)^{-1}$ $(1 + (1 - \tau_{k2})(1 + \tau_{s2})r_1)^{-1} \ldots (1 + (1 - \tau_{kt})(1 + \tau_{st})r_{t-1})^{-1}$, and wealth, W_0, is

$$W_0 = \sum_{t=0}^{T} d_t \left[(1 - \tau_{wt})w + (1 - \tau_{kt})(r_k - \theta)K_t - (1 - \tau_{It})I_t \left(1 + \frac{b}{2} \frac{I_t}{K_t} \right) \right]$$

$$+ d_T (1 - \tau_{kT})aK_T - [1 + (1 - \tau_{k0})(1 + \tau_{s0})r_{-1}]B^p_{-1}.$$

The investment equation, I_t, is obtained by a maximization of wealth, W_0, with respect to investment, I_t. This yields

$$-(1 - \tau_{It})d_t \left(1 + b\frac{I_t}{K_t} \right) + \sum_{s=t+1}^{T-1} d_s (1 - \theta)^{s-t-1} \left[(1 - \tau_{ks})(r_k - \theta) + \right.$$

$$\left. (1 - \tau_{Is})\frac{b}{2} \left(\frac{I_s}{K_s} \right)^2 \right] + d_t (1 - \theta)^{T-t-1}(1 - \tau_{kT})(r_k + a - \theta) = 0 \quad (A.6)$$

Equation (A.6) represents an implicit investment rule. The negative term is equal to the marginal cost of investment in period t while the positive terms are equal to the marginal benefits consisting of the rise in output resulting from the increased capital stock (the terms with r_k and a) and the fall in future costs of investment (the terms associated with $(b/2) \cdot (I/K)^2$). To illustrate in the two-period case the investment function implied by equation (A.6) is

$$I_0 = \frac{1}{b} (\alpha_1 \frac{(1 - \tau_{k1})}{(1 - \tau_{I0})} (a + r_k - \theta) - 1)K_0.$$ (A.6a)

Equation (A.6a) together with the assumption that $(a + r_k - \theta)$ exceeds unity (an assumption necessary for a positive level of investment in the two-period case) implies that the level of investment rises with the initial capital stock, K_0, with the effective (tax-adjusted) discount factor, α_I, with the rental rate net of depreciation, $r_k - \theta$, and with the consumption coefficient, a, attached to the final-period capital. On the other hand, investment falls with an increase in the cost-of-adjustment parameter, g. Substituting equation (A.6a) into (A.5) yields the corresponding value of wealth (A.5a):

$$W_0 = \sum_{t=0}^{1} d_t(1 - \tau_{wt})w + q_0 k_0 - [1 + (1 - \tau_{k0})(1 + \tau_{s0})r_{-1}]B^p_{-1} \quad \text{(A.5a)}$$

where q_0 denotes the tax adjusted market value of a unit of the capital stock (Tobin's q):

$$q_0 = (1 - \tau_{k0})(r_k - \theta) + \alpha_1(1 - \tau_{k1})(m + 1 - \theta)(r_k + q - \theta)$$
$$- (1 - \tau_{I0})m(1 + gm/2)$$

where

$$m = [\alpha_1((1 - \tau_{k1})/(1 - \tau_{I0}))(r_k + a - \theta) - 1]/g.$$

14.8   Appendix B: Tax on International Borrowing

In this appendix we extend the tax structure to include a tax on international borrowing, denoted by τ_b. With this added tax, the periodic budget constraint in equation (14.1) of the text becomes[24]

$$(1 + \tau_{ct})C_t + (1 - \tau_{wt})w(1 - l_t)$$

$$= (1 - \tau_{wt})w + (1 - \tau_{kt})((r_k - \theta)K_t) - (1 - \tau_{It})l_t\left(1 + \frac{b}{2}\frac{I_t}{K_t}\right)$$

$$+ (1 - \tau_{bt})(B^p_t - B^p_{t-1}) - (1 - \tau_{kt})(1 + \tau_{st-1})r_{t-1}B^p_{t-1}. \quad \text{(B.1)}$$

As formulated, the international borrowing tax applies to the accumulation of external debt. Letting total debt be $B^P = (1/(1 - \tau_b))B^{HP} + B^{FP}$ and applying the arbitrage condition, by which the after-tax rates of return are equal so that $r_F = (1 - \tau_b)r_H$, yields the last two terms on the right-hand side of equation (14.1). Analogously, the lifetime present-value budget constraint applicable to the two-period case becomes

$$
C_0 + \alpha_c C_1 = \left\{\frac{1 - \tau_{w0}}{1 + \tau_{c0}}\right\} \{wl_0 + \alpha_L wl_1\}
$$

$$
+ \left\{\frac{1 - \tau_{I0}}{1 + \tau_{c0}}\right\} \left\{\alpha_I(r_k - \theta) - \left(1 + \frac{b}{2}\frac{I_0}{K_0}\right)\right\} I_0
$$

$$
+ \left\{\left(\frac{1 - \tau_{b0}}{1 + \tau_{c0}}\right)(r_k - \theta_k)\left[\frac{1 - \tau_{k0}}{1 - \tau_{b0}}\right.\right.
$$

$$
+ \frac{1 - \tau_{k1}}{1 - \tau_{b1} + (1 - \tau_{k1})(1 + \tau_{s1})\tau_0}\left.\right]\right\} K_0
$$

$$
- \left\{\frac{1 - \tau_{b0} + (1 - \tau_{k0})(1 + \tau_{s0-1})r}{1 + \tau_{c0}}\right\} B^p_{-1}, \tag{B.2}
$$

where

$$
\alpha_c = \frac{(1 + \tau_{c1})}{(1 + \tau_{c0})}\frac{(1 - \tau_{b0})}{1 - \tau_{b1} + (1 - \tau_{k1})(1 + \tau_{s1})r_0},
$$

$$
\alpha_I = \frac{(1 - \tau_{k1})}{(1 - \tau_{I0})}\frac{(1 - \tau_{b0})}{(1 - \tau_{b1} + (1 - \tau_{k1})(1 + \tau_{s0})r_0},
$$

and

$$
\alpha_L = \frac{(1 - \tau_{w1})}{(1 - \tau_{w0})}\frac{(1 - \tau_{b0})}{(1 - \tau_{b1}) + (1 - \tau_{ki})(1 + \tau_{s1})r_0}.
$$

The formulation of the periodic budget constraint illustrates the *equivalence relation* existing among the taxes on consumption, (cash flow) income, and international borrowing. Indeed, the real effects of any given combination of the three taxes can be duplicated by a policy consisting of any two of them. Denoting the cash flow income tax by τ_y the budget constraint is

$$
(1 + \tau_{ct})C_t = (1 - \tau_{yt})Y_t + (1 - \tau_{bt})(B^p_t - B^p_{t-1}),
$$

where Y_t denotes income net of investment. Now consider an initial situation with a positive consumption tax rate, $\bar{\tau}_c$, and zero income and international borrowing tax rates. If the consumption tax was eliminated and the income and international borrowing taxes were both set equal to $\tau_c/(1 + \bar{\tau}_c)$, then the *effective* tax rates associated with this new combination of taxes are zero income and international borrowing taxes and a positive $(\bar{\tau}_c)$ consumption tax. It follows that the real equilibrium associated with the new tax pattern $(\tau_c = 0, \tau_y = \tau_b = \bar{\tau}_c/(1 + \bar{\tau}_c))$ is identical to the one associated with the initial tax pattern $(\tau_c = \bar{\tau}_c, \tau_y = \tau_b = 0)$.

Table 14.4
Effects of a 10 percent point rise in the international borrowing tax rate between Europe
and the rest-of-the-world (percentage deviations from baseline)

Variable	Budgetary balance obtains through VAT		Budgetary balance obtains through cash flow income tax	
	SR	MR	SR	MR
r_c^E	$+0.30$	-0.20	0	0
r_y^E	0	0	$+0.23$	-0.20
r	-0.23	-0.20	-0.24	-0.18
I^E	-0.6	$+3.5$	-0.5	$+3.0$
I^R	$+3.4$	$+2.5$	$+3.0$	$+2.5$
L^E	$+3.2$	-3.0	$+3.0$	-2.7
L^R	-6.0	$+5.4$	-5.2	$+5.2$
Y^E	$+1.3$	-1.3	$+1.4$	-1.2
Y^R	-2.5	$+3.4$	-2.0	$+3.0$
C^E	-1.0	$+0.8$	-0.9	$+0.7$
C^R	$+1.5$	-1.4	$+1.4$	-1.3
S^E/Y^E	$+0.02$	-0.02	$+0.02$	-0.02
S^R/Y^R	-0.04	$+0.06$	-0.03	$+0.05$
B^E/Y^E	-0.07	-0.10	-0.06	-0.10
U^E	0.1	-2.0	0.1	-2.0
U^R	-0.1	$+2.4$	-0.1	2.7

Note: European and foreign variables are designated by superscript E and R, respectively.
SR and MR are defined as in table 14.2 and 14.3. The welfare change is measured by the
percentage factor by which the posttax consumption path must be raised to bring utility up
to the pretax level.

This analytical framework of taxes on international borrowing can be
used to examine the effects of a removal of impediments on capital movements within Europe of 1992 (while maintaining the impediments between
Europe and the rest of the world) on the key economic variables within and
outside Europe. In table 14.4 we present preliminary simulations of such an
experiment. Specifically, we consider the effects of an introduction of a
common tax by the two countries forming the single market on international borrowing from the rest of the world (country R). In conducting the
simulations we assume that the periodic budget balance in Europe (country
E) is maintained through appropriate adjustments of either VAT or of cash
flow income taxes. To highlight the external effects we chose to focus the

simulations on the case in which the domestic and foreign economies (forming the single European market) are identical. The opposite welfare implications of such a tax for Europe and the rest of the world underscore the international concern regarding the specific modalities of the integration process.

15

Spillover Effects of Budget Deficits

The analysis in chapter 14 focused on changes in the composition of taxes, while maintaining in each period a given value of total tax revenue. Such revenue-neutral tax restructuring ensures that the tax conversion policies do not affect the budgetary imbalances. In this section, we use the same analytical framework to shed light on the domestic and international macroeconomic consequences of changes in the timing of taxes and provide dynamic simulations.

15.1 Budget Deficits in a Two-Country World Economy

Consider the effects of budget deficits arising from a current tax cut. Of course, the intertemporal government budget constraint implies that, as long as government spending remains intact, the current tax cut must be followed by a future rise in taxes. The main conclusion of the analysis is that the effect of budget deficits depends critically on whether it arises from changes in the timing of consumption or income taxes.

Consider first a budget deficit arising from a current-period consumption tax cut (followed by a corresponding rise in future consumption taxes). As is evident from the definitions of the effective discount factors in equation 15.2 such a tax shift raises the effective discount factor governing consumption decisions, α_c, while leaving the discount factor governing investment decisions intact. These changes induce a substitution of demand from future to current consumption and induce rightward shifts of the domestic (and the world) relative demand schedules in figure 15.1 while leaving the relative supply schedules intact.

Figure 15.2, which was used for the analysis of tax conversion from income to consumption tax systems, is also fully applicable for the analysis of the budget deficit under the consumption tax system. Accordingly, the budget deficit raises the world rate of interest and crowds out domestic and

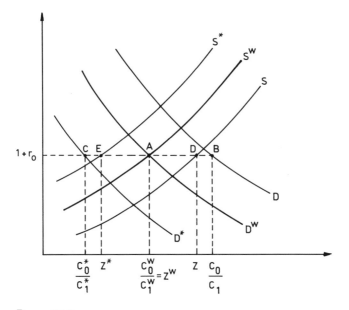

Figure 15.1
Relative demands, relative supplies, and world equilibrium

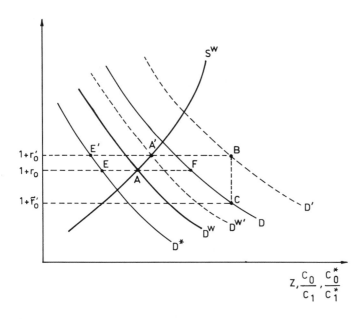

Figure 15.2
The effects of a revenue-neutral tax shift from income taxes to consumption taxes with an initial-period domestic trade-balance deficit

foreign investment. It also lowers the growth rate of domestic consumption while raising the growth rate of foreign consumption.

By the same reasoning, a budget deficit arising from a cut in current income tax rates (and followed by a corresponding rise in future income tax rates) yields results similar to those obtained under a revenue-neutral tax conversion from consumption to income tax systems. Again, as is evident from the definitions of the effective discount factors in equation (15.2), this change in the timing of income tax rates lowers the effective discount factor governing investment decisions, α_I, and discourages domestic investment while leaving α_c intact. In terms of figure 15.1, these tax changes induce a rightward shift of the domestic (and the world) relative supply schedule while leaving the relative demand schedules intact. As a result, the world rate of interest falls, foreign investment rises, and the domestic investment is crowded out. At the same time, the lower world rate of interest lowers the growth rate of both domestic and foreign consumption.

15.2 Dynamic Simulations of Budget Deficits

The simulations that allow for a variable labor supply in a multiperiod model illustrate the key relations implied by the theoretical model: they underscore the critical importance of the underlying tax system in determining the macroeconomic effects of budget deficits. They also provide further insights into the dynamic consequences of budget deficits.

Figures 15.3 and 15.4 contain selected simulations of the dynamic effects of current-period budget deficits under a consumption tax system and under an income tax system, respectively. We assume that the current-period deficit arises from a 10 percent reduction in tax rates, which is made up for by a permanent rise in tax rates in all future periods. By and large, the directions of changes in the various variables in the two figures are opposite to each other. The underscores the key proposition of the theoretical analysis. In addition, the simulations show that the effects of the budget deficit on the qualitative characteristics of the time path of employment and output also depend critically on the underlying tax system. Specifically, under a consumption tax system, a domestic budget deficit exerts recessionary effects on the contemporaneous levels of domestic employment and output and expansionary effects on the corresponding levels abroad. These employment and output effects are reversed in all future periods. In contrast, under an income tax system, the same budget deficit induces a contemporaneous expansion at home and a recession abroad. These

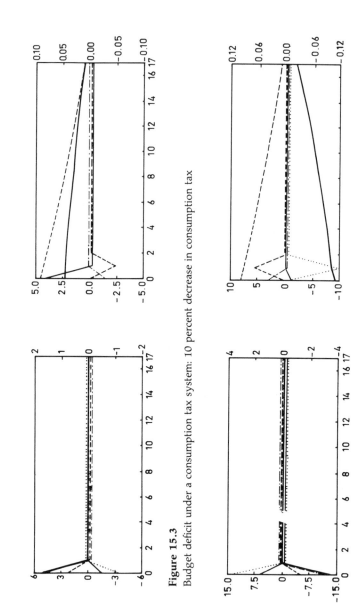

Figure 15.3
Budget deficit under a consumption tax system: 10 percent decrease in consumption tax

Figure 15.4
Budget deficit under an income tax system: 10 percent decrease in income tax in year 0

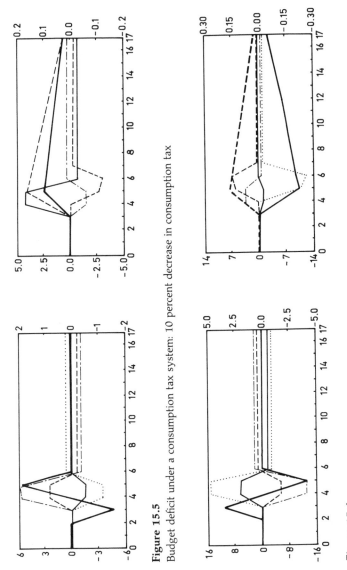

Figure 15.5
Budget deficit under a consumption tax system: 10 percent decrease in consumption tax

Figure 15.6
Budget deficit under an income tax system: 10 percent decrease in income tax in years 4 and 5

(Percentage deviation)

——— Home output
– – – Foreign output
········· Home labor
– · · – Foreign labor
——— Interest rate (right scale, basis points)

········· Home investment
– · – · – Foreign investment
——— Home consumption
– – – Foreign consumption
– · – · – Home government debt (right scale, level)
——— Home external debt (right scale, level)

changes are reversed in subsequent periods. In general, the international transmission of the effects of budget deficits is shown to be negative in both the short and the medium run.

We also note that the current-period budget deficit exerts opposite effects on the levels of domestic and foreign consumption. Under a consumption tax system, the deficit raises current-period domestic consumption and lowers the corresponding level of foreign consumption. These changes are reversed in subsequent periods. In contrast, under an income tax system, domestic consumption falls in the current period while foreign consumption rises, and, as before, these changes are reversed in subsequent periods. Again, in terms of the correlations between domestic and foreign consumption, the simulations demonstrate the negative transmission of the effects of domestic budget deficits.

The effects of the budget deficits on the time paths of consumption and leisure influence the levels of domestic and foreign welfare. Using the utility function specified in equations 15.3 and 15.4, our simulations show that the current period budget deficit, arising from a 10 percent reduction in the consumption tax rate, raises the level of domestic welfare (by about 2 percent) and lowers the level of foreign welfare (by about 1.5 percent). In contrast, if the current-period budge deficit arises from a 10 percent reduction in the income tax rate, then the level of domestic welfare falls (by about 3 percent) while the corresponding foreign welfare rises (by about 3.5 percent). These opposite changes in the levels of domestic and foreign welfare reflect the negative transmission of the effects of budget deficits.

The effects of an expected future-period budget deficit are shown in figures 15.5–15.6. These simulations show the consequences of an expected 10 percent tax cut in periods 4 and 5 that is then made up for by a permanent rise in tax rates in all subsequent periods. As before, they reveal the central role played by the tax system. They also reveal the general feature of a negative transmission. However, since the various changes in tax rates occur only in the more distant future, our simulations show that their effects on the levels of domestic and foreign utility (viewed from the standpoint of the current period) are small.

VIII

Epilogue

16

Analytical Overview

In this book we have attempted to develop a unified conceptual framework suitable for the analysis of the effects of government expenditure and tax policies on key macroeconomic aggregates in the interdependent world economy. The analysis was motivated by the major developments occurring in the world economy during the 1980s: changes in national fiscal policies were unsynchronized, real rates of interest were high and volatile, and real exchange rates exhibited diverging trends and were subject to large fluctuations. Furthermore large fiscal imbalances resulted in drastic changes in public debt and were associated with large imbalances in current-account positions and with significant changes in the international allocations of debt. Though these real-world developments provide the impetus for the analysis, the orientation of the book is theoretical. It aims at clarifying the complex economic mechanisms underlying the international transmission of the effects of macroeconomics policies. An empirical implementation of the theory developed throughout the book is highly complex. Without attempting to launch on such a challenging endeavor, we provide in section 16.1 some illustrative computations of the intertemporal model and compare the results with the actual data. Section 16.2 highlights key differences between the income-expenditure and the intertemporal models as reflected in the economic mechanisms underlying the main channels of the international transmission of fiscal policies. Finally, section 16.3 contains a brief discussion of suggested extensions.

16.1   An Illustrative Computation

In this section we use the analytical model developed in section 13.2 to compute the predicted paths of domestic and foreign consumption that are implied by the actual paths of the exogenous macroeconomic variables. We then compare these predicted paths of consumption with the paths that have actually been followed. In addition we compute the correlations between the predicted paths of consumption and the actual paths of the other variables and compare these correlations with those actually observed in the data. Though these computations should not be viewed as the empirical counterpart to the theoretical model, they nevertheless are suggestive of the potential applicability of the theoretical approach.

The illustrations used in this section center around the paths of consumption since the comovements of these paths with the other key economic variables were the focus of the theoretical analysis. In performing the computations, we have assumed specific values for the key parameters. These parameter values along with the actual paths of the exogeneous variables were substituted into the model yielding the solution paths of the endogenous variables.

Tables 16.1 and 16.2 report the actual and the predicted annual growth rates of private-sector consumption in the United States and in the rest-of-the-world for the period 1956 to 1984. For this illustration the rest-of-the-world is defined as the Group of Seven major industrial countries excluding the United States. This group comprises Canada, France, Italy, Japan, the United Kingdom, and West Germany. The computation of the model necessitates the conversion of all data for various countries into common currency units. In view of the sharp changes in exchange rates that have occurred during the sample period, the choice of the common numeraire may have significant consequences for the relations among the various time series. Therefore, to allow for this possibility, we have computed all series for two alternatives. The first expresses the data in constant German prices, and the second in constant U.S. prices.

The growth rates reported in both tables exhibit considerable correlation between the actual and the predicted time series. For example, the actual mean annual growth rate of U.S. private-sector consumption (in constant German prices) is 2.84 percent with a standard deviation of 7.4 percent, whereas the predicted mean and standard deviation are 2.24 percent and 7.60 percent, respectively. The correlation between the predicted and actual rates of growth of consumption is 0.75. A similar pattern (with a somewhat lower correlation) emerges for the series that are based on constant U.S. prices. In that case the means of the actual and of the predicted growth rates are reasonably close to each other, being 2.99 and 3.10 percent, respectively, but the standard deviations of the two series are further apart from each other, being 2.23 and 6.36 percent, respectively. The correlation coefficient corresponding to these two series is 0.61.

Table 16.1
Predicted and actual U.S. consumption: 1956−1984 (annual percentage growth rates)

Year	In constant German prices		In constant U.S. prices	
	Actual	Predicted	Actual	Predicted
1956	2.21	1.97	3.21	1.89
1957	3.26	−1.30	1.99	−1.46
1958	1.00	−7.96	0.30	−6.30
1959	6.23	8.74	6.25	7.97
1960	2.94	5.91	3.03	6.61
1961	−3.29	−8.45	1.95	−0.95
1962	2.17	−1.22	4.76	1.96
1963	2.34	3.66	3.96	5.03
1964	4.37	7.38	5.62	8.91
1965	4.01	5.46	5.62	6.89
1966	4.30	−1.63	4.66	−1.14
1967	3.68	−4.95	2.52	−6.47
1968	7.51	3.44	4.97	1.18
1969	4.72	6.23	2.72	6.97
1970	−4.33	−8.42	0.95	1.40
1971	−1.88	−5.11	3.65	2.50
1972	−5.30	0.82	5.81	11.27
1973	−14.69	−2.08	3.75	16.69
1974	−0.95	−6.65	−1.43	−5.29
1975	−1.34	−5.63	0.68	−3.60
1976	8.50	14.36	4.83	9.93
1977	−1.15	2.95	4.20	8.81
1978	−6.02	2.93	3.82	14.58
1979	−1.97	0.57	0.62	5.78
1980	4.07	2.56	−2.53	−0.34
1981	25.97	23.23	0.41	−4.07
1982	9.06	0.29	1.19	−8.20
1983	10.10	12.09	5.07	6.41
1984	16.73	15.80	4.06	2.86
Mean	2.84	2.24	2.99	3.10
Standard deviation	7.40	7.62	2.23	6.36
RMSE		5.25		5.21
Correlation		0.75		0.61

Note: In aggregating the six non-U.S. countries into the rest-of-the-world we have used two alternative methods. The first expressed all quantities in German marks deflated by the German GDP deflator; the second expressed all quantities in U.S. dollars deflated by the U.S. GDP deflator. The parameters used in forming the predicted series are $\gamma = \gamma^* = 0.99$, $\delta = \delta^* = 0.95$, $\varepsilon_n = \varepsilon_n^* = \beta_n = \beta_n^* = 0.40$ and $\theta = \theta^* = 0.25$.

Table 16.2
Predicted and actual rest-of-the-world consumption: 1956–1984 (annual percentage growth rates)

Year	In constant German prices		In constant U.S. prices	
	Actual	Predicted	Actual	Predicted
1956	6.14	2.84	7.13	2.55
1957	5.23	−0.38	3.96	−0.75
1958	2.05	−5.74	1.36	−4.20
1959	1.72	9.39	1.73	8.30
1960	7.76	7.17	7.85	7.57
1961	1.73	−7.04	6.97	0.33
1962	5.27	−0.12	7.86	2.90
1963	6.76	4.49	8.38	5.67
1964	6.45	8.28	7.70	9.60
1965	6.02	6.98	7.63	8.20
1966	5.08	0.70	5.44	0.98
1967	5.78	−2.17	4.62	−3.91
1968	4.45	6.01	1.91	3.41
1969	6.42	8.32	4.43	8.62
1970	0.15	−5.84	5.43	3.57
1971	3.49	−2.21	9.02	5.02
1972	5.43	3.20	16.54	13.25
1973	−1.82	−1.55	16.62	16.57
1974	1.06	−7.30	0.58	−5.98
1975	5.12	−5.54	7.14	−3.52
1976	3.54	13.18	−0.14	9.38
1977	2.02	3.66	7.37	9.78
1978	6.43	3.46	16.27	14.88
1979	1.31	−2.57	3.90	1.95
1980	5.75	−2.66	−0.86	−6.72
1981	11.85	18.54	−13.71	−8.01
1982	−1.60	−2.02	−9.47	−10.46
1983	4.24	8.96	−0.78	3.32
1984	7.92	16.41	−4.74	3.93
Mean	4.34	2.63	4.49	3.32
Standard deviation	2.99	6.87	6.73	6.88
RMSE	5.73		5.11	
Correlation	0.61		0.72	

Note: The rest-of-the-world comprises a weighted average of the non-U.S. G-7 countries (Canada, France, Italy, Japan, the United Kingdom, and West Germany). See the note to table 16.1.

Table 16.3
Correlations between annual growth rates of U.S. consumption and key economic variables: 1956–1984

Actual growth rates in	In constant German prices		In constant U.S. prices	
	Actual	Predicted	Actual	Predicted
Y	0.98	0.81	0.84	0.69
I	0.81	0.90	0.81	0.76
C	1.00	0.75	1.00	0.61
G	0.93	0.53	0.03	−0.47
T	0.84	0.75	0.37	0.39
WPI/CPI	−0.50	−0.23	−0.18	0.27
Y^*	0.62	0.73	0.32	0.65
I^*	0.30	0.48	0.32	0.62
C^*	0.57	0.57	0.39	0.61
G^*	0.50	0.39	0.11	0.45
T^*	0.35	0.29	0.05	0.45
WPI^*/CPI^*	−0.40	−0.28	−0.24	0.04
$C + C^*$	0.97	0.78	0.62	0.71

Note: See the note to table 16.1.

The relation between the actual and the predicted growth rates of private-sector consumption in the rest-of-the-world is shown in table 16.2. When expressed in constant U.S. prices, the mean and the standard deviation of the actual series are 4.49 and 6.73 percent, respectively, whereas the corresponding mean and standard deviation of the predicted data are 3.32 and 6.88, respectively. The correlation between the actual and the predicted series is also significant, being 0.72. When the data are expressed in constant German prices, the correlation between the two series is also relatively high (even though somewhat less pronounced), being 0.61.

The correlations between the growth rates of private-sector consumption and the growth rates of the key economic variables are shown in tables 16.3 and 16.4. In these tables we report the correlations between the *actual* growth rates of consumption and the other macroeconomic variables and compare these correlations with the corresponding correlations between the *predicted* growth rates of consumption and the same macroeconomic variables. As is evident, especially for growth rates of series expressed in constant German prices, there is considerable similarity between the actual and the predicted correlations. This similarity which is exhibited by figures pertaining to U.S. consumption (in table 16.3) and to the rest-of-the-world

Table 16.4
Correlations between annual growth rates of rest-of-the-world consumption and key economic variables: 1956–1984

Actual growth rates in	In constant German prices		In constant U.S. prices	
	Actual	Predicted	Actual	Predicted
Y	0.60	0.76	0.36	0.73
I	0.58	0.92	0.33	0.78
C	0.57	0.70	0.39	0.72
G	0.53	0.47	0.01	-0.33
T	0.65	0.73	0.20	0.40
WPI/CPI	-0.27	-0.28	0.37	0.21
Y^*	0.92	0.75	0.98	0.74
I^*	0.69	0.55	0.90	0.72
C^*	1.00	0.61	1.00	0.72
G^*	0.81	0.34	0.94	0.53
T^*	0.49	0.24	0.82	0.51
WPI^*/CPI^*	-0.48	-0.28	-0.01	0.02
$C + C^*$	0.75	0.75	0.96	0.83

Note: See the note to table 16.2.

consumption (in table 16.4) is reflected in both the relative magnitudes and signs of the various correlations.

Overall, the computations reported in tables 16.1 through 16.4 indicate considerable conformity between the actual and predicted growth rates. They exhibit similar patterns of correlations between the actual growth rates of consumption and of key macroeconomic variables, on the one hand, and between the predicted growth rates of consumption and the same variables, on the other hand. These results indicate the potential usefulness of the analytical framework developed in this book. It is important to reiterate, however, that the purpose of these computations has only been illustrative and should not be viewed as a substitute for a thorough empirical implementation of the model.

16.2 Interest Rates and Terms of Trade: Differences between Models

In this section we highlight some of the key differences between the predictions of, and the economic mechanisms underlying, the income expenditure model and the intertemporal model. The integration of both

Table 16.5
The effects of fiscal policies on the current rate of interest: the income-expenditure and the intertemporal models

Effects of	Income-expenditure model		Intertemporal model	
	Fixed exchange rates	Flexible exchange rates	Tradable goods	Nontradable goods
Debt-financed rise in government spending				
Current	+	+	+	+ (for $\sigma_{nx} > \sigma$) − (for $\sigma_{nx} < \sigma$)
Future	0	0	−	− (for $\sigma_{nx} > \sigma$) + (for $\sigma_{nx} < \sigma$)
Permanent	+	+	+ (for $CA > 0$) − (for $CA < 0$)	$\left.\begin{array}{c} + \\ - \end{array}\right\} a$
Tax-financed rise in government spending				
Current	+ (for $A > 0$) − (for $A < 0$)	0	+	+ (for $\sigma_{nx} > \sigma$) − (for $\sigma_{nx} < \sigma$)
Future	0	0	−	− (for $\sigma_{nx} > \sigma$) + (for $\sigma_{nx} < \sigma$)
Permanent	+ (for $A > 0$) − (for $A < 0$)	0	+ (for $CA > 0$) − (for $CA < 0$)	$\left.\begin{array}{c} + \\ - \end{array}\right\} a$
Current tax cut	+	+	+	+

Note: A rise in the world rate of interest is indicated by a +, and a fall by a −. The signs corresponding to the income-expenditure model are based on the assumption that exchange-rate expectations are static and that there are no revaluation effects; those pertaining to the intertemporal model presume that taxes are nondistortionary. $A = s/M_y - s^*/M_y^*$, CA denotes the current account position, and a indicates that the result depends on the interactions between the current account position and the sign of the difference between the intertemporal elasticity of substitution, σ, and the temporal elasticity of substitution, σ_{nx}.

goods and capital markets in the world economy implies that the key channels through which the effects of fiscal policies are transmitted internationally are the temporal and the intertemporal prices—that is, the world rates of interest and the commodity terms of trade. Accordingly, in what follows we choose to illustrate the differences between the two approaches developed in the preceding chapters by focusing on, and summarizing, the interest-rate and the terms-of-trade effects of fiscal policies. The different predictions of the two alternative models concerning the effects of fiscal policies on the current world rate of interest and on the current terms of trade are summarized, respectively, in tables 16.5 and 16.6.

Table 16.6
The effects of fiscal policies on the current terms of trade: the income-expenditure and the intertemporal models

Effects of	Income-expenditure model	Intertemporal model
Debt-financed rise in government spending		
Current	$+$ (for $\tilde{B} > 0$) $-$ (for $\tilde{B} < 0$)	$+$ (for $J > 0$) $-$ (for $J < 0$)
Future	0	$-$
Permanent	$+$ (for $\tilde{B} > 0$) $-$ (for $\tilde{B} < 0$)	$\left.\begin{array}{c}+\\-\end{array}\right\}a$
Tax-financed rise in government spending		
Current	$+$	$+$ (for $J > 0$) $-$ (for $J < 0$)
Future	0	$-$
Permanent	$+$	$\left.\begin{array}{c}+\\-\end{array}\right\}a$
Current tax cut	$+$ (for $\tilde{D} > 0$) $-$ (for $\tilde{D} < 0$)	0

Note: A rise in the relative price of importables in terms of exportables is indicated by a $+$, and a fall by a $-$. The signs corresponding to the income expenditure model are based on the assumptions that the exchange rate is flexible, that exchange-rate expectations are static, and that there are no revaluation effects. The signs pertaining to the inter-temporal model are based on the assumption that all goods are internationally trad-able. $\tilde{B} = e_t(M_y/M_r)[\tilde{a}^* + \tilde{s}^*(1 - a^g)] - (M_y^*/M_r^*)[\tilde{a} + \tilde{s}a^g]$, $\tilde{D} = e_t(M_y/M_r)(\tilde{a}^* + \tilde{s}^*) - (M_y^*/M_r^*)\tilde{a}$, $J = \beta_m^g - \beta_m(1 - \gamma_s)$, and a indicates that the result depends on the interactions between the current-account position and the sign of the difference between the shares of importables of the private sector, β_m, and of the government β_m^g.

The interest-rate effects are shown in table 16.5. The results pertaining to the income-expenditure model are based on the analysis in chapter 3 and those pertaining to the intertemporal model are based on the analysis in chapter 11 extended (on the basis of chapters 7 through 8) to allow for a finite horizon. The key characteristics emerging from table 16.5 are the significant differences in the predictions of the various models. Furthermore, for those cases in which a given policy may either raise or lower the rate of interest, the key factors governing the actual outcome differ drastically across the two models. In the income-expenditure model these key factors reflect relative magnitudes of parameters measuring the effects of changes in income on spending and on money demand. In contrast, in the intertemporal model the key factors reflect intertemporal parameters, both the temporal/intertemporal substitution elasticites and the current-account positions. It is also relevant to note that for the cases in which the *directions* of predicted interest-rate changes do not differ across the two models, the *magnitudes* of the changes may differ sharply since the mechanisms that operate in the two models are not the same.

A similar inference applies to the comparison of the predictions of the two models concerning the terms-of-trade effects of fiscal policies, shown in table 16.6. Due to the assumed fixity of GDP deflators in the income-expenditure model, the changes in the terms of trade pertaining to this model arise from exchange-rate changes (under the flexible exchange-rate regime) and are based on the analysis in chapter 3. The results pertaining to the intertemporal model are based on those analyzed in chapter 11 extended (on the basis of chapters 7 through 8) to allow for a finite horizon. As examples of the difference, consider the effects of a debt-financed rise in current government spending on the current terms of trade. Both models imply that the current terms of trade may either rise (deteriorate) or fall (improve). However, the factors determining the actual outcome differ significantly. In the income-expenditure model the actual result depends on the relative sensitivities of the domestic and the foreign rates of interest to income changes (arising from the fiscal policy). These relative sensitivities underly the sign of the parameter $\tilde{B}$. In contrast, in the intertemporal model the actual result depends on the difference between the government and private-sector's propensity to spend on current importables out of wealth. These propensities underly the sign of the parameter J.

The examples shown in tables 16.5 and 16.6 were based on simplified versions of the models chosen to highlight differences between some of their predictions. The more complex versions analyzed in the preceding chapters allow for mechanisms and factors that may generate additional differences. These include debt revaluation effects arising from terms-of-trade changes, exchange-rate expectations in the income-expenditure model of chapter 3, details of the nominal exchange rate regime underlying the intertemporal model of chapter 11, and distortionary taxes. The latter factor is of special interest since it plays a unique role in determining the effects of tax policy in the intertemporal model. Specifically, as shown in chapter 11, the various types of taxes can be classified into those for which a current tax cut raises the world rate of interest (e.g., as a value-added tax) and those for which a current tax cut lowers the world rate of interest (e.g., an income tax).

For ease of exposition, the summary provided in tables 16.5 and 16.6 considers only the effects of policies on the *current* values of the interest rate and the terms of trade. As such it focuses on the current channels of the international transmission of fiscal policies. Throughout the discussion in this book we emphasized that current policies also have profound effects on the *future* values of the interest rates and the terms of trade. The two models also differ sharply in their predictions of these future values. The differences reflect the fundamental distinction between the models. The intertemporal model is based on forward-looking behavior of individuals and governments whose current and future decisions must obey intertemporal budget constraints. No such features characterize the dynamics of the income-expenditure model.

Finally, the analysis in this book also highlights differences between the models that are not summarized in tables 16.5 and 16.6. These differences are reflected in the current and the future levels (and growth rates) of domestic and foreign private-sector consumption, investment, outputs, and real exchange rates.

16.3 Conclusions and Extensions

The Modern Intertemporal Approach

A key feature of the modern approach to the analysis of fiscal policies in open economies is the great attention given to microeconomic foundations, in which behavior is forward looking. Intertemporal considerations, therefore, play a major role in determining the effects of fiscal policies. In contrast with the traditional approach, the modern intertemporal optimizing approach also provides a framework suitable for a normative analysis of the domestic and international welfare implications of government spending and tax policies.

The stylized model of a small open economy that underlies the neoclassical theory of fiscal policy in open-economy macroeconomics is presented in figure 16.1. Investment spending is measured in a leftward direction, from the point measuring the endowment of the country (consisting of the sum of current period GDP, $F(K_t, L_t)$ and previous-period capital stock, K_{t-1}). The economy can produce present (public and private) consumption, G_t and C_t, according to the transformation schedule, TT. Point A represents zero current investment while point M represents an economy which fully mobilizes its resources for investment. The intermediate point, B, represents the efficient level of investment, at which the domestic marginal rate of

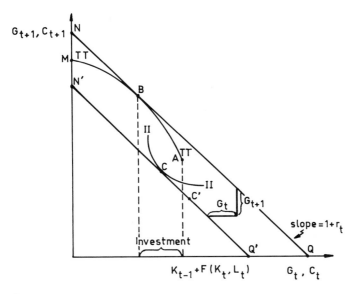

Figure 16.1
The general equilibrium of consumption, investment, and the trade balance

transformation is equal to the corresponding world marginal rate of transformation (one plus the rate of interest). The (public and private) consumption possibility frontier is portrayed by the line NBQ, whose slope is equal
to one plus the world rate of interest, r_t. Subtracting from the consumption
frontier a vector consisting of present and next period public consumption
yields the private consumption possibilities frontier, $N'Q'$. An efficient
consumption allocation point is the one at which the intertemporal marginal
rate of substitution is equal to the world marginal rate of transformation,
point C. If taxes are not distortionary, the stylized model yields the celebrated Ricardian Equivalence Proposition which states that government
finance, namely the debt-tax composition of the government budget, is
irrelevant (see Barro 1974).

Government spending influences the private sector through two channels:
it absorbs resources that otherwise would have been available for consumption (the "tax effect"), and it may influence the marginal evaluations of
private goods (the "consumption tilting effect"). In operating through the
resource-withdrawal channel, government spending policies generate a
transfer of purchasing power between the private and public sectors and
the international economic effects of the fiscal policy are therefore akin to
the "transfer problem," familiar from the international trade literature (see
Samuelson 1952). A temporary rise in government spending implies a

transfer from a sector with high saving propensity (the private sector) to a sector with low saving propensity (the government), since the temporary government spending can be viewed as an intertemporal shift in the pattern of government spending toward the present. Consequently, national savings falls and the current account of the balance of payment must deteriorate. If the country enjoys some market power in the world capital markets the world rate of interest must rise. If, on the other hand, the rise in government spending is viewed as permanent, national saving would not be affected (provided that the intertemporal composition of public and private consumptions are the same), since the transfer then involves sectors with equal saving propensities (see Frenkel and Razin 1987b).

The stylized intertemporal model features government debt neutrality, stating that shifts between lump-sum taxes and debt have no real consequences. With intergenerational altruism this property is extended to infinite horizon models (see Barro 1974). The requirements for the Ricardian equivalence of interior transfers may not, however, be satisfied, and consequently shifts from tax finance to debt finance may not be neutral. Furthermore, even if interior intergenerational transfers take place, strategic behavior implies that income distributions across generations are not neutral even with intergenerational altruism (see Kotlikoff, Razin, and Rosenthal 1990). Evidently the use of distortionary taxes weakens the key implication of the neutrality proposition, the private-sector saving offsets changes in public-sector saving, and the current account balance is not significantly affected by budgetary imbalances.

The predictions of the Mundell-Fleming model concerning the effects of budget deficits on relative prices, employment, and deficits on the current account contrast sharply with the implications of the international-intertemporal model. Within the context of the latter model, if taxes are lump-sum and nondistortionary, it follows that the timing of taxes and the path of budget deficits do not affect the real equilibrium. In contrast, in the Mundell-Fleming framework with fixed exchange rates budget deficits are a powerful instrument of policy.

Budget deficits play a meaningful role in the international-intertemporal model if an overlapping-generations structure is incorporated into the model (see Samuelson 1958) or distortionary taxes are admitted. Blanchard (1985) demonstrates that a tax cut tends to raise the current account deficit through a wealth effect if the overlapping generations have finite horizons (see also Frenkel and Razin 1987b for two-country extensions that also involve relative price adjustments). Similarly, Weil (1987) analyses a variant of the overlapping-generations model with a growing population. In these models, budget deficits in effect generate a transfer between generations with unequal saving propensities. With finite horizons a tax cut followed by a future tax rise (so as to maintain the government solvent) amounts to a transfer from the future generation (whose propensity to consume in the present is zero) to the current generation (whose propensity to consume in the present is positive). Consequently, current absorption must rise and the current account position must deteriorate. A similar mechanism (akin to the transfer problem criterion) also operates with population growth if there are weak altruistic links between old and young generations, as in Weil (1987).

The effects of budget deficits on the current account operate through a different mechanism if taxes are distortionary. To demonstrate this point consider alternatively consumption and income tax systems. If a current tax cut, followed by a future tax hike (to maintain government solvency) is carried out under a consumption tax system, the budget deficit policy operates through an intertemporal substitution of consumption to advance consumption spending from the future to the present. Consequently, the current account position deteriorates. Figure 16.2 portrays the domestic, D, foreign, D^*, and the world, D^W, relative demand curves, that is, ratios of present and future consumption spending, for a two-country world economy. The corresponding relative supply curves are denoted by S, S^*, and S^W. Schedule D^W is a weighted average of schedules D and D^*, while schedule S^W is a weighted average of schedules S and S^*. The effects of domestic budget deficit policies under the income tax system can be dem-

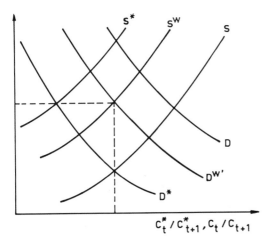

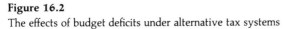

Figure 16.2
The effects of budget deficits under alternative tax systems

onstrated by a rightward shift in the domestic and world relative demand curves, resulting in a deterioration in the domestic current account position and a rise in the world rate of interest, r_t. If, however, the budget deficit arises under the income tax system, the effect on the current account operates through intertemporal substitution in investment, creating incentives to raise current output net of investment, at the expense of the corresponding future net output. Consequently, the current account position improves. In terms of the diagram in figure 16.1 the domestic budget deficit policy would cause a rightward shift in the domestic and world relative supply curves, resulting in an improvement in the domestic external balance and a fall in the world rate of interest (see Frenkel and Razin 1987b).

International Taxation

The objectives of fiscal policies may be accomplished in a variety of ways and means. A leading example is the elimination of fiscal frontiers in Europe of 1992. The trade-creating incentives that can result may, however, be mitigated if domestic-based taxes that exert equivalent effects are changed in an offsetting manner (see, for example, Gordon and Levinsohn 1990). The international taxation literature has uncovered a long list of such tax equivalences which have important policy implications (see Frenkel, Razin and Sadka 1991). Notable examples are: the equivalence between import and export taxes (for static models, see Lerner 1936 and for dynamic models, Razin and Svensson 1983); the equivalence between consumption taxes and taxes on income from labor, profits, and returns on the pre-existing capital (Atkinson 1977); and the equivalence between indirect taxes (such as source-based value-added tax) and income taxes (such as cash-flow income tax).

The economic integration of the world goods market and capital markets transforms tax bases from national to global, although each national tax jurisdiction remains independent. Imports and exports of goods and services may be subject to double taxation, first at the origin and second at the destination, even if border tax adjustments (such as import tariffs or export taxes) are not allowed. Broadly-based indirect taxation, such as the value-added tax, could be levied by both the importing and the exporting country. Similarly, even if international borrowing and lending taxes are allowed, foreign-source capital income of a country's residents may be subjected to taxes by the home country while the same income may be taxed at the source by the foreign country. The interactions between sovereign jurisdictions in an integrated world economy have immensely important implications for the allocation of savings and investment among countries, as well as for the location of production and consumption of goods and services.

To alleviate the problem of double taxation the various tax systems in most of the industrialized countries follow one of the two dual principles: the residence and the source principles (in the case of income taxation) and the destination and origin principle (in the case of indirect taxation). According to the residence (destination) principle, foreign-source incomes of residents (imports of goods) are taxed by the home country, while they are exempt by the foreign country, which is the source (origin) country. According to the source and origin principles, foreign-source income and imports of goods are tax exempt by the home country while they are subject to the income tax and indirect taxes by the foreign country, respectively. Giovannini (1989) and Frenkel, Razin, and Sadka (1991) show that the residence principle, if used universally (with country-specific income tax rates to accommodate the country revenue needs), generates an efficient allocation of world investment among countries. At the same time, however, the allocation of world saving is inefficient. Similarly, the destination principle of indirect taxation generates an efficient allocation of the production of goods and services across countries but the geographical distribution of consumption may be inefficient. In contrast, the source principle of income taxation and the origin principle of indirect taxation, if adopted universally (but with country-specific rates) distort the international allocation of investment and production while maintaining an efficient international allocation of world saving and consumption. These basic principles are useful as a guide for the design of optimal tax systems.

The optimal taxation model (see Diamond and Mirrlees 1971) yields the aggregate production-efficiency result. It specifies that the tax-ridden economy must operate on its consumption possibilities frontier, TT, in figure 16.2. Optimal tax wedges should be used to separate consumers' marginal rates of substitution from producers' marginal rates of transformation but not to separate marginal rates of transformation across production units. The equilibrium of the optimum tax system is shown by points B and C' in figure 16.2. Based on this model the key implications of optimal taxation for international economic policies are that: (1) impediments to trade in goods and services and capital flows should be removed; (2) direct taxation should adopt the residence principle; and (3) indirect taxation should adopt the destination principle.

Due to the distortions caused by direct and indirect taxation in a world economy with uncoordinated national fiscal authorities, an important issue is whether there are gains from harmonizing tax policies of the individual tax authorities. Evidently if fiscal authorities can manipulate the terms of trade to gain national advantages the resulting Nash equilibrium must be inefficient, as known from the prisoner's dilemma game (see Dixit 1985). However, in an integrated world economy each individual country may not enjoy significant market power. Frenkel, Razin, and Sadka (1991) demonstrate that if the world prices are beyond the influence of an individual country, then in a Nash equilibrium each government adopts the residence-based taxation as an optimizing strategy. Thus, the competition among national tax authorities generates an efficient allocation of the world stock of capital. If instead of competing, national fiscal authorities jointly determine the optimal design of taxes, the most that they can achieve with the distortionary taxes at their disposal is an efficient allocation of capital, as implied from the production efficiency proposition. Such an allocation is, however, achieved anyway through tax competition. Thus, there are no gains from an international tax harmonization if governments cannot manipulate the terms of trade in the design of their tax systems.

Deviations from this benchmark could, however, arise if domestic authorities cannot enforce taxes on the foreign source income of their residents. Such enforcement failure generates incentives to restrict capital exports (see Frenkel, Razin, and Sadka 1991).

Dynamic Inconsistency and Fiscal Policy

Fiscal policy is dynamically inconsistent if in absence of new information, future policies deviate from the original plan due to altered incentives on the part of the government. Kydland and Prescott (1977) and Calvo (1978) first demonstrated that the supply elasticities of capital, or money balances, vary during the process of asset accumulation and, consequently, government incentives to tax income from assets very over time, leading to dynamically inconsistent tax policies.

In a dynamically inconsistent setting a Phillips curve monetary policy game has been developed by Barro and Gordon (1983) to explain inflationary biases. In the Barro-Gordon one-period game the private sector chooses first the expected inflation (through the wage contract). Once the private sector has committed itself to this rate the government may choose the rate of inflation so as to minimize a loss function, featuring inflation and unemployment. If the government target level of output exceeds the natural rate (the private-sector target) then the Nash equilibrium, in which the inflation expected by the private sector is in fact implemented by the government, is an inflationary-biased solution for the game.

Dynamic inconsistency is invoked to explain situations in which international harmonization may be inferior to the international competitive equilibrium (which is also less costly to implement). An important example is developed by Rogoff (1985), who applies the Barro-Gordon framework to the issue. The inflationary effects associated with exchange rate depreciations, which arise only if monetary expansions are uncoordinated, tend to restrain the government in its pursuit of the high-employment–low-inflation objective. In comparison, if monetary expansions are coordinated, depreciations of the exchange rate are absent. Consequently, coordinated-policy inflation rates exceed the noncoordinated rates, while output levels are the same. In this example, therefore, coordination is undesirable.

Kehoe (1989) provides a similar example where the ability to coordinate policies would exacerbate the credibility problem of each government vis-à-vis its own private sector for the case of fiscal policy. Using a standard two-period neoclassical model, in which the objective function of each country's policymaker coincides with the objective function of its residents, Kehoe assumes that national tax authorities make the policy decision before the private-sector decisions on the precise international allocation of its saving are made. He demonstrates that with international policy coordination the joint policy must tax away all the return on savings. Anticipating the low return prospect, investors would not invest at all. In the alternative case of international tax competition, low taxes on income from saving are used by each government to attract world saving. It then follows that taxes on the returns on savings would be relatively low and forward-looking investment must be high. Thus, international cooperation is, again, undesirable.

Canzoneri and Diba (1991) consider the beneficial effects of international coordination. They show that if governments have access to the world capital market a rise in government spending generates a smaller increase in the rate of interest compared to the financial autarkic situation. Consequently, the amount by which the payment on existing debt rises is smaller, and the costs associated with the rise in taxes to finance the increase in spending are diminished, relative to financial autarky. Thus financial integration of the capital markets induces a government spending bias. This mechanism generates the classic benefits from coordination, since if an individual government makes its spending decisions it internalizes the costs to other governments associated with debt servicing.

Evidence on the Twin Deficits

In testing the hypothesis about the irrelevance of the timing of taxes and the neutrality of government debt, the traditional approach is to regress the current account deficit on real exchange rates, interest rates (as 'price variables') and output, government spending, taxes, government debt and money creation (as 'income variables'). The typical regression uses mostly current variables, except that lagged output is added so that with current output they both form a proxy of permanent income. Traditional studies test debt neutrality by the restriction that the coefficients of taxes and debt are not significantly different from zero. However, none of the future expected variables suggested by the intertemporal model are explicitly included in the estimated equation.

The reduced-form equation of the current account sur-plus is not likely to provide the relevant information on the validity of the debt neutrality proposition, because, if current taxes are good predictors of future government spending, the fact that the tax coefficient is significantly different from zero is evidently in line with the neutrality proposition; this is contrary to the above-mentioned interpretation.

A more recent approach in empirical tests of the proposition is based on rational expectation estimations of structural (saving-investment balance) models (see, for example, Aschauer 1985 and Leiderman and Razin 1990). In these models the behavior equations arising from the intertemporal optimization of consumers are estimated jointly with the underlying exogenous stochastic processes, which characterize the behavior of spending and taxes. The null hypothesis is specified by a set of cross-equation nonlinear restrictions on the parameters, implied by the theory.

The empirical findings about the neutrality of government debt are, so far, mixed. Although there exists substantial evidence that private-sector savings tend to offset, to some extent, changes in public-sector saving, a full offset (indicated by government-debt neutrality) is rejected.

A drawback of existing approaches is the inability to account for fiscal regime changes. An increase in the stock of government bonds may signal future increases in taxes, so as to service the new debt. But the rise in debt may also signal future monetary accommodation, or future fall in government spending. The current econometric approach cannot distinguish between the different forms of regime change, and thus it is incapable of providing more decisive answers to the debt-neutrality puzzle (see Blejer and Leiderman 1988).

Evidence on International Policy Coordination

The interdependence among economies highlighted by the theoretical models has been subjected to numerous econometric examinations employing large-scale models of the world economy. While results differ across models, the fundamental point that fiscal actions undertaken by a large country are transmitted to the rest of the world is evident. In most international macroeconometric models a fiscal expansion by the United States worsens the U.S. balance of trade, appreciates the foreign exchange value of the U.S. dollar, puts upward pressures on interest rates, and stimulates foreign output (see Bryant et al. 1988).

The interdependence among economies, which intensified with the growing integration of world capital markets, has led to the development of the international policy coordination process of the Group of Seven industrial countries (G7), as well as to an intensification of multilateral surveillance through the International Monetary Fund (IMF). The coordination process is aided by the use of "objective indicators" related to policy actions and economic performance (such as fiscal positions, GNP and demand growth, monetary conditions, and the balance of payments). The indicators can be used *ex ante* in formulating objectives and policies, as well as *ex post* in monitoring progress and assessing outcomes.

The literature on the costs and benefits from international policy coordination is abundant (see, for example, Branson, Frenkel and Goldstein 1990). Among the obstacles that are frequently cited are that countries do not share the same objectives, they are not subject to the same political constraints, their economic systems differ from each other, policy instruments of some are the policy objectives of others, the econometric models are not viewed as a reliable guide for policies, policy commitments are hard to enforce, and the like. Nevertheless, a consensus emerges that the highly integrated world economy requires some degree of policy coordination, at least in the form of an ongoing process of cooperation in which information is exchanged to yield a joint assessment of the economic situation and prospects.

Gauging the effects of policy coordination, the literature compares the value of a welfare function under the assumption that each country maximizes welfare independently, with the value obtained under the alternative assumption that the countries maximize a joint welfare function. The early findings reveal that the gains from coordination are likely to be small (see Oudiz and Sachs 1984) and, if policymakers cannot precommit themselves to a policy rule, then coordination could be counterproductive (see

Canzoneri and Henderson 1988, Kehoe 1989, and Rogoff 1985). More generally, if coordination attempts to reinforce "bad" policies, it will be welfare-reducing (see Feldstein 1988). However, some of the negative findings obtained by this strand of analysis need to be qualified. First, the relevant comparison is frequently between suboptimal uncoordinated policies with suboptimal coordinated policies rather than between optimal coordinated and uncoordinated policies. Second, some of the gains from coordination may be unobservable and spread beyond the area of fiscal policies. Third, empirical estimates of gains from coordination have typically compared policies that do not exploit the incentive governments may have not to adhere to agreements in the light of changed circumstances on one hand, and the incentives to stick to agreements to enhance their reputation, on the other hand.

The debate on the need for, and the modalities of, coordination of fiscal policies within Europe has come to the fore with the progress toward the creation of a single market within Europe as part of the 1992 process of European economic integration. Two notable examples are tax harmonization and the constraints that a European Monetary Union imposes on the conduct of fiscal policies. The key issue in the debate on tax harmonization arises from the great diversity of tax rates among the members of the European Community and the diverging welfare implications of a greater convergence of tax rates (see Frenkel, Razin, and Sadka 1991). The key issues in the debate on the fiscal consequences of a European Monetary Union are the constraints that need to be imposed on member countries' fiscal deficits, including the "no bail-out" guarantee and the prohibition on monetizing deficits, fiscal transfers among member states designed to reconcile the gap between the international incidence of economic shocks and the increased centralization of policy, and the distribution of seignorage from centralized money creation.

17

Bibliographical Notes

Throughout this book we have not dealt with the large body of literature bearing on the subjects covered in the various chapters. In this chapter we provide selected bibliographical notes. We do not present a comprehensive survey of the voluminous work underlying the development of economic thought and analysis of fiscal policies in the world economy. Rather, our purpose is to indicate some linkages between the ideas and concepts developed in this book and the work that precedes it. We do not refer here to our own earlier work which is cited in the preface to the book.

17.1   Selected Notes on the Literature

Part II of the book is devoted to the presentation of traditional approaches to international macroeconomics, with special emphasis given to the role of fiscal policies. It opens with a model of international economic interdependence which is based on the Keynesian analysis of the foreign-trade multiplier as developed, among others, by Metzler (1942a), Machlup (1943), and Robinson (1952).

Throughout the book we analyze the international mechanism of adjustment in terms of the transfer-problem criterion. This criterion was developed originally in the context of post-World War I discussions about the German reparations, and it was debated among Keynes (1929), Ohlin (1929), and Rueff (1929). This concept was further clarified by Metzler (1942b), Meade (1951), Samuelson (1952), Johnson (1956), and Mundell (1960).

The basic model used throughout our analysis of the traditional approach to international macroeconomics is the income-expenditure model. In specifying this model, we have employed elements from the absorption approach to the balance of payments, as developed by Alexander (1952), and from the monetary approach to the balance of payments, as presented by

Polak (1957), Johnson (1958), Prais (1961), Mundell (1964), Frenkel and Johnson (1976), and IMF (1977).

The increased integration of world capital markets led to the development of models in which international capital mobility plays a pivotal role. A pioneering treatment of international capital mobility appears in Iversen (1935). The incorporation of capital movements into the main corpus of international macroeconomics was carried out in a series of class articles in the 1960s by Mundell (collected in Mundell 1968 and 1971), and by Fleming (1962). The so called Mundell-Fleming model is still the main workhorse of traditional open-economy macroeconomics. This model has been extended in several directions. Among them is a long-run analysis by Rodriguez (1979); a stock (portfolio) specification of capital mobility by McKinnon (1969), Floyd (1969), Branson (1970), and Frenkel and Rodriguez (1975); an analysis of the debt-revaluation effects induced by exchange-rate changes by Boyer (1977) and Rodriguez (1979); and an analysis of expectations and exchange-rate dynamics by Kouri (1976) and Dornbusch (1976). A critical evaluation of the Mundell-Fleming model is provided by Purvis (1985).

Expositions of the income-expenditure models for alternative exchange-rate regimes and for different degrees of international capital mobility are presented in Swoboda and Dornbusch (1973) and Mussa (1979). The diagrammatic analysis used in chapters 2 and 3 builds in part on these two expositions.

Surveys of various issues covered by the traditional approaches to open-economy macroeconomics are contained in Frenkel and Mussa (1985), Kenen (1985), Marston (1985), and Obstfeld and Stockman (1985), and a comprehensive treatment is provided in Dornbusch (1980).

Part III of the book (chapters 4 and 5) provides an exposition of the basic elements of intertemporal macroeconomics. The intertemporal approach extends Fisher's (1930) analysis to the entire spectrum of macroeconomic decision making, including saving, investment, and labor. Examples of such extensions, in the context of consumption-savings decisions are Modigliani and Brumberg (1954), Friedman (1957), and Hall (1978). Examples in the context of investment theory are Lucas (1967), Uzawa (1968), Tobin (1969), Lucas and Prescott (1971), Abel (1979), Hayashi (1982), and Abel and Blanchard (1986). Other examples in the context of dynamic labor supply and demand are Lucas and Rapping (1969), Heckman (1974), Ghez and Becker (1975), and Sargent (1978). Integrations of the various elements into a general equilibrium model of closed-economy business-cycle theory are contained in Barro (1981a) and Lucas (1981).

Elements of the intertemporal approach that we develop in chapter 4 have been used in the context of open economies, with special emphasis given to the theory of international borrowing and the current account of the balance of payments. Examples of writings in this approach are Bruno (1976, 1982), Eaton and Gersovitz (1981), Sachs (1981, 1984), Razin (1984), and Penati (1987). In chapter 5 we develop the relations between temporal and intertemporal prices and their effects on the time profile of spending and the current account. This analysis is based on Obstfeld (1982), Dornbusch (1983), and Svensson and Razin (1983), who in turn reexamine the older problem of the effects of changes in the terms of trade on savings as analyzed by Harberger (1950) and Laursen and Metzler (1950).

The intertemporal approach to fiscal policies in the world economy is presented in part IV of the book (chapters 6 and through 8). Our analysis of the effects of government spending in chapter 6 builds on a model embodying the Ricardian neutrality property, according to which intertemporal shifts of lump-sum taxes do not influence the economic system. Typically, this proposition is ascribed to Ricardo, even though, as documented by O'Driscoll (1977), Ricardo himself while anticipating its logic denied its practical validity. Analyses of elements underlying the Ricardian proposition originate in Buchanan (1958), Modigliani (1961), Bailey (1962), and Patinkin (1965), and its modern revival is due to Barro (1974).

Early discussion of the long-term effects of fiscal policies in a Keynesian closed-economy context is contained in Blinder and Solow (1973). In the context of the intertemporal approach Barro (1981a) highlights the distinction between permanent and transitory government spending.

Our discussion of budget deficits (chapters 7 and 8) deals with the dynamic effects of fiscal policies in models of overlapping generations. The first formulation of the model in a closed-economy context is due to Samuelson (1958), and the detailed analysis of public debt and capital accumulation within this model is found in Diamond (1965). Examples of open-economy applications of this model are Buiter (1981), Dornbusch (1985), and Persson and Svensson (1985). Aspects of welfare are highlighted in Fried (1980) and Persson (1985). In chapters 7 and 8 we adopt another formulation of the overlapping generations model, based on Yaari (1965) and due to Blanchard (1985). In this model the finiteness of the horizon stems from lifetime uncertainty. An application of the model to a two-country framework is found in the first edition of this book (Frenkel and Razin (1987) and in Buiter (1987). The role of population growth in a similar model is treated by Weil (1987).

Chapter 11 is devoted to the analysis of the effects of current and anticipated future fiscal policies on the term structure of the world rate of interest and the dynamics of the real exchange rates. Examples of related works dealing with similar issues are Blanchard (1984), Branson (1986), Dantas and Dornbusch (1986), and Helpman and Razin (1987). Dynamic patterns of real exchange rates induced by resource changes rather than fiscal policies are analyzed in the context of the so called "Dutch Disease." Early examples of such analyses are Gregory (1976), Corden and Neary (1982), and Purvis and Neary (1985).

Part V of the book deals with the international effects of distortionary taxes. The exposition of tax equivalences in the open economy, in chapter 9, draws on Auerbach, Frenkel, and Razin (1988). The symmetry of import and export taxes was first noted by Lerner (1933). An extension of the symmetry argument to dynamic setting is found in Razin and Svensson (1983). Kotlikoff (1989) addressed the issue of tax equivalences in the context of debt-tax finance. He argues that in many policy-relevant circumstances measured budget deficits may not be an economically meaningful concept. Gordon and Lavinsohn (1990) provide an empirical analysis of the use of domestic tax instruments to offset the reduction in border taxes. Another useful equivalence, the relationship between taxes on international borrowing and the dual exchange rate system, is analyzed in Frenkel and Razin (1988) and Mendoza (1990).

Our discussion of distortionary taxes in chapters 10 through 12 is related to earlier research emphasizing intertemporal considerations in a closed economy framework. Examples of such research are Diamond (1970, 1975), Diamond and Mirrlees (1971), Mirrlees (1972), Barro (1974, 1979, 1981b), Feldstein (1974, 1977), Atkinson and Stern (1974), Atkinson and Stiglitz (1976), Sadka (1977), Dutton, Feldstein, and Hartman (1979), Kydland and Prescott (1980), Brock and Turnovsky (1981), Balcer and Sadka (1982), Dixit (1985), King (1983), Lucas and Stokey (1983), Gordon (1986), and Judd (1987). In the international context examples of analyses of various aspects of distortionary taxes are found in Razin and Svensson (1983), Aschauer and Greenwood (1985), Greenwood and Kimbrough (1985), Kimbrough (1986), and van Wijnbergen (1986).

Chapter 12 is devoted to the taxation of capital income in the open economy, based on Razin and Sadka (1991). A comprehensive treatise of various aspects of international taxation is found in Frenkel, Razin, and Sadka (1991). Examples of the literature bearing on this subject are Dixit (1985), Gordon (1986), Musgrave (1987), Giovannini (1990), Lucas (1990), and Sinn (1990).

Part IV of the book deals with the international effects of stochastic fiscal policies. Uncertainty elements appear in various branches of economics and play a central role in the financial economics and in modern macroeconomics. Arrow (1963–64) emphasized the role of elementary securities in the allocation of risk. Following Arrow's insight, Diamond (1967) developed a general-equilibrium model of a stock market economy. Helpman and Razin (1978) applied the stock market model to international trade in the presence of uncertainty. Examples of relevant literature in finance, using stochastic processes in the analysis of markets for equity and debt, are Merton (1971), Pitchford and Turnovsky (1977), Ingersoll (1987), Svensson (1988), and Faig (1991).

Part VII of the book is devoted to dynamic simulation analyses of international spillovers of fiscal policies. Among the literature bearing on this subject are Auerbach and Kotlikoff (1987), Cnossen and Shoup (1987), Pechman (1988), Tait (1988), Tanzi and Bovenberg (1989), and Perraudin and Pujol (1991).

Chapter 16 of part VIII of the book is devoted to overall summary of the intertemporal approach to international economics and extensions in three areas: (1) international taxation; (2) dynamic inconsistency; and (2) the evidence on the twin deficits and international fiscal policy coordination. Examples of the literature on international taxation are Frenkel, Razin, and Sadka (1991), Giovannini (1990), Gordon (1986), Sinn (1990), and Slemrod (1988).

The constraints on the conduct of fiscal policies may give rise to difficulties associated with time inconsistency of government actions. Such issues are dealt with in Calvo (1978), Kydland and Prescott (1977), Lucas and Stokey (1983), Fischer (1986), Calvo and Obstfeld (1988), and Persson and Svensson (1986). A related issue concerns the formulation of a positive theory of government policy, as analyzed by Barro and Gordon (1983) in the context of an inflation-biased economy. Accordingly, in situations for which policy makers are unable to commit their course of future actions, the game-theoretic equilibrium may be suboptimal, as in the well-known "prisoner's dilemma" game. Recent literature adopts the intertemporal approach and develops a positive theory of economic policy in an alternative institutional environment. Examples of this political economy literature are Persson and Tabellini (1990) and Metzer, Cukierman, and Richard (1991).

Empirical analyses of the effects of fiscal policies on private-sector spending are ample. Examples are Kochin (1979), Feldstein and Horioka (1980), Barro (1981), Feldstein (1982), Kormendi (1983), Aschauer (1985), Aschauer and Greenwood (1985), Leiderman and Razin (1989, 1991), and Mendoza

(1991). A survey of key issues relevant for empirical testing is Leiderman and Blejer (1988). Simulations of models based on consumers with finite horizons are found in Blanchard and Summers (1984), Hubbard and Judd (1986), and Poterba and Summers (1986). The intertemporal approach to macroeconomics has also been subjected to numerous empirical tests. Examples are Hall (1978), MaCurdy (1981), Altonji (1982), Mankiw, Rothemberg, and Summers (1985), and Leiderman and Razin (1985). A modification of saving behavior allowing for life cycle characteristics is contained in Auerbach and Kotlikoff (1987) and Modigliani (1987). A further modification of the saving behavior arising from an altruistic bequest motive that is not operative is examined by Barro (1974), Drazen (1978), Feldstein (1986), Nerlove, Razin, and Sadka (1988), and Kotlikoff, Razin, and Rosenthal (1990).

Kydland and Prescott (1982) simulate a theoretical dynamic model, using assumed parameter values, and are able to generate stochastic behavior that closely resembles economic time series. For an application to international economics, see Mendoza (1991).

The interdependencies among countries provide incentives for strategic behavior by individual countries. Analysis of the implications of such strategic behavior is contained in Hamada (1976, 1985). The interdependencies among countries may call for harmonization and coordination of economic policies. Early analyses of these issues are contained in Cooper (1968, 1985). Examples of analyses of this issue within a game-theoretic approach are Oudiz and Sachs (1984), Rogoff (1984, 1986), Canzoneri and Gray (1983), and Canzoneri and Henderson (1987). Additional examples of the empirical literature on the costs and benefits from international policy coordination are contained in Branson, Frenkel, and Goldstein (1990).

The 1980 debt problem generated a renewed interests in the analytics of international debt management. Examples of the ample literature on this issue are Eaton and Gersovitz (1981), Kletzer (1984), Sachs (1984, 1985), Cohen and Sachs (1986), Krugman (1985, 1990), Bulow and Rogoff (1988), Dooley (1990), and Helpman (1990).

The following list of references also contains recent applications of the intertemporal approach to open-economy macroeconomics that are applicable to the problem sets.

Chapter 4

1. See also Caballero 1991.

Chapter 5

1. An alternative (dual) way to characterize the price index, P, is as follows:

$$\underset{\{c_x, c_m\}}{\text{Min}}\ z = c_x + pc_m \quad \text{subject to } C(c_x, c_m) \geqslant \bar{C}.$$

Necessary conditions for a minimum are

$$1 - \lambda C_1(c_x, c_m) = 0,$$

$$p - \lambda C_2(c_x, c_m) = 0,$$

$$C(c_x, c_m) = \bar{C},$$

where λ is the Lagrange multiplier that is associated with the constraint in the minimum problem.

Thus, the minimum cost of obtaining utility level $\bar{C}$ is $z = c_x + pc_m = \lambda[c_x C_1(c_x, c_m) + c_m C_2(c_x, c_m)] = \lambda\bar{C}$, and λ is therefore equal to the corresponding *unit* cost, the price index, $P(p)$.

It is easy to check that $\partial z/\partial p = c_m$. Thus, $[dP(p)/P(p)]/[dp/p] = [d(z/c)/dp]/[p/(z/c)] = pc_m/z$. Accordingly, the price elasticity of $P(p)$ is equal to the share of importables in consumption.

Chapter 9

1. This chapter draws on Alan Auerbach, Jacob A. Frenkel, and Assaf Razin, "Notes on International Taxation," IMF, January 1989. We thank Alan Auerbach for the permission to reproduce the work.

Chapter 10

1. Recent tax-reform proposals advocate the adoption of a consumption-tax system as proposed by Fisher (1930). In specifying the implementation of the consumption tax and its virtues over the conventional income tax, they use the closed-economy equivalence relation between a consumption tax and a cash-flow income tax (capital income tax with expensing plus a labor income tax). Being confined to a closed-economy framework, they abstract from the role that taxes on international borrowing play in this tax-equivalence relation. For a comprehensive discussion of the closed-economy tax-equivalence proposition, see Auerbach and Kotlikoff (1987).

2. Our specification in equations (10.1)–(10.4) did not allow for government bond selling to the domestic private sector. This simplifying assumption was made for convenience only and does not affect the analysis. To illustrate this point, let $-B^p$ denote foreign bonds purchased by the domestic government; A^R, domestic government bonds purchased by the domestic private sector; and $-B^R$, foreign bonds purchased by the domestic private sector. In the presence of a tax on international borrowing, arbitrage between government bonds and foreign bonds implies

$(1 + r_0 - \tau_{b1})/(1 - \tau_{b0}) = 1 + r_0^g, \quad (1 + r_{-1} - \tau_{b0})/(1 - \tau_{b-1}) = 1 + r_{-1}^g,$

where r^R is the market rate of interest on government bonds sold to the domestic private sector. Accordingly, we can subtract $[A_0^g - (1 + r_{-1}^g)A_{-1}^g]$ from the right-hand side of equation (10.1) and add $[(1 + r_0^g)A_0^g]$ to the right-hand side of equation (10.2). Correspondingly, we can add the term $[A_0^g - (1 + r_{-1}^g)A_{-1}^g]$ to the right-hand side of equation (10.3) and subtract $[(1 + r^g)A^g]$ from the right-hand side of equation (10.4). The reader can verify that these changes do not affect the results, and, for simplicity, we henceforth set $A_{-1}^g = A_0^g = 0$.

3. Under the assumption that the initial equilibrium was undistorted, the real income effects induced by the departure from the flat tax pattern are dominated by the substitution effect.

4. To verify this point we note that

$$\hat{D}^w = \left(\frac{C_0}{C_0 + C_0^*}\right)\hat{D} + \left(\frac{C_0}{C_0 + C_0^*} - \frac{C_1}{C_1 + C_1^*}\right)\hat{C}_1.$$

Accordingly, the proportional change in the world relative demand is composed of two components. The first consists of the product of the proportional change of the domestic relative demand and a fraction (the relative share of current-period home consumption in world consumption), and the second consists of the product of the proportional change in future-period consumption and a term measuring the difference between the relative shares of current-and future-period home consumption in world consumption. This latter term reflects the difference between the domestic and foreign saving propensities. If the current-period trade balance deficit arises from a relative low domestic saving propensity, then this is positive. We also note that $\hat{C}_1$ is negative, since the change in the time profile of consumption taxes induces a substitution away from future-period consumption. It follows that under such circumstances $D^w < D$ and, therefore, the displacement of the D schedule exceeds that of the D^w schedule.

5. Differentiating the domestic and world supply ratios at a given world discount factor yields

$$\hat{S} = \left[\frac{I_0}{\overline{Y}_0 - I_0 - G_0} + \frac{F'(I_0)I_0}{\overline{Y}_1 + F(I_0) - G_1}\right](-\hat{I}_0)$$

and

$$\hat{S}^w = \left[\frac{I_0}{\overline{Y}_0 - I_0 - G_0 + \overline{Y}_0^* - I_0^* - G_0^*}\right.$$
$$\left. + \frac{F'(I_0)I_0}{\overline{Y}_1 + F(I_0) - G_1 + \overline{Y}_1^* + F^*(I_0^*) - G_1^*}\right](-\hat{I}_0),$$

respectively. Evidently the proportional change in S (in absolute value) exceeds the corresponding change in S^w (in absolute value).

6. The specification of the tax structure in equation (10.6) presumes, for simplicity, that the tax rates applicable to labor income and capital income are the same. The present analytical framework can be easily used to examine the consequences of

differential tax rates, as would be the case in the presence of a corporation income tax.

7. The S^w schedule is drawn with a positive slope for convenience. In fact, changes in the rate of interest affect the intertemporal prices of leisure and of ordinary goods as well as wealth. These changes may alter the supply of labor in a way that more than offsets the effect of the induced changes in investment on z. In that case the S^w schedule is negatively sloped, but, as long as it is steeper than the world relative demand schedule, our subsequent analysis remains intact.

Chapter 11

1. The government present-value intertemporal budget constraint is

$$(G_{x0} + p_{n0} G_{n0}) + \alpha_{x1}(G_{x1} + p_{n1} G_{n1}) = T_0 + \alpha_{x1} T_1 - (1 + r_{x-1})B^g_{-1},$$

where G_{xt} and G_{nt} denote, respectively, government purchases of tradable and nontradable goods, and where B^g_t denotes government debt in period t. Consolidating the private-sector lifetime constraint (1) with that of the government (2) and imposing equality between consumption and production of nontradable goods in each period yields the economy's consolidated constraint:

$$c_{x0} + \alpha_{x1} c_{x1} = (\overline{Y}_{x0} - G_{x0}) + \alpha_{x1}(\overline{Y}_{x1} - G_{x1}) - (1 + r_{x-1})B_{-1},$$

where $B_t = B^p_t + B^g_t$ denotes the economy's external debt in period t.

2. In general, these parameters may vary over time because they may depend on the time-varying relative prices. Equation (11.6) corresponds to an initial situation in which relative prices are stationary. In what follows, we consider the case in which the temporary elasticity of substitution, σ_{nx}, is close to unity, so that changes in relative prices do not have an appreciable effect on the expenditure share, β_n. Clearly, under such circumstances we can fully characterize the world economic system in terms of percentage rates of growth of the endogenous variables (prices and quantities).

3. Here and in what follows we assume that the initial level of government spending is zero and we denote the rise in the discounted sum of government spending by dG.

4. This interpretation suggests that the effects of government spending on the interest rate and on the time path of real wages depend critically on the relative importance of wages in the government budget. For the remainder of this section we continue to assume zero government spending.

5. Thus, the expression specifying the world relative supply is the analogue to equation (11.8) modified to allow for a variable labor supply with zero government spending.

6. Again, in the present case the N and N^* schedules are adjusted for the dependence of the relative output of nontradable goods on the percentage growth rate of the real exchange rate.

7. This can be verified by recalling that the effective discount factors are $\alpha_{xt1} = [(1 + \tau_{c1})/(1 + \tau_{c0})]\alpha_{x1}$ and $\alpha_{nt1} = [(1 - \tau_{y1})/(1 - \tau_{y0})]\alpha_{c1}$.

Chapter 12

1. This chapter draws on parts of "Vanishing Tax on Capital Income in the Open Economy," by Assaf Razin and Efraim Sadka, NBER Working Paper No. 3796, 1991. We thank Efraim Sadka for permission to use parts of the paper in the book.

2. A tax credit is usually given against taxes paid abroad on foreign-source income, to achieve an *effective* tax rate on income from all sources. See Frenkel, Razin, and Sadka (1991) for a modern treatise on international taxation.

3. We assume that these tax rates apply symmetrically to both interest income and interest expenses.

4. The issue of tax arbitrage is not unique to open economies. Tax arbitrage emerges also in closed economies if the relative tax treatment of various assets differs among individuals. In the open economy case tax arbitrage becomes more serious if different types of financing are treated differently. This enables inviduals and corporations to arbitrage across different statutory tax rates. Another factor that increases the scope of the tax arbitrage is the interaction between inflation and exchange rates, on the one hand, and differential tax treatments of inflation and exchange rate gains and losses, on the other.

5. Efficiency emerges when corporate and individual taxes are fully integrated and interest income faces the same tax rate as equity income. Evidently, a nonuniform treatment of different components of the capital income tax base would violate efficiency.

6. If rents cannot be fully taxed or if the country can manipulate world prices, the choice of whether to adopt the source principle or the residence principle (or a mixture of the two principles) would depend on the interest rate elasticities of saving and investment. (See Giovannini 1989; see also Gordon 1986, Musgrave 1987, and Sinn 1990. Dixit 1985 demonstrates a related result by showing that the production efficiency proposition implies no border taxes, such as import or export taxes).

Chapter 13

1. The present model is the two-period one-good version of the stock market model in Helpman and Razin (1978, ch. 11). The endowment θY includes labor income.

2. If, for example, the utility function is logarithmic, the ratio of the marginal propensity to spend in state one to the corresponding propensity in state zero, $[\partial G_1(1)/\partial G]/[\partial G_1(0)/\partial G]$, is equal to $[\pi(1)/\pi(0)p]$. Thus, the propensity ratio depends on the relative price and the probability ratio, but not on government resources.

Chapter 14

1. This chapter draws on Jacob A. Frenkel, Assaf Razin, and Steve Symansky. "International VAT Harmonization Macroeconomic Effects," *IMF Staff Papers*, December 1991. We thank Steve Symansky for the permission to reproduce the paper.

2. Zero-rated products involve the reimbursement of taxes levied on inputs with the result that the final good is completely untaxed.

3. Until the end of 1992 the only permissible changes in the standard rates must be within the 14−20 percent range, or, if the rates lie outside the range then only changes towards the range are allowed. The final agreement on the rate structure is planned to be reached by the end of 1991.

4. For a recent broad survey of the international practice and problems in the area of VAT, see Tait (1988).

5. Such a proposal is still under review by the commission. For a further examination of the various proposals and considerations, see Cnossen and Shoup (1987).

6. The analytical framework underlying the international intertemporal approach to open economy macroeconomics is based on Frenkel and Razin (1987, 1988b). A fuller analysis of international taxation is contained in Frenkel, Razin, and Sadka (1991). For an analogous approach developed in a closed economy context, see Auerbach and Kotlikoff (1987); for an analogous approach developed in the context of a two-country world economy, see Bovenberg and Goulder (1989); and for an extension to a model with borrowing constraints, see Perraudin and Pujol (1991). For a discussion of supply-side policies, see Tanzi and Bovenberg (1989). In the present formulation capital markets are assumed to be integrated through the free access to credit markets; in appendix B we consider taxes on international borrowing. To simplify we exclude direct foreign investment, which is analyzed in Frenkel and Razin (1989).

7. Our formulation reflects the assumption that except for the final period, bolted capital cannot be consumed. However, in the final period, the capital stock, K_T, can be transformed into consumption at the rate equal to aK_T, where $0 \leqslant a \leqslant 1$. This assumption serves to mitigate abrupt changes in the behavior of the economy arising in the final period of the finite horizon model. Accordingly, the budget constraint applicable to the final period (period T) is analogous to the one shown in equation 14.1 with an added term on the right hand side equal to aK_T.

8. Obviously, with more than two periods, these discount factors are replaced by the appropriate present value factors.

9. The expression for α_L reveals an added dynamic effect whereby a rise in the capital income tax, τ_k, induces intertemporal substitution toward future labor supply.

10. The tax systems in many countries include incentives to saving and investment and, thereby, contain important features of the cash flow income tax system. Such

a system was advocated recently for the United States by Feldstein (1989). For a recent comparative analysis of capital income tax systems in various industrialized countries, see Pechman (1988).

11. To verify this point we note from equation (14.1) that, under a destination-based value-added tax system, the tax rate $1 - (1/(1 + t_c)$ applies to the value of GNP (net of investment) minus exports, plus imports; thus in effect, imports are taxed while export taxes are rebated. In contrast, the cash flow income tax applies only to GNP (net of investment); thus, in effect imports are not taxed, while export taxes are not rebated. Hence this tax system is equivalent to a value-added tax system which is source based. We are indebted to Sijbren Cnossen for providing us with this interpretation of the relation between the various VAT systems.

12. This latter property is more general and not confined only to the benchmark case.

13. In the present model, the tax structure affects the economic system through altering the inter- and intra-period margins of substitution as well as by altering wealth. An additional mechanism would recognize that in the context of over-lapping generations model, intertemporal-offsetting shifts of tax revenue of equal present value may alter private sector behavior through changes in the inter-generational wealth distribution.

14. The intertemporal labor supply elasticity, indicated by a, is 0.3, the coefficient of cost of adjustment for investment, indicated by b, is 40, and the intertemporal elasticity of substitution for consumption is unitary. In fact, in searching for the Ramsey's (second best) tax structure for this range of parameter values we find that income tax is superior to VAT. To examine the sensitivity of the results with respect to the values of the elasticities we also simulated the model with a lower cost-of-adjustment coefficient and a higher labor supply elasticity. Under these circumstances the welfare cost of VAT diminished relatively while the welfare cost of income taxes increased relatively.

15. The consequences of VAT harmonization accompanied by compensatory adjustments of the cash flow income tax can shed light on the likely effects of transforming a VAT system that is destination-based to a system that is source-based (since the cash flow income tax is equivalent to the source-based VAT). Under the destination-based system, the cross-country location of production of tradable goods is undistorted, while that of consumption is distorted. The opposite outcome holds under the source-based system. See Frenkel, Razin, and Sadka (1991).

16. To highlight the pure effects of tax conversions, we only consider cases of revenue neutrality. In the absence of revenue neutrality the tax conversion results in periodic budgetary deficits and surpluses.

17. The simulation analysis relaxes these assumptions by considering multi-period simulations with a richer tax structure that allows for the various taxes and incentives specified in the previous section.

18. We note that even though the effective tax-adjusted discount factors do not change following the first component of the tax conversion, the intratemporal tax ratio $(1 - r_w)/(1 - r_c)$ rises. As a result the supply of labor in each period rises.

19. More precisely, since under the cash flow formulation the income tax base is the level of output net of investment and the VAT base in the level of consumption, the difference between the two tax bases is the primary current account, that is, the current account net of debt service.

20. The foregoing analysis assumed that revenue neutrality obtains through appropriate changes in income taxes. If, on the other hand, budgetary corrections obtain through changes in consumption tax rates, then the effective discount factor governing investment and labor supply decisions would not change while the effective discount factor governing consumption decisions would change the supply of labor (the direction of the change would depend in an obvious way on the initial current account position). In that case, the domestic (and thereby the world) relative demand schedules in figure 14.1 would shift while the relative supply schedules would remain intact. For an analysis of such changes see Frenkel and Razin (1989).

21. Intuitively, the rise in the home country VAT accompanied by an equiproportional fall in the income tax broadens the tax base and raises tax revenue in the current period if the home country runs a current account deficit. To restore tax revenue, the income tax rate must be lowered. The opposite changes occur in the future period in which the current account position is in surplus, reflecting the intertemporal budget constraint. Similar considerations imply that the path of income tax abroad also steepens. As a result, the tax incentives to investment decline, yielding a fall in the world rate of interest.

22. As an example for induced changes in the functional distribution of income, consider the left-hand column of table 14.3. There, the VAT harmonization raises the share of labor and lowers the share of capital income in the domestic economy for both the short and medium runs while inducing opposite redistribution in the economy.

23. Our preliminary simulations of such an extended three-country model reveal that if the two countries joining the single market differ from each other significantly in terms of their saving and investment propensities, then the VAT harmonization impacts significantly on the levels of investment, employment, output, and welfare in the rest of the world (the third country). Furthermore, with some configuration of parameters, the presence of a third country affects some of the qualitative changes within the countries forming the single market. In order to examine some dimensions of the debate on "fortress" versus "open and enlarged" Europe, we report in appendix B some simulations of the effects of taxes on international borrowing within a three-country world. The simulations reveal that impediments to capital mobility between Europe and the rest of the world could exert significant negative welfare effects on the rest of the world.

24. Equation (14.1) implicitly incorporates both external and internal debt. To verify, denote internal debt by B^{HP} and the corresponding rate of interest by R_H. Analogously, denote the external debt by B^{FP} and the corresponding rate of interest by r_F. Debt flows in the budget constraint for period t are then

$$B_t^{HP} - B_{t-1}^H - (1 - \tau_{kt-1})(1 + \tau_{st-1})r_{Ht-1}B_{t-1}^{HP} + (1 - \tau_{bt})(B_t^{FP} - B_{t-1}^{FP})$$
$$- (1 - \tau_{kt-1})(1 + \tau_{st-1})r_{Ft-1}B_{t-1}^{HP}.$$

As formulated, the international borrowing tax applies to accumulation of external debt. Letting total debt be $B^P = (1/1 - \tau_b))B^{HP} + B^{FP}$ and applying the arbitrage condition, by which the after-tax rates of return are equal so that $r_F = (1 - \tau_b)r_H$, yields the last two terms on the right-hand side of equation (14.1).

17.2   Selected References

Abel, Andrew B. 1979. *Investment and the Value of Time*. New York, Garland.

Abel, Andrew B., and Blanchard, Olivier, 1983. The Present Value of Profits and Cyclical Movements in Investment. *Econometrica* 51 (May):675–692.

Adams, Charles, and Greenwood, Jeremy. 1985. Dual Exchange Rate Systems and Capital Controls: An Investigation. *Journal of International Economics* 18 (February):43–63.

Alexander, Sidney S. 1952. Effects of a Devaluation on a Trade Balance, *IMF Staff Papers* 2, No. 2, (April):263–278.

Altonji, Joseph G. 1985. The Intertemporal Substitution Model of Labor Market Fluctuations: An Empirical Analysis. *Review of Economic Studies* 49, no. 5 (special issue on unemployment), 783–824.

Arrow, Kenneth, J. 1963–64. The Role of Securities in the Optimal Allocation of Risk Bearing. *Review of Economic Studies* 31:91–96.

Aschauer, David A. 1985. Fiscal Policy and Aggregate Demand. *American Economic Review* 75 (March):117–127.

Aschauer, David A., and Greenwood, Jeremy. 1985. Macroeconomic Effects of Fiscal Policy. In *The New Monetary Economics,' Fiscal Issues and Unemployment*, edited by Karl Brunner and Allan H. Meltzer. Carnegie Rochester Conference Series on Public Policy 23, Autumn, 91–138.

Auerbach, Alan J., and Kotlikoff, Laurence J. 1987. *Dynamic Fiscal Policy*. London: Cambridge University Press.

Azariadis, Costas. 1978. Escalator Clauses and the Allocation of Cyclical Risks. *Journal of Economic Theory* 18 (June):119–155.

Bailey, Martin J. 1962. *National Income and the Price Level*. New York: McGraw-Hill.

Barro, Robert J. 1974. Are Government Bonds Net Wealth? *Journal of Political Economy* 82 (November/December):1095–1117.

Barro, Robert J. 1979. On the Determination of Public Debt. *Journal of Political Economy* 87 part 1 (October):940–971.

Barro, Robert J. 1981a. Output Effects of Government Purchases. *Journal of Political Economy* 89 (December):1086–1121.

Barro, Robert J. 1981b. *Money, Expectations, and Business Cycles: Essays in Macroeconomics.* New York: Academic Press.

Barro, Robert J., and Gordon, David B. 1983. A Positive Theory of Monetary Policy in a Natural Rate Model. *Journal of Political Economy* 91 (August):589–610.

Blanchard, Olivier J. 1984. Current and Anticipated Deficits, Interest Rates and Economic Activity. *European Economic Review* 25 (June):7–27.

Blanchard, Olivier J. 1985. Debt, Deficits, and Finite Horizons. *Journal of Political Economy* 93 (April):223–247.

Blanchard, Olivier J., and Summers, Lawrence H. 1984. Perspectives on High World Interest Rates. *Brookings Papers on Economic Activity* 2:273–333.

Blinder, Alan S., and Solow, Robert M. 1973. Does Fiscal Policy Matter? *Journal of Public Economics* 2 (November):319–337.

Boyer, Russell S. 1977. Devaluation and Portfolio Balance. *American Economic Review* 67 (March):54–63.

Bovenberg, Lans A. 1989. The Effects of Capital Income Taxation on International Competitiveness and Trade Flows. *American Economic Review* 79 (March):70–89.

Bovenberg, Lans A., and Goulder, Lawrence. 1989. Taxes on Old and New Capital Under International Capital Mobility: An Intertemporal General Equilibirum Assessment. Unpublished manuscript, International Monetary Fund, August.

Branson, William H. 1970. Monetary Policy and the New View of International Capital Movements. *Brookings Papers on Economic Activity* 2:235–262.

Branson, William H. 1986. Cases of Appreciation and Volatility of the Dollar. In *The U.S. Dollar-Recent Developments, Outlook, and Policy Options.* Kansas City: Federal Reserve Bank of Kansas City, 33–52.

Branson, William H., Frenkel, J. A., and Goldstein, M. (eds). 1990. *International Policy Coordination and Exchange Rate Fluctuations.* Chicago: The University of Chicago Press.

Brock, William, and Turnovsky, Stephen 1981. The Analysis of Macroeconomic Policies in Perfect Foresight Equilibrium. *International Economic Review* 84 (February):179–209.

Bruno, Michael. 1976. The Two-Sector Open Economy and the Real Exchange Rate. *American Economic Review* 66 (September):566–577.

Bruno, Michael. 1982. Adjustment and Structural Change under Raw Material Price Shocks. *Scandinavian Journal of Economics* 84:199–221.

Bryant, R. C., Henderson, D. W., Holtham, G., Hooper, P., and Symansky, S. A. 1988. *Empirical Macroeconomics for Interdependent Economics.* Washington, D.C.: The Brookings Institution.

Buchanan, James M. 1958. *Public Principles of Public Debt.* Homewood: Irwin.

Buiter, Willem H. 1981. Time Preference and International Lending and Borrowing in an Overlapping-Generations Model. *Journal of Political Economy* 89 (August): 769–797.

Buiter, Willem H. 1987. Fiscal Policy in Open Interdependent Economies. In *Economic Policy in Theory and Practice,* edited by Assaf Razin and Efraim Sadka. London: Macmillan, 101–144.

Buiter, Willem H. 1988. Death, Birth, Productivity Growth and Debt Neutrality. *The Economic Journal* 98 (June):279–293.

Buiter, Willem H. 1988. Structural and Stabilization Aspects of Fiscal and Financial Policy in the Dependent Economy. *Oxford Economic Papers* 40:220–245.

Bulow, Jeremy, and Rogoff, Kenneth. 1988. The Buyback Boondoggle. *Brookings Papers in Economic Activity* 2:675–698.

Bulow, Jeremy, and Rogoff, Kenneth. 1990. Cleaning Up the Debt Crisis Without Getting Taken to the Cleaners. *Journal of Economic Perspectives* 4:31–42.

Caballero, Ricardo J. 1991. "Earnings Uncertainty and Aggregate Wealth Accumulation." *The American Economic Review* 81 (September), 859–871.

Calvo, Guillermo A. 1978. On the Time Consistency of Optimal Policy in a Monetary Economy. *Econometrica* 46 (November):1411–1428.

Calvo, Guillermo A. 1987. On the Costs of Temporary Policy. *Journal of Development Economics* 27:245–261.

Calvo, Guillermo A. 1988. Costly Trade Liberalizations: Durable Goods and Capital Mobility. *IMF Staff Papers* 35 (September):461–473.

Calvo, Guillermo A., and Obstfeld, Maurice. 1988. Optimal Time-Consistent Fiscal Policy with Finite Lifetimes. *Econometrica,* forthcoming.

Canzoneri, M. B. and Diba, B. T. 1991. Fiscal Deficits, Financial Integration, and a Central Bank for Europe. NBER-TCER-CEPR Conference on Fiscal Policy in Open Macroeconomies, Tokyo, January.

Canzoneri, Matthew, and Gray, Jo Anna. 1985. Monetary Policy Games and the Consequences of Noncooperative Behavior. *International Economic Review* 26 (October):547–564.

Canzoneri, M. B. and Henderson, D. 1988. Is Sovereign Policymaking Bad. *Carnegie Rochester Conference Series on Public Policy* 28:93–140.

Canzoneri, Matthew, and Henderson, Dale, 1991. *Monetary Policy in Interdependent Economies*. Cambridge, Mass.: MIT Press.

Clower, Robert W. 1967. A Reconsideration of the Microfoundations of Monetary Theory. *Western Economic Journal* 6 (December):1–8.

Cohen, Daniel, and Sachs, Jeffrey, 1986. Growth and External Debt Under Risk of Debt Repudiation" *European Economic Review* 30 (June):529–558.

Cooper, Richard N. 1968. *The Economics of Interdependence*. New York: McGraw-Hill.

Cooper, Richard N. 1985. Economic Interdependence and Coordination of Economic Policies. In *Handbook of International Economics*, Vol. 2, edited by Ronald W. Jones and Peter B. Kenen. Amsterdam: North Holland, 1195–1234.

Corden, W. Max, and Neary, J. Peter. 1982. Booming Sector and De-Industrialization in a Small Open Economy. *Economic Journal* 92 (December):825–848.

Cnossen, Sijbren, and Shoup, Carl S. 1987. Coordination of Value-Added Taxes. In Cnossen Sijbren (ed.) *Tax Coordination in the European Community*. Antwerp: Kluwer Law and Taxation Publishers.

Dantas, Daniel V., and Dornbusch, Rudiger. 1984. Anticipated Budget Deficits and the Term Structure of Interest Rates. NBER Working Paper Series No. 1518, December.

Devereux, Michael. 1987. Fiscal Spending, the Terms of Trade, and Real Interest Rates. *Journal of International Economics* 22:219–236.

Devereux, Michael. 1988. Non-Traded Goods and the International Transmission of Fiscal Policy. *Canadian Journal of Economics* 21 (May):265–278.

Diamond, Peter A. 1965. National Debt in a Neoclassical Growth Model. *American Economic Review* 55 (December):1126–1150.

Diamond, Peter A. 1967. The Role of a Stock Market in a General Equilibrium Model with Technological Uncertainty. *American Economic Review* 57:759–776.

Diamond, Peter A., and Mirrlees, J. 1971. Optimal Taxation and Public Production. *American Economic Review* (March):8–17; (June):216–78.

Dixit, Avinash 1985. Tax Policies in Open Economies. In *Handbook of Public Economics*, edited by A. Auerbach and M. Feldstein. Amsterdam: North Holland.

Djajic, Slobodan. 1987a. Effects of Budgetary Policies in Open Economies: The Role of Intertemporal Consumption Substitution. *Journal of International Money and Finance* 6:373–383.

Djajic, Slobodan, 1987b. Temporary Import Quota and the Current Account. *Journal of International Economics* 22:349–362.

Dooley, Michael P. 1990. Market Valuation of External Debt. In *Analytical Issues in Debt*, edited by Jacob A. Frenkel, Michael P. Dooley, and Peter Wickham. Washington, D.C.: International Monetary Fund, 75–82.

Dooley, Michael P. 1991. Market-Based Debt Reduction Schemes. *Analytical Issues in Debt*, edited by Jacob A. Frenkel, Michael P. Dooley, and Peter Wickham. (Washington, D.C.: International Monetary Fund, 258–278.

Dornbusch, Rudiger. 1976. Expectations and Exchange Rate Dynamics. *Journal of Political Economy* 84 (December):1161–1176.

Dornbusch, Rudiger. 1980. *Open Economy Macroeconomics*. New York: Basic Books.

Dornbusch, Rudiger. 1983. Real Interest Rates, Home Goods, and Optimal External Borrowing. *Journal of Political Economy* 91 (February):141–153.

Dornbusch, Rudiger. 1985. Intergenerational and International Trade, *Journal of international Economics* 18 (February):123–139.

Dornbusch, Rudiger. 1986. Special Exchange Rates for Capital Account Transactions. *The World Bank Economic Review* 1 (September):3–33.

Eaton, Jonathan, and Gersovitz, Mark. 1981. Poor-Country Borrowing in Private Financial Markets and the Repudiation Issue. *Princeton Studies in International Finance* 47 (June).

Edwards, Sebastian. 1989. *Real Exchange Rates, Devaluations and Adjustment*. Cambridge; Mass.: MIT Press.

Emerson, Michael, Aujean, Michel, Catinat, Michel, Goybet, Philippe, and Jacquemin, Alexis. 1988. Fiscal Barrier. *The European Economy* (March):45–107.

Engel, Charles, and Kletzer, Kenneth. 1990. Tariffs and Saving in a Model with New Generations. *Journal of International Economics* 28:71–91.

Faig, Miguel. 1991. A Simple Economy with Human Capital: Transitional Dynamics, Technology Shocks, and Fiscal Policies. Working Paper No. 9121, May, Institute for Policy Analysis, University of Toronto.

Feldstein, Martin. 1988. Distinguished Lecture on Economics in Government: Thinking about International Economic Coordination, *Journal of Economic Perspectives* 2 (Springer):3–13.

Feldstein, Martin S. 1974. Tax Incidence in a Growing Economy with Variable Factor Supply. *Quarterly Journal of Economics* 88 (November):551–573.

Feldstein, Martin S. 1977. The Surprising Incidence of a Tax on Pure Rent: A New Answer to an Old Question. *Journal of Political Economy* 85 (April):349–360.

Feldstein, Martin S. 1982. Government Deficits and Aggregate Demand. *Journal of Monetary Economics* 9 (January):1–20.

Feldstein, Martin S. 1986. The Effects of Fiscal Policies When Incomes Are Uncertain: A Contradiction to Ricardian Equivalence. NBER Working Paper Series No. 2062. November.

Feldstein, Martin, and Horioka, C. 1980. Domestic Saving and International Capital Flows. *Economic Journal* 90:314–329.

Fischer, Stanley. 1986. Contracts, Credibility and Disinflation. In *Indexing, Inflation and Economic Policy*. Cambridge, Mass: MIT Press, 221–246.

Fisher, Irving. 1930. *Theory of Interest*. New York: Macmillan.

Fleming, J. Marcus. 1962. Domestic Financial Policies under Fixed and under Floating Exchange Rates. *IMF Staff Papers* 9 (November):369–379.

Flood, Robert P. 1978. Exchange Rate Expectations in Dual Exchange Markets. *Journal of International Economics* 8 (February):65–78.

Floyd, John E. 1969. International Capital Movements and Monetary Equilibrium. *American Economic Review* 59, part 1 (September):472–492.

Frenkel, Jacob A., and Johnson, Harry G., eds. 1976. *The Monetary Approach to the Balance of Payments*. London: Allen & Unwin.

Frenkel, Jacob A., and Mussa, Michael L. 1985. Asset Markets, Exchange Rates and the Balance of Payments. In *Handbook of International Economics*, Vol. 2, edited by Ronald W. Jones and Peter B. Kenen. Amsterdam: North Holland, 680–747.

Frenkel, Jacob A., and Razin, Assaf. 1985a. Government Spending, Debt and International Economic Interdependence. *Economic Journal* 95 (September):619–639.

Frenkel, Jacob A., and Razin, Assaf. 1985b. Fiscal Expenditures and International Economic Interdependence. *International Economic Policy Coordination*, edited by Willem H. Buiter and Richard C. Marston. Cambridge: Cambridge University Press, 37–73.

Frenkel, Jacob A., and Razin, Assaf. 1986a. The International Transmission and Effects of Fiscal Policies. *American Economic Review* 76 (May):330–335.

Frenkel, Jacob A., and Razin, Assaf. The International Transmission and Effects of Fiscal Policies. 1986b. *American Economic Review* 76 (May):330–335.

Frenkel, Jacob A., and Razin, Assaf. Fiscal Policies in the World Economy. 1986c. *Journal of Political Economy* 94, Part I (June):564–594.

Frenkel, Jacob A., and Razin, Assaf. 1986d. Real Exchange Rates, Interest Rates and Fiscal Policies. *The Economic Studies Quarterly* 37 (June):99−113.

Frenkel, Jacob A., and Razin, Assaf. 1987a. The International Transmission of Fiscal Expenditures and Budget Deficits in the World Economy. In *Economic Policy in Theory and Practice*, edited by Assaf Razin and Efraim Sadka. London: Macmillan, 51−96.

Frenkel, Jacob A., and Razin, Assaf. 1987. The Mundell-Fleming Model: A Quarter Century Later. *IMF Staff Papers* 34 (4), December 567−620.

Frenkel, Jacob A., and Razin, Assaf. 1987c. *Fiscal Policies in a World Economy: An Intertemporal Approach*. Cambridge, Mass.: MIT Press.

Frenkel, Jacob A., and Razin, Assaf. 1988a. Exchange Rate Management Viewed as Tax Policies. *European Economic Review* 33 (December):761−781.

Frenkel, Jacob A., and Razin, Assaf. 1988b. *Spending, Taxes and Deficits; International-Intertemporal Approach*. Princeton, N.J.; Princeton Studies in International Finance No. 63, International Finance Section.

Frenkel, Jacob A., and Razin, Assaf. 1989. International Effects of Tax Reforms. *The Economic Journal* 99 (March):38−59.

Frenkel, Jacob A., and Razin, Assaf. 1992. Fiscal Policies in Open Economies. In Peter Newman (ed.), *The Now Pelgrave Dictionary of Money and Finance*. London: Macmillan Press.

Frenkel, Jacob A., Razin, Assaf and Sadka, Efraim. 1991. *International Taxation in an Integrated World*. Cambridge, Mass., MIT Press.

Frenkel, Jacob A., Razin, Assaf, and Symansky, Steve. 1990. International Spillovers of Taxation. In *International Aspects of Taxation* edited by A. Razin and J. Slemrod. Chicago, Ill.; University of Chicago Press.

Frenkel, Jacob A., Razin, Assaf, and Symansky, Steve. 1991. The International Macroeconomic Effects of VAT Harmonization. *IMF Staff Papers* (December):38.

Frenkel, Jacob A., and Rodriguez, Carlos A. 1975. Portfolio Equilibrium and the Balance of Payments: A Monetary Approach. *American Economy Review* 65 (September):674−688.

Froot, Kenneth A. 1988. Credibility, Real Interest Rates, and the Optimal Speed of Trade Liberalization. *Journal of International Economics* 25 (August):71−93.

Fried, Joel. 1980. The Intergenerational Distribution of the Gains from Technical Change and from International Trade. *Canadian Journal of Economics* 13 (February):65−81.

Friedman, Milton. 1957. *A Theory of the Consumption Function*. Princeton: Princeton University Press.

Ghez, Gilbert R., and Becker, Gary S. 1975. *The Allocation of Time and Goods over the Life Cycle*. New York: Columbia University Press.

Giovannini, Alberto. 1989. National Tax Systems vs. European Capital Market. *Economic Policy* 9 (October):345−386.

Greenwood, Jeremy. 1983. Expectations, the Exchange Rate and the Current Account. *Journal of Monetary Economics* 12 (November):543−569.

Greenwood, Jeremy, and Kimbrough, Kent P. 1985. Capital Controls and Fiscal Policy in the World Economy. *Canadian Journal of Economics* 18 (November):743−765.

Greenwood, Jeremy, and Kimbrough, Kent P. 1986. An Investigation in the Theory of Foreign Exchange Controls. Duke University, Working Paper, No. 86 (13).

Gregory, R. G. 1976. Some Implications of the Growth of the Mineral Sector. *The Australian Journal of Agricultural Economics* 20 (August):71−91.

Gordon, Roger H. 1986. Taxation of Investment and Saving in a World Economy. *American Economic Review* 76:1087−1102.

Gordon, Roger H. and Levinsohn, James. 1990. The Linkage Between Domestic Taxes and Border Taxes. In *Taxation in the Global Economy*, edited by A. Razin and J. Slemrod. Chicago: University of Chicago Press.

Hall, Robert E. 1978. Stochastic Implications of the Life Cycle-Permanent Income Hypothesis: Theory and Evidence. *Journal of Political Economy* 86 (December):971−987.

Hamada, Koichi. 1976. Strategic Analysis of Monetary Interdependence. *Journal of Political Economy* 84, part 1 (August):677−700.

Hamada, Koichi. 1985. *The Political Economy of International Monetary Interdependence*, Cambridge: MIT Press.

Harberger, Arnold C. 1950. Currency Depreciation, Income and the Balance of Trade. *Journal of Political Economy* 58 (February):47−60.

Hayashi, Fumio. 1982. Tobin's Marginal q and Average q: A Neoclassical interpretation. *Econometrica* 50 (January):213−224.

Heckman, James J. 1974. Shadow Prices, Market Wages and Labor Supply. *Econometrica* 42 (July):679−694.

Helpman, Elhanan. 1981. An Exploration in the Theory of Exchange Rate Regimes. *Journal of Political Economy* 89 (October):865−890.

Helpman, Elhanan. 1991. The Simple Analytics of Debt-Equity Swaps and Debt Forgiveness. *American Economic Review* 81 (March):20−35.

Helpman, Elhanan, and Razin, Assaf. 1978. *A Theory of International Trade under Uncertainty*. New York: Academic Press.

Helpman, Elhanan, and Razin, Assaf. 1979. Towards a Consistent Comparison of Alternative Exchange Rate Regimes. *Canadian Journal of Economics* 12 (August): 394–409.

Helpman, Elhanan, and Razin, Assaf. 1982. A Comparison of Exchange Rate Regimes in the Presence of Imperfect Capital Markets. *International Economic Review* 23 (June):365–388.

Helpman, Elhanan, and Razin, Assaf. 1984. The Role of Saving and Investment in Exchange Rate Determination Under Alternative Monetary Mechanisms. *Journal of Monetary Economics* 13 (May):307–325.

Helpman, Elhanan, and Razin, Assaf. 1987. Exchange Rate Management: Intertemporal Tradeoffs. *American Economic Review* 77 (March):107–123.

Hubbard, R. Glenn, and Judd. Kenneth L. 1986. Liquidity Constraints, Fiscal Policy, and Consumption. *Brookings Paper on Economic Activity* 1:1–50.

Ingersoll, Jonathan E., Jr. 1987. *A Theory of Financial Decision Making.* Rowman and Littlefield Publishers, New York.

International Monetary Fund. *International Financial Statistics.* Washington, D.C.: International Monetary Fund, various issues.

International Monetary Fund. *World Economic Outlook.* Washington, D.C.: International Monetary Fund, various issues.

Inversen, Carl. 1935. *Aspects of the Theory of International Capital Movements.* London: Oxford University Press.

Johnson, Harry G. 1956. The Transfer Problem and Exchange Stability. *Journal of Political Economy* 59 (June):212–225.

Johnson, Harry G. 1958. Towards a General Theory of the Balance of Payments. In *International Trade and Economic Growth,* by Harry G. Johnson, London: Allen & Unwin, 153–168.

Judd, Kenneth L. 1987. A Dynamic Theory of Factor Taxation. *American Economic Review* 77 (May):42–48.

Kehoe, Patrick. 1989. Policy Cooperation Among Benevolent Governments May Be Undesirable. *Review of Economic Studies* 56:289–96.

Kenen, Peter B. 1985. Macroeconomic Theory and Policy: How the Closed Economy Was Opened. In *Handbook of International Economics,* Vol. 2, edited by Ronald W. Jones and Peter B. Kenen. Amsterdam: North Holland, 625–677.

Keynes, John M. 1929. The German Transfer Problem. *Economic Journal* 39 (March): 1–7.

Kimbrough, Kent P. 1986. Foreign Aid and Optimal Fiscal Policy. *Canadian Journal of Economics* 17 (February):35–61.

King, Mervin A. 1983. The Economics of Saving. NBER Working Paper Series No. 1247, October.

Kletzer, Kenneth, M. 1984. Asymmetries of Information and LDC Borrowing with Sovereign Risk. *Economic Journal* 94 (June):287–307.

Kochin, Levis. 1974. Are Future Taxes Discounted by Consumers? *Journal of Money, Credit, and Banking* 6 (August):385–394.

Kormendi, Roger. 1983. Government Debt, Government Spending, and Private Sector Behavior. *American Economic Review* 73 (December):994–1010.

Kotlikoff, Lawrence, J., Razin, Assaf, and Rosenthal, Robert W. 1990. A Strategic Altruism Model in Which Ricardian Equivalence Does Not Hold. *Economic Journal* 100 (December):1261–1269.

Krugman, Paul R. 1985. International Debt-Strategies in an Uncertain World. In *International Debt and the Developing Countries*, edited by Gordon W. Smith and John T. Cuddington.

Krugman, Paul R. 1990. Market Based Debt-Reduction Schemes. In *Analytical Issues in Debt*, edited by Jacob A. Frenkel, Michael P. Dooley, and Peter Wickham. Washington, D.C.: International Monetary Fund, 258–278.

Kydland, Finn E., and Prescott, Edward. 1980. A Competitive Theory of Fluctuations and the Feasibility and Desirability of Stabilization Policy. In *Rational Expectations and Economic Policy*, edited by Stanley Fischer. Chicago: University of Chicago Press, 169–198.

Kydland, Finn E., and Prescott, Edward C. 1982. Time to Build and Aggregate Fluctuations. *Econometrica* 50 (September):1345–1370.

Laursen, Svend, and Metzler, Lloyd A. 1950. Flexible Exchange Rates and the Theory of Employment. *Review of Economics and Statistics* 32 (November):281–299.

Leiderman, Leonardo, and Blejer, Mario I. 1988. Modelling and Testing Ricardian Equivalence: A Survey. *IMF Staff Papers* 35 (March):1–35.

Leiderman, Leonardo, and Razin, Assaf. 1988. Testing Ricardian Neutrality with an Intertemporal Stochastic Model. *Journal of Money Credit and Banking*

Leiderman, Leonardo, and Razin, Assaf. 1991. Determinants of External Imbalances: The Role of Taxes, Government Spending and Productivity. *Journal of the Japanese and International Economies* 5 (December).

Lerner, Abba P. 1936. The Symmetry Between Export and Import taxes. *Economica* 3 (August). 306–313.

Levy, H., and Markowitz, H. 1979. Approximating Expected Utility by a Function of Mean and Variance. *American Economic Review* 69:308–317.

Lopez, Ramon, and Rodrik, Dani. 1990. Trade Restrictions with Imported Intermediate Inputs: When Does the Trade Balance Improve? *Journal of Development Economics* 34 (November):329–338.

Lucas, Robert E., Jr. 1967. Optimal Investment Policy and the Flexible Accelerator. *International Economic Review* 8 (February):78–85.

Lucas, Robert E., Jr. 1978. Asset Prices in an Exchange Economy. *Econometrica* 46:1429–1445.

Lucas, Robert E., Jr. 1980. Equilibrium in a Pure Currency Economy. *Economic Inquiry* 18 (April):203–220.

Lucas, Robert E., Jr. 1981. *Studies in Business Cycle Theory*. Cambridge: MIT Press.

Lucas, Robert E., Jr. 1982. Interest Rates and Currency Prices in a Two-Country World. *Journal of Monetary Economics* 10 (November):335–359.

Lucas, Robert E., Jr. 1990. Supply Side Economies: An Analytical Review *Oxford Economics Papers* 42:293–316.

Lucas, Robert E., Jr., and Prescott, Edward C. 1971. Investment under Uncertainty. *Econometrica* 39 (September):659–681.

Lucas, Robert E., Jr., and Rapping, Leonard A. 1969. Real Wages, Employment and Inflation. *Journal of Political Economy* 77 (September/October):721–754.

Lucas, Robert E., Jr., and Stokey, Nancy L. 1983. Optimal Fiscal and Monetary Policy in an Economy Without Capital. *Journal of Monetary Economics* 12:55–93.

Machlup, Fritz. 1943. *International Trade and the National Income Multiplier*. Philadelphia: Blakiston.

MaCurdy, Thomas E. 1981. An Empirical Model of Labor Supply in a Life Cycle Setting. *Journal of Political Economy* 89 (December):1059–1085.

Mankiw, Gregory N. 1987. Government Purchases and Real Interest Rates. *Journal of Political Economy* 95 (April):407–419.

Mankiw, Gregory N., Rotemberg, Julio J., and Summers, Lawrence H. 1985. Intertemporal Substitution in Macroeconomics. *Quarterly Journal of Economics* 100 (February):225–251.

Marion, Nancy P. 1984. Nontraded Goods, Oil Price Increases, and the Current Account. *Journal of International Economics* 16 (February):29–44.

Marston, Richard C. 1985. Stabilization Policies in Open Economies. In *Handbook of International Economics*, Vol. 2, edited by Ronald W. Jones and Peter B. Kenen. Amsterdam: North Holland, 859–916.

McKinnon, Ronald I. 1969. Portfolio Balance and International Payments Adjustment. In *Monetary Problems of the International Economy*, edited by Alexander K. Swoboda and Robert A. Mundell. Chicago: University of Chicago Press, 199–234.

Meade, James E. 1951. *The Theory of International Economic Policy: The Balance of Payments*, Vol. 1. London: Oxford University Press.

Merton, R. C. 1971. Optimum Consumption and Portfolio Rules in a Continuous-Time Model. *Journal of Economic Theory* 3 (December):373–413.

Metzer, Allan H., Cukierman, Alex, and Richard, Scott F. 1991. *Political Economy*. New York: Oxford Economic Press.

Mendoza, Enrique. 1991. Real Business Cycles in A Small Open Economy, *American Economic Review* 81 (September):797–810.

Mendoza, Enrique. (1991a). A Quantitative Examination of Current Account Dynamics in Equilibrium models of Barter Economies, the IMF, draft.

Metzler, Lloyd A. 1942a. Underemployment Equilibrium in International Trade. *Econometrica* 10 (April):97–112.

Metzler, Lloyd A. 1942b. The Transfer Problem Reconsidered. *Journal of Political Economy* 50 (June):397–414.

Modigliani, Franco. 1961. Long-Run Implications of Alternative Fiscal Policies and the Burden of the National Debt. *Economic Journal* 71 (December):730–755.

Modigliani, Franco. 1987. The Economics of Public Deficits. In *Economic Policy in Theory and Practice*, edited by Assaf Razin and Efraim Sadka. London: Macmillan, 3–44.

Modigliani, Franco, and Brumberg, Richard. 1954. Utility Analysis and the Consumption Function: An Interpretation of Cross Section Data. In *Post-Keynesian Economics*, edited by Kenneth K. Kurihara, New Brunswick: Rutgers University Press, 383–436.

Mundell, Robert A. 1960. The Pure Theory of International Trade. *American Economic Review* 50 (March):67–110.

Mundell, Robert A. 1964. A Reply: Capital Mobility and Size. *Canadian Journal of Economics and Political Science* 30 (August):421–431.

Mundell, Robert A. 1968. *International Economics*. New York: Macmillan.

Mundell, Robert A. 1971. *Monetary Theory*. Pacific Palisades: Goodyear.

Murphy, Robert G. 1986. Tariffs, Non-Traded Goods and Fiscal Policy. *The International Trade Journal* 1 (Winter):193–211.

Musgrave, Peggy. 1987. International Tax Competition and Gains from Tax Harmonization. HBER Working Paper No. 3152 (October), Cambridge, Mass.

Mussa, Michael L. 1979. Macroeconomic Interdependence and the Exchange Rate Regime. In *International Economic Policy: Theory and Evidence*, edited by Rudiger Dornbusch and Jacob A. Frenkel, Baltimore: Johns Hopkins University Press, 160–204.

Neary, J. Peter, and Purvis, Douglas D. 1982. Sectoral Shocks in a Dependent Economy: Long-Run Adjustment and Short-Run Accommodation. *Scandinavian Journal of Economics* 84:229–253.

Nerlove, Marc, Razin, Assaf, and Sadka, Efraim. 1988. A Bequest-Constrained Economy: Welfare Analysis. *Journal of Public Economics* 37, 203–220.

O'Driscoll, Gerald P. 1977. The Ricardian Nonequivalence Theorem. *Journal of Political Economy* 85 (February):207–210.

Obstfeld, Maurice. 1982. Aggregate Spending and the Terms of Trade: Is There a Laursen-Metzler Effect? *Quarterly Journal of Economics* 97 (May):251–270.

Obstfeld, Maurice. 1986. Capital Controls, the Dual Exchange Rate and Devaluation. *Journal of International Economics* 20 (February):1–20.

Obstfeld, Maurice, and Stockman Alan C. 1985. Exchange Rate Dynamics. In *Handbook of International Economics*, Vol. 2, edited by Ronald W. Jones and Peter B. Kenen. Amsterdam: North Holland, 917–977.

Ohlin, Bertil. 1929. The Reparation Problem: A Discussion. *Economic Journal* 39 (June):172–178.

Ostry, Jonathan D. 1988. The Balance of Trade, Terms of Trade, and Real Exchange Rate: An Intertemporal Optimizing Framework. *IMF Staff Papers* 35 (December):541–573.

Ostry, Jonathan D. 1989. Government Purchases and Relative Prices in a Two-Country World. IMF Working Paper 89/28 (April).

Ostry, Jonathan D. 1990. Tariffs and the Current Account: The Role of Initial Distortions. *Canadian Journal of Economics* 23 (May):348–356.

Ostry, Jonathan D. 1991a. Tariffs, Real Exchange Rates, and the Trade Balance in a Two-Country World. *European Economic Review* 35 (July):1127–1142.

Ostry, Jonathan D. 1991b. Trade Liberalization in Developing Countries: Initial Trade Distortions and Imported Intermediate Inputs. *IMF Staff Papers* 38 (September):447–479.

Ostry, Jonathan D. 1992a. Trade Restrictions with Imported Intermediate Inputs: A Comment. *Journal of Development Economics*, forthcoming.

Oudiz, Gilles, and Sachs, Jeffrey D. 1985. International Policy Coordination in Dynamic Macroeconomic Models. In *International Economic Policy Coordination*, edited by Willem H. Buiter and Richard C. Marston. Cambridge, Mass.: Cambridge University Press, 274–319.

Pechman, Joseph, A., ed. 1988. *World Tax Reform: A Progress Report*. Washington, D.C.: The Brookings Institution.

Penati, Alessandro. 1987. Government Spending and the Real Exchange Rate. *Journal of International Economics* 22 (May):237–256.

Perraudin, W. P. M., and Pujol, T. 1991. European Fiscal Harmonization and the French Economy. *IMF Staff Papers*, October.

Persson, Torsten. 1984. Real Transfers in Fixed Exchange Rate Systems and the International Adjustment Mechanism. *Journal of Monetary Economics* 13 (May): 349–369.

Persson, Torsten. 1985. Deficits and Intergenerational Welfare in Open Economies. *Journal of International Economics* 19 (August):1–19.

Persson, Torsten, and Svensson, Lars E. O. 1985. Current Account Dynamics and the Terms of Trade: Harberger-Laursen-Metzler Two Generations Later. *Journal of Political Economy* 93 (February):43–65.

Persson, Torsten, and Tabellini, Guido. 1990. *Macroeconomic Policy, Credibility and Politics*. New York: Harwood Academic Publishers.

Pitchford, John, and Turnovsky, Stephen J., eds. 1977. *Applications of Control Theory of Economic Analysis*. New York: North-Holland.

Polak, Jacques J. 1957. Monetary Analysis of Income Formation and Payments Problems. *IMF Staff Papers* 6 (November):1–50.

Poterba, James M., and Summers, Lawrence H. 1986. Finite Lifetimes and the Crowding-Out Effects of Budget Deficits. NBER Working Paper Series No. 1955.

Prais, S. J. 1961. Some Mathematical Notes on the Quantity Theory of Money in an Open Economy. *IMF Staff Papers* 8 (May):212–226.

Purvis, Douglas D. 1985. Public Sector Deficits, International Capital Movements, and the Domestic Economy: The Medium-term Is the Message. *Canadian Journal of Economics* 18 (November):723–742.

Razin, Assaf. 1984. Capital Movements, Intersectoral Resource Shifts and the Trade Balance. *European Economic Review* 26 (October/November):135–152.

Razin, Assaf. 1990. Fiscal Policies and the Integrated World Stock Market. *Journal of International Economics* 29:109–122.

Razin, Assaf, and Sadka, Efraim, eds. 1987. *Economic Policy in Theory and Practice: Essays in Memory of Abba P. Lerner*. London: Macmillan.

Razin, Assaf, and Sadka, Efraim. 1991. Efficient Investment Incentives in the Presence of Capital Flight. *Journal of International Economics* 31:171–181.

Razin, Assaf, and Svensson, Lars E. O. 1983. The Current Account and the Optimal Government Debt. *Journal of International Money and Finance* 2 (August):215–224.

Razin, A. and Svensson, L. E. O. 1983. Trade Taxes and the Current Account *Economic Letters*, 13, no. 1:55–58.

Robinson, R. 1952. A Graphical Analysis of the Foreign Trade Multiplier. *Economic Journal* 62 (September):546–564.

Rodriguez, Carlos A. 1979. Short- and Long-Run Effects of Monetary and Fiscal Policies Under Flexible Exchange Rates and Perfect Capital Mobility. *American Economic Review* 69 (March):176–182.

Rodrik, Dani. 1987. Trade and Capital Account Liberalization in a Keynesian Economy. *Journal of International Economics* 23 (August):113–129.

Rodrik, Dani. 1989. Promises, Promises: Credible Policy Reform via Signalling. *Economic Journal* 99 (September):756–772.

Rogoff, Kenneth. 1985. Can International Policy Coordination be Counterproductive? *Journal of International Economics* 18 (May):199–217.

Rogoff, Kenneth. 1986. Reputational Constraints on Monetary Policy. NBER Working Paper Series No. 1986, July.

Rueff, Jacques. 1929. Mr. Keynes' Views on the Transfer Problem: A Criticism. *Economic Journal* 39 (September):388–399.

Sachs, Jeffrey D. 1981. The Current Account and Macroeconomic Adjustment in the 1970's. *Brookings Papers on Economic Activity* 1:201–268.

Sachs, Jeffrey D. 1984. Theoretical Issues in International Borrowing. *Princeton Studies in International Finance* 54 (July).

Sachs, Jeffrey D. 1985. External Debt and Macroeconomic Performance in Latin America and East Asia. *Brookings Papers on Economic Activity* 2:523–574.

Samuelson, Paul A. 1952. The Transfer Problem and Transport Costs: The Terms of Trade When Impediments Are Absent. *Economic Journal* 62 (June):278–304.

Samuelson, Paul A. 1958. An Exact Consumption-Loan Model with or without the Social Contrivance of Money. *Journal of Political Economy* 66 (December):467–482.

Sargent, Thomas J. 1978. Estimation of Dynamic Labor Demand Schedules under Rational Expectations. *Journal of Political Economy* 86 (December):1009–1044.

Sinn, Hans-Werner. 1990. Tax Harmonization and Tax Competition in Europe. NBER Working Paper No. 3263 (February), Cambridge, Mass.

Stockman, Alan C. 1980. A Theory of Exchange Rate Determination. *Journal of Political Economy* 88 (August):673–698.

Svensson, Lars E. O. 1981. Oil Prices, Welfare and the Trade Balance. *Quarterly Journal of Economics* 94:649–672.

Svensson, Lars E. O. 1988. Trade in Risky Assets. *American Economic Review* 78.

Svensson, Lars E. O., and Razin, Assaf. 1983. The Terms of Trade and the Current Account: The Harberger-Laursen-Metzler Effect. *Journal of Political Economy* 91 (February):91–125.

Swoboda, Alexander K., and Dornbusch, Rudiger. 1973. Adjustment, Policy, and Monetary Equilibrium in a Two-Country Model. In *International Trade and Money*, edited by Michael G. Connolly and Alexander K. Swoboda. London: Allen & Unwin, 225–261.

Tait, Alan A. 1988. *Value Added Tax: International Practice and Problems*. Washington, D.C.: International Monetary Fund.

Tanzi, Vito, and Bovenberg, Lans. 1989. Economic Interdependence and the International Implications of Supply-Side Policies. In *A Supply-Side for Germany*, edited by G. Fels, and George M. von Furstenberg. New York, 153–80.

Tobin, James. 1969. A General Equilibrium Approach to Monetary Theory. *Journal of Money, Credit, and Banking* 1 (February):15–29.

Uzawa, Hirofurni. 1969. Time Preference and the Penrose Effect in a Two-Class Model of Economic Growth. *Journal of Political Economy* 77, part 2 (July/August): 628–652.

Van Wijnbergen, Sweder. 1986. On Fiscal Deficits, the Real Exchange Rate and the World Rate of Interest. *European Economic Review* 30 (October):1013–1023.

van Wijnbergen, Sweder. 1987. Tariffs, Employment and the Current Account: Real Wage Resistance and the Macroeconomics of Protectionism. *International Economic Review* 28:691–706.

Weil, Philippe. 1987. Overlapping Families of Infinitely Lived Agents. *Quarterly Journal of Economics*, forthcoming.

Yaari, Menahem E. 1965. Uncertain Lifetime, Life Insurance, and the Theory of the Consumer. *Review of Economic Studies* 32 (April):137–50.

Index

Adjustment path, and short-run equilibria, 39–40
Aggregate consumption, 204, 252
  dynamics of, 205–208
Aggregate consumption function, 195, 219
  described, 196, 201–204
Aggregate wealth, 219
  composition of, 202–204
Allocation of spending, temporal and intertemporal, 139–140
Analytical framework. *See also* Income expenditure model; Intertemporal macroeconomic model; Overlapping-generations model
  distortionary taxes in, 278–280
  in multiple-good world, 137–140
  real exchange rate in, 291–293
Asset demands, characteristics of, 345–347
Assets, 51–52, 348–349

Balanced-budget policies, 223, 227–228, 241
Balance of payments, 65, 123, 225
  current account of, 228–229
  short and long run, 25–26, 47
Balance of trade, 22–23, 36, 157, 184, 282
  and budget deficit, 287–288
  output and consumption in, 206–207
  and supply shocks, 112, 122–124, 187–188
  surplus and deficits in, 116–117
  and terms of trade, 145–151, 152(table)
Barro-Gordon one-period game, 414–415
Benelux countries, 359
Bond-financed government spending. *See* Government spending, debt-financed rise in

Borrowing, 290
  and consumption motives, 118–122
  taxes on, 153, 278, 386–389
Budget constraints, 58, 322, 427n1
  and capital-income taxes, 269–270, 271–272
  and consumption, 326–327
  formulation of, 359–361
  household, 259, 263–264, 267–268
  multiple-good world, 138–140
  periodic and lifetime, 278–279
  private-sector lifetime, 291–292
Budget deficits, 1, 24, 85, 277, 309
  and consumption, 210–211
  and consumption taxes, 280–282, 391–393
  and current account, 411–412
  and distortionary taxes, 195, 329
  dynamic simulations of, 393–396
  and government spending, 252–253
  impacts of, 243–249
  with income tax, 282–285
  and international-intertemporal model, 410–411
  policies of, 234–235
  and rate of interest, 288–289
  and taxes, 212–213, 240, 301–303, 305
  and variable labor supply, 285–288
  wealth effects of, 208–212, 235–236
  and welfare, 241–242

Canada, 2, 6, 10, 400
Capital, 286, 324, 429n7
  and budget constraints, 263–264, 267–268
  and production, 258–259
  return to, 320–321

Capital accumulation, 267
Capital Asset Pricing Model (CAPM), 342–343, 350
Capital markets, 320, 410, 412, 415
access to, 116, 285
and assets, 51–52
integration of, 49, 51, 315, 333, 384
Capital mobility, 49, 319, 327, 340
and fixed exchange rates, 53–65, 105–106
and flexible exchange rates, 65–80, 81–82, 106
Cash flow taxes, 365(fig.), 371, 376, 387, 429–430n10
Capital tax system, and VAT harmonization, 367–369(figs.)
CAPM. See Capital Asset Pricing Model
Consumer price index, domestic, 105
Consumption, 10, 115, 117, 126, 157, 188, 253, 284, 333, 361, 362, 382, 387, 413, 429n7
and budget constraints, 326–327
and budget deficits, 195, 210–211
factors of, 263–265
of foreign goods, 249–251
generational, 211–212
and government spending, 344–345
growth rates of, 230, 289–290, 400–404
of importables and exportables, 155–156
and income, 111, 118
and income tax, 271, 278
and marginal rate of substitution, 165–166
paths of, 251–252, 399–400
and portfolio selection, 347–348
private sector, 162, 172, 293, 295
relative demands for, 286–287
and stock market model, 349–350
and supply shock, 112, 122–124
and tax cuts, 212–213
and terms of trade, 158, 175
of tradable and nontradable goods, 309–311, 325–326
variability of, 112–113
and world output, 131–132
Consumption augmenting, 111
Consumption-augmenting motive, 118, 120–121
Consumption-based price index, 139. See Price index, consumption-based
Consumption demand, elasticity of, 292–293
Consumption equation, 214–218
Consumption function, 219

Consumption-saving choice, 356
Consumption smoothing, 111
Consumption-smoothing motive, 118, 119–120, 121(table), 211
Consumption taxes, 270–271, 284–285, 308, 309, 328, 425n1. See also Value-added taxes
and budget deficits, 391–393, 393–396
conversion to, 306–307
deficits with, 280–282
Consumption tilting, 111
Consumption-tilting channel, 165–166, 167
Consumption-tilting motive, 118, 120, 121(table)
Current account, and budget deficits, 411–412
Current-account adjustment, 15
Current account imbalances, and tax conversions, 372–375
Current-account positions, 6, 384

Debt, 15, 51, 80, 111, 252, 275, 410, 416, 431–432n24
accumulation of, 195, 203
and domestic output, 70–71
life insurance and, 196–197
private-sector, 72–73, 74, 75, 101–102
public-sector, 8, 73–74
redistribution of, 133, 231–232
Debt commitment, 138
Debt-revaluation effects, 72
Debt service, 278
Deflator effect, 142, 144, 147
Demand, 180, 184, 220, 221
for goods, 238–239, 297
and interest rate, 223, 229–230
and world debt, 231–232
world relative, 294, 302, 304
Demand schedule, 231, 304, 305
Denmark, 357
Discount factor, 154, 157, 303, 431n18
and current investment, 373–374
effective, 279, 281
and investment, 375–376
real, 140, 141, 151
and tradable goods, 292, 309–311
and world interest rate, 324–325
Distortionary taxes, 288
in analytical framework, 278–280
and budget deficits, 277, 329
Dividends, 272–273
Dynamic inconsistency, 414–415

EC. *See* European Community
Economic integration, of European
    Community, 257–258
Economic variables, comovements of,
    10–15
Economies, interdependence of, 417–418
Elasticities of substitution, 200, 297, 312
Employment. *See* Labor supply
Equilibrium, 118, 220, 221, 232, 277, 298,
    320, 414
    goods-market, 32, 66, 77
    and income-expenditure model, 53–54
    money-market, 76, 78, 93
    trade-balance, 95–96
    of world economy, 126–128, 294, 339,
    345
Equilibrium, long-run, 29–31, 41, 42, 47,
    59, 74, 98
    and fixed exchange rates, 86–88
    in two-country world, 92–93
Equilibrium, short-run, 26–29, 32, 34–35,
    42, 55, 71, 78, 112
    and flexible exchange rates, 93–98
    and import propensity, 37–38
    and rise in government spending, 61–65
    in two-country world, 89–92
Equilibrium values
    and wealth, 244–246
    and world economy, 220–224
Europe, 8–9
    VAT harmonization in, 357–359
European Community (EC), 355, 418
    economic integration of, 257–258
    market integration in, 357, 359
    tax harmonization of, 260–261, 358(table)
European Monetary Union, 418
Exchange rate, 4(fig.), 5(fig.), 86, 308
    changes in, 51–52, 106–107
    domestic real, 299–300, 303
    expectations of, 98–103
    and fiscal policies, 55–61
    and government spending, 296–297
    real, 241, 242, 291
Exchange rate, fixed, 22, 50–51, 107
    and capital mobility, 53–65, 82–83,
    105–106
    and long-run equilibrium, 86–88
    and output, 103–104
Exchange rate, flexible, 49–50, 51, 83–84,
    107
    and capital mobility, 65–80, 81–82
    and short-run equilibrium, 93–98

Exchange rate, real, 1, 2, 6, 15, 427n6
Excise taxes, 259–260
Expenditure shares, 178–179
External shock, 10

Fiscal policies, 1–2, 15, 38, 44, 219, 345,
    355, 405. *See also* Budget deficits;
    Government spending
    dynamic inconsistencies of, 414–415
    modern intertemporal approach to,
    408–412
    real exchange rates, 291–293
    small country, 55–61, 67–76
    two-country, 61–65, 76–80
    welfare effects on, 233–235
Fiscal shocks, 333, 343–344
Fixed exchange rate. *See* Exchange rate,
    fixed
Fixed price model, and government
    spending, 104–105
Flexible exchange rate. *See* Exchange rate,
    flexible
France, 2, 6, 10, 400

GATT. *See* General Agreements on Tariffs
    and Trade
GDP. *See* Gross domestic product
GDP deflators, 51–52, 105, 407
    and exchange rates, 65–66, 99
GDP effect, 146
General Agreements on Tariffs and Trade
    (GATT), 258
Germany, 2, 6, 10, 400
GNP, 6, 8, 9, 12, 14, 115
Goods, 112, 221, 228, 315, 355, 427nn1,7.
    See also Nontradable goods; Tradable
    goods
    consumption of, 249–251
    domestic vs. foreign, 35–36
    exportable goods, 1, 155–156, 180
    private sector demand for, 169–170
    taxation of, 258–259, 429n2
    world market for, 237–240
Goods markets, 412
Government (public sector) consumption,
    10, 11(fig.)
Government finance, neutrality of,
    335–336
Government spending, 16, 21, 81(table),
    85–86, 229, 237, 244, 293, 295, 329,
    334, 338, 427nn1–5
    analytical framework of, 161–165

Government spending (cont.)
  balanced-budget rise in, 35–36, 37, 39,
    40–42, 43, 44–45, 91–92, 95–96,
    227–228, 230
  and consumption, 162, 344–345
  current and future, 226–231
  and debt, 252–253
  debt-financed rise in, 59–60, 68–69,
    73–74, 75, 82–83, 90–91, 96–97, 102,
    107
  and exchange rates, 71–72, 296–297
  and fixed price model, 104–105
  future, 154, 230–231, 341–342
  and GDP, 154–155
  and interest rate, 167–172, 173(table),
    241, 298–299, 339–340
  and investment, 182–185
  optimal path of, 185–186
  past, 231–232
  and private sector, 409–410
  propensities for, 180–181, 188–189
  rise in, 297–298
  short-run equilibrium, 26–28, 61–65
  in small open economy, 165–166
  and taxes, 163–165, 247–249
  tax policies and, 308–309
  tax-financed rise, 60–61, 69–70, 74,
    75–76, 79–80, 82, 83–84, 97, 103
  and terms of trade, 172, 174–182
  in United States, 14–15
  unit rise in, 36, 56–57
Gross domestic product (GDP), 33, 148,
    207, 284, 288
  and balance of trade, 187–188
  and consumption variability, 112–113,
    124
  and government spending, 154–155, 165
  growth rates, 125, 129–130
  and short-run equilibrium, 27, 28
Group of Seven, 400, 417

Importable goods, 180
  and composition of spending, 174–175
  consumption of, 155–156
  price of, 146–147
Import propensity, 36
  and short-run equilibrium, 37–38
  and world output, 38–39
Imports, 41, 258
Income, 73, 176, 260, 322, 356, 362, 383
  capital, 268–269, 271, 315
  and consumption, 111, 118
  disposable, 75, 162, 170, 246–247, 338,
    342
Income-expenditure model, 43, 85–86,
    406
  analytical framework of, 19–25, 52–53
  Keynesian version of, 25–29
  of output determination, 45–48
Income taxes, 260, 278, 308–309, 316,
    375, 383, 430n14
  and budget deficits, 282–285, 305, 393,
    393–396, 411–412
  cash flow, 371, 376, 387, 431n19
  and consumption, 271, 382
  vs. consumption tax, 306, 307
Insurance, life, 196–199
Interest rate, 137, 198, 223, 304, 307, 311,
    328, 417n7, 428n6. See also Interest rate,
    world
  and budget deficits, 246–247
  and debt, 202, 203, 431–432n24
  and demand, 229–230
  domestic, 78–79
  effective, 212, 281–282, 284, 303, 309
  equilibrium, 93–94, 112
  and government spending, 166–172, 241,
    427n4
  growth-adjusted, 213–214
  and marginal utility of wealth, 199–200
  money-market clearing, 76–77
  and present-value factor, 322–323
  and terms of trade, 404–408
Interest rate, real (consumption-based), 1, 6,
    140–141
  short- and long-term, 2, 3(fig.), 15
  and terms of trade, 143, 148,
    180–182
Interest rate, world, 62, 66, 185, 219,
    220, 239, 281, 282, 295, 410. See
    also Interest rates
  and budget deficits, 196, 242, 288–289,
    391
  determination of, 124–133
  and discount factor, 324–325
  equilibrium value of, 128–129, 184
  and exchange rate, 49–51
  and government spending, 173(table),
    297–299, 339–340
Interest-rate parity, 49–50
International transmission mechanisms,
    171–172
Intertemporal allocation of investment,
    model of, 112–114

Intertemporal macroeconomic model, 406–407. *See also* Overlapping-generations model
open-economy, 112–118
Intertemporal macroeconomics, 111
and fiscal policies, 408–412
Intertemporal ("true") price effect, 142, 144, 147
Intertemporal price ratio, 311
Intertemporal stochastic model, 334–335
Intertemporal substitution, 277, 282, 288
Investment, 9(table), 13, 281, 287, 321, 362, 383, 429–430n10, 431n19
costs of, 112–113, 268
and discount factor, 373–374, 375–376
endowment through, 151–153
and GDP growth, 129–130
and government spending, 182–185
international allocation of, 320, 413
in intertemporal macroeconomic model, 112–118
and maximization of wealth, 385–386
private sector, 14(fig.), 15
and supply shock, 112, 124
taxation of, 267, 268–269, 270–271, 272–273
Investment incentive system, 369(fig.), 371
Investment plans, 356
Investment spending, 114–115
Investment technology, 112–113
Ireland, 357, 359
Italy, 2, 10, 400

Japan, 2, 6, 8–9, 10, 400

Keynesian model, 49
and fixed price model, 104–105
of income-expenditure, 25–26

Labor, 258–259, 286, 315
Labor income, 287
Labor-leisure choice, 356
Labor supply, 374, 427n5
budget constraints and, 263–264
and consumption, 361, 362
elasticity of, 303, 430n14
foreign, 287–288
variable, 285–288, 393
Labor tax system, 371
Lagrange multiplier, 322, 323
Laursen-Metzler-Harberger effect, 145, 151
Leisure, 287, 321, 427n7

Lending, and consumption motives, 118–122
Lerner's symmetry proposition, 261
Levels of output. *See* Output
Life insurance. *See* Insurance, life
Loans, life insurance, 196–197
Luxembourg, 357

Macroeconomics, 49, 399, 408
Macroeconomics, intertemporal. *See* Intertemporal macroeconomic model
Marginal propensities, 36
Marginal propensity to consume, 199
Marginal propensity to hoard, 58
Marginal propensity to import. *See* Import propensities
Marginal propensity to save. *See* Saving propensity, marginal
Marginal propensity to spend. *See* Spending propensity
Marginal rate of substitution. *See* Substitution rate, marginal
Markets
incomplete, 338–342
integration of, 355, 357, 359
Maximization problem. *See also* Budget constraints; Utility function, maximization of lifetime
Microeconomics, 111
Money, demand for, 55–56, 100
Money holdings, 83
Money-market equilibrium, 75
Money supply, 34, 39, 106
distribution of, 47–48, 54
and output, 103–104
Multiperiod simulation model, 311–313
Mundell-Fleming model, 49, 106, 410

National income accounting, 115
Nominal exchange rates. *See* Exchange rates
Nontradable goods, 236–237, 244–245, 296, 297, 300, 312–313
consumption of, 309–311, 325–326
market for, 292–293

Output, 236, 281
and balance of trade, 206–207
distribution of, 33, 42
domestic, 40–41, 64–65, 70–72, 75, 77–78, 90
equilibrium levels of, 25–31
and exchange rate, 99, 103–104

Output (cont.)
  and fixed prices, 104–105
  foreign, 38, 41, 44
  and money demand, 55–56
  and private sector debt, 72–73
  shocks to, 133–135
  world, 38, 42, 127, 129, 131–132, 154,
    170, 182, 192, 220
Output determination, 49
  income-expenditure model of, 45–48
Output multipliers, short- and long-run, 80,
  82, 84
Overlapping-generations model, 410–411

Payments, balance of. See Balance of
  payments
Phillips curve monetary policy game,
  414–415
Portfolio selection, and consumption,
  347–348
Portugal, 357
Present-value (PV) factors, 265–266, 321,
  322–323
Price index, 142, 425n1
  consumption-based, 139, 189–192
Price ratio, intertemporal. See Intertemporal
  price ratio
Prices, 86, 155, 180, 333
  fixed, 104–105
  of importables, 146–147
  relative, 137, 241, 291
  and taxes, 259–260
  and trade policies, 262–263
Price vectors, 262
Private goods, 187, 188
Private sector, 161, 162, 315, 336, 427n2
  demand for goods, 169–170
  government spending and, 409–410
  spending of, 170–171, 415
  spending propensity of, 180–182,
    188–189, 226, 227
  wealth of, 164–165
Private-sector consumption, 9, 13(fig.)
Private-sector debt, 202
Private-sector spending, 1, 13, 43, 44, 293
  and budget deficits, 240–241
  and world output, 38–39
Production, factors of, 258–259, 264–265,
  413
Production function, 322
Productivity, permanent, 343–344
Profit maximization, 117–118

Propensity to import. See Import propensity
Propensity to save. See Saving propensity
Propensity to spend. See Spending
  propensity
Public debt. See also Budget deficits
Public goods, 186, 188
Public sector, 188–189. See also
  Government; Government spending
Public-sector consumption, 8–9
Public-sector spending. See Fiscal policies;
  Government spending
PV. See Present-value factors

Ramsey (second-best) taxation, analytical
  principles of, 316–319
Rate of interest. See Interest rate
Rate of substitution, marginal. See
  Substitution rate, marginal
Real exchange rate. See Exchange rate, real
Real interest rate. See Interest rate, real
Real spending. See Spending, real
Real wealth, consumption-based 137, 140
Relative-price structure, internal, 295
Resource allocation, 350
Resource-withdrawal channel, 165, 167
Revenue neutrality, 431n20
  and tax conversions, 372–375
Ricardian equivalence of interior transfers,
  410
Ricardian Equivalence Proposition, 409
Ricardian neutrality proposition, 333
Risk
  and assets, 348–349
  international allocation of, 333, 336–342
Risk-adjusted interest rate. See Interest rate,
  effective
Risk aversion, 158
Risk-free interest rates. See Interest rate
Risk sharing, 334

Saving incentive system, 368(fig.)
Saving propensity, 33, 45, 170, 177,
  188–189, 211, 232, 376. See also
  Spending propensity
  and government spending, 226–227, 410
  marginal, 58, 112, 177, 227
  and value of wealth, 200–201
Savings, 38, 177, 182, 342, 383, 362,
  429–430n10
  international allocation of, 320, 333,
    355–356, 413
  and taxation, 266, 267, 272, 274

Second-best taxation. *See* Ramsey taxation
Securities, 338, 341
Services, 315, 355
Shocks
  random, 135
  transitory, 133–135
Slutsky decomposition, 142, 310
Spain, 357
Spending, 293, 297, 334, 362
  allocation of, 21, 415
  composition of, 174–175
  foreign and domestic, 223, 225–226
  and international allocation of risk,
    336–342
Spending, government. *See* Fiscal policies;
  Government spending
Spending, 38
  private-sector, 61, 226, 227, 295–296
  real, 141–145, 292
Spending function, 20, 141
  real, 20–21, 157
Spending policies
  and Capital Asset Pricing Model, 342–343
  and incomplete markets, 338–339
Spending propensity, 33, 45, 61, 180,
  188–189, 200. *See also* Saving propensity
Spending shocks, 334
Stock markets, 333, 334, 349–350, 351
Stock prices, valuations of, 336–338
Stocks, intertemporal stochastic model,
  334–335
Subjective discount factor, defined,
  118–119
Substitution
  and discount factor, 373–374
  margins of, 363, 430n13
Substitution, elasticity of. *See* Elasticities of
  substitution
Substitution, intertemporal. *See*
  Intertemporal substitution
Substitution bias, 296
Substitution rate
  marginal, 165–166, 186–187, 325
  tradable, 253–254, 291
Subutility function, 292
Supply, 294, 296, 303–304
Supply schedule, 231, 283–284
Supply shocks, 112, 149
  intertemporal adjustment to, 122–124
  permanent, 187–188

Tariffs, 155, 156, 157

Tax-adjusted discount factor. *See* Discount
  factor, effective
Taxation, 266, 429n2. *See also* Ramsey
  taxation
  capital-income, 267, 315
  direct and indirect, 257, 258
  international, 319–321, 412–414
  one-period model, 258–263
  optimal, 321–325
Tax bases, 260, 306, 374, 375
  and economic integration, 412–413
Tax conversions, 430n16
  impacts of, 372–377
  revenue-neutral, 305–308, 393
Tax cuts
  and budget deficits, 288–289, 301–302,
    309
  and consumption, 212–213
  and welfare, 233, 234
Tax equivalences, 412
Taxes, 51, 153, 156, 252, 253, 287, 364,
  416, 426–427n6, 428nn2–6. *See also by
  type*
  ad valorem, 155, 278
  and budget deficits, 195, 208–209, 240,
    243–244
  capital-income, 268–272, 325
  cash-flow, 273–275
  on consumption, 265–266
  and current period wealth, 209–210
  distortionary, 235, 236
  and government spending, 85–86,
    163–165, 247–249
  on international borrowing, 386–389
  international trade, 261–262
  lump-sum, 315–316
  and output, 103–104
  time profile of, 302–303, 356, 361–362
  types of, 259–261
Tax harmonization policy, 260–261
Tax model, and VAT harmonization,
  355–356
Tax policies, 16, 246, 257, 267, 355, 415
  and budget deficits, 301–305
  and government finance neutrality,
    335–336
  impacts of, 290, 300–301
  wealth effects of, 235–236
Tax reform, revenue-neutral, 305–308
Tax revenues, 375
  growth rates of, 10–12, 16
  and VAT harmonization, 357, 431n21

Tax systems, 430nn13, 17. *See also by type*
  conversion of, 306–307
  and VAT harmonization, 365–369(figs.),
    370(table)
Terms of trade, 125, 157, 382, 414
  and balance of trade, 145–151, 152(table)
  deterioration of, 148–149
  and government spending, 172, 174–182
  and interest rates, 404–408
  and real spending, 141–145
  temporal and intertemporal, 188–189,
    192–193
  and tradable goods, 327–328
Time aggregation procedure, 220, 242–243
Time preference
  rate of, 168–169
  subjective rates of, 125–126, 170,
    178–179
Tradable goods, 253–254, 291, 292, 308
  consumption of, 309–311, 325–326
  and terms of trade, 327–328
Trade, 126, 156, 173(table), 264
Trade, terms of. *See* Terms of trade
Trade account, 22, 290. *See also* Balance of
  trade
Trade balance. *See* Balance of trade
Trade policy
  and domestic policies, 262–263
  and taxation, 261–262
Transfer-problem analysis, 132–133
Transfer-problem criteria, 176, 188, 193
Transformation rate, marginal, 186, 409

United Kingdom, 2, 6, 8, 10, 400
United States, 2, 6, 10, 417
  consumption rates in, 400–404
  government spending, 14–15
  investment growth rates, 13–14
  public-sector consumption, 8–9
Utility, 234
  expected, 196, 198, 254
  marginal, 199–200
Utility function, 153–154, 174, 186, 219,
  323, 362, 428n2
  and consumption, 253, 326
  instantaneous, 321–322
  maximization of lifetime, 138–140,
    161–162, 285–286, 292, 312, 384–385
  in multiperiod simulation model,
    311–312
  and stock market model, 349–350

Value-added taxes (VAT), 258, 260–261,
  266, 280, 359, 430n11. *See also* VAT
  harmonization
  impacts of, 301, 431n19
  as tax base, 374, 430n14, 431n21
Valuation of equities, 334
VAT. *See* Value-added tax
VAT harmonization, 355–356
  current account imbalances and, 375–383
  in Europe, 357–359
  implications of, 383–384, 430n15,
    431nn22, 23
  simulations of, 363–372
Vietnam War, 10

Wage rate, 321–322, 427n4
Wage tax system, 366(fig.)
Wealth, 122, 157, 182, 202, 223, 234, 239,
  249, 351. *See also* Aggregate wealth;
  Real wealth
  aggregate changes in, 244–246
  components of, 203–204
  equilibrium values of, 221–222, 238
  and government spending, 169, 180
  human, 198–199
  marginal utility of, 199–200
  maximization of, 385–386
  private sector, 164–165
  and saving propensity, 200–201
  and taxes, 209–210
Wealth deflator, 180–182. *See also* Deflator
  effect
Wealth effects, 142, 144, 147, 242
  and budget deficits, 208–212, 235–236,
    277
Welfare, 155, 396
  and budget deficits, 241–242
  and economic integration, 417–418
  and fiscal policies, 186, 233–235
  redistribution of, 371–372
  and tax cuts, 233, 234
Welfare effects, 382
West Germany. *See* Germany
World rate of interest. *See* Interest rate,
  world